Buddhism Transformed

Buddhism Transformed

RELIGIOUS CHANGE IN SRI LANKA

BY

Richard Gombrich

Gananath Obeyesekere

PRINCETON UNIVERSITY PRESS

PRINCETON, NEW JERSEY

Published by Princeton University Press, 41 William Street,
Princeton, New Jersey 08540
In the United Kingdom: Princeton University Press, Guildford, Surrey

Library of Congress
Cataloging-in-Publication Data

Gombrich, Richard Francis.
Buddhism transformed: religious change in Sri Lanka /
Richard Gombrich and Gananath Obeyesekere.
p. cm. Bibliography: p. Includes index.
ISBN 0-691-07333-3 (alk. paper)
1. Buddhism—Sri Lanka—History—20th century.
I. Obeyesekere, Gananath. II. Title.
BQ374.G65 1988 294.3'09549'3—dc19 88-12656

This book has been composed in Linotron Garamond

Clothbound editions of Princeton University Press books
are printed on acid-free paper, and binding materials are
chosen for strength and durability. Paperbacks, although satisfactory
for personal collections, are not usually suitable for library rebinding

Printed in the United States of America by Princeton University Press,
Princeton, New Jersey

Designed by Laury A. Egan

For Sanjukta and Ranjini

CONTENTS

PREFACE

The two authors of this book have for many years been interested in the history and anthropology of Buddhism, especially in the Theravāda Buddhism practiced in Sri Lanka. Collaboration between an anthropologist sympathetic to history and Indology and an Indologist sympathetic to anthropology is hardly strange nowadays. But we must add that we have long been friends and that we undertook this book as a result of our friendship. Though socialized in different ways, we not only have intellectual interests in common but also share a deep respect for the Buddhist doctrinal tradition and a sympathy for its various embodiments in Sri Lankan history and village society. There is no senior or junior authorship to this volume and we take joint responsibility for the whole of it. Like good social and cultural anthropologists, we have both done our stint of fieldwork in villages. But unlike many of our tribe, we rapidly became dissatisfied with those horizons. In modern times political and economic power have more and more become centralized in Colombo—not a big city by contemporary Asian standards, but the home of social classes, the bourgeoisie and the proletariat, who are quite alien to the traditional agrarian society in which most Sinhalas have practiced Buddhism for over two millennia. Ideas and values have been diffusing from Colombo to the towns, from the towns to the villages, till almost everyone has been in some measure affected. We became interested in the historical background of the new middle-class and working-class variants of Sinhala Buddhist religion, and while we were pursuing these interests ever more startling facts kept forcing themselves on our attention. We owe a special debt of gratitude to Mr. Godwin Samararatne, a true *kalyāṇa-mitra*, for having directed our attention to some of them. Though we collected the bulk of the data ourselves, we are also grateful to two research assistants: Mr. Lionel Gunasekara not only helped collect data we asked for (mainly for Chapters 2 and 3) but also exercised his initiative most fruitfully; and Mr. N. Shanmugalingam translated Tamil material for us, since neither of us knows Tamil. We are also grateful to the Virginia and Richard Stewart Lectureship Committee for inviting one of us (Richard Gombrich) to visit

Princeton in the fall of 1986. This effectively gave us the opportunity to complete this book. We must also thank Margaret Case of the Princeton University Press for her friendship and the tolerance she exhibited when our manuscript inadvertently began to break the bounds of decent size! Finally our thanks and gratitude to Mrs. Pauline Caulk for typing with the skill of a craftsman and the patience of a saint.

Circumstances have made the compilation of this book all too sporadic. Most of the fieldwork for it was done in the 1970s, along with that for *Medusa's Hair*. Our plan was—and remains—that the two books should to some degree complement each other, *Medusa's Hair* dealing with its material from the angle of the individual, this book using instead a broader historical and social perspective. Having agreed in 1976 to write the book together, we nearly completed a first draft in 1978 and 1979. *Medusa's Hair*, benefiting from single authorship, was then finished and published. Meanwhile our paths diverged for several years: one of us was working in Princeton, the other in Oxford; we both had other commitments and were unable to coordinate leaves or visits to Sri Lanka. We managed to get back together in 1985. Since then we have added most of Chapters 4, 7, 11, and 12 and revised the rest. We have not entirely refrained from adding points right up to the time when the book went to press; on the other hand, some sections preserve an ethnographic present that dates back ten years and more. Had we kept revising, the book would never have appeared. We have tried to ensure that nothing is lost by the temporal inconsistency. At the same time we are acutely aware that as we write the most important fact about Sri Lanka is the ethnic conflict that has escalated into a civil war since 1983. This year (1987) a "peace accord" was signed between India and Sri Lanka in the hope of terminating the civil war. This book almost totally ignores these events: we do not mention the civil war in our account of socioeconomic concerns and only touch on it (in Chapters 11 and 12) in our account of religion. The ethnic riots of 1983 and the angry Sinhala reaction after the peace accord produced, among other things, a new brand of political monks. In 1983 monks actively incited laity to acts of violence; in 1987 they actually burned buses and government property. The Sinhala lay opinion that they were mostly youthful revolutionaries disguised as monks is poor consolation, since monks belonging to the established fraternities were also involved. Violence has taken root in the heart of the Buddhist establishment. But we believe that even if experience of terrorism and war has made Sinhala religion take a new turn, that itself will not be intelligible without awareness of the earlier developments that we document and analyze here. And if this book appears, somewhat unfashionably, to be full of detailed (and colorful) facts, we would reply, "Theories date rapidly, but documents, like diamonds, are forever."[1]

Here is a brief chart to guide the reader over the sea of our ethnography. In Part One we summarize the main features of Sinhala Buddhism as traditionally practiced and show how they relate to the doctrine of the scriptures. This background is intended to equip the reader for our discussion of the changes in the two parts of the religion of Sinhala Buddhists—the spirit religion, which deals with this life, and Buddhism in the strict sense, which is concerned mainly with salvation. We also adumbrate the general direction of these changes. Part Two is devoted to the spirit religion, especially in and around Colombo. We focus on the loss of community and the development of surrogate kin groups which we label "cult groups"; on the conversion of demonic beings of village religion into divine beings for city dwellers; and on the legitimation of changes in the spirit religion at Kataragama, the great pilgrimage center at the southeast corner of the island to which most of our subjects repair at least once a year. No discussion of Sinhala spirit religion can omit Kataragama, for it is here that Hindu theistic devotion is reworked and appropriated by Sinhalas, not only into their spirit religion but also, indirectly, into the more austere tradition of Buddhism.

Part Three deals with the recent evolution of that Buddhism. We begin with the religious reform movement of the late nineteenth century which we label "Protestant Buddhism." We illustrate this new strain of Buddhism through the ideas of its first great Sinhala protagonist, Anagārika Dharmapāla, who may be said to be for modern Sinhala Buddhism what Kataragama is for the spirit religion. Protestant Buddhism formulated a new set of values for the new bourgeoisie. It began to undermine the hierarchies on which Sinhala Buddhism was traditionally built, such as the rigid distinction between clergy and laity (Anagārika was in fact a role halfway between, introduced to Buddhism by Dharmapāla) and the corresponding distinction between things pertaining to salvation and things of this world. We illustrate the results of this new value orientation in Chapter 7, which presents Sarvōdaya, a recent movement for socio-

[1] E. H. Gombrich, *Reflections on the History of Art*, Oxford: Phaidon, 1987, p. 32.

economic reform that consciously follows Dharmapāla's lead, and the unself-conscious creation of a Buddhist wedding ceremony on the Christian model. The latter upsets the traditional hierarchy of values in the ritual sphere just as Sarvōdaya does in the economic sphere: traditionally monks did not work, and the Buddha had nothing to do with marriage. Chapter 8 then deals with the revival of monasticism for women. This is connected to the improved education and rising, but often frustrated, expectations of Sinhala women.

The nuns' movement is largely a middle-class phenomenon and a part of the Protestant Buddhist revival. But the end of Chapter 8 is the first point at which our two main currents of change begin to mingle: a few nuns are mixing up their Buddhism with the spirit religion. To delve deeper into such syncretism, we turn from institutions to individuals. First we devote a chapter to a pillar of the Buddhist establishment, a venerable monk who not only has connections with—and views on—Protestant Buddhism, but is obsessed with a concomitant phenomenon, astrology. His remarkable views owe nothing to Hindu theism or the spirit religion; but we can trace those influences in the still more remarkable views and activities of the three small Buddhist movements, all outside the pale of the established monastic order, which occupy Chapter 10. These movements, which we examine mainly through their leaders, also illustrate how Protestant tendencies, taken to extremes, lead to the fragmentation of religious authority. Though these radical movements are small, most of their members are educated and some occupy influential positions, notably as educators.

In the last part of the book we broach the question: towards a new synthesis? Chapters 11 and 12 present cases in which the changes in Sinhala spirit religion have also affected Buddhism. The *Bōdhi pūjā*, a recently invented Buddhist ritual, is infused with a devotional spirit. Contrary to the intention of the monk who founded it, it is now on the one hand being adapted to the spirit religion and on the other being used to express Sinhala political solidarity. This political strain comes out even more strongly in the new myths being developed at Kataragama to claim the shrine as exclusively Sinhala cultural property and to assert that its god is not Hindu but pure Buddhist. In our final chapter we place the recent changes in the context of the religious history of greater India in order to peer into the future. What we think unlikely to change is the identification of the Sinhala people as Theravāda Buddhists, meaning that they will not turn to

Mahāyāna and that the Buddha will continue to reign supreme as the only guide toward spiritual liberation. Religion is so much affected by social and political conditions, which we cannot predict, that we hesitate to go further; but we conclude by showing that even if the rise of Hinduistic devotion leads to what from the traditional Theravādin point of view look like inconsistencies and contradictions, Indian religion has been here before.

We make no claim that this book, long though it is, is in any way exhaustive. On the contrary, we feel we have uncovered only a fraction of what is going on, and we hope to stimulate others to do research and find more, not only in Sri Lanka but also in other Theravādin societies. But we are also aware that our data will probably make the book controversial in Sri Lanka. We hope that it will not merely interest Sri Lankan intellectuals, but worry them, because we find some of the transformations we record troubling in their departure from the rational and humane tradition of Buddhism. For the same reason, we would like to see the book translated in Sinhala. Meanwhile we hope that this English edition may interest not only our academic colleagues and their students, but a wider public too. For the issues raised by our narratives are not only intellectual and not only local; they concern many of the problems of living in the world today.

A NOTE ON TERMINOLOGY

To limit the number of foreign words in the text, while avoiding lengthy explanations and circumlocutions, we must introduce some technical vocabulary. We present here only traditional terms, well known to Sinhala Buddhists; neologisms will be discussed in the text.

Sinhala Buddhists normally refer to their Buddhism in one of two ways. Its content, the truth that the Buddha rediscovered, is the **Doctrine** (*Dhamma, Dharma*). By preaching the doctrine, the Buddha founded the **Teaching** (*śāsana, sāsana, sasuna*)—the term denotes Buddhism as a historical phenomenon. Buddhism is preserved by the monastic **Order** (*Sangha*), traditionally held to embody the teaching.

The Order's members (*bhikṣu, bhikkhu, hāmuduruvō, himi*) are known in Sri Lankan English as "priests," but as we require this term elsewhere we adopt the traditional Orientalists' translation and call them **monks**. Monks have received the **higher ordination** (*upasampadā*); before that they are **novices** (*poḍi hāmuduruvō, sāmaṇēra*). Both monks and novices are **clergy** (*mahaṇa, pävidi*). It requires a monk to ordain a novice. As the higher ordination for women is extinct, there cannot any longer be nuns (*bhikṣuṇī*) or even **female clergy** (*meheṇi*) in the strict sense; but in Chapter 8 below we discuss the closest female counterpart, women who have taken the **ten precepts** (*dasa sil*), and for convenience we call them **nuns**, as do some of their supporters. The term **supporter** is quasi-technical and translates *dāyaka* (literally "donor"); **chief supporter** translates *käpakaru dāyaka*. The terms **pious layman** and **pious laywoman** are also technical and translate the assumed statuses of *upāsaka* and *upāsikā* respectively. The pious laity expresses its piety mainly by undertaking certain observances on Buddhist **holy days** (*pōya*), the quarter days of the lunar month.

By normal Western usage monks should live in a **monastery**; but we have reserved this term to translate the term for the actual house inhabited by a monk or monks (*pansala*) and follow local Sinhala usage in calling the complex of monastic buildings (*vihāra, ārāma*) a **temple** or **Buddhist temple**. In this complex the building that houses a consecrated Buddha image and is thus the site of certain rituals we call a **Buddha shrine** (*vi-*

hāragē, budugē). A monk may choose an ascetic life style and formally become a **forest dweller** (*vanavāsī, araññavāsī*). He then lives not in a monastery but in a **hermitage** (*araññasthāna*) and the actual room he occupies, which usually constitutes a separate building, is a **cell**, *kuṭi* (literally "hut"), whatever its size or construction.

A Sinhala building for **gods** (*deriyō, deyiyō*), whether or not it is on the premises of a Buddhist temple, we call a **shrine** (*dēvālaya, dēvāle*). Its Hindu equivalent (*kovil*) we call a **Hindu temple**; this term implies both Tamil Hindu ownership and considerable architectural and organizational independence.

The officiant at a Sinhala shrine is known by terms (*kapuvā, kapurāḷa*) that literally denote a "go-between" and thus indicate the mediumistic character of his performance: he acts as a vehicle for a deity, who on certain occasions possesses him and speaks through him. It was tempting to borrow the spiritualist term "medium" as the most literal rendering available, but the connotations are too misleading; so it is for the *kapuvā* that we have reserved the term **priest**. His counterpart who officiates at a Hindu temple, the *pūsārī*, we call a **Hindu priest**.

The *pūsārī* derives his name from *pūjā*, the formal **act of worship** carried out before a god or a Buddha image. Priests, and others whom we shall discuss, **deliver oracles**. It is by this term that we translate *śāstra kiyanavā* and *pēna kiyanavā*. Strictly speaking, the latter term denotes only clairvoyance, but in practice the two terms are nowadays confused and loosely cover many different "techniques." Sinhala oracles involve supernormal knowledge of past, present, and future: in particular, the specialist normally tells the client (for whom there is no special term) what it is that the client has in mind to ask and gives him advice on how to gain his end or avert misfortune. The practice of magic is covered by the general term *yantra mantra; yantra* means **charms** (as physical objects), especially mystic diagrams, and *mantra* means **spells**.

We translate *yakā/yakṣa* (feminine: *yakinī/yakṣiṇī*) as **demon**. The ritual controller of demons (*kaṭṭāḍiyā, kaṭṭāḍirāḷa*) we call an **exorcist**. *Dēvatā* we translate "**godling**"; the term is explained in Chapter 1.

Some technical terms of Buddhist meditation are introduced in Chapter 1.

For further explanations, readers may consult the Glossary on pp. 339–48 of Gombrich's *Precept and Practice: Traditional Buddhism in the Rural Highlands of Ceylon*.

PART ONE

A New Religious Orientation

CHAPTER 1

The Subject Defined

The Contemporary Religion of Sinhala Buddhists

In this book we aim to describe, analyze, and interpret recent changes in the religious life of Sinhala Buddhists. By Sinhala Buddhists we mean those who identify as such—a matter on which there is nowadays no ambiguity. By their religious life we mean something broader than Sinhala Buddhism. Their identity implies that the defining and major component of that life is the Buddhist tradition (*Buddhāgama*). That remains, as it has been for many centuries, the Theravāda Buddhism that derives its authority from the teachings of the Buddha as given in the Pāli Canon and interpreted by commentators, culminating in Buddhaghosa (fifth century A.D.); as further preserved and interpreted by the Sangha (monastic order) of Sri Lanka; and as practiced and understood in its monasteries and villages. But if we work with the Western conception of religion as involving belief in and action directed toward supernatural beings, we must add that the religious life of Sinhala Buddhists has always (except for a few individuals) included such belief and action: worship of gods and propitiation of demons, belief in and attempted manipulation of supernatural powers—things for which the Buddhist scriptures give no specific authority and which the actors themselves have generally considered to form no part of Buddhism, though perfectly compatible with it. This distinction, crucial within the culture, will be further explained below. Here it suffices to say that this non-Buddhist part of the religion of Sinhala Buddhists has no name, no unifying label within the culture, and as we need to refer to it we shall give it a label of convenience and call it "spirit religion." Like Theravāda Buddhism, Sinhala spirit religion has its own traditional roles and institutions.

CHAPTER 1

Three Kinds of Sinhala Buddhist Religion

The contemporary Sinhala religion described in this work springs from conditions in urban society. By "urban" we do not refer just to towns and cities, but more broadly instead to middle- and working-class people who live in an urban life style, even though they may be physically located in what people call a "village." By aspiration and life style they are clearly differentiated from "peasants." Their forms of religion cannot be understood except in relation to traditional village religion and the changes that were brought about in village religion in the nineteenth century through the movement that we have called "Protestant Buddhism." Thus in this book we shall talk of three kinds of Sinhala religion: traditional village Buddhism, Protestant Buddhism, and the contemporary religion of urban Buddhists. Sometimes we use the more inclusive term "Sinhala Buddhism" as a convenient shorthand for "the religion of Sinhala Buddhists."

Traditional Sinhala Buddhism we see as a system of belief and action, with a distinctive ethos, integrated within a Buddhist framework that traces its history all the way back to the introduction of Buddhism into the island from the Indian mainland in ca. 250 B.C. From about the turn of the Christian Era various external influences, such as foreign invasions, have brought upheavals and vicissitudes but few major changes in the religion's essential character. Periods of decline, measured primarily by the state of the Sangha, have been ended by self-conscious revivals, usually under royal patronage, directed towards models provided in literary sources: the scriptures and the island's Buddhist chronicle, the *Mahāvaṃsa*.[1] The most permanent setback, from the Buddhist point of view, is that the Order of Nuns became extinct by the eleventh century. A notable revival of traditional Buddhist ideals has been taking place in recent years and is admirably documented in Michael Carrithers's book, *The Forest Monks of Sri Lanka*.[2] Buddhist readers who find in the ensuing pages a

[1] The latter part of the *Mahāvaṃsa* has been published in the West under the title *Cūlavaṃsa*. The chronicle is translated into English in 3 vols.: *Mahāvaṃsa: The Great Chronicle of Ceylon*, trans. Wilhelm Geiger assisted by Mabel H. Bode (London: Pali Text Society, 1912); *Cūlavaṃsa, Being the More Recent Part of the Mahāvaṃsa*, 2 vols., trans. into English by Mrs. C. Mabel Rickmers from the German trans. by Wilhelm Geiger (Colombo: Department of Information, 1953).

[2] Michael Carrithers, *The Forest Monks of Sri Lanka* (Delhi: Oxford University Press, 1983).

distressing record of departures from orthodoxy will find that book a refreshing counterweight to ours.

Traditional Buddhism was the religion of a rice-growing peasant society—not only in Sri Lanka but also in the Theravādin societies of continental Southeast Asia: Burma, Thailand, Laos, and Cambodia. Its central institutional feature is the distinction between the laity and the Sangha. The role of the laity is to give material support to the Sangha, whose members are recruited from their ranks; the Sangha embodies their ideals and preserves the scriptures that provide the charter for those ideals. The religious goal of the laity is to be good enough to be reborn in a pleasant station, in heaven or on earth; anyone who has more spiritual ambitions joins the Sangha, who represent the ideal of detachment from both pain and pleasure.

In an earlier book[3] Gombrich attempted to depict this form of religion as it was to be found twenty years ago in a traditional Sinhala village.[4] By now it has been the subject of a good deal of scholarly literature. Since that literature provides an adequate background, we shall recapitulate (later in this chapter) only those facts about it which are relevant to our present argument, and for a wider understanding refer readers to that earlier work.

We are not assuming that traditional Buddhism was static. We are aware how easy it is to be misled by such clichés as the timeless East, the Asiatic mode of production, hydraulic society; historical sources record that Buddhism in Sri Lanka has undergone many vicissitudes. On the other hand, those very sources also reveal persisting themes. The *Mahāvaṃsa*, composed by monks under royal patronage, tends to see Buddhism from above and to be concerned with its fortunes at the state level. But for a worm's eye view we have not only more popular literature but Robert Knox, who had to live in Kandyan villages from 1659 to 1679; he has left us the earliest document comparable with modern ethnography concerning village life anywhere in South Asia.[5] Knox's more willing successors of recent times have agreed that his account of popular religion could still

[3] Richard Gombrich, *Precept and Practice: Traditional Buddhism in the Rural Highlands of Ceylon* (Oxford: Clarendon Press, 1971), chap. 5.

[4] That village has now been submerged by a development project: all too literally has that community disappeared.

[5] Robert Knox, *An Historical Relation of the Island of Ceylon* (London: Richard Chiswell, 1681), p. 83.

characterize at least the remoter Kandyan villages. Against this background, we claim that the changes discussed in this book have been more rapid and far-reaching than any before. Even today, the basic structure of Buddhist soteriology is intact: the Buddha is still above the pantheon, and the goal he set, Enlightenment, transcends worldly concerns. But many rarely give these facts a thought, many more interpret their implications in completely new ways. Nor is it surprising that such dramatic change should accompany the demise of traditional agricultural society.

In the late nineteenth century, under British colonial domination, a new Sri Lankan social class developed. This urbanized, often English-educated, and partly Westernized elite was the forerunner of the contemporary middle class; and among the Sinhala Buddhist segment of this middle class arose a new form of Buddhism. Even when we did our fieldwork in 1964–1965, this form of Buddhism, although it lacked self-definition, was so evidently distinct from village Buddhism—if only because it was the Buddhism of local English-language sources—that we found it necessary to begin our account of the latter by contrasting it with the former. Although this distinction had already been drawn by the Anglican Bishop of Colombo in 1892, the first scholar to publish an adequate account of the new Buddhism was Heinz Bechert. In his three-volume work, *Buddhismus, Staat und Gesellschaft in den Ländern des Theravāda Buddhismus*,[6] he called it "Buddhist modernism" ("Buddhistischer Modernismus"); he was concerned primarily with its ideology and its relation to politics. Since Bechert wrote in German, his book unfortunately did not have the impact on Sri Lankan studies that it deserved; however, over the years he has distilled some of its conclusions into several English articles. In 1970 Obeyesekere published an article in which he coined the term "Protestant Buddhism."[7] This term was accepted by Kitsiri Malalgoda for his masterly account of the movement's origins.[8] His history of Protestant Buddhism,

[6] Vol. 1, Frankfurt and Berlin: Alfred Metzner, 1966; vols. 2 and 3, Wiesbaden, 1967 and 1973.

[7] Gananath Obeyesekere, "Religious Symbolism and Political Change in Ceylon," *Modern Ceylon Studies* 1, no. 1 (1970), reprinted in *Two Wheels of Dhamma*, ed. Bardwell Smith, AAR Monograph no. 3 (Chambersburg, 1972). For more recent developments of this argument see Obeyesekere, "Sinhala-Buddhist Identity in Ceylon," in *Ethnic Identity: Cultural Continuities and Change*, ed. George de Vos and Lola Ross (Palo Alto: Mayfield Publishing Company, 1975).

[8] Kitsiri Malalgoda, *Buddhism in Sinhalese Society, 1750–1900* (Berkeley and Los Angeles: University of California Press, 1976).

however, only takes the story up to the entrance of its greatest figure, Anagārika Dharmapāla (1864–1933). In Obeyesekere's article and elsewhere, we have written on the life and thought of Dharmapāla and their impact on modern Sri Lanka. Thus, though Buddhists themselves still do not articulate Protestant Buddhism as a separate phenomenon, let alone agree that it can be contrasted with traditional Sinhala Buddhism, its character has been documented and its label become current in scholarly literature.

The utility of the label "Protestant Buddhism" lies in its double meaning. It originated as a protest against the British in general and against Protestant Christian missionaries in particular. At the same time, however, it assumed salient characteristics of that Protestantism. We shall further explore its Protestant character below. Here it suffices to say that Protestant Buddhism undercuts the importance of the religious professional, the monk, by holding that it is the responsibility of every Buddhist both to care for the welfare of Buddhism and to strive himself for salvation. The traditional monastic monopoly in withdrawal from the world is called into question, while those monks (the majority) who do not become meditating hermits are criticized for lack of social involvement. The distinction between Sangha and laity is thus blurred, for religious rights and duties are the same for all.

For the best part of a century, Protestant Buddhism was limited to a small emerging middle class, consisting of minor government officials educated in Sinhala and living in the village (though not of the village) and constituting an educated elite, and a larger number of people, some of them English-educated, concentrated in Colombo and smaller cities like Galle and Kandy. Those living in cities had been cut off from their village roots and had no experience of other kinds of community living. But since Independence (1948) the pace of social change has quickened. Indeed we can no longer talk of traditional village communities of the sort described by Leach, Obeyesekere, and Yalman.[9] More importantly, owing to the development of education and an expanding economy, the native bureaucratic elite of colonial times has expanded into a bourgeoisie whose influence, supported as it is by the modern educational system, is out of all propor-

[9] E. R. Leach, *Pul Eliya: A Village in Ceylon* (Cambridge: Cambridge University Press, 1961); Nur Yalman, *Under the Bo Tree* (Berkeley: University of California Press, 1967); Gananath Obeyesekere, *Land Tenure in Village Ceylon: A Sociological and Historical Study* (Cambridge: Cambridge University Press, 1967).

tion to its size. Modern changes emanate from urban centers, and even if changes stem from proletarian sources, their larger acceptance does require bourgeois validation. The bourgeois culture of Protestant Buddhism exerts hegemonic sway over larger areas of the nation.

As social historians of religion, we believe that great social change will, in due course, entail great religious change, however complex the causal process. It therefore comes as no surprise that when the mass of the Sinhala population is experiencing dramatic change in its material circumstances its religious life too is being transformed. The loss of traditional community, which for several generations had affected only a small upper middle-class bourgeois elite, has now become the common lot. But naturally the cultural correlates of moving from being a farmer to being a city businessman or bureaucrat have not been replicated when the peasant has become an urban slum dweller or a landless laborer.

The changes that concern us must have become visible in the forties; but we think that they became widespread and important only in the 1960s and 1970s. Most of them have started in Colombo, with its slums and its middle-class districts, its mixed population of Sinhala and Tamil, of Buddhists, Śaivite Hindus, Muslims, Roman Catholics, and various Protestant denominations. In addition to Colombo we must include the pilgrimage centers, notably Kataragama in the southeast of the island, to which a large number of the inhabitants of Colombo probably pay at least one visit a year. From Colombo the changes spread into its penumbra, the commuter belt that by now includes almost the whole of the southwest coastal region; and from there to small towns and even to rural areas in the rest of the country. A good half of the Sinhala population no longer lives in the stable village communities so convenient for anthropologists, and "how the other half lives" has so far gone practically unrecorded.

The greatest single catalyst of change has been population growth. The figures tell their own story. Population figures for ten-year intervals from 1931 are as follows: 5,307,000 (1931), 5,981,000 (1941), 7,776,000 (1951), 10,030,000 (1961), 12,608,000 (1971) and 14,800,657 (1981); the population has nearly trebled over a fifty-year period. Inevitably there is mass unemployment and underemployment, and the country has been pauperized: enormous numbers of people have suffered a dramatic decline in their living standards, and that within a single generation, so that they are vividly aware of their deprivation—though usually not of its causes. Frustration and bewilderment are widespread. They have been compounded by the centralization and sometimes arbitrary use of political power. Other important factors, operating over a rather longer term, have been the spread of literacy and a gradual change in the status of women—itself the product of such factors as female education and urbanization. Moreover, social changes have produced changes in the structure and nature of the family and so impinged on people's intimate emotions.

We see in many Sinhala Buddhist milieus a disoriented society with a new religious culture—which it is the purpose of this book to characterize. We can call this new Buddhism "post-Protestant," but the precise label is unimportant, and even its delineation as a third and separate stage we regard merely as a convenient label. Since this religious culture is not demarcated, like Protestant Buddhism, by a new view of the religious roles of Buddhist laity and Sangha, but rather accepts the Protestant view of this matter, it may at first sight seem like a continuity of Protestant Buddhism and the spirit cults into modern times. The reader of the early chapters of this book may receive from them the impression that just as traditional religious life has two parts, the strictly Buddhist and the spirit religion, we are merely recording separate developments in each of those two parts: that just as Buddhism changed in the hands of the new urban middle class, the spirit religion has changed in the hands of the urban poor. For Dharmapāla, the model Protestant Buddhist, the spirit religion was a mass of superstition in which no true Buddhist should believe or indulge; for many Colombo slum dwellers, Buddhism is something lofty to which one pays lip service when occasion demands and which helps them to assert a social and political identity, but which is too abstruse to be comprehensible and too detached to be relevant to the struggle for a living. If one thus considered the two developments in isolation, one would no more expect to meet a middle-class exorcist or firewalker than to come across a Buddhist monk who had grown up in a city slum. But as they read on, readers will see that although the two developments can be described separately, they are complementary, and even more than that: they intermingle. Whether any boys who grew up in the city slums have been ordained in the Sangha we do not know; we do, however, record the case of a slum dweller who became a pseudomonk and recruited disciples from the same milieu. On the other hand, there are certainly exorcists and firewalkers of middle-class origins. As this asymmetry in our data suggests, it is the new developments in the spirit religion that have been influencing Protestant Buddhism, rather than vice versa. But what began in the late nineteenth century as the Protestant Buddhism of the emerging middle class has moved down the social scale to embrace a far wider range of people, while coming under influences which for the most part arise from below. It is this new synthesis—inchoate, multiform, and disorganized though it is—that we try to describe in this book.

Contemporary Religion and Social Class Formation

One way of framing our view of recent religious changes is in terms of class structure. On the broadest level we relate the changes in religion to a phenomenon new to nations like Sri Lanka—the emergence of a large bourgeoisie and an urban proletariat. Specific social and demographic changes, such as rapid population growth and universal free education, have little significance on their own unless they can be related to the larger socioeconomic forces operative in the society, such as the formation of social classes. Population growth in Sri Lanka has had distinctive features. As Kearney and Miller have noted, there has been no rush to the cities on the scale found elsewhere in South and Southeast Asia, since internal migration seems to have been preferred.[10] Those who have moved into the cities (primarily Colombo) have formed the base of the middle and lower classes. Owing to the smallness of the country, many living in the penumbra of the city continue to do so, others from the hinterland move elsewhere. Universal free education has had similar effects. Not only has education been free since Independence; reasonably good schools have been established over most of the country. A striking feature of Sri Lankan society has been the rise of peasant ambitions for white-collar and professional jobs for their children through education. The educational system has pumped more and more persons into the modern class structure, especially the bourgeoisie. The dramatic growth of population and expansion of education, without matched growth in the economy, underlie the massive frustration of expectations seen in the nation today.

None of these observations are new. Though the facts are well known, what they imply for religion has not been analyzed before in the detail

[10] For a detailed analysis of patterns of internal migration see Robert N. Kearney and Barbara Diane Miller, *Internal Migration in Sri Lanka and Its Social Consequences* (Boulder, Colo.: Westview Press, 1987).

presented in this book. Furthermore the beginnings of the bourgeois formation, we shall show in Chapter 6, lay in Protestant Buddhism. Thus as a religious reform movement Protestant Buddhism not only had a strong anticolonialist bias, but also provided a value system to the Sinhala elite that in turn expanded, through population growth and education, to constitute the modern bourgeoisie. In fact one can argue, though we cannot demonstrate it here, that schools were the prime vehicle for the continuity of Protestant Buddhist values and their spread into village society. These values in turn have come to constitute a reference for ordinary peasants and larger and larger sectors of society are orienting themselves to the new value system.

This diversity is new to Sinhala Buddhism. Earlier there was no real hiatus between the values of the aristocracy and those of the peasants they ruled. By contrast the religious values and ethos that spring from the bourgeoisie and the urban proletariat are not only different from one another but also contrast with traditional village Buddhism. Historically viewed, the crucial components of bourgeois religious values come from Protestant Christianity, especially its Victorian forms. Proletarian religious values, we suggest, at the risk of some oversimplification, go counter to the puritan ethos of the bourgeoisie and find their primary expression in an emotional religiosity derived from Hinduism. The two value systems react on each other. Hindu theistic devotionalism (which is known by the Sanskrit term *bhakti*) has interacted with Sinhala religion in the past as well. Yet our times are characterized by the sheer intensity and spread of *bhakti* religion; and while it starts among the urban poor, it gets accepted by others as a reaction to the fundamentalism and the puritan ethics of Protestant Buddhism. Some of the social forms described here, such as Sarvōdaya, show the influence of the new Buddhism; others, such as the cults emerging from Kataragama, show the influence of *bhakti*. To put the issue differently: if Buddhism has been profoundly affected by Protestantism, Orientalism, and Theosophy, the spirit cults have been influenced by *bhakti*. But other movements among urban Buddhists show the two forces in tension or in reconciliation as contemporary Buddhists strive to define an ontology and world view in the face of rapid social change and economic uncertainty. What we depict in the following pages is religious forms and movements in the making. We have had to freeze them in time, but these forms of life continue to change and grow as we are writing this book.

Cultural Influences

Foreign influences have always played a major part in Sinhala cultural change, and naturally the greatest source of external influence has been India. While Sri Lanka was colonized by European powers, the cultural interchange with India was hampered; this was especially so under the British, who ruled India and Sri Lanka from different ministries and so enhanced the Sinhala sense of separateness from India (see also below). One theme which will recur in this book, however, is how Western—especially British—cultural influence on Buddhism, first evident in the nineteenth century but surviving Independence, is matched by Indian influence on the spirit cults. Since about a quarter of the Sri Lankan population are Tamil Śaiva Hindus and members of virtually all Sri Lankan communities mingle in the Colombo slums, this is hardly surprising. Besides, terrorists are not the only Tamils who cross the twenty-two miles of sea between Sri Lanka and India. Though not all the Hindu influences on our subjects come directly from Tamil Hindus, a great many do. The irony of this will not be lost on our readers.

Interwoven with the theme of Hinduization and with each other are two further themes that will often recur in these pages: the increasing religious prominence of women and the widespread value attached to what we have called hypnomantic states[11] and others have called altered states of consciousness, whether these be classified as possession or meditation. Professor Ioan Lewis has recently[12] pointed out that in many cultures exorcism is the abortion of priesthood. This succinct formulation has great relevance to our material. As we shall show, possession was not infrequent in traditional Sinhala culture but was defined as a malady to be cured by exorcism; those who resisted cure were defined as mad. Now, however, some of the resisters succeed in new roles as ecstatic priests and priestesses.

Professor Lewis's thesis has a second half. Typically, he says, exorcists are male and their patients female. He has drawn examples from Islamic, Christian, and Buddhist cultures to show how the males, acting in the name of a literate culture, a world religion, control a parallel but unofficial religion, centering on possession states, which tends to be only for women

[11] Gananath Obeyesekere, *Medusa's Hair: An Essay on Personal Symbols and Religious Experience* (Chicago: University of Chicago Press, 1981), pp. 169–82.

[12] In a paper delivered to a conference on religious pluralism at Bristol, United Kingdom, in April 1987.

(plus perhaps a few deviant men). Some parts of his model fit our Sinhala material: the exorcists have always been male, and so, for the last thousand years, have the Buddhist religious specialists, the monks (though monks and exorcists have kept well apart); on the other hand, not all those possessed, either the traditional patients or those who have recently resisted "cure," have been women. Nevertheless we would agree that there must be a connection between improvements in the position of women—widespread female literacy and female paid employment, both rare before this century—and the recovery (Buddhist nuns) and invention (priestesses) of public religious roles for women.

Rationality and Post-Protestant Buddhism

Another way of looking at the recent history of Sinhala Buddhism is in terms of rationality. This concept has more than one meaning in the social sciences. Weber himself wrote of "rationality": "It means one thing if we think of the kind of rationalization the systematic thinker performs on the image of the world: an increasing theoretical mastery of reality by means of increasingly precise and abstract concepts. Rationality means another thing if we think of the methodical attainment of a definitely given and practical end by means of an increasingly precise calculation of adequate means."[13] Weber also uses the term "rationality" in a weaker sense to describe coherent, systematic thought;[14] but we avoid this use of the term, as virtually all human thought could be claimed to be at least partly rational in this sense.

The Buddha was rational in Weber's first sense: he gained theoretical mastery of reality by using precise and abstract concepts. Traditional Sinhala religion integrated a spirit religion into the Buddhist ethical and cosmological framework; it was coherent but not rational in either of Weber's strong senses of the term.

Like Western Protestantism, Dharmapāla's thought favored a practical or instrumental rationality. He wrote: "Europe is progressive. Her religion is kept in the background for one day in the week and for six days

[13] Max Weber, "Social Psychology of the World Religions," in *From Max Weber*, ed. Hans Gerth and C. Wright Mills (New York: Oxford University Press, 1976), p. 293. We have slightly emended the translation.

[14] Weber, "Social Psychology," pp. 293–94.

her people are following the dictates of modern science. Sanitation, aesthetic arts, electricity, etc. are what made European and American people great."[15] Castigating what he saw as superstition, Dharmapāla, for all his nativist rhetoric and invention of tradition (of which more below), wished to enlarge the sphere of the secular and of instrumental action. Even Buddhism he saw as contrasted to Christianity (and other religions) by the very fact of its rationality; hence the Protestant Buddhist claim that Buddhism is not a religion but a philosophy. Early Protestant Buddhists tended to follow Dharmapāla at least in favoring rationality in the Weberian sense, for instance in economic life. Many of them clung to parts of the traditional cosmology, as for example the belief in planetary influences, but claimed them to be science congruent with modern Western science. Though the claim is unjustified, it nevertheless represents an attempt at the theoretical mastery of reality. Consequently, Protestant Buddhism in its pure form may be characterized as generally rational in both senses.

The recently evolved Sinhala religion we find rational in neither sense, though it might eventually develop rational forms. In the first place, the incompatible views of the world, and especially of its causal processes, which lingered in the minds of some halfhearted Protestant Buddhists have proliferated and brought confusion to the minds of those from largely traditional backgrounds to whom some modern ideas have percolated. Such confusion is hardly surprising when children from homes that have never repudiated the traditional cosmology receive a few years of formal education predicated on a completely different view of the world and for indoctrination into that new view are virtually dependent on a few Sinhala textbooks. Besides, as we shall show, the traditional cosmology no longer seems to fit the world of daily experience. The resultant cognitive confusion allows for little theoretical rationality in Weber's sense. Second, reinforcing the cognitive confusion, is the increasing difficulty of coping with scarcity and want. This is especially true of urban proletarians and dwellers in the grim neighborhoods of Colombo. A proletarian ethic parallel to the bourgeois ethics of Protestant Buddhism has not developed in the city's working class, and in spite of many years of left politics, Marxist ideology has not taken root as a proletarian ethic. When the inner world makes little sense in terms of rational thought and the outer world of physical

[15] Anagārika Dharmapāla, *Return to Righteousness*, ed. A. Guruge (Colombo: Government Press, 1965), p. 717.

and social reality is grim, one may well resort to other modes of dealing with it. One method of retreat, available in the Buddhist tradition, is to withdraw one's attention from the external world and meditate. Another is to evade the harsh realities of daily life in ecstatic emotion, the love of a god. The former, being a way of restraint, has more appeal to the middle class; the latter, less quiescent, appeals readily to the comparatively uneducated. Both responses we might call, in answer to Weber, remystification.[16] Though the two responses are quite different, our data will show that they can be and sometimes are combined.

We must make clear at this point that we are not suggesting that Buddhist meditation, whether as preached by the Buddha or as understood in the Theravādin tradition, tries to mystify the world or to flee reality; it sets out to do precisely the opposite. Buddhist meditation, as defined in the orthodox tradition, was articulated to the rational life style of the monk who has renounced the lay social world. Modern bourgeois Buddhists attempt to reconcile radical Buddhist meditation with the ordered reality of everyday social life, a reconciliation that is theoretically impossible in Buddhist doctrinal terms.

The next section will expound the traditional Sinhala Buddhist view of the world in both its cognitive and its affective dimensions, its cosmology and its ethos, in such a way as to show its coherence and contrast it with what is taking its place. In the course of this exposition we shall explain the religious roles available in this tradition and give its view of altered states of consciousness. To begin this account it is best to return to the point where we came in: the traditional distinction between what is Buddhism and what is not.

Traditional Sinhala Buddhism

Cognitive Dimensions: Soteriology

Traditionally Sinhala Buddhists believe in gods (and magic); yet, as monks have repeatedly told us, for them "belief in gods has nothing to do with

[16] Gananath Obeyesekere, "Social Change and the Deities: The Rise of the Kataragama Cult in Modern Sri Lanka," *Man*, n.s. 12 (December 1977): 377–78. See also Daniel Bell, "The Return of the Sacred," in *The Winding Passage* (New York: Basic Books, 1980), pp. 324–54.

religion." Like the other religious traditions that began in ancient India, Theravāda Buddhism makes a sharp distinction between the worldly (*laukika*) and the supramundane (*lōkōttara*). The supramundane, the truly "religious," is what concerns and leads to release from worldly existence. Thus what our monastic informants very reasonably equate with Western "religion" (translated in Sinhala as *āgama*) is soteriology, the teaching and practice that lead from the pains of the cycle of rebirth (*sasara dukin*) to salvation. The quest for salvation cannot be conducted through intermediaries. Each of us can only save himself, by following the path proclaimed by the Buddha. That path consists of morality, meditation, and wisdom. It leads to the goal of "seeing things as they are"—ever changing, unsatisfactory, devoid of ultimate essence. These three epithets characterize all phenomenal things, both physical and mental; but in particular they apply to the individual, who is to see himself as ultimately nothing but a bundle of processes kept in concerted motion by the drives arising from his moral and cognitive imperfection. His failure of understanding will be corrected by the realization that "this [i.e., anything; e.g., a sensation] is not I," just as his selfishness will be eliminated in realizing that "this is not mine"; for his existence as a self, as a person, is no more than a pragmatic, worldly convention. To realize this is to experience *nirvāṇa*, the "blowing out" of the fires of greed, hatred, and delusion. This extinction of ignorant craving (*not* of the self, for that never existed, it was but a figment of the imagination) means that there is nothing left to be reborn and so experience further suffering. The Enlightened Being lives out the remainder of his natural life in equanimous benignity, without the normal false sense of involvement in what he observes.

One of the constituents of every living being is will, in particular moral will. It is fundamental to the Buddha's teaching that each of us has free will and can act virtuously or wickedly—though of course moral habits may be hard to reverse. And equally fundamental is the belief that the universe runs according to a moral law that will produce rewards for virtue and punishments for vice—unless the whole process is terminated by the attainment of *nirvāṇa*. For a wicked creature such attainment is however impossible. Since morality consists in acts of will, good intentions, it is itself the necessary first stage in that purification and refinement of the mind which constitutes what the West calls spiritual progress. Denying the existence of a soul, Buddhist doctrine considers the mind to be the instrument of salvation.

The Buddhist doctrine (Dhamma) is always the same and always valid, whether anyone knows it or not. It is periodically rediscovered and preached by exceptional beings, Buddhas, who by that preaching found what Buddhists call a *sāsana*, literally a "Teaching." A *sāsana* is the empirical appearance of Buddhism among men, and each *sāsana* is of limited duration. We are living in the *sāsana* of Gotama Buddha; he is "our" Buddha: thanks to his preaching we can attain Enlightenment. A being who takes a vow that he too will become a Buddha and found a *sāsana* is called a *bodhisattva*.

Cognitive Dimensions: Cosmology

In every society that adopted it, Buddhism has always been associated with a rich and complex cosmology. The cosmologies of all traditional societies tend to equate the natural order with the social order and both with the moral order; and probably none have done so more thoroughly than that of classical India, in its Hindu, Buddhist, and Jain variants. Sinhala Buddhism has inherited that classical Indian cosmology and added only minor local modifications. Thus, on the one hand, it holds that the world is devoid of religious value or significance; it is mere uncreated space, without beginning or end in time. On the other hand, all the beings that populate it reflect the moral order, which *is* the natural order. Wicked beings are beneath us in hells, virtuous beings above us in heavens, we humans and other orders of beings in whom good and bad are more evenly mixed are roughly in the middle; and even our human social order is but a reflection of vice and virtue in past lives. However, the mixture of pleasure and pain which is the human lot is essential to attaining salvation. Lower beings are suffering too much to think with sufficient clarity, gods are too comfortable to be fully aware of suffering and hence feel no urgency about escaping from it. Only men and women can rise above gods to leave the cycle of existence forever.

Gods and demons are, like us, evanescent inhabitants of this ever-changing cosmos. Like us, they are subject to decay, death, and re-becoming. Indeed, in a sense they *are* us, for if we are good, we may be reborn as gods, if bad, as meaner spirits—in due course to die again. For the universe is a moral hierarchy: power, comfort, and longevity all increase as one ascends the universe, an ascent that is itself the result of virtue. All, however, are irrelevant to salvation, for that is something which no being has the power to grant or withhold. If a god favors you or a demon punishes you, that is only what you deserved. Beings who give others pleasure or pain are from the point of view of the recipient mere instruments of the karmic process (so that demons are rather like cosmic policemen); from their own point of view, on the other hand, they too are moral agents with free will who will be rewarded and punished for their intentional acts.

It is important to understand that in this traditional Buddhist cosmology any god, such as Viṣṇu, is really performing a *role*, like "the king of this country." The present Viṣṇu will eventually die, and then some other being will be reborn as Viṣṇu, with the same powers and attributes. The life of a god like Viṣṇu is so long that this is of no practical consequence for one's dealings with him. But knowledge of his limitations does color one's attitude towards him, for since being Viṣṇu is really a role, the being in that role can be expected to act like Viṣṇu, not in some arbitrary or capricious manner. These gods do not "move in a mysterious way."

In this view of the world there is no such thing as unjust suffering: Buddhism provides a solution to the "problem of evil."[17] This coherence can be seen as reassuring or daunting. It is no doubt reassuring that the world is a perfectly just place—unless you feel yourself less than perfect. In *Precept and Practice* the ways in which Theravādin Buddhists have tried to mitigate the rigor of the system without contravening orthodoxy have been discussed.

The most important of these ways is what is generally known in English, rather misleadingly, as transfer of merit. When one does something virtuous (*pina*), such as feeding monks, one invites the gods to empathize in the merit. Since virtue is a mental state, someone who merely observes a good deed may become as virtuous as the doer, or even more so. The idea—which goes as far back as the Pāli Canon—is that in gratitude to the doer for calling their attention to his good deed the local deities will protect and help him.

This is the main doctrinal link between Buddhism and the spirit religion. It offers a charter for recognizing the existence of gods and even for interacting with them, though not for worshipping them. That however it does not prohibit. The converse position is also acknowledged. If the

[17] Buddhism has no theory of evil strictly comparable with the Christian. The "problem of evil" referred to here is that of the "theodicy."

gods do men favors, they are acquiring merit like any other moral agent. This is recognized in rituals of the spirit religion by stating the fact (*pin dīma*) and thus in effect saying thank you, but it is not of great practical importance for religious behavior.

There is another ancient link between Buddhism and spirits; this one concerns malevolent or potentially malevolent spirits. The only truly Buddhist way to deal with such spirits is to preach to them and convert them to benignity. Certain canonical texts do just this. They form the nucleus of a body of texts for apotropaic protection (*pirit*) that Buddhist monks (or rarely laity) recite on various culturally determined occasions to avert misfortune.

All this serves to illustrate that the Buddhist universe is not deterministic. Sometimes when people comment on an unexpected turn of fortune, "that's my *karma*," the remark may sound fatalistic; but it is no more so than the Western "just my luck." One cannot know what acts in past lives may produce results in this one; but one is responsible now for fashioning one's future. Among the acts that may serve to improve the future is winning the favor of the powerful, both human and divine. And just as one can normally approach a lord only through an intermediary, one normally uses the services of an intermediary to approach a god. It is no accident that the basic Sinhala word for a priest of gods, *kapuvā*, means precisely "go-between." (The term is usually extended by some minor honorific, e.g., *kapurāḷa*.)

Authority in the Cosmos

The traditional Sinhala Buddhist pantheon had a clearly articulated authority structure. It was legitimated in the ancient chronicle, the *Mahāvaṃsa*. According to this text the Buddha entrusted the care of his religion (*sāsana*), which he predicted would survive in Sri Lanka, to Śakra, the king of the gods, and Śakra in turn gave charge of it to Viṣṇu. Thus, although the Buddha is conceived of as no longer in the world or active in its affairs, his authority is still effective by delegation through warrants (*varam*). The Buddha gave a warrant to Śakra and he gave one to Viṣṇu, and all authority, even that of demons, is thus handed down from the top.

The system, as we understand it from precolonial sources, is modelled on the administrative structure of the Kandyan Kingdom. Viṣṇu shares the overlordship of Sri Lanka with three other deities; the territory is partitioned among them. The idea that there are four guardian deities is found in many societies, because there are commonly considered to be four main directions in the compass. What distinguishes the traditional Sinhala Buddhist pantheon is the structure of the system. Thus, although there have always been four such guardian deities (often called the Four Warrant Gods), their precise identity has not been stable through space and time.

A set of Twelve Gods below the Four Gods in the hierarchy derive their warrants from them.[18] Again, the enduring feature is the number; the personnel vary. These gods are less powerful and less moral than the Four. Their moral ambivalence puts them in the category below god and above demon, the interstitial category of "godling" (*dēvatā*). Such "godlings" are often referred to as gods out of politeness, but are definitely a cut below the true gods. While most of the higher gods historically derive from India, the Twelve Gods are (whether in myth or fact is hard to determine) deified local lords (*baṇḍāra*). These minor gods are thus morally on much the same level as human beings. They in their turn license the demons and other evil spirits.

The traditional spirit religion of Sinhala Buddhists is carried on with the aid of professional intermediaries, mostly hereditary specialists. Just as the spirits are in hierarchic categories, so their priests are in corresponding categories with distinct names. The priests, who are paid for performing their roles, usually put their clients in touch with the spirits they serve by having the spirits possess them. Though such possession is sometimes called "shamanic," there is a distinction to be made here. The classic shaman detaches his spirit from his body and goes on journeys; he returns, reanimates his body, and can tell of his experiences. This kind of mind-body dissociation has not been culturally normal in Sri Lanka and is not part of any role performance. In possession, on the other hand, another spirit enters the body and takes over; it commonly holds conversations with clients in something called "gods' language," normal Sinhala sometimes mixed with nonsense. What happens to the possessed person's normal mind/spirit/personality during possession is a question people do not think to ask. There is a common procedure for becoming possessed—

[18] For a recent discussion of the Twelve Gods see Gananath Obeyesekere, *The Cult of the Goddess Pattini* (Chicago: University of Chicago Press, 1984), pp. 285–93.

swinging the head and breathing fast and deeply so as to hyperoxygenate. The onset of possession is marked by violent trembling, which usually begins in the legs.

The traditional spirit religion offers no professional roles to women. This fits the fact that for the purposes of this religion various "impurities" are considered to make one unfit to be in communion with the gods, and menstruation and childbirth are among these impurities. Buddhism takes no cognizance of such impurities. Thus a menstruating woman may visit a monk or attend a Buddhist temple, but she may not approach a shrine of the gods.

There is some correspondence between the spirit hierarchy and the human caste hierarchy of the specialists who act as their intermediaries. The *kapurāḷa*, the priest for the "godlings," comes from the dominant caste (in Kandyan areas normally the *goyigama*); the *kaṭṭāḍirāḷa*, the priest from the demons, is usually low caste (typically *beravā*), though a higher-caste male may exercise that profession if he chooses.[19]

We have seen that spirits can be worshipped or propitiated for worldly ends, just like powerful people, and indeed much of the terminology of worship is common to transactions with spirits and with human beings. Traditionally Sinhala Buddhist villagers have not been all that respectful to their deities and have stuck to their view of the relationship as based on quid pro quo. The marooned British sailor Robert Knox recorded in the late seventeenth century that when a godling failed to deliver the villagers said: "What manner of god is he? Shit in his mouth!"[20] Lesser spirits may suffer even worse than abuse and neglect. A class of unpleasant spirits called *prēta*, though they are in theory likely to be one's own (not very virtuous) ancestors, or even parents, are exorcised by such ignominious devices as trapping them in a box which is then thrown down the privy or into the ocean. All this is a far cry from the attitudes now becoming prevalent.

Corresponding and closely related to the moral hierarchy of categories of beings in the universe is the logical hierarchy of levels of causation. The Buddhist *karma* provides an overarching causal framework which determines one's station and basic attributes (especially moral propensities) at

[19] The distinction between *kapurāḷa* and *kaṭṭāḍirāḷa* is very clear in the Low Country, but these roles overlap elsewhere. Related terms are *yakdessā* and *anumätirāḷa*.

[20] Robert Knox, *Historical Relation*, p. 83.

birth. Within one's life one's good or bad fortune (one's karmic deserts) is instantiated, again on a broad scale, by the planetary influences that may be predicted or diagnosed by astrology. Within this operate the other influences that we may consider both natural and supernatural. An example may make this clear. If I have an upset stomach, this may be because I have eaten bad food or because a hungry person unwittingly cast an envious eye on me while I was eating—or both. The latter is the kind of explanation I am more likely to get if I consult some "go-between" (*kapurāḷa*). I can take medicine from a doctor and/or have a small white magic ritual performed by a minor specialist. I fail to get better. An astrologer determines that this is an inauspicious planetary period for me. I can sit it out or try to improve matters by holding a *bali* ceremony, with rather grander specialists and more expense. If I get well, that diagnosis was correct and the remedy worked. If I die, I must be paying for the sins of a former life—perhaps I once poisoned someone. I died because I ate bad food; but behind that explanation lies the question why I ate the bad food; there lies in fact a series of questions—and answers. The various causal explanations are integrated into the overarching framework of *karma*. By contrast, among the exemplars of modern-day Buddhism, both questions and answers often seem eclectic, random, and arbitrary, offering no grounds either for choosing between alternative explanations or for relating them to each other.

Traditional Religion in Action: The Ritual Function

In most societies religion performs several functions. As a soteriology, it provides life with meaning and a sense of purpose; that is the function of Buddhism in Sinhala society. Then it answers to practical individual predicaments as they occur; we have noted how the spirit religion has this thaumaturgic function for Sinhala Buddhists. It also serves to mark and celebrate events of communal importance, whether they involve everyone in the community at once, like calendrical festivals, or concern the individual as he passes through the statuses that are stages in the life cycle. For the most part, these communal functions in traditional Sinhala society are the province of the spirit religion, not of Buddhism. There is a major Buddhist festival at Vesak, the annual commemoration of the Buddha's birth, Enlightenment, and death (all on the same day), and we shall see that the lunar calendar is of some liturgical significance; but such communal events as harvest festivals and such communal crises as threats of epidemic tend to be signalized by performances in the spirit religion and center on the shrine of the local guardian deity. What is even more striking is that Buddhism has very little to do with the individual life cycle. Only at death, the ideal occasion for recalling impermanence, does Buddhism provide anything analogous to a sacrament; only at and after the funeral do monks officiate. Birth, puberty, marriage, etc. are traditionally secular (*laukika*) events for Sinhala Buddhists.

Buddhist Roles and Patterns of Practice

Essential to the traditional Theravādin view of the world is the distinction between the religious statuses of monk and layman. While Buddhism is not esoteric and its doctrines are accessible to all, those who wish to put those doctrines into practice beyond a certain point are expected to join the Sangha, and so renounce all sexual and economic activity. Slightly oversimplifying, one may say that the laity are to practice morality, the first of the three components of the Buddhist path to salvation, but to practice concentration they need to join the Sangha; and without meditation one cannot hope to attain wisdom. (The precise relation between concentration and meditation will be explained below.)

The fact that monks embody the values of the whole society is given symbolic expression in the dignity they are accorded. They are habitually addressed and referred to as "lords," with further honorific vocabulary; and even the highest layman in the land—once the King, now the President—accords them formal precedence.

In theory the Sangha is open to all. In practice, since the Order of Nuns has died out, it is not open to women; and at times it has not been open to men of low caste. Though the modern Sangha consists of fraternities that largely follow caste lines, the order as a whole has for well over a century admitted men of virtually any caste status, so that is no longer a major issue. It has, however, been assumed in traditional Buddhism that because of the institutional decay of Buddhism—a development predicted in the scriptures—the higher stages of spiritual progress are in practice virtually inaccessible to women, there being no institutional setting in which they could learn to meditate. One may add that the same theory of decline has tended to the view that even males in these degenerate times no longer attain Enlightenment: it has been widely held that even members of the Sangha are mostly *puthujjana*, ordinary unenlightened beings who are not yet assured of realizing *nirvāṇa* even within the next seven lives.

This pessimism about the state of Buddhism relates to an ancient distinction within the Sangha. Monks formally assume one of two "burdens," i.e., responsibilities. They either take up the "book burden" or the "insight burden." Only the latter devote themselves wholeheartedly to the practice that leads directly to Enlightenment. The majority have assumed responsibility for "books," that is, the scriptures, which they are to copy out, memorize, preach, and teach, thus keeping Buddhism alive and so preserving for others the chance to seek Enlightenment. This distribution of duties has tended to coincide with a later formal distinction between "village-dwelling" and "forest-dwelling" monastic lineages. The monks with whom villagers come into daily contact are the village-dwelling fraternity, who are not aiming themselves to attain Enlightenment in this life and who in most cases perhaps do little or no meditation.

Theravāda Buddhism has a traditional list of "ten good deeds": generosity, morality, mental development, transferring merit, empathizing in the merit transferred, doing service (to elders), respectful behavior, teaching, listening (to religious teaching), holding right views. Although all are strictly relevant to the third, mental development, in as much as that is the same as religious progress, it is commonly more narrowly understood as meditation; we postpone its discussion.

The two that are most important for the laity are the first two. Generosity is traditionally understood in both a wide and a narrow sense, the latter referring particularly to the material support of the Sangha. The role of "donor" (*dāyakayā*) is ascribed to a village householder by virtue of his membership in a community that supports a village monk or monks. Morality is understood as observance of what the West has come to call the "precepts." The five that are always binding are not to kill, steal, be unchaste (not further defined), lie, or take intoxicants that may lead, through carelessness, to infringing the first four. On the quarter days of the lunar calendar, and especially on full-moon days, it has been customary for those who could spare the time (mostly old people and some housewives) to take what are known as "eight precepts": sexual activity is completely barred for the twenty-four-hour period, and one takes no solid food after noon, watches no shows or entertainments, wears no adornments, and avoids luxurious beds.

There is also a list of "ten precepts" that adds to the eight only foreswearing the use of gold and silver (which is taken to include all money). By tradition, these ten precepts are taken by two categories of person. They constitute the code of conduct of novices, that is, those who have entered the Order but have not yet received the higher ordination (for which the minimum age is twenty); and indeed they embody the moral principles applicable to *all* monks. (In fact, one might say that only the first four are really principles; the rest are rules of abstention.) The ten precepts are also taken by a few elderly people, one might say "retired" people, who then habitually wear white clothes and spend most of their time in religious activities, usually at temples. Though the classical (Pāli) term for a Buddhist layman (*upāsaka*, feminine: *upāsikā*) strictly refers to anyone, by custom it has been reserved as a temporary or permanent designation for those who take the eight or the ten precepts respectively. It is significant that in common parlance such people have been commonly known as "mother" and "father" (*upāsikammā*, *upasākappacci*[21]); they are of the older generation and indeed often widowed.

The highest religious status traditionally open to women is thus to be a "ten-precept mother" (*dasa sil māṇiyō*). In Chapter 8 below we shall explain how this status system has recently been adapted to new circumstances.

Meditation

At this point we need to explain some fundamental technicalities of Buddhist meditation (*bhāvanā*). Though the ultimate authoritative texts are all to be found in the Pāli Canon, their content has been systematically presented in a fifth-century A.D. compendium, the *Visuddhimagga* ("Path of Purification") by Buddhaghosa,[22] and it is to this medieval work that subsequent teachers and meditators most commonly have referred. Though meditation is thus described in books, according to the (pan-In-

[21] This Kandyan term is perhaps not widespread: *upāsaka unnähe* is commoner.

[22] Translated as *The Path of Purification* by Bhikkhu Ñāṇamoḷi (Kandy: Buddhist Publication Society, 1964).

dian) tradition one can only learn it from a teacher with whom one has a stable and intimate relationship, so that he knows one's character and capacities. Meditation is taught one-to-one; and in the Buddhist context this means by one monk to another.

According to the *Visuddhimagga* there are two kinds of meditation: "calming" (*samatha*) meditation and "insight" (*vipassanā*) meditation. The former aims to culminate in a state of absorption (*samādhi*), the latter in "seeing things as they are" (*yathā-bhūta-dassana*), which is tantamount to *nirvāṇa*. The former is thus nothing but a propaedeutic for the latter; it is normally a necessary preparation, but exceptionally gifted people may undertake insight meditation directly without the preliminary training of calming. The early stages of this insight meditation consist in practicing "awareness" (*sati*) of one's body, feelings, states of mind, and thoughts. This awareness leads one on to the realization that all phenomenal things, both physical and mental, are impermanent, unsatisfactory, and without essence: the three characteristics are inseparably intertwined. This (as explained above) is to realize *nirvāṇa*. Such a realization is far more than normal understanding, but it involves no alteration in normal consciousness. On the contrary, it is a state of supreme lucidity. The meditator is aware of everything available to his senses but completely controls his attention.

If we go by the texts alone, it is unlikely that even "calming" meditation aims at anything but increasing suppression of the instinctive emotions and control over one's attention. The part of the *Visuddhimagga* devoted to calming meditation discusses *techniques*—there are forty possible objects to work on (*kammaṭṭhāna*) in order to attain absorption—while the part devoted to insight meditation is philosophical; but this difference in approach reflects only what is appropriate to the different stages of one's progress. At this preliminary stage the meditator's aim is complete "one-pointedness of mind" (*cittassa ekaggatā*); but this should be attained without loss of lucidity. However, here the tradition contains a certain ambiguity which is of great importance for this book.

In developing and formulating his meditative path, the Buddha was working within the general tradition of Indian yoga. The term *samādhi*, which we have translated "absorption," is common to all branches of this tradition, and there is no doubt that in Hindu tradition this term denotes what we generally call a trance, in which consciousness is altered and awareness of the normal world of sense experience is much diminished or even abolished. The Buddha divided progress along the path to absorption into four stages (called *jhāna*),[23] in which normal discursive thought (*vitakka-vicāra*) is progressively eliminated. By comparing Pāli texts with early Hindu texts, Michael Barnes[24] has shown that the Buddha's concept of absorption was distinctive in that for him the gaining of concentration did not imply a loss of awareness and lucidity. Empirical discussion of the states of mind of bygone meditators is obviously risky. But the most cursory acquaintance with the pan-Indian tradition suffices to show that *in fact* this path to absorption does very easily lead the meditator to a trance state. Discussions with contemporary lay Buddhists who are serious meditators show us that they do tend to experience hallucinations (of any of the senses) and other sensations one can roughly label as characteristic of "trance." We shall show in our last chapter that this seems to be the opinion of greater experts than ourselves and is of considerable importance for understanding the contemporary religious scene.

Little or none of the above is known to the traditional laity who practice "meditation" by reciting Pāli verses at temples on holy days. These verses are in fact on some of the *topics* of meditation, and by concentrating on their meaning the laity are practicing elementary calming meditation—elementary in the sense that they have no expectation of attaining even the lowest classified stage of absorption, the first *jhāna*. The "calming" topics on which the laity have customarily meditated are loving-kindness (*maitrī*), the virtues of the Buddha (*Buduguṇa*), and the repulsiveness of the body, which inevitably decays and dies. The last of these was especially appropriate to the old people who traditionally have taken the ten precepts in order to end their lives well.

The Traditional Buddhist Ethos

Buddhism is an ethic of intention that sees as the highest goal of life a dispassionate lucidity. Even at its least sophisticated level the Sinhala Buddhist tradition has been informed by these values. It harmonizes with the ethic of intention that the only formulation of what is binding on all

[23] Like other technical terms in this section, *jhāna* is Pāli. Some of our informants used the Sanskrit equivalent, *dhyāna*.

[24] Michael Barnes, "The Buddhist Way of Deliverance: A Comparison between the Pāli Canon and the Yoga Praxis of the Great Epic" (M.Litt. thesis, Oxford, 1977).

Buddhists, the "five precepts," is presented not as commandments but as undertakings that function as ethical guidelines. Within these guidelines it has been possible to incorporate the diverse moral codes and cultural norms indigenous to the societies that have accepted Buddhism. The undertaking not to kill, for example, has not generally been so interpreted as to impose vegetarianism—never a norm for Sinhala Buddhists. Again, the third precept enjoins abstention from illicit sexual behavior, but Buddhism nowhere attempts to define the right kind of marriage for laymen, and Buddhist societies have permitted monogamy, polyandry, and polygamy—all of which have indeed been customary in various segments of Sinhala Buddhist society. This indifference to lay mores, so long as they did not violate the precepts, explains the fact mentioned above, that neither monks nor Buddhist sacred objects have been involved in rites of passage in traditional Sri Lanka—excepting only death rituals. On the other hand, where lay customs violated Buddhist principles the religion has changed them; for example, animal sacrifice was almost completely eradicated from Sinhala Buddhist society.

We have seen that Buddhist ideology puts a premium on awareness and self-control. For instance, drunkenness is condemned in as much as it leads to a loss of self-control. In accordance with this principle, Sinhala Buddhists have traditionally considered possession to be an undesirable state, for one possessed has no self-control but acts at the will of another being. Normally someone who becomes possessed (*āvēśa*, *ārūḍha*) is considered to be ill, a "patient" (*āturayā*) who must be exorcised, and from this it follows that spirits who possess people are not good spirits but demons (*yakku*) or ghosts (*prētayō*, *maḷa prētayō*, or *maḷa yakku*) and bad ghosts at that.

The one exception in which the culture has allowed possession is that of the priest who becomes possessed by a minor deity or godling in order to give the god's answer to the human clients' problems, an activity known as delivering oracles (*śāstra kiyanavā*). That this proves the rule is demonstrated by the stringent prohibition against becoming possessed on a holy day, that is, on a day that should be devoted to Buddhist religious observance; thus priests do not even open their shrines on that day. (They traditionally explain their abstention by saying that on holy days the gods meet in assembly and so are too busy to come down to earth and attend to our affairs.) Note that even priests become possessed only by minor, local deities, never by gods of high rank, like the four guardian deities. The functionaries of lower spirits—exorcists and devil-dancers—may also become temporarily possessed during the performance of their duties. But all these possessions are recognized to be *controlled* phenomena, induced at will by a specialist in the course of discharging his function. Anything further is regarded as an aberration requiring remedy.

The temper of traditional Buddhism is opposed to strong emotion in any form, even if the object of that emotion be religious or divine. Kindness is extolled, but not enthusiasm. The highest term of praise for a person in Sinhala society is *śānta dānta*, meaning "calm and controlled." This is not to say that the religion is without emotional content. Every Buddhist occasion begins with "taking refuge" in the "Three Jewels": the Buddha, the Dhamma, the Sangha; the Buddha image and other sacred objects are worshipped; even the word *bhaktiya*, the Hindu term for religious devotion, is occasionally used (though normally in the form *bätiya*). But the state of mind induced by Buddhist devotional exercises is a serene joy, a tranquillity the very opposite of ecstasy. This is the nub of what has changed.

Important Departures from Tradition

Reserving lengthy case studies for later chapters, we shall now offer some data to characterize the new religious climate; our aim is to draw a contrast with the older patterns of thought, practice, and feeling presented in the above pages. Before we embark on what is bound to appear an account of confusion and discontinuity, we must remind the reader that one central feature of traditional Buddhism has survived almost unscathed. Buddhism is still seen as the only true soteriology: gods, magic, and other agencies may provide benefits for this life, but only following the way taught by the Buddha will finally solve the miseries of worldly existence. We have come across one man who prays to the god Kataragama that he may attain *nirvāṇa*, but we believe that this is still exceptional. If that central distinction between the worldly and the supramundane should be broken down and people come to believe that a god can grant them salvation, it will be difficult to claim that they remain Theravāda Buddhists in any meaningful sense.

What we are describing goes on, as it were, beneath the canopy of the Buddha's doctrine of salvation. We are concerned with "practical religion," as Bryan Wilson has explained it:

> Whilst the higher religions at their most elevated and philosophical levels may provide a set of intellectual propositions that answer (in the religion's own terms—which are not terms that need convince an outsider) "ultimate questions," practical religion, religion at the everyday level, has been preoccupied with other issues. . . . These ultimate concerns may be of limited consequence in the everyday life circumstances of those who, nominally, embrace the teachings of one of the higher religions. The social significance of religion has rather lain in the provision of categories and symbols that facilitate simultaneously man's comprehension of his circumstances and his capacity to evaluate them and to cope with them emotionally.[25]

The Changing Pantheon

We begin with changes in the pantheon. The traditional cosmology does not explicitly envisage change in the divine hierarchy, but scholars know that it has occurred; the structure, however, has remained constant. Thus, historical evidence shows that while Sri Lanka has always had four guardian deities, they have not always been the same four. The three to join Viṣṇu (whose place is presumably guaranteed by the *Mahāvaṃsa*) have varied, but come from a list of five: Nātha, Pattinī, Saman, Vibhīṣaṇa, Kataragama. The god Nātha, who was associated especially with Sinhala royalty, became virtually obsolescent when the Sinhala monarchy was destroyed in 1815; he is often identified with the next Buddha, Maitreya, though it has been suggested that originally he was identified with the Bodhisattva (i.e., future Buddha) Avalokiteśvara.[26] There is no inconsistency in a god's being a future Buddha, for all gods must die, and so they too may be on the way to a final existence (in however remote a future) as a Buddha. In fact there is a structural reason why all Four Warrant Gods should be Bodhisattvas: they guard the Buddha's Tooth Relic in Kandy and thus also the welfare and stability of all Buddhists in Sri Lanka. Though their ultimate attainment of Buddhahood can be considered sure, they must be at very different stages along the path. Viṣṇu is unambigu-

[25] *Religion in Sociological Perspective* (Oxford and New York: Oxford University Press, 1982), p. 10.

[26] Senarat Paranavitana, "Mahayanism in Ceylon," *Ceylon Journal of Science* 2, no. 1 (1928): 35–71.

ously very good and is thus felt to be a Bodhisattva. Pattinī has the problem of being female; before becoming a Buddha she will have to be reborn as a male. At the bottom end of the scale is Kataragama, who is traditionally held to be capable of bad acts and so has a long way to go to achieve release; structurally he is a Bodhisattva, but he does not have the virtuous and compassionate character normally associated with that status.

The substitution of one god for another in the status of guardian of Sri Lanka may occur simply through confusion resulting from the breakdown of accepted conventions regarding iconography. Sometimes there is a blending of two deities—a process familiar in comparative mythology. We have seen in recently constructed temples such anomalies (in terms of the traditional mythology) as the iconic confusion of Nātha (Maitreya) with Saman: Nātha acquires Saman's mount, the elephant, and/or Saman acquires Nātha's lotus (held in the right hand). To be specific, let us cite but one temple, Bellanvila. This wealthy temple in a Colombo suburb, which has thousands of visitors every week, has a series of shrines built since the mid-1950s. Here Nātha's mount is a grey elephant. The priest who showed us around said, when questioned, that this was not like Saman's elephant, because the latter was white; however we saw that the elephant accompanying Saman's image was in fact grey, though the one painted on the curtain in front of the image was white. At the same temple both Hūniyam and Däḍimuṇḍa (see below) have horses as mounts, which presumably both reflects the fact that some people confuse the two and promotes that confusion. Moreover, at this temple Vibhīṣaṇa, who is not generally an important deity nowadays, *also* is shown with a horse mount, which is untraditional; perhaps he acquired it because like Hūniyam he has small fangs or tusks. The iconography at the big Colombo temples is widely copied by the professional craftsmen who design and decorate temples throughout the island.

What is more interesting than these simple iconographic confusions and has not previously been commented on is that there is a process of upward mobility in the pantheon, a mobility that need not destroy its structure. Gods who at one time are low enough to take an interest in human affairs gradually move up into a kind of honorary retirement as "great gods"; minor deities of rather mixed or neutral character move up to full godhead; their place as "godlings" (*dēvatā*) is taken by (ex-) demons. Canonizing gods by calling them future Buddhas is an aspect of this process. This upward mobility has existed since ancient times; for instance, the gods who inhabit the lowest heaven, that of the Four Great Kings,[27] were once active interveners in human affairs, but now serve only to decorate the front walls of Buddhist shrines. The mobility is fueled by the internal logic of the traditional Buddhist ideology: the more favors a god grants, the more compassionate (and powerful) he must be; so in this Buddhist universe, where virtue is its own reward, the good god drifts ever higher up the scale of being and thus loses direct contact with the world of men. At the same time he loses his punitive aspect and so must be replaced as "the man on the spot" by someone inferior in the cosmic administration, probably by a member of his retinue (*pirisa* or *pirivara*). When in the eighteenth century the god Viṣṇu moved from his shrine at Alutnuvara to Kandy, where he was in official residence as one of the four guardian deities, his local servant Dädimuṇḍa took over the main shrine, acquired Viṣṇu's title of Alutnuvara Deviyō ("God of Alutnuvara"), and became far more important. It is clear from Kandyan folk poetry (e.g., *Galakäpu Sähälla*) that Dädimuṇḍa was earlier a godling commonly known as Dēvatā Baṇḍāra, a euphemistic title meaning "Chieftain of the Godlings."[28]

Having pointed out this dynamic, we may add that this cosmology will normally lead to certain correlations from the observer's point of view. These covariable characteristics of a deity are on the one hand certain empirical features: antiquity, geographical diffusion, and extent of mention in literature; and on the other hand certain ascribed characteristics: association with Buddhist doctrine, logical consistency of mythology, concern for ethics, and lack of interest in thaumaturgy. Our formulation further implies that time creates its own dynamic, as mere antiquity makes a god drift up and out of the pantheon with which man may interact.

What we now seem to be witnessing is a breakdown of the whole traditional structure of the pantheon, especially of its authority structure. What best symbolizes this breakdown is the rise of the personal guardian deity (*iṣṭa dēvatā*). The very concept may not be a recent import into the Sinhala Buddhist world; its popularity certainly is. In Hinduism the idea is ancient. A Hindu is free to choose a particular deity, or particular form of a deity, whom he adores and who will in turn be his loyal patron. The relationship between god and devotee is at the same time asymmetrical and extremely emotional: analogies commonly employed are the relations

[27] These were Dhṛtarāṣṭra, Virūḍha, Virūpākṣa, Vaiśravaṇa.

[28] On Dēvatā Baṇḍāra alias Dädimuṇḍa see Obeyesekere, *Pattini*, esp. pp. 312–21.

of owner to slave and of (polygamous) lover to pining mistress. God cannot be constrained by his devotee's devotion (*bhakti*); but the very term, which comes from "sharing," indicates that he is sure to reciprocate by extending his grace. In Hindu *bhakti* religion, this grace may extend from trivial worldly favors to ultimate salvation. One's relations with one's "chosen deity" (the literal meaning of the Sanskrit term *iṣṭa dēvatā*) are intimate and personal and need not affect one's public religious life or one's duties as a member of society. They do not normally subvert or call into question the moral order.

The *iṣṭa dēvatā*—it seems significant that the Sanskrit term is still being used—does not merely represent the creation of a private sphere of religious emotion disconnected from traditional Buddhism and the fragmentation of religious authority. What is most important, from a Buddhist perspective, is that the three deities from whom the vast majority of the people we have studied are selecting their guardian deity are all traditionally considered of dubious moral character. They are Kataragama, Kālī, and Hūniyam. We shall here merely indicate enough of the character of each to suggest that making them one's protector and object of adoration, rather than relying on the moral order inherent in the cosmos, has disturbing implications for the moral order (or lack thereof) of contemporary society.

We have already shown elsewhere that in practical religion nowadays Kataragama has eclipsed Viṣṇu and the other members of the group of Four Warrant Gods. A study of their four shrines in the center of Kandy, the precolonial capital, showed that Kataragama is receiving several times as many requests (and hence offerings) as the other three gods together.[29] This is because the other gods are associated either with curing diseases for which modern medicine provides surer remedies or with general benevolence; but what most people want is help in coping with the particular stresses of modern life, for which they tend to think that a god as morally scrupulous as Viṣṇu may not be the most effective patron. The rise in importance of the god's main shrine at Kataragama (whence this version of Śiva's son Skanda derives his local name) is even more spectacular and will concern us below; we attribute it to the same causes.

Of all the national guardian deities, Kataragama is the only one who by tradition could be approached for immoral purposes (black magic); indeed

[29] Obeyesekere, "Social Change," p. 392.

his moral tone used to be so low that an old Kandyan monk could describe him to us as a demon in charge of cemeteries! This is an extreme view; but certainly informants from a traditional background could concur in ascribing to Kataragama (and to him alone of the major deities) the epithet "harsh" (*sära*). His immorality appears also in his having two wives, or rather, a wife and a mistress (*hora gǟni*, literally "stealth woman"), a fact which his annual festival celebrates. Yet there is no doubt that for masses of Sinhala Buddhists, whether or not they consider Kataragama their personal deity, he has quite eclipsed all the other traditional gods.

Two other gods, lower down the scale than Kataragama, are rising meteorically. One of them is Kālī, the great Indian goddess who is most commonly shown slaying a buffalo (demon). She has long been worshipped by Tamils, but until recently she had a clear Hindu identity and was not considered a significant member of the Buddhist pantheon at all; at the most, she was a demoness. It could hardly have been otherwise, because those Buddhists who knew anything about her at all were aware that she receives blood sacrifices (*bili*), which for them could only be the attribute of a demon. At Munnēssarama we have seen self-confessed Buddhists bring cockerels and goats as sacrifices to be slaughtered for Kālī in payment of a vow. Some lodged in the nearby Buddhist temple with their prospective victims, and one lady with a cockerel wore the white clothes appropriate for Buddhist religious observances, a startling visual paradox. The vast majority of Buddhists, however, aware of the first precept of Buddhism, still regard such sacrifices with horror.

Kālī is sometimes divided into two, Bhadra ("Auspicious") Kālī and Sohon ("Cemetery") Kālī, thus isolating her benign and her terrible aspects in a way reminiscent of her treatment in Hinduism—compare the division into (benign) Durgā and (awful) Kālī in Bengal. We shall see, however, that the situation is complicated, for it may be the terrifying goddess who has the greater power to help and to bless (Chapter 4). The most important shrine to Kālī in Sri Lanka is that at Munnēssarama, and she is acquiring many new shrines in the Colombo area.

The other deity whose influence has shown a remarkable increase is Hūniyam/Sūniyam.[30] (In Sinhala there has been a historical phonetic shift of

[30] In Sinhala a final *m* is pronounced as a pure nasal sound, much like English *ng*. If a word beginning with a *t* or *d* follows closely, as in *Hūniyam dēvatā*, this is pronounced as *n*. We have preserved the historically correct spelling, as the written sources tend to do.

s to *h* before a vowel, and in many words both forms are extant; to use the *s* tends to sound more formal.) The etymology of *hūniyam* has been long debated; but it is certain that the word means "sorcery" or "black magic," and the spirit bearing that name is the personification of black magic. Traditionally he is thus a demon (*yakā*). He has always been patronized principally in the Low Country, though he is not unknown elsewhere and his principal shrine is at Käbällāva in the Kurunägala District. From ca. 1950 to ca. 1975 he had a famous residence at the Kataragama temple at Lunāva, just south of Colombo. He was installed there shortly after Independence and gained fame especially through the obsequious devotions of a governor of the Central Bank who was removed from office and threatened with prosecution on a criminal charge (he would perform menial tasks at the shrine and crawl round it on all fours). A major Hūniyam shrine that was founded as an offshoot of Lunāva will be described in Chapter 3. The shrine of Hūniyam at Bellanvila (see above) is also extremely popular.

While Kataragama is a deeply ambivalent figure, both Kālī and Hūniyam are prima facie dreadful. Kālī is usually depicted sticking out her tongue, engaged in the gory decapitation of the buffalo demon; Hūniyam has tusks and matted locks, both apparently dread attributes, and is wreathed in poisonous snakes. What emotions these three deities actually evoke will concern us later. Here we are concerned with their relation to the structure of the pantheon. First, we may remark that even these popular gods are exhibiting the upward drift discussed above. Kataragama's fearsome aspect is soft-pedalled by many of his devotees, who claim that the dirty work of black magic is done by lesser deities in his retinue, such as Kaḍavara and Kurumbara, who appear as collectivities of seven. In other words, Kataragama is on the way to being perceived as a Bodhisattva very like Viṣṇu in character. The new Buddhist myths about Kataragama (see Chapter 12) display a similar tendency. There does of course remain a difficulty about his love life; this can be evaded by claiming that there are really two Kataragamas, a moral Buddhist deity and a later Hindu intruder with whom the Buddhist Kataragama has been confused and who has tarnished his reputation. Kālī's very arrival on the Buddhist scene is already a step up from her position as a demoness, and her split into two, Bhadra Kālī and Sohon Kālī, seems analogous to the morally ambivalent *dēvatā* ("godling") stage. Hūniyam, whom Buddhists have long known as a straight demon, has shown a similar progress and we shall discuss his remarkable rise in Chapter 3. Here we wish only to record a point that represents yet a further distortion of the traditional structure. Some of his devotees now call him Gambāra Deviyō. This means "god in charge of a/the village." Traditionally a local deity (a *dēvatā*) could be so called as an *epithet*, but the reference would be to a particular village. In isolation the title is a solecism, for Hūniyam is not the official guardian deity of any village, let alone of Colombo, where most of his devotees live. When a traditional demon is accorded the title of god and said to be in charge of a village but in fact made a personal protector, a guardian god, the moral ordering of the traditional Sinhala Buddhist view of the world has come into question.

Possession

In many of our case studies the guardian deity manifests himself or herself by possessing the devotee. This brings us to the heart of the new religious complex—the positive evaluation of possession. This in turn is intimately connected to the new religious roles that have arisen, notably for women.

We have explained above that the loss of self-control led traditional Buddhist culture generally to look askance at possession. The only people the culture allowed to be possessed, the professional intermediaries between men and spirits of the rank of "godling" and lower, guarded their monopoly. If anyone, male or female, became possessed outside traditional role performances by recognized specialists, this could only be something bad: the possessing spirit must be a demon (*yakā*) or malign ancestral spirit (*prēta*). Exorcists had a material interest in invalidating the claims of amateur competition. Moreover, the traditional *kapurāḷa*s, who tend to be the theoreticians of the spirit religion (some even use the term *dēva-sāsana*, corresponding to *Buddha-sāsana*), have so categorized the universe that the status of the possessing spirit is defined a priori by context. A true god, like one of the four guardian deities (such as Kataragama), is too pure to enter a human body, even a male one, let alone that of a woman. If the priests preserve certain taboos, they may themselves be possessed, on set occasions, by the morally ambiguous deities "of little power" (*alpēsākya*) whom they serve. A spirit who possesses a woman must ipso facto be low/impure; if it claims (through her mouth) to be higher, this is the kind of lie you can expect from such a spirit.

Sporadic possession seems to have been fairly common in traditional Sinhala society, especially among women. But the person possessed was defined as ill (*ātura*) and every attempt was then made to exorcise the spirit. If all failed, the person was considered mad (*pissu*) and alienated from society. So far as we know, there were no such people operating as self-recruited free-lance exorcists. A male might possibly manage to become attached to a professional specialist; but we know of no case in traditional society of a woman's possession being considered socially acceptable through recognition of the benign character of her possessing spirit, let alone of her becoming a professional medium.

Perhaps the most striking recent change in the Sinhala religious scene has been the widespread acceptance of possession as something positive. This is not to say that exorcisms no longer occur. Typically, when a person first becomes possessed relatives try to have him or her exorcised. But when the attempts at exorcism wholly or partially fail, things no longer proceed as they used to. The possessed person (the following sentences apply to members of either sex) often manages to impose on those around her the belief that she is an accredited vehicle of a god. Usually she claims that she is possessed by a powerful deity—commonly Kataragama, Kālī, or Hūniyam. This does not settle the issue, because an inferior spirit can lyingly claim to be a god. But the possessed person authenticates her claim by some successful role performance, such as miraculous knowledge of the past or future, or maybe by sheer force of personality. (Of course these are not exclusive alternatives, being explanations on two different levels.) To effect such an authentication, she must in fact have considerable control over her mental state: she cannot be possessed all the time but must to some extent routinize the attacks; and even during possession there are some limits to permissible behavior, to transgress which (e.g., to undress in public) would establish that the possessing spirit was evil. The subsequent career of such a possessed person follows a set pattern: she establishes a shrine, at first at home; then, if she prospers, she may construct a separate building or move to one already in existence. Occasionally such a possessed person, if male, may succeed to a position as priest of a shrine in a temple; so far as we know, this has not yet been done by a woman, though we record a case below of a woman who was appointed as the first full-time priest of a temple shrine. In this milieu of the possessed and their clientele, nominal religious affiliation is of no account; we found quite a few, especially among the women, who were born as Sinhala Roman Catholics. But only those Catholics crossed our path who considered themselves possessed by Hindu-Buddhist deities (though not necessarily exclusively by them); the other possessed Catholics, those who remain within the community of their coreligionists, are still taken to be exorcised.

Those possessees, necessarily males, who are drafted to be priests at established shrines, thereby fit into an established role, though their method of recruitment is (we think) new. But two new roles emerge from the phenomena described above. Female priests are a novelty, and even the Sinhala language has trouble coping with them. They are known as "go-between mothers" (*kapu mǟṇiyō* or *kapu ammā*), but the term is so new that to many Sinhala people it is still completely unfamiliar. Perhaps partly because the collocation sounds so strange, some simply use the term *mǟṇiyō*, a very formal word for "mother." We have heard of one old lady who ran a shrine to the goddess Pattinī in the mid-1950s; and another lady who officiated at Lunāva from 1950 to 1960 (see below); but we are sure that until the 1970s priestesses were very rare indeed. The *kapu ammā*, we repeat, is the feminine counterpart of a *kapurāḷa*, a gods' priest, but almost always works at a shrine she herself has founded (except that we can already see second-generation *kapu ammālā* emerging!).

The other new role, a kind of masculine counterpart to the *mǟṇiyō*, is the *sāmi*. The Sinhala *sāmi* is a kind of urbanized, Hinduized, self-recruited priest. Strictly speaking, *sāmi* is more a title than a role; the same could be said of *mǟṇiyō*, when the word *kapu* is not used. The word *sāmi* is the Tamil form of the familiar Sanskrit word *svāmi(n)*, and we think that Kataragama is the locus of its transfer into Sinhala. It literally means "master, lord,"[31] and sounds much grander than *kapurāḷa*, the traditional term; in usage it indicates not so much that its bearer works at a shrine—though he invariably does—as that he is the chosen vehicle, or mediator on behalf, of one of our three "modern" deities, most commonly Kataragama. The title *sāmi* is not adopted by those whose deity is perceived as more Buddhist than Hindu. By this we do not mean the apparent converse—that the deity is necessarily perceived as Hindu rather than Buddhist; we mean that the *sāmi* usually does not make such a distinction.

A *sāmi* or a *mǟṇiyō* may also be possessed by the spirit of his or her dead

[31] *Svāmin*, with the further honorific affix *vahansē*, is a traditional form of address or reference (though not a formal title) for a Buddhist monk. This book could aptly, if obscurely, be titled, "From *svāminvahansē* to *sāmi*."

relative. That such a spirit may be defined as good represents another radical innovation, parallel to the redefinition of possessing deities as major (*mahēsākya*, literally "of great power," to use a traditional term that goes all the way back to the Buddhist Canon). Traditional interaction with the dead is as follows: when a family member dies, the head of the household organizes first the funeral and later certain *pirit* ceremonies at which merit is specifically transferred to the dead person. (Such ceremonies may be repeated annually.) The theory is that if he has not been very virtuous he may have been reborn as a hungry ghost, a *prēta*, a class of being that has virtually no chance to make merit on its own initiative. The merit it obtains from empathizing with the feeding of monks at the *pirit* ceremony may suffice for it to be reborn in a better state. Disgruntled *prēta*s sometimes return (like Western ghosts or poltergeists) to their former habitat, smell bad, and cause other trouble, such as possessing people, so that they have to be exorcised. Dead members of the family who have better *karma*, on the other hand, are reborn elsewhere, on earth or in a heaven, and one has no further contact with them at all.

With the breakdown of the village community and hence of traditional forms of social control, claims that possession is a sign of some kind of divine grace can no longer be quashed by defining the possession as malign and insisting on exorcism. As instances of benign possession multiply, the traditional norms are forgotten and the phenomenon ceases to appear anomalous. The creation of the category of benign spirits of departed relatives (for which there is as yet no standard word—the term *prēta*[32] retains its negative connotations) is a particularly interesting piece of reinterpretation. Such reinterpretation occurs at the pilgrimage centers of the new religious complex, notably Kataragama, where the *māṇiyō* and *sāmi* congregate. We feel certain that the category of good dead relative emerged in this milieu as a compromise. Some possessed people claim that their trance is due to good gods; traditional bystanders say that that is impossible: it must be a *prēta*. So the possessee backs down a bit and says that it is a *good* kind of *prēta*. We shall record below several cases of what is obviously the next stage (which could supervene immediately): this good departed spirit is acting as a mediator between the priest (or client) and the major god who is his or her personal deity.

[32] *Maḷa yakā*, "demon of the dead," has slightly less pejorative connotations, and nowadays people might say that the benign ancestor is a *maḷa yakā* and not a *prēta*.

If the question is then asked, in what cosmological category is this good spirit, the answer must be (since it is good) that it is a deity in the "godling" category. Traditionally, godlings are local spirits and the deities of village community religion. With the loss of the village community, that sense too is lost. The benign dead are entering that vacant space in the scheme of things and endowing the category with new meaning.

To illustrate this, here is the statement of a thirty-year-old priest, a *sāmi* in the making, who works at a Colombo shrine. The term *ārūḍē* is derived from the Sanskrit *ārūḍha*, which literally means "mounted"; the spirit "rides" the person it possesses, as in the Western theory of the succubus but without differentiation according to sex, for the term has no sexual connotation. The *ārūḍē* is the gift of becoming possessed. The word *bhūta* is traditionally used for any kind of low, nasty spirit, whether a dead ancestor (*prēta*) or a demon (*yakā*, *yakṣa*). The priest is trying to carve out a new significance for the word.

> I have not yet received the *ārūḍē* of the gods. Light readers[33] as well as possessed priests have told me that this will be given to me soon. Astrologers who saw my horoscope also said that I'd obtain it in January 1976. Sometimes people get the impression that they have the *ārūḍē* of the gods. But it is not the gods who give *ārūḍē*. There is *ārūḍē* by *prēta*s [*prētārūḍē*], then *ārūḍē* by gods [*dēvārūḍē*], and thirdly *ārūḍē* by demons [*yaksārūḍē*]. Ordinarily people obtain *ārūḍē* from *bhūta*s.[34] If you wish to obtain *ārūḍē* of the gods you must depart for the forest, eating the leaves, tubers, roots, and bark of trees. You must drink milk. You must live thus, meditate, and obtain *dhyāna* powers. Then like a magnet attracting metal the gods' *ākarsana* [magnetism] draws the penitent.
>
> However, the *ārūḍē* I hope to obtain is from *bhūta*s. Generally the power of *bhūta* [*bhūta-balaya*] we get is from a member of the family well disposed to us who says, "Anē! who is there to succor this child?" Thus saying, the person dies and from this person's *ātma* [self] we obtain *bhūta*-power. One of my grandfathers died. That grandfather is now a tree deity [*vṛkṣa-dēvatā*]. . . . I was told this in several oracles. But even that tree deity does not enter into my body.

[33] Those who do *anjanaṃ eliya*, in which a diviner peers into a light and sees a deity (generally Hanuman) who tells the future.

[34] *Bhūta* is another term for *prēta*.

When my principles become nobler, when I engage in pure activities, and when my bad astrological times go away, I shall get encouragement from that tree deity to do divine work. By that power I will be able to cure the sick and destroy the dangers caused by evil spirits.

The theory of divine possession enhances the self-respect of the possessed person and becomes a source of "liberation" (increased dignity, social independence, earning power) for women and indeed many other people who see no hope of other success or fulfillment. Once the break to benign possession has been made, the traditional logic is followed through: a divine spirit gives one the power to do good. That they are working for the benefit of the world is the universal rhetoric (and no doubt belief) of *mǟṇiyō* and *sāmi*. To the outsider this work appears at first sight to take a bizarre form: they firewalk and practice a variety of penances. But these are all performances to authenticate their roles by reassuring themselves and others that their deities really are protecting them and giving them abnormal powers. The good of the world is effected in practice by giving oracles, that is, advising clients. *Mǟṇiyō* who come (as most do) from the poorer segments of the population normally charge for their services (either on a fixed scale or just by asking for voluntary contributions); it is perhaps this feature that sets the seal on the professional role. The *sāmi*, being attached to a shrine, naturally does the same. A few middle-class women behave in just the same way, but they provide their services free; this may be expressed by saying one has not put up a signboard (*bōḍ ekak dālā nǟ*).

The Effects on Buddhism Proper

The above exposition has shown that change in the cosmology and the creation of new religious roles are interconnected matters. The changes we have dealt with so far all concern the spirit religion. However, this book will show that strictly Buddhist ideas, roles, and institutions have not remained unaffected by the new trends. In the latter half of the book we shall discuss two Buddhist roles that have not been so much invented as exhumed—the roles of Buddhist nun and of self-ordained monk. The reemergence of a monastic role for women picks up the theme of women's liberation, their emergence into greater social prominence. The self-ordained monk explicitly and flagrantly defies the established structure of authority. Indeed, what the two roles obviously have in common is that they stand outside the traditional Buddhist hierarchy; and this common feature underlies other characteristics that they turn out to share. Though the roles are formally not new, they have been reinvented in and for modern urbanized Sri Lanka. However, neither of these two roles correlates with a change in Buddhist cosmology.

For the traditional pantheon to retain its integrity, what must not be infringed is the Buddha's position at the top of (albeit outside) the pantheon and the monk's position at the top of (and also in a sense outside) society. Although we do not think that either of these positions is *commonly* compromised even now, some steps have been taken in that direction.

Impairment of the Buddha's supremacy is never stated in so many words, but can be deduced from symbolic arrangements. At exorcistic ceremonies it is customary to raise an arch in honor of the deities; this arch does not traditionally carry any representations of deities. The Buddha is duly mentioned at the beginning of all ceremonies but plays no further part in such rites as exorcisms. At a recent exorcism (*tovil*) in Colombo we not only saw an arch bedecked with cheap store-print pictures of the gods, but even noted a similar picture of the Buddha included among them. Though he was highest on the arch, this introduction of the Buddha into a ceremony dealing with demons is utterly out of place and compromises his dignity.[35]

The spatial and timing arrangements of ritual at Bellanvila, an extremely rich and popular temple in a Colombo suburb, afford a good example of slippage from traditional orthodoxy; and they are particularly interesting because many regular visitors to the temple premises are middle class and educated. Traditionally, certain higher gods (i.e., *deviyō*), typically members of the group of six from which the four guardian deities of Sri Lanka are recruited, could have statues inside a Buddhist shrine and/or shrines of their own in the temple compound. Any more dubious characters, like Hūniyam or Däḍimuṇḍa, would have a very subordinate po-

[35] This type of "symbolic shift" must be distinguished from others in the history of popular Buddhism (and other religions also). In Laggala, where we did research in 1958–1960, within living memory of the informants it had been customary to propitiate the local deities *before* a Buddhist ritual (*pin kama*) was held. When we were there the procedure had been reversed. But none of these procedures compromised the Buddha's dignity.

sition, rarely dignified by a statue; if they had a separate shrine at all it would be a small one somewhere to the side. At Bellanvila the buildings include a huge new Buddha shrine, in architecture a copy of the twelfth-century Lankātilaka Vihāra at Poḷonnaruva. What attracts the thousands of visitors, however—and presumably has provided the money to build the Buddha shrine—is the other complex of buildings (a main one and smaller structures), which now comprises, rather irregularly dispersed, two small Buddha shrines and shrines for ten deities: Viṣṇu, Īśvara, Gaṇeśa, Pattinī, Nātha, Saman, Vibhīṣaṇa, Kataragama, Hūniyam, and Däḍimuṇḍa. We are told that the first shrines were to Viṣṇu and Kataragama, though the present Kataragama shrine is a new one: his old one was too small and has been reallocated to the Buddha. The twin shrines to Hūniyam and Däḍimuṇḍa were erected by a donor (giving the merit to his dead wife) in 1952; their incumbent priests do a roaring trade in black magic, as they freely admit. The other shrines are more recent. What is most striking to the observer interested in symbolic space, however, is that in the main building the shrine to Viṣṇu is dead center in the front wall, the shrines to the Buddha to the side (one of them around the corner). From the traditional point of view this is unconventional, to say the least. The spatial relations are mirrored in the timing of the ritual. It is customary to place evening refreshment (*gilampasa pūjāva*) before the principal statue of the Buddha in a shrine, and this is supposed to happen at 6 P.M. (Some urban temples, however, now have the *gilampasa pūjāva* later, to give people a chance to go home from work, wash, and dine before coming to the temple.) At Bellanvila it is the evening *pūjā* (strictly known as *tēvāva*) to Viṣṇu that starts at 6 P.M. precisely.

Far more radical displacements of the Buddha occur in some of the case histories related below; but they no longer relate to the traditional pantheon, for that has been completely left behind. We shall meet a university lecturer who in his private shrine puts the Buddha image lower than a picture of the feet of Sai Baba, whom he considers to be a Buddha; and in due course encounter the Sun Buddha, who considers himself to have superseded the Moon Buddha, as he calls Gotama Buddha, and to be the Buddha for our age. We shall, however, show that such extremes of unorthodoxy are confined to individuals and small sectarian groups.

What about the role of Buddhist monks? Their rule forbids them to assume other religious roles. One reason for this is that monks are altogether forbidden worldly occupations: they are not supposed to earn (ideally, not even to touch) money, and that prohibition merely epitomizes the principle that they should reduce contact with secular life to a minimum. There is also another less obvious but equally important reason why a monk may not become a priest of the gods or an exorcist: the exercise of these roles involves entering states of possession and trance (generally known in Sinhala as *māyam*) which are the polar opposite of that awareness (Pāli: *sati*), to gain which is the paramount aim of Theravāda Buddhists and, a fortiori, of Buddhist monks. Obviously it is also illegitimate for a monk to practice black magic, whether he is paid for it or not, simply because harming others is sinful.

As early as 1965 we visited a small shrine on the premises of a temple near Amparai in Eastern Province, where the incumbent monk assured us that he acted as the god's priest—but did *not* get possessed. His excuse for undertaking this office was that it normally runs in families, but in this new colony there happened to be no one among the settlers with hereditary qualifications. He ran the shrine by displaying a tariff with fees for particular services (*pūjā* and prayers)—itself a feature perhaps borrowed from Hindu temples (*kovil*). In the same period, in a rural part of the Western Province, we came across a monk who performed exorcisms just as a lay specialist would, with some Hindu trappings (e.g., sounding of bells).

But the Venerable Ratmalāne Siddhārtha of Kataragama has scaled yet further heights of unorthodoxy. He lives on the hill called Väḍahiṭikanda, where the god first settled down. That he has a great reputation as a magician does not much concern us: he claims that knowledge of how to compose spells (*vas kavi*) is in his pupillary succession (*guru śiṣya paramparāva*), and we would judge that this ability, which is coupled with hypnotic powers, yields him a substantial income. But this is interesting only as a background to what follows.

Though dates are a little vague, we are clear that for many years after the Second World War Väḍahiṭikanda, then a remote hill covered in jungle, was principally inhabited by a Tamil holy man called Sangarapillai Sāmi. Sangarapillai, according to Siddhārtha, was brought to Sri Lanka from South India as a child and worked most of his life as a paid *pūsārī* ("priest"), among other places at a Pattinī *kovil* ("shrine")[36] in Negombo and lastly at the Tēvānī *kovil* at nearby Sella Kataragama. In 1960 Ratmalāne Siddhārtha, after practicing Buddhist meditation (*bhāvanā*) on Gaṇadevi Kanda, a hill at Deṭagamuva, came to Väḍahiṭikanda and em-

[36] These are Tamil words; the Sinhala equivalents are *kapurāḷa* and *dēvālē*.

ployed Sangarapillai as his *pūsārī*. "I had to worship my deity, didn't I?" he said to us in explanation; and went on to specify that everyone has a guardian deity (*iṣṭa dēvatāva*), a personal (*paudgalika*) deity, who is more or less powerful (*mahēsākya* or *alpēsākya*), good or bad, according to the individual. He did not pay Sangarapillai cash, he said, but fed him and looked after him till his death in 1963. In other words, he behaved as pupil does to *guru*; and indeed he added that Sangarapillai taught him the rituals of worship (*pūjā vidhi*) from a Hindu book. Siddhārtha has himself published a book called *Kandakumāra Pūjāmālāva* ("The Garland of Worship to the Mountain Prince"), based on Sangarapillai's teaching. When we asked Siddhārtha what he used *pūjā* for, he said that he did not expect, like Hindus, to get the *nirvāṇa* of the gods (*deviyangē nirvāne*) (a bizarre expression by which he must have meant that he did not have the Hindu theistic concept of salvation) but that it was fine to use these rites to get what one wanted (*iṣṭa karaganṭa*). We must have looked surprised, for he added in justification that in the time of the Buddha Ānanda did *pūjā* to the gods and that when a novice called Sānu had a stomachache the Buddha prescribed a charm (*yantra*) for him. (We do not know whether this justification is based on an older source or is Siddhārtha's invention; it certainly does not come from classical scripture.)

Ratmalāne Siddhārtha seems to us to have earned an individual niche in the history of religion. Himself heavily Hinduized, he embodies also the Buddhist takeover of Kataragama to which we shall return in Chapters 5 and 12. For he took full possession of the hill of Väḍahiṭikanda on Sangarapillai's death and has consolidated his hold despite a Tamil lawsuit to oust him. According to Ammā Sāmi, a Sinhala holy man who is himself a pupil of Sangarapillai, the latter was Siddhārtha's pupil because Siddhārtha administered the five Buddhist precepts to him, while Siddhārtha was Sangarapillai's pupil because Sangarapillai taught him the rites of divine worship. By this latter pupillary relationship Siddhārtha acquired proprietary rights (*ayitivāsikama*) in the site. Ammā Sāmi also informed us that the divine worship (*dēvapūjā*) in the monastery was now (in 1975) performed by an illiterate carpenter who had been recruited by becoming possessed.

We owe most of our information on another interesting monk to the unpublished research of Dr. Tamara Gunasekera.[37] The Venerable Galkisse

[37] Tamara Gunasekera, "Deity Propitiation in Urban Sri Lanka" (M.A. thesis, Edinburgh, 1974).

Śrī Visuddhānanda[38] was born Lucimen Franco Fernando on 16 August 1911, into a well-to-do family. His family was Buddhist, but he had both Catholic and Protestant relatives, and he lived in an area with a large and dominant Christian population. He was educated at a leading Anglican school in Colombo, St. Thomas' College. In his late teens he became a Buddhist novice. In 1930, while studying at the Buddhist monastic university of Vidyodaya, he took up residence at the small Buddhist temple of Lunāva, on the main coastal road a few miles south of Colombo. In 1938 he received his higher ordination as a monk in the Amarapura fraternity and we deduce that he became the incumbent of the monastery at about that time. He later attained the rank of Nāyaka Thero and was the senior monk in charge of twenty-nine temples of his fraternity in the Moraṭuva area in which Lunāva is situated. He died recently (26 January 1983) and with his death the institution we are about to describe lost its importance.

Gunasekera writes:

> The [temple] . . . developed remarkably in size and prestige after the arrival of a middle-aged lady—Mrs. C. E. de Silva of Moratuwa—in 1942. Both she and her husband, who were devout Buddhists, worked untiringly for the improvement of the [temple]. She organized many of the projects, while her husband, a contractor by occupation, designed and planned the edifices that were put up after 1942. Between 1942 and 1946 the [stupa], the new [image house] (until then it remained on the upper floor of the [monk's quarters]), and a new monks' residence, were built. The *devale* itself, constructed in the latter part of the 1940's, was the last to be built. Mr. D. S. Wijemanne, a retired schoolteacher, Pali scholar, and longtime friend of 'the monk', claims that it was built on insistence of certain worshippers, who felt the spot was hallowed by the *devas*. The monk however, asserts that it was built on his own initiative after the deity Sooniyam [Hūniyam] asked him to do so in a dream.
>
> In 1950, Mrs. C. E. de Silva became the first regular *kapurala* of the *devale*. This was a clear divergence from the practice in the village where it would be considered inconceivable for a woman to become a *kapurala*. Mrs. de Silva had great faith in the gods. When 'the monk' was present and asked the deity Sooniyam to manifest himself in her,

[38] Gunasekera spells him Visudhananda, which would be abnormal; we have taken the liberty of emending it.

she would get the *arude* as she gave *puja* and recited the *Karaniya-metta Sutta* (a Buddhist stanza which preaches universal love and goodwill). She was believed to be favoured by the gods and was herself a powerful personality, second only to the monk. Mrs. de Silva was the chief *kapurala* at Lunawa for ten years. In 1960 she died unexpectedly of diabetes.[39]

Mrs. de Silva is the earliest "ecstatic priestess" of whom we have record. We may observe that our case history of Uttama Sādhu (Chapter 10) has parallel features which suggest that there must have been a symbiosis between the monk and the priestess. This implies no impropriety: it is simply that she had the trances while he successfully presented himself as being in control of what was happening—as he continued to do with her successors after her death, though they were male.

The shrine soon became incomparably more important than the temple, even in the eyes of the incumbent. In this he was extremely heterodox. "Visudhananda Nayake Thero sees himself, as do the laity, not as the chief incumbent of the *vihare* but of the *devale*."[40] The Buddha shrine was kept locked most of the day, whereas the *dēvālē* was open from 5 A.M. to 8:30 P.M. Visuddhānanda never preached or taught and there was no meditation at the temple. He participated in the Buddha *pūjā* only twice a year, at the major festivals of Vesak and Poson. There was only one Buddha *pūjā* a day, that at midday (*daval pūjā*), and it was offered by the priest of the Kataragama shrine (*kapumahatmayā*). On the other hand, Visuddhānanda made charms (*yantra*).[41]

The main deity of the shrine was nominally Kataragama, and the shrine held an annual procession for Kataragama (a *perahära*) on the monk's birthday—which, being in mid-August, fell at about the time of other Kataragama festivals. There were also shrines for Viṣṇu, Pattinī, Śiva, and the monk's maternal uncle. This uncle, who had brought him up, was the shrine's guardian deity (*ārakṣaka dēvatāva*) as well as being his own personal deity (*iṣṭa dēvatāva*). The largest shrine, however, is a room reserved for Hūniyam.[42]

Visuddhānanda said that with his uncle's help he "caught" Hūniyam,

[39] Gunasekera, "Deity Propitiation," p. 28.

[40] Ibid., p. 67.

[41] Ibid., pp. 66–67.

[42] Ibid., p. 26.

winning him over by firmness to do good works. Hūniyam appeared to him in a dream and asked him to build the *dēvālē* and also directed him to a spot on the premises where he would (and did) find a buried image of Hūniyam. He continued to see Hūniyam in dreams and Hūniyam addressed him as "son." Despite this, Visuddhānanda spoke disrespectfully to Hūniyam during séances, interrupted him, told him to repeat, and so forth; he claimed he had a special power over Hūniyam (rather than the other way round).[43] Hūniyam manifested himself through the *kapumahatmayā* ("Mr. Go-Between"). However, this manifestation, according to Visuddhānanda, could take place only at his behest. He "has usurped control over *devale* activities. Consequently there is a decrease in the degree of spiritual prowess the *kapurāḷas* are allowed to possess. Visudhananda, and not the *kapurāḷas*, is believed to have spiritual powers and influence over the gods. . . . [His] superiority would be seriously undermined if the *kapumahatmayās* could get into the trances on their own."[44] During Gunasekera's fieldwork, the chief priest insisted to her that he could get possessed even in the absence of the monk; it was probably this claim that led to his dismissal.[45] His assistant, more prudent, accepted that he could only operate as an instrument of the monk.

Like Väḍahiṭikanda, Lunāva was a highly visible public institution patronized by leading public figures. Gunasekera writes: "During the period 1950–60 many politicians and important public figures were associated with the *devale*. . . . Their number included the President of the Senate [and] the former Governor of the Central Bank. . . . Even the Prime Minister of the time, Mr. S.W.R.D. Bandaranaike, was a devotee of the *devale*. His wife, the present Prime Minister, used to take an active part in the ceremonies held every Saturday night in honour of the gods."[46] In the late 1950s the shrine received considerable press coverage.

To illustrate the kinds of rituals in which the Venerable Visuddhānanda played a central role, we summarize one of Gunasekera's case studies.[47] A recently bereaved widower came to ask after the whereabouts of his dead wife. The monk arranged a private ritual at which the priest became possessed by the dead lady, who announced through him that with the help of the merit transferred to her by her relatives "and also through the help

[43] Ibid., pp. 68–70.
[44] Ibid., p. 75.
[45] Ibid., pp. 75–76.
[46] Ibid., p. 30.
[47] Ibid., pp. 106–7.

of Sooniyam *devatava*" she had been reborn as the tree spirit in the *bō* tree right there at Lunāva. The monk then said that he would see to it that some member of the family received her spirit within three months. After consultation, the family selected the lady's youngest son for this mediumship; and when Gunasekera last saw him he was visiting the shrine three or four times a week to do *pūjā*s, transferring the merit to his mother, and waiting for her to possess him. However, he had no plans to utter oracles: it was just to keep his mother in touch with her family. But the role of the monk remained crucial: their expectation was that when they needed the mother's help they would have to ask *him* to tell the spirit to talk through the son. In other words, the son would (they hoped) talk and the monk would interpret the message.

In our chapter on Hūniyam below we shall discuss the Hūniyam shrine at Baseline Road in Colombo, which Visuddhānanda founded as a branch establishment from his Lunāva headquarters. Our principal concern in this introductory section is to document involvement of a monk with spirit religion in a way that runs counter to traditional ideas of hierarchy and propriety. We are aware that, though it is condemned by Buddhist scripture, for a monk to be involved with magic is not entirely new. According to popular Sinhala tradition the fifteenth-century monk Toṭagamuve Śrī Rāhula, a poet and scholar, practiced black magic and composed versified spells (*vas kavi*); moreover, it is said that in his academy the subjects included astrology and Tamil. Tamil, astrology, and black magic is a collocation of topics in the Sinhala imagination that frequently recurs in our material. Unlike Ratmalāne Siddhārtha, who became the pupil of a Tamil *sāmi*, Visuddhānanda does not seem to have compromised his preeminence in the hierarchy of religious roles; on the contrary, by claiming to control the possession states of others he went to great lengths to preserve it. However, his relationship to Hūniyam and other spirits was highly ambivalent; and his whole involvement with the spirit religion was in stark contrast to his neglect of the temple to which the spirit shrines were attached. His career represents an intrusion of the spirit religion into Buddhism and begins to look like a takeover.

Indian Influence

The above two cases bring to an end our opening account of how the traditional cosmology has been disrupted. Both cases show influence from outside the Sinhala Buddhist tradition. Visuddhānanda was strongly influenced by Catholicism, as our account of the shrine at Baseline Road will demonstrate. Siddhārtha furnishes a clear example of how Tamil religiosity has been injected into Sinhala Buddhist religion. At this point we shall say something more about recent Indian influence, especially as evident in language. Some of this influence has been mediated by Sri Lankan Tamils; most of it is directly from India. We are not concerned with differentiating between the two routes: so many Tamils in Sri Lanka have close links with India that that would be impossible. To anyone who just looks at the globe or summarily surveys the entire course of Sri Lanka's history, Indian influence will hardly come as a surprise; nevertheless, there is an irony to it. The Sinhalas have always been extremely concerned (at least in public life) about emphasizing their distinctness from India, and this concern has been accentuated since Independence. Until 1978 the Tamil language did not figure in the Sinhala school curriculum, and when the government belatedly introduced it, the regulation remained almost a dead letter because it was so hard to find Sinhala people who knew enough Tamil to teach it. This ignoring of India extends beyond Tamil: even now (1985) Mahatma Gandhi is not mentioned in the Sinhala school syllabus. But it is especially Tamil influence on Sinhala history and culture that is soft-pedalled by officialdom. Even to recall that several Kandyan Sinhala noblemen signed the Kandyan Convention in 1815 in a Tamil script is politically daring. Since 1956 there has been fairly consistent communal tension between Sinhalas and Tamils, tension that for twenty years led only occasionally to bloodshed, but now alas has become a war. Some may be tempted to postulate that the political discrimination against the Tamils by the Sinhala majority has some causal connection with Tamil prestige in matters occult; magical powers, compensating for lack of sociopolitical power, are ascribed to oppressed minorities the world over. On the other hand, India has a reputation as the haven of the occult—a reputation that has reached middle-class Sinhalas via the West. Of course, these two ideas may combine. Whatever the reason, it is poignant that Mrs. Bandaranaike, the leader of the principal Sinhala nationalist party (which during the 1970s was the one major party with very little Tamil support), was generally believed to rely on the advice of Tamil astrologers. Even more interesting—though it is obviously not a development for which she can be held directly responsible—is that at a huge party rally held in Kandy on 3 September 1976 and headed by Mrs. Bandaranaike, many Sinhala supporters of the SLFP did *kāvaḍi* dancing (see below) in the procession, and a few people, who also were to all appearances Sinhalas, even had spikes (*kaṭu*) through their cheeks. Both these practices are traditional Tamil ways of honoring Kataragama and have recently entered Sinhala culture through that source; to act thus at a political demonstration is not only a kind of de-secularization but also suggests that Mrs. Bandaranaike was being honored after the fashion of an Indian god.

Recent Indian influence, however, is not simply Tamil. A brief linguistic discussion seems a useful way of broaching this subject. Sinhala language is basically derived from Sanskrit (with much Dravidian influence), and at a previous period of intense Indian influence, the Poḷonnaruva period, the language was heavily re-Sanskritized. Very many words in the language can now be used in either pure Sinhala forms or re-Sanskritized forms, so that, for example, a school can be a *pāsäla* (pure Sinhala) or a *pāṭhaśālāva*. By and large, to use the Sanskritic forms sounds more pompous and impressive; this explains why, although the liturgical language of Sinhala Buddhism is Pāli, monks tend to be in the habit of using Sanskrit forms. (There is some analogy with the use of Latin-derived, as against Anglo-Saxon, words in English.) This will be relevant when we come to consider Uttama Sādhu in Chapter 10. The Sanskritic terms that we are about to discuss are not completely new, but their use in the common parlance of uneducated people is new, and they are being used with new meanings, or at least new resonances.

One Sanskrit term has probably entered Sinhala via English! *Sādhu* is a Sanskrit word meaning "good"; it is traditionally used in Sinhala as an exclamation of approval and participation in the context of a Buddhist ritual, but is not traditionally applied to people. The word has entered English as a designation for an Indian "holy man," though the term is not used so specifically in Sanskrit. Buddhist monks are traditionally referred to and addressed by a title literally meaning "lord" or "master," and with this title go certain other linguistic conventions, for example, special verbs for coming, going, speaking, eating, and sleeping. But the word *sādhu* does not necessarily evoke such honorific concomitant terms; and laity tend to use the word lightly of monks. On the other hand, the followers of Uttama Sādhu (see Chapter 10) simply substitute "Sādhu" for the more traditional titles and retain the panoply of honorifics. The same (predominantly middle-class) milieu is much given to heavily Sanskritized Sinhala, as we shall see, and the leading lady lay disciple is known in the movement by the Sanskrit word for "mother" plus the Sinhala nominal ending—"Mātāva." This word, though readily intelligible to a Sinhala, is a neologism; its only more general use is in the phrase *sil mātāva*, which is a modern synonym for *sil mäṇiyō*, the title of the ladies whom for convenience we are calling Buddhist nuns. A whole Sanskrit terminology pervades the milieu of firewalkers and possessees which we shall discuss in Chapter 5, and thence is entering urban Sinhala. Possessed people become "mounted" (*ārūḍha*) or "entered" (*āvēśa*); they then show their "devotion" (*bhaktiya*) to their "chosen deity" (*iṣṭa dēvatāva*) by firewalking, which gains them the god's "favor" or "grace" (*prasādaya*) so that he grants them "magnetism" (*ākarṣaṇaya*); but before they can walk on the fire they are smeared with the god's "sacred ash" (*vibhūtiya*), a word which also signifies "divine power." They earn their living by delivering oracles (*śāstra*). All the italicized terms used in the above six lines are Sanskrit words (some with Sinhala endings added) which are constantly on the lips of these devotees (*bhaktimanta aya*). The word *bhakti*, for example, is not foreign to Sinhala vocabulary in the sense of "religious devotion," but the kind of devotion a Buddhist may show to the Buddha or to a god is a very mild and sober emotion and is usually referred to by the Sinhala derivative *bätiya*. The moment the Sanskritic form *bhaktiya* is used the resonances change completely: this is nothing less than love and adoration. Similarly, *śraddhāva* is a term not alien to the Sinhala Buddhist tradition, but there it means "trust" (basically, in the validity of Buddhism) and might also mean "piety"; whereas the new usage is in the sense of unreasoning faith.

In stressing the new emotional tone of contemporary religion, we are not claiming that emotional religiosity and ritualized catharsis were unknown to the world of the traditional Sinhala Buddhist. They found their place in exorcisms and in some of the rituals for gods, events that were, however, structured by the culture and confined to prescribed times and places. In this regulated mode, there was even one point of contact between Buddhism and possession. The text that forms the climax to a full-scale *pirit* ceremony is the *Āṭānāṭiya Sutta*; it addresses all spirits in the Buddha's name, and this is traditionally held to excite them. Someone listening—typically a young woman—may start trembling or show some other sign of possession; then the rest of the recitation will exorcise her or, if that has not worked, another exorcism will be held later.

However, states so rigorously controlled by society cannot be equated with what we are describing, if only because the value put on them is so different. The breakdown of traditional structures of authority and meaning is associated with a radical shift in religious affect. The new climate of religious emotion is a response to these changes, a refuge from a harsh and often unintelligible reality, and at the same time promotes these alterations; for the violent love, the overpowering intimacy between the worshipper and his god, bypasses and ignores all structures as irrelevant complications. It is in this light that we must observe the devotion that some Sinhala Buddhists now feel for Sai Baba.

Sai Baba is a contemporary Indian religious leader who simply preaches the love of God and performs miracles in the central tradition of Indian holy men. Whether he himself is God is ambiguous, in that the ultimate is not a person, and yet if a personal symbol is wanted he will do very well. As ultimately all is one, no religion is false—unless, presumably, it denies the authenticity of Sai Baba's miracles. This religion might look like the polar opposite to Theravāda Buddhism. Yet more and more urban middle-class Buddhists (imitating their Hindu neighbors) are worshipping Sai Baba in private shrine rooms, chanting his hymns (*bhajan*) of praise to God, and seeing their highest bliss in any opportunity to prostrate themselves at His blessed feet.

Some Buddhist devotees of Sai Baba ritually combine their two allegiances in daily devotions as follows: after taking the Buddhist Three Refuges and five precepts they sing hymns to Sai Baba and end with the usual Pāli verse by which Buddhists invite all deities to empathize with the merit gained by their religious activities.[48] Some of these devotees hold that Sai Baba is the Buddhist god Nātha. The meaning of this ascription is that Nātha is traditionally considered to be the current incarnation of the next Buddha, Maitreya. These Buddhists have thus assimilated Sai Baba into the Buddhist pantheon and made him a Bodhisattva.

Similarly, the son of an extremely famous Protestant Buddhist, himself notable for his Buddhist activities, surprised us when we called on him in Colombo to interview him about his late father. He told us that he worships Kataragama twice a day, "not forgetting his brother" Gaṇeśa. His mother and sister are devout followers of Sai Baba, whom they were recommended to visit by the Venerable Balangoḍa Ānanda Maitreya (see Chapter 9), while the informant too declares that Sai Baba "preaches absolutely pure Buddhism."

[48] Personal communication from Mr. Dias Gunawardhana.

We have encountered a more extreme claim for Sai Baba, one that does not accommodate to Buddhist ideology but directly conflicts with it. A university don, a man of intelligence and sophistication, told us (in English) that he asked only to devote his life to Sai Baba, whom he considered "a Fully Enlightened One"—a Buddha. For him, "the traditional sense of meditation does not obtain." Why? Because after producing a *lingam* from his mouth for all to see, Sai Baba had assured a crowd in which he was present that "those whom I have invited to be present shall not be born again," an assurance that coincided with a Pāli verse that was running through his head to the effect that this was his last birth. In his shrine room, among the pictures of Sai Baba (including two of just his feet) were little plastic moldings of the Virgin Mary and Jesus, Buddha images, photographs of Ramakrishna, and a store print of Piṭiya Deviyō (one of the Twelve Gods and the "village guardian" of what is now a suburb of Kandy, where the lecturer lives). All are aspects of the divine, though the pictures of Sai Baba, which allegedly emanate holy ash (*vibhūti*) and "a yellow substance," must in a sense be more divine than the others. More astonishing than this syncretism is the spatial arrangement: the Buddha images are in an open-fronted box on a low table/altar, with cult objects resting on the box and pictures hanging above it. Fundamental to Buddhist consciousness is the feeling that nothing must be placed higher than the Buddha, but when we drew attention to this arrangement the lecturer replied that here "the question of high and low doesn't arise."

In periods of enthusiasm, before it becomes routinized and institutionalized, the ideology of Hindu *bhakti* does entail a spiritual egalitarianism under the aegis of the *guru* (who may be a form of God). But among devotees we have met it not only breaks down customary hierarchies but also ordinary perceptions of reality and in particular of causation. This, as we have remarked, is most important evidence of the remystification of the world. When we asked the lecturer what help he had received from Sai Baba he launched into a long account of his trip to India to get *darśan*,[49] an account in which every circumstance of his progress, no matter how trivial, was ascribed to Sai Baba's aid. That his application forms to leave Sri Lanka went through the Colombo offices without a hitch is no doubt a miracle, and that this should be so is a sad comment on the local bureaucracy. But when at the end of the day he had to return from Colombo to

[49] A pan-Indian word that means "the sight of a god or charismatic person."

Kandy, he arrived at the bus stand to find it deserted. "All of a sudden" (words that constantly recurred in his account) "a bus came from nowhere as it were, the conductor announced that he was going to Kandy, and that if anyone cared to join him he was welcome." We found this interplay of sophisticated irony with rapt credulity disconcerting in an intellectual. At the same time we were reminded of an earlier conversation with a female servant in Colombo, who said that when she thought of Kataragama things went right and the bus came quickly. City life has its daily tribulations, but lest readers get the wrong impression we wish to place on record our admiration for the bus service provided by the Sri Lanka Transport Board.

One can of course argue a difference between miracles, which a god produces by his grace to favor his devotees, and magic, a technique by which humans can coerce unseen powers. But when the miracle-working god takes human form, the distinction becomes blurred; and when an ordinary Buddhist layman produces a Buddhist version of Sai Baba's act, as has been reported to us, and materializes relics of the Buddha, is that a miracle or magic? There are several priests and priestesses in the western and southern parts of Sri Lanka who miraculously produce relics and other religious objects. Relics appeared between the hands of one lady whenever she folded them in worship. Some were skeptical, whereupon the relics began to arrive on a jasmine flower. They were examined by monks and their authenticity approved. The lady's late father had become a *bhummaṭṭhā dēvatā* and supplied the relics by his power. *Bhummaṭṭhā dēvatā* is a Pāli expression meaning "earth-dwelling deity"; it would correspond to "godling" in the traditional cosmology. But of course such godlings do not traditionally have the power to supply Buddha relics. Be that as it may, about a dozen relics produced by this lady were taken to Kataragama by three bus loads of devotees and enshrined there in the Kiri Vehera, the Buddhist stupa near Kataragama's shrine.

Miracles and magic both bypass normal, ordinary causal processes; and belief in both is burgeoning in Sri Lanka. While the miracles recall the rise of emotional *bhakti* religiosity in India in the first millennium A.D., the increased preoccupation with magical means to attain material ends recalls *tantra*, the vast and ill-defined magico-religious complex that developed in the same period and that, in combination with *bhakti*, has dominated Hinduism to this day. As a philosophical system *tantra* developed sophistication and a soteriological nobility, but most people have always regarded it primarily as magic. This ambivalence is essential to *tantra*, for it is distinguished by the doctrine that the same observances may yield either material benefits (*bhukti*)—notably power—or salvation (*mukti*); indeed, until the final stage of the practice, when one must make a choice, it advances both, so that in it magic and religion are inextricably interwoven. In practice, Tantric culture systematically ignores the contrast between the worldly and the supramundane, the distinction expressed in the Sinhala saying, "The Buddha for refuge, the gods for help" ("Budungē saraṇayi, deyiyangē pihiṭayi").

This fundamental feature of *tantra* has old Indian roots: the Buddha, like other teachers of yoga, warned his disciples not to be diverted by the wonder-working powers that would come their way as they made spiritual progress, but to see them as an inessential byproduct that might distract them from the path to salvation. This dichotomy is recalled today, but often in garbled form: an educated and enthusiastic pious layman told us that after attaining the fourth *jhāna*, the highest level of calming meditation, one could choose between the supernormal powers and the path to *nirvāṇa*. This formulation implied that the mere possession of these powers was a great spiritual attainment. Spiritual progress implies magical power, and conversely the display of supernormal power for benign ends indicates spiritual progress.

Means and Ends

In religion, as elsewhere, the same institutions may answer disparate ends. Classical *tantra*, modern firewalking, and even Buddhist meditation furnish us with examples. Conversely, the same individual needs may find expression (and fulfillment or frustration) in diverse practices, and the same practices surface within different institutions, thus drawing our attention to significant similarities. It may be more important to note the tone of devotionalism than to mark its object. As the family of the late Buddhist leader may suggest to us, a worshipper may derive the same satisfactions from worshipping Kataragama and Sai Baba. In either case he seeks the blessed vision of his god; in either case he ascribes any and every piece of luck, however trivial, to the god's protection.

Similarly, behavior may persist while its interpretations change. Let us take a case of glossolalia as an example. A Kandyan village lady in her forties, mother of ten children and wife of a humble shopkeeper, became possessed by Bhadra Kālī. The family was Buddhist. People visited her for oracles, and she thus supplemented her income. This went on for about three years. But her improved fortunes attracted the jealousy of neighbors, even of her own brothers, and the family suffered continuous troubles; obviously her relatives were practicing sorcery against her, hoping to destroy Mother Kālī's power. Trying to counter the sorcery, she first visited Kuḍāgama, where a Roman Catholic priest, Father Jayamanna, exorcises patients and blesses hordes of visitors. But even four visits to Kuḍāgama were fruitless. They then answered an advertisement placed in an occult newspaper by an astrologer calling himself Prince of Fire (Agnikumāra), but he replied that he could not save them. Then a son of hers picked up a leaflet headed, "Demons We Reduce to Ashes" (*Yakṣayō Api Aḷu Karanavā*) and as a result wrote to Colombo for a correspondence course called "Life Eternal" (*Amaraṇīya Jīvitaya*). The son took this course and went on to attend the Pentecostal Theological College and become a minister; but an earlier result of the contact was a visit from a minister to their home. Just before he arrived, the lady says, she heard a voice say several times, "Proclaim thou my name" (*Magē nama elidarav karapan*), and she realized that it was Jesus. God had been speaking through her secretly, disguised as Kālī's voice. Whether or not the sequence of events was just as she remembers it, the theory that God was speaking through her in Kālī's voice had been broached earlier to her daughter by a Christian lady. The family were converted to Pentecostalism. They now attend church in Kandy on Sundays; on Saturdays there are regular meetings in their village home. At all these meetings the lady manifests the gift of tongues (*anyabhāṣāva*) and prays for herself and others. She will also pray for people at other times if they ask her to, but only if they have faith. Only those of pure soul (*suddhātmaka*) may use the gift of tongues at meetings, but it appears that most of those present do so. The lady has since converted a local exorcist who came as a client and stayed as a fellow Christian. The variety of means to which the lady resorted when she felt herself in difficulties gives us the flavor of religion in contemporary Sri Lanka, its "cultic milieu," which through the press and other modern means of communication reaches out even into quite rural areas.

Several other examples of the reinterpretation of altered states of consciousness according to their institutional context will further illustrate our point. A young man runs a shrine to Kataragama at Dehiwela, an inner suburb of Colombo. He is middle-class and well-educated, having passed the school certificate (G.C.E. "O" level) in seven subjects; his father is a Justice of the Peace, and his lowly occupation embarrasses his parents; there are several Buddhist monks in the family. He first became possessed and went firewalking at the age of eleven; he is possessed by his maternal grandmother, who was a Buddhist "nun." On leaving school at the age of eighteen he went and lived by himself in the country as a Buddhist hermit, practicing the classic Buddhist meditation on kindness (*maitrī bhāvanā*). He attained the higher states of consciousness known as *jhāna* (see above). This accomplishment enabled him to help people by mind reading and giving advice. During this period, which lasted three years, he was not possessed. But his parents insisted that he get married, so he had to return to Colombo. On his marriage his powers were "broken" (*käḍunā*). He returned to possession and firewalking and made them his profession. He derives his income mainly from delivering oracles, an activity that again consists of mind reading and giving advice (which is based on paranormal knowledge of the future). It does not seem far-fetched to suggest that this man is doing the same thing when he mind reads on the basis of Buddhist meditation as when he mind reads through possession. The difference for him is that he can only operate qua meditator when he is chaste, and sexual activity forces him into a socially less prestigious style of life; the main difference for his clientele is that the meditator's services are free while the priest works for fees. Nor does it seem absurd to go further and posit that this young man's experiences of *jhāna* and possession have something in common and that both relate to a problem about his sexuality. We could then connect culture and personality by suggesting that both *jhāna* and possession, being traditionally unusual and inappropriate states for a young man of respectable family to get into, are becoming so much more widespread because of more puritanical attitudes towards the libido and its socialization in urban middle-class culture.

In most (not all) of the cases we have encountered, the subjects retain a traditional sense that the behavior appropriate to meditation is different from that in possession. This was clearly stated by an English-speaking *māṇiyō* whom we came across at the Kālī shrine at Mōdera in north Colombo (see below). She explained that her state of possession (*ārūḍē*) was a permanent condition but she didn't "take" it during meditation—that's quite different. On the other hand, she acquired her "spirit powers" (possession by Viṣṇu-Kataragama),[50] with concomitant ability to give oracles, *by* Buddhist meditation: "after some *bhāvanā* the person is perfect and can understand all this world." She regularly meditates in a special room at home and goes into a *jhāna* (she used the parallel Sanskrit term, *dhyāna*) as a preliminary to entering a possessed trance. Moreover, for this lady and other Buddhist *mǟṇiyō* the ethical situation is isomorphic to the psychological one: their powers are acquired and maintained as a reward for Buddhist merit, a boon requiring the "transference" of that merit to the gods, and are both an expression of their virtue and an instrument for enhancing it, in that they use their powers for the good of the world.

Our final example has interesting parallels to the case of the Dehiwela priest noted above. The vice-principal of a school near Colombo, a follower of the self-ordained monk Uttama Sādhu (see chapter 10), told us that under Uttama Sādhu's guidance he used to attain *jhāna*, in which state he had various paranormal powers; on his marriage all these powers were broken (he used the same word as the Dehiwela priest) and he attained no more *jhāna*, but he discovered that he was able to cure people of all kinds of complaints by the practice of "hypnotism" (he used the English word), the "Indian method" of which he learned from a Sinhala book. The objective similarity between his activities may not be quite as close as in the previous case (we do not know whether he used his *jhāna* to effect cures, though we know that his teacher did); but their significance for the man's social standing and self-image seems obvious; and the connection with sexuality is again almost explicit. The preoccupation with hypnosis, whether with Western or, as here, with Indian prestige, is another phenomenon typical of the widespread flight to the occult.

The Cultic Milieu

This flight to the occult has other manifestations besides those on which we focus. Many seek security in such "sciences" as astrology and palmistry. Astrology we postpone for later (Chapter 9). A palmist in a Colombo suburb charges (in 1978) thirty rupees for a half-hour appointment, which is comparable to the fifty dollars an American psychoanalyst may charge for

[50] Hyphenating the two gods in this manner is to place them in a single category in respect of a particular quality or characteristic, for example, status.

an hour of his time. In Colombo are published at least four Sinhala newspapers dealing with astrology and the occult, newspapers that convey to a wide readership (circulation figures would tell us little, as the papers pass from hand to hand) an amazing mishmash of occult beliefs. A study of this press could constitute a separate monograph; we present but one article and one advertisement. *Situmiṇi* of 24 September 1976 carries the front-page headline (in English): LATE PRIME MINISTER OF SRI LANKA—Mr. B—OR—GOD MANGALANATHA, and then in Sinhala the words "Bandāranāyaka—Sēnānāyaka—Dēvarahasa." The first two of these words are the names of the two major political leaders of Sri Lanka who died in the previous twenty years, and their photographs appear under their names; *dēvarahasa* means "secret of the gods." The whole front page and half of the back page are devoted to a pair of articles under this joint heading, which is, however, misleading because both articles are devoted exclusively to Mr. Bandaranaike's reincarnation as the god Mangalanātha. Dudley Sēnānāyaka appears only to give political balance; one gathers that his reincarnation as a god called Jayanātha figured in an earlier issue. The first article begins with a statement, couched in Buddhist doctrinal terms, that the main difference between men and gods is that men have five constituents (i.e., body, sensations, perceptions, volitions, and consciousness) but gods only have two of these, sensations and perceptions, and have very subtle bodies. This is clearly counter to Buddhist doctrine, according to which *all* beings have volitions and consciousness as well. The article then rambles over to Kataragama, where it appears that an (unnamed) "distinguished company" on 2 March 1967 saw a peacock dancing on Väḍahiṭikanda. (The peacock is Kataragama's mount.) This phenomenon was apparently arranged by Mr. Bandaranaike in his present divine existence and somehow portended his party's election victory in 1970. The main point of the article, however, is that while (the same?) distinguished company was sitting around reciting Buddhist texts at 9:48 P.M. on 13 September 1966, one of them received by automatic writing the message contained in the headline. When he complained to Mangalanātha (the late Prime Minister) that he knew no English, the god wrote in reply (still in English), "Oh," and then, switching to Sinhala, instructed the company to dedicate blue curtains decorated with lotuses in nine shrines to Viṣṇu. For good measure he added a Sinhala verse that translates, "The blue curtain and the lotus flower; the Mahaväli goes and the water flows"—an allusion to the government's major irrigation scheme. This summary may well seem inconsequential, but then so does the article. Automatic writing is not a traditional ingredient of Sinhalese necromancy; it is just as much a Western import as the "spiritboard" that the same article refers to as a "puerile method."

A common thread that runs through many of our case studies is coping with a language one cannot understand. Here it is English. Urban Sri Lanka is full of people taking English lessons and examinations in the search for employment and advancement. Our sample advertisement gives an idea of the typical problems with which people are trying to cope by fair means or foul. The newspaper *Iraṇamaya* ("Fate") of 23 August 1978 carried this notice (in Sinhala):

> "We accept challenges from anyone"
> Considering that it is meritorious to serve,
> *free* to those who cannot raise the money
>
> Extinguishing the fire of anguish of poor wretches with nowhere to turn, making to tremble with fright the sorcerers who have bewitched you, making the earth quake, binding the demons, the valuable
>
> Koṇḍādeniyē Black Magic of the God of Death.
> See for yourselves! No mistake!! True!!! Confidential
> Confidence-inspiring magical power.
>
> Bring under your spell within 36 hours anyone you please. Speed up marriage by overcoming the objections of elders. Bring to your feet the one who has abandoned you. Write both names and ask for details.
>
> Honours! Honours!! Pass your exam with honours!!!
>
> This time pass the exam you are taking with top results. Ask for free details, with either your time of birth or a number below 72. You who have not studied, you who have failed 2 or 3 times, dispel malign astral influence, evil eye, evil tongue, and take the exam with no doubt or fear.
>
> Do you lack the merit to find gems or to make progress?
>
> I give you the necessary to dispel all kinds of black magic, evil eye, evil tongue, malign planetary influence, and so acquire wealth. In-

quire, writing in the time at which you write the letter and a number under 108.

We did in fact visit this gentlemen at Koṇḍādeniya. He appeared to be in his forties. He had been a monk for fifteen years but had left, he said, because public opinion was against monks' doing black magic. He had learnt his magic from a monk (his monastic teacher) and himself had a monk pupil who also practices sometimes. He regards it as the Dhamma of Māra, the classical Buddhist personification of death. A famous Pāli verse says:

Sabbapāpass' akaraṇaṃ kusalass' upasampadā
Sacittapariyodapanaṃ etaṃ Buddhāna sāsanaṃ

("Avoidance of all sin, performance of right, purifying one's thoughts: this is the teaching of the Buddhas.")

Māra's doctrine, he said, was different:

Sabbapāpassa karaṇaṃ akusalass' upasampadā
Sacittāpariyodapanaṃ etaṃ Mārānusāsanaṃ.

("Doing all sin, performance of wrong, not purifying one's thoughts:[51] this is the teaching of Māra.")

This inversion of *sacralia* for magical purposes recalls Satanism in the Christian context. Details of this gentleman's magic would for the most part take us from our theme. But it is relevant that he worked from a Sanskrit book (in Sinhala script) and seemed familiar with the six maleficent acts (*ṣaṭ karma*) of Hindu *śākta tantra*. He worked mainly through Kālī, and many of his clients were local Roman Catholics. He was about to visit the main Kālī shrine at Munnēssarama, though not to offer blood sacrifice there. He did not believe that possession was a genuine phenomenon; firewalking was done either by saying spells (*mantra*) or by mental concentration (*cittekāgratā*). His traditional skepticism about possession reflected the fact that conceptually this gentleman inhabited a comparatively rational world. Both as monk and as technician, albeit of magic, he was fulfilling traditional roles, roles that supplied him with two explanations (for different cases) of firewalking. However, the mental concentra-

[51] We are not quite sure about the third quarter; we were not allowed to write this verse down in the magician's presence.

tion that is the goal of "calming" meditation is not traditionally supposed to be used for such purposes.

One more example of the cultic milieu must here suffice. We were taken by a monk to visit a wealthy middle-class clairvoyant who claimed to operate by looking into a (mystic) television set. This man called in an old retainer, said a few syllables, and the old man became possessed, that is, he shook all over and began to gibber; his master then gave another abrupt order and the possession stopped as suddenly as it had begun. The fortuneteller explained to us that he had a personal spirit who did his bidding and whom he could cause to possess others. This idea, familiar to us maybe from the Arabian Nights or from science fiction, has absolutely no antecedents in Indo-Sri Lankan civilization; the fortuneteller, a fairly educated man, probably picked it up from some book or newspaper article.

At the end of the session the clairvoyant offered to give us his name and address, but we said we already knew it. "How did you learn it?" he asked in great amazement. We had read an envelope lying on his desk. This little story illustrates an important point. Many of these people are living in a world in which they see few or no common-sense explanations, no ordinary causation. Anything the least bit unusual is attributed to a supernatural cause: if a bus comes quickly, Kataragama (or Sai Baba) sent it; if a stranger impinges on one's life, he must, on reflection, have been a deity in disguise. These people are not like the Azande described by Evans-Pritchard, who accept normal causation *plus* witchcraft (I bumped into a post because I did not look out, and I did not look out because I was bewitched); they tend to ignore normal causation. One might even say that their world has become "de-rationalized."

What do traditional Buddhists think of all this? Immediately after visiting the clairvoyant we happened to visit a monastic school (*piriveṇa*) headed by Buddhist monks of the old style to chat about our research with the principal and vice-principal. They agreed that there was an amazing upsurge in the worship of gods, and each ventured a one-word explanation. The old culture looked at the new. "Entertainment" (*vinōde*), said the young vice-principal. "No," corrected his senior, "folly" (*mōḍakama*).

PART TWO

Changes in the Spirit Religion

CHAPTER 2

Re-creating Community: Cult Groups of the Spirit Religion

In this chapter we present a case study of a shrine in a Colombo suburb. We aim to show why people visit it, and how some of the visitors crystallize into a stable core congregation, a cult group. The recently founded urban shrines may thus serve as a focus for a new kind of association, a surrogate for the traditional community life of the village and its kin groups. In the last part of the chapter we shall show how some members of the cult group go on to become priests or priestesses and may in due course lead cult groups themselves. The phenomenon of cult groups around shrines and shrine leaders is not uniquely Sri Lankan but has been widely reported for similar resurgent spirit cults in urbanized sectors of the Caribbean and South America.[1]

In the following three chapters we shall examine in turn the three deities around whom most of these cults have crystallized: Hūniyam, Kālī, and Kataragama. In each of these four chapters of Part Two we shall summarize the socioeconomic changes that seem to us most relevant to understanding the religious change under discussion. Thus we hope to build up a picture of the sea change that has overtaken the mass of Sinhala society, the poor, and how, in interaction with cultural and individual factors, it has affected the spirit religion they practice.

The Decline of the Village Community and Extended Kinship Ties

Traditional Sinhala Buddhist society was based on peasant agriculture. Most people passed their lives in villages or hamlets with a clear communal

[1] See, for example, Alfred Metraux, *Voodoo in Haiti* (New York: Schoken, 1972), pp.

identity. These villages or hamlets in turn consisted mainly of kin groups. Most traditional households consisted of nuclear families, and newly married couples settled in either the husband's or the wife's village (the two were in fact very often the same), rarely in a third place. The nuclear family was embedded in a wider network of kin. The kinship system was a presumptive framework of responsibilities, a structure to guide and support (as well as constrain) the individual.

This pattern of life is eroded by two demographic trends: population growth and mobility. Between the eve of Independence in 1946 and 1981 (most of our fieldwork data antedate this year) the population of Sri Lanka increased from 6,657,339 to 14,850,001 and the Sinhala population from 4,620,507 to 10,985,666. The annual rate of growth between 1971 and 1981 was down to 1.7percent; that still adds more than 250,000 persons a year to the total population. This rate of growth in what remains predominantly an agricultural economy has meant not only impoverishment. In the more thickly populated areas—the whole western and southern littoral and the central area around Kandy—villages have expanded till they converge and the boundaries between them are mere lines drawn on the map for administrative purposes. The area thus demarcated is administered by a government official appointed from the center, the optimistically titled *grāma sēvaka* ("village servant"). He is often a newcomer to the area and sometimes remains personally unacquainted with most of the villagers. He replaced the traditional headman (*gam āracci*) as the local representative of central state authority in 1958. These attempts at administrative rationalization would alone have sufficed to diminish villagers' sense of community.

Only in remote parts of the island do traditional village communities now survive. On the west and south coast, roughly from Chilaw to Matara, and for miles inland and in the central provinces around Kandy, the countryside is so full that it looks like city overspill even though those who live there may rarely even visit the cities. But the landless young villagers are hangers-on of urban life, lounging around the small market towns waiting for something to turn up, a semirural lumpen proletariat. It is universal experience in Sri Lanka that geographic and social mobility have taken on

61–69; Seth and Ruth Leacock, *Spirits of the Deep* (New York: Anchor Books, 1975), pp. 98–121; and especially Victor Turner, "Conflict in Social Anthropological and Psychoanalytical Theory: Umbanda in Rio de Janeiro," in *On the Edge of the Bush* (Tucson: University of Arizona Press, 1985), pp. 125–26.

a new order of magnitude.[2] Marriage partners are now frequently chosen from distant places (often through such impersonal means as newspaper advertisements) and many of the resultant new households are neo-local, set up away from the parents-in-law and other kin. We postpone to Chapter 5 discussion of the fact that the age of marriage is rising because many people are just too poor to marry.

Mobility has been between villages, into "colonies," and into cities. The "colonies" have been formed in waves ever since Independence (a few even earlier), by government action. They are resettlement schemes for landless villagers. Some of them are on relatively small pieces of land alienated from large landholders (notably estates) and parcelled into plots. The conspicuous majority are in the large areas opened up for paddy cultivation in the dry zone of the country. The inhabitants of most of these colonies have been selected (by political patronage) from all over the Sinhala countryside; they arrive with few previous ties or acquaintance. In recent years the government has realized that such random assemblages have acute social problems, and villagers displaced by irrigation schemes have been moved en bloc; this may be expected to mitigate the psychological dislocation, but community is alas not so easily transplanted into a new ecological and economic environment.

Urbanization is the change most obvious to the casual visitor—and yet more far-reaching than is obvious. It is not just a matter of villagers moving to towns as they look for jobs. Many of those who live in what superficially look like villages within a radius of as much as sixty miles of Colombo commute to the capital for regular or casual employment. (The same is true, on a smaller scale, of the smaller cities such as Kandy, Galle, and Matara.) Socially, the many villages within about twenty miles of Colombo have in fact become suburbs. These villages have little or no social cohesion. Their inhabitants are urbanites: many of them have moved house more than once; others have lost touch with the relatives who remain in their villages of origin. Where these urbanites are comparatively well-to-do, middle-class people, they and their houses have displaced the homes and inhabitants of the older village. Nāvala, the erstwhile village with which this chapter is most concerned, is like this. The smart urban-style residences built in the last thirty years have displaced the original villagers, who have dispersed—we know not to where. The priest's little

[2] Kearney and Miller, *Internal Migration*.

wattle-and-daub house now looks like an archaic anomaly; and he has no relatives living in the area.

In traditional communal rituals (*gammaḍuva*) the whole village is a congregation; there are no cult groups of selected individuals. In such a ritual, the village assembles for a yearly ceremony of thanksgiving or first fruits and disperses after the celebrations are over. Cult groups (if that is not too strong a term) have been associated with the activities of the Buddhist temple rather than the god's shrine. There are small groups of pious people (*upāsaka*) who in old age have renounced most lay activities and responsibilities to devote themselves to religion. On Buddhist holy days (*pōya*) these groups of *upāsaka* may gather in the temple to listen to sermons, read and discuss Buddhist texts, "meditate" (by chanting verses), and participate in the temple rituals. By contrast, urban society all over Sri Lanka has now produced another kind of cult group, new to Buddhist Sri Lanka: that associated with a god's shrine. Practically every shrine in urban Sri Lanka has two classes of clients: those who come for help from the gods as occasion demands, and others who form a stable core of believers under the leadership of the priest (*kapurāḷa* or *sāmi*) of the shrine.

The Nāvala Shrine

In September 1968 we studied a shrine in Nāvala, already then a suburb, a few miles outside the city limits of Colombo. The shrine itself is a tiny, unimpressive building with a large sandy compound that serves as a dancing area for large-scale rituals of exorcism. The priest (*kapurāḷa*) lives with his mother, two "wives" (modelling himself in this respect on the god Skanda), and several children in a tiny thatched wattle-and-daub house across from the shrine on the other side of the compound. These unimpressive features stand in sharp contrast to the large houses of middle-class professional people in the neighborhood. However, none of the rich neighbors ever visits it. It is unobtrusively located in a quiet cul-de-sac, though the periodic beat of drums announces its presence.

To the right of the shrine is a large *bō* tree with several "altars" for lighting lamps and offering flowers to the Buddha. The formal suzerainty of the Buddha is always recognized in that no rituals for the gods can take place in the shrine without preliminary permission from the Buddha, who is worshipped at the *bō* tree.

Inside the shrine are altars for the gods Viṣṇu, Gaṇeśa, Skanda, Vibhīṣaṇa, Dēvatā Baṇḍāra, and the goddesses Pattinī and Kālī. The chief deity of the shrine is Īśvara (Śiva). Neither Īśvara nor Gaṇeśa nor Kālī was normally thought of as a member of the traditional village pantheon. Īśvara's suzerainty is a noteworthy innovation. In Sri Lanka it is Viṣṇu who is viewed as the chief god, since he has been charged with protecting Sinhala Buddhism. His subordination to Śiva is a striking departure from the Sinhala tradition. The reason for the change is not too difficult to see. In this shrine, as elsewhere in urban Sri Lanka, the god Skanda is viewed as the most powerful deity, capable of helping the devoted worshipper to achieve his goals, as we show in Chapter 5. With the importance of Skanda worship, the priests have become more interested in the myths associated with him, most of which are Hindu. In Hindu mythology Skanda is the son of Śiva; if so, the father must occupy a position of prestige superior to the son and the other deities who are on the son's level in the pantheon. Thus Śiva presides over the shrine as its head.

The priest of the shrine inherited the office from his father. His brother too has a shrine, in Maharagama, an outlying suburb of Colombo.

The shrine, like many in urban Sri Lanka, has two standard services it renders to its clientele.

1. Every morning at 11:05 A.M. the priest or an assistant goes into a trance and acts as a vehicle for one of the deities in the pantheon, male or female. This again is a departure from tradition. In village Sri Lanka a priest may get possessed by the spirit of *one* of the lower gods (known collectively as the Twelve Gods), but here the *kapurāḷa* can act as a vehicle for any of the major (higher) gods housed in the shrine. Clients visit the shrine and tell the priest their problems. He often utters *śāstra*s, "divine utterances" or "oracles" from the deity. These *śāstra*s in general diagnose the client's troubles, prescribe medicine if he is sick, and give advice for that and other problems.

2. In addition to these regular sessions, the priest holds occasional rituals of countersorcery to cure clients who have been ensorcelled and performs rituals to exorcise persons possessed of evil spirits and demons. Such rituals start at around 6 P.M. and continue until 9 or 10 A.M. the next day. They are known as *käpilla*, "cutting," since in most instances their aim is to "cut" the evil bondage of the sorcerer's magic. We tape-recorded every ritual session held in the *dēvālē* during the period 17 September to

18 October 1968. During this month seventeen regular sessions were held at the *śāstra* hour of 11:05 A.M.; and two major *käpilla* rituals were held. The *käpilla* rituals we have described elsewhere;[3] they are not relevant to the theme of this chapter.

The Clientele and Cult Group

Only seventeen regular sessions were held during the period of research. Sessions were missed either because the priest was busy at a *käpilla* ritual or because no clients came. Many clients have the traditional belief that the best days for invoking the gods are *kemmura* days (Wednesdays and Saturdays) and tend to patronize the shrine on those days. During this period fifty-four clients paid seventy visits to the *śāstra* sessions. All the clients were briefly interviewed and each session was fully tape-recorded. The following basic information comes from the interviews.

1. Practically all the clients came from the suburbs of Colombo or one of the smaller townships within a radius of about thirty miles from the city. As would be expected, none of them were traditional peasant farmers from the villages. Three occupational categories were noted. First, a few were well educated and economically reasonably well off; they either occupied stable government jobs, such as those of Sinhala-educated schoolteachers, or were small businessmen. One client had a son and another had two daughters who were college graduates. A second category, of those employed in minor jobs in the government or city bureaucracy, like police constable, office peon, mechanic, had earnings of about 200 rupees per month (in 1968). A third category was of those in highly unstable jobs (laborer, vendor) or jobs carrying low prestige (lavatory coolie).

There were no wealthy upper-class persons or elite in the sample. Only three clients in the first category had any surplus wealth. Most of them, including all the clients in the second and third categories, were barely able to make ends meet and were living at subsistence level. They were neither peasant cultivators nor fully integrated into urban bourgeois culture.

[3] Gananath Obeyesekere, "Psychocultural Exegesis of a Case of Spirit Possession from Sri Lanka," in *Contributions to Asian Studies* 8: 42–89, reprinted in *Case Studies in Possession*, ed. Vincent Crapanzano and Vivian Garrison (New York: John Wiley, 1977), pp. 235–64.

2. Clients either came for their own problems or on behalf of someone else. Sometimes several people came together, but only the chief person in the group was recorded as the "client." Thus a classification by sex and age may not be too significant. However, out of a total of seventy client visits there were thirty-four males and thirty-six females. Age did not seem particularly significant. No client was under twenty (this was an artifact of the sample), and over half the clients were between twenty-five and forty-five.

3. We found a large proportion of regular clients, defining regulars as those who came to the shrine regularly for over a period of a year in order to cope with their problems. New clients were those who had come to the shrine for a few weeks only. The proportions were as follows:

	Regular	vs.	New
No. of client visits	43	:	27
No. of persons visiting	35	:	19

At least three of the new clients were on their way towards becoming "regulars" and thought of themselves as "members" of the cult group. If we consider these three cases as regular also, the proportion between regulars and new clients is 2:1. The sociological significance of regulars will be discussed later.

The distinction between new clients and regulars comes out clearly when we examine their respective reasons for visiting the shrine, given in table 1. In table 1 we have classified the major reason for the client visit. In column 1 we have listed clearly stated and identifiable illnesses, including those caused by spirits ("spirit intrusion"). By "spiritual reasons" (col-

Table 1
Main Reason for Visiting Nāvala Shrine, by New Clients and Regulars

	Illness	Spiritual reasons	General misfortune	Evil magic	Other	No info.	Total
New clients	6	0	11	0	1	2	20
Regulars	14	11	4	2	2	2	35
TOTAL	20	11	15	2	3	4	55

umn 2) we refer to two types of requests to the deity: to grant either some kind of spiritual power or nonspecific blessings. "General misfortune" (column 3) refers to a series of misfortunes that seems to hit the individual and/or members of his family, such as loss of a material object, desertion by a spouse. "Evil magic" is the belief that the client is a victim of sorcery; he seeks confirmation and help from the deity.

Analysis of table 1 shows some striking differences between regulars and new clients.

1. New clients come for two basic reasons: they have some specific illness, or they seek relief from the misfortunes that seem to be piling on them. By contrast regular clients come for a variety of reasons, including spiritual reasons often of an expressive rather than an instrumental or pragmatic character.

2. The importance of columns 1 and 3 is reversed in the case of new clients and regulars: new clients are greatly concerned with general misfortune whereas only four of the regulars seem concerned about it. Regulars are preoccupied with specific problems: illness, spiritual problems, sorcery.

3. This contrast comes out even more clearly when we consider specifically the illnesses in column 1. When we broke down the data we found that new clients were all victims of serious illnesses, whereas regulars had minor ones. Of the six new clients in column 1, three were possessed by evil spirits and all of them displayed bizarre "hysterical" behavior; one patient had severe anorexia and migraine; another patient was extremely pale, could hardly speak, and was probably suffering from a serious illness; the sixth client's daughter had been suffering from a severe pain in the right side of her abdomen for the last two years. By contrast almost all of the regular clients came for simple illnesses, for example, stomach disorder (two cases), swelling of joints, sores on legs, cold (two cases), worms, pimples(!). We had only two cases here that we considered serious illnesses: the "madness" suffered by a client's sister and anorexia. Both of these clients expressed the view that their specific illnesses were part of a larger series of misfortunes that had hit them.

What then is the implication of these differences between regular and new clients? New clients are potential regulars; the priest is fully aware of this and looks upon new clients as recruits. (He simply cannot make a living without a body of regular clients.) Let us examine the stages (not the processes) by which new clients are converted into regulars.

1. The new client either has a serious illness or is beset by constant misfortune. He seeks a *śāstra* ("prophecy," "divination") from the priest. The *śāstra* deals with a diagnosis of the misfortune and interpretation of it. It also deals with a "cure," generally herbal medicines combined with ritual prescriptions.

2. Two types of client reaction follow the *śāstra* session. Most clients go home and do not come back, either because the medicine has worked, or because it has not and they are therefore dissatisfied customers. A few, however, return to the shrine in order to complete their cure. The priest tells them that the cure will entail several visits; or the client may feel that several visits are required before success is ensured; or—and this is the truly significant reason—the priest while in trance tells the client that his misfortune is due to sorcery (or some other serious supernatural cause), and he must get a *käpilla* ("sorcery-cutting ritual") performed in an elaborate all-night ceremony. Sometimes the priest prescribes a less elaborate ritual in the shrine. We suspect that he does this when he feels a client cannot afford a *käpilla*.

3. If the *käpilla* is successful and the client is "cured," he, and sometimes members of his family, become regular members of the cult group and visit the shrine whenever they suffer illness or any other kind of misfortune. This accounts for the fact that regular clients in our sample visit the shrine for more specific reasons than new clients. Regular clients tend to be ardent believers; almost all of them have told us that they never go to Western doctors or Ayurvedic physicians for their illnesses, but instead obtain medicines from the shrine.

Typical Case of a New Client

The client, a woman thirty years old, came with her husband to ask for a *śāstra* from the priest, who on that day acted as a medium for the god Īśvara (Śiva). The clients came from Welikada, a suburb of Colombo. They said that they were beset by constant misfortune—illness in the family and poverty. Although the husband worked very hard the family led a hand-to-mouth existence. Everyone in the family was restless and constantly quarrelling. A neighbor who was a regular client advised them to consult this *śāstra* ("oracle"). They came here in the hope of receiving the gods' aid to overcome their misfortunes.

The clients go into the shrine at 11:05. They first worship the Buddha and then go into the shrine with a basket of offerings—generally flowers, fruit, and cash (one rupee). The priest, after various preliminary invocations, goes into a trance state in which he is possessed by (the spirit of) Īśvara. With Īśvara's trident in his hand he faces the clients and utters his *śāstra*. We quote portions of the *śāstra*.

> Ah! Verily! you do good to everyone but though you do good, especially I say, your fortune had gone downwards—why this is the case, I will unravel this mystery in great detail today. . . . Verily a group of your close kinsmen think, "Here look how serenely they live, they conduct their lives with propriety, they are becoming more prestigious than us, they live in more glory [*jaya*, 'victory'] than we do"—thus they think, and will it thus. . . . It was three years in terms of years, plus six months in terms of months and in terms of days seventeen days from this day when this darkness befell you.
>
> During this period of darkness, ah, verily, they have joined up with a sorcerer from Malaya [i.e., from Kerala].

The priest goes on to say that this Malayali sorcerer used the spirit of a dead female relative to cast an evil spell on the household. This woman has

> rotten smells emanating from her mouth, she is bald on the top of her head, verily she laughs loudly and vacuously. . . . She has been used by the sorcerer and however much you live in glory that glory gets enshrouded in darkness, troubles wherever you go, troubles wherever you come, especially a woman [spirit] is the chief cause, yes, such that whatever glorious life you lead, such glory will be enshrouded in darkness, troubles wherever you go, wherever you come, things you think and do get lost in a maze. With the will to destroy you the Malayali sorcerer has enlisted others [spirits] also, and with this intention, verily I say, to destroy you all wherever you are, wherever you'll be, even if you are living like kings, to confuse you all . . . with these intentions this sorcerer has taken two bones from the body of a man who had died of heart disease . . . has in-

> scribed your names on the bones; and especially[!] he has inscribed also the names of the following demons: Maru Kāma [demon lover of death], Pillu Kāma [love demon of sorcery], Pali Kāma [demon lover of revenge], Bili Kāma [demon lover of the sacrificial offering]; and then put these two bones aside for a while. Then, verily, having taken a black wild yam, he has carved an image on the yam and, especially, he has pricked thorns of five varieties into the hands, head, and feet of the image and has brought into this spell, has trapped as many demons and demonesses into the spell[?], he has taken six lengths of black thread, made seven knots [i.e., he has uttered a spell and tightened the knots to trap demons], tightened them, and has tied this string on the neck of the image . . . and making the wish [in the spell] that the lady of this place be ruined . . . he has taken these objects to a grave for a period of seven days and has made these objects "alive."

The priest goes on to say that the sorcerer placed these charmed objects under a plank covering a drain over which the client walks. The client had walked over it at an inauspicious time. After this the human bones were thrown in the ocean. As a result of this the client experiences "more troubles tomorrow than today, more troubles the day after tomorrow than tomorrow, more troubles the day after and the day after that." Thereafter, the yam image was thrown into a muddy marsh, so that the client's life goes continually downwards, the client can't raise her head, the body weakens, becomes thin. "Not only this: periodically you have mental pains, pains in the chest. . . . Not only this: you eat, drink, and your wealth is lost, and your life is fruitless." And so it goes on and on in this vein, "not only this . . . not only this. . . ." Having stated the underlying causes of the client's misfortune and the dire effects that are yet to come the priest holds out hope for the future and prescribes a cure. "In the life span allotted to you, you have time yet to rise to glory, you can rise to three statuses. . . . [Your present failure] is due to the deadly thorns stuck by others . . . will that the ill effects of the thorns may end, look between the north and the east, will with joy that new bounty may arise, and the misfortunes may be done with—finished." The god now commands the patient to offer the following items:

> seven betel leaves, one silver coin, one ash melon fruit, eight pins made of five metals, five ornaments [for deities]; six red stones and

> blue stones on them, and with incense, and with nine red coconuts offer these at this place [the shrine] for three consecutive days, and at the end of the third day I will end your misfortunes and bring you glory. Since I [i.e., Īśvara] will bring you success and victory, bring the following offerings to the Prince Skanda, the god Däḍimuṇḍa, and mother Bhadra Kālī; no need for other offerings, since we [i.e., the gods] only require the meritorious acts of humans. . . . But on that day bring five types of sweets, five types of fruits, seven types of seeds, one torch, two coconut flowers, five bottles of oil, one and a half measures of incense, and also four yards of yellow cloth, that is all(!) that's necessary for the *pūjā*. But for the well-being of those who work in this place you must offer ninety-seven rupees and twenty-one cents. . . . I will end the period of darkness, I will create new glories for you, peace, blessing, contentment, joy—I will show you the paths to achieve these.

The case of the *śāstra* quoted above is utterly typical of new-client problems. The priest's response is based on a series of evaluations—the nature of the client's complaint, the financial status of the client, and finally the client as a potential recruit. For example, if the client is possessed by a spirit and is given to "hysterical" behavior the priest would almost inevitably recommend a night-long *käpilla* for exorcising the demon irrespective of the financial status of the client, because these clients (we shall show later) are sure recruits. In the case quoted above the priest told us that the clients would not be able to afford a night-long *käpilla*, so he had recommended a minor one. Here too the intention is to *cut* (*käpilla*) the effects of sorcery: this is generally done by cutting the ash melon fruit in half at the conclusion of the ritual.

The priest's technique is a simple yet powerful one. He interprets the misfortunes of the client as due to sorcery, a kind of interpretation that is always in the back of the minds of all who come here. His statement is authoritative, for it comes from the god Īśvara. By it the client's suspicions are confirmed; or if he did not consciously suspect sorcery, the idea is now established in his mind. The belief that misfortune is due to sorcery is comforting: one is absolved from personal responsibility for one's "fate." Furthermore, in this case, as in almost all of the cases in which sorcery is diagnosed, the priest identifies the sorcerers (or those who hired a sorcerer) as kinsmen or neighbors of the client who are practicing black magic out of envy, spite, or revenge. This gives the client an opportunity to search out among his kinsmen and neighbors those whom he (the client) hates, and he projects his own hostility onto others, who then become "scapegoats." He can then make a delayed rationalization and justification of his hatred toward his kinsmen or neighbors: "I have a perfect right to hate them since they have practiced sorcery on me." Thus the displacement of responsibility from self to other, the projection of one's own hostility, are reasons why new clients are more receptive to sorcery explanations than to alternative explanations of a more general sort (like the *karma* theory) that are also available in the culture.

The priest's *śāstra* is highly specific regarding the details of sorcery (the actual demons are named, places and times are specific), as well as unverifiable, general, and unspecific regarding those who did it (the nature of the enemy is not specified—references to the spirit of an old lady, who could be any old lady, and so forth). The specific details give a ring of authenticity and factuality to the sorcery, and the general references help the client to fill in with his own projections. All this helps to persuade the client of the truth of the *śāstra*. The *śāstra* also immediately raises the anxiety level of the client: the horrible portents of sorcery and the dire consequences yet to follow frighten the client, who has experienced enough frustration and misfortune. Having scared the client, the *śāstra* offers hope for the future. The evil can be eliminated, and a bright future awaits the client—provided that the ritual is held and payment made to those who work there (the priest makes explicit that the deity himself is not interested in such materialistic things).

The Formation of the Cult Group

If the patient feels that the *käpilla* has been successful, he may become a member of the cult group. Once he joins the cult group, the compensations of cult membership are so great that he rarely leaves, unless perhaps to join another group. Thirteen of the regulars interviewed volunteered the information that their faith in the priest was due to a *käpilla* he had performed; one client said that while in a trance he had cured her sick child with a medical prescription. In some *käpilla* there are much more dramatic ways of incorporating the client into the cult group. These *käpilla* rituals are elaborate exorcisms for persons who have been possessed by the spirit of a dead ancestor. The patient acts out in the temple compound, behaving like a demon—hooting, shouting, and dancing with the priest. At a late stage in the ritual, before the ash melon is cut, the following rite is performed. The priest and patient are dancing in the temple compound to the beat of drums. A chair is brought into the dancing area and the priest's assistant stands on it with a cane in his hand. The priest points a coconut flower at the patient and then at the chair. The patient crawls under the chair, going to-and-fro several times. The priest directs the patient: to-and-fro he crawls, sometimes for ten minutes, abjectly grovelling on the floor, literally eating the dust. This is a crucial episode in the ritual of exorcism and it has several meanings. One symbolic meaning of the ritual is clear: it is a rebirth rite. The patient crawls under the assistant priest and is symbolically reborn as a member of the cult, subject to the authority (symbolized by the cane) of the priests of the shrine. These patients eventually become ardent and devoted members of the cult organization.

The *käpilla* is not only a curing ritual but also acts as an initiation into the cult group. Once the client becomes a regular visitor to the shrine he usually undergoes an involuntary change of name. This is interesting because there is no formal rule that an initiated member must change his name. Name changing nevertheless occurs, so that the client's formal name—associated with a variety of secular statuses—is never used. Rather an intimate name or a nickname is used, for example, Pot Mahatmayā ("Mr. Book," for the bookseller), Mudalāli ("merchant"), "Teacher" (the English word is used for Miss Perera, a schoolteacher), Sōmā (a diminutive for Sōmāvatī). Thus the regulars become members of an intimate, exclusive group. The cult acts as a kind of substitutive kin group in which individuals can depend on each other for mutual sympathy, nurturance, and comradeship. However, it is not an egalitarian organization: the priest is the acknowledged leader, and the wealthier members of the group act as a kind of committee that handles the financial and organizational aspect of the cult, its diverse religious and social activities. Though only the priest is formally a leader, members of the cult committee are highly respected and often exercise leadership roles.

The sense of cult exclusiveness is fostered by certain formal rules that the members must obey. These are commands issued by the god through the priest. Many of the rules pertain to canons of propriety and decorum while in the shrine premises. The rules are revised periodically and new ones introduced. Two rules are specially important: one a rule of strict vegetarianism and the other a rule of ritual behavior that each client has to observe as a part of his daily routine.

1. Vegetarianism

A regular is a strict vegetarian. Sociologically viewed, the food taboo demarcates the cult as a group apart from the outer world, where "impure" food habits prevail. Members are pure as opposed to the impure mundane society round them. On the individual level it is a deliberate act of renunciation that establishes the individual's strong commitment to the deities of the cult. It is strongly believed that violation of the taboo may cause illness or perhaps death. Even involuntary violation may cause grave anxiety. For example, Nōnā Hāmī (age forty-two), a regular client, is a vegetable seller in a suburban market. Her husband, who is not a member, brought cooked beef from a small restaurant and ate it with his dinner, though she had forbidden the eating of any kind of meat or fish in the house. She went several times to the shrine to get herself purified but every time the god (i.e., the priest) passed her by without a word. She came again a few days later suffering from severe stomach pains. This time the deity uttered a *śāstra* for her and told her that she had to perform a special *pūjā* in the shrine to cleanse herself of this impurity and appease the anger of the gods.

2. Ritual Routine

At home each client has to perform a regular religious routine in accordance with specific *śāstra* injunctions. The rituals involve facing in a particular direction and uttering a special prayer to the deity. Psychologically viewed, these rituals are like the compulsive acts of neurotics and they are performed in a rigorous, obsessive-compulsive manner.[4] They act as substitutes for neurotic compulsive "rituals" and as a defense against anxiety.

The food taboo and the ritual routine symbolize a unique personal contract with the deity and express the commitment of the client to the deity

[4] It is in relation to these kinds of rituals that one sees a parallelism between religion and obsessive compulsive neurosis, rather than ritual or religion in general, as Freud believed. See his paper, "Obsessive Acts and Religious Practices" (1907), in *The Standard Edition*, vol. 9 (London: Hogarth Press, 1959), pp. 117–27.

and the cult. Similarly, the talisman most clients wear around their necks or arms serves as a badge of cult membership.

Other Colombo Shrines

The Nāvala shrine is a small one and is typical of the many shrines that have mushroomed in and around the city of Colombo. It is easy to demonstrate that it is no isolated case and that cult groups have arisen all over urban Sri Lanka, in particular in the city of Colombo. In 1976 we collected some basic information from ten shrines associated with Buddhist temples in probably the most urbanized area in the capital—Colombo 9 and 10. Here we are concerned only with the clientele; for other details see Chapter 3. Almost all these shrines have both classes of clients: new clients and regulars. Clients come every day of the week, but there is an increase in numbers on *kemmura* days. We asked the priests to estimate the numbers of new clients and regulars in their shrines. We have not verified the ac-

Table 2
Estimated Client Visits on Kemmura *Days in Shrines Located in Ten Buddhist Temples*

Name of temple	Estimated client visits per day	*Kemmura* days	Regulars
Mahā Visuddhārāmaya	25	30	10
Śrī Jayasēkarārāmaya	30	50	10
Purāna Śrī Mahā Vihāra	25–30	50	10
Śrī Nāgamanārāmaya	7	12	2
Mallikārāmaya	15–25	25	5
Vikramasiṃhārāmaya	10–15	—	10
Ñāṇavimalārāmaya	no estimates: priest visits shrine twice weekly		
Vēḷuvanārāmaya	no priest		
Bauddha Madhyasthānaya	no priest		
Dakṣiṇārāmaya	no special shrine, only pictures of gods		5

curacy of these statements. It is likely that the numbers are inflated, though our interviews suggested the importance of the cult groups in several of these shrines. It is at least clear that the numbers forming these cult groups are smaller than at the Nāvala shrine. This is not surprising. These shrines serve only small local areas. Moreover:

1. Several of the chief monks do not personally believe in spirit worship or are indifferent to it. Most monks stated that they agreed to establish the shrines because of pressure from clients and/or the intercession of the priest.
2. Some of these shrines simply have no room to expand. Two monks told us that they would like to add shrines to their temples (which lacked them) but were hampered by lack of space.
3. Some of the priests themselves discourage possession by clients, especially their claim to being possessed by divine beings.
4. Several of these shrines, we shall soon show, were but recently founded and are run by young priests. It is likely that some of them will become popular in due course.
5. Most important, many clients are drawn to new, large, and highly specialized shrines in and near Colombo. Examples of such shrines are the Kataragama shrine at Lunāva, the Bellanvila temple with its many shrines, the Mōdera shrine for the goddess Kālī, and the Hūniyam shrine at Baseline Road, Demaṭagoḍa, which we studied (see Chapter 3). These major shrines serve every sector of society from the richest to the poorest. They receive financial support from rich businessmen, professional people, and high-ranking bureaucrats. All these places have regulars who form cult groups of the type we have described for Nāvala. These cult groups assemble for the ceremonies that are held on special days (like *kemmura* days and shrine festivals).

Regulars and New Clients at the Lunāva Shrine

The Lunāva shrine is credited with many miracles (*hās kam*) and is patronized by every segment of urban society—from the wealthy elite to the urban poor living at or near subsistence level. Generally thirty to forty people visit the shrine on weekdays and sixty to eighty-five on Sundays.

The distinction between regulars and new clients comes out very clearly in Gunasekera's study. She interviewed fifty-one clients during a ten-day period in July to August 1973. Initially she tried to interview every third client but this was not often possible. The data, though not strictly random, probably represent a fair cross section of the people who patronize the shrine.

Gunasekera defines regulars as those who visit the shrine at least "twice a week even when they do not have an immediate problem" and have patronized the shrine for at least a year.[5] She goes on to say: "This is very different from the peasant attitude to the spirit cult. Peasants will not visit the shrine unless they have a specific problem."[6] In the sample interviewed, there were thirty-five regulars to sixteen new clients. Of the regulars only ten came for specific problems (such as illness). Twenty-five came for the following reasons: to transfer merit to the gods, to give thanks to the gods, to get the blessings of the gods. In fact, all those who sought nonspecific blessings of the gods were regulars; furthermore, all those who came for spiritual (expressive) reasons (generally seeking power through possession) were also regulars. By contrast, all the new clients came here for some specific misfortune—marital problems, lost property, illness, etc. It is true that eight regulars came here for illness as against three new clients. Yet, as in Nāvala, the new clients had acute or serious illnesses whereas the regulars came for minor complaints—coughs, colds, stomach disorders.

One of Gunasekera's interesting findings is the relationship between client residence and regularity of visits. Twenty-four regulars came from the area near the shrine, particularly from the large town of Moraṭuva, eleven from outside. By contrast, out of sixteen new clients only three came from Moraṭuva; thirteen came from outside. New clients came from long distances (some from about one hundred miles away), attracted by the fame of the shrine. Moreover, there were five Christians among them (their proportion in the general population), which indicated that the popularity of the shrine, and especially of its deity Hūniyam, attracted both Buddhists and Christians.

The implication of this pattern is clear. Regular visits to the shrine take both time and money; hence only those who live near the shrine can visit it easily. This is confirmed by comparison with the eleven regulars who

[5] Gunasekera, "Deity Propitiation," p. 55.

[6] Ibid., p. 55.

live outside Moraṭuva: eight of them are from the elite, or at least hold stable jobs, and so could afford to pay regular visits to the shrine. What then happens to most new clients from outside the area? They presumably tend to become regulars at a shrine closer to their homes, or join other kinds of cult groups, or help to establish one if none is available.

The Cult Group as a Surrogate Kin Group

A cult group functions (among other things) as a kind of fictional kin group. It is a voluntary association under the leadership of the priest. We have remarked above how in such areas the nuclear family has been physically isolated and removed from its traditional base as a part of a larger kinship network. Poverty and the housing shortage often mean that the household is larger than the typical nuclear family in the West, which consists of a married couple and their unmarried children. Nevertheless, the urban household depends on its own economic and moral resources. As in the West, family members have to interact more intensively. In the village other kinsmen often intervene to settle conflict in the family; here they are no longer available to act as peacemakers. Given conditions of urban poverty and limited good, conflicts are inevitable between spouses, between parents and children, and between siblings. On the other hand, Colombo also contains many lonely people (mainly but not only men) who have left their families in the village and come to the city to earn a living. Some visit their families periodically, the less successful cannot afford to.

These strains of urbanization are familiar all over the Third World today. The West experienced them long ago. In his account of Protestant sects during the British civil war, Christopher Hill writes that London's "population may have increased eightfold between 1500 and 1650. . . . There was more casual labour in London than anywhere else, there was more charity, and there were better prospects for earning a dishonest living."[7] (Incidentally we note that then too the flight to the cities was due to the push of rural impoverishment rather than the pull of industrialization.) For the new arrivals "the sects . . . provided social insurance in this world as well as in the next."[8]

[7] Christopher Hill, *The World Turned Upside Down* (London: Temple Smith, 1972), p. 33.

[8] Hill, *World*, p. 34.

We shall have more to say on these matters later, but here let us emphasize the kin nature of the cult groups. In this sense they are different from clubs and other voluntary associations in the West.

The lack of client kin ties comes out clearly when we compare the *käpilla* rituals in Nāvala with similar exorcistic rituals in the villages. Traditionally an exorcistic ritual is held in the village of the patient. During the ritual members of the kin group assist the afflicted family in various ways and, as anthropologists have noted, this type of kin support has a profound effect on the patient's morale. By contrast, most *käpilla* rituals at Nāvala and other urban shrines are held in the shrine, not in the house of the patient. The patient's more distant relations are conspicuous by their absence. In some cases even members of the patient's immediate family (siblings, parents) are not present. If the patient is married, the spouse and children and an occasional relative may be present; if unmarried, the parents and a few unmarried siblings may attend. Assistance in the ritual is not provided by kinsmen but by the cult regulars, many of whom visit the shrine for the *käpilla*. This cooperation by "outsiders" must be apparent to the client and his family and must serve as a further impetus for them to join the cult themselves. The cult group represents a response to social change on the "urban" level—a unique type of voluntary association modelled on the basis of kin and family ideology and operating within the framework of a religious belief system.[9]

We note one difference from comparable circumstances in, say, seventeenth-century London—the results of medical advance. There, effective medical help was rarely available: there were few doctors; they normally had to be paid; and even they often did more harm than good.[10] In Sri Lanka today the medical conquest of certain diseases has rendered obsolete the cults that traditionally aimed to control them (see Chapter 3). Moreover, everyone in Colombo has some access to modern medical services, including free hospitals. The illnesses for which people visit shrines are conceptualized under the category of *dōsa*, "afflictions," which is wider than disease. It ranges from physical diseases that are still incurable, such as cancer, through vivid disorders of clearly emotional origin, to feelings

[9] Victor Turner, "Umbanda," makes the same point. "My argument is that for Umbandist stargroupers, the cult center is, in the atomistic urban environment, a surrogate family" (p. 126). His "stargroup" is roughly equivalent to our "cult group."

[10] Keith Thomas, *Religion and the Decline of Magic* (London: Weidenfeld and Nicolson, 1971), pp. 5–14.

of malaise that may or may not manifest themselves in physical symptoms, feelings that among these clients are typically ascribed to sorcery.

Specific Functions of the Cult Group

Urban shrines have a whole program of activities that are both social and religious, drawing clients closer to each other and increasing their faith in the cult. We may broadly divide the activities that the shrines perform and foster for regulars into five categories.

1. Outpatients' Clinic

Regulars come to the shrine often, sometimes to visit and gossip and at other times to consult the *śāstra*. They come for very specific and sometimes trivial complaints. The priest always prescribes medicines. We have carefully collected the priest's prescriptions over a month and can affirm that the medicines he prescribes come straight from the Ayurvedic medical tradition; they are of the type prescribed by native physicians and presumably efficacious for the minor ills with which clients are afflicted. But there is a crucial difference from consulting a doctor: the prescription comes from the deity himself and the physical medicine is always associated with ritual prescriptions. The psychological effect is obvious. In many clients hypochondriacal tendencies are satisfied. The *śāstra* are also good therapy for psychosomatic illnesses. Nevertheless, illness seems to be mainly a pretext for visiting the shrine. The important reason is the visit itself, to gossip, meet members of the group, and break away from the routine of everyday activity.

2. Pilgrimages

One of the most popular and exciting events regularly organized by members of the cult is a pilgrimage to traditional Buddhist places of worship and/or the central shrines of the major deities. About six such pilgrimages are organized every year; the group members hire a bus for the purpose. The most frequent and popular pilgrimages are to Kataragama, the central shrine of the god Skanda, and to Alutnuvara, the shrine of Däḍimuṇḍa. During visits to the Däḍimuṇḍa shrine the Nāvala priest puts the whole group en masse into a trance! In addition, the priest may recommend that an individual or a smaller group visit one of these shrines to fulfill vows or undergo penances.

3. Rituals at the Shrine

Regulars often visit the shrine to witness rituals. The Nāvala shrine also holds a large-scale annual festival in which all regulars participate. This festival is, among other things, the annual thanksgiving to the gods of the shrine for the benefits they have bestowed on the cult group. Practically every urban shrine has such an annual festival of thanksgiving.

4. Discussions of Religious Topics

When he is in a trance state, the priest often utters sermons. If, for example, he is possessed by the god Viṣṇu, he will preach a sermon on Buddhism, since Viṣṇu is the guardian of the Buddhist church. At other times a deity will speak through the priest and mention episodes from his (the deity's) life. Sometimes the priest (i.e., the deity speaking through him) may even "emend" historical accounts given in Sri Lankan chronicles like the *Mahāvaṃsa*.[11] This stimulates members of the cult group to discuss the sermons.

These trances also provide opportunity for the priest to introduce new religious ideas (typically they are Hindu in character) that he may have picked up from discussions with other religious professionals or enthusiasts. Such discussions take place informally at pilgrimage centers or houses of friends, though we have at least one case of a priest at a Colombo shrine who summons other priests for regular seminars and discussions of religious topics.

5. Spiritual Development and Uplift

Practically all the regulars admit that participation in the activities of the shrine helps them in their spiritual development. Everyone is aware of the spiritual benefits the shrine brings to them, but the nature of these benefits varies widely. While group members have common spiritual interests, some also have individual spiritual goals. In table 1 we showed that eleven regular clients came to the Nāvala shrine for spiritual reasons. Of these four came specifically to ask the deity for power to utter *śāstra* or (what in practice comes to the same) to obtain the power to be possessed by a deity of the shrine. One person came because he was in communication with the god Skanda, who gave him special messages and spiritual

[11] For other attempts at revising history see chap. 12.

instructions. Since these spiritual goals are an important dimension of client aspiration, let us discuss them further.

From Patient to Priest

In this section we shall deal with the spiritual aspirations of two categories of clients: a category of regulars or would-be regulars who have been possessed by evil spirits and have undergone a *käpilla* ritual; and those regulars who have come to seek power, that is, the ability to utter *śāstra* and sometimes *pēna* ("prophecy," "visions"). This quest for spiritual power is so common nowadays as to constitute the prime motivation of many regular visitors to urban shrines.

In Nāvala the curing of individuals (generally women) possessed by evil spirits is one of the most important occasional rituals performed by the priest. We are not concerned in this chapter with the psychological problems expressed in the idiom of spirit possession[12] but with one aspect of the client's spiritual experience—possession. Every client who is diagnosed by the priest as being possessed by spirits has experienced temporary seizures during which he shouts, utters obscenities, and manifests other kinds of "strange" behavior. During the exorcism the following types of activity are standard:

1. The priest goes into a trance state in which he is possessed by the spirit or essence of a major deity of the pantheon. During the course of the ritual he acts as medium to three of the following gods or goddesses: Skanda, Viṣṇu, Īśvara, Däḍimuṇḍa, Vibhīṣana, Kālī, Pattinī. The deity (i.e., the priest) and the evil spirit (i.e., the patient) dance in the ritual arena at various points in the ritual. For the patient this experience is profoundly moving. She, or the spirit within her, is dancing with the deities, interacting with them face to face. During this interaction the patient sometimes verbalizes her inner conflicts through the idiom of the demon possessing her; then the god who is confronting her promises to banish the demon from her body. At other times the patient acts out—

[12] For a discussion of this problem see Gananath Obeyesekere, "The Idiom of Demonic Possession: A Case Study," in *Social Science and Medicine* 14: 97–111, reprinted in *Labelling Madness*, ed. Thomas T. Scheff (Englewood Cliffs, N.J.: Prentice Hall, 1975), pp. 135–51.

dances violently, shouts, yells, abuses, may threaten to assault people or tear her clothes off, and sometimes (we guess) achieves an orgasm. These are what Wallace calls cathartic strategies.[13] At other times the priest (deity) gives the patient (demon) a bunch of coconut flowers (serving as a whip). The patient beats herself with it; on other occasions the priest beats the patient. This may serve both cathartic functions (if the patient is masochistic) and control functions, with the latter instilling obedience in the patient (demon).

2. The priest employs other symbolic means to bring the patient under control. We have described how the patient crawls under a chair on which an assistant priest stands and is "reborn" as a member of the cult group. The patient is humiliated and shamed. She expresses her self-abnegation and subservience to the priests of the shrine. After this is over, she is brought before other authority figures: the Buddha, the gods housed in the shrine, her parents, and perhaps her husband. She is made to bow low before them and seek their forgiveness.

These experiences have profound psychological effects. The patient interprets them in a religious idiom. Having been confronted with evil spirits, having those spirits exorcised by the priests of the shrine, having interacted with the gods, it is not easy for the patient to revert to the drab routine of her workaday life. No wonder that the erstwhile patient wants to become a priest and relive, in a more orderly and controlled fashion, those intense spiritual experiences.

Once cured, the patient joins the cult group or else is converted into a priest or priestess of the Nāvala shrine. The latter happens as follows. In the early hours of the morning, at the very conclusion of the *käpilla*, the deity announces through the priest that the patient has the *ākarṣaṇa balaya* of a particular named deity or deities. *Ākarṣaṇa balaya* is the "magnetic power" of the spirit or essence of a deity. This is a message to the patient that she can participate directly in the rituals of the shrine as a priestess. After the ritual is over, she can ponder over this message and make her decision. If her decision is positive, the priest gives her a series of instructions that culminate in a large-scale, formal ritual of initiation (a modified *käpilla*) in which he, as the vehicle of the deity concerned, formally be-

[13] A.F.C. Wallace, "The Institutionalization of Cathartic and Control Strategies in Iroquois Religious Psychotherapy," in *Culture and Mental Health*, ed. M. K. Opler (New York: Macmillan, 1959), pp. 63–96.

stows power on the erstwhile patient by giving her the *āyuda* ("insignia" or "weapon") of the deity she must serve. The client is now converted into a junior priestess, who generally acts as a medium for a goddess, Kālī or Pattinī, during *käpilla* rituals and during the annual festival of the shrine. In some cases, the patient may set up her own shrine in a room in her house and seriously adopt the vocation of priestess and prophetess.

Men take a similar road to priesthood, but they bypass the patient stage. Such men interpret their seizures as indicating potentiality for some sort of power. They would like to get the magnetism (*ākarṣaṇa balaya*) of a deity and visit the shrine regularly for divine help to achieve their goal. The priest in his trance may then state that the client in fact has the power: he gives further instructions and the client is soon converted into a priest in much the same manner as the female clients. During the one month of our survey three male clients visited the shrine seeking for power. Two women came for similar purposes during the same period, and we have information on six more cases from subsequent research on the Nāvala shrine.

Two Priestesses: An Illustration

We have detailed case histories of several patients who progressed into the priesthood—their early and later lives, the history of their illnesses and methods of coping with them, and a full tape recording of the exorcisms and subsequent installation rituals. However, here we shall just use two cases to outline the journey from patient to priestess.

Sumanāvatī is a forty-five-year-old woman married to a postman working at Piliyandala, ten miles from Colombo. She had had several spirit attacks since puberty, but the serious ones started in 1966 when her dead grandmother—whom she loved very much—possessed her. Several *śāstra*s and rituals were held to banish the spirit but to no avail. Eventually she was taken to Nāvala and during the *śāstra* the priest, with considerable insight, told her that she had the magnetism (*ākarṣaṇa balaya*) of the goddess Pattinī. She is not only possessed of the spirit of her dead grandmother but she also had the propensity to a Pattinī *ārūḍē*, that is, the capacity to be possessed by a good deity. Indeed, for several past births she had been meditating on this wish and she would realize it in her present life. An exorcism was performed for her on 24 September 1968. In the early part of the ceremony the priest became the medium for Īśvara. About 8:15 P.M. a dialogue ensued between god and evil spirit, acting through the bodies of priest and patient. We quote excerpts from this dialogue:

God Īśvara: With joy I say that the reception of the garland of magnetism [*ākarṣaṇa mālāva*] of the Seven Pattinī is near and, as a result, when you leave this human body you can achieve a great deal of merit. . . . From the vast store of merit you too will have your share. . . . Hence you must swear that you will leave this human body at 4:20 in the morning as you promised us earlier.

Spirit: God, I will leave [this body] for a period of three years.

God Īśvara: Verily! not for just three years. Hah! This human body has to be consecrated to Pattinī and so, especially, that Seven Pattinī Goddesses' magnetism will raise this body into high [status]. . . . Will you [therefore] leave this body? Hah! Speak at once [He orders roughly].

Spirit: Is that true? Is that true? Will you raise me [my status]?

God: Yes!

Spirit: Lord God, are you saying the truth? [!]

God: Yes . . .

Spirit: If that is true I'll leave [this body] for good. . . .

God: Yes! Verily I am the immortal Īśvara, yes! I don't lie . . . from the time the world existed I have never told a lie. . . . Yes! Meditate on my truthfulness, yes! Are you going to respect this rise [in status]?

Spirit [humble tones]: I respect it.

[An assistant brings a picture of the Buddha and Īśvara asks the spirit to swear before the Buddha that it will leave the body of the patient.]

God: Again place your hands together on your head and swear that this human body is now consecrated to the goddess Pattinī. Touch [the picture] three times and say that this body is consecrated to the goddess Pattinī. Hah! Verily I say that this body is consecrated to the goddess Pattinī. Swear three times!

Spirit: This human body is consecrated to the goddess Pattinī.

God: Saying in that manner won't do. You must touch this "Buddha-picture-shadow" . . . touch this shadow and swear. . . .

Spirit: I am loath to leave, O lord God.

God: If so, I'll have to punish you. . . . Swear and say that this body will take on a noble character.

Spirit: May this human body take on a noble character.

God: . . . you must swear and say that never again will you inhabit this mortal body.

Spirit [touching the picture of the Buddha]: Never again will I enter this human body!

God: Yes, especially say, "As long as this human body exists I will not cause it suffering." Yes!

Spirit [swears]: As long as life lasts in the body I will not inflict suffering on this human body.

God: Verily may this noble human body be consecrated to the goddess Pattinī.

Spirit [swears]: May this noble human body be consecrated to the goddess Pattinī.

After this the god Īśvara gave a series of ritual instructions, interdictions, and medicines for the patient. Three days after the exorcism (27 September 1968) Sumanāvatī sent her brother for further instructions during the 11:05 sessions; again she came personally for instructions on 3 October 1968 and 10 October 1968. An important incident occurred on the latter date. The priest was possessed by Gaṇeśa and while he was uttering *śāstras* Sumanāvatī got possessed again, but the deity told Sumanāvatī (since the grandmother's spirit was no longer in her) that she was ready for the Pattinī *ārūḍē*. "The time for keeping the company of the dead is over, now finally . . . time for keeping the company of the goddess." In his *śāstra* he instructed her in precise detail to sew a gown, belt, blouse, etc., to wear as the vestment of the deity. He told her that within thirty days she would have a "great victory," that is, *mukha varam* or "mouth warrant," the power to utter *śāstra*. The reference is to the formal installation: within thirty days the woman will be given permission to speak on behalf of the deity.

On the day of Sumanāvatī's exorcism a classificatory brother's daughter was present. This girl, Kusumāvatī (twenty years old), had a similar history of possession. During her aunt's exorcism she too got into a trance and started yelling and dancing. According to the priest she had a similar power. Thus she too had an exorcism. During Kusumāvatī's exorcism her aunt got possessed again and danced in the ritual arena with the priest, who looked upon it as a Pattinī *ārūḍē*. Kusumāvatī was also given instructions similar to those given her aunt, and she was formally installed as a priestess about three months later.

Both were highly intelligent women. Initially each worked as a priestess for one or two days of the week in the Nāvala shrine; subsequently they got instructions to establish shrines in their own houses. Kusumāvatī's parents at first objected to this, but the deities, speaking through the girl, forced them to agree. When we interviewed them on 1 June 1970, both women were fully involved in their new roles. Our impressions of the two women were then as follows:

> When Sumanāvatī was a patient she could not bear to hear the sound of drums or Buddhist chanting of Buddhist texts (*pirit*). Now she can, and she has never got "ill" again. She now utters *śāstra* and practices *käpilla*; she speaks with pride of her achievements. Since obtaining *mukha varam* ("mouth warrant") she has uttered over one hundred *śāstra*s and has performed seven *käpilla* rituals. She described them well: she told us that two of her patients—a thirty-year-old and an eighteen-year-old female—will acquire power from the god Kataragama! Her husband stated that he was pleased with her transformation, not to mention the added income.
>
> When we met Kusumāvatī as a patient, she was extremely thin, shy, withdrawn, and looking very depressed and lethargic. The contrast now was truly impressive: she was energetic, talkative, and spoke to us with considerable self-assurance. Also she was no longer thin; she looked physically attractive and had a healthy complexion. Her new role had given her a new self-image and also enhanced her status and given her fame. Two weeks ago, she said, many people came to see her in an *ārūḍē* of the goddess Sarasvatī. She no longer fell ill and could calmly hear drumming and *pirit* chanting.
>
> We noted that she started with a Pattinī *ārūḍē*; now she could take the *ārūḍē* of any deity. During her *ārūḍē* people from neighboring villages come for *śāstra*; she prescribes medicines, utters prophecies, gives the blessings of the deities during these sessions. She told us that she has performed at least four *käpilla* rituals during the last few months, assisted by her aunt, Sumanāvatī. All these rituals were performed in her (parents') house: the Nāvala priest was present, but

only as a "witness." She, however, offered him the client fees from the *käpilla* rituals as a token of her gratitude.

Kusumāvatī's mother said that she has had four proposals for marriage and that the parents will soon select a suitable partner for her. Kusumāvatī also wants to get married and settle down. She said that when she gets married she will give up her priestly role and settle down to a "normal" existence.[14]

On the basis of the preceding discussion we may infer certain principles underlying the conversion of patient to priest or priestess.

1. The individual's propensity to possession by a demon is utilized in the post-*käpilla* proceedings. The evil demon is expelled and a positive deity is substituted.

2. The patient is given a new role and a higher status. For a woman the status change is striking: she has a new freedom. This is a "role resolution" of a psychological conflict: in her new role she can put her conflicts to creative use. Her earlier sickness had impaired her role performance; the new status provides an opportunity for role performance more congruent with her inner needs.

3. The individual has, in her own estimation, developed spiritually. She lives in a spiritual world to which few have access and continues to interact with the deities of the shrine. This gives meaning and direction to her life.

4. Not all patients take over the priestly role; some simply join the cult group and get into occasional trances during celebrations at the shrine or on trips to pilgrimage centers. Some who become priests or priestesses may eventually give up the role, as Kusumāvatī planned to do after marriage. In such a case, the exorcism and investiture help the patient overcome a personal crisis and allow her to function normally again.

The conversion of patients into priests is constantly going on in urban shrines. Even allowing for those who later give up the role, this means that priests and priestesses must be proliferating. The Nāvala priest aimed to produce 108[15] priests and priestesses who would establish their own shrines in various parts of the country!

[14] There is a widespread, but not universal, belief among recent priests and priestesses that celibacy is necessary for the proper performance of the priestly role.

[15] One hundred and eight is a standard magical number coming into Sri Lankan tradition from India, where it dates as far back as the *Atharvaveda*.

CHAPTER 3

Social Change and the Deities

Changes in the Pantheon

The Second World War brought massive economic and political changes to Sri Lanka. Most obviously, in its wake came Independence in 1948. During the war malaria was virtually eradicated, with dramatic effects on the mortality rate. The rise in the world price of rubber produced an economic boom that was prolonged by the Korean War. The boom enabled Sri Lanka to import consumer goods on a large scale, creating an atmosphere of material prosperity.

In this atmosphere the government laid the foundations of a welfare state—universal free education (1947) and a free national health service operating through a network of hospitals in country towns. Soon almost every baby was born in a maternity ward. In the war many Sri Lankans served abroad with the British forces.

In the general election of 1956 there was a massive swing to a new populist party, the MEP.[1] This party was a coalition of forces who appealed to the Sinhala Buddhist identity. The year happened to be the 2500th anniversary of the Buddha's death by traditional computation. The previous government had tried to capitalize on this event in its own preparation for the election, but was identified by many of the electorate with the colonialist past and Christian hegemony, so that its propaganda backfired and its leader, Sir John Kotelawela, though himself a Sinhala Buddhist, became an object of ridicule. His victorious opponent, Mr. S.W.R.D. Bandaranaike, wore the recently invented "national dress" in public, and this soon became de rigueur for politicians. His vote was mobilized by the cultural heirs of Anagārika Dharmapāla, the local Buddhist intelligentsia, above all the schoolmasters. In this populist upsurge the new class of Sin-

[1] MEP = Mahajana Eksat Peramuna ("Peoples United Front").

hala-educated white-collar workers, who were in the village but not of the village, were joined by the traditional intelligentsia with firm local roots, the monks and Ayurvedic physicians. Though research has suggested that economic issues were at least as important as cultural ones in determining the electoral swing, we shall take this year as paradigmatic for our synoptic view of economic and cultural change.

The MEP called itself a socialist party. The Sinhala term for socialism is *samāja-vāda*, literally "the social doctrine," which has ineluctable positive moral overtones. No political party since has been able to exist without claiming to be *samāja-vādin*. Government subsidies to the consumer had begun earlier, but the MEP began really large-scale intervention in the economy. It nationalized the port, the buses, and the oil companies and brought the cooperative movement, and with it much wholesale and retail trade, under government control. The Paddy Lands Act (1958) gave the actual cultivator of rice fields virtual permanency of tenure on favorable terms. More and more bureaucrats were appointed, so that increasingly the population looked to government not only for economic assistance in consumption, but also for jobs. The government came to be seen as a providential agency supplying both material and cultural needs. The public considered that it was the government's moral duty to provide. Private business might incur the stigma of greed, but the government operated through salaried officials; they might be imperfect, but their individual moral faults could not be attributed to the government. The entrepreneur (*mudalāli*) became the embodiment of the antithesis to *samāja-vāda* and thus represented the evil system of exploitation associated with colonialism and capitalism.

By 1971 the changes begun in 1956 were so firmly entrenched and had gone so far that no one could safely articulate opposition to *samāja-vāda*. Even the rightist party, the UNP, was only trying to outbid the ULF, the successor to the MEP, with promises of ever-larger consumer subsidies.[2] The real opposition came from the left. Relatively educated young men and women of the Sinhala Buddhist majority, the very section of the population to whom Mr. Bandaranaike had appealed, organized an armed revolt that was suppressed with much bloodshed by the armed services and police. Losses on the government side were probably under one hundred (mainly police killed in the first few days of the uprising); unofficial esti-

[2] ULF = United Left Front; UNP = United National Party.

mates of insurgents killed (mostly executed) range from five to ten thousand. The political response of the ULF government was to intensify its economic intervention. It nationalized the estates and put a fifty-acre ceiling on landholdings. Every branch of the economy except the retail trade was completely dominated by the government; even large sections of the retail trade worked through government suppliers, and the erstwhile local cooperatives were manned and controlled from the center. The government passed a law enabling it to take over any commercial enterprise by administrative action, and there was no right of appeal against any such decision. Not only were all state appointments (and therefore most jobs) accessible primarily through political influence; it was official policy, to some extent embodied in the new constitution (1972), that all government servants, including the judiciary, must be responsive to the will of the "people," which was the will of the political party elected to power. Despite the proliferation of bureaucrats, all semblance of rational bureaucratic administration was abolished by the creation of virtually all-powerful "local political authorities," who were in fact government MPs. Almost all local governments were suspended by government decree. No government job could be had without a letter from the MP. In some cases (such as selection of trainee teachers) such rational procedures as competitive exams were abolished; in others they remained, but merely as a formal charade. Thus both the traditional Kandyan bureaucracy and the rational bureaucratic principles brought in by the British were abolished in favor of the exercise of a political influence that had no clearly perceived formal structure.

Since 1977 the UNP government under President J. R. Jayawardene has reversed economic policy to favor private enterprise and introduced a new constitution, but done nothing to restore an orderly and effective administrative system. Arbitrary government interference has continued, even when it runs counter to the ideology of laissez-faire capitalism. The electoral process has been tampered with and the referendum of December 1982 witnessed a new level of intimidation and interference with the right to vote. Even in the private sector most jobs are available only through political patronage. Although MPs and their thugs are for most practical purposes above the law, one further step towards the centralization and derationalization of power is that the President holds signed and undated letters of resignation by all MPs of the ruling party. It is small wonder if to most people the world no longer seems to be organized on the principle that power and morality must ultimately coincide.

The First Phase: The Rise of Kataragama

The article "Social Change and the Deities: The Rise of the Kataragama Cult in Modern Sri Lanka"[3] has demonstrated that Kataragama/Skanda has virtually supplanted his three colleagues in the set of Four Warrant Gods; in practical terms he alone now holds the place previously held jointly by the four. These practical terms we measured in 1968 by finding out the numbers and purposes of those who visited the shrines of the four gods in Kandy. Hardly anyone now seeks a favor of Nātha; we believe that this is because Nātha was closely associated with Kandyan kingship, and with the fall of the kingdom in 1815 he had obviously failed and indeed lost his main raison d'être. Even more striking, however, is our finding that over a ten-day period Kataragama had nearly three times as many visitors as Viṣṇu and Pattinī *together*. We were able to show that Kataragama is visited by different people for purposes different from the other gods. Their visitors were more rural than urban, his the reverse. But the clearest distinction between Kataragama on the one hand and Viṣṇu and Pattinī on the other was in the reasons people gave for coming to them. While Kataragama was more frequently visited than any other god for every kind of purpose, he was most preeminent in modern spheres of activity: passing examinations, getting on in business, finding employment. We suggested that Pattinī, whose mythology associates her with heat, is still primarily thought of as effective against infectious diseases and drought (both traditionally connected with heat), areas in which she has rivals in modern medicine and irrigation. She and Viṣṇu have strongly Buddhist and hence moral associations. Kataragama was traditionally a war god; the main classical Hindu myth about him is that he was begotten by Śiva to lead the gods in battle against the antigods (*asura*). It is also essential to his mythological character that he has two wives or rather, in the Sinhala view, a legal wife and a mistress (*hora gǟni*). (His legal wife is a colorless personification of the divine army [Dēvasēnā, Tamil: Tēvānī],

[3] Gananath Obeyesekere, "Social Change and the Deities: The Rise of the Kataragama Cult in Modern Sri Lanka," *Man*, n.s. 12 (December 1977): 377–96.

but Sinhalas are not aware of that.) Kataragama is therefore ineluctably associated with both violence and unchastity and must, by the same token, still be a long way from the ultimate sanctity of attaining Buddhahood. We argued that on the one hand he had lost his specific role as a war god in Sri Lanka because peace made that function otiose, so that he was free to take up the new specific functions of modern life; while on the other his moral ambivalence made him seem a more sympathetic and useful ally in the zero-sum games of modern competitive existence.

Our hypothesis, to put it simply, is that people want a lot of things and no longer see rational or practical ways of getting them. Universal education has meant that they want new things: the children of peasants now aspire to white-collar jobs. That the successful can now afford modern luxuries, such as television, has also led to what moralists castigate as "consumerism" and to what sociologists see as "relative deprivation." But of course people also want the things they have always wanted and most want, such as the capacity to earn a basic living and lead a stable family life, and these goods too are in increasingly short supply. At the best of times it is not easy to see what practical steps one should take to achieve such goals as family harmony, and we have suggested in the previous chapter that traditional means of coping with such problems are failing as family groups scatter. But a disordered modern society contains many other bafflements and frustrations. The police are not always readily available to recover lost property and the legal system is not always perceived as accessible to all and impartial in its workings. However hard one studies, the published examination results are not always free from suspicion of tampering by interested parties; moreover, even those who have equipped themselves with qualifications are passed over for employment or promotion by those less qualified but better connected or more adept at winning politicians' favors.

People quite correctly perceive that in modern Sri Lanka rational action to better oneself or one's family is not always crowned with results, especially if one is not a member of the elite. On the other hand, the comparatively stable hierarchy of patron-client relationships of a former era is also a thing of the past; one might in fact argue that the forms of egalitarian democracy and even the alternation of parties in power, however admirable from other points of view, have further confused people's perceptions and destabilized the patronage structure. Recourse to supernatural aid has been one reaction; another was the revolt of 1971, which was predominantly manned by the educated unemployed; the Sinhala burning and looting of Tamil homes and businesses in July 1983 was (among other things) a manifestation of the same confused frustration.

The recent career of Kataragama and the spectacular rise of his main shrine have been documented and explained elsewhere,[4] and we shall return to the latter topic in Chapter 5. Since we are anxious to present new material, we shall concentrate here on the concomitant rise of other deities.

Śiva, who in Sinhala is usually called by his alternate name Īśvara (originally a Sanskrit epithet meaning "Lord"), has probably risen not merely because he is the supreme deity in the soteriology of most Sri Lankan and many Indian Tamils, but more specifically because he is in myth the father of Skanda. We have already seen Īśvara's prominence at the Nāvala shrine, and shall meet him again at many shrines in Colombo. His veneration by Sinhala Buddhists reverses tradition. In the fifteenth century the great monk Vīdāgama in his poem the *Budugunālankāraya* ("The Garland of the Buddha's Virtues") ridiculed Śiva and his cult. For Vīdāgama, as for much public culture to this day, Śiva belongs to Tamil religion. Sinhala Buddhists have traditionally invoked Hindu gods, including Śiva, in exorcisms and esoteric magic; but in the cult of gods he at best received formal mention in a list of gods invoked. This has now changed. Thus, for example, a Kandyan young lady who had failed to find a job appropriate to her high-school education and was working as a domestic servant in Colombo told us that Hinduism is the mother of Buddhism and that (correspondingly) while Kataragama is a Buddhist his father Īśvara is a Hindu. She told us that she had read a newspaper article by a monk who had conversed with Kataragama and reported that the god had told him that while his father was a Hindu, the Buddha had entrusted the care of Buddhism to him. While this view that Kataragama has usurped what we (and most Sinhalas) know to be Viṣṇu's traditional role is no doubt idiosyncratic, it fits in with the elevation and Buddhicization of Kataragama that we shall later report and shows how some relatively articulate people are fitting Śaiva Hindu influence into their world view.

[4] Obeyesekere, "Social Change"; Gananath Obeyesekere, "The Firewalkers of Kataragama: The Rise of Bhakti Religiosity in Buddhist Sri Lanka," *Journal of Asian Studies* 37, no. 3 (1978): 457–76.

CHAPTER 3

The Pattern of Shrines in a Colombo Slum

To provide some concrete data on the current complexion of the pantheon we conducted a survey in seventeen Buddhist monasteries in a predominantly proletarian part of Colombo (Colombo 9, which is Demaṭagoḍa, with adjacent parts of Colombo 10, Maradāna). This area contains large slums in which the very poor, both Sinhala and Tamil, live in dreadful conditions. It also has areas inhabited by people with regular employment but low income, as well as a few better-off people in government and business. Some of the wealthy businessmen with economic interests in the area live elsewhere, but patronize local temples and shrines.

The country's two most famous monastic training colleges (*piriveṇa*), Vidyōdaya and Vidyālaṃkāra, were founded here in the late nineteenth century. There are also several temples belonging to the Amarapura Nikāya, a monastic fraternity founded with reformist intentions early in the nineteenth century. Three temples belong to a later wave of reform, in the 1920s, which made little impact outside Colombo; they derive their ordination traditions from the puritanical Sulagandi and Sveggin fraternities of lower Burma. In Burma these two fraternities objected to the worldliness of the dominant fraternity, in particular to wearing silk robes and sandals, to handling money, and to holding noisy functions in temples.[5] The oldest and largest Buddhist fraternity in Sri Lanka, the Siyam Nikāya, is generally considered conservative, but in this area their temples too were in the forefront of the late nineteenth-century Buddhist revival.

In other words, the Buddhist temples of the area are a rather unrepresentative sample in that most of them are associated with reform movements, movements with purist and fundamentalist intentions, including a wish to take a distance from spirit religion. One would expect the incumbents of these temples to resist the building of shrines on their monastery premises and certainly to discourage spirit cult activity there. We found that indeed a few have held out, but most have succumbed to the pressure of *bhakti* religiosity which is so powerful in the neighborhood.

We were interested in the spirit religion and assumed that religious change would be reflected in the physical structures on the temple premises. We drafted questions accordingly and administered a questionnaire to the incumbent monks. Where shrines existed in the temple premises

[5] See E. M. Mendelson, *Sangha and State in Burma* (Ithaca and London: Cornell University Press, 1975), p. 10.

we administered another questionnaire to the priest. The presence or absence of shrines (*dēvālēs*) in the temples surveyed is as follows:

1.	Shrines with resident or part-time priest: in all but one of these cases the shrines were physical structures separate from the Buddhist image house; in one the pictures of gods were painted within the image house, the monk having resisted the construction of a separate shrine.	8
2.	Shrines exist but no regular officiating priest	3
3.	No shrines at all	6
	Total	17

Table 3 shows the temples with active shrines:

The implications of the above data are readily apparent.

1. It is clear that in all but two cases the temple (*vihāra*) was built long before any of the shrines (*dēvālēs*). Those who founded these temples viewed them as exclusively Buddhist places of worship. There are two exceptions. In one (no. 8) there was a Kataragama shrine but the monk was unable to date it except to state that it was old. In the other a shrine for the Four Gods was constructed in 1937 along with the temple.

2. All temples except one had installed in the shrine at least the Four Gods of this region: Viṣṇu, Saman, Vibhīṣaṇa, and Kataragama. This indicates that after the temples were built, the monks made concessions to lay needs but in a way that stuck to tradition.

3. Six temples had other deities also housed in the shrine; in four, these latter deities were housed after the Four Gods had been installed. In all six cases the latter deities were installed after 1964.

4. Of the latter deities the most important is Hūniyam, who appears in all six of the shrines noted in number 3 above. Gaṇeśa appears in three places (we shall explain why later), and a cluster of six other deities appears together in one shrine (no. 2).

Thus a stratigraphy of the structures can be observed:

Buddhist temples	(1800–1937)
The Four Gods	(1920–1967)
Hūniyam and others	(1965–)

Several monks stated explicitly that they were yielding to public demand in constructing shrines for gods. Almost all monks affirmed the doctrinal position: they were otherwise indifferent to the gods but trans-

Table 3

Temples with Dēvālēs with Incumbent Priests in Colombo 9 & 10 in 1976

Name of temple	Date of construction	Dēvālē for Four Gods	Date	Hūniyam?	Date	Other dēvālēs and date
1 Mahā Visuddhārāmaya	1920	Viṣṇu, Saman, Vibhīṣaṇa, Kataragama	1947	Hūniyam	1969	Pattinī: 1969 Gaṇeśa: 1975
2 Śrī Jayasēkarārāmaya	1923	Viṣṇu, Saman, Vibhīṣaṇa, Kataragama	1920	Hūniyam	1965	Däḍimuṇḍa, Nātha, Pattinī, Mahā Brahma, Sarasvatī, Īśvara, Gaṇeśa: 1969
3 Purāna Śrī Mahā Vihāra	1925	Viṣṇu, Saman, Vibhīṣaṇa, Kataragama	1965	Hūniyam	1965	Gaṇeśa: 1965
4 Ñāṇavimalārāmaya	1922	Viṣṇu, Saman, Vibhīṣaṇa, Kataragama	1945	Hūniyam	1976	None
5 Mallikārāmaya	1935	Viṣṇu, Saman, Vibhīṣaṇa, Kataragama	1949	Hūniyam	1973	None
6 Vikramasiṃhārāmaya	1930	Viṣṇu, Saman, Vibhīṣaṇa, Kataragama	1967	Hūniyam	1967	None
7 Dakṣiṇārāmaya	1937	Viṣṇu, Saman, Vibhīṣaṇa, Kataragama	1937	None		None
8 Śrī Nāgamanārāmaya	1800	Kataragama	?	None		None

ferred merit to them in order to help them. Only one monk stated his firm belief in Hūniyam. (By contrast most monks dabbled in astrology, either helping laymen to interpret horoscopes, or consulting their own in times of trouble, or both. This is because astrology can be more easily rationalized with *karma* theory than the belief in the gods can.[6]) While the monks themselves were traditionalist, they nevertheless yielded to popular demand. This included two temples founded by the ascetic fraternities, Mahāvisuddhārāmaya by the Sveggin and Ñāṇavimalārāmaya by the Sulagandi. While temples had installed the Four Gods after 1920, at least one of these gods, Vibhīṣaṇa, was moribund and Saman too was almost otiose. Viṣṇu has all along been viewed as a benevolent deity at the head of the pantheon. It is very likely that the shrines for the Four Gods were built as a result of the increasing importance of Kataragama, but instead of having a separate shrine for him the monks followed tradition in installing the Four Gods collectively.

About the period since 1965 we need not speculate: clearly Hūniyam has risen into prominence. His rise in popularity must have been well under way by 1965 for monks to have permitted his installation.

We have information on two of the three temples with shrines but no priests. Both fit the pattern:

1. Vēḷuvanārāmaya (built in 1923) has Viṣṇu and Kataragama, both installed in 1940 by the then incumbent monk. But the present monk is uninterested in this aspect of popular religion.

2. Bauddha Madhyasthānaya (built in 1948) has a Viṣṇu and Kataragama shrine built in 1963. Here is a clear case of monk yielding to public demand by building a shrine for interested worshippers but refusing to have a resident priest.

Our historical survey shows that gods have intruded into temple premises and especially that Hūniyam is rising fast, but it does not by itself show confusion of traditional categories. For that we must take a closer look.

The monks are aware of traditional categories, such as the sets of Four and Twelve Gods, but under popular pressure they seem sometimes to be

[6] For the relation between *karma* and astrology see Gananath Obeyesekere, "Theodicy, Sin, and Salvation in a Sociology of Buddhism," in *Dialectic in Practical Religion*, ed. E. R. Leach (Cambridge: Cambridge University Press, 1968), pp. 7–40.

pouring new wine into old bottles. Consider Jayasēkarārāmaya in table 3. The four gods were established in 1920 and the other eight between 1965 and 1969. There is however order in the establishment of the later eight. Pattinī and Nātha, deities of the same class as the Four Gods (in Kandy they are members of that set), are installed on the right side of the Buddha (the propitious side), and next to them are gods moving up to divine status, Hūniyam and Däḍimuṇḍa (alias Dēvatā Baṇḍāra or the God of Alutnuvara). On the left of the Buddha are the Brahmanical gods newly introduced from South India, Sarasvatī and her consort Mahā Brahma, Gaṇeśa and Īśvara. The total now is twelve, a traditional number. But, as we have explained, the older category of the Twelve Gods consisted of minor gods distinct from the Four Gods. Only two deities in the above pantheon approximate to the lower status: Hūniyam and Däḍimuṇḍa.

This survey did not include shrines that have no association with any temple or monk; but we have observed that in such shrines tradition recedes even further. In Colombo most of them are in the charge of the new type of priest, self-recruited, known as *sāmi* (see Chapter 1). Whereas the traditional priest arranged his shrine in accordance with more or less formalized texts and the instruction of his teachers, the ecstatic *sāmi* derives a considerable part of his knowledge from direct inspiration (in trance or in dreams), a source that brooks little argument.

A temple in our survey where the *sāmi* (or his predecessor) has evidently exerted influence is Śrī Vikramasiṃhārāmaya in Kuppiyavatta (Colombo 9). Our table shows that the Four Gods and Hūniyam were installed there in 1967; it does not show that they are all treated alike in spatial terms. In a row, enclosed within a larger building, stand five shrines of equal size. (Neither five nor any multiple of five plays any part in the traditional pantheon.) Each shrine is dedicated to a god and contains his statue; on the side walls of each shrine are labelled paintings of other deities. We move from spectator's left to right and add in brackets some glosses supplied by the priest. The five gods with shrines are Viṣṇu, Vibhīṣaṇa, Saman, Hūniyam, and Kataragama. Viṣṇu has painted on his side walls the nine planets and Śriyā Kāntāva [Lakṣmī]; Vibhīṣaṇa has Pattinī and Däḍimuṇḍa; Saman has Gaṇa Deviyō [Gaṇeśa] and Met Bōsat [Nātha]; Hūniyam has Kalukambili Dēvatāva (one of a group of seven demons) and Kālī [Bhadra Kālī]; Kataragama has Īśvara [Śiva] and Vallī Ammā. This is (from the traditional point of view) higgledy-piggledy: Kataragama does not even have Tēvānī, his lawful wife!

When we revisited this temple in 1975 we saw the following. Just outside the major entrance to this building (which is opposite the Kataragama shrine) was a trident (traditional emblem of Śiva) stuck in the ground, with a small rectangular fenced enclosure behind it; in this was a stone on which to smash coconuts. Behind the stone were altars to Bhadra Kālī and Hanuman, on which were framed popular prints of those deities. Hanuman is the Hindu monkey god who helped Rāma conquer Lankā in the Hindu epic, the *Rāmāyaṇa*. This is the first time we have come across Hanuman on Buddhist temple premises in Sri Lanka—a piece of Hindu influence. It is also the first appearance of Kālī in that context of which we are aware. At a ritual that happened to coincide with our visit, an English teacher, born a Roman Catholic but converted to Buddhism, was making offerings to Kataragama, Hūniyam, and Kālī to gain revenge on enemies who had bewitched him.

One may safely assume that such innovations arise from the priests' experiences or rather their interpretations of their experiences. In this case the priest told us that he becomes possessed by all the gods (*dēva-samāgama*) in turn; he particularly mentioned Kataragama and Hanuman. Sometimes he finds that while in trance he has been jumping and cavorting; then it was possession by Hanuman. This priest was a young man, but not all innovators are young. The priest of Dakṣiṇārāmaya, age sixty-one, told us he could get possessed by eighteen deities. He learnt his art from a South Indian *sāmi*, Vaḍivel Samiyar, who lived in Kañdavala Estate, Ratmalāna (a Colombo suburb).

A Major Hūniyam Shrine

The above data concern shrines on the premises of Buddhist temples. There are many other shrines in Demaṭagoḍa. The biggest of them is the Hūniyam Dēvālē on Baseline Road. This was founded in 1958, seven years before we think Hūniyam was installed in any local temple. No doubt it influenced religion in the area, but we think it could not have succeeded had it not also reflected an existent popular sentiment.

Hūniyam's shrine at Baseline Road was founded by a monk. When a shrine is founded on temple premises the monk takes no part after granting permission. But this unorthodox monk, whom we have already met, is the Venerable Visuddhānanda. At Lunāva he had founded a shrine to Kataragama and then a subsidiary shrine to Hūniyam. In choosing these deities, he clearly had his finger on the pulse of popular religiosity in the

Chart 1

Plan of Hūniyam Shrine, Demaṭagoḍa, Colombo 9

BY LIONEL GUNASEKARA

1. Bō tree.
2. Stone for smashing coconuts (1958).
3. Gaṇēśa shrine (1958).
4. Buddha image with altar for flower offerings (1958).
5. Kaḷu Devatāvun vahansē (the Ven. Black Deity) (7 September 1975).
6. Statue of the demon (*yakṣa*) Hūniyam. (This image, made of white marble, was imported from India and offered by Cyril de Zoysa in 1958.)
7. Statue of door guardian (1958).
8. Statue of the god (*dēva*) Sūniyam. Eight feet tall, in a glass case (1965).
9. Statue of door guardian (1958).
10. Large photograph of the incumbent monk of Lunāva monastery, the Ven. Visuddhānanda (1965).
11. Statue of Sihavaṭuka (1958).
12. Dhṛtarāṣṭra (one of the four warranted [*varam*] gods) (1965).
13. Protector god (7 September 1975).
14. Virūḍha (warranted god) (1965).
15. Kataragama (1965).
16. The Lady Śrī (Śrī Kāntāva) (1965).
17. Sarasvatī (1965).
18. Viṣṇu (1965).
19. Pattinī (1965).
20. Däḍimuṇḍa (1965).
21. Saman (1965).
22. Kālī (1965).
23. Gaṇa Deviyō (Gaṇēśa) (1965).
24. Nātha (1965).
25. Virūpākṣa (warranted god) (1965).
26. Vibhīṣaṇa (1965).
27. The Buddha (1965).
28. Īśvara (1965).
29. Vaiśravaṇa (warranted god) (1965).
30. The Lady Śrī (Śriyā Kāntāva) (26 March 1966).

The monks' residence etc. dated 25 December 1958.

Colombo area. We present here a schematic plan of the shrine's layout (chart no. 1). There are twenty-one gods portrayed, as well as the Buddha (two statues) and the Venerable Visuddhānanda (a large photograph). The only sacred feature without a date of installation is the *bō* tree. We deduce that the monk chose this site because of the tree: a shrine on that spot

PLAN OF HŪNIYAM DĒVĀLĒ, DEMAṬAGOḌA

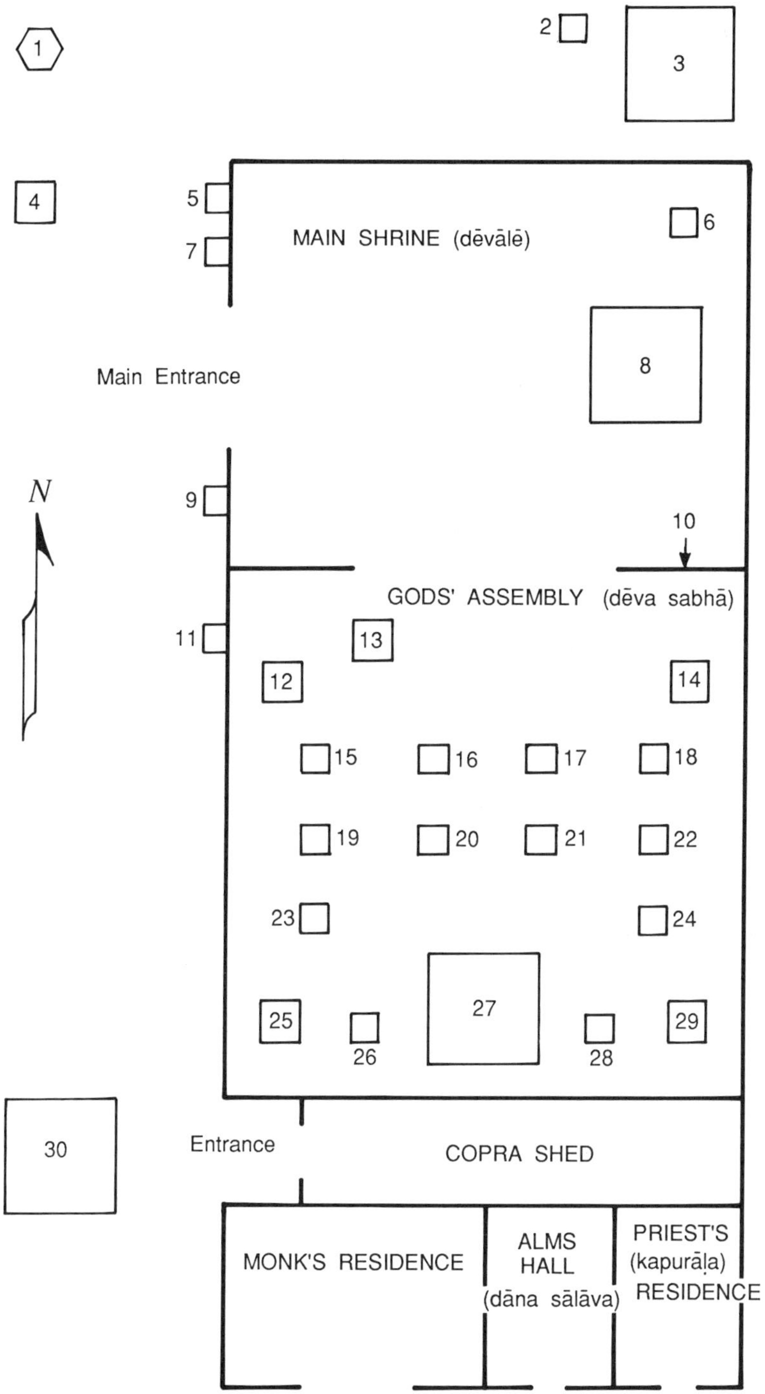

would have symbolic Buddhist legitimation. Next to the *bō* tree is a modern (ugly) statue of the Buddha with a flower altar.

As this shrine was founded from the Kataragama shrine at Lunāva, one might have expected a Kataragama image there from the start. But the monk seems to have sensed that Kataragama was less popular locally then Hūniyam. The main image now is an image of Hūniyam as a god, eight feet high. As principal image it has superseded the one on its right, a marble statue of Hūniyam as a demon (*yakṣa*). It is this rise in Hūniyam's status that will occupy most of the rest of this chapter, so we postpone discussion of these images. Here we shall discuss other untraditional features of the shrine, in particular how they betray Hindu and Roman Catholic influence.

The rising popularity of Gaṇeśa—whom our chart also showed to be installed at three temples and we also found at Vikramasiṃhārāmaya—is comparable to that of Īśvara: as Īśvara is Skanda/Kataragama's father, Gaṇeśa is his elder brother, and so rises through a family connection. In Hinduism he is the lord of beginnings, the deity who overcomes obstacles, and so should be installed first and be the god closest to the entrance. This Hindu tradition has been followed at Baseline Road.

Two guardians stand at the entrance of the main shrine for Hūniyam. While there is Sinhala Buddhist precedent for this, generally traditional Sinhala shrines were simple structures that did not have anything as elaborate as guardians of shrine premises; such guardians were usually reserved for Buddhist image houses. Guardians (generally Bhairava) are, however, commonplace in Hindu temple architecture, from little village *kovils* to more elaborate temples. Structure 11 is a large sculpture of Śiva in his demonic form, known as Sihavaṭuka. Sihavaṭuka images were sometimes erected in village *bali* rituals for warding off bad planetary influences, but we have never seen a permanent statue for Śiva as demon erected in any traditional Sinhala shrine or Buddhist temple. However, we have seen paintings of Sihavaṭuka in other shrines of the new ecstatic priests and priestesses. It is again very likely that this image of Śiva reflects Hindu influence.

The last structure to be erected is that of *āraksaka deviyō*, "the protector god." This is a deceased ancestor (mother's brother), who helped the monk to "catch" (*allanavā*, i.e., to employ, to tame, to capture) Hūniyam. Here he is elevated to the status of a deity. This highly idiosyncratic feature parallels another—the monk's inclusion of himself. In 1965, when the demon Hūniyam gave way as the main focus of the shrine to Hūniyam the god, the monk installed himself to flank the god Hūniyam, balancing his original favorite and so suggesting some kind of equipollence. The monk must have seen himself as an actual or potential deity, or at least as a most accomplished magician, something like a Hindu *siddha*[7] who by esoteric means has mastered all forces.

In the same year the monk added an extra room to house what he called "the assembly of the gods" (*dēva-sabhāva*). This is not a wholly untraditional concept, but it has been untraditionally applied. In Sinhala tradition the gods number thirty-three *kōṭi*, which is 330 million, so of course they are never represented. However, many ecstatics nowadays seek the vision of the "divine assembly." Perhaps the version here presented was ideated by some of the priests or priestesses whom the monk employs.

Superficially, traditional Buddhist arrangements are respected. The Buddha presides from the center over a set of Four and a set of Twelve Gods. But the contents of these forms are again completely new. The set of Four Gods, standing at the four corners of the assembly (nos. 12, 14, 25, 29), are the Four Great Kings, World Protectors (*lokapāla*), from the Pāli Canon; it is traditional to represent them on the entrance walls of Buddhist image houses to act as guardians, but they play no other part in the culture—they are remembered as nothing but names. Into the category of the Twelve Gods have been poured (as nos. 15–24, 26, and 28) twelve members of the modern urban pantheon. Yet the salient feature of the arrangement of statues in this shrine is that it is unlike anything in Buddhist shrine construction, but is modelled on the Roman Catholic grotto.

Protestantism, which had a profound impact on Buddhism, has had no impact on the new spirit cults. This is easy to explain: Protestantism in Sri Lanka has been an urban bourgeois movement (if we except Pentecostal churches, still very small), whereas the changes that we have noted have mostly sprung from lower-class urban roots. Moreover, Protestantism (and even Roman Catholicism) severely discouraged the spirit religion and hence could not affect the development of the spirit cults. In general, it is working-class Catholics who are attracted by the new cults. Often Catho-

[7] Hūniyam is called *siddha*, which in Sanskrit means "perfected being." Actually he is *siddhi*, "possessor of magical powers." Since Hūniyam is *not* a perfected being, we think that he is given that title either as an honorific or simply because it is easier to say *siddha* Hūniyam than *siddhi* Hūniyam in Sinhala.

lics subsequently become Buddhists via the spirit cults. In one case a Buddhist woman whose husband was a nominal Catholic had a vision of Jesus Christ, but this is rather exceptional in our data.

The Catholic influence on Venerable Visuddhānanda is further discernible in two great ritual innovations. Every year a procession leaves the Lunāva shrine on Christmas Day and arrives ceremonially at the shrine at Baseline Road. The gold image of Hūniyam is brought here, kept in state for twenty-one days, and then taken to the mother shrine at Lunāva. It is difficult to assess the significance of this innovation. Perhaps it is intended to make Hūniyam relevant to Christians as well as Buddhists; perhaps it simply recognizes that he (like Kataragama before him) is relevant to Buddhists, Hindus, and Christians. (The proportion of Christians to Buddhists in our sample of visitors to the shrine was 7:47.)

Even more innovative are the songs following the *pūjā*s offered to Hūniyam. Traditionally in Sinhala (and Hindu) culture the ritual songs and invocations are uttered by the priest on behalf of his client or congregation. Here the priest and audience (generally the cult group) *jointly* sing the ritual songs in honor of the god. These are called *stōtra*s ("hymns of praise"); they are simply the texts sung in the main shrine (*mūlika dēvālē*) at Lunāva. Such choral singing probably raises the emotional tone of the cult group. It is a form of devotional activity that comes from Christianity, not from anything in Sinhala or South Asian culture.

From Demon to Divinity: The Rise of Hūniyam in Urban Religion

Divine Obsolescence

In Chapter 1 we expounded the internal logic of the traditional Buddhist pantheon and argued that a god who is too good can become otiose by promoting himself beyond the sphere of mundane affairs. Moreover, by granting a great many favors, provided they are moral favors, a god risks being perceived as *too* beneficent and thus no longer being called on to help out in mundane exigencies. It is our hypothesis that in some quarters this has happened to Kataragama. Many modern Sri Lankans are so devoted to him that for affective purposes he has become for them a kind of supreme deity.

We are not, however, hypothesizing that a god who is too good at granting his suppliants' wishes is rapidly abandoned; that would be strange indeed. We think that what has happened to Kataragama is in a sense the reverse. We have shown his phenomenal popularity in recent years. No deity can possibly supply the wants of such a mass of followers. While people clamor to him for favors—jobs, promotions, success in business—many must suffer disappointment, for such things as jobs are strictly limited by the nature of an impoverished economy. The god must necessarily fail to meet many of the instrumental needs of his devotees, though he may still succeed in meeting their expressive (spiritual or psychological) needs. Yet since many go to the god for the former reason, some expectations must inevitably be frustrated. Moreover, gods like Kataragama are feared and held in awe by most devotees—unlike some peasants in South India, who scoff at the deity when he does not deliver the goods.[8] Thus if I fail to achieve my goal, I dare not attribute this failure to the god Kataragama; I find some other cause: my unworthiness, my unfavorable horoscope, *karma* which nothing can avert, a taboo violation, or whatever. But if another deity is moving up, I can now transfer my allegiance to the latter in the hope that he, being more powerful and more involved in the world, can deliver the goods. This means that erstwhile devotees of Kataragama will switch their allegiance to Hūniyam (not, of course, in any deliberate or conscious manner). This action may then be justified by the classic rationalization that Kataragama, by virtue of his increasing benevolence and saintly nature, can have no say in the affairs of the world. This must also be the reason for the fact that while in the past gods became otiose gradually and slowly, nowadays the pace has accelerated.

In our survey of monks and priests in Colombo 9 and 10 several of them articulated this classic rationalization, at least indirectly. One priest said: "People increasingly offer *pūjā*s to god Sūniyam because he generally associates (moves) with human beings. Gods like Viṣṇu and Saman have moved away from men, and they find it hard to help us. God Kataragama is also like that and that is why those who believe in Kataragama also light a lamp for god Sūniyam."

[8] M. N. Srinivas, *Remembered Village* (Berkeley: University of California Press, 1976), p. 327. See our chap. 1, n. 20, for a parallel example from Sri Lanka. We have not come across this form of abuse of gods or godlings in our current research. However, priests in Laggala, where Obeyesekere did fieldwork in the late fifties, often tell their deities, "It is a disgrace (*nindāvayi*) that you do not help us . . ."; "Aren't you ashamed. . . ." This perhaps is a development from the blunter statements quoted earlier.

One Buddhist monk (at Mallikārāmaya), who professed lack of interest in the gods, explained the significance of the four shrines built on his temple premises in 1949 and the Hūniyam shrine built in 1973 in the following manner: "The Gods of the Four Dēvālēs are for *set sānti* ("blessings") while Hūniyam is for problems like conflicts in the family, court cases, and conflicts in general." Another priest put it thus: "The god Sūniyam moves very closely with people. He observes their good and their bad. Viṣṇu is a very tranquil being (*sānta kenek*), one who wants to acquire merit (*pin*). Gods like Viṣṇu and Kataragama are *mahēsākya* (of great power, i.e., of the higher class). They are filled with kindness (*maitrī*). Therefore they have removed themselves somewhat from people. Beings like God Sūniyam are servitors of Viṣṇu-Kataragama."

These are very widespread notions of Hūniyam and are also held by his ordinary devotees. Almost all devotees in addition see Hūniyam as powerful, full of strength (*sakti sampanna*). He can punish; therefore it is necessary to have him as your protector and enlist his aid to curse or punish your enemies. A mechanic (age fifty) in the Railway Department said, "Hūniyam is the one god among all the gods of Lankā who can cause frightening punishments."

If one looks at these statements critically, one sees that just such sentiments have been expressed by his devotees about Kataragama. Kataragama is powerful, a vanquisher of antigods; he "moves with people," he administers punishments. However, for these urban people in Colombo, Kataragama by and large has become more benevolent, very much like Viṣṇu. Indeed, the two terms are often conjoined to form a doublet, so that people will refer to "Viṣṇu-Kataragama gods." This is a category that fills roughly the same conceptual space as did the old Four Warrant Gods; the other members of that set are now too unimportant for most urbanites to take any account of them, and there are even people who cannot produce their names if asked. But the doublet has a further significance: these are the "powerful" (*mahēsākya*) gods, future Buddhas, who are too lofty to involve themselves directly with our mundane practical human needs.

Hūniyam's Unique Advantage

If Kataragama is no longer the god to whom many city dwellers feel they can turn for practical help, why have they chosen Hūniyam? Of course, demons are obvious candidates for promotion to the limelight because by definition they are wholly involved with the world. Nevertheless, there are other spirits in the traditional Sinhala pantheon who have much the same character and attributes as Hūniyam. Take some of the demons who are propitiated, with Hūniyam, in village exorcisms. Rīri yakā, the blood demon; Sanni, who sometimes takes the apparition of a god; Mahāsōna, who frightens people by his size and occasionally assaults them; Kaḷu Kumāra, an attractive, black, erotic possessor of females. All these are powerful beings, and like any demon, they are felt presences, that is, "they move among the people." Yet none of these is a candidate for apotheosis in urban society.

Even more striking is the case of Dēvatā Baṇḍāra, the god of Alutnuvara, who has already moved from *dēvatā* to divine status.[9] He seems on the face of it an ideal candidate, since he is the tamer of demons, a powerful god who stood by the Buddha during his battle against Māra, the personification of death, when all other deities fled aghast. He cures persons possessed by demons, and hundreds of possessed patients go to his shrine in Alutnuvara—as they have been doing at least since the end of the nineteenth century.[10] Yet Dēvatā Baṇḍāra is losing his hold on townspeople, both specialists and ordinary devotees. He is well known by name but clearly not relevant to their needs.

In our fieldwork among devotees of Kataragama we found that for their more practical needs some of them invoke demons, such as Kaḍavara and Gini Kurumbara, who in the traditional pantheon are members of his retinue. However, the deity in the best position to take over the dirty work is Hūniyam. This is because his name means Black Magic and he personifies it. However, the extraordinary thing is that despite this name, clearly denoting maleficence, Hūniyam is rising up the cosmic scale. We shall chart his transformation from demon, via godling, to god.

Hūniyam as Demon

The historical origin of the name Hūniyam has been long debated. Geiger derived the word from old Sinhala *hū-niyam*, which would mean "thread method."[11] However, if he were a true Sinhala one would rather expect

[9] For an account of the rise of this deity see Obeyesekere, *Pattini*, pp. 312–31.

[10] H.C.P. Bell, *Report on the Kegalle District* (Colombo: Government Printing, 1892), pp. 46–48.

[11] Wilhelm Geiger, *Culture of Ceylon in Medieval Times* (Wiesbaden, 1960).

him to have acquired a final *a* and have become Sūniyama, but that form of the name never seems to occur. The final *m* sounds Dravidian. Our doubts about Geiger's etymology are intensified by discovering Sūniyam in the sense of "sorcery" in South India. Here also *sūniyam* refers to black magic caused by a sorcerer sending an evil spirit (*pisasu*) to attack a victim. "Powerful *mantiravathi* are able to incite the *pisasu* to attack others. The technique is called *suniyam pisasu*. . . . The only possible defence agains [*sic*] *suniyam pisasu* is counter magic. . . . But most often there is no defence at all, because, presumably, *suniyam pisasu* is most often an *ex post facto* explanation of apparently 'unnatural' deaths."[12] It is of course possible that the Tamil term *sūniyam* was borrowed from the Sinhala or that both were derived from Malayalam.

Let us first consider the myths of this deity in the repertoire of traditional exorcists (*kaṭṭāḍirāḷa* or *yakädurā*). In an account written in 1865 Dandris de Silva Gooneratne says:

> Oddig Cumara Hooniyan Dewatawa is the son of Susiri, queen of Sagalpura in Maduratta. He always rides on a horse. He has six different apparitions; in the first he is called Cala Oddisey, or demon of incurable diseases; in the second, Naga Oddisey or demon of serpents; in the third, Cumara Oddisey or demon prince; in the fourth, Demale Oddisey or Tamil demon; in the fifth, Gopadu Oddisey or Royal demon. He is the principal demon that has much to do in that department of sorcery called Hooniyan.[13]

Gooneratne also tries to explain (not very satisfactorily) why he is also addressed as *dēvatā*, a "godling," when he is in fact a *yakā* ("demon"). "Though *dewatawa* is a term which is applied to the inferior classes of gods, and to the superior classes of demons, that do not inflict diseases on men, yet it is also sometimes used by Cattadiyas, as in the text, to inferior or malignant demons."[14] A better explanation may be that *dēvatā* is used as an honorific to flatter and cajole a demon, particularly if that demon is born of royalty. Thus Hūniyam Yakā, Sanni Yakā, and Kalu Yakā are sometimes addressed as *dēvatā* in traditional practice. In some myths and

[12] Goran Djurfeldt and S. Lindberg, *Pills against Poverty*, Studentlitteratur (London: Curzon Press, 1975), pp. 146–47.

[13] Dandris de Silva Gooneratne, "On Demonology and Witchcraft in Ceylon," *Journal of the Ceylon Branch of the Royal Asiatic Society* 4 (1865): 26–27.

[14] Gooneratne, "On Demonology," p. 26 (n.).

ritual dramas these demons appear in the guise of royalty or as godlings (*dēvatā*), two of their well-known apparitional forms. They take these apparitional forms to lure people to doom.

The term Oddisey or Oddissi strongly suggests that Orissa was the original homeland of this deity.

Paul Wirz, writing in the 1930s, recorded two well-known myths of Hūniyam from the Southern Province, which we quote below.[15]

1. The Sūniya-yakka is, like the Maha-sohona, Hiri-yakka, Kalu-kumāra, and Saniya-yakka, one of the most dreaded yakku. He has eight different names: Sri Adhnata-kumāra, Naga Oddissa-kumāra, Sanniya Oddissa-kumāra, Garunda Oddissa-kumāra, Velamba Oddissa-kumāra, Sūniya-dēvatavā, and Sūniya-yakshini, but he is usually just called Sūniya- (or Hūniya-) yakka.

Also this yakka may appear in ten different forms (avatāra), namely: as raksha, Yogi, donkey (būruvā), naga, narasingha, wolf (vrkayā), god (dēva), viper (polanga), "Tamil [who] has five tresses of hair hanging down his back" (demalā sedapolu pahak), and finally as a woman shadowed by a cobra (nāgakanyā = serpent-maid).

The Sūniya-yakka is always addressed by the edura in the most respectful and deferential manner as "Sūniya-dēvatavā."

Moreover, it is said that this yakka has twelve wives, all yakkiniyo, who always accompany him and help him to make people ill. Their names are Takari, Makari, Yamī yama, Dutti, Kala-raksha, Asēni-visēni, Irugalkandi, Nanahrupi, Puspakumāri, and Tiloka-dēvi.

Sūniya-yakka is pictured as riding a white horse, surrounded on all sides with cobras and with numerous snakes which wind themselves around his body, with a sword in his right hand and brazier in his left (text fig. 1). This representation is based on the following legend about him:

A long time ago there was a town in Northern India, called Dēvunuvara. Here reigned a king named Panduhas-rajjuruvo with his queen Tuserin-bisavun. One day, in the eighth month of her pregnancy, she went to the lotus pond to bathe. There she saw a large beautiful lotus flower, floating on the water. She picked it and enjoyed its fragrance. And thus it came to pass that the child she was bearing grew up to be an extremely handsome boy. After her bath, the queen returned home. Then, all kinds of queer desires began to take hold of her (dola dukha).

[15] Paul Wirz, *Exorcism and the Art of Healing in Ceylon* (Leiden: Brill, 1954), pp. 30–34. Though some names appear garbled, we have not emended them.

She longed to copulate with cobras and other snakes, and she took a huge cobra with her into her bedroom. The king came to know about this and was very much disturbed. He called a brahman to consult him. The brahman said, "The child will grow up to be a very cruel person. Everyone will go in fear of him and he will be the horror of the whole population."

A second and a third brahman were asked but they both answered the same. Then the king enquired about his own fate and the brahman replied, "When the child is seven years old, he will disappear into the forest and capture all kinds of snakes, drink their blood, and absorb their venom. Through this he will acquire supernatural powers. After this, your son will set off for another country, wage war and kill people. Six kingdoms will he conquer, among them that of his father, whom he will kill to make himself lord of the country."

Such were the words of the brahman, but the king would not believe his prophecy.

The child was born and grew up. He was extremely handsome and was the pride of his father. However, when he was seven years old, he secretly left his father's house and went into the jungle to a big termite's nest (humbāha). Here there lived four times four and twenty cobras. The lad caught them and wound them around his waist, arms, and legs. Then he caught a viper, raised it to his mouth and drank the blood and venom, thus becoming endowed with supernatural powers. He wound another very long snake, a "mahakala naga," round his whole body from feet to neck, and another one round his loins. Thus equipped, he mounted a white horse which was eight feet tall and fifteen feet long, took in his right hand a sword fifteen feet long and in his left a fire-pan, and resolved to return home and overthrow his father. In the meantime he had become a powerful yakka. The god Sakradēviyo saw him coming and asked him what his intentions were. He said he was going to Naraloka to kill people. Sakra begged him to desist from his purpose, but in vain. Finally, Sakra promised to endow him with a power to make people ill, but at the same time he must promise to revere Buddha and to obey him. Further, he must promise to restore to health the people whom he made ill, when they brought him an offering. After much resistance he agreed, and Sakra endowed him with the promised power (varanuduna). So he became Sūniya-yakka, but his proper name is *Adhanta Oddisa* or shortly Oddi.

2. In the time of Kashyāpa Buddha, there was born in Sagala Puranura (near modern Madras) a yakka. At that time there reigned a king, Sagala

Narendrarajjuruvo, whose consort was named Tusarinam-bisava. Their child grew up to be a yakka. Even as a small boy he distinguished himself by his unusual behavior and gifts. From his infancy he had a great preference for snakes of all kinds, which were his only playfellows. When he grew up he set out for the Himalayas. There he discovered a termite's hill, from which he took a lot of cobras and wound them round his body, so that it was entirely wreathed in snakes. In his mouth he placed two vipers (polanga), took a fire-pan in one hand and in the other a mighty sword, fifteen feet long and as broad as a banana-leaf. Thus supplied, he mounted a white horse and assembled seven thousand yakku round him, who appointed him to be their leader.

During this time, Kashyāpa used to preach in his temple which had four gates. One day he was preaching as usual, Sūniya-yakka came in one of the gates and began to roar terribly. He had come to entreat Buddha to give him a power which would enable him to make people fall ill. Mugalang-Hāmuduruvō, one of Buddha's disciples, went to see who was making the noise. Seeing the yakka at one of the gates, he asked him what he wanted. "I have come," answered the yakka, "to ask Buddha for a power to make men ill, so that they will present me with offerings." "You have come in vain," replied Mugulang, "for my master will never fulfill your wish. You had better return to where you came from." He then had the door of the temple shut, and the yakka went back to the Himalayas. But he returned on one of the following nights and showed himself at another gate of the temple. Once more he began to roar terrifically. Buddha heard the noise and sent Mugalang to see who was there. "There is a man at the gate, the same who came several nights ago," answered Mugalang. "He has come to ask you for the power to make men ill so that they will present him with offerings." "Tell him to leave," said Buddha, and ordered the temple-gates to be closed again. Once more, Sūniya-yakka returned to the Himalayas, but reappeared a few nights later for the third time at the temple door, making a loud noise, as before. But this time he asked for food, pretending to be suffering from continual hunger. Buddha, however, had him put in irons and sent to the *avīchiya narakadiya*, the bottommost hell, where the devils were to torment him.

While Mulanga [*sic*] went to execute Buddha's order, Buddha changed his mind and was sorry to have issued such a command, for he could not hurt anybody. He therefore called Mulanga [*sic*] back and said to the yakka, "You shall not suffer, and your wish will be fulfilled, but only on one condition: There is a place, Tammananuvara, where all the yakku live. There you shall go. In that place there lives a certain edura who possesses a certain mantra. You will do whatever this edura tells you to do. If he recites his mantra to summon you, you will come at once and receive the offering presented and restore immediately the health of the person you made ill. The edura will say the following mantra: 'Dēviyanga, Buddhunga! Vesamunu-rajjuruvo anakiya (to forbid) yak-edura (exorcist) dolaha (twelve) pidenni (offerings) devi (divine),' at the same time keeping at hand the offering prepared for you."

The yakka promised to do as Buddha told him and went away. Sūniya-yakka is able to produce the most diverse diseases, especially internal ailments, indigestion and intestinal disorders, accompanied by nausea and convulsions. Above all, he like to harass women, causing internal indispositions, sterility, and complaints during pregnancy. However these things are mostly ascribed to the Kalu-kumāra and his accomplices.

It should be apparent that according to traditional accounts there is no ambiguity regarding Hūniyam's demonic status. This comes out in practically every ritual text we have seen. Consider the first three verses of one traditional exorcist's invocation to Hūniyam:

> In order to suck and eat blood and heart's flesh
> He prepares to arrive, biting a viper.
> Take a mass of cobras and tie them round your waist!
> Powerful Sūniyam Yakā has set out to come here.
>
> His various vehicles are elephants, buffaloes, horses, bulls.
> Unsparingly he destroys cattle and crocodiles.
> Invariably he has a fire pot, mace, and sword.
> Sūniyam Yakā is coming to this world of men for offerings.
>
> Taking a mace in his right hand, and the fire pot in his left,
> Wearing a red dress and riding a white horse,
> Eating peoples' liver and drinking their blood,
> This is the cruel manner in which the Sūniyam demon comes.[16]

There is no ambiguity here: in the Sinhala tradition Hūniyam is simply a demon, a *yakā* or *bhūta*. The last stanza is especially significant because

[16] The Sinhala originals of these stanzas are in Michael Egan, *The Configurational Analysis of a Sinhalese Ritual* (Ph.D. thesis, Cambridge University, 1969), chap. 2, pp. 153–55.

it fits the iconography of Hūniyam in contemporary prints. However, in these prints he is Hūniyam *dēvatā* ("godling"), not demon. Hence the question: How is it that an erstwhile demon has acquired semidivine and more recently fully divine status?

Hūniyam as Godling

Before Hūniyam became a popular god on the urban level he had become, by the beginning of the twentieth century, the personal guardian of exorcists and other ritual specialists. Exorcists who were engaged in cutting the effects of sorcery or *hūniyam* (*hūniyam käpilla*) were themselves vulnerable to ensorcelling by rival practitioners. In fact, one well-known explanation for the failure of *any* ritual is that rival sorcerers are doing evil magic to counter its success. Thus the solution: if the demon of sorcery can be enlisted to protect the individual, then evil sorcery directed against him is of no avail. Indeed, such protection is more effective than the talismans generally worn by ritual specialists. So Hūniyam became the personal guardian of exorcists, perhaps even during this century. But a demon cannot in Sinhala cultural logic and linguistic usage be an *iṣṭa dēvatā* or personal guardian. Hence Hūniyam in his guardian role must be converted into a *dēvatā*. We noted above that like Sanni *yakā* he was sometimes called *dēvatā* as an honorific. Thus Hūniyam's form as *dēvatā* became important and part of a contrastive set: he was both *yakā* (as demon of sorcery) and *dēvatā* (as personal guardian or *iṣṭa dēvatā*).

Exorcists may have been the first to take Hūniyam as their personal deity, but lots of people living in and around the city have followed suit. One of the impressive features of the current social situation is that more and more people seem to be attributing personal misfortune to sorcery practiced by jealous neighbors. In our field data this appears not only in interviews but also in the predictions and utterances of mediums and seers like the Nāvala priest. The most frequent interpretation of client illness and misfortune is sorcery. This pervasive fear of sorcery is endemic in crowded "villages" and wards in and around Colombo. Often informants say that neighbors are jealous of their well-being and practice sorcery to bring them down. At other times family dissension is attributed to sorcery by outsiders. Sorcery is the symbolic idiom that expresses the conflicts endemic in urban society. At the end of the chapter we shall discuss the underlying cause for its increase in urban Sri Lanka.

Feeling himself surrounded by the threat of sorcery, the individual seeks the protection and patronage of the sorcery deity, Hūniyam, who is thus converted into an *iṣṭa dēvatā*. We have seen this process occur in several hamlets near Colombo. For example, Ihala Biyanvila, ten miles from Colombo, is a "village" that has lost much of its traditional homogenous base. Many people living here work in Colombo as dockers and in other low-paid manual and office jobs. Many houses in Biyanvila have a spirit shrine for Hūniyam erected outside the main residence. Several people we interviewed explicitly stated that they did so because Hūniyam was their *iṣṭa dēvatā* who could protect them from their enemies.

A protective deity is by definition benevolent to his devotee, but malevolent toward his enemies. It is, of course, difficult to reconcile *any* kind of benevolence with the traditional Hūniyam Yakā (demon). Thus an ingenious theory has been invented in the city that Hūniyam is *both* demon and *dēvatā* (a "godling"): during the waxing (*pura*) of the moon he is a *dēvatā*, and during the waning (*ava*) a demon (*yakā*). This ingenious myth can link Hūniyam, somewhat tenuously to be sure, with astrological thought, for the waxing (*pura*) and waning (*ava*) of the moon are related in astrology to the upward and downward flow of bodily energies. Furthermore, the needs of the devotee can also be resolved in this fashion: one can invoke Hūniyam in his good form to give *pihiṭa* ("help") and in his bad form to curse (*avalāda*) or practice sorcery against one's enemies.

One consequence of the elevation of Hūniyam to protector status is that individuals almost never refer to him as *yakā* ("demon"), even though he is demon during the waning (*ava*). His predominant status is that of "personal guardian" and hence that part of the verbal set is stressed. But people are aware of his demonic status: often individuals would say that you must light lamps daily for Hūniyam *dēvatā*; if you fail he may cause you some misfortune—the underlying threat from his being a demon.

For priests and magicians the demonic visage of the deity during the waning of the moon has clear uses. The *demon* Hūniyam is indispensable for practicing sorcery, *vas kavi* ("poison verses"), and other kinds of magic for which there is a client demand and financial remuneration. Clients not only want to be protected, they also want to have revenge on those who do them ill. Furthermore, the public perception of the power of the deity is related to his demonic form.

Several linguistic changes must occur when Hūniyam becomes a *dēvatā*. The term *hūniyam* means "sorcery" in common parlance: how can we call this protector "a sorcery *dēvatā*," a contradiction in terms? One solution is to change the *h* in Hūniyam into *s* since, as explained above, the *s* sounds more formal. Thus the colloquial *h* is used to refer to the deity as demon—Hūniyam Yakā—while the higher-sounding *s* is used to designate his *dēvatā* status—Sūniyam Dēvatā. Nevertheless, the *s* is substituted in formal contexts (invocations, etc.) only. In everyday parlance he is referred to as Hūniyam.

Hūniyam is addressed by his true devotees as Siddha Hūniyam/Sūniyam Dēvatāvun Vahansē, "the Perfect Lord—Dēvatā Sūniyam," or even as Nambukara Mahēsākya Deviyō, "Honorable God of the Higher Class." With these kinds of epithets and honorifics Sūniyam can be further removed from the pejorative connotations of the word *hūniyam*. For the true devotee Sūniyam is really a god, as we shall soon show, and he covers up the obvious linguistic discrepancies by multiplying honorifics and exalted modes of address. But for the *sāmis*, the priests who are theoreticians of the cult, this is not possible. Their solution is to give the deity an alias. This is a classical device in Sinhala mythology for helping a deity to move from demonic to divine status. Thus Dēvatā Baṇḍāra (his name conveys his status in the *dēvatā* or godling class) has several aliases: Vāhala; then, more elevated, Däḍimuṇḍa; finally Alutnuvara Deviyō.[17] Similarly, Sūniyam is given an alias that has no pejorative connotation: Gambāra Deviyō, "the God in Charge of Villages." Gambāra Deviyō in all likelihood was simply a category term that referred to the *grāma dēvatā*, the guardians of villages well known in Indian literature and ethnology. Such village guardian deities have become defunct in Sri Lanka. Now a defunct category term used to designate "a god in charge of villages" is used as an alias for the deity who is a personal guardian. It certainly helps resolve the problem raised by the term Hūniyam.

Yet as long as Hūniyam has these two separate aspects, he must on the ideological level remain a *dēvatā* in spite of all the aliases or honorifics given to him. For him to be truly a god he must divest himself of the demonic form or incorporate it within the divine (as in the case of Kataragama). To renounce the demonic form is no easy matter because his history as a demon is recent and widely known. Thus at this point most

[17] Obeyesekere, *Pattini*, pp. 317–21.

priests view him as god during the waxing of the moon and demon during its waning. Yet this is clearly a stage in the continuing evolution of the god and his cult.

Hūniyam as God

Irrespective of the cultural theory of Hūniyam as *dēvatā*, this is not how he is perceived by devotees. We noted in several previous quotations that priests refer to him as Hūniyam Deviyō, "the God Hūniyam." The impetus to full deification is there, though when questioned priests will affirm his dual nature. While priests refer to him both as *deviyō* and *dēvatā*, lay devotees most often simply call him Hūniyam Deviyō. This comes out clearly in a questionnaire we administered to twelve devotees, randomly picked at the Hūniyam shrine at Baseline Road on a *kemmura* day, 13 August 1975. We asked a simple straightforward question: Is Hūniyam a god (*deviyek*), a *dēvatā*, or a demon (*bhūta*)? All except one considered him a god; the only exception thought of him as a *dēvatā*; none referred to him as a demon. In addition, during the more open part of the interviews practically everyone referred to him as Hūniyam Deviyō, one informant saying *dēva hāmuduru vahansē* ("Elevated Lord God"). It seems inevitable that soon Hūniyam must shed his demonic guise and that priests must evolve new myths to give Hūniyam the elevated status his devotees demand. Let us see whether there are any such trends among the priests of our sample.

A Modern Myth of Hūniyam

We present a recent myth of Hūniyam from a young priest (age twenty-two) of Vellampiṭiya. He communicated the myth to devotees while in a trance.

> The father of Sūniyam Deviyō was a king who lived in India [Dam̆badiva] during the time of the Buddha. That king had seven sons, and the youngest was Hūniyam Dēvatā Vahansē. The father asked his Brahman [astrologers] about his youngest son. The Brahman told him that some day Prince Hūniyam would kill his father and broth-

ers. The king thought of destroying him. But instead the king and the other sons suffered death from Hūniyam. Then the citizens decided to destroy Hūniyam. But Hūniyam came to know about this and fled the country. Then he took to the forest in wrath like a demon. Since there wasn't enough food in the forest he started eating cobras. One day, while existing in this manner, he came to the Lord Buddha as he was preaching. The citizens were frightened by his appearance because he had wrapped cobras and vipers around his neck. The people tried to kill this prince, but the Buddha told them to desist and not be frightened. He was like Angulimāla, the brigand who was tamed by the Buddha. Prince Sūniyam advanced to kill the Buddha. The people then got hold of him and tied him to a pillar [*gaḍol kanuva*] and molested him. The Buddha saw with his divine eye that Prince Sūniyam had a great store of [past] merit, and accordingly one day would become a *pratyekabuddha*.[18] The Buddha then told the citizens not to molest him. The Buddha tried to tame him by his sermons. Yet Hūniyam remained recalcitrant. Then the Buddha thought that it was not wise to allow him to remain in India. The Buddha asked him, "What do you really want?" Prince Sūniyam replied, "I need blood sacrifices [*bili pūjā*]." The Buddha then sent Prince Sūniyam to Lanka. He came to Devundara and met the Lord Mahā Viṣṇu. He told Mahā Viṣṇu that he was sent here by the Buddha. Yet Prince Sūniyam continued to frighten people and destroy villages and hamlets. Then Viṣṇu summoned him and told him, "Do not accept *bili* ['sacrifices'] but take *bali* ['offerings'] instead." Then he was made [by Viṣṇu] commander in chief of all demons under the authority of God Däḍimuṇḍa of Alutnuvara. He was ordered to protect the four monastic libraries of Lanka and all temples and stupas therein. Thus Prince Hūniyam, who arrived in Lanka as Oḍḍissa, now got the title Gambāra Deviyō ["God in Charge of Villages"].

When he first came to Lanka he used to live in Käbällǟva rock and kill and eat humans. Even today you can see the blood marks. After some time he went to the Srīpāda forest and started to meditate. In this state he eventually became a *dēva*. It is then that the God Viṣṇu asked him to protect villages. After that he obtained the power that

[18] *Pratyekabuddha* is one who has achieved Buddhahood, but does not proclaim his message to the world (Pāli, Pacceka Buddha; Sinhalese, *pasē budu*).

when he opens his eyes for a moment he sees the 140,000 *kovil* and temples through his divine gaze. While he cast his protective gaze over these, he also began to watch over the good fortune and suffering of noble and decent folk. Thereafter he was given the authority to make a report of the good and bad of all human beings and submit it to the assembly of gods. It is because he must submit details about humans to the divine assembly that god Hūniyam comes close to people. He associates with men more than any other god. The god Sūniyam appears at *pura* in the guise of a *dēva*, and at *ava* as a *yakṣa*. At the *pura* period he does *sānti karma* [good acts]; at *ava* he practices woe.

Near the Buddha are four powerful persons. These four are saints [*ṛṣis*]. These four are the lords of all the magical knowledge in the whole world. [The Buddha] has given god Sūniyam the charge of protecting magical knowledge. That is why before one commences any magical act one must light a lamp for god Sūniyam.

I was given this information through "a garland of possession" [*ārūḍē mālāva*] in 1970. I have the "look" of my dead grandmother. She also protects me. If I need it I can summon her for a *dēva ārūḍē*.

The myth advances Hūniyam further in his career toward deification and gives him legitimacy in the Sinhala Buddhist pantheon. The latter is obtained initially through his relationship to the Buddha and then through warrant from Viṣṇu, the guardian of the Buddhist church in Sri Lanka. According to this myth he is a god who takes two forms, rather than a *dēvatā* composed of two forms—an important difference. He is however a special type of god, one who mediates between humans and the divine assembly. Finally, the interesting invention of the Four Ṛṣis near the Buddha simply is an indication of the importance of magic in contemporary urban culture and the role of Hūniyam as the god of magic.

At this point we can return to look at the icons in the Hūniyam shrine on Baseline Road as depicted in our chart. Our feature 6 is a marble statue of Hūniyam as a demon. It was the original centerpiece of the shrine. According to the priest in charge, it was commissioned to be made in India and presented by the Buddhist philanthropist Sir Cyril de Zoysa. The late Sir Cyril, one-time President of the Young Men's Buddhist Association (the "Young" is a dead letter), is perhaps best known for his development of the site of a *bō* tree near the bridge in Kalutara, Western

Province, into a large Buddhist complex. Practically every motorist on the main coastal road feels compelled to stop there, worship the *bō* tree, and make a cash donation. At the same time Sir Cyril, like many other businessmen, was an ardent supporter of the gods, especially Kataragama and Hūniyam. He also endowed the Hūniyam shrine at the rich suburban temple of Bellanvila.

By 1965 Hūniyam the god had come into vogue, so the demon had to be moved to one side and a new image, shorn of demonic attributes, installed in the middle. This spatial shift neatly symbolizes the development we have described.

But the matter has another aspect. Building a shrine to a demon and erecting a marble statue to him is not traditional Sinhala behavior. Already in 1958 Hūniyam was not purely demonic, though his ambiguity had not found iconographic form. Gunasekera's study of Lunāva shows that the Venerable Visuddhānanda considered himself to have a close relationship with Hūniyam, who in his dreams addressed him as "son"; probably he thought that Hūniyam would protect him from his enemies. Our survey disclosed another case of a monk who was an active devotee of Hūniyam. According to the present incumbent, the former chief monk of Vikramasiṃhārāmaya, now deceased, regularly lit lamps for Hūniyam's demonic form (*yakṣa avatāra*), who he believed would bring progress and prosperity to the temple. This fits the fact, recorded above, that in this temple we found Hūniyam installed on a par with the Four Warrant Gods.

Hūniyam's Clients

When we interviewed twelve priests in shrines in Colombo 9 and 10, all asserted categorically that the major reason for client visits to their shrines was family conflicts, generally conflicts between husband and wife or desertion by a spouse. One priest said: "People come here to resolve conflicts in the family or fights in the home. Occasionally they come for children's illnesses." Another: "Most people come here not so much for illnesses but for lies and dissension (*bhēda-bhinna*) in the family. Women often come here and say that their husbands have deserted them, or left them in anger, or forsaken them for another woman."

It is interesting that while all priests stated family dissension as the prime cause of client visits (followed by illness and obtaining of blessings), not one mentioned the jobs or court cases so common in Kataragama shrines.

We tried to check whether the priests' assessment of the situation was correct. We asked forty out of ninety-two clients who visited the Hūniyam shrine at Baseline Road on 13 August 1975 the purpose of their visit. They answered: obtaining of general blessings (9); family conflict (8); jobs and business enterprises (7); illness (4); cursing enemies (4); redress in court cases or property thefts (3); success in marriage proposals (3); "just came" (2). It is clear that, contrary to the priests' opinions, clients visit the Hūniyam shrine for a variety of reasons. This is indeed what one might expect since Hūniyam is an important god for most of these people, having taken the place of Kataragama in their allegiance. In the above sample the largest number came for no special purpose; they were members of the cult group who came to seek the god's blessings. But after this were those who came to resolve family conflicts, an impressively large number. It is this feature, peculiar to urban society, that had impressed the priests whom we interviewed.

The Increase in Black Magic

Let us now attempt to characterize the social and resultant psychological situation that has led so many people to worship and even adore the personification of black magic. In an earlier paper we have shown that it is reasonable to think that the practice of black magic has greatly increased in recent years, and we found that the clients at three famous centers for its practice are almost all in nontraditional occupations.[19] Moreover, those who practice it (or, more accurately, pay to have it practiced on their behalf) are a mere fraction of those who fear that it is being practiced against them. Why should this be?

One need not be a romantic about Sri Lanka's rural past to believe that the traditional social system saw to it that no one starved. Seen from the point of view of the majority caste, the cultivators who owned the land or had usufruct of it, the system worked like this. In the village society of organized inequality, the minority "service castes" were treated as one's

[19] Gananath Obeyesekere, "Sorcery, Premeditated Murder, and the Canalization of Aggression in Sri Lanka," *Ethnology* 14, no. 1 (1975): pp. 1–23.

social inferiors, but they were also to some extent dependents with a claim on one's sympathies. So long as they did not surpass one's own standard of living—which under conditions of rural isolation was hardly conceivable—one felt no inhibitions about giving them a hand when times were hard. So far as one's social equals were concerned, they were usually kindred toward whom one had similar obligations. A kin group in general rose or fell together. If an individual tried to better himself without sharing out his gains, his guilt externalized itself in the belief that his neighbors had the evil eye or the evil tongue. Those who have the evil eye or tongue are unaware of the fact: to have them is not morally reprehensible because there is no malign intention. The evil eye in this case is simply the guilt the more fortunate feels toward the less fortunate.

The breakdown of the structure of the traditional and relatively self-contained village began nearly a century ago. The Paddy Lands Ordinances from 1840 to 1867 produced a market in land and social mobility that noticeably affected the western and southern coastal areas.[20] Here the weakening of kinship obligations began earlier than in the Kandyan area, and the practice of black magic was indeed mainly associated with the Low Country in the first half of the century. With social mobility, economic expectations naturally rose. For a while these expectations were not unrealistic, and many people benefited, especially members of the lower castes, who were enabled to escape from their position of dependence; the forfeiture of the cultivators' patronage was no great loss while their services and abilities commanded a better price in the open market. But population and poverty have greatly increased in recent years; the changes have permeated most of the country and social disintegration has accelerated.

The situation must have become acute in the mid-fifties. It became unrealistic to expect that those better off should use a part of their wealth to subsidize the less well off; there were simply too many mouths to feed. Each man had too many dependents in his own household to be able to care for other households too; and the other households naturally proliferated as well, so that most villages came to contain many people one did not even know personally. The village community has gone and with it most of the community rituals and the social mechanisms for redistribution. The gap between the ideology of mutual kin support and reality now yawns wide.

[20] Obeyesekere, *Land Tenure*.

But the widespread inequality—especially of course its darker side—leaves people with a great sense of unease. The better off feel guilty and look for justification; the poor require some explanation for their undeserved misery. One option for the poor is to absolve oneself of responsibility by blaming society or in particular the capitalist class. But the justification that suits rich and poor alike is the attribution of jealousy (*īrṣyāva*)—usually to one's neighbors, who may be identified by oracles. To attribute jealousy is by no means irrational in these crowded areas, which are full of theft, violence, and abuse. The widespread ethos of suspicion that is created is not the true paranoia that stems from personal pathology but a sociological phenomenon of urban anomie.

Unlike the traditional evil eye and evil tongue, jealousy is conscious and therefore a sin; one's neighbors are thus morally reprehensible and their jealousy is not to be assuaged by a gift—which might only inflame it further.

To the putatively jealous is attributed black magic. This black magic is a marvellous explanation for any misfortune one may suffer. We see the attribution of black magic to others as fulfilling four functions. First, it provides a cognitive explanation for misfortune. Second, it shifts responsibility for that misfortune from oneself to one's neighbors. If economic effort is not rewarded with success—which in fact is probably due to economic forces outside individual control—the failure is attributed to jealous neighbors. Third, since the jealous neighbors are morally culpable it assuages one's guilt at not helping the less well off. Finally, one can project onto others one's own jealousy and indeed more generalized feelings of hostility.

Of course, jealousy must really be common. But it does not work in the way culturally ascribed to it. The jealous man is not usually engaged in black magic against his neighbor. The neighbor is suspicious and uses protective white magic to calm his own fears. There is indeed plenty of black magic about, but that is used to avenge concrete wrongs, real or fancied. One does not *initiate* hostilities with black magic, one uses it to get one's own back against the man who has insulted one, stolen one's goods, or wronged one's daughter. Moreover it is the response of the man who because of his social position and his fear of the law is too cautious or too timid to hit back openly. If you stab your aggressor you may hang for it; if he dies of a wasting disease, no one will blame you. Even if your victim suspects you, he cannot effectively take revenge, as the practice of black magic is not a punishable crime—as it was under the laws of the Kandyan Kingdom.

Expansion and Prognosis

The god Hūniyam originated from the village cults of the demon Hūniyam as a response to the needs of urban proletarians. Once established in Colombo the cult began to expand into other small towns in Sri Lanka. Thus there are shrines for Hūniyam emerging in many parts of Sri Lanka, especially those areas that have been subjected to increased demographic and societal change. We were especially struck by a very elaborate building put up for Hūniyam in Aluvihāra, a famous Buddhist temple on the outskirts of Mātalē, a large market town in the Central Province. According to tradition Aluvihāra was the place where the Buddhist scriptures were committed to writing in the first century B.C. Thus Hūniyam has moved into an old and traditional Buddhist temple. Furthermore Aluvihāra also draws many pilgrims from all over the nation. Hence it is likely that it will serve as a conduit for the dissemination of the Hūniyam cult into village areas. Within a short radius of Aluvihāra is also a large number of old villages, rapidly becoming overcrowded, with increasing social differentiation, factionalism, and conflict, their economic resources being fast depleted. It is likely that the Hūniyam cult will appeal to these villages and similar ones in the Western, Southern, and Central Provinces. Not only this: urban middle-class people have also shown considerable interest in the Hūniyam cult, though for the most part they remain adherents of the Skanda cult. The elaborate shrine complex for Hūniyam on Baseline Road attracts businessmen, white-collar workers, and professionals as well as the urban proletarians for whom it was primarily established. The malaise and frustration are spreading.

We have shown that since Hūniyam personifies black magic, to placate him will serve both purposes: defense and attack. Hence his dual nature, half god, half devil. Hūniyam's future seems to us to be in the balance. Two forces are at work. We have shown the dynamic in Sinhala Buddhist ideology that pushes gods upwards: the more Hūniyam protects, the more he risks honorary retirement and promotion out of active service; he may get kicked upstairs. On the other hand, if the above analysis is right, there will be a continuing need to placate a god of sorcery. Here Hūniyam holds the unique advantage of actually being *called* "black magic," so he may not be easy to replace. A possibility is that these two developments may *both* occur: a part of Hūniyam under one of his other names, such as Gambāra Deviyō, may rise to the position of a higher god, imitating the recent career of Kataragama, while the black-and-white, Jekyll-and-Hyde Hūniyam may continue just where he is. There seems to be a permanent slot for a black protector, maybe as the nominal minister of a higher god. But in either case to attribute autonomous power to a black deity runs counter to the traditional Buddhist ideology that correlates power and morality in the universe.

In recording the shift of power and influence from the Four Warrant Gods to Kataragama and from Kataragama to Hūniyam we are not claiming that this takes place all over Sri Lanka or even all over urban Sri Lanka at a uniform pace or even that each shift is in due course inevitable. We are tracing a line of development that has taken place in some contexts and among certain rather numerous individuals; and we would not be surprised if it continued. To extrapolate with such precision as to predict, for example, just what will happen to Hūniyam is impossible, if only because one cannot predict the social history of Colombo. But we do not see the line of development as ending even here. It extends to our next topic—the rise of Kālī.

CHAPTER 4

Kālī, the Punitive Mother

Kālī is a major goddess of Hindu mythology, probably known to every Hindu villager. The Goddess (Sanskrit: Devī) has both benign and terrible forms. Theologically, these forms are aspects of the one goddess; in myth, some are distinct characters. The classic myth about Kālī is that when the Goddess in her form as Durgā fought a great battle to destroy the Buffalo Demon (Mahiṣāsura) a demon called Blood Drop (Raktabīja) posed a terrible threat because as soon as a drop of his blood touched the ground it turned into a living replica of himself. Kālī came to the Goddess' aid; with her great tongue she licked up the blood even as it fell. Triumphant, she rampaged over the battlefield, garlanded with severed heads, brandishing her sword and trampling on corpses. Because she was fighting against a malevolent demon for a just cause she is Bhadra ("Auspicious") Kālī; because she filled the battlefield with corpses she is Śmaśāna ("Cemetery") Kālī.[1]

In Sinhala awareness there is probably no distinction between Kālī and Durgā as slayer of the Buffalo Demon (Mahiṣāsura-mardinī), and the same may well be true of her Tamil devotees. In the Kālī shrine at Munnēssarama near Chilaw in Sri Lanka we saw hanging two pictures that from the classical point of view depicted Durgā in that role. One of the hymns sung at that shrine also refers to Kālī as decapitating the buffalo. This conflation does not disturb the sense of the classic myth. But Kālī has a lolling tongue and other horrendous attributes which the classical Durgā lacks.

The protruding tongue is perhaps Kālī's most distinctive iconographic feature. In her other most common iconic representation this tongue is often reinterpreted. She is shown standing on a body which is that of her husband Śiva. In the classical myth recounted above she has no husband; this is a conflation that probably originated in North India. In Tantric

[1] In contemporary Sinhala religion this is Sohon ("Graveyard," "Cemetery") Kālī.

theology the Goddess personifies God's Power (Śakti). God is her locus. Iconically this is shown as the divine couple in sexual embrace, the Goddess seated on the God. Kālī is thus seated on the aspect of Śiva called Sadāśiva ("Eternal Śiva") as a personification of his potency. Then by conflation with the battlefield image she comes to be standing on him; in early depictions his member is erect even in this pose. Finally prudery eliminates that feature and reinterprets the protruding tongue as showing Kālī's embarrassment at her faux pas in standing on her husband![2]

Since Kālī's cult has long been widespread in South India, it could hardly have remained unknown to Sinhala culture. After Indo-European speakers had introduced the forerunner of the Sinhala language, Sinhala Prakrit, into the island some time around the middle of the first millennium B.C., virtually all later migrations into Sri Lanka came from various parts of southern India. Physically the Sinhala people are a Dravidian population. Their basically Indo-European language has been heavily influenced by Tamil, especially in its syntax. Though their language and their Buddhist religion gave the Sinhalas a distinct cultural identity, such fundamental institutions as kinship are Dravidian in form, and so are many aspects of the traditional spirit religion. In fact, were a comprehensive historical and comparative study of Sinhala and South Indian (Tamil and Kerala) popular religion to be undertaken, we suspect that it would emerge that it was the features of Sinhala spirit religion that were *not* related to Dravidian religion that were exceptional and stood in need of further explanation; and moreover that the explanation for those differences would be found to lie in Buddhism.

Of these differences the cult of Kālī furnishes an excellent illustration. The Kālī we have described, who literally thirsts for blood, is too ghoulish to be accepted into the divine hierarchy of Sinhala Buddhism; she must be demoted to the position of demoness or else converted. Let us give examples of both treatments.

There is a very old story in Sinhala culture about the conversion of the demoness (*yakṣiṇī*) Kālī into a benign spirit. It first occurs in a fifth-century Pāli text, the commentary on the *Dhammapada*. It is probable that this version of the story was itself based on an even older original in Sinhala Prakrit, but if so, that version has been lost. The Pāli version was translated into Sinhala, with additions, by the Sinhala monk Dharmasēna in

[2] Sticking out one's tongue is a gesture of embarrassment in South Asian culture.

the thirteenth century as part of his *Saddharmaratnāvaliya*.[3] This Sinhala version has been analyzed in some detail elsewhere.[4] Here we shall just summarize Burlingame's translation of the Pāli[5] so as to show Kālī's moral progress. This illustrates the karmic logic, explained above, that underlies upward mobility through the Sinhala pantheon and thus shows that such mobility is a phenomenon "of long duration," as Braudel would say, in Sinhala history.

The story is told in the commentary to illustrate the famous verse: "Hatred is never appeased by hatred. Hatred is appeased by nonhatred. This is the eternal law."

> A hunter, on the death of his father, had a hard time continuing his father's occupation and coping for his widowed mother. She urged him to marry so he would have help at least with the household chores. At first he refused but finally agreed. Unfortunately the wife proved to be barren so the mother nagged him to get another wife, but again he refused. The barren wife felt that the husband would yield eventually to his mother's request and also felt that a second wife of his mother's choice might treat her badly. She therefore decided to pick a second wife for her husband herself and keep the woman as her subordinate. This she did but, lest the second wife bear a child and thereby pose a threat, she pretended friendship and asked to be told when the second wife conceived. The woman did so and the barren wife secretly introduced dangerous medicines into the food she prepared for her co-wife and this caused a miscarriage. She conceived again, and again the barren wife caused her foetus to be aborted. The co-wife was now warned by her neighbors and took precautions not to tell her rival about her third pregnancy. But the barren wife saw her belly and asked her co-wife why she wasn't told of her conception. The co-wife replied, "It was you who brought me here, and twice you have caused me to suffer a miscarriage; why should I tell you?" The barren wife knew that she was lost and se-

[3] *Saddharmaratnāvaliya* by Dharmasēna Mahāsāmi, ed. Kiriällē Gnānavimala (Colombo: Gunasena and Company, 1971), pp. 101–9.

[4] Ranjini and Gananath Obeyesekere, "The Story of the Demoness Kālī: A Thirteenth-Century Text on 'Evil,' " *History of Religions*, forthcoming.

[5] E. W. Burlingame, *Buddhist Legends*, pt. 1 (London: Routledge and Kegan Paul, 1979 [1921]), reprinted for the Pali Text Society, pp. 170–75.

cretly administered a poison that caused the babe in the womb to be lodged horizontally when the hour of delivery arrived. The foetus was destroyed and the mother died. Before she died she swore vengeance, to be born as an ogress and devour her enemy's children.

And so in the next birth the second wife was born as a cat and the barren wife as a hen. When the hen laid her eggs, three times in succession the cat ate them up. The hen vowed revenge and was born as a tigress while the cat was born as a deer. Three times did the tigress eat the deer's offspring and so the deer vowed revenge. Then the tigress was born as the daughter of a noble family in Sāvatthi. She married and bore a son. The deer was born as a demoness who, taking the guise of a friend, came to the woman's bedchamber and devoured the child. A second child was eaten in the same manner. On the third occasion the woman, fearing a repetition, went to her parents' house to deliver the child. Meanwhile the demoness searched for her high and low but with no success. The woman delivered the child and was returning to her husband's home when she was pursued by the demoness. She ran into a temple—a temple where the Buddha was resident.

The woman fell at the feet of the Buddha and begged protection for her child. The Buddha told Ānanda, his personal attendant, to summon the demoness. The woman was terrified but the Buddha told her not to be afraid. The demoness came forward and the Buddha tamed her by his compassion and delivered a homily that expressed the ethics of the *Dhammapada*. "Why do you return hatred for hatred? Hatred is quenched by love, not by hatred." With this the demoness was established in "the fruit of conversion."

Now the Buddha asked the noblewoman to give her child to the demoness. She was terrified but the Buddha calmed her. The demoness held the child, kissed and caressed it, and then wept. The Buddha told the noblewoman to take the demoness home. "Let her live in your own house and feed her with the choicest rice porridge."

Let us now quote the conclusion in full from Burlingame's translation.

So the young wife took the ogress home with her, lodged her on the central rafter of the hut, and fed her with the choicest rice-porridge. Now when the rice was threshed and the flail was raised, she feared that it would strike her head. So she said to her friend, "I shall not be able to live here any longer; lodge me elsewhere." She was lodged successively in the flail-hut, the water-chatty, the bake-house, the storeroom for nimbs, the dust-heap, and the village gate. But she refused to live in any of these places, saying, "Here the flail rises as if it would split my head in two; here boys empty out slops; here dogs lie down; here boys attend to nature's needs; here they throw away sweepings; here village boys practice fortune-telling." So they lodged her in a quiet place by herself outside of the village, and there they brought her the choicest rice-porridge.

The ogress said to her friend, "This year there will be abundance of rain; therefore plant your crops in a dry place. This year there will be a drought; therefore plant your crops in a moist place." Other people's crops were destroyed either by excessive moisture or by drought, but the crops of the young wife flourished above measure.

People asked the young wife, "Woman, your crops are destroyed neither by excessive moisture nor by drought. When you plant your crops, you seem to know in advance whether the season will be wet or dry. How is this?" The young wife replied, "I have a friend, an ogress, who tells me whether the season will be wet or dry; and I plant my crops according to her directions on high or low ground. Don't you see? Every day the choicest rice-porridge and other kinds of food are carried out of our house; to her are they carried. Do you also carry the choicest rice-porridge and other kinds of food to her and she will look after your crops also."

Straightway all the residents of the city rendered honor to her. On her part, from that time forth, she looked after the crops of all. And she received abundant gifts and a large retinue. Subsequently she established the Eight Ticket-foods, which are kept up even to this present day.

The *Saddharmaratnāvaliya* was composed in the thirteenth century after the old capital of Sri Lanka, Polonnaruva, had been sacked by Māgha of Kalinga, who invaded Sri Lanka in 1214. While Māgha held sway over the ancient northern kingdom, Vijayabāhu III established a separate Sinhala kingdom in Daṁbadeniya, from which he launched attacks against Māgha and defeated him. Vijayabāhu's son, Parākramabāhu II (1236–1270), a great patron of letters, continued to rule from Daṁbadeniya. Māgha came from Kalinga in the northeastern part of India (present-day Orissa), but according to Sinhala chronicles his force consisted of South Indian mercenaries. Wherever Māgha's forces came from, it is likely that some of them settled in Sinhala territory. They may have brought popular cults, including that of Kālī, from the Indian mainland.

In his version, Dharmasēna gives the good village guardian deity at the end of the story a name, Kālī Barāṇḍhi. Presumably he is thus matching the classical story to a village deity of his day.

The *Daṁbadeni Asna* ("The Daṁbadeni Message"), another text written during this period, lists the various officers and service corps of the Sinhala kings. One group listed here are *kālī naṭannō*, "those who dance Kālī."[6] We think this refers to ritual specialists who were possessed by Kālī, either to bring or predict victory. It would have been appropriate to propitiate this fierce deity for help in battle. It is also possible that this corps of "Kālī dancers" was introduced by the forces of Māgha.[7] If our speculation is correct (and it is a speculation), then the fierce Kālī was a presence in this region of Sri Lanka.

Kālī's simultaneous presence in a local culture in two forms, one demonic and the other benign, would not be paradoxical; on the contrary, it is a recurrent feature of her history in Hindu culture. The same pattern has been found among Sinhalas living at the edge of the Tamil area of northern Sri Lanka. In the late nineteenth century Nevill recorded two Sinhala texts from the Nuvarakalāviya District.[8] Both texts immediately reveal the deity's Tamil origin by using the Tamil form of her name, Patrakālī, for the Sanskrit/Sinhala Bhadra Kālī. They convert her into a Buddhist deity: "She watched at the foot of the Siri Ma Bo tree, when Budu attained Buduship." But other texts collected in the same region[9] identify her with a demoness of disease, Vaduru Mā Dēvī, as has been done in texts of the Pattinī cult in the Western, Southern, and Sabaragamuva Provinces.

[6] We have obtained this reference from M. B. Ariyapala, *Society in Medieval Ceylon* (Colombo: Government Press, 1968), p. 166. The interpretation is ours.

[7] The tradition of men and women dancing on the battlefield was well known in the Cankam literature. So was the custom of an offering to Koṭṭavai (Kālī) of rice balls soaked in blood. See Elamkulan Kunjan Pillai, *Studies in Kerala History* (Kottayam: National Book Stall, 1970), pp. 28–36.

Fully to understand the Kālī cult in Sri Lanka systematic research of available historical sources must be undertaken. We have not dealt with the history of the cult but with historical *processes* involved in the transmission, transformation, and acceptance of the cult by Buddhists.

[8] Hugh Nevill, *Sinhala Verse* (Colombo: Government Press, 1952), 3: 250–51.

[9] L. D. Barnett, "Alphabetical Guide to Sinhalese Folklore from Ballad Sources," *The Indian Antiquary* 45 (1916): 1–116.

In the exorcistic rituals of this region there are no special rites for Kālī, though her name appears in spells (*mantra*) and invocations. On the other hand, in the elaborate *gammaḍuva* rituals for the goddess Pattinī, Kālī again appears in two different forms. In the ritual drama known as *Killing and Resurrection*,[10] Pattinī quells Vaduru Mā Dēvī, a demoness of pestilences (*vaduru*). (We have noted that in India Dēvī is often a synonym for Kālī.) On the other hand, Kālī, identified by that name, appears in the same drama as a harmless servant of Pattinī. It looks as if there has been a debate between the officiants of two ritual traditions: the priests of the Pattinī cult have tried to downgrade and render innocuous the fierce demoness of the exorcists. They do not want Kālī to compete with Pattinī; but their texts still have to accommodate Vaduru Mā Dēvī as a Kālī-like figure under another name. Finally, the same region offers evidence of Kālī's more overt Buddhicization in a text quoted by Nevill.[11] The *Kālī Yakinī Kavi* ("Songs of the Demoness Kali") was apparently recited to cure people of rabies. In it she is portrayed as the daughter of a *nāga* (divine cobra) king and queen, subservient to the Buddha. Here is a sample stanza:

> We offer rightful oblations to the demoness.
> She gives blessings on the patient and gets ready to depart.
> She sheds her canine guise and is ready to leave.
> By the command of the Buddha, the demoness is about to leave.

So far as we know, Kālī played very little part in the traditional religion of the Kandyan area (the contemporary Central and Uva Provinces).

In sum, the traditional Sinhala view of Kālī was that she was a demoness. Some traditions held that she had been tamed by conversion to Buddhism, but at considerable cost to her power: she was at best a marginal figure.

Kālī in Contemporary Religion

We have not come across a single Sinhala shrine for Kālī founded before the 1960s. This situation has changed dramatically in recent times in the

[10] See Obeyesekere, *Pattini*, pp. 245–82.

[11] Nevill, *Sinhala Verse* 2: 28.

city of Colombo and other urban areas, so that nowadays there are many Sinhala Buddhist priestesses who have tiny shrines for her or propitiate her along with other deities in their shrines. Only a few Buddhist monks have thus far built shrines for her within temple premises. There is no Sinhala Buddhist center for Kālī like those for other emerging deities, for example, for Hūniyam at Käbällǟva and for Dēvatā Baṇḍāra at Alutnuvara. No major shrines on the scale of the Hūniyam shrines at Demaṭagoḍa and Aluvihāra have appeared yet. This may of course change, but currently the major centers for Kālī worship are in Tamil Hindu temple complexes patronized by Sinhala Buddhists. Kālī is however very popular with the Tamil populations in the tea country of the highlands, and many well-known Tamil *sāmi*s in Kataragama have been devotees of both Kālī and Murugan (Skanda). It is likely that these *sāmi*s influenced their Sinhala Buddhist counterparts in Kataragama, as they did in respect of the Skanda cult and *bhakti* religion in general.

The main shrine for this goddess is at Munnēssarama (Munneśvaram), near Chilaw, about forty miles north of Colombo. The temple for Munneśvaram, a form of Śiva, is highly venerated by the Hindus of Sri Lanka, but Sinhala Buddhists are more drawn to the Kālī temple located outside the sacred premises and controlled by non-Brahman priests (*pūsārī*, *sāmi*). The location of the Kālī shrine outside the main premises and its control by non-Brahmans are due to the polluting animal sacrifices that were performed there. In 1980, however, animal sacrifices at Hindu temples were banned.[12]

The ritual cursing and sorcery for which the Kālī shrine at Munnēssarama is famous are described elsewhere.[13] Briefly stated, a person pays a fee to the priest and then slaughters a goat or chicken in order to wreak vengeance on an enemy. Most persons who come there are in fact Sinhala Buddhists, and there is a recently built Buddhist temple nearby to cater to their more orthodox needs. A Buddhist may sacrifice a goat or chicken to Kālī in her shrine and then go to the Buddhist temple for orthodox worship. What is striking is, of course, the failure or refusal of Buddhists to recognize the blatant contradiction here, since Sinhala ritual rarely practiced animal sacrifices. In exorcistic rituals, for example, the chicken is only symbolically killed.

[12] A cabinet decision was taken to ban all animal sacrifices in Hindu temples on 24 June 1979. Government officers were asked to enforce this decision on 16 January 1980.

[13] See Obeyesekere, "Sorcery, Aggression."

Insofar as the goddess Kālī of Munnēssarama is associated with sorcery and cursing, her rise in urban Sri Lanka must be seen in relation to Hūniyam, who is also a village-society demon associated with sorcery. Thus one could argue that the urban acceptance of Kālī as a goddess parallels the acceptance of Hūniyam as a god, and the rise of their respective cults must make sense in relation to conditions of urban anomie sketched in this book. In both instances powerful demonic figures are being converted into powerful *divine* figures. However, if Hūniyam has been split into demonic and divine forms, Kālī still retains both. There are several forms of Kālī being placated, at least by priests and priestesses, and some are more malevolent than others (e.g., Sohon Kālī, Madana Kālī, Bhadra Kālī), but all of them still contain the demonic.

As we said earlier, Kālī is propitiated all over urban Sri Lanka by the new priests and priestesses. Since these shrines are very small, attracting a few individuals only, let us shift our focus to Hindu shrines of the goddess in order to demonstrate the continuing Hindu influence on Buddhists and, at the same time, her importance for them. In June–July 1983 we studied a *kovil* or shrine in Mōdera, a suburb of Colombo. This is a Hindu temple complex owned by Colombo merchants. The main shrine is for Gaṇeśa, but once again there is a large shrine for Kālī on the side facing the narrow street, beyond which is the ocean. The officials are all Brahman priests, but they tolerated animal sacrifices at the Kālī shrine till very recently.

The Mōdera temple exemplified two religious orientations—those of Sinhala Buddhists and Tamil Hindus. The latter came primarily to worship Gaṇeśa, the major deity of the temple, and other Hindu deities, including Śiva and Pārvatī. Some of them also came to Kālī, but having propitiated her they would also perform rituals at the other shrines. By contrast about eighty percent of the clients who visited the Kālī shrine were Sinhala, according to rough calculations we made. For Sinhala Buddhists the visit to the Kālī shrine was the primary goal; some of them then offered *pūjā* at the main temple, often very perfunctorily. Only one Sinhala Buddhist whom we interviewed came to worship Gaṇeśa exclusively rather than Kālī. The Brahman priests were well aware of the economic (and perhaps even the political) importance of Sinhala clients. Consequently they have given some of the Hindu gods Sinhala names. Thus Pārvatī has a name board in Sinhala which tells us that she is Pattinī and Bhairava is Hūniyam. Most Sinhalas who go into the main shrine ignore Śiva and utter invocations to Hūniyam-Bhairava, wonderfully illustrating the prevailing religious eclecticism.

Before 1980 the Kālī shrine here was famous for its animal sacrifices; Sinhala Buddhist priestesses congregated here and performed services for their clients. There were about a dozen who regularly got into trances and uttered invocations on behalf of clients, and some actually participated in sacrificing chicken and goats. With the ban on sacrifice, there was also a further ban on ecstatic trances. Most of the priestesses went back to their own shrines in the city and its outskirts and occasionally came to Mōdera with a client who had a specially difficult problem. One woman known as Nāvala Mā̄ṇiyō ("the mater from Nāvala") was designated by the Brahmans as the official priestess, though others also perform here unofficially. Nāvala Mā̄ṇiyō gives a portion of her income to the Brahman priests.

The official *pūjā*s for the goddess are performed by a Brahman priest. The Sinhalas and others congregate here and offer baskets of flowers and fruit, and some may bring an animal (nowadays not for slaughter but as a gift to the goddess). The worshipper then silently prays to the deity and asks that the request be granted. Some may go a step further and ask Nāvala Mā̄ṇiyō (or any other Sinhala priest or priestess present) to perform a special invocation for a fee in the compound outside the shrine. The priestess does this while facing the ocean. The invocation uttered aloud is a public plaint to the deity stating the nature of the client's problem and asking for her help. There are varieties of plaints and *pūjā*s, and graded fees, depending on the seriousness of the problem. Many problems require repeated visits, either daily or once or several times a week (generally on Wednesdays and Saturdays, the *kemmura* days) for a designated period of time. At the conclusion of the invocation the client performs a standard act done by all who visit here—smashing a coconut on a stone slab in the compound. If the coconut breaks with the white kernel facing up, it is a good sign; if the coconut faces down, it is considered inauspicious, though the latter omen hardly seemed to bother most people.

It was difficult for us to estimate the numbers that visit this Kālī shrine. However, Wednesdays and Saturdays, the special *kemmura* days that are suitable for propitiation of deities, draw well over a hundred people from all walks of life in urban society—from the wealthy in their large Mercedes-Benz cars to indigent proletarians. Interviews were difficult and some were reluctant to talk, since many came here for very intimate reasons. During our visits in summer 1983 we interviewed forty-four Sinhala clients, all Buddhists except for two Catholics. We have information on the backgrounds of thirty-three persons and they break down as follows:

39 percent (13) were clearly working class; 18 percent (6) were in petty jobs and could be roughly categorized as lower-middle class; 33 percent (11) came from middle-class backgrounds; 9 percent (3) were extremely well off. What was impressive in the sample was that there was only one peasant farmer; all the others were town or city dwellers or educated middle-class people (businessmen, teachers) living in villages. This was partly because the shrine was located in the city, but this cannot explain the absence of ordinary villagers, since the shrine drew people from a thirty-mile radius. We think the sample clearly indicates that the goddess Kālī is primarily a deity of urban people. The data also give a very clear picture of the problems that beset people who come here. Almost all of them come either for the resolution of personal conflicts (21 cases) or for jobs and for ensuring prosperity (18 cases). Most job requests are by people seeking employment in the Middle East (8 cases). Two people were victims of thefts and came for revenge, three for marriage proposals, and two for illness. It is clear that typically Kālī primarily helps resolve interpersonal conflicts such as marital ones, insult by neighbors, and hostility on the part of fellow workers. Since considerable numbers of persons came to Kālī for help in getting jobs or ensuring prosperity in their profession, one can infer that Kālī's role has been generalized recently. The overwhelming number of people who came to the Kālī shrine in Munnēssarama in 1969 came for sorcery and vengeance;[14] here at Mōdera in 1983, they also came to seek her aid for jobs. Though Kālī's role is not as generalized as Hūniyam's, it is very likely that her rise into divine status is very much like the latter's, that is, a powerful demoness associated with sorcery has been converted into a powerful goddess who can help one in a variety of ways. People would articulate this idea, as they did in respect of Hūniyam. A thirty-two-year-old woman said: "I very much want a job in the Middle East. So I come to Kālī Mā̰ṇiyō and make a vow (*bāra venavā*). Kālī Mā̰ṇiyō is very stern (*darunuyi*). She brings quick results." Nevertheless, as with Hūniyam, her earlier demonic status is reflected in the cases of conflict and theft. In these the individual not only asks for redress, but also wants the evildoer punished. It is likely that many more people came for reasons of personal conflict and the wish to wreak vengeance than the data suggest. Many refused to be interviewed; they simply said they came to Kālī "because of a trouble" (*karadarayak nisā*). We feel that underlying this euphe-

[14] Ibid., p. 9.

mism are interpersonal conflict and hope of revenge. Moreover, as with Hūniyam, supplicants when interviewed would say that in general people come to the Kālī shrine for cursing and the resolution of conflict. But in fact they came for a variety of other reasons also. It is as if there is a lag between an earlier view of Kālī's role and a newly emergent one.

The mere figures do not give a feel for the complexity of the cases that come to the Kālī shrine. Some of the cases are very simple, for example, revenge for hurt or desire to get a visa for the Middle East, but others are more complex and require a fuller presentation. Let us first present a few simple, typical cases and then some more complex ones that lead us to the themes of this book.

Case A., female, Buddhist, age twenty-eight, from Rājagiriya near Colombo.

She came here, without informing her parents, in the company of friends, one of whom had got a job thanks to Kālī. She wants a husband. She has passed the general certificate of education (G.C.E. "O" level) but has no job. She has had several marriage proposals but they came to naught. Now there is a proposal from someone she really likes. She wants Kālī to fulfill her wishes. If her wishes are fulfilled she will offer the goddess a garland of flowers plus a *pūjā* of fruit. She has to come every Tuesday for seven days.

Case B, male, Buddhist, age fifty-two, from Matara but living in Kohuvala near Colombo.

This man, a worker in the Health Department, complained that a young relation of his abused him in front of his wife and daughter. He says he doesn't want to go to the police because things may then get out of hand. Moreover, he says, he is not the type who will engage in verbal or physical violence. So he has come here to ask the deity to have revenge on his enemy.

Case C, male, age forty-five, a well-to-do shop owner from Piliyandala, a suburb ten miles from Colombo.

One evening while she was out walking someone insulted his daughter by throwing excrement at her. He knows that this place is famous for redress in these matters. So he has come here to plead that they are blameless and to curse those who cause them trouble (*karadara*).

He had complained to the police about this matter, but was told that he must have suspects, with their names and addresses! "We live and eat well and we have motor vehicles, and so someone has done this through jealousy. We like to help people in the village, though."

First he went to Munnēssarama. But his younger sister told him about this place since she has had success here. Moreover, this place is easily accessible.

Comment: The three cases are very typical of the ordinary supplicants who came here. In case A we have a twenty-eight-year-old woman, well educated (high school graduate), but with no job and no husband. The bleak statistics on marriage and the economic conditions underlying them have come alive.[15] Case B illustrates the tensions between kinfolk and the lack of mechanisms for resolving these conflicts. The motive for revenge is stark and clear in this case: the supplicant is not the type that will confront his enemy directly; therefore he comes to the shrine to ask the deity to wreak vengeance on his foe. This case is very typical of clients who come to Munnēssarama and other sorcery shrines in Sri Lanka. Case C in fact had gone to Munnēssarama but then decided to come here for pragmatic reasons. Very typically one comes to a shrine after getting advice from someone (a sibling in this case) who has had success. Case C also illustrates the conditions of urban anomie and interpersonal conflicts that exist there. "We live and eat well and we have motor vehicles," says the supplicant. We have noted that "jealousy" is the motivation attributed to others who wish to harm someone doing well[16]—in this case surreptitiously throwing excrement at a businessman's daughter, and in other cases also practicing evil sorcery against well-to-do neighbors. In case D below we have a much more complex instance of revenge.

Case D, male, age thirty-four, bakery owner in Koṭahēna, a suburb of Colombo.

He is a father of four children. His wife was given magical medicine (*vaśi*) by a group of people who took her away and then "raped" her. He firmly believes that some *vaśi* or "jumping of the lines" (*iru pänumak*), a form of sorcery, was done to her. When she came back home after a few days, he beat her. She said she knew nothing of it and that she was not abused.

[15] See chap. 5 for a discussion of these problems.

[16] See chap. 3.

Owing to the love magic her body has swelled. She says her feet also feel lifeless. Later her husband got someone to charm some king coconut (*tämbili*) for her to drink and she recovered. Then he came to this *dēvālē*, uttered poison songs (*vas kavi*), and cursed those who harmed her. Consequently one of those people, while engaged in a brawl, died, and seven of the others were taken into custody by the police. Now the others in the family (suspecting sorcery) are planning to attack him. So he has come to punish them and also to ensure that no harm will befall his family.

Comment: In case D the revenge motive is clear, but not the supplicant's other motivations and rationalizations. The husband says that his wife was raped, but she denies it. He does not say that his wife voluntarily left home, but that she was forced to do so as a consequence of sorcery practiced by her seducers. The man has come to this shrine previously and as a result of his curse one of his enemies has died and others have suffered misfortune. This form of success in sorcery is very typical: when some calamity strikes an acquaintance it is attributed to the success of sorcery. The further consequences that resulted from this definition of the situation may either be real or a product of the supplicant's paranoid fantasy.

We shall now interpret two cases of persons involved in the Middle East job market.

Case E, male, Buddhist, age twenty-four, married with one child, lives in Kosgoḍa, forty-five miles south of Colombo.

Mr. E is a worker in the government Plywood Corporation. He has three sisters working in the Middle East (as domestic servants). He also would like to go there with his wife. Therefore two months ago he came here to make a plea to the goddess to get them both to the Middle East. The effort (as far as the wife is concerned) is successful, because she will leave in two weeks. He came here to fulfill that vow and also to ensure that she will work there without trouble for the next two years. He believes it is the deity who helped his wife, since his sisters did not help her. It is because of the goddess' *pihiṭa* ("help").

He heard of this place originally from his sisters, who also invoked the deity's help for their jobs abroad. They regularly send money for *pūjā*s for Kālī in gratitude. We too will offer a grand *pūjā* when we come back, he says.

"My wife worked at Asoka Garments in Chilaw. Now she has another job in a garment factory. We have one child," he adds.

This is a straightforward case of a man who believes that the goddess is so powerful that she can help find jobs for him and his wife. Underlying this case is, of course, a common tragedy of contemporary Sri Lankan life. Dire economic circumstances force the breakup of family life. The husband's home is Kosgoḍa, and the wife works in Chilaw at the other end of the island. The wife probably lives in a cramped boardinghouse while the husband's family looks after their child. In this situation the lure of the Middle East is to earn a large sum of money very fast and then return home to a more stable family life. Europeans have often noted how South Asians leave their families and go abroad as students or professionals. This feature is now endemic in Sri Lankan life. Many Sinhalas of all social strata suffer separation from their families, not because of the looseness of family ties, but because of their strength. Short-term separation to earn money ensures long-term family welfare. Most people are aware of the dangers that can befall women in the Middle East, since newspapers often recount these horror stories. It is here that the favorite deity comes in: the deity not only finds the job but ensures her protection during the dangerous sojourn in a foreign land. The kind of danger involved is illustrated in our next case, F.

Case F.

A woman (age forty-eight) has come here with her husband to make a *bāra* ("vow") on behalf of her daughter. While this girl was working in the Middle East, she became pregnant. She tried unsuccessfully to destroy the foetus by jumping from the top story of the house and broke her legs. Her parents have come here to implore the deity to destroy the foetus and also to help her recover from her injuries. They also implored the deity to permit her to stay her full two and one-half years (either because she has an income or because of the shame). The daughter is twenty-four.

They have travelled daily for seven days from Piliyandala (twenty miles from the shrine) to utter invocations through Nāvala Mā̄ṇiyō, the Kālī priestess. The woman offered an egg in a basket with lit camphor, and the priestess uttered the invocation. Then she smashed the coconut on the slab while thinking about her problem. If the goddess delivers the promise, she will give her a goat as a gift.

We quote below the invocation to the goddess Kālī uttered by Nāvala Māṇiyō.

Invocation to Kālī

There is a foetus in her womb. O immortal mother having destroyed it, without insult or calumny, O mater who with the power of *devas*, who resides facing the ocean, O immortal mother, I your servant have served you for forty-nine years, O lord justice of the courts, I am like the court interpreter, and please, your worship, witness my making this plaint with your divine eye, hear with your divine ear, and stretch your hand in sympathy to our suffering, and if we are in fault forgive us a thousand times over and help [*pihiṭa*] us and light up the life of that innocent child. And also fulfill the thoughts in the minds of these parents. They have brought here for you a goat as a life [*prāṇaya*]. They have also [promised] a garland of flowers for decking you, a good *pūjā* of fruit, and a sari for you to wear, see how lovely they [these promised gifts] look! Forgive us and grant our wishes. [She sings]:

Wearing white shawls, head with matted hair, with lights (in her
hand) she shows her might.
In the left hand a sacrifice (*billak*), a sword in the right hand, and
decked with a garland of heads,
Expeditiously she displays her power; she watches over injustice and
decides cases.
O mater, quickly listen to our words, O wondrous Kālī, O goddess.

Comment: This case illustrates some features of Kālī worship, especially in relation to ethics. In general the fundamental ethic in Sinhala Buddhist thought is that deities will mete out punishment only if your case is just. Kālī, however, is somewhat different, since South Indian myths about her emphasize her wrathfulness and capacity for unprincipled wreaking of vengeance. These ideas have influenced Sinhala thought also, so that the belief is that Kālī, especially her dark apparitions like Sohon ("Graveyard") Kālī, can help you irrespective of the justness or morality of the cause. Case F is a morally dubious one: an old couple want to get the daughter's foetus destroyed. They promise a goat to the goddess as a gift; earlier it would have been sacrificed. The killing of the goat would please the bloodthirsty goddess who would have by then killed the foetus. In all of this the priestess is the mediator: she is, says Nāvala Mā̄ṇiyō, "like the court interpreter,"[17] while the goddess is the judge. But she is not an ordinary judge. She has matted hair; she carries a sacrificed animal in one hand, a sword in the other; she wears a garland of decapitated human heads; she is a most unusual mother!

We shall now present a series of cases that will take us further into the themes of this book.

Case G, female, age eighteen, Colombo 2 (Slave Island). The girl came to the shrine accompanied by her grandmother, who gave us the following account.

> Her granddaughter has sudden fits of fainting and tends to froth at the mouth. When the family took her to Western medical practitioners, they said she did not suffer from any disease. They have gone to distant places and tied magical threads and done other treatments. Still there wasn't a complete cure, though she was better than before. Then she went to the Middle East for a job, but she had fainting spells again and had to be brought back to Sri Lanka. In hospital she was once again told that she does not suffer from a disease.
>
> Subsequently they came to this *kovil* and made a vow for Kālī Ammā. It is Nāvala Mā̄ṇiyō who helped them. Since then her fainting spells only occur on *kemmura* days, that is, Wednesdays and Saturdays. They come on these days and light lamps for Hūniyam and Pattinī. Now for the last three weeks she has had no fainting spells.

Comment: This is probably a case of hysteria brought about by sexual repression and the burgeoning sexual needs of a young woman. Western doctors say that she is not ill, and the family seeks religious help. Here they make a vow or *bāra* for Kālī. We have translated *bāra* as vow, but the word literally means "in charge of." The patient is in the deity's charge and if she gets well she will honor the deity with a *pūjā*. She will thus fulfill her vow.

Note the strategy of the cure. The priestess initially controlled the fainting spells by limiting them to *kemmura* days, when the power of the deities

[17] A key official in the courts who "translates" the Sinhala of witnesses into English for the judge. Nowadays this procedure has been reversed as courts mostly conduct their proceedings in Sinhala.

is especially active. The priestess deliberately gets the girl possessed on these days, and after some time this act becomes routinized and the patient's fainting spells are confined to these occasions alone. Subsequently the priestess helps the patient to establish fuller control over her illness, so that when we met her she had not had her attacks for three weeks. One can predict that if her illness is not cured, she will end up by becoming a priestess of the Kālī cult herself.

Case H, male, Buddhist, age forty-eight, from Kōṭṭe, owner of motor car repair shop.

> He came to the shrine to fulfill a vow. His sister has gone to the Middle East, and she had vowed to give a *pūjā* for the deity from her first salary. Yesterday she sent him the money and he came here today to fulfill the vow. He has come here previously also, for surgery that he had to undergo. That too was successful, and he will soon come here to fulfill that vow as well.

In an interview with us this man spelled out his faith in the gods.

> At first I had no belief in the *deva*s, but after I married this changed. My wife has an *āvēśa* ("possession by a spirit"). Her mother possesses her and appears in her dreams and talks to her. If anyone in our house or among our neighbors wants to ask a question, she provides a full answer. Some days she goes on making prophecies for hours on end. She studied only for the second grade and cannot even read a letter. But sometimes she utters excellent Buddhist sermons. It is after this experience that I had faith in the *deva*s.
>
> Every day we light lamps in our house on behalf of the *deva*s. When *I* light lamps and invoke the gods, my work does not prosper the next day. But when she does it my business prospers, and so it is she who does all of this now. Now on certain days she gets possessed by the spirit of her father who also resides in her. Her parents are reborn in the state of *maḷa yakṣa* ("male spirit of the dead") and *maḷa yakṣinī* ("female spirit").[18] They inform her in great detail about the worlds in which they live. They also tell her how to conduct rituals.
>
> I am a Buddhist and I go to temple on *pōya* days and light lamps for the Buddha.

[18] See chap. 1, n. 32 and the Note on Terminology.

Comment: Here is a man who came to fulfill a vow on behalf of his sister. He himself is a devotee of Kālī and of the gods in general. Note how his belief comes about. He is initially a skeptic, but his wife gets possessed by the spirit of her mother. The wife's accomplishments prove the reality of the spirit world and help to convert him. Once again we are dealing with urban people. Their beliefs do not clash with traditional Buddhism insofar as the fundamental relation between the Buddha and the gods are concerned: the Buddha is supreme over man's salvation and the gods are for this world. Hence the businessman's final affirmation that he is in fact a good Buddhist. Finally it should be noted that this man shrewdly utilizes his wife's spiritual powers to further his business interests. Here, as in an overwhelming majority of cases, it is the woman who gets possessed: the man has a more pragmatic role, whether he is managing his own business or the business of ritual. Some of the priestesses have men (either a husband, a relation, or a companion) to manage their affairs. When the men take a more spiritual role, they may have a woman to take on the managerial role, as do Uttama Sādhu and the Sun Buddha.[19] These divisions may be based on a far more fundamental distinction between instrumental and affective roles in the family and, more generally, in all forms of human task activity.[20]

Case I, female, Buddhist, age thirty-eight, from Ukuvala off Kandy (near Mātalē, Central Province). We shall quote verbatim from our interview with this interesting informant.

> I had a *diṣṭi* ["look," "essence"] of the gods about one year ago. In order to obtain this I suffered greatly for eight years, with inability to eat and pains in my back. Then suddenly I got possessed [i.e., got the *diṣṭi*] and I wanted to run away from home to the forest. Family members thought I was possessed by a demon and tied a charmed thread, but I untied it and in a part-conscious state [*avasihiyen*] I lit a lamp. I said that it was not a demon [possession]. Apparently I had told people that it was a *diṣṭi* that I obtained from my mother, and I am now possessed by Mother Kālī. Then a *kapurāḷa* living nearby came and uttered a chant.
>
> Subsequently I established a shrine (*dēvālē*) and did *set sānti* ("bless-

[19] See chap. 10.

[20] Morris Zelditch, "Role Differentiation in the Nuclear Family," in Talcott Parson and Robert Bales, *Family Socialization and Interaction Process* (Glencoe, Ill.: Free Press, 1955).

ings") for people. People came to ask questions of me and I gave them answers. I did not practice evil magic. I was successful but my enemies had (magically) imprisoned my *diṣṭi*. I do get possessed, but the *diṣṭi* has no power [i.e., "I cannot prophecy accurately"]. My clients diminished, and my work came to a complete stop. I have spent 25,000 rupees to build the shrine, and to go to Kataragama [to legitimate her possession], and to buy the ornaments [sacra] of the deity. Hence our fortunes have declined and family problems have arisen.

My elder sister is at present living in Kaḍavata [near Colombo]. She advised me to come to this shrine. I made a vow that the warrant [boon] from the deity be given back so I can start work again. I have come all the way from Kandy for this purpose. My husband is a businessman and I have three children.

Today is the fourth Sunday I've been here. I feel some benefit already. I feel that my domestic problems have diminished. And more persons are coming to my shrine. I have dreams of getting my possession back, but I won't tell anyone those secrets [conveyed in dreams]. In my dreams I am told about my own future. I have no doubt that I'll get my powers back.

Comment: In our statistical breakdown we listed this case under the rubric of "jobs and for ensuring prosperity." But the case is much more interesting and complex than such a listing suggests. After an arduous eight-year effort the woman in this case achieved possession. Typically her case was diagnosed as demonic possession and typically she resisted this interpretation and claimed that she was possessed by the spirit of her dead mother. With the help of her mother she got the warrant of Mother Kālī, and she set up a business as a priestess of Kālī in Ukuvala, a small town near Mātalē. But a not unusual mishap occurred. She lost her gift of prophecy, her income diminished, her domestic problems (no doubt conflict with her husband over money matters) started. Again very characteristically, she blames this on jealous enemies who have magically imprisoned her power. We are back to a variety of themes central to this book: possession by dead ancestors, the rise of new priestesses, the emergence of the Kālī cult in small towns, the attribution of sorcery to the machinations of jealous neighbors. What is pathetic but not unusual in this case is the loss of the woman's powers in a period of one year in spite of enormous effort and expenditure. But she is not easily defeated. She confronts the goddess in her shrine at Mōdera and the goddess indicates to her in her dreams that her powers may be restored to her.

Case J, male, Buddhist, age forty-eight, from Morontuḍuva, about thirty miles from Colombo, middle class and English educated.

Mr. J wore Western clothes and was accompanied by his attractive wife. He told us that he had come here to curse (*paliyak*) those persons who came to his residence drunk and destroyed the outside altars (*mal yahan*) he had constructed for the gods. It is true that those people repented and came back and repaired them, but Mr. J wants to show them the power of the gods. He was especially angry that they had apparently kicked the altar of God Hūniyam (Hūniyam Deviyō). He started to light lamps for Kālī Mater and pleaded with her. He asked her, "Are you trying to become an *arhant*[21] without punishing those who do wrong?"

Question: Is it after this event that you developed faith in Kālī Mā̄ṇiyō?

Mr. J: I did believe in her from the very beginning, but it is only just over a month ago that I started placing lamps in her honor. It is the goddess Kālī herself who appeared before me and told me to light lamps and "hit revenge" [*pali gahanavā*, *pali* meaning "curse" or "revenge" and *gahanavā* "hit," since the smashing of the coconut is involved]. It is today that I cursed and smashed a coconut. It broke into pieces. I could say from the manner in which it broke that there were four people involved. Four pieces fell face down and this means that the four persons will be punished; the ones representing the pieces that fell face upwards will be exonerated. There are four persons involved in the desecration of my altars, including one child.

Mr. J readily responded to our questions about his relationship with his parents. He said that both parents were harsh (*särayi*) and punished their children. There were three boys and three girls in the family. "If we did anything wrong father used to hit us." He added, "Since our father

[21] *Arhant* or *arhat* is a person, generally a monk, who has achieved *nirvāṇa*. *Arhant*s are entirely benevolent and therefore cannot punish. This example again shows the "karmic logic" accepted implicitly by ordinary people.

brought us up we must respect him and treat him well." Mr. J's mother had only a grade-school education. She was equally stern. "Even now, though we are grown up, she is like that. Recently I had an argument with her and she tried to hit me." Mr. J told us that he had not thought of marrying for a long time. His intention was to devote all his spare time to his work with the gods. But he relented and married a friend's younger sister in 1968.

Question: Isn't the married life a hindrance to the work of the gods?

Mr. J: Yes, but there are special days allotted for sexual intercourse and domestic activity. Tuesdays, Wednesdays, Fridays, and Saturdays are suitable for the work of the gods. Mondays, Thursdays, and Sundays are given to my personal life.

Mr. J is a clerk in a government department, but his true interest is in the work of the gods. Let us briefly recount some of his past history insofar as it is relevant to the themes of this book.

It was in 1967 that Mr. J received his first instruction from the gods. He was told in a dream to go to a Buddhist *stūpa*, the Kiri Vehera at Kataragama, and meditate. "This happened when I was lighting lamps for the gods at my residence. I was told to go there with god Viṣṇu's permission, worship the *stūpa* at Tissa on the way to Kataragama, and once there meditate and observe the precepts for seven days at Kiri Vehera. I lay beneath the *ähäla*[22] tree near the "King Stupa" and was in deep meditation. Then I saw the god Kataragama in his live form [*jīvamānava*]. This was no dream. He appeared in youthful guise wearing a garland of *eramiṇiyā* flowers.[23] His breast was bare and he was wearing a red cloth around his waist. I then bowed low and said, 'Why have you rubbed off the *tinnur* ["sacred ash"] from your forehead?' Then the person who was wearing red replied, 'Child, lower yourself and look again.' I did so and then noticed that the mark on the forehead and the color of the body were the same [that's why it was not seen at first]."

Question: Who was it you saw?

Mr. J: That was the god Kataragama. That day was also the first time I had that god's *ārūḍē* ["gift of possession"].

Question: Was the *ārūḍē* like a fainting spell?

[22] *Ähäla*, Cassia fistula.

[23] *Eramiṇiyā*, Zizyphus napeca.

Mr. J: No, no, I have no recollection whatever. I saw him and then blank. It was about 2 A.M. and no one was around. I was also unmarried at that time. There was a man named Baṇḍaiyā in the temple premises. He had gone and told the monk that the *upāsaka unnähä* [i.e., a Buddhist who has taken the eight or ten precepts] had fainted. Apparently [in trance] I had told the monk that I saw such a person and obtained an *ārūḍha* from him and that he had told me that it was my *diṣṭi* ["look," "essence"]. After I regained consciousness, the monk gave me all the details. The monk also said that I was told to reside [go on pilgrimage or meditate] at such and such places.

Question: Who do you think gave you those last instructions?

Mr. J: That I do not know since the monk did not tell me. Accordingly I resided at *sellam dūva* ["the island where they sported"]. [This is the place where, according to myth, the god and his mistress "sported."] *Sellam dūva* is about nine miles from Sella Kataragama [where the god first met his mistress] in the heart of the forest. There are *yogi*s there. I meditated along with these people. A person named Velupillai Sāmi [a Tamil] helped me [as preceptor]. Thereafter I haven't gone to Kataragama. But this year I plan to go and, if the god gives permission, I also plan to walk the fire. Then I went to Väḍahiṭikanda [the peak sacred to Kataragama]. One morning I rang the bell hung on the tree and then uttered *stōtra*s ["praise verses"], but as I did so I felt that I was about to lose consciousness—and I did. [After I awoke] the monk who was there asked me to serve the god ritually [*āvatēva karanna*]. Then I went to Vallimalai [the residence of Vallī Ammā, the god's mistress]. And then came back to Väḍahiṭikanda. The Buddhist monk Siddhārtha[24] wasn't there then. I stayed there five days. Later I returned and helped Venerable Siddhārtha to build the *dēvālē* and stayed there for one year. After one year I was told (in a dream) to go to the main shrine at Kataragama. I went there on the Sinhala New Year's Day and received *ābharaṇa* ["ornaments," "insignia"] from the priest there. I have [temporarily] sequestered those insignia at a shrine in Kōṭṭe, with my teacher, Selliah [also a Tamil].

Question: How did you acquire your knowledge of the occult arts?

[24] For an account of Siddhārtha see chap. 1.

Mr. J: My brother used to live in Rājagiriya [a Colombo suburb] and I lived at his place for a while. They used to go to a place where prophecies were uttered. Subsequently I also went there every day and served the deity. I also studied under Selliah, whom my sisters regularly consulted. He was a Tamil, about forty-five years old, and unmarried. I do not know his background but he works at a Hindu temple, cuts the effects of sorcery, and practices medicine. He also had a job with the Colombo Municipality and lived in Ätul Kōṭṭe. I learnt *stōtra* from him.

Question: These *stōtra*—were they in Tamil or Sanskrit?

Mr. J: There are some in Sanskrit and others in Tamil. I do not know Tamil, but I have memorized them.

My interest in the gods started in 1964 after I got my job. I felt the effect of Vibhīṣaṇa first. I used to light lamps daily for Viṣṇu, Kataragama, Saman, Vibhīṣaṇa, Däḍimuṇḍa, and Sūniyam—and also for Bhairava. Right now there is an impurity in our house [childbirth?] and I don't light lamps. Its effect will last for two months. I have also had visions of Kālī Māṇiyō with her tongue protruding about nine inches and blood colored. I see blood on her tongue. Vibhīṣaṇa has hair about ten inches long and also protruding canines [lit. tusks], and I have been frightened by that sight. The God of Alutnuvara, Däḍimuṇḍa, has three colors—rose, white, and blue—and he is dressed like a king. Pictures depict him with a beard, but I saw him with thick moustaches curled upwards.

Recently Mr. J has been asked to observe *sil* (the eight precepts) forty-one times to obtain ornaments (*ābharaṇa*) from Alutnuvara, the residence of Däḍimuṇḍa. The *kapurāḷa* of that shrine should give them; if he does not, Mr. J will perform *satyakriyā* (lit. "power of the truth";[25] in fact it means he's going to stay outside the shrine and perhaps even fast till his wishes are met). Each full moon he has to observe *sil* for forty-one moons and then go there. "I have only done *sil* three times thus far. It must be done without a break."

Question: Why are you told to observe *sil*?

Mr. J: The gods essentially require merit (*pin*). *Pūjā*s and service

[25] For the traditional meaning of this term see Gombrich, *Precept and Practice*, p. 224.

> aren't essential. It is the gods' retinue who accept *pūjās* on behalf of the gods, and it is they who accept the vow (*bāra*) and help you. The Buddha has asked us to give merit to the gods. After all, the gods expect to achieve eventual Buddhahood.

Comment: In statistical terms Mr. J was someone who came to the Kālī shrine to resolve a personal conflict, but his case history is enormously complex and interesting. Mr. J appears as an ordinary, well-dressed middle-class person with a nice wife. Yet he spends most of his leisure doing the work of the gods. Let us enumerate some striking features of his case history.

1. Here is a clear case of an educated person getting an *ārūḍha* or gift of possession. But his path to achieving this state is quite different from most others who are possessed by the spirit of a dead ancestor. Mr. J achieves his trance through meditation, and in this meditative trance he has a vision of Kataragama. Kataragama says that Mr. J has his *diṣṭi* ("look," "essence") and he should go to the centers of the other gods, meditate there, and obtain their *diṣṭi* also. We believe he has taken a path that suits his class background and perhaps even his gender. Women are much more susceptible to possession than men, and they can better achieve orgiastic convolutions of the body than men. In Mr. J's case he is not only a male, but an educated middle-class person. The lower-class path of possession trance is not for him; thus he achieves "contemplative trance." But the goal of his contemplative trance is completely unsoteriological and consequently un-Buddhist. It is generally accepted among Buddhists that the purpose of meditation is not to have a vision of the gods; if such visions occur they must be superseded in order to achieve a higher soteriological condition. In Mr. J's case, he takes to meditation not because of a personal salvation quest but because of instruction received in a dream vision. This is of course characteristic of such ecstatics. Once he achieves *ārūḍha* in this thoroughly bourgeois fashion he is given the *diṣṭi* of the gods directly. No mediating ancestral spirit is required.

2. Nevertheless, Mr. J is in the same class as the *sāmi*s discussed in this book and in *Medusa's Hair*. At Kataragama he came under the influence of the unorthodox monk, Siddhārtha, and especially Velupillai Sāmi, a well-known Tamil priest who became his preceptor. Later he learnt more about ritual procedures from another Tamil guru, Selliah Sāmi. Even though he does not know Tamil he has memorized Tamil texts and invocations.

3. His case once again reflects the breakdown of moral values in Sinhala culture. We do not know whether Mr. J's accusation of his neighbors is true, but it is likely that it is. In any case J retaliates with black magic in order to destroy them, even though one of them is a child. We have pointed out that in the process of upward mobility, gods tend to be saintly figures and consequently not very useful. This is implicitly recognized by Mr. J's plea to Kālī: "Are you trying to become an *arahant* without punishing those who do wrong?" If Kālī is to be effective she must be stern or *särayi*; but there is always the danger that her very popularity and the merit transfer of her devotees might convert her into a benevolent figure. J recognizes this Buddhist dynamic very clearly in his closing statement: "The Buddha has asked us to give merit to the gods. After all, the gods expect to achieve eventual Buddhahood." As far as Kālī is concerned he seems to say, "but not yet." Kālī must be *särayi* or "stern," "angry" in order to be effective. It is even likely that the angry Kālī Mater is rooted in Mr. J's infantile experience of his own mother, though we do not have enough evidence to be sure. He does say, however, that his own mother is *särayi* and that she recently attempted to hit him in an argument. The relationship between the divine mother and human mothers remains an important one and will be explored in the remainder of this chapter.

The Social-Psychological Backdrop of the Kālī Cult

The rise of Kālī from the status of a demoness to that of a goddess (though not a benevolent one) in urban society is perhaps sociologically even more significant than the parallel rise of Hūniyam. Both cults are related to the historical and sociological changes we have discussed. But Kālī is a female deity and Hūniyam a male one; female deities are scarce in the Sinhala pantheon, and Kālī's rise from relative obscurity to urban prominence merits further investigation.

The preeminent and popular mother goddess in Sri Lanka, especially in the Western and Southern areas, is the goddess Pattinī.[26] In addition there were the Kiri Ammā ("Milk Mothers") propitiated as a cluster of seven deities or as a single deity in the remoter regions. Pattinī was a deity of

[26] Obeyesekere, *Pattini*, esp. chap. 1, pp. 1–49.

the same class as the four guardian deities whereas Kiri Ammā was a goddess of the lower *dēvatā* or godling class. Pattinī was unequivocally moral and fundamentally benevolent. She can be stern, but her anger, when roused, is directed toward maintaining a just and rationally grounded social order. She was both wife and mother, and her cult had a great deal of emotional appeal to men. In addition, her cult, like that of other gods, was related to the achievement of practical this-worldly goals—fertility, welfare of man and beast, prevention and care of infectious diseases, etc. Thus, in the Sinhala Low Country infectious diseases and children's illnesses were cured by Pattinī. In other areas this role was taken over by the Kiri Ammā; sometimes the Kiri Ammā were viewed as servants of Pattinī, sometimes (though more rarely) as manifestations of her.[27]

The last thirty years have seen a dramatic decline in the Pattinī cult, and the once ubiquitous priest of the cult is virtually nonexistent today. In line with the strategy of analysis in this book we shall not try to isolate causal variables, but instead highlight two major reasons for the decline of her cult. These reasons must be seen in the larger context of modern Sri Lankan history, already recounted.

1. Population increase and limited land resources have resulted in a pattern of internal migration and competition for land. The relative homogeneity of village society has been upset. The complex ritual cycles for Pattinī held after harvest required the mobilization of labor resources and the cooperation of villagers. None of that is now possible. Leadership patterns have also changed, and the new government-appointed headmen are outsiders who cannot command the respect of villagers. Changing patterns of education have perhaps altered taste, so that younger generations find the music, dance forms, and ritual dramas of the Pattinī cult old-fashioned.

2. As far as disease is concerned, free universal medical treatment, a reasonably good system of hospitals, and compulsory universal inoculation for smallpox have eliminated serious pestilences and have provided people with a technology for coping with them. Smallpox has been virtually nonexistent for the last forty years. The threat of famine consequent on drought is not as serious a problem as it was before. Traditionally there

[27] Obeyesekere, *Pattini*, pp. 293–96; R. Gombrich, "Food for Seven Grandmothers," *Man* 6, no. 1 (March 1971): 5–17.

was no known technology to cope with these problems, and only symbolic solutions were available through propitiation of the deity.

Thus the Pattinī cult had an emotional component and a practical one: she was the "good mother" and the ideal wife, and people propitiated her for the welfare of crops and for freedom from disease. We noted that the second role has become redundant. Pattinī is a future Buddha and it is impossible to solicit her aid for cursing or sorcery. But to account for the decline of her cult does not fully account for the parallel (and perhaps concomitant) rise of Kālī. Why should Kālī, a relatively insignificant demoness for Sinhalas but a goddess for Tamil Hindus, become popular in urban Sri Lanka? South Indian specialists helped introduce the cult to Sinhala priests and priestesses, who in turn helped disseminate the cult among large sectors of urban society. Nevertheless one still has to account for the popular *acceptance* of the cult. Kālī, it should be noted, does exactly the same things as Hūniyam: she deals with sorcery, personal and familial conflicts, jobs, etc. If so, why must people propitiate her when they could as easily propitiate Hūniyam? Both cults came into prominence around the same time. Yet Hūniyam had clear advantages over Kālī since his cult was not associated overtly with South Indian Hinduism, and he has been better incorporated into Sinhala Buddhism. To understand the choice of Kālī one must move from the practical aspect of her cult to the emotional: she is both goddess *and mother*. It is the maternal and emotional role of the deity that clearly differentiates her from Hūniyam and is relevant to understanding her rise and contemporary cultural significance.

The good mother image used to be institutionalized in the public pantheon in the goddess Pattinī. The "bad mother" appeared in the image of evil demonesses, including Kālī, but none of them were prominent. These demonic figures were activated in exorcistic rituals and they helped account for certain kinds of demonic illnesses and evil that befell individuals. If Kālī (and other demonesses) related to individual afflictions, the goddess Pattinī was institutionalized in both individual *and* group rituals. Can this leap in popularity be related to the greater preoccupation with the "bad image" of the mother in the consciousness of modern Sinhala Buddhists? If so, can one suggest social changes that might make the "bad image" of the mother more prevalent?

Let us sketch the role of the mother in two ideal-typical situations. We acknowledge that approximations to these ideal types cannot be statistically determined and that obviously they do not exclude other maternal role types. But our thesis is that in traditional, agrarian Sinhala society the role of the mother had one consistent feature: she had no say in pushing the son to achieve. Before the modern school system, there were only a few occupations that permitted status mobility and achievement—monks, priests, Ayurvedic physicians, etc. Most sons followed in the footsteps of their fathers, and the contours of the individual's life cycle were largely predictable. There was no great gap between aspiration and achievement. The socioeconomic situation was coordinate with the ideal role of the mother as benevolent and nurturant. Individual mothers may have been different, but the *mother's role* in the family was supported by the larger socioeconomic order. The socioeconomic changes sketched in this book have tended to alter this radically: between the socioeconomic order and the mother's role a gap has opened up. Education became an extremely important avenue for mobility. Caste and kinship were no insuperable bar to achievement, and consequently there developed an increasing preoccupation at every level of society with achievement and mobility through education. The rising aspiration levels have affected all familial roles, but the effect on the maternal role has been dramatic. The mother can no longer be exclusively nurturant and loving: she must push the son to achieve. It is she, and not the father, who is out working, who must instill in her child the values demanded by modern society. The changed role of the mother is especially conspicuous in urban life. Here the family is cut off, partially or wholly, from the context of larger kinship ties and other village loyalties. In child rearing the support that a woman receives from her kinsmen is diminished in the urban setup, though a servant may help with the physical aspects. In any case the aspirations of urban families are much higher than those of rural ones, and insofar as the father is absent from home for most of the day, it is the mother who must instill in her child the new motivation for upward mobility. She can no longer be mostly nurturant: love must be conditional on the child's willingness to study and to achieve in school, and this may even entail physical punishment. In proletarian society the same motivation may be present, but even when it is not, the mother is quite different from that of our ideal-typical village family. She herself works and is away from home; sheer poverty, lack of physical help in child rearing, and the burden of an ever-increasing number of children may also convert her from the loving mother to a wayward, unpredictable, and cruel one in the eyes of the growing child. In this situation the cruel image of the mother that develops in the mind of the child can be projected onto Kālī. If confronted with the question, people will say that Kālī is not a demoness but a goddess. Yet the term "*deviyō*" is not spontaneously applied to her. In ordinary discourse she is referred to and addressed as Kālī Māṇiyō or Ammā ("Kālī Mother"), never Kālī Deviyō (the "goddess Kālī"). By contrast Pattinī is both Māṇiyō or Ammā ("mother") and Pattinī Deviyō ("goddess"). This suggests that Kālī, even more than Pattinī, is tied closely to the infantile perception of the mother.

We are not suggesting, however, that the good mother image is totally moribund; it still exists but is no longer projected onto Pattinī, since Pattinī no longer can combine in a single image both the emotional and the practical. The loving mother is projected onto another omnipresent being in the public pantheon—the Buddha himself. The Buddha, as contrasted with Pattinī, has little say over man's material interests: people do not ask him for health, wealth, or freedom from disease. The purely loving aspect of the mother can be canalized into the figure of the Buddha, who appears in the contemporary *Bōdhi pūjā* cult as the "mother Buddha."[28] By contrast Kālī, like the old Pattinī, combines the pragmatic and the emotional. In this context it is surely inevitable that the sphere of Kālī's influence must widen. In this connection let us note that over the last few years "tutories" for coaching people for government examinations and for teaching English have mushroomed everywhere and have even reached remote villages. We would not be surprised if Kālī too follows the path of these tutories into the villages of contemporary Sri Lanka.[29]

[28] See chap. 11.

[29] These tutories and typing schools (and at one time weaving and embroidery schools) serve an important unrecognized motive and function in providing an opportunity for sexually frustrated young men and women to flee home (temporarily) and seek the company of the opposite sex.

CHAPTER 5

Kataragama, a Center of Hindu-Buddhist Syncretism

The Popularity of the Shrine

In modern Sri Lanka the religious center that attracts the most indigenous visitors and is the greatest focus of interest and emotion is Kataragama, an ancient shrine situated far from any city in the scrub jungle in the extreme southeast corner of the island. Its annual festival, starting on the first day of the new moon (*pura pǟlaviya*) of the month of Äsaḷa (generally July–August) and ending with "water cutting" and "water sports" on the morning after the full moon (*ava pǟlaviya*), is also the most important religious occasion of the year. The pageant of the Temple of the Tooth in Kandy, which symbolically expresses the Buddha's suzerainty over the nation and its gods and which is held during the same season, is a great international tourist attraction, and hordes of Sinhala people, especially from the surrounding Kandyan villages, go to watch it; but that is nowadays more a cultural spectacle and an entertainment than an object of piety. Most religious festivals and places of pilgrimage offer entertainment as well as spiritual solace, and Kataragama offers entertainment too; but going there is considered a serious business. Moreover, Kataragama is now busy throughout the year and is visited by people of all social classes and all nominal religious affiliations. An extremely wealthy upper-class lady,[1] born an Anglican but now claiming to have "no religion," told us that whenever she and her husband planned to go "in a frivolous spirit" something went wrong; for instance, when her husband planned to be back for a certain horse race, an accident delayed them. One is not to presume that

[1] She is classed as a Burgher (a person of mixed indigenous and European descent), now married to a Sinhala.

one can time one's journey or otherwise control it without Skanda's help. On the other hand, her journeys when seriously undertaken always went well. Once a close relative had been charged with involvement in an attempted coup d'état. She promised Skanda, just in her mind, not by any overt act, that if he was released from prison within a certain time, she would walk the twelve miles from Kataragama to Tissamahārāma. He was, and she did it, though (she claimed) she had never before walked more than the three miles of a golf course; nevertheless, she felt as fresh at the end as when she started.

The lady's walk is not the usual way of fulfilling a vow to the god of Kataragama; it recalls the "sponsored" activities with which many people of good will in the modern West "earn merit" and raise money for charities. Traditional Tamil Hindu devotees might shave their heads or roll in the hot dust around the god's shrine; both they and Sinhala Buddhists might bring offerings. Nowadays one can witness more spectacular activities—firewalking, hanging from hooks, pulling carts by means of hooks fastened into one's back—though the motivation for these acts is not necessarily retrospective (fulfilling a vow) but may also be prospective (acquiring the power bestowed by the god's grace). Nevertheless, the point we are making is that there are very few households in Colombo where one could now feel surprised to be told at any time of year that family members were making the trip to Kataragama. Christians have no official excuse in terms of their own affiliation. Muslims, on the other hand, have a shrine there to a holy man (*pir*) called Pālkuḍibāva, and they claimed to us that the mosque, which has local associations, was three hundred years old.[2] In this Muslim enclosure during the Äsaḷa festival members of the Rifai sect cut themselves with knives and stick spikes into their skulls. Non-Muslims rarely enter this enclosure and play no part in its proceedings. On the other hand, some of the hook hangers in the main area are Muslims; and the mosque used to rent out the carts that hook hangers hire for their purposes—as one can see from the little green Muslim flags attached to the scaffolds.

Kataragama is well endowed with Buddhist *sacralia*. Tissamahārāma, twelve miles away, is one of the traditional sixteen sites of Buddhist pil-

[2] For accounts of the Muslim shrine see Paul Wirz, *Kataragama: The Holiest Place in Ceylon*, trans. from the German by Davis Berta Pralle (Colombo, 1972), and M.C.A. Hassan, *The Story of Kataragama, Mosque and Shrine* (Colombo: United Printers, 1968).

grimage in Sri Lanka and is rich in historical associations. It is from this part of the island, according to national chronicles, that King Duṭugämuṇu in the second century B.C. set out on his successful venture to reconquer his capital, Anurādhapura, and the whole island from the Tamil invaders. Another large Buddhist stupa, the Kiri Vehera, stands less than a quarter of a mile from the Kataragama shrine (locally called Maha Dēvālē, "the Great Shrine," though physically it is small), and the shrine itself stands virtually in the shade of a large *bō* tree. The shrine's popularity with Buddhists is recent. It was connected to Tissa by a paved road in 1949 and by bus in 1952. It was after this that Buddhists arrived en masse and soon came to outnumber Hindus. In 1973 the official estimate was that 800,000 pilgrims visited the shrine. This might be an exaggeration and our own estimate, admittedly tentative, is that about 550,000 pilgrims visited Kataragama during the whole of 1973, which means about one in every twenty-seven people.[3] However, the numbers visiting Kataragama during the festival season vary from year to year, depending on political and economic vicissitudes.[4]

The Atmosphere[5]

The sacred area of Kataragama is across a small river, the Mäṇik Gaṅga, and is noted for its associations with the god and his mistress. As the pilgrim approaches the river he notices the large number of shops and stands selling *pūjā vaṭṭi*, or trays of offerings, generally consisting of various kinds of fruit. The fruits and other religious wares are colorfully displayed, and the shops are decorated with the god's color, red. At another point of the river crossing are the *kāvaḍi* stands where one can rent a *kāvaḍi*, a peacock arch of the god. The devotee generally bathes in the river and joins a *kāvaḍi* group, who then dance all the way up to the god's shrine (and other shrines) to the accompaniment of exuberant dance music.

Once one crosses the river, itself a symbolic act, one is in the larger area of the Kataragama shrine premises. The main shrine of the god is a small, unimpressive building; next to it is a yet smaller shrine for the god's elder

[3] For details see Gananath Obeyesekere, "Social Change," pp. 377–96.

[4] For example, in some recent seasons the numbers have been drastically reduced by political unrest.

[5] This section has been reproduced with a few changes from Obeyesekere, *Medusa's Hair*.

brother, Gaṇeśa, and close to Gaṇeśa's shrine are two recently constructed shrines for Viṣṇu and the Buddha. The area of the main shrine is connected to the shrine of the god's mistress Vallī Ammā by a narrow street a few hundred yards long. The back of the main shrine is connected by a similar street to the ancient Buddhist stupa, the Kiri Vehera, with its beautiful white dome dominating the landscape. On the left of the god's shrine, but physically separate, is the shrine of his legitimate spouse Dēvasēnā or Tēvānī Ammā. This shrine is of considerable importance for Hindus, but not for Buddhists. There are many other subsidiary shrines scattered over the sacred premises. The mosque is near the Vallī Ammā shrine.

The central drama of the annual festival is the grand procession that leaves the main shrine for the Vallī shrine every night for fifteen days. It celebrates the god's joyous union with his mistress Vallī Ammā. A notable feature of this pageant is that the god does not visit the shrine of his first wife and legitimate spouse, Tēvānī Ammā (Dēvasēnā).

The fortnight's pageant culminates with the ritual of water cutting, which ordinary people believe commemorates the washing of the deity's clothes, polluted by sexual intercourse. (Originally the rite was intended to control the element of water in the environment.) After the water cutting the assembled throng let themselves go. They sport in the water (*diya keliya*) and splash themselves and each other, and there is a cathartic and exuberant display of emotion. The pageant celebrates the god's passion and sensuality; it is a glorification of the life of the senses. So are the recently introduced *kāvaḍi* dances; the people dance before the god, men and women together in groups, young and old, many of them lost in ecstasy. In contrast with these is another feature of Kataragama: a number of penitents suffer in abject humiliation and self-torture before the god. These piacular activities are no longer confined entirely to Hindus and Muslims; but for the most part the Buddhists remain awed spectators. For the typical Sinhala Buddhist the most significant aspect of the festival is the passion and the sensuality, the celebration of the god's illicit love life.

But Kataragama cannot be studied in isolation from the Buddhist part of the complex. The pilgrim pays the conventional homage to the deity, an offering of fruit, and then he goes to the Kiri Vehera (the Buddhist stupa). To do so he must go past the back entrance of the Kataragama shrine premises along a street that connects the shrine with the Buddhist stupa. As soon as the pilgrim passes the gate he is confronted with beggars and destitutes lining the street to the Kiri Vehera. Here are the lame, the decrepit, bodies riddled with sores, the sick and the aged hovering near death's door.

The contrast in ethos is dramatic: the pilgrim is confronted with another aspect of worldly life—suffering, impermanence. He passes on and then comes to the shops of vendors selling almost nothing but white and red lotuses, Buddhist symbols of purity. Then he reaches the Kiri Vehera, an impressive white stupa. The pilgrim now recites Pāli verses praising the Buddha and recalling the impermanence of all physical things, which are compared to the fading flowers with their evanescent scent. There is a very different atmosphere here—serenity, calm, stillness. The noise and bustle of the god's shrine are not heard here, not even the cacophony of the loudspeakers that the Sinhalas aptly call the "iron mouth."

If the predominant color of Kataragama is red, the color of the Kiri Vehera is white; if one place represents the celebration of the senses, the other celebrates their subjugation and transcendence. Underlying all of this is the powerful "myth model" of the Buddha's own renunciation of the world: his enjoyment of a life of hedonism; his confrontation with the four signs—sickness, old age, death, and the model of their transcendence in the yellow-robed mendicant; his final achievement of salvation—a calm, a blowing out, *nirvāṇa*. The pilgrim also has made his full progress: he crosses the river and leaves the everyday reality of mundane existence; from there he goes on to the passion and sensuality of Kataragama, then to the shock of life's suffering and misery, and finally to a realization of release from both passion and misery—all aspects of impermanence—into the serenity and calm of the Kiri Vehera.

This relationship between the shrine and the temple is central to understanding Kataragama as a collective representation. Even the beggars' position in the appropriate street (*vīdiya*) is not due to conscious design, but to the operation of myth models subscribed to by most Sri Lankans, including the beggars, who know where to place themselves. In the last few years this collective representation of Kataragama has changed with the extensive renovations and alterations at the premises. The embourgeoisement at Kataragama, for example, has pushed the beggars out of the streets into more segregated spots within the premises, but much of the collective meaning is still retained.

The physical layout of Kataragama has one unusual feature. The pilgrim must cross the river and enter the shrine premises: this forces him to pay attention to the god before the Buddha since the Kiri Vehera, the Buddhist part of the complex, lies well beyond the god's shrine (*dēvālē*). This seems to violate the norm that one must worship the Buddha before going to the *dēvālē*. But in spite of the distance to the Kiri Vehera the pilgrim in fact *can* pay homage to the Buddha before Skanda: the Buddha has been brought into the *dēvālē* premises. In the shrine room to the right of the god's shrine stands a large Buddha sculpture. And a Buddhist temple has recently been built almost at the very entrance of the shrine. Once inside the shrine's premises the pilgrim also has a chance to pay homage to the Buddha at the large *bō* tree behind the shrine of the god. This is supposed to be a sapling from the sacred *bō* tree at Anurādhapura, itself a sapling of the very tree under which the Buddha achieved Enlightenment; and hence the *bō* tree represents the Buddha himself or is at least a symbol of the Enlightenment. But in reality the physical layout practically forces the pilgrim to pay homage to Skanda before the Buddha. As he enters the premises he immediately faces the shrine of the god: it is not possible to ignore him and bypass him to go to the Buddha. One must at least smash a coconut on the rock slab in front of the shrine and acknowledge the god's awesome presence.

Kataragama: A Catalyst for Change

In the shade of the great *bō* tree behind the main shrine, during the final days of the Äsaḷa festival, congregate the ecstatics and religious innovators, the *sāmi* and the *māṇiyō* ("mothers"). It is in their discussions that are forged and from that assemblage that are diffused both theories and practices of the new religious orientation of the spirit religion. For example, though the role is so new to their culture, there are now quite a few Sinhala *sāmi* who are acting as "leaders" at new-style firewalking ceremonies at various Sinhala shrines up and down the country. It is almost as if every Sinhala shrine that holds an annual pageant (*perahära*) thinks it necessary to include firewalking. When we spoke to one such gentleman, the aptly initialled T.N.T. Sirisēna Dissānāyaka, at the end of June 1975, he was engaged as chief firewalker at a series of festivals for most of the following three months. In fact firewalking, like *kāvaḍi* dancing, has even been commercialized and is frequently staged at hotels and nightclubs to entertain foreign tourists, so presumably it now affords some people a living.

Kataragama has become a great melting pot of Sri Lankan society. It is the one place where all the religions of the nation—Buddhist, Hindu, Muslim, Catholic, and Protestant—meet and mutually influence one another. The different kinds of groups who congregate here are receptive to all sorts of new ideas, some transient, some lasting, some trivial, some profound. Let us give a trivial example. In 1979 we were completely taken aback when several firewalkers, including women, shook hands with us in the European fashion instead of using the South Asian form of greeting with palms together. They also shook hands with each other. Clearly the new custom had developed since our previous visit in 1977. It seemed very likely that the custom was picked up from foreign tourists both at Kataragama and elsewhere. They readily accepted the custom because the handshake seems conducive to the warmth and close camaraderie sought by the ecstatics. A more significant example we will discuss in Chapter 11: how in 1981 a young man performed a new Buddhist ritual known as the *Bōdhi pūjā* at the *bō* tree behind the main shrine. The traditional priests (*kapurāḷas*) of the god (not the new *sāmis*, mind you) were so impressed by this that they urged him to stay on and conduct the new ritual. One of the priests got the young man to perform a *Bōdhi pūjā* blessing for his own mother. The examples could be multiplied.

The strangest behavior is not only tolerated at Kataragama, but even encouraged—if it is given a religious dressing. People wear bizarre costumes; some talk to themselves; others let themselves go. Men and women cry, rage, laugh, dance; women in particular are constantly getting possessed. Visions are experienced both in dreams and in hypnomantic states not only by ecstatics but also by ordinary devotees; some of them give rise to myths. People talk about their experiences, and others recount the strange experiences of others. Most of them pertain to the vision of the god, whom some see walking across the fire before his human devotees. For many others he appears as an old man. (Indeed, if any venerable-looking old man were to speak to a devotee, this might be interpreted as a direct vision of Skanda.) The Buddhist monk Siddhārtha told us that on three occasions the god appeared to him in a dream as a small boy and urged him to occupy the mountain of Väḍahiṭikanda! We shall see below that he has similarly appeared to the Venerable Ānanda Maitreya and to a Sinhala judge, whom he even persuaded to adjudicate against Hindu priests in favor of Buddhist monks. Such experiences and their continual recounting have their influence far beyond the boundary of Kataragama and set a decisive stamp on contemporary Sinhala religiosity.

At Kataragama ecstatic worship of the god takes two emotional directions. Joy, celebration, and catharsis are to be seen in the *kāvaḍi* dancing and the water cutting; tension and agony in the firewalking, rolling in the hot sands, and even more violent forms of self-mortification and mutilation. During the period for which we have good evidence, the last couple of centuries, the latter type of practice used to be confined to Hindu penitents and Muslim Sufis. To account for them, Buddhists had a myth (which may not be old) that the god was torturing Tamils to punish them for betraying him during the war between the Tamils and the Sinhalas in King Duṭugämuṇu's time.

However, during the period of our fieldwork this myth was fast losing its popularity because some Sinhalas were adopting these uncomfortable practices. At the same time, the erotic character of the god's worship has intensified and involved increasing numbers of Sinhala people. The combined effect of these two developments has amounted to a virtual takeover of Kataragama by the Sinhalas.

The invasion of Sinhala religious life by Tamil *bhakti* religiosity is a major theme in our account of cultural change. In this chapter we shall describe the past of Kataragama in myth and history, to draw the contrast with what has recently taken place. We shall then show how and why Sinhalas have largely taken control of Kataragama's institutions, formal and informal. This will lead us back to the joyful and erotic side of the god's worship. That worship is a mass phenomenon, and we follow the pattern of the preceding three chapters by suggesting an explanation for it in the socioeconomic changes that have affected most of the Sinhala population, especially the poor.

One major feature of the Sinhala takeover we postpone, however, to Chapter 12. The background to the Sinhalicization of the firewalk is treated here as part of the recent history of the shrine, and we shall have something to say of the rank and file of Sinhala firewalkers. But the individuals who have led this takeover, as "leaders" (a technical term) of the firewalk, are mostly drawn from the middle class and to explain their background and attitudes we need first to describe Protestant Buddhism. An account of them and of the new mythology for which they are responsible therefore belongs in the book's concluding section, in which we illustrate and discuss how the new trends in the spirit religion and in Buddhism proper appear to complement and influence each other.

The Myths of Kataragama: Skanda and Vallī Ammā

Those myths of the god Skanda with which people in Kataragama are familiar are basically common to South India and Sri Lanka and to Hindus and Buddhists alike. The Sanskrit myth that deals with the god's leading a divine army to conquer the *asura* ("antigod") Śūrapadma is barely known to Buddhists. For them the starting point of the mythological tradition is the god's coming to Sri Lanka and his falling in love with the woman of the wilds, Vallī Ammā ("mother Vallī"). Why did Skanda leave India for Sri Lanka? A pan-Indian myth has it that his mother Umā summoned him and his brother Gaṇeśa to circle the world and told them that whoever won the race would be rewarded by a golden mango. Skanda impulsively went around the world on his peacock vehicle, while Gaṇeśa simply circled around his mother. Naturally, Gaṇeśa, who is mama's darling, wins the mango, and Skanda, chagrined, leaves his mother and his legitimate spouse Dēvasēnā (known in popular parlance as Tēvānī Ammā, "mother Tēvānī") and comes to Sri Lanka. Here the myth tradition of Skanda's relationship to his illegitimate spouse Vallī takes over.

This tradition is an ancient Dravidian one first recorded in *Naṟṟiṇai* 82:4, which is part of the bardic (*sangam*) corpus of Tamil poetry compiled in the first few centuries of the Christian Era.[6] The sacred geography of the god's erotic exploits is localized around various shrines of the god in South India (such as Palani) and at Kataragama. The standard version is found in the popular Tamil *Kantapurāṇam* of Kacciyappacivācāriyar and is summarized by Shulman:[7]

> Two daughters of Viṣṇu performed *tapas* ["austerities"] . . . to be wed to Murukaṉ. By the grace of Murukaṉ, one of them was born as the daughter of Indra and raised by his white elephant; hence she was named Tĕyvayāṉai.[8] After the war in which Murukaṉ defeated Śūrapadma, Indra gave his daughter in marriage to Murukaṉ. . . .
>
> The second daughter was born to a deer impregnated by the lustful

[6] Kamil Zvelebil, "The Beginnings of *Bhakti* in South India," *Temenos* 13 (1977): 233.

[7] David Shulman, *Tamil Temple Myths* (Princeton: Princeton University Press, 1980), pp. 275–78. Reprinted with permission of Princeton University Press. We have omitted a few details and added a few words in square brackets.

[8] This is a folk etymology based on *yāṉai*, "elephant"; in reality Tam. Tĕyvayāṉai is undoubtedly derived from Devasenā [Shulman's note].

glance of the sage Śivamuni, who was performing *tapas* on Vaḷḷimalai. Seeing that the girl, who was born with bangles of fine workmanship on her arms, was not of her own kind, the deer abandoned her in the pit in which she had given birth, and there she was found by the lord of the Kuṟavar hunters, Nampi, who longed for a daughter. The hunter chief adopted her and named her Vaḷḷi, since she was born in a pit from which old men scrape the roots of the *vaḷḷi*.

When Vaḷḷi reached the age of twelve, she was sent to guard the ripening millet from a raised platform . . . ; she frightened away birds and beasts with a sling-shot and the cry of "*ālolam.*" To grant her grace, Murukaṉ came from Kantavarai to Taṇikai. There he was met by Nārada, who sang the praises of Vaḷḷi. Murukaṉ sent Nārada away and placed within himself the grievous disease of love. Taking the form of a hunter, the love-sick god went to the millet fields and there beheld Vaḷḷi. He said to her, "Lady, hear me—did Brahmā fail to provide those barbarians with knowledge, that they have made you sit here guarding the millet? Tell me your name; or, if you will not say, tell me the name of your village; or, if you will not tell me even that, then show me the way thither." As he was pleading, her father suddenly arrived with his retinue of hunters, and Murukaṉ transformed himself into a *veṇkai* tree. Nampi gave his daughter some *vaḷḷi* roots, mangoes, honey, and the milk of a wild cow. Then the hunters noticed the new tree. "This tree was never here before; no good will come of it," they said, and made preparations to cut it down and dig up its roots. Nampi stopped them. "How did this tree come to be here?" he asked, scrutinizing the face of his daughter. Alarmed, Vaḷḷi said, "I do not know how it came; it appeared, I think, like magic (*māyam*). I have been trembling at the thought that something that was not here before has sprung up so suddenly."

"Be not afraid; the tree came here to be a sweet companion for you," said the hunter, and left with his men. Murukaṉ resumed human form and said, "Daughter of the Kuṟavar, I shall never leave you. How could anyone depart from you, who are like life to a body? My life is in your hands. Watching the fields is low, demeaning work; come with me, and the very women of heaven will worship you, and I will give you perfect gifts."

The daughter of the hunters understood. "I am but a humble girl who guards the fields of millet," she said, ashamed. "You are a leader who rules the whole world. Is it not wrong . . . for you even to speak of embracing me?"

Suddenly the drums of the hunters were heard. Vaḷḷi urged Murukaṉ to flee; instead he transformed himself into an old ascetic. He bowed to Nampi, and the hunters' lord asked what he desired. "I have come to rid myself of age and my heart of its delusion; I wish to bathe in the Kumari (spring) of this, your mountain," replied the god. Said Nampi, "Father, bathe in that *tīrtha* ["sacred bathing place"] and be a companion to our daughter, who is all alone." He gave Vaḷḷi fresh fruits and millet and departed.

The old man asked Vaḷḷi for food, and, when she had given him from her honey and fruits, he complained of thirst. She told him of a spring on the mountain, on the other side of seven hills; he asked her to show him the way there. He drank from the spring as if parched by the heat; then he asked her to satisfy his desire. "You are saying things which must not be said; if the hunters knew, they would cause you harm. Are you mad, that you speak without understanding?" Saying this, Vaḷḷi hastened away. Murukaṉ, watching her go, thought of his elephant-headed brother Gaṇeśa. Gaṇeśa took the form of a wild elephant in Vaḷḷi's path. She fled back to the arms of the old man: "Save me and I will do as you wish!" Murukaṉ embraced her and revealed to her his true form.

Vaḷḷi returned to the millet fields. Her companion noticed the change in her manner. Murukaṉ appeared again as a hunter and asked the companion if she had seen a wild elephant go past. Guessing he was really seeking Vaḷḷi, she told him to leave, lest the fierce hunters take his life. He threatened to mount the *maṭal* hobby-horse[9] and ride through the streets of the village if he were not allowed to meet Vaḷḷi; succumbing to this threat, the companion became an accomplice to their secret union.

When the millet was ripe, the hunters, preparing for the harvest, sent Vaḷḷi back to the village. She pined for her lover, and her foster mother . . . and her mother noticed that she was not well. They locked her in the house and consulted women (skilled in divination).

[9] According to the *akam* conventions, a rejected suitor might ride a hobby-horse fashioned from the leaves of the palmyra palm in a public place in order to shame the beloved into accepting him [Shulman's note].

> "She is possessed by the spirit (*cūr*) of these mountain slopes," they said, not knowing her to be possessed by the enemy of Cūr.[10] The hunters therefore held a ceremony of ecstatic dance . . . for Murukan̲. During the dance, the god descended upon the wild dancer . . . and indicated by signs that he had taken possession of Vaḷḷi while she was out in the fields, but that her sickness would depart if he were worshiped. No sooner was this uttered than Vaḷḷi arose restored; her foster mother and mother praised Murukan̲.
>
> Not finding Vaḷḷi in the fields, Murukan̲ lamented and wandered over the mountain. At midnight he stood outside the hut of Nampi. Vaḷḷi's companion saw him there and urged him to elope with his beloved; with her help the couple were united and fled the village.
>
> In the morning they were pursued by the angry Kuṟavar, who found them in a grove. They showered arrows at Murukan̲, but at the crow of his cock they all fell dead. Vaḷḷi mourned her relatives and, at Nārada's urging, Murukan̲ revived them and agreed to their request that he return to the village and marry Vaḷḷi in a proper ceremony.

The Väddas, Sinhalas, and Tamils of Sri Lanka have all localized the myth in Kataragama. The idea that the events in the myth occurred at Kataragama is also well known in South India and has influenced their traditions. Zvelebil persuasively argues that in the earliest Tamil literature Skanda was known as Ceyon and later as Murugan (youthful), a deity associated with the mountain regions. It was much later that he was fused with the Sanskritic deity Skanda, alias Kumāra.[11] It should be noted that the Sinhalas have always interpreted Kanda not as a Sinhalicization of Skanda, but as the Sinhala word for "mountain," and Sinhala mythology refers to his six separate heads being put together by his mother (or father) into a "mountain of heads" or *is-kanda* that then became the Sinhala folk etymology for "Skanda." The Seligmanns persuasively argue that Skanda was fused with the attributes of a popular mountain deity of the Sinhalas and Väddas known as Kande Deviyō ("the god of the mountain") and suggest that the unimposing shrine for Skanda once may have been a

[10] Cūr (Skt. Śūrapadma) is in the Tamil tradition the major enemy of Murukan̲ [Shulman's note].

[11] Zvelebil, "The Beginnings of *Bhakti*," pp. 245, 249.

shrine for Kande Deviyō.[12] One might add that the identification may have been facilitated by other cultural conditions. Even in South India popular shrines for Skanda like Palani are located in mountains and (maybe more importantly) among mountainous or wild people. Many scholars have noted that the marriage of Vallī Ammā, the wild woman, with Skanda *on one level of symbolic meaning* might well indicate an articulation of hunters ("wild people") into the larger society through the mythic and ritual order dominated by peasant cultivators. This union of people radically alters the Sanskritic orientation of the cult as expressed, for example, in the *Skanda Pūraṇa*. Note that in Kataragama the god is ritually offered venison, and at one time, it is said, was even given iguana meat. Before the Protestant Buddhist embourgeoisement of Kataragama after the fifties and its official conversion into a sacred city in 1961, venison and other meat of wild animals (except the peacock, which represents the god's mount) were freely available in Kataragama. Zvelebil clearly shows that the god's consumption of meat is an ancient tradition stemming from the period when he was more or less exclusively the god of South Indian mountain folk.[13] It is after all Vädda women, sixteen in all, their breasts covered only with the drape of their saris, who attend the god on his furtive journey to his mistress. These women symbolize the Vädda lineage of Vallī Ammā. The senior priests of the god's shrine also claim descent from the same lineage. Thus even today, in spite of Buddhicization and Sanskritization, the cult maintains its association with "wild people" of the mountains. It is, of course, impossible to determine whether the myth of Skanda and Vallī Ammā was diffused into the Vädda country from South India or whether it was a part of an ancient myth shared by the wild people of both South India and Sri Lanka and continued through oral tradition among contemporary Väddas. It is clear, however, that this myth was *not* introduced into Kataragama by the recent South Indian plantation workers. A text in the nineteenth-century Nevill collection entitled *Kaňda Sura Varunā* ("Praise of God (S)kanda") reiterates the basic myth quoted above. Nevill dates it to A.D. 1642 or 1542, though it could be later.[14] This text describes the city of Palaniya, the abode of the god, but betrays no aware-

[12] C. G. Seligmann and Brenda Z. Seligmann, *The Veddas* (Cambridge: Cambridge University Press, 1911), pp. 187–88.

[13] Zvelebil, "The Beginnings of *Bhakti*," p. 230.

[14] Nevill, *Sinhala Verse* 2: 188.

ness that Palaniya is Palani, an important shrine (city) of the god in South India.

Kataragama: A Synoptic History

The sources do not permit us to trace the vicissitudes of the Kataragama cult in ancient and medieval times, but the deity has long been known in Sri Lanka. The first clear reference to the god in the *Mahāvaṃsa* dates from the seventh century; while uttering incantations to the god, a prince angered him so that the peacock on which the god was riding pecked out his eye.[15] We have heard the identical story told of a magician in the Kalutara District many years ago. This image of the god has changed little; then as well as now the god can give magic power to his devotees, but any slight lack of devotion or inadvertent irreverence will provoke his wrath. But up to the fourteenth century there is little reference to his popularity as a member of the public pantheon or as one of the guardian deities. Paranavitana in his discussion of the civilization of medieval Sri Lanka says that references to Viṣṇu (Upulvan), Saman, Vibhīṣaṇa, and Skanda are found in the literature and inscriptions of the fourteenth century.[16] The Lankātilaka inscription of the mid-fourteenth century refers to images of this god and others to be installed in that temple. Other fourteenth-century references like the *Nikāya Saṃgraha* clearly refer to Skanda Kumāra along with Upulvan (Viṣṇu), Saman, and Vibhīṣaṇa as the four guardians of the land.[17] By the fifteenth century the deity is well known, and there are references to him in the *Sandēśa* (epistolary poem) literature of the time. This literature and popular religious songs also refer to a shrine dedicated to him in the fifteenth-century kingdom of Kōṭṭe, south of that city. From the sixteenth century onwards reference to Skanda increases, and there is no question of his importance in the Sinhala pantheon. The *Jinakālamāli*, written in Siam in 1516, refers to Khattagāma (i.e., Kataragama) as one of the guardian gods of Sri Lanka.[18] It is also clear that by this period the

[15] *Cūlavaṃsa*, p. 193, chap. 57, verses 8–9.

[16] S. Paranavitana, "The Civilization of the Period: Buddhism," in *History of Ceylon*, vol. 1, pt. 2 (Colombo: University of Ceylon Press, 1960), p. 765.

[17] N. Mudiyanse, *The Art and Architecture of the Gampola Period (1341–1415 A.D.)* (Colombo: M. D. Gunasena, 1965), p. 10.

[18] Paranavitana, "The Civilization," p. 764.

god was known by the name of his central shrine at Kataragama. Earlier he was known as Kumāra or Mahāsēna or Kanda Kumāra.

Let us briefly consider the importance of this deity in the Kandyan Kingdom (1474–1815). For Knox, Skanda is the "great God" "who striketh such terror into the Chingulayes, that those who otherwise are Enemies to this King [Rajasiṃha II of Kandy] and have served both Portuguez and Dutch against him, yet would never assist either to make Invasions this way."[19] The awe in which Skanda was held was a continuous phenomenon. John Davy in the early nineteenth century also said that the god was not loved but feared and he could not get an artist to draw his picture.[20] His role as a god of war becomes prominent in the Kandyan period. In about the year 1765 the Dutch governor Falk, who was at least nominally in control of this region, wrote an account of Kandyan religion based on a questionnaire that he sent to Buddhist monks about religious matters, including the cult of the god of Kataragama. This account makes no reference to penances or firewalking, but describes the main procession in his honor, the visits to Vallī Ammā culminating in water cutting and water sports.[21] This account links the god to Buddhism, for he is said to have made obeisance to the Buddha and obtained his permission to help humans. The account also explicitly states that he is one of the "inferior gods."[22] He is said to be a "god of the earth," living under the sea just above the world of the *asuras* ("antigods," an archaic category inherited from Hindu mythology). The Buddha ordained that "men should respect but not worship him, as one of the powerful inferior Gods."[23] But his shrine at Kataragama was obviously popular, since the king himself not only sent presents to it, but permitted his subjects to visit it in great numbers through pilgrim routes, well known even today though now little used. In the city of Kandy itself Skanda ranked with Nātha, Viṣṇu, and Pattinī as one of the four guardian deities of the realm and of Bud-

[19] Knox, *Historical Relation*, pp. 6–7.

[20] John Davy, *An Account of the Interior of Ceylon and of Its Inhabitants with Travels in That Island*, London, 1821, reprinted in the *Ceylon Historical Journal* 16 (1969): 169, 314.

[21] "Kataragama Deviyo and the Ritual of Worship," Johnson manuscript no. 13 of the Colombo Museum, in P. E. Pieris, *Sinhalē and the Patriots, 1815–1818* (Colombo: Colombo Apothecaries, 1950), pp. 695–701.

[22] Elwood Upham, *Budhist Tracts* (London: Parbury, Allen, and Company, 1833), p. 147.

[23] Pieris, *Sinhalē*, p. 695.

dhism. Yet the Skanda shrine in Kandy has a curious feature: it is the only Sinhala shrine where a Tamil Brahman priest, not a Sinhala *kapurāḷa*, officiates. The reason for this apparent anomaly lies in a major feature of the Skanda cult, one which helps to explain its increasing popularity since the fifteenth century: the cult has been the focus of interaction between popular Hinduism and Buddhism.

The Brahman priest of the Skanda shrine, we believe, served very important religious needs of the court of Kandy, which became increasingly dominated by the South Indian Nayakkars of Madurai. Beginning with Rājasiṃha II (1635–1687), Kandyan kings married South Indian princesses and soon South Indian Nayakkars became an influential aristocracy in the Kandyan court. In 1707 the kingship of Kandy passed completely into the hands of the Nayakkars. The Nayakkars embraced Buddhism, but it is likely that they extended their patronage to the popular South Indian god of their homeland, Murugan. Even Kīrti Śrī Rājasiṃha, the patron of the great Buddhist revival of the mid-eighteenth century, was also a Śaivite (and no doubt a Skanda devotee) in private life, since he used to daub himself with sacred ash in the Śaivite fashion.[24] Buddhist monks clearly resented this practice of the king, perhaps because they doubted his true allegiance to Buddhism. The pejorative remarks about Skanda by the monks who responded to the questions posed by Governor Falk in 1765 should perhaps be seen in this political context.

Other influences from South India strengthened the cult of Skanda. Immigrants such as the *karāva* and *salāgama* castes, who mostly came from South India, may have increased its popularity. More important than these, we think, were priestly and ascetic devotees of the Skanda cult—the *paṇṭāram*s and *āṇḍi*s.

1. *Paṇṭāram* is a label given to a large number of groups in South India, including semitribal groups, the hill *paṇṭārams*.[25] However, some in Tamil Nāṭu belong to non-Brahman Śaivite castes of priests (*vellāla* and *palli*, according to Thurston) and tend to be vegetarians. There are also

[24] L. S. Dewaraja, *The Kandyan Kingdom, 1707–1760* (Colombo: Lake House Publishing Company, 1972), p. 111. See also K.N.O. Dharmadasa, "The Sinhalese-Buddhist Identity and the Nayakkar Dynasty in the Politics of the Kandyan Kingdom, 1739–1815," *Ceylon Journal of Historical and Social Studies*, n.s. 6, no. 1 (1976): 1–23.

[25] E. Thurston, *Castes and Tribes of Southern India* (Madras: Government Press, 1909), 6: 47.

mendicant *paṇṭāram*s who come from a variety of castes; some of them eat meat, and others adopt a highly ascetic mode of existence, wearing matted locks and sandals with spikes.[26] Little detailed sociological information is available on *paṇṭāram*s, but Dewaraja says that two well-documented waves of *paṇṭāram* immigration entered Sri Lanka in the thirteenth and fifteenth centuries. According to Dewaraja these were high-caste *paṇṭāram* managers of Śaiva temples, who were absorbed into the Sinhala aristocracy.[27] Dewaraja also states that the title *baṇḍāra*, used later to designate Kandyan nobility, was derived from the term *paṇṭāram*. It should be noted that both Kandyan aristocrats and high-caste *paṇṭāram*s claim that the terms *baṇḍāra* and *paṇṭāram* are both derived from the Sanskrit *banḍāra*, meaning "treasury."[28] According to Thurston a subcaste of the *paṇṭāram*s served as priests of the Nāṭṭukōttai Cettiars, who both in India and in contemporary Sri Lanka are devotees of Skanda.

2. *Āṇḍi* are wandering mendicant devotees of Murugan. Thurston notes that some *āṇḍi* come from subdivisions of the *paṇṭāram*,[29] but others do not. King Rājasiṃha of Sitavaka (1581–1593), the apostate Sinhala king who espoused Hinduism, settled a large number of *āṇḍi*s in the Hevahäṭa area, but it is likely that they were, like the *paṇṭāram*s, constant visitors to Sri Lanka. Place names like Āṇḍiambalama ("the resting place for *āṇḍi*") indicate their presence. The popular Sinhala folk play, *Sokari*, parodies and ridicules a figure known as *āṇḍi guru*. Skanda himself is known in Palani, his most famous South Indian shrine, as Palani Āṇḍi ("the *āṇḍi* or ascetic of Palani"). One of the Tamil operators of spikes in Kataragama today also has the surname Palani Āṇḍi and comes from a family of recent immigrants to a rubber plantation in the Galle District. It is clear that *āṇḍi*s have been a continual presence in Sri Lanka and also without doubt at Kataragama.

If the Kandyan kings gave Skanda their patronage, the mendicants from South India would have brought with them the devotional and mortificatory aspects of Śaivite worship. But it is doubtful whether they could fundamentally alter the Sinhala Buddhist orientation of the Skanda cult. This orientation meant that: (a) Skanda was one of the four guardian gods and

[26] Ibid., p. 49.

[27] See also Thurston, *Castes and Tribes*, p. 49.

[28] Ibid., p. 47.

[29] Ibid., p. 48.

a protector of Buddhism and the nation; (b) that he was an aspirant to Buddhahood, but unlike the other guardians, he had a long way to go to reach that goal; (c) the ritual specialists of the cult, outside the central shrine in Kandy, were Sinhala priests known as *kapurāḷa*, and Buddhist monks had no ritual role there; (d) self-mortification was not an official part of the formal cult, though individual South Indian mendicants practiced it; (e) the main ritual of the annual festival was the parade of the deity to his mistress culminating in water cutting and water sports and not, as almost everywhere in South India, the enactment of Skanda's victory over the antigods.

The central shrine at Kataragama was an important pilgrimage center in Kandyan times; also for the inhabitants of the Low Country this function was perhaps even more significant because the Portuguese had destroyed the great pilgrimage center for Viṣṇu in Devinuvara in 1588. Yet the impact of the cult on the popular level was in no way comparable with South India. In village life the deity propitiated in annual collective rituals was the goddess Pattinī. Kataragama myths were also sung at these rituals and he was formally propitiated, but he was not a central figure in these collective festivals nor was he associated, as Pattinī was, with the agricultural cycle. Probably then, as now, people who were confronted with difficult tasks made a "vow" (*bāra*) to him which they fulfilled at his annual festival at Kataragama. He may have had another attraction for Sinhalas. In the village the annual ritual dramas enacted the chastity of the goddess, her marital fidelity in the face of the fickleness of her consort. In the rituals at Kataragama we noted the enactment of the opposite theme: the consort deserts his wife for his mistress. The themes of village morality are overturned in the pilgrimage center. The deep motivational significance of this enactment has been discussed elsewhere.[30] By contrast the theme of Skanda's victory over *asura*s, so important for South Indian religiosity, meant nothing to Sinhalas on the level of either personality or culture. Even today Sinhala firewalkers we have interviewed are ignorant of this latter myth. Hindus have been unable to introduce the *asura* war into the dramatic enactments at Kataragama. Nevertheless they have invented their own myth: they have labelled the Buddhist stupa, the Kiri Vehera, the fortress of Śūrapadma, the *asura*!

The nineteenth century saw a dramatic decline in the popularity of the

[30] Obeyesekere, *Pattini*, pp. 470–74.

cult. The Kandyan Kingdom, the last stronghold of Sinhala sovereignty, fell into the hands of the British in 1815. This crippled the cult of Nātha, the guardian of Kandyan sovereignty. Skanda was the god of war but his help had proved useless. After the conquest there were several rebellions against the British, the most serious one by Vilbāvē, who launched his campaign at the shrine of Kataragama in 1817 with the god's blessings. But Skanda failed again: the rebellion was easily crushed and the pretender executed. We noted that John Davy, a British army surgeon who visited Kataragama soon after the rebellion, around 1819, recounted the fear that people felt for the god. The shrine itself he found so decayed and neglected that he predicted the imminent demise of the pilgrimage and the cult: "The number of pilgrims now is annually diminishing, and the buildings are going to decay. In a very few years, probably, they will be level with the ground and the traveller will have difficulty in discerning their site."[31]

Demoralized by conquest, the Sinhalas did indeed neglect the Kataragama shrine throughout the nineteenth century. It is very likely that it was patronized by the few Sinhalas living in that remote area, as described by Leonard Woolf in *Village in the Jungle*, and by the Tamil people of the East Coast. Around the middle of the century, however, the cult got a fillip from the newly arrived South Indian plantation workers. These people, alienated physically, socially, and psychologically from their native land, sought solace in their popular deity, Murugan. They virtually took over the shrine in the latter part of the nineteenth century. In addition to these proletarians, the only group of people who regularly patronized the shrine was the powerful merchants and financiers of Colombo, the Tamil-speaking Nāṭṭukoṭṭai Cettiars. These merchants had two major shrines for Skanda in Colombo, but like true devotees they felt obliged to make the annual pilgrimage to the central shrine at Kataragama. In any case the numbers at Kataragama were not large: government statistics collected by the British official in charge at the annual festival (for Tamil and Sinhala combined) were 3,500 (1871), 4,000 (1872), 6,000–7,000 (1873). These may have been underestimates, but people were afraid of a new scourge, cholera, in addition to the malaria that was now endemic in that region. The government reacted in 1873 by introducing restrictions that limited the pilgrims to a stay of four days, including the days of arrival and departure, and enforced their registration. The numbers dropped drastically:

[31] John Davy, *An Account of the Interior*, p. 315.

1,200 (1874), 53 (1875), 44 (1877). In the next year the British Government Agent could state: "I hope this may be regarded as a defunct institution."[32] The numbers were so small that in 1875 the annual procession could not be held.[33]

In the early twentieth century the pilgrimage slowly rose in popularity, but not in proportion to the population of the country. In 1910, Leonard Woolf, at that time a British official in Sri Lanka, visited Kataragama and noted 3,000–4,000 pilgrims during the whole season, at a time when the general population was about 4.5 million. It was also a period when the government had relaxed the permit system (finally abolished in 1925). Cholera and smallpox were by then under control, though malaria remained a serious problem. These numbers were more or less constant till the early 1930s when, according to informant interviews, there were about 10,000–15,000 pilgrims annually, most of them Hindus from Sri Lanka or South India. In 1949 Kataragama was connected to the southern coastal road by a main road, and in 1952 buses were introduced on this route. Within twenty-five years, as noted above, annual pilgrim traffic was exceeding half a million.

The Hindu-Buddhist Confrontation at Kataragama

The shrine at Kataragama and the cult of its eponymous god have undergone many vicissitudes, but none comparable in quantity or quality to those of the last forty or fifty years. It is to this period, within living memory, that we now turn our attention. Since about 1950 most of the pilgrims to Kataragama have been Buddhists. One of our most reliable informants, an ex-official at the temple, put it this way: "In 1926 about 5,000 people were present at the final day of the procession, and one-quarter were Buddhists; in 1950 there were many more and the proportions were reversed." With the increase in popularity of the cult the procession also became more elaborate. According to the same informant, in 1926 the procession contained one elephant, two *davul* drummers, and the officials of the cult, but in 1936 an influential politician introduced Kandyan dancers, more drummers, and elephants and this process of elab-

[32] *Administration Reports: Report of the Assistant Government Agent, Hambantoṭa District* (Colombo: Government Press, 1975), p. 32.

[33] Ibid.

oration has been going on ever since. The main annual ritual of Kataragama has always been in Sinhala hands; the priests of the main shrine have been Sinhala, as have the lay trustee (Basnāyaka Nilamē) and the managers of the extensive properties owned by the temple. However, there has also been a Śaiva presence. The shrine of Dēvasēnā, who plays no role in Sinhala ritual, is Hindu and so are the shrines for a variety of Śaiva deities—Śiva himself, Kālī, and Gaṇeśa. (We have already noted the Sufi presence and a mausoleum for the Muslim saint.)

The Tamil Hindu visitors who came, both from India and from within Sri Lanka, brought with them their traditional Śaiva practices. Some of these, such as hanging oneself from a scaffold on hooks passed through the back, had been forbidden by the British administration in India, but never completely died out. Śaivas in many parts of India stick pins through their tongues, cheeks, the flesh of their arms and upper bodies; at Kataragama these pins commonly have the form of a spear, the god's emblem. They also walk on shoes studded with nails pointing sharp end upwards.

Those who provide the paraphernalia for these ritual observances are still mainly Tamils. They own the scaffolds, the carts, the spears; and they both hire them out and fix up the devotees as they wish, passing the hooks or spikes through their flesh with such dexterity that one rarely sees any blood. In 1975 the cost of a cart was one-third of the takings or sometimes a cash payment of a few rupees. The takings come from clients who press around the cart puller once he is up on the main concourse and ask for oracles; to get a hearing they must put money in a tin can held by an assistant of the cart's owner. As for *kāvaḍi*, by 1975 most stalls were owned by Sinhalas. The arrangements for dancing *kāvaḍi* were as follows: the owner provided the band to play for each group of dancers and sent them off in groups of fifteen to twenty, whom he charged a few rupees each; if they wanted to go in smaller groups, it naturally cost more per person.

Perhaps the most spectacular Śaiva ritual associated with Kataragama is firewalking. Those who wish to walk the fire are supposed to register their names with the lay trustee the previous day. The lay trustee also appoints the "leader" (*nāyakayā*), also known as the "chief firewalker." This is a prestigious and coveted position. The leader is the last to cross; he is at the head of the fire trench and checks each firewalker as he or she is about to step onto the fire; he then permits the person to proceed by smearing some sacred ash (*vibhūti*) on the forehead as a blessing—a common Śaiva practice.

One could say that while formal control of the ceremonies has always been in Buddhist hands, the substance of what goes on at the shrine has for the most part been Tamil Hindu by culture—and until recently has been guided and executed by Tamil Hindus. The Tamil religious leaders were generally given the title of *sāmi* ("lord"). This title was given to priests of Murugan among the Tamil plantation laborers. The priests of the wealthy Nāṭṭukoṭṭai Cettiar of Colombo were also known by this term.[34] Some of these *sāmi*s resided permanently in Kataragama. Some lived in the main shrine premises, others in Sella Kataragama (where Murugan met Vallī) and Väḍahiṭikanda (where he first landed). These latter places were effectively taken over by *sāmi*s, who built small shrines there. A few lived in caves dotted around the desolate mountains and forests of Kataragama. Kataragama is the only place in the Sinhala-speaking areas of Sri Lanka that is a locus of a non-Buddhist, Śaivite form of asceticism.

The Tamil *sāmi*s of Kataragama have had an enormous influence on the contemporary religiosity of Sinhala Buddhists. Several of them were charismatic persons held in high esteem by Sinhalas who came under their influence. We have noted the case of Sangarapillai Sāmi, who influenced not only Venerable Siddhārtha but also a large number of senior Sinhala Buddhist firewalkers of today. Many older Sinhala *sāmi*s we have interviewed were pupils of well-known Tamil priests; these Sinhala *sāmi*s in turn have trained a whole generation of Sinhala priests and priestesses. In reference to the latter, one should remember that traditional Sinhala priests (*kapurāḷa*s) and exorcists did not accept the doctrine of divine possession by women. Not so with some of the Tamil *sāmi*s; they, without hesitation, interpreted female possession as a sign of possible grace. The efflorescence of priestesses in contemporary Sri Lanka was made possible by the liberating influence of the *sāmi*s of Kataragama.

The Tamil Hindus imprinted their piacular and emotional ethos on Kataragama. But they could only control its shrines and practices as long as Sinhalas refrained from coming there in large numbers. But Sinhalas started once again to patronize Kataragama in the thirties and we have noted that their visits increased dramatically after the main road was constructed in 1949. (It would be foolish to see the construction of the road as the cause of the deity's rise; it is the rise of the deity that was responsible

[34] For the role of the Nāṭṭukoṭṭai Cettiar in Kataragama see Don Handleman, "On the Desuetude of Kataragama," *Man* n.s. 20, no. 1 (1985): 156–57.

for the road.) As we noted in Chapter 3, this rise was due to the inability of an increasingly educated populace to gain their legitimate goals (especially jobs), since the desired goods are scarce and their attainment without political patronage virtually impossible. As has happened the world over, they tried to achieve the new goals by traditional means—in this case the intercession of a deity. But why Skanda?

Of the deities of the traditional pantheon, Skanda is best suited to the new situation. He is par excellence the resourceful deity, the vanquisher of the *asura*s, the deity who could overcome obstacles. Furthermore, the actor's psychological and social relationship to the deity is very important. When frustrations accumulate it is comforting to place oneself in dependence on a strong authoritarian figure—be he natural or supernatural—who will act on one's behalf. Skanda is such a strong character: the ideology underlying his worship is based on filial piety; the son submits to the father, who then rewards him by granting his wishes and acting on his behalf. Moreover, amidst the confusion of rapid social change there seems to some to be no clear-cut body of norms defining the legitimate means for goal achievement. Others become willing to reach their goals by normatively nonsanctioned or even immoral actions, as Merton pointed out of American society.[35] Here again, Skanda fits in best. Unlike Viṣṇu, who is unequivocally a moral deity, Skanda is willing to do *anything* to help his devoted adherent. Hence he is the god of the politician, the businessmen, and big-time crooks in the city of Colombo. We have known of professional people competing with their colleagues for promotion who visit the Skanda shrine at Kataragama and dramatize their submission to the deity by rolling bare-bodied on the sandy floor around the temple premises.

We believe that what we have said here accounts for the preoccupation of even educated members of the elite with traditional forms of supernaturalism. Thus political leaders in Asia and Africa may resort to sorcery to destroy political opponents or use white magic for more positive political purposes. In Sri Lanka practically every politician—left and right—propitiates the deity Skanda in order to win an election or ensure the national electoral success of the party. Prime ministers and cabinet ministers have been devotees of the cult. Before any general election large motorcades from the political parties visit Kataragama.

[35] Robert K. Merton, "Social Structure and Anomie," in *Social Theory and Social Structure* (Glencoe, Ill.: Free Press, 1957), pp. 121–60.

But one question still persists. How did Skanda, who seemed discredited by defeat and was practically rejected by the Sinhalas in the nineteenth century, resurface so dramatically in the middle of the twentieth? We think the Hindu *sāmi*s of Kataragama have had a decisive role. They were responsible for resurrecting the prowess of the deity by their acts of asceticism and penance. Most important in this regard is the firewalk, which they introduced to Kataragama probably in the early part of this century. The Sinhalas have forgotten Skanda's failure to defeat the British, a failure in any case largely eclipsed by Independence; meanwhile they have been confronted by an entirely new set of socioeconomic problems.

Political relations with the Tamils also took a new turn. The Tamil settlements in the hill country created an alien community in the middle of the Sinhala area. Traditionally Tamil and South Indian immigration was a well-known phenomenon; powerful caste groups like the *karāva* and *salāgama* came from the Tamil country and Kerala. But they were eventually assimilated into the Sinhala social structure. Not so the plantation Tamils; they retained their language, forms of social organization, and even kinship ties with their original home. To complicate matters further there were increasingly vociferous political demands by the older Tamil communities in the northern and eastern areas of the country for greater political participation in the nation state. These demands interacted with the increased Sinhala Buddhist national consciousness that was articulated around the turn of the century by the great Protestant Buddhist leader Dharmapāla. Dharmapāla saw the nation as an entirely Sinhala Buddhist one, with no room for Tamils, Muslims, or other ethnic and religious minorities. In this context the Sinhala Buddhist reaction to the Tamil Hindu presence was perhaps inevitable. This reaction meant emphasizing and legitimating the Sinhala as well as the Buddhist character of Kataragama—the deity as well as the place. We are about to see, however, that in this process the Sinhala Buddhists assimilated the values of the Tamil religion.

The Buddhist takeover of Kataragama began in the early forties. We have noted (see Chapter 1) the takeover of Väḍahiṭikanda by the Venerable Siddhārtha from the ascetic Sangarapillai Sāmi. It is not unknown for a monk to start a temple by an established shrine of the spirit religion and gradually to acquire control over its functioning. In this case, however, the monk absorbed the values of the Hindu priest. The Venerable Siddhārtha retained the services of his Hindu *sāmi*, but when Sangarapillai died in 1963 his mantle fell on the new Sinhala *sāmi*s of Kataragama.

Another group of monks has built a Buddhist shrine at the very entrance to the main premises of the deity. This temple, the Abhivanārāmaya, does a roaring trade from the offerings of the devotees who pray there—rarely to the Buddha, mostly to the gods! Finally the extensive premises of Sella Kataragama, associated with the erotic life of the god and his mistress, were taken over by another group of monks. Here the resident Hindu priests, assisted by powerful Hindu organizations, resisted and filed an action in the courts, claiming the rights of trusteeship. Though many predicted their victory, they were mistaken. The god himself appeared before the Sinhala judge in a dream vision and ordered him to give judgment in favor of the Sinhalas—which he did.

However, Sinhala control of the local institutions is not (at least, not yet) complete. Tamils still control some of the shrines, especially those near the main shrine. Moreover, Hindu pilgrims have hardly ever been physically harmed or intimidated on the sacred premises; the general atmosphere is one of tolerance and egalitarianism.

As Sinhala Buddhist monks have taken control of the sacred areas, the Sinhala Buddhist laity has adopted Tamil ritual forms. A few go so far as to have their bodies perforated with an array of small spears and hooks before putting on nailed shoes and pulling carts by using hooks passed through their backs. A great many dance *kāvaḍi*—the topic of our next section. A certain number—at most a couple of hundred per year—walk the fire at the annual firewalking, which is held on a night toward the end of the major festival.

We have explained above why we must postpone a detailed account of the Sinhala individuals who have led this takeover of the firewalking. Here, however, we complete our picture of the shrine's recent historical evolution by giving the background to that takeover.

Though not practiced in Kataragama until the present century, firewalking was well known in South India and was practiced by the Tamil-speaking Hindus of the east coast of Sri Lanka as well as by the Tamil workers in the tea plantations. According to the traditions of the senior priests at Kataragama, at the beginning of this century minor firewalking rituals were occasionally performed by South Indian mendicants fulfilling vows. One of these mendicants, Anakutti Sāmi, instituted firewalking on a more regular basis in about 1912. In order to overcome the resistance of the Sinhala priests, the ritual was performed as a personal vow rather than as a public proceeding. It did not occur annually; sometimes no firewalking ritual was held for several years. However, around 1926 Selliah Sāmi, another Hindu mendicant, took over the firewalking arrangements. From that time onward, firewalking probably occurred every year without interruption. Even so, the firewalkers were rarely more than seven in number, all Hindu males—women being excluded on account of their inferior ritual status.

That firewalking was not an old, accepted custom seems clear from the attitude of the Sinhala priests (*kapurāḷa*) at Kataragama. Their role was minimal; the firewalking arrangements were in the hands of Hindu *sāmis*. After walking the fire the devotee entered the main shrine, where the *kapurāḷa* gave him some sacred water. This was the practice till 1976 when, for the first time, an attempt was made to involve the *kapurāḷa* in the rites for lighting the fire.

The Hindu monopoly of firewalking was broken by a young Sinhala Buddhist now known as Vijeyaratna Sāmi, who became interested in the "occult sciences" in India. When he came back to Sri Lanka, he determined to test his occult knowledge by walking the fire at Kataragama. In 1942 he brashly crossed the fire pit without seeking permission from the chief firewalker, the mendicant Selliah Sāmi. The latter was outraged; he doused the fire and put a stop to the proceedings. However, the lay trustee of Kataragama, a Sinhala Buddhist aristocrat, reconciled the two. Vijeyaratna fell on his knees and asked forgiveness from Selliah Sāmi, who then with great magnanimity took Vijeyaratna as his first Sinhala pupil. While Vijeyaratna Sāmi was the first Buddhist to walk the fire, we shall see below that it was another Sinhala Buddhist, Mutukuḍa Sāmi, who was responsible for converting the ritual into one dominated by Sinhala Buddhists.

To understand the dramatic nature of the Sinhala Buddhist takeover consider the following figures. According to a very reliable informant, in 1941, the year before Vijeyaratna Sāmi walked, there were not more than seven firewalkers, all Tamils. Mutukuḍa Sāmi told us that in 1949 there were about thirteen, but only two Sinhalas. By the time Mutukuḍa became chief firewalker (in 1951 or 1952) there were thirteen Sinhalas and fifteen Tamils. When he resigned in 1962 the numbers had increased, the largest being seventy-one persons. In 1973 there were about 250 walkers, of whom about 175 were Sinhala Buddhists. We checked on the social background of twenty-eight of them and found that only one came from a peasant family, and even he was not a typical farmer but had brothers in government service.

The Sinhala Buddhicization of the firewalk began to alienate the Tamils. This was exacerbated by the increasing political tensions between the two ethnic groups. Some Tamils began to organize their own firewalk at Sella Kataragama, a few miles away from the main shrine, while many increased their patronage of the firewalks in temples in the Tamil regions. In 1975 about 160 persons walked the fire and we could identify only a few Tamils. From this time onwards Tamils were conspicuous by their absence and the main firewalk at Kataragama had become an almost exclusively Sinhala Buddhist ritual.

The Bhakti Ethos of the Firewalk

Almost within one generation, walking the fire at Maha Kataragama (the main shrine complex) has changed from being an exclusively Tamil Hindu practice to being an exclusively Sinhala Buddhist preserve. Few Sinhalas are fully aware that firewalking in this sense is new to their culture. There is a traditional rite in Sinhala spirit religion called "firewalking" or, more strictly, "fire trampling," but it is quite different: essentially a priest stamps out some embers.[36] Though the same term is used for the new practice, there is no question of stamping out the fire at Kataragama. Wood is stacked about four feet high in a trench some thirty feet long and attendants keep brushing off the layer of ash that accumulates on top, so that the surface is red hot. The walkers go over one at a time at a pace and gait of their own choosing—the styles are completely varied.

The overwhelming majority of the firewalkers with whom we have talked over a fifteen-year period have stated that *bhakti*, "devotion" to the god, is absolutely essential. Moreover, these firewalkers are ardent *kāvaḍi* dancers—and betray no trace of Buddhist puritanism. They say that in the *kāvaḍi* one can combine both possession trance and *bhakti* devotion. This rank and file of firewalkers, unlike their innovating leaders, are generally of low socioeconomic standing and come from the urbanized areas of Sri Lanka. They have adopted the *bhakti* ethos of Hinduism and extol possession trance.

[36] For an account of the traditional firewalk see Obeyesekere, *Pattini*, pp. 41–44.

Why do these Sinhala people firewalk? Some are fulfilling vows—for example, if they or a family member have recovered from a serious illness—the sort of reason for which Hindus have long undertaken such arduous practices. But for most firewalkers these mundane vows are subordinate to a deeper motive—their devotion (*bhakti*) to the god. These are the new-style ecstatic devotees who constantly appear in the pages of this book. They are for the most part Sinhala Buddhist *sāmi*s, or those aspiring to become *sāmi*s; they come here year after year to seal a compact with the deity or to renew their power. For a variety of reasons, including situational factors, devotionalism may commence with faith in a deity other than Skanda—Saman, Kālī, Hūniyam, Pattinī. For example, while climbing Srī Pāda (Adam's Peak), a woman experienced a vision of Saman, the god of that mountain. Yet all firewalkers agreed that the gift of possession (*ārūḍē*), be it by Skanda or any other deity, must be sanctioned by Skanda. It is Skanda who grants this boon to the devotee, who then must visit Kataragama in order to obtain the boon from the god himself. This means that, in all cases, Skanda validates the devotee's experience of divine possession as a genuine one. The firewalking experience constitutes the deity's imprimatur, divine authorization. He is the only deity in the Sinhala Buddhist pantheon who can validate the experience, since there is no theory of *bhakti*, no underlying philosophy or ideology that has yet developed in respect of the other gods. Kataragama is the locus of *bhakti* ideology. It is also here (and at other Skanda shrines that have recently developed on the same lines) that the free expression of *bhakti* religiosity is permitted.

The firewalkers clearly agree on one thing: all of them walk the fire to renew their power. Part of this power is the capacity to be possessed or imbued with the essence of the deity. It is also the power to utter prophecies, cure the sick, and banish evil spirits. Walking the fire gives the devotee *ākarṣaṇa*. It is difficult to define this Sanskrit word, which literally means "attraction," "pull." The firewalkers often say it is "like a *kāndama* ('magnetic force')"; some refer to an electrical charge in the body, using the popular English term "current." *Ākarṣaṇa balaya* ("power of *ākarṣaṇa*") or *ākarṣaṇa mālāva* ("garland of *ākarṣaṇa*") is the *śakti* ("essential power") of the god reaching the body of the devotee. *Ākarṣaṇa* can also come through other acts of devotion (e.g., meditation on the god, hanging on hooks); but for these Sinhala Buddhists, firewalking is the finest way, a combination of meditation and penance. *Ākarṣaṇa* is what induces trances at curing rites; thus it is imperative that this magnetism be maintained and renewed.

Inner devotion must be expressed in outer acts such as a pure life style, exemplified by vegetarianism. Whenever possible, there should be a special abode or shrine or at least a separate room in the household reserved for the deities. Lamps must be lit for them every evening. The firewalking sets the seal on the relationship between the person and the deity whom he or she especially favors. The deity in turn aids the devotee and reads her innermost thoughts and protects her in times of inner turmoil and personal travail.

Joy, Play, and Eroticism: A Cult for the Masses

What most Sinhala pilgrims derive from a visit to Kataragama is an experience rather less intense than that of the firewalkers and perhaps not so completely new to their culture. We have seen that the main public rituals—described already in 1765—are the enactment of Skanda's visits to his "secret woman" (*hora gǟni*) and the water cutting and water sports that form the festival's culmination. In many South Indian temples Skanda openly has two wives: their images are to either side of him in his shrine.[37] But for Sinhalas the relationship with Vallī Ammā has the glamour of adultery. In the evening procession of the god they are celebrating his illicit love life, and when his secret visits have passed successfully (as they must), they celebrate by jumping into the water and splashing around in joyous abandon.

This Sinhala core of the festival is, we believe, as intrinsic to Kataragama for Sinhalas even today as is the expiatory aspect for Hindus. The joyous, playful dimension of the god's cult is responsible for a word that is commonly uttered in Kataragama—*vinōda* ("joy," "diversion"). In ordinary language *vinōda* has secular connotations of pleasure, as for example

[37] Clothey in his account of the Skanda-Saṣti festival in South India says: "On the seventh day the festival is terminated. This day is highlighted in the evening by a re-enactment of the god's marriage to Devasena and Valli. . . . The god is rewed to his consorts." Fred W. Clothey, "*Skanda-Saṣti*: A Festival in Tamil India," *History of Religions* 8, no. 3 (1969): 236–59. See also Fred W. Clothey, *The Many Faces of Murukan* (The Hague: Mouton, 1978), p. 138. What is striking in Kataragama is the *absence* of celebration of Skanda's marriage with his legitimate spouse.

the *vinōda* I get when I see a show, attend a festival, go on a picnic. This word is simply transferred to Kataragama to describe the joyous ethos associated with the god's love affair so that devotees will often say that they came to Kataragama for *vinōda*. It is easy for Westerners, subscribing to the radical distinction between secular and sacred, to be misled by the use of this term to imply that Sinhalas go to Kataragama for *vinōda* (glossed as "entertainment") and *not* for religious purposes, as one scholar does.[38] In the Sinhala consciousness *vinōda* does not contradict the "sacred" aspects of Kataragama but is intrinsic to the latter.

Not only foreign anthropologists but also Protestant Buddhists look askance at this phenomenon, as the following newspaper excerpt suggests:

> *An Appeal to Pilgrims*
> *by A. B. Dionysius De Silva.*
>
> . . . As a Buddhist and a devotee of God Skandha I have had the fortune to participate in the Annual Esala Festival for the past forty or more years regularly. I have to mention with deep regret that the faith and devotion of pilgrims have been degenerating annually and the pilgrimage is undertaken now more as a pleasure trip than a pilgrimage. This has resulted in many pilgrims having to experience more and more hardships and calamities after their return than getting the Blessings of God Kataragama or accruing any merits.
>
> Being a Buddhist religious leader who has cured free of charge many incurable ailments such as asthma insanity etc. and rendered relief from worries and tribulations, I have come across that "Deva Aprasadaya" or displeasure of Gods has come upon people for failure to fulfil their vows completely or for fulfilling them improperly.

The author then indignantly cites "drinking orgies, improper or forbidden behaviour or even taking beef, ham, bacon, pork, etc. . . . multi-coloured miniskirts and gorgeous shirts and bell-bottoms." He tells pilgrims first to visit the Kiri Vehera, then to visit the *bō* tree (by the Maha Dēvālē), and "having gained merit, bestow it on God Kataragama by making any type of offerings at the Maha Devale."[39]

[38] M. C. Hodge, *Buddhism, Magic, and Society in a Southern Sri Lankan Town* (Ph.D. thesis, Victoria University of Manchester, 1981), p. 299.

[39] *Ceylon Observer*, Thursday, 10 July 1975, p. 2.

It is rare that a person comes to Kataragama simply to have a good time, though a few, especially among the young, no doubt do. In the fifties a famous singer, Sunil Sānta, sang a song on Radio Ceylon in the style of the "poison verses" of black magic and used Kataragama's name; he lost his voice and hence his career as a result. By contrast in the mid-1970s a pop group called the Super Golden Chimes made a hit record called *Kanda Surim̆duni*, "O Lord God of the Mountain," the words of which are a hymn of praise to the god Kataragama as they might be uttered by a pilgrim at the shrine: the refrain goes, "I have come to worship you, I have come to see you." The words alone could sound solemn, but the music is utterly secular, an extremely cheerful lilting dance rhythm. No divine retribution is known to have afflicted Clarence Wijewardene and his band presumably because, unlike Sunil Sānta, they did not use the lord's name in vain.

Kanda Surim̆duni adopts a conventional genre. Its cheerful music and pious sentiments come from the practice of *kāvaḍi* dancing. This is a traditional devotional practice of Śaiva Hindus to honor Skanda. The *kāvaḍi* is an arch decorated with peacock feathers (real or artificial) that the devotee carries on his shoulders. It represents the peacock, which is Skanda's mount, so that by carrying it one becomes the vehicle of the god's vehicle. The dance honors the god by entertaining him and maybe was originally thought of as imitating the dance of the peacock. In any event, it is nowadays thought to imbue the dancer with the god's "magnetism," which in turn shows itself in the irresistible urge to dance.

Kāvaḍi dancing is today the most common and visible form of ecstatic religiosity in Kataragama, as well as in Skanda temples all over Sri Lanka. Every year thousands of men and women bear the peacock arch on their shoulders and dance ecstatically to the sound of drums and flutes. The music is completely nonreligious, often modern Sinhala or Hindi film music. The dance is based on *baila*, a swinging dance style (originating in Portugal) popular among the urban working class. Our investigations show clearly that *kāvaḍi* dancing was rarely practiced by Sinhala Buddhists until after the 1940s; it became popular only in the 1960s. Furthermore, the first to adopt *kāvaḍi* dancing were urban proletarians in Colombo and elsewhere. The lower classes "created" the new institution. This is often the case with radical cultural innovations; they spring from a relatively small, often low-status group, since such groups are comparatively unaffected by such constraints as shame or social disapproval. (Compare the development of colorful dress styles by blacks in the United States and the

West Indies or the sexual mores and life styles of the hippies in the sixties.) Once created, the innovation is accepted by the larger society, including the middle classes, if it serves their needs.

Thus today *kāvaḍi* dancing is enormously popular; it is the only instance we know in recent Sri Lankan history where men and women engage in communal dancing—not with a partner, but in a group led by a band of musicians playing secular music. The institution can be accepted by the larger culture since it is under the aegis of the powerful lord of Kataragama. Thousands of men and women—young and old, belonging to every stratum of society—dance the *kāvaḍi*, thereby presenting a new kind of "cultural model" before the assembled populace. It is as if people are being acclimatized to the idea of close intersex communication and interaction, traditionally frowned upon by the culture. Many people, including some of the officials at Kataragama, are puzzled by the new phenomenon; they condemn the short skirts and swing music as immoral, holding up as true devotees of Murugan the Hindus from the north who practice a more sedate form of *kāvaḍi* with religious music. However, those Hindus have in turn become influenced by the Sinhala example.

What the Sinhalas did was to take over *kāvaḍi*, a Hindu Tamil *bhakti pūjā* associated with *bhajan*s, or verses praising god, and develop it in a very Sinhala direction, influenced by the ethos of *vinōda* at Kataragama. Like the ritual enactment of the Skanda-Vallī relationship, the *kāvaḍi* dance is compounded of eroticism and devotionalism, and like the former it has a hint of the illicit. After all, in spite of Mr. Dionysius de Silva (whose name could not possibly be symbolic) and the Protestant Buddhists who control Kataragama, groups of men, women, and children, who sometimes do not even know each other, dance together ecstatically in honor of the god, and some may even move out of the circle of dancers, lost in a possession trance. Moreover, over the last ten years, even small children carrying miniature *kāvaḍi* dance with adults. They are being socialized not only into the worship of Skanda but also into a more relaxed sexual ethic. It is not unusual nowadays to see a village woman or a middle-class matron swaying her reluctant buttocks to the swinging music of the *kāvaḍi* dance.

The erotic aspect of the main festival is then clear: the god is the lover, but his love life is with his mistress and not with his wife. (In Sri Lanka this theme is enacted only in Kataragama and in some Hindu temples on the East Coast. It is possible that Kataragama was the source of its diffusion to South India.) Traditionally some Tamil couples have come to re-enact their marriages before Kataragama, as they do in South India. Some Sinhala couples now do the same. We infer that this bestows erotic glamour on marriage, an institution that traditionally emphasized fidelity and procreation, not eroticism. The faces of the crowd attending the procession as Kataragama goes to make love to his mistress have fortunately been recorded for posterity by a sensitive camera.[40] They make extraordinary viewing. Eyes glisten with tears. Both men and women seem beside themselves with bliss. Yet no one seems to be aware that they are celebrating the violation of one of their society's most cherished norms.

Skanda has become a figure very like Kṛṣṇa in some sects of Hindu Vaiṣṇavism.[41] Kṛṣṇa is a handsome youth of infinite erotic charm. Moreover, most of his lovemaking is with other men's wives. This religious tradition, which is more than a thousand years old, has found its explicit theoretical justification: it is adulterous love (*pārakīya*) that is the most intense experience and hence the fitting model for the love of god, which should ignore all earthly and conventional constraints.[42] The eroticism of Skanda has not yet found any such theological justification in Sinhala, probably because nothing could be further from the ethos of Buddhism.

What the *kāvaḍi* dance has done is to increase the level of joyous eroticism or *vinōda* in a certain direction—into small groups dancing together to the sound of (often) secular music. We must now inquire into the social conditions that led to this new formation.

Economy, Society, and Eroticism in Bhakti

During the last decade, twenty to thirty percent of the labor force of Sri Lanka have been unemployed or drastically underemployed. Despite the free enterprise policies pursued by the present government since 1977, a recent analysis is grim: the poor are getting poorer.[43] "Even today 50 per-

[40] "Kataragama: A God for All Seasons," Granada TV, England, 55 minutes.

[41] Shulman, *Tamil Temple Myths*, pp. 282–83.

[42] The classic text is the Sanskrit *Bhāgavata Purāṇa*, composed in South India ca. A.D. 900, esp. book 10. See Friedhelm Hardy, *Viraha-Bhakti: The Early History of Kṛṣṇa Devotion in South India* (New Delhi: Oxford University Press, 1983). See also chap. 13 below.

[43] For an excellent (and grim) account of rural poverty see W. Gooneratne and P. J. Gunawardena, "Poverty and Inequality in Rural Sri Lanka," in *Poverty in Rural Asia*, ed.

cent of the country's population receive food stamps of some sort and are officially considered as belonging to households whose incomes are inadequate to meet the basic necessities of life."[44]

The economic situation has had profound effect on the age of marriage. People are too poor to marry, which for Sinhalas normally implies setting up a household. Statistics show that between 1946 and 1971 there have been large and increasing numbers of never-married persons in the population. (Unfortunately we have no separate figures for the Sinhala or the Buddhist population.) Abeysekera has also pointed out[45] that the problem is worse in the wet zone, the densely populated part of the country where education and aspiration levels are highest—and consequently where the religious changes we are documenting are taking place. We append three tables from the 1971 census report.[46]

What are the implications of these statistics for the widespread existence of sexual frustration? The census report states in respect of table 4: "The most striking feature to be noted is that the female age at marriage has risen from 20.7 years in 1946, through 20.9 in 1953 and 22.1 in 1963 to 23.5 in 1971 respectively, while that of the male had registered only a

Table 4

Mean Age at Marriage (1946, 1953, 1963, and 1971 Censuses)

	Average age at marriage (in years)		
Census year	Males	Females	Difference
1946	27.0	20.7	6.3
1953	27.2	20.9	6.3
1963	27.9	22.1	5.8
1971	28.0	23.5	4.5

Azizur Rahman Khan and Eddy Lee (Bangkok: International Labour Organization, 1984), pp. 247–71.

44 Gooneratne and Gunawardena, "Poverty and Inequality," p. 247.

45 Dayalal Abeysekera, "Being Realistic about Age at Marriage and Fertility Decline in Sri Lanka," *Ceylon Journal of the Social Sciences* 5, no. 1 (1982): 9.

46 *Census of Population 1971, Sri Lanka: General Report* (Colombo: Department of Census and Statistics, 1978), pp. 99–101.

Table 5

Proportion of Women Currently Married and Never Married by Age Groups (1946, 1953, 1963, and 1971 Censuses)

Age of women	1946		1953		1963		1971	
	Currently married	Never married	Currently married	Never married	Currently married	Never married	Currently married	Never married
15–19	23.9	75.3	23.7	75.7	14.8	85.0	10.3	89.5
20–24	68.4	29.4	65.7	32.5	57.6	41.3	45.9	53.1
25–29	84.4	11.8	84.4	12.8	81.0	17.1	73.5	24.6
30–34	87.1	6.6	87.8	7.5	88.6	8.3	85.9	10.9
35–39	85.5	4.3	86.5	5.4	89.8	4.8	89.3	5.6
40–44	78.4	4.1	80.7	5.0	86.1	4.3	87.8	4.3
45–49	71.4	3.4	73.8	4.4	81.6	3.9	84.9	3.6

Table 6

Proportion of Men Currently Married and Never Married by Age Groups (1946, 1953, 1963, and 1971 Censuses)

Age of men	1946		1953		1963		1971	
	Currently married	Never married	Currently married	Never married	Currently married	Never married	Currently married	Never married
15–19	1.2	98.7	0.9	98.7	0.9	99.0	0.6	99.4
20–24	18.9	80.5	15.8	83.5	15.0	84.7	13.6	86.3
25–29	55.1	43.4	53.3	45.4	49.0	50.5	46.9	52.6
30–34	75.3	22.4	76.4	21.7	72.8	26.1	73.7	25.5
35–39	84.3	12.5	85.4	11.8	85.2	13.1	84.9	13.7
40–44	85.9	9.3	87.2	8.7	87.0	10.4	88.7	9.4
45–49	86.0	7.6	86.5	7.6	88.6	7.2	89.3	7.9

slight increase from 27.0 years in 1946 through 27.2 in 1953 and 27.9 in 1963 to 28.0 in 1971."[47] The mean age at marriage of previously unmarried women in Sri Lanka in 1975, according to the World Fertility Survey, was 25.1, a further rise.[48] There is some controversy about this figure and Dayalal Abeysekera has suggested that it should be around 20.0, though this we think is an underestimate.[49]

Though the rise in the age of marriage is very significant if contrasted to a traditional society in which most people married in their early teens, it cannot provide a clue to the incidence of sexual frustration. One must consider the number of unmarried persons as given in tables 5 and 6.[50] For present purposes we shall ignore sex differences. According to the 1971 census, traditional early marriage is now practically nonexistent: 92 percent of [6.4 million] persons under the age of 19 were unmarried. While this is a significant finding, we cannot make inferences regarding sexual frustration from this datum, since the population is still very young. But in the 20–24 age group 68.7 percent (of 1,270,689 people) were unmarried; and in the 25–29 age group 38.6 percent of nearly a million people remained unmarried. These patterns were formerly unheard of in South Asia or for that matter in any traditional society. It is clear that parents are finding it increasingly difficult to find spouses for their children. The proportion of unmarried persons declined abruptly in the older age groups—18.2 percent in the 30–34 age group and 9.6 in the 35–39 group. It seems likely however that, unless dramatic economic development occurs, the older cohorts will in years to come include many more unmarried persons.

Consider the age group 25–44. Even on a conservative estimate these people would legitimately expect to be married. But of nearly three million people in this age group, 600,000 or 20 percent had never married. The same percentage obtains for the ages 25–54, if we include those who have been widowed (divorces and separations being rare in Sri Lanka). This amounts to about 800,000 people. Given the limited opportunities for the satisfaction of sexual needs outside marriage, the number of persons

[47] Ibid., p. 99.

[48] Quoted in Abeysekera, "Being Realistic," p. 1.

[49] Ibid., p. 8.

[50] Abeysekera rightly points out that the crucial factor in the reduction of fertility in Sri Lanka is not the age at marriage but the large number of unmarried persons in the population.

in the contemporary population whom we may surmise to suffer from acute sexual frustration must be very large.[51]

For the parental generation the obligation to find a spouse for one's child is still very strong; but this is often not possible owing to unemployment or the inability to find a dowry. Nor can the children be expected to find mates for themselves, since intersex interaction among adolescents and unmarried adults is extremely restricted. The need to associate with members of the opposite sex is important for the children's generation not only because they suffer sexual frustration but also because, given their modern education, they often cannot intellectually justify the traditional arranged marriage. Furthermore, sex education in the schools only helps to exacerbate their frustrations. Yet no new institutions such as courtship, intersex communal activity, or dating have developed. It is difficult to expect these institutions to be developed by the middle classes owing to their conservatism and the rigidity of their mores, as well as their fear of social disapproval. In other words, there is both a social and a psychological need for the development of new institutions.

The *kāvaḍi* dance, originally a Hindu form, has been given a Sinhala meaning in response to socioeconomic change. This new cultural form illustrates the complicated interrelation between base, superstructure, and personality. The changes in the economic infrastructure affect rational decision making regarding marriage, which results in delaying marriage and increasing the number of unmarrieds in the population. Given the current conservative sexual mores, this situation produces sexual frustration that in turn is related to the development of the *kāvaḍi* dance. It is no accident that ecstatic dancing developed in a religious context, for this is the only context in which it would be generally acceptable. The *kāvaḍi* dance is not only a cultural and aesthetic expression of sexual frustration but also a protest against the domination of Protestant Buddhist moral norms. It might even herald a more relaxed sexual ethic in the nation at large.

[51] The above analysis is taken substantially from Obeyesekere, "The Firewalkers of Kataragama," pp. 473–74.

PART THREE

Buddhist Developments

CHAPTER 6

Protestant Buddhism

Origins of the Movement

Protestant Buddhism has its roots in the latter half of the nineteenth century and the encounter between Sinhala society and the British colonial power.

Malalgoda has brilliantly documented and analyzed the early impact of the British government on Buddhism.[1] In 1815, when the British became the first colonial power to win control of the whole island, they signed the Kandyan convention, which promised: "The Religion of Boodhoo professed by the Chiefs and Inhabitants of these Provinces is declared inviolable, and its rites, Ministers and Places of Worship are to be maintained and protected."[2] They never explicitly repudiated this undertaking nor did the government as such mount a frontal attack on Buddhism; but from the first that article of the treaty was attacked by Protestant evangelicals, and the government soon felt obliged to dissociate itself from Buddhism. The traditional bond between Buddhism and the government of the Sinhala people was effectively dissolved by about 1850. On the other hand, while not all Governors and other British officials were personally enthusiastic about the activities of Protestant missionaries, official policy favored them. The building of Anglican churches very close to Buddhist temples symbolized the supersession of the old established religion by a new one. Though Anglicanism itself was disestablished in 1880, after which time Sri Lanka had a secular government, already by then conversion to Christianity was almost essential for those who wished to join the ruling elite. Buddhism had lost its prestige and Buddhists their power.[3] The demoralization of the Sinhala Buddhist peasantry is shown by the millenarian

[1] Malalgoda, *Buddhism*.

[2] Cited in ibid., p. 109.

[3] Ibid., p. 235.

myth of Diyasēna that became popular in the last century. Diyasēna will arise as a Sinhala Buddhist hero who will kill all Christians and nonbelievers and reestablish the glory of Buddhism. Probably the last period in which this myth was current was in the late 1950s, when some attempt was made to identify the Sinhala Buddhist Prime Minister S.W.R.D. Bandaranaike with Diyasēna.

Protestant Buddhism can be traced back to two sets of historical conditions, the one more specific and the other more general. The more specific concern the activities of the Protestant missionaries, to which Buddhists began to react in the quarter century 1860 to 1885; by the latter date the foundations of the movement were all in place. The more general causes were the results of close contact with the West: the arrival of modern knowledge and Western-type education, printing and increased use of literacy, and the rise of a Sinhala middle class and the embourgeoisement of Sinhala society. We shall see below that while the features of Protestant Buddhism that reflect the specific Sinhala experience of British colonial domination have gradually lost their importance since Independence, the others are set in long-term and probably irreversible trends that find echoes in many parts of the world and yet produce quite distinctive results in a Buddhist context.

Educated as they were in the Christian tradition of martyrdom, the missionaries from the first expected and indeed hoped to excite hostility among the Buddhists. At first they were disappointed by the Sangha's eirenic response, which they tended to interpret as religious indifference. Their persistent provocation did at last elicit some response in kind, a counterprotest; "Thanks be to God, battle is joined at last," wrote the Methodist Spence Hardy in 1863. In 1862 the monk Mohoṭṭivatte Guṇānanda founded the Society for the Propagation of Buddhism in imitation of the Society for the Propagation of the Gospel, and on a press originally imported by the Church Missionary Society began to print replies to Christian propaganda.[4] In 1865 the first of a series of public debates between Christians and Buddhists was held; in most Guṇānanda led for the Buddhists.[5] The most important event in Christian-Buddhist encounter proved to be a two-day debate held at Panadura, south of Colombo, in

[4] Ibid., p. 220.

[5] Ibid., p. 224.

1873.[6] An account of the Panadura debate, which was a triumph for Guṇ-ānanda, was published in the English-language press and read by Colonel H. S. Olcott.[7]

Olcott was an American who, with Madame Blavatsky (born Helene Hahn von Rottenstern), had organized the Theosophical Society of New York in 1875. Its headquarters moved to Adyar, near Madras, in 1879 and have been there ever since. Olcott arrived in Sri Lanka on 17 February 1880, a day which for a while in Independent Sri Lanka was celebrated as Olcott Day. He stayed five months on that occasion and founded the Buddhist Theosophical Society, with both clerical and lay branches. Blavatsky, a spiritualist medium and thaumaturge, was responsible for Theosophy's ideology, Olcott, who had military and judicial experience, for its institutionalization. Theosophy claimed to supersede, or rather to subsume, all currently established religions; but at the same time it strongly criticized contemporary Christianity and held that the truth was to be found in the spiritual Orient. Though they at first knew next to nothing about Hinduism and Buddhism, the founders of Theosophy were prejudiced in their favor. The prejudice was reciprocal. Olcott seemed a kind of antimissionary missionary. America of course appeared in those days as the great anticolonialist Western power, the successful rebel against British rule, so Olcott was welcomed as a political and cultural ally who could assist the Sinhalas in their struggle and also bring to bear the organizational skills of the West.

Some of Olcott's innovations, though influential for a time, had a chiefly symbolic value: he invented a Buddhist flag[8] (that in due course became the emblem of the international Buddhist movement),[9] formu-

[6] Ibid., pp. 225–26.

[7] Ibid., p. 230.

[8] "Colonel Olcott felt the need for a symbol to rally the local Buddhists. To meet this need, he designed a flag for the Buddhists from the aura that shone around the head of the Buddha. The first five stripes of the flag are blue, yellow, red, white, pink; the sixth colour is a mixture of the five, but for design, it has been broken up into its constituents." Buddhadasa P. Kirthisinghe, "Colonel Henry Steele Olcott, the Great American Buddhist" (pp. 1–20), in B. P. Kirthisinghe and M. P. Amarasuriya, *Colonel Olcott: His Service to Buddhism* Buddhist Publication Society, Wheel Publication no. 281 (Kandy, 1981), p. 12. When Olcott died in 1907, his corpse was carried to his cremation covered by the Buddhist and American flags. Ibid., p. 20.

[9] Ibid., p. 13.

lated a Buddhist "catechism"[10] in terms to which he felt (wrongly) all Buddhists could assent,[11] persuaded the government to declare Vesak a public holiday,[12] and encouraged Buddhists to celebrate it with songs modelled on Christmas carols—whence further developed the custom of sending Vesak cards on the analogy of Christmas cards. But besides imparting a Christian style to Buddhist civil religion, he founded institutions that had a more solid impact. Probably the most important function of the Buddhist Theosophical Society was that it founded and ran Buddhist schools to emulate those founded by the Christian missions. It was clearly Olcott's inspiration that led to the founding of the Young Men's and Young Women's Buddhist Associations and the Buddhist Sunday schools, which came to be held in almost every village and were supplied with textbooks and an examination structure by the Young Men's Buddhist Association. The society's schools were taken over by the government in 1961, but they still exist and so do the Sunday schools.

Despite all these achievements, Olcott should perhaps be seen rather as the patron than as the true founding father of Protestant Buddhism. From the point of view of this book he is overshadowed by his Sinhala protégé, who was born in 1864 as Don David Hēvāvitarana and died in 1933 as the Venerable Devamitta Dharmapāla, but is generally known as Anagārika Dharmapāla. The name Dharmapāla means "Defender of the (Buddhist) Doctrine." The style Anagārika was an innovation. The word is a Pāli term meaning "homeless" and is a classical epithet of a monk. Dharmapāla used it, however, to denote an interstitial role that he created to stand between layman and monk as traditionally conceived; he used it to mean a man

10 "The *Catechism* was first published in Sinhalese on 24th July 1881, and later in English and several other languages." Kirthisinghe, "Colonel Henry Steele Olcott," p. 12.

11 He was however more successful in formulating "Fourteen Fundamental Buddhistic Beliefs," to which Buddhist representatives from Japan, Burma, Sri Lanka, and Chittagong (now in Bangladesh) gave formal assent at a meeting in Adyar, Madras, in 1891; Mongolian Buddhists too are said to have accepted all of them but the date of the Buddha. Kirthisinghe, "Colonel Henry Steele Olcott," pp. 13–18.

12 H. S. Olcott, *From Old Diary Leaves: Olcott Commemoration Volume*, ed. S. Karunaratne (Colombo: Gunasena Press, 1967), p. 60, quoted on p. 727 in Sarath Amunugama, "Anagarika Dharmapala (1864–1933) and the Transformation of Sinhala Buddhist Organization in a Colonial Setting," *Social Science Information* 24, no. 4 (1985): 697–730. Amunugama gives Dharmapāla a hand in formulating the catechism and promoting the Vesak carols, but the initiative apparently came from Olcott.

without home or family ties who nevertheless lived in the world, not in the isolation of a monastery. We shall further discuss this idea below.

Dharmapāla was from a Buddhist home in Colombo but was educated at Christian mission schools, for there were hardly any others. His father, a wealthy businessman, had come to Colombo from southern Sri Lanka. As a child Dharmapāla heard the Panadura debate. In his early teens he passed Guṇānanda's temple daily on the way to school, and it was from him that he learnt of the Theosophists, even before their arrival in the country.

He met them in 1880, when he was only sixteen, and when they returned to Sri Lanka in 1884 he persuaded Olcott to initiate him into the Theosophical Society. Despite paternal objections he went with Olcott and Madame Blavatsky to the Theosophist headquarters in Adyar near Madras. Here he wanted to study occultism with Madame Blavatsky, but she persuaded him instead to study Buddhism and to learn Pāli, the classical language of its scriptures. Returning the same year to Sri Lanka, he became manager of the Buddhist Theosophical Society and worked for it, with some interruptions, till 1890. He also edited and produced the society's newspaper, *Sañdaräsa*. By then Madame Blavatsky had died, and he and Olcott were drifting apart; they finally separated in the early 1900s, when Olcott claimed that the tooth relic in Kandy was an animal bone. This relic had served for centuries as the palladium of Sinhala royalty, and its symbolic importance has hardly diminished in modern times; Olcott's rationalistic (Protestant) view of relics was too much for Dharmapāla's Sinhala Buddhist sentiment.

From 1889 to 1906 Dharmapāla travelled widely: first to Japan with Olcott; then to India, Burma, Thailand, Europe, and the United States, where he represented Buddhism at the World Parliament of Religions in Chicago in 1893. He became the founder of international Buddhism, both in the sense of making Buddhists in different Asian countries aware of each other and in starting propaganda for Buddhism in the West. In 1891 he founded the Maha Bodhi Society, whose primary goal was to regain control of the site of the Buddha's Enlightenment at Bodh Gaya in India; however, it is also this society, now based in Colombo, that sponsors all Sinhala Buddhist monasteries outside Sri Lanka and is thus responsible for Sinhala Buddhist missionaries (*Dhammadūta*) in the West. It therefore represents the reality, rather than the rhetoric, of a world Buddhist movement in this century.

From 1906 to 1915, when he was exiled to Calcutta, Dharmapāla lived mainly in Sri Lanka, and his Sinhala Buddhist nationalism intensified. In 1906 he started his own newspaper, *Siṃhala Bauddhayā* ("The Sinhala Buddhist"), and carried on polemics against the Buddhist Theosophical Society, which he now wished to purge of Theosophy in name as well as substance.

Dharmapāla's political legacy has been brilliantly explored by Professor Bechert.[13] Moreover, although Dharmapāla's views were somewhat distinctive, Sinhala Buddhist nationalism has a long continuous tradition. Since we aim in this book to discuss only what seems to us really new, we shall here say little of Dharmapāla's political activity and impact.

The Impact of British Colonial Rule: Education and Embourgeoisement

Our main concern is with Dharmapāla's specifically religious views and legacy, but they cannot be adequately understood unless seen against the background of the rise of the Sinhala middle class and his influence upon it. The interaction between Dharmapāla's personality and the cultural dilemmas of his time have been explored elsewhere;[14] here we confine ourselves to public matters.

We must first consider education and literacy. The Sangha were both the traditional intelligentsia and the traditional educators of the Sinhala laity. There is some evidence[15] that male literacy in Sri Lanka in the early nineteenth century was as high as in Britain. But the use of that literacy must have been very restricted in Sri Lanka, as there was nothing printed in Sinhala except a few productions of presses imported by the Dutch and British. Monasteries kept manuscripts; and popular literature was mainly preserved orally, though some families possessed palm leaf manuscripts. The average layman had no direct access to written texts of his scriptures. A sine qua non of Christian Protestantism was that the layman had his own Bible, in his mother tongue, but to this day (as we shall further ex-

[13] Bechert, *Buddhismus*.

[14] Gananath Obeyesekere, "Personal Identity and Cultural Crisis: The Case of Anagarika Dharmapala of Sri Lanka," in *The Biographical Process*, ed. Frank Reynolds and Donald Capps (The Hague: Mouton and Company, 1976), pp. 221–52.

[15] Davy, *An Account of the Interior*, p. 176.

plain in Chapter 13) the Sinhala Buddhist has few Buddhist scriptures available in his own language. The means for the layman to develop his own selection and interpretation of the sacred texts, apart from the hierarchy, were therefore limited: Protestant Buddhism has been a Protestantism virtually without a Bible.

During the first fifty years of British rule the small village temple school apparently continued to flourish in the Low Country, but not in the Kandyan provinces. In any case these schools, with their traditional curricula and lack of English, could not compete with the English-medium schools opened by the missionaries. In 1869 the mission schools lost their monopoly of modern education with the opening of the government Department of Public Instruction; and in the same year a Buddhist monk organized the opening of the first nonmonastic Buddhist school in the country, with a headmaster who was a convert from Christianity and had been educated in a mission school. But it remained the case till well after Independence that education at an English-medium school was the sole point of entry to the ruling elite.

Inevitably, every pupil at such a school was brought into contact with the world view conveyed in English textbooks. He and she became aware of the world of modern knowledge and scientific advance. Evidently the Sangha did not know everything that seemed worth knowing. The monk lost his place as intellectual leader to the schoolteacher.

Modern education is more than the acquisition of modern knowledge. It involves the realization that the past knew less than we do and that knowledge is constantly growing. Recognizing the limitations of ancient wisdom is an important part of demystifying the world of the past. At the same time, as Elkana has written, "The conscious effort to demystify the world is not only about the world; it is also an effort to guide one's thoughts; it is thinking about thinking."[16]

It is an open question to what extent this cognitive rationality permeated the English-educated who constituted the Sri Lankan middle class in the nineteenth century and among whom Protestant Buddhism was born. On the one hand, the acceptance of English mores in this class went unusually deep. At Independence many middle-class households in Co-

[16] Yehuda Elkana, "The Emergence of Second-Order Thinking in Classical Greece," manuscript, 1984, p. 1. German version published in Y. Elkana, *Anthropologie der Erkenntnis* (Frankfurt, 1986), p. 344.

lombo and other major towns spoke English at home and used Sinhala ("the vernacular") only to the servants and were literate only in English; in this respect Sri Lanka was more like a French colony in Africa than a part of South Asia, for in India hardly any Hindu or Muslim households adopted English as their mother tongue. On the other hand, the influence of Christianity was rarely more than skin-deep: despite the best efforts of the missionaries, only a minority even of the pupils at mission schools became Christians. As the middle class expanded, it included an ever-higher proportion of Buddhists (and of course Hindus among the Tamils). The majority of schoolchildren were in the same situation as the young Dharmapāla: they attended Christian scripture lessons at school and were examined in their knowledge of the Bible, but returned home to Buddhist households. This is stranger by Christian than by Buddhist standards. In South Asia it is commonplace for the same person to apply different "religions" (for want of a better term) to different contexts; of this the traditional Sinhala partition between Buddhism for the next world and the spirit cult for this ("The Buddha for refuge, the gods for help")[17] affords an example. The Sinhala anglophone class must have come to regard Christianity as the civic religion of the day—Christianity for public life, Buddhism for private.[18]

There is of course an important difference between this division and the one between Buddhism and the spirit religion. The latter division is hierarchized, the former is not. The traditional religion integrated Buddhism and the spirit religion into a logically coherent framework. But to accept both Buddhism and Christianity involves cognitive inconsistency, even if one chooses to ignore the fact. It lays open the way to a somewhat schizoid attitude to religion, which may also apply to rationality: rationality is to operate in one part of life, not in another. (There is of course nothing particularly unusual about that.)

The "schizoid" attitude of modern educated Buddhists is much in evidence when it comes to the spirit religion. Dharmapāla, who was interested in the occult and deeply influenced by Theosophy, had no time for the traditional spirit religion with which he, as a member of the Colombo haute bourgeoisie, presumably had little early contact. But in this respect

[17] "Budungē saraṇayi, deviyangē pihiṭayi."

[18] This is beautifully illustrated in the history of the Ilangakōn family of Galle. See P. E. Pieris, *Notes on Some Sinhalese Families, Part IV: Ilangakon* (Colombo: Times of Ceylon Company, n.d.).

he was much more rational than most of his followers. It is common for contemporary Buddhist intellectuals to say, "Of course, *as a Buddhist* I don't believe in those things," but this is not intended as a complete disavowal—quite the contrary. Even the minority who are completely skeptical about spirits usually accept astrology because that is considered to be "scientific."

What was affected was not the belief in the spirit religion but the style of its practice. Worship of the gods has been affected by the more serious spirit hitherto generally reserved for worship of the Buddha. Middle-class notions of propriety have superseded the licensed obscenity and other forms of unbuttoning typical of village communal rituals. Rather than act out his emotions (or watch others do so) the middle-class Buddhist approaches gods with private prayer and inner devotion. The decorum inculcated by Dharmapāla's code (see below) is extended to every realm of behavior, but cannot of course touch the needs that take people to the spirit cult.

What could English-educated Buddhists find to read about their religion? For the first time in history the complete Pāli Canon was printed in Thailand in 1893, and that was in Thai characters. In the nineteenth century very few Pāli texts were printed in Sinhala script; and there was no demand for them, as the English-educated learned Latin at school, not Pāli. So the Sinhala elite depended almost as heavily on Western, and especially British, Orientalism as they did on Western books for modern subjects. In 1881 T. W. Rhys Davids, who had been a colonial administrator in Sri Lanka, founded the Pāli Text Society in London; many of the early subscribers were Sinhala. The Pāli Text Society began to publish not only Pāli texts in Roman type—it finished producing the Canon early in the present century—but also English translations of the texts. These were relatively expensive books, and their contents were not always particularly easy reading, but for the educated Sinhala laity they were the main path of access to the Canon. One wonders how many people actually read them.

Traditionally the more abstract doctrines of Buddhism were reserved for monks. The laity was edified and entertained with the story literature, tales of the Buddha and of his former births—the latter are called *Jātaka* tales. These tales were collected and retold in the medieval Sinhala classics; but although their language is relatively simple, few English-educated Buddhists can have understood it. Printing gradually came to serve rather what had hitherto been a largely oral literature, the popular ballads on the same themes. Early in this century such ballads came to be printed in cheap leaflets called *kavi koḷa* that were sold in markets and at pilgrimage centers by vendors known as "umbrella men" because they laid their stock out on the ground and sheltered it under a big black umbrella. But again, the buyers of this literature were mainly not the middle class, but the wider population who were filling the state school system. But paradoxically, in recent years this market has again been eroded and the "umbrella men" are fewer. It is possible that the demand for the older *kavi koḷa* has been sapped by the same school system that has made literacy almost universal, for it teaches a Buddhism that has been much influenced by Protestant tendencies. The *Jātaka* ballads have been superseded on the one hand by modern pulp novels and on the other by magical and astrological texts that cater to the great upsurge in demand for occult literature.

The diffusion of Protestant Buddhism, albeit in a diluted form, through the Sinhala population by way of the Sunday schools and the state school system has run parallel to that gradual embourgeoisement of Sinhala society in terms of ideology (though not, sadly, of living standards) to which we referred in Chapter 1. This chapter is concerned to trace the origins of Protestant Buddhism in the late nineteenth century and then discuss another period of rapid change, the last few years. But of course Sinhala society did not stand still between 1900 and 1950. Dharmapāla grew up among a small, largely anglophone middle class, an haute bourgeoisie, but he influenced and in some sense helped to create a much broader class, a petite bourgeoisie. The acquisition of bourgeois values in a society that had consisted of a small aristocracy ruling a large peasantry is a process that needs to be documented by historians, but its outlines are reasonably clear. Dharmapāla initially influenced a stratum of Sinhala society consisting of the village intelligentsia and the Buddhist entrepreneur class emerging in the cities. The village intelligentsia was to a large extent created by the colonial regime—state employees like headmen, coroners, registrars of births and deaths, and above all, village schoolmasters. These joined traditional elites like Buddhist monks and Ayurvedic physicians. An influential stratum of this type had existed in traditional society also, but its numbers were now greatly increased. In the cities and towns there arose a new group of entrepreneurs who, like Dharmapāla's parents, were moving into small businesses. Both groups were educated in Sinhala medium schools. They had high ambitions but were socially alienated in two fundamental ways. First, they were cut off from political power, which was controlled by the British and the native anglophone and partly Christian elite. Second, they were alienated from peasant society itself. The entrepreneurs had left the village and resided in Colombo and large towns. The village intelligentsia, while living in the village and often having kin ties with ordinary villagers, were still separated from them by education, aspiration levels, and increasing differentiation of life styles. These groups could identify with Dharmapāla and accept his ethic of this-worldly asceticism and the new morality he envisaged. His political message was quickly and eagerly accepted, since these people were self-consciously Buddhist and could easily be swayed to accept Dharmapāla's view of the past and his resentment of the British and the missions. Dharmapāla's social morality and his adapting Buddhist doctrinal values as an everyday ethic (see below) fitted their hopes of bettering themselves and permitted their children to move into the same elite group as the Christians and compete with them for jobs in the upper echelon of the administration and the professions. In the village society in which they lived, Dharmapāla's code of morality helped them to differentiate themselves from the mass of peasants. In turn these elites provided a model for the villagers, a model that the latter began increasingly to accept in the middle of the twentieth century when universal free education (started in 1947) made peasant mobility a reality. Perhaps the key figure in the diffusion of the new Sinhala Buddhist bourgeois morality into the village was the Sinhala schoolteacher. He more than anyone else was the missionary of the new ethic into village society, and it was not unusual to come across schoolteachers, as late as the late fifties, taking upon themselves the duty of orienting peasant children to the new values, which they saw as quintessentially Buddhist values. It is this stratum of village elites, constituting a local leadership, that mobilized the village vote in 1956 and so brought the SLFP into power and radically altered the face of the Sri Lankan polity. It is no exaggeration to say that 1956 was symbolic, among other things, of the radical embourgeoisement of Buddhism.

Dharmapāla's Protestant Ethic

Let us now try to summarize Dharmapāla's cultural legacy. His campaign against British imperialism had little practical success, but it greatly enhanced Buddhists' self-respect. He drew effective attention to the moral failings of missionaries, especially where they could be starkly contrasted with Buddhist values—their consumption of meat and alcohol, their lack of a norm against killing animals. At the same time, like many effective political leaders, he blew hot and cold: he often castigated the Sinhala for their laxity, which he interpreted as a degeneracy from ancient ideals. The continuation of the passage on practical or instrumental rationality quoted in Chapter 1 reads: "Asia is full of opium eaters, *ganja* smokers, degenerating sensualists, superstitious and religious fanatics. Gods and priests keep the people in ignorance."[19]

Such remarks are not confined to his public utterances. Even more than his published writings, Dharmapāla's diary (which he kept in English) reveals a man full of painful ambivalences. He refers to "the increase of drunkenness among the Sinhalese"[20] and writes "the Ceylon Buddhists are ignorant."[21] These deficiencies could of course be attributed to colonial suppression.

His politicization of Buddhism involved castigating all the non-Sinhala communities in Sri Lanka, but he directed his fiercest vituperation at Indian merchants (Borahs and Parsis), Muslims (whom he contemptuously referred to as *hambayō*), and "filthy Tamils" (*häḍi demalu*).[22] He considered these groups to be aliens who exploited the Sinhalas economically. This exploitation could only be overcome, he thought, if the Sinhalas adopted an ethic of thrift and hard work; if they emulated Western capitalism by engaging in business; if they educated themselves and learned languages, including Hindi and English; and above all if they adopted a proper code of civilized conduct, such as the one he invented and propagated.

In the Buddhist scriptures the rules of conduct for the Order are minutely regulated, great emphasis being placed upon personal decorum and good manners. For the laity, by contrast, ethical principles are laid down, but no specific rules. This lack of specificity facilitated the spread of Buddhism among peasant societies with diverse and even mutually incompatible moral codes. However, in 1898 Dharmapāla published a Sinhala pamphlet entitled *Gihi Vinaya* ("The Daily Code for the Laity"). When the

[19] Dharmapāla, *Return to Righteousness*, p. 717.

[20] Diary entry, 29 July 1898, in *The Maha Bodhi* 69, no. 9, September 1961, p. 278.

[21] Diary entry, 9 May 1899, in *The Maha Bodhi* 72, no. 2, February 1964, p. 35.

[22] Anagārika Dharmapāla, *Dharmapāla Lipi* (Dharmapāla Letters), ed. Ānanda W.P. Guruge (Colombo: Government Press, 1963), pp. 61–64.

nineteenth edition appeared in 1958, nearly fifty thousand copies of this work had been sold. There were detailed rules on the following subjects:[23]

The manner of eating food (25 rules)
Chewing betel (6)
Wearing clean clothes (5)
How to use the lavatory (4)
How to behave while walking on the road (10)
How to behave in public gatherings (19)
How females should conduct themselves (30)
How children should conduct themselves (18)
How the laity should conduct themselves before the Saṅgha (5)
How to behave in buses and trains (8)
What village protection societies should do (8)
On going to see sick persons (2)
Funerals (3)
The carter's code (6)
Sinhala clothes (6)
Sinhala names (2)
What teachers should do (11)
How servants should behave (9)
How festivities should be conducted (5)
How lay devotees (male and female) should conduct themselves in the temple (3)
How children should treat their parents (14)
Domestic ceremonies (1)

There are thus 200 rules guiding lay conduct under twenty-two headings. The pamphlet is addressed to a literate Sinhala bourgeoisie. The rules proscribe behavior that peasants are generally given to, for example, "bad" eating, dress, and lavatory habits; indiscriminate betel chewing; use of impolite forms of address (though Dharmapāla uses those same forms in a letter to one of his servants). Consider the code that he devised for Sinhala women. Among the thirty rules enunciated for them are the following: to keep the house and personal belongings, clothes, and the body clean; to beautify the garden with flowering plants; not to bask near the fire or indulge in siestas; to wear saris and shun blouses that expose the midriff;

[23] Ibid., pp. 31–46.

not to address children or servants with pejorative pronouns; not to spend time lazily chewing betel; not to comb one's hair or pick lice in the presence of others. Clearly what is occurring here is a reformation of peasant habits. But at the same time Dharmapāla is trying to introduce Buddhist practices from the doctrinal tradition into everyone's daily round. Soon after waking one should utter Buddhist prayers and take the five precepts along with one's children; one should observe the eight precepts on *pōya* days and attend temple once a week to listen to sermons. This kind of Buddhist routine has been firmly adopted in many bourgeois households.

Dharmapāla, one might say, formulated a code for an emerging Sinhala elite. But note that the condemnation of peasant manners is based on Western notions of propriety. In some instances Western norms are directly advocated as, for example, eating with fork and spoon and using toilet paper before water during ablutions. Thus Dharmapāla attempted to formulate a code based on the norms prevalent in the wealthy society in which he was reared. Some points do not conflict with tradition; but by and large Protestant and Western norms have been assimilated as pure and ideal Buddhist norms. Sociologically viewed, Dharmapāla's social reform provided a value system to a new class, an emerging bourgeoisie. In many non-Western nations nineteenth-century Western values, generally Victorian, have been assimilated into the fabric of indigenous bourgeois society. In India Victorianism found a happy home in Brahmanic values; in Middle Eastern nations like Egypt and Turkey it was harmonized with Islam and in Sri Lanka with Buddhism. The Sri Lankan case is especially striking since the new value system was articulated into a powerful ethic of this-worldly asceticism. We have labelled this value system Protestant Buddhism, not only because of its incorporation of Protestant values but also because of its radical protest against traditional Buddhism, which in Sri Lanka was essentially geared to a peasant society and economy and a peasant moral code.

Salient Features of Protestant Buddhism

The essence of Protestantism as we understand it lies in the individual's seeking his or her ultimate goal without intermediaries. In Christianity this means rejecting the priest and the saint as essential links between men and god; in Buddhism it means denying that only through the Sangha can one seek or find salvation, *nirvāṇa*. The most important corollaries of this rejection are spiritual egalitarianism, which may or may not have consequences for practical life, and an emphasis on individual responsibility that must lead to self-scrutiny. Religion is privatized and internalized: the truly significant is not what takes place at a public celebration or in ritual, but what happens inside one's own mind or soul. At the same time religion is universalized: its injunctions apply to everyone at all times and in all contexts.

The following brief extracts from Dharmapāla's diary for May 1899 go to the heart of the matter.

> 5th:—In Bodhgaya. Spent the noon under the shade of the sacred Bo tree. Oh, the bliss of solitude. When will I attain to the sublime condition of the passionless when there will be absolute calm in the mind?
>
> 6th:—In Gaya. Wish to remain permanently in the holy place at Bodhgaya and practise Dhyāna Bhāvanā.[24] . . . The hot winds are blowing. But by Dhyāna processes the internal could be modified.
>
> 8th:—I . . . preached the Doctrine of Righteousness to many. Poor in body but rich in mind I returned after having done useful work. Still there lurks [*sic*] in me signs of passion. But I will destroy every vestige of it without delay.[25]

However many Buddhists have sought *nirvāṇa* through the ages, we can be sure that none before Dharmapāla articulated their quest to themselves with quite that flavor of sensibility. The intimate anguish, the self-criticism, the courting of hardship (it was 107°), and above all the assumption of responsibility for the spiritual progress of both himself and others are eloquently expressed in the idiom of the Protestant missionary.

The hallmark of Protestant Buddhism, then, is its view that the layman should permeate his life with his religion; that he should strive to make Buddhism permeate his whole society; and that he can and should try to reach *nirvāṇa*. As a corollary, the lay Buddhist is critical of the traditional norms of the monastic role; he may not be positively anticlerical but his respect, if any, is for the particular monk, not for the yellow robe as such. As an Anagārika, Dharmapāla wore white and did not shave his head; he

[24] See chap. 1 n. 23.

[25] *The Maha Bodhi* 72, no. 2, February 1964, p. 34.

thus felt free to live in the world to fight for Buddhism in the social and political arena; but by taking the eight precepts for life he had undertaken an ascetic, celibate existence.

Dharmapāla derived the outward form of the *anagārika* role from traditional Hinduism via Theosophy. There is some irony in this, for he reviled traditional Hinduism just like a Victorian missionary: the Śaiva monastery at Bodh Gaya was a "Hindu fakir establishment" that had disfigured the temple with "monstrous figures of Hindu deities."[26] But the fact remains that since ancient times Hinduism has had a permitted role for a young man of upper caste (usually Brahman) called *naiṣṭhika brahmacārin*, "perpetual religious student"; such a person did not end the period of religious studentship (which involved chastity and moderate asceticism) prescribed for all high-caste males by marrying, but vowed to remain celibate for life. He entered no monastic establishment, was free to move around, and would probably have worn white.

Some Indian Theosophists professed this role. Amunugama writes: "Dharmapala was aware that there were 'chelas' (disciples) in the Theosophical movement like Damodar Mavalankar who had taken the vows of Brahmachari in the cause of Theosophy (*Diary*, p. 51). Indeed, Mavalankar seems to have been the *ideal* of Dharmapala at the time and in Theosophical circles Dharmapala was spoken of as Ceylon Damodar."[27]

As for the meaning he gave to the role (which he himself called "the brahmachari life"[28]), Dharmapāla later wrote in his diary that he intended to "renounce the world and work for the welfare of humanity. This idea I got from three sources—the life of Bodhisat Sumedho, *The Light of Asia* by Edwin Arnold and HPB's writings."[29]

Historically, then, the *anagārika* role derives from a social status traditional in Brahmanism as interpreted by late nineteenth-century Theosophists who were heavily influenced by the Western Protestant tradition. But it came to mold and epitomize a new cultural ideal for a whole class, most

[26] Dharmapāla, *Return to Righteousness*, p. 689, quoted in Amunugama, "Anagarika Dharmapala," p. 710.

[27] Amunugama, "Anagarika Dharmapala," p. 725.

[28] Dharmapāla, *Return to Righteousness*, p. 702.

[29] Amunugama, "Anagarika Dharmapala," p. 724. "HPB" is Madam Blavatsky. Sumedho occurs in the introduction to the *Jātaka* book; probably Dharmapāla read it in the English translation by Rhys Davids. This in turn suggests that he knew Rhys Davids's *Buddhism* and its peroration quoted in n. 33 below.

of whom naturally have had no inkling of these complex origins. It is their understanding of their role as Buddhist laymen that is our central theme here, and to this theme we shall return below.

But first we must briefly explore certain other characteristics of Protestant Buddhism. These are:

(1) It abandoned Buddhism's traditionally eirenic treatment of other religions and decorous style of presentation for a polemical stance.
(2) It had a fundamentalist approach to Buddhism.
(3) It claimed that Buddhism was not a religion but a philosophy.
(4) Intertwined with all the above, especially the last—it depended on English-language concepts.

While the central theme can be related most closely to what we called at the outset the more general causes, those connected with education and the rise of the middle class, the above features derive directly from the specific circumstances of Sri Lanka in the late nineteenth century. To some extent they so depend on those circumstances that they have faded away as the circumstances have changed. Thus the four features have been listed in decreasing order of evanescence: the first is now virtually obsolete, whereas the fourth can probably never be quite obliterated. We shall say a few words about each.

(1) When Guṇānanda undertook public debates with the Christian missionaries, in most important respects he was doing nothing new. Buddhism has a tradition of public debate, though it had died out in Sri Lanka at that time. As a monk Guṇānanda was keeping religious leadership where it traditionally belonged. And the contents of what he said and wrote about Buddhism seem to have been traditional. However, his style and presentation were new, being modelled on those of his Christian opponents. His use of the press was a novelty. And he was perhaps the first monk to move out of the temple and take to the public platform. To see monks on public platforms is now so common that it comes as a surprise to recall that the custom is perhaps not much more than a century old. On the other hand, Guṇānanda's street preaching in imitation of the missionaries is now, like public religious debate, completely obsolete. When he talked, Guṇānanda acted the publicist, not the quietist. He would walk about and make large gestures. Olcott wrote of him: "Some of the more meditative monks habitually drop their eyes when conversing with one, but he looked you square in the face, as fitted the most brilliant polemic

orator of the island, the terror of the missionaries. One could see at a glance that he was more wrangler than ascetic."[30]

Traditionally the preaching monk sits on a higher level than the laity (who normally sit or squat on the floor) and speaks to them in an even tone from behind a fan; thus there are no histrionics and the audience cannot even see his face. Most monks still give sermons in the traditional style, but when they appear on political platforms or sometimes on other public occasions, as when they are trying to raise funds for their temples at festivals, they may assume a more strident tone. The contemporary public recognition of the new polemical style is reflected in the two statues of Guṇānanda erected in Ambalangoḍa and Panadura. In both he is depicted with his right hand raised and the index finger pointing outward in an imperious gesture. The identical gesture is found in the statue of Vāriyapola Śrī Sumangala recently erected in the premises of the Palace of the Tooth Relic. On 2 March 1815 British troops hoisted the Union Jack prior to the signing of the Kandyan Convention that ended Sinhala sovereignty. Tradition has it that this monk dragged down the flag, insisting that it should not fly until the convention was actually signed!

Polemical content, on the other hand, is now rare. In terms of religion the enemy was always Christianity (for Tamils and Muslims are differentiated and attacked in ethnic or linguistic, rarely in religious, terms), and that has vacated the field. In the Panadura debate Guṇānanda held the biblical account of the creation up to ridicule. The early Protestant Buddhists made eager use of the anti-Christian writings of Western rationalists; Dharmapāla made a list of such writings that he recommended to Sinhala youth for study.[31] But it is striking that later anti-Christian fervor shifted its object from Protestants to Roman Catholics—after Independence they seemed the more threatening. Here is a late (and rather mild) example of such a polemic; it dates from 1955 and is written under the pseudonym Himavantavasi ("Dweller in the Himalayas") in *The Maha Bodhi*, the English-language monthly magazine founded by Dharmapāla in 1892.

> Himavantavasi feels pretty certain that if interplanetary transport ever does become a reality, among the first batch of space-travellers

[30] Amunugama, "Anagarika Dharmapala," p. 719.

[31] Dharmapāla, *Dharmapāla Lipi*, p. 178; quoted from *Siṃhala Bauddhayā*, 21 October 1922.

to land on Mars will be an emissary of the Vatican. Dr. Billy Graham would no doubt be not very far behind. What a disappointment it would be if the Martians greeted them not with *Ave Marias* and *Hallelujahs* but with *Namo Buddhaya*!

Himavantavasi's readers will probably join him in smiling at the fanatical proselytizing zeal of the Christian, especially the Catholic, Church. But let them reflect that if Mars, even, is threatened with invasion, how great is the danger that looms over their own easily accessible Buddhist homelands here on earth![32]

(2) The Protestant missionaries who were the models for the first Protestant Buddhists were fundamentalists; in the Christian tradition the rejection of clerical intermediacy normally implies going "back to the Bible," which each man has the right and duty to read for himself. We have seen that for Buddhists in practice this has not been at all easy. But the fundamentalist suspicion of "later accretions" has been influential. The missionaries sometimes conceded certain qualities to the Buddha and his teachings but claimed that contemporary Buddhism was degenerate and moribund; Protestant Buddhists generally accepted this evaluation.

Furthermore, Protestants defined their position vis-à-vis Roman Catholicism, which they caricatured as a mass of ritual and superstition. In the eyes of Protestant Buddhists, Mahāyāna holds an analogous position: the pristine simplicity of the faith has been obscured by mumbo jumbo. This unfortunate (and absurd) analogy, which has contributed to anti-Mahāyāna prejudice in Sri Lanka, goes back to the extremely widely read (and generally excellent) book by T. W. Rhys Davids, *Buddhism*, in which he equates Lamaism with popery.[33] Rhys Davids, though himself probably a humanist, was the son of a nonconformist (Congregationalist) minister.

Westerners who had views on Buddhism, whether hostile or sympathetic, derived those views from the study of texts and, in particular, after its publication in England, of the Pāli Canon. The view is now widespread in Sri Lanka—and hardly surprising in an educated population—that even religion can be learned from books directly without the need for living teachers.

[32] *The Maha Bodhi* 63, no. 12, December 1955, p. 485.

[33] T. W. Rhys Davids, *Buddhism* (London, 1887), p. 250; see also p. 247. "The study of Lāmaism" throws light on "the intimate connection of superstitious dogma, gorgeous ritual and priestly power."

One must be careful at this point not to overdraw the contrast. In traditional Buddhism the earliest scriptures, "the word of the Buddha," have of course always been ultimately authoritative. The state of Buddhism is held to be sinking, and periodic restitutions and "purifications" are undertaken by recourse to the scriptures. Their maintenance is held to be the sine qua non for the presence of Buddhism on earth, and they are indeed copied, memorized, and studied. Fundamentalism in this positive sense is thus nothing new to Buddhism, and in the negative sense of rejecting tradition it has become less clearly articulated as the new ideas have spread through the population. But there are points of clear contrast. Traditionally meditation can only be learned from a teacher; Dharmapāla studied it from a book.

The conscientious fundamentalist tries to read his scriptures in the original language. Dharmapāla records that it was Madame Blavatsky, at the Theosophical headquarters in Adyar, who persuaded him "that I should study Pali, where all that is needed is found."[34]

(3) As early as 1847 a Sinhala Christian wrote, in an essay entitled "On the Corruptions of Buddhism . . . ," "It is to be hoped that if Buddhism can be brought back to its early principles and doctrines, it will be simply a kind of abstruse and metaphysical philosophy."[35] This combines our second and third features: Buddhism as actually present in Sri Lanka is analyzed into ancient philosophy plus folk superstitions. Dharmapāla virtually accepted this dichotomy. It was persuasive because religion was defined (as it still often is) as belief in God (or gods, alas), and from the first the West had defined Buddhism as atheistic. Protestant Buddhists accepted the contrast drawn by Christian missionaries between the two religions: Christianity was theistic, Buddhism atheistic; Christianity rested on faith, Buddhism on reason. Positively, it was agreed, Buddhism rested on its enlightened ethics.

It is of course true that the Buddha appealed to reason and stressed a humane ethical code, just as it is true that he preached that ritual was useless for salvation. But earlier no need had been felt to justify the rationality of Buddhism, let alone to posit a contrast between religion and philosophy: the Dhamma was both.

[34] Dharmapāla, *Return to Righteousness*, p. 702, quoted in Amunugama, "Anagarika Dharmapala," p. 706.

[35] Cited in Malalgoda, *Buddhism*, p. 257.

The now widespread view that Buddhism is "a philosophy not a religion"—people trot out the formula at every turn—has, we shall see, some rather bizarre consequences. The view has probably flourished because it has cut loose from its missionary origins and represents a reaction to the phenomenon of religious pluralism. If Buddhism is not a religion like Christianity, Hinduism, or Islam, that leaves open the possibility that it moves on a higher level of generality, a more exalted plane. It can overcode mere "religions," include them under its mantle. It may have learned this trick from Theosophy. Theosophy means "God Wisdom." It was itself an attempt to cope with the bewilderment of religious pluralism by claiming that all religions were really one—exactly what that one is being explained by the Theosophists. This attempt to deny and explain away all differences between religions has remained popular in India, where it struck a chord in the indigenous tradition. Dharmapāla's temperament was not so eirenic; but he too, even after he had quarrelled with the Theosophists, held Theosophical beliefs that he evidently regarded as perfectly compatible with Buddhism. On 6 August 1897 he recorded in his diary: "In 1900 the Masters will again appear publicly and teach the Dharma. Buddhism will spread in the United States."[36]

Protestant Buddhists thus lift Buddhism out of the ruck of religions by claiming that it is not a religion but something else; and sometimes they further claim that all mere religions are compatible with this something else. Sometimes the something else is a practice. But the commoner claim is that Buddhism is rational, scientific. "The Buddha was the first great scientist," wrote the eminent Buddhist intellectual G. P. Malalasekere.[37] The late Professor K. N. Jayatilleke, whose London Ph.D. thesis aimed to demonstrate that the Buddha had anticipated logical positivism,[38] was much concerned to show that rebirth, as predicated by Buddhist doctrine, could be proved scientifically, and he wrote or sponsored demonstrations that the Buddha had anticipated what was of value in the discoveries of Marx and Freud.[39] His newspaper articles and radio talks in the 1960s impressed middle-class Buddhists, though no doubt such claims are not widely understood in detail and heeded only insofar as they contribute to

[36] *The Maha Bodhi* 65, no. 7, July 1957, p. 297.

[37] Cited in Bechert, *Buddhismus*, p. 63.

[38] Published as *Early Buddhist Theory of Knowledge* (London: Allen and Unwin, 1963).

[39] See, for example, *Facets of Buddhist Thought* (Kandy: Wheel Publications, 1971), pp. 162–64.

a sense of national worth. But middle-class Buddhists come out with various set phrases in English to exemplify the "scientific" character of Buddhism. For example, in a temple in a Colombo slum we encountered a middle-aged teacher of English, who had come to make offerings to Kataragama, Hūniyam, and Kālī in order to feel better and revenge himself on those who were making him feel bad. Born a Roman Catholic, he explained that he had converted to Buddhism because it is the only religion to teach "action and reaction."

(4) At this point the discussion shades over into our fourth feature, the influence of the English language, on which something has already been said in Chapter 1. Protestant Buddhism has never been confined to the English medium: though English was his first language (he began learning Sinhala at the age of eight),[40] even Dharmapāla used both English and Sinhala. Nevertheless, the influence of the English language on the movement is pervasive and sometimes decisive.

Symptomatic of Protestant Buddhist attitudes is a remark by Sri Lanka's future prime minister, S.W.R.D. Bandaranaike, whose sweeping election victory in 1956 was the turning point in the modern history of Sinhala Buddhist nationalism. In 1944 J. R. Jayawardene, the present President, and a colleague proposed in the state council that Sinhala be made the only national language, the very program that later swept Bandaranaike's SLFP to power. Opposing this, Bandaranaike said that a previous speaker "thought that the Sinhalese language was necessary from the point of view of a closer study of the Buddha's teaching, culture, doctrine, and so on. For that purpose English may be more useful than Sinhalese. At least one would have to know Pali."[41]

Nowadays English is no longer commonly used as the medium for talking and writing about Buddhism; and yet the influence of English usage may still be paramount. The Sinhala of Protestant Buddhism is often what linguists call a "calque" on English: Sinhala words are used not in their earlier or more general senses but as translations of underlying English words. For example, Protestant Buddhists frequently resort, as we shall see below, to *bhāvanā madhyasthāna*—literally "meditation centers," the term being translated from English into highly Sanskritized Sinhala.

This is not a mere curiosity, but of fundamental importance. How does

[40] Amunugama, "Anagarika Dharmapala," p. 709, quoting Dharmapāla's *Diary*.

[41] Cited in Bechert, *Buddhismus*, p. 310.

one deny, in Sinhala, that Buddhism is a religion? The modern Sinhala word for religion is *āgama* and for Buddhism is *Buddhāgama*. In 1965 the Ministry of Education published a new primer for teaching Buddhism in schools, the first book in a projected series. In the first paragraph of this book, intended for six-year-olds, is a sentence that one can only translate literally as "The Buddhist religion is not a religion."[42] The writer goes on to explain that it is a way of life; but this is hardly enough to compensate for the apparent self-contradiction. That awkwardness must have arisen because the writer tried to translate his English idea word-for-word into Sinhala.

If Buddhists are not following a religion but a philosophy, a science, or a way of life, this poses problems not merely for their practice of the spirit religion, as mentioned above, but indeed for all forms of activity that would normally be considered "religious practice." The case histories in Chapter 10 will show to what doings these conceptual confusions can lead.

To conclude this section we can summarily illustrate this legacy of the colonial missionaries by means of two quotations taken from the *Buddhist Annual of Ceylon* for 1932. The French Theosophical "Buddhist" Alexandra David-Neel wrote: "There exists a Buddhist mysticism, but it is a rational mysticism. . . . In truth, a Buddhist religion can be found only where the primitive Buddhic doctrine has been corrupted by the masses who were incapable of raising themselves to its height."[43] (There is no word in Pāli or Sinhala even remotely corresponding to "mysticism.") Some pages on, the Sinhala lawyer H. Sri Nissanka writes: "Whether we pray or not, we suffer and die leaving all we love behind, and taking along with us, be it even to the very gates of Paradise, a terrible desire to be reunited with all that we have left behind. All the great Masters have sounded the chord of sorrow. Sorrow is an awful pebble that, once thrown into the pool of Life, ripples and ripples into what our Lord has described as the circles of conditioned existence."[44] This restatement of the Buddha's First Noble Truth in startlingly Christian terminology opens an article in which Sri Nissanka describes the founding of a forest hermitage for meditating monks at which "distinctions of caste, creed, or sect play no part in the choice of an applicant"; evidently the direct quest for *nirvāṇa* is superordinate to religion as conventionally understood.

[42] "Buddhāgamaya āgamayek novē." See Gombrich, *Precept and Practice*, pp. 62–63.

[43] *Buddhist Annual of Ceylon* (Colombo, 1932), pp. 123–24.

[44] Ibid., p. 206.

Effects of Protestantization on the Buddhist Monastic Role

It is in its view of the relative religious statuses and roles of clergy and layman that Protestant Buddhism has deviated most sharply, most permanently, and most influentially from Buddhist tradition. Here it truly mirrors Protestant Christianity. Let us first look at the negative side of the question.

To criticize the condition of the Sangha, to claim that monks have fallen from their ideal, is a perpetually recurrent feature of traditional Buddhism. Traditionally such criticism comes from within the Sangha itself and leads to internal reform. The Sangha has again and again persuaded the king to "purify the Sāsana" by expelling bad monks and encouraging the good; the initiative has come from within and the lay power has merely been the executant. After the British had conquered the whole of Sri Lanka in 1815 the lay power gradually withdrew, insisting on the dissociation of state power from non-Christian religions; the first constitution of independent Sri Lanka was for a secular state; and though since 1972 Buddhism has constitutional recognition as the religion of the majority, the state still will not uphold the *Vinaya*; in other words it will not enforce ecclesiastical decisions. Thus purification of the Sangha can now only be carried out voluntarily by the Order itself. It is in this light that we must see the modern movements in which monks detach themselves from the Nikāyas, the organized body of the Sangha, and go off into the "wilderness" to practice a stricter regimen. These "forest-dweller" monks of modern Sri Lanka have recently been sensitively studied by Michael Carrithers,[45] who stresses that there is nothing essentially untraditional about such reform movements.

The ambivalence of Protestant Buddhism toward the Sangha lies deeper. Again to take Dharmapāla as an example: his advocacy of Buddhism could hardly ignore its traditional human vehicle. And his nationalism, with its romantic view of ancient Sinhala kingdoms and of traditional peasant society, could not exclude from that vision the inhabitants of the monasteries that had depended on the former and still proliferated throughout the latter. Yet his Protestant anticlericalism made him incredulous that the local Buddhist clergy, most of whom knew no English and had little or no modern learning, could have respectable ethical or spiritual

[45] Carrithers, *Forest Monks*.

values. His ambivalence erupted in such remarkable statements as "Gods and priests keep the people in ignorance."[46] "The Bhikkhus in Ceylon are indolent and ignorant of the *Paramattha Dhamma* [Ultimate Truth], and they keep up their position by a smattering of Pāli grammar and Sanskrit prosody."[47] "The Hedonism of Kalidasa [the great Sanskrit poet] will be their ideal."[48]

All this however could still be construed as mere criticism of the actual state of the Sangha. Though no traditional Buddhist layman would have dared to publish a reference to "monks who exist only to fill their spittoons,"[49] the point at issue is rather the Protestant Buddhist attitude toward the monk's role. Up to a point Dharmapāla himself took the traditional view that the religious roles of monk and layman are strictly complementary. As far back as 1930 he declared, "It is no business of the bhikkhu to take part in politics, for it spoils the Brahmacariya (celibate life) and when that is lost the bhikkhu can be regarded as a layman."[50] He lived as a layman because he regarded his political and organizational activities as incompatible with the *Vinaya* and hoped to create conditions in which monks could live up to their ideals.

It is the village monk who is the target of Dharmapāla's criticism. Dharmapāla affirmed the *arhat* ideal but considered that the ordinary monk did not live up to it. The monk was concerned with his own welfare (*ātmārthakāma*), not with working for the welfare of the world (*lōkārtha dāyaka vāḍa*).[51] Here Dharmapāla's criticism repeats that made by Mahāyāna Buddhism of the Theravādin monk; but it is more likely that he was influenced by the missionaries. It is still the commonest Christian criticism of Buddhism that it is selfish to devote oneself to the quest for one's own Enlightenment: a truly religious man should dedicate his life entirely to the welfare of others. For Dharmapāla, as for the Christians, such dedication involves far more than the traditional contact of the Buddhist

[46] Dharmapāla, *Return to Righteousness*, p. 717.

[47] Ibid., p. 520.

[48] Ibid., p. 521.

[49] David Karunaratne, *Anagārika Dharmapāla* (in Sinhala) (Colombo: M. D. Gunasena, 1964), p. 125. A closer translation of the whole sentence would be: "Doing no work for race or nation, forever laying waste the Teaching, filling their spittoons, the venerable monks should have those spittoons hung around their necks."

[50] Cited in Bechert, *Buddhismus*, p. 68, n. 202.

[51] Karunaratne, *Anagārika Dharmapāla*, p. 47.

monk with laity, namely giving religious instruction: it involves social and political activity. He resolved the dilemma by creating a new role, the Anagārika. He chose the title and dress to dramatize and give visible effect to his decision to renounce ordinary lay life—crucially in that he renounced sex and family life—while yet remaining active in the world.

By inventing this interstitial role, Dharmapāla was able to preserve the clear distinction between the roles of monk and layman. But though he himself entered the Sangha at the end of his life, his propaganda and example encouraged the monk to become involved in the world. The Anagārika role that he invented has, for reasons suggested below, found very few imitators, but his ambivalence toward the Order did, and there is widespread feeling among Buddhists, both monks and laity, that monks have responsibilities to others than themselves.

Protestant Buddhism seems to have produced two new role models for monks; both tend in the same direction but have slightly different consequences. Both contrast sharply with the traditional ideal, exemplified in the eremitical forest dwellers. The monk can now pattern himself after a Protestant clergyman or after a (good) Buddhist layman. These role models are not articulated or clear-cut, but are summary ways of expressing the developments we are about to discuss.

Buddhist monks may now find themselves criticized unless they actively seek pastoral involvement. Obvious direct Christian influence can be seen in the creation of Buddhist chaplaincies—to prisons, hospitals, and military establishments—and a Buddhist mission to seamen. In recent years a monk has headed the Nurses' Trade Union[52] (but not, we gather, worked as a nurse). English-speaking Buddhists sometimes address and always refer to the monk as "Reverend." Where the monk's concern is with one local community, his pastoral role may bear a superficial resemblance to the traditional concern of a "village-dwelling" (*grāmavāsin*) monk, but there is a distinct difference in the type of concern thought to be appropriate. Even in the village that we have studied, the incumbent has been moved since we first wrote to sponsor a new institution, grandly entitled a Kalāyatana ("Arts Institute"), at which village children of both sexes are taught Kandyan dancing in the temple preaching hall, often under his benevolent eye. This type of involvement, which is considered "cultural,"

[52] Amunugama, "Anagarika Dharmapala," p. 729, n. 5.

is now widespread, and few object that it contravenes the prohibition on monks' watching dancing and other shows.

An even more important aspect of Christian influence on the monk's role performance is to demand that monks now bless and even officiate at all kinds of undertakings with which they have not customarily been associated. Traditionally monks bless people who engage in merit-making activities or just come to see them (they use some simple formula such as "May you be happy" or "May you attain the reward of your merit"), but even monks who undertook worldly activities were not called upon specifically to bless the functions they attended. Now few important public functions begin without some such blessing, so that monks are to be found everywhere from the opening of Parliament to the inauguration of a new bus depot. The blessing most commonly takes the form of reciting certain Pāli texts called *pirit*. The spread of *pirit* has been discussed by others. Here we will just mention two facts. Radio Ceylon's Sinhala service begins every day with five minutes of *pirit* chanting and a short sermon. Thus Buddhism is purveyed to the layman, brought to him in his own home, instead of his having to seek out the monk. Second, Buddhist monks now chant *pirit* before the firewalking at the Kataragama festival; this represents a wish to Buddhicize not merely ordinary secular enterprises but even the activities of the spirit religion.

A startling innovation is the occasional involvement of monks with weddings. Traditionally the only life-crisis ceremonies that concerned monks were those connected with death; birth, puberty, marriage, etc., were strictly secular affairs. The gradual Buddhicization of the Sinhala wedding has come hard on the heels of its Westernization, and indeed the two trends appeal to the same social strata. Since we devote half of the next chapter to the modern Buddhist wedding we postpone till then discussion of the monk's role in it.

Having dealt with the influence on modern Sinhala monks of the role of the Protestant minister, we turn to consider the current opinion that holds that monks should get fully involved with the world, thus minimizing the difference between monk and layman. A very important aspect of this involvement is the political one, but we omit that topic, not only because it has been so well covered by Professor Bechert and others. There is considerable room for argument about how Protestant or modernist such involvement is. When the Venerable Hēnpiṭagedara Ñāṇasīha, an outstanding modernist monk,[53] is imprisoned after being convicted of conspiring to overthrow the government in 1966, one is tempted to see a radical departure from tradition until one remembers that in 1760 the Venerable Välivița Saranaṃkara, author of the great Buddhist revival of that century, was banished from Kandy for the very same reason. Thus the issue is somewhat complicated. However, one can confidently assert that, on the whole, public opinion favors the traditional quietist attitude and that most readers of *Dinamiṇa* will have been startled on 28 October 1976 to see the same Venerable H. Ñāṇasīha saying that the monastic robe is no bar to ministerial office. "If monks are appointed as ministers," he is reported as saying, "they will not fail to do the job. So give them the posts and see what happens." His exhortation has not yet been heeded. But in the 1977 general election a monk actually ran for Parliament from the Karadeniya seat in the Southern Province. He stood as an independent and lost his deposit.

The main issue in the modernistic laicization of the clergy is whether a monk can take a salaried job. That this is contrary to the *Vinaya* is indisputable; those who want to argue the matter can only say that the *Vinaya* should be adapted to modern conditions. (Inscriptional evidence shows[54] that in the tenth century monks were paid for teaching Buddhist scriptures, but this precedent is little known.) For at least twenty years monks have held paid positions as schoolteachers: this seemed a natural reversion to their traditional role as the educators of Sinhala children. The state pays the schoolmaster; whether the monk keeps the salary or passes it on to his monastery is up to him. In fact the salary gives many monks economic independence and with it geographic mobility, so that they need no longer be attached to temples in any meaningful sense. For monks to have other jobs than teaching is still rare, but the newspapers have reported a startling development.[55] A monk called Nakulugamuve Sumana, having been through law college, applied to enroll as an attorney at law. His applica-

[53] Besides having a very active and eccentric political career, he published books on the Buddha's anticipation of such modern scientific discoveries as quarks and argued that the great Mahāyānist philosopher Nāgārjuna propounded the purest Buddhism. He would earn a fuller place in this book if we knew of anyone who was influenced by his idiosyncratic opinions; but he did play a part in the Sarvōdaya movement (see chap. 7).

[54] Walpola Rahula, *History of Buddhism in Ceylon: The Anurādhapura Period* (Colombo: M. D. Gunasena, 1956), p. 137.

[55] *Ceylon Observer*, 14 July 1978, p. 3.

tion was refused by a bench of five judges of the Supreme Court, but only on the ground that he was improperly dressed. What might seem weightier objections were brought forward by several lay Buddhist organizations (as well as a private individual objector) but were overruled by the judges by a majority of four to one. These objections were: "(1) That the applicant was not a person of good repute and therefore not a fit and proper person to be admitted and enrolled. (2) That the applicant was acting in contravention of the *Vinaya Pitaka* and therefore in the large interest of Buddhism, this court in the exercise of its discretion should refuse to admit and enrol him. (3) That the rules of *Vinaya Pitaka* had acquired the force of customary law and therefore this court could not admit and enrol the applicant. (4) That by reason of the fact that by Sect. 6 of the Constitution of Sri Lanka [the state] had undertaken to protect and foster Buddhism this court cannot admit and enrol the applicant."

The Chief Justice said that "we must in no way be understood to condone the proposed action," but he could "see nothing in the Civil Law which disentitles the applicant to be admitted and we are powerless to prevent it." He stated in effect that the state's patronage of Buddhism was too vague to permit the court's approving the latter three objections. Thus the secular character of the state was upheld. Arguments concerning the first objection are not reported, but an editorial in *The Buddhist* (the journal of the Young Men's Buddhist Association, one of the objecting bodies at the hearing) argues that a person "prepared to violate the code of conduct of one society to which he belongs" may break another, so that a monk who is violating the *Vinaya* may not be an ethical lawyer. Whatever we may think of this argument, it comes oddly immediately after the statement, "The legal profession has become as venial [*sic*] as any other." The editorial, which is entitled "The Bhikkhu in Secular Employment," argues that the "disappearance of the self-contained village unit" compels monks to get employment to support themselves; it thus seems to condone some forms of secular employment for monks as a necessary evil.[56]

The unsuccessful applicant at the bar has been given a job in the state bureaucracy. While technically teachers too are civil servants, this does seem to widen the range of salaried employment open to monks. Public opinion may be divided on the issue, but clearly those with the power to give monks these jobs are willing to consider them on the same footing as

[56] *The Buddhist* 48, no. 3, October 1977, pp. 2–3. The editor was C.D.S. Siriwardane.

laymen. Nor are we aware of any attempt by monastic authorities to force a showdown by imposing a penalty on a salary earner as prescribed in the *Vinaya*.

The Role of the Protestant Buddhist Layman

In 1904 a *Memorial of the Sangha of Ceylon to King Edward VII* stated, "By the laws of Buddha the laity form no part of religion."[57] One of the signatories was the president of the monastic branch of the Buddhist Theosophical Society, Hikkaḍuvē Sumangala. He and his cosignatories were evidently reacting against the rising pretensions of the local laity. Taken out of that context, the statement perhaps goes slightly too far. Even though Theravāda means "the Doctrine of the Elders" (i.e., of the Sangha) and its history until modern times can be identified with the history of the Sangha, we have explained above that it offers the laity the roles of *upāsaka/upāsikā* and of *dāyaka/dāyikā*. But these roles are bounded by context, a context furnished by the Sangha. In particular we have noted above that meditation, the assault on the summit that is *nirvāṇa*, has normally been reserved for members of the Sangha. Moreover, monks traditionally learn meditation from a teacher, another monk; and so far as we can tell such teaching has normally been given informally, one to one. We shall see below how all this has changed.

Max Weber called the ethic of Calvinists "inner-worldly asceticism." They worked conscientiously and amassed wealth, but rather than use that wealth to buy pleasures they reinvested it to become still richer, hoping to discover from such worldly success whether they were among God's elect. A similar puritan tendency is discernible in Protestant Buddhism, for all that it has no similar theological roots. Dharmapāla encouraged thrift and hard work for straightforward rational reasons, to promote the material well-being of his countrymen. Thrift and hard work were likewise recommended to the laity by the Buddha. These bourgeois virtues coincided with the aspirations of the new class of entrepreneurs and village elites to whom Dharmapāla was primarily addressing himself. They are less prevalent among today's greatly expanded middle class of bureaucrats, teachers, and clerical workers. But something analogous to this "inner-

[57] Cited in Bechert, *Buddhismus*, p. 67.

worldly asceticism" persists as a hallmark of their ethos. What "asceticism" means in a Buddhist context is in general to behave like an ascetic, which means a monk, and in particular to meditate—for in Sinhala the very term "to practice asceticism" (*tapas rakinavā*) refers precisely to meditation. Thus a layman is to be both a layman and monk at the same time—to live in the world and yet strive to leave it.

This is true Protestantism, for it recalls the revolt against the Catholic church's claim that there is no salvation outside the church (*extra ecclesiam nulla salus*). In the Christian context this led to the conclusion that every man is to be his own priest. We shall see in the next chapter that a few Buddhists have gone as far as the Calvinists and see no need in their quest for salvation to have any dealings with the Order at all. Most Protestant Buddhists, however, are prepared and indeed eager to continue supporting the Order and listening to its preaching. The big step that they have taken—and this cannot be overemphasized—is to believe that their religious responsibilities go much further and that without necessarily entering the Order they can and must—men and women, old and young—strive to make progress toward *nirvāṇa*.

The Buddhist Order traditionally distributes among its members two duties: the duty to preserve the doctrine, mainly by preaching; and the duty to meditate. These two activities were traditionally the prerogatives of monks alone; laymen have now encroached upon both preserves. But lay Protestant Buddhist activity also has a wider aspect that again originates in imitation of Christianity: the validation of lay work to advance social welfare in general and Buddhist causes in particular.

Dharmapāla dramatized this validation of the "calling" to be a Buddhist layman by assuming the role of Anagārika. It seems that the role did not catch on because it became redundant: more and more middle-class Buddhists began devoting themselves to good causes. Yet approximation to the role, attempts (whether sincere or not) to recapture its spirit, have become a commonplace in modern Sri Lanka. One can meet them any day in the newspapers, as the following excerpt indicates: "From my younger days I have a special liking towards the Buddhasasana. And recently I made up my mind to live a celibate life for the service of mankind, thus going on the path taken by Anagarika Dharmapala. But my relations and friends do not encourage this idea of my being a bachelor for life. Anyway, I would not change this idea." These sentiments were expressed by Mr.

Ryter Tillekesekera, the MP for Ambalangoḍa, at the Kahatapiṭiya Hermitage, Baṭapola, addressing a meeting after planting a Bodhi sapling.[58]

The extreme Protestant Buddhist (like his Christian forebear) is anticlerical, holding that the clergy's corruption is so deep as to be irremediable and their function hence palpably obsolete. A lay movement founded in 1941, the *Vinayavardhana Samitiya* (the title could be translated "Association for the Improvement of Buddhist Discipline"), was anticlerical.[59] On the model of the late nineteenth-century debates between Buddhists and Christians, the *Vinayavardhana Samitiya* would challenge monks to public debate and attempt to belittle both their knowledge of canonical doctrine and their purity of conduct. This movement went so far in questioning the monastic role that members took up the function of preaching—believing that in doing so they were sweeping away the accretions of medieval custom and returning to pristine canonical orthodoxy. The heyday of the movement's influence was probably in the 1950s; one rarely hears of it now. Just as the role of Anagārika has become virtually redundant because what it embodies has become so commonplace, the *Vinayavardhana* movement has fallen a victim to its own success. In its anticlericalism it was more extreme than the average Protestant Buddhist, who is content to allow monks to preach and officiate in traditional ways; but we shall see that some recent movements are similarly extreme.

The vast majority of Protestant Buddhists do not go the whole way and renounce family life or moneymaking occupations, but they dedicate their spare time to religious concerns and assume symbols of asceticism: they wear white clothes very frequently when about worldly business, take alcohol "only for medicinal purposes," and even become vegetarians or at least give up eating beef. The consumption of beef, which is cheaper in Sri Lanka than in most other countries in the world, was perhaps unusual in premodern times when the country was within the Hindu cultural sphere, but at least since the mid-nineteenth century it has been the meat most widely available to the Sinhala population and very widely consumed. However, when a Sinhala Buddhist has renunciatory tendencies, beef is the first food to be cut out of his diet. Dharmapāla travelled in a truck

[58] *Sun*, 4 September 1978, p. 8.

[59] For a full account of the movement see Steven Kemper, "Buddhism without Bhikkhus: The Sri Lanka Vinaya Vardhana Society," in Bardwell L. Smith, *Religion and the Legitimation of Power in Sri Lanka* (Chambersburg: Anima Publishers, 1978); M. C. Hodge, *Buddhism, Magic*, pp. 139–46.

bearing the slogan, "Eat beef and become an outcaste," a piece of Hinduism that may have lingered in the indigenous tradition. He also wrote in his diary: "To eat the flesh of the tender calf, cow and bull one must be devoid of kindness. How can the mother who has love to her children eat the tender flesh of calf?"[60] Nevertheless, from the traditional point of view it is striking that when in 1979 President Jayawardene celebrated the introduction of a new constitution that he claimed inaugurated an "Era of Righteousness" (*Dharmiṣṭha Yugaya*), he did so by banning for two days the sale of alcohol and *beef* and the slaughter of *cattle*.

The pious Buddhist laity has organized itself into committees and associations on the Western model. Professor Bechert has devoted a chapter to these associations,[61] and their activities and publications recur throughout his volume, so we need only mention that the most important ones are the Buddhist Theosophical Society (founded in 1880—we saw above that originally it had two branches, but only the lay branch survived); the Young Men's Buddhist Association, founded in 1898 by an ex-Catholic; and the All-Ceylon Buddhist Congress, an offshoot of the Young Men's Buddhist Association. These are island-wide organizations, albeit heavily based in Colombo. No less significant are the small committees that proliferate locally. People who give food to the temple, who were never organized except ad hoc, now usually form themselves into a Donors' Committee (Dāyaka Sabhāva). The officeholders of these committees are usually men even if their wives do the work. But these male-dominated committees now have feminine counterparts. All over the world there is a kind of middle-class lady who rejoices in committee work, committees that engage in the small, pleasant tasks of providing food, decorations, and other amenities for festive occasions, and Sri Lanka is certainly no exception. A lady colleague who lives in Colombo has told us that every temple in the country now has a Ladies' Committee (Kāntā Samitiya, Mahilā Sabhāva); this is certainly not true of the deep countryside, but it may be true of the towns and suburbs. As an indication of the rising importance of women (as our colleague would have it) these committees are no more striking than are Women's Institutes in Britain; but they do indicate the embourgeoisement of Sinhala society and the concomitant spread of Protestant Buddhism as an ethic of the bourgeoisie.

[60] Diary entry, 2 August 1897, *The Maha Bodhi* 65, no. 7, July 1957, p. 294.

[61] Bechert, *Buddhismus*, pp. 300–305.

The advancement of Buddhist causes is a somewhat vague rubric; but in actually teaching Buddhism the laity has improved its religious status in a clear-cut way. There is no doubt that educated laymen existed in Sri Lanka before modern times. A popular text, *Gaṇadevi hǟlla*, written in the reign of Narendrasiṃha (1707–1739), refers to lay teachers. This is hardly surprising in a society where monks are permitted to disrobe and revert to lay life. Yet it would be a rare layman who was a teacher of the doctrine in any formal sense. But the lay teaching of Buddhist doctrine was probably almost inevitable when Buddhism came to be a subject taught in state and other lay schools. Other institutions too have fostered the practice. The Young Men's Buddhist Association has always had propagandist aims and began early to sponsor Buddhist Sunday schools, for which it provided the textbooks and an all-island examination with certificates and prizes. Such Sunday schools were to be found in almost every village in the areas of our fieldwork in 1965. They are headed by the incumbent of the village temple, but he frequently leaves their conduct to others, for instance to a local schoolteacher. Moreover, they are divided into ten classes. The junior classes are usually taught by successful senior pupils. The schools even have a kind of internal career structure, for the Department of Cultural Affairs (which has taken over responsibility for the schools from the Young Men's Buddhist Association) grants a qualification called Teacher of Buddhist Doctrine (Bauddha-Dharmācārya). This examination can be taken by a pupil who has passed through the ten classes of a Sunday school and presents a certificate of worthiness from the local incumbent. It is free and can be taken any number of times. At present (1979) the examination consists of six papers, five on aspects of Buddhism and one on "other religions" (*samayāntarajñāna*); it is hard to pass on the latter paper as there are no adequate textbooks for it. To gain the qualification, which is widely recognized, one must pass in all six subjects at one sitting.

Lay preaching is also on the increase. Traditionally lay preachers were old virtuosi (*upāsaka*) who read popular religious texts to their peers on holy days and provided simple exegesis. Contemporary lay preachers often focus on the importance of meditation. As an example we may take Mr. C. Koḍikarnāracci. Mr. Koḍikarnāracci is lecturer in *abhidharma* (systematic Theravādin philosophy) at the Dharmapīṭha at Anurādhapura. This is itself interesting because the Dharmapīṭha is a university founded in 1966 exclusively for monks, since the government of the day felt that the older monastic universities, Vidyōdaya and Vidyālankāra, had become too secularized to serve as seminaries. In recent years Mr. Koḍikarnāracci has been much in demand. He gives regular weekly classes in Colombo, Kandy, and several other cities, which means that he is constantly on the move. These classes are based on a slim volume that he distributes, a selection from the Pāli *Abhidhamma* texts; he also offers for sale to his pupils a little book called *Taraha Yathā Mānasika Diyunuva* ("Anger and Mental Progress"). The latter book lists mainly vices—anger, sloth, jealousy, etc.—and defines them in simple language. The *Abhidhamma* indeed consists mainly of lists of constituents of the universe classified in various ways, most of them psychological. Mr. Koḍikarnāracci's course of classes (*panktimālāva*) lasts about two years. In that time he explains to his classes the Pāli terms in his book. Though the burden of *Abhidhamma* is analytical rather than normative, Mr. Koḍikarnāracci uses the class as a vehicle for moralizing. He gives simple everyday examples and talks with humor, but his popularity is not due to any originality of content. His classes are in most respects typical products of Protestant Buddhism: he wears white "national dress," arrives and ends punctually, and addresses a sedate middle-class audience. The audience sits on benches (or on the floor), takes notes: it is halfway between a sermon and a lecture. He was invited to Kandy on the initiative of the organization of laymen (Sāsana Sēvaka Sabhā) attached to a certain temple and speaks in that temple, with a couple of monks on the platform listening to him. Every week a member of the class gives thirty rupees to cover his expenses. A famous local doctor tape-records every lesson.

In one respect, however, we must note that Mr. Koḍikarnāracci's teaching is not Protestant at all: there is no protest left. As the title of a famous book has it, a church may comfort or challenge. Commonly religious movements begin with the latter mission but end up with the former. Dharmapāla, like all religious reformers, often tried to make his audience uncomfortable. Nothing could be further from Mr. Koḍikarnāracci's intention. He preaches some of the puritan values of Protestant Buddhism: absolutely no alcohol; smoking and meat eating are bad for the breath; parents should not allow their daughters to wear miniskirts. But this kind of puritanism has become merely formal, and the injunctions are but the repetition of what an urban middle-class audience, predominantly middle-aged, considers to be pious verities, as obvious as that couples should live in harmony and children should obey their parents. This is religion as reassurance. There are no references to current affairs or to anything that will be morally problematic. When he had been preaching in Kandy for about a year the classes had to be interrupted because of the 1977 race riots in which Sinhalas looted Tamil shops and homes. So far as we can discover, Mr. Koḍikarnāracci made no allusion to these events when he resumed his classes.

Lay Meditation

The widespread practice of meditation by laity is the greatest single change to have come over Buddhism in Sri Lanka (and indeed in the other Theravādin countries) since the Second World War; and in our final chapter we shall attempt to link it to some of the developments recorded in the first half of the book.

Meditation is traditionally held to be a somewhat hazardous affair, so that the novice requires the constant supervision of an experienced teacher. Serious progress in meditation was held to require the instruction of a meditation master and constant practice over a period of years. However, in 1890 Dharmapāla discovered a Pāli manuscript on meditation and with the help of that text and others devised his own meditational exercises. He thus became perhaps the first Buddhist to learn meditation from a book. (This fundamentalist proceeding may also have been an attempt to find a short cut to Enlightenment.)

Most lay Buddhists who meditate, however, still learn from a master. They may learn to meditate at temples, but frequently they go to "meditation centers" (*bhāvanā madhyasthāna*). These meditation centers may give weekly classes (typically on Sundays and/or Buddhist holy days) and they may run short residential meditation courses. The meditators then go home and practice meditation by themselves, unsupervised. A surprising number of middle-class Buddhists—and most meditators are middle class—have rooms set aside in their own homes for meditation, to which they retire daily. The untraditional nature of such daily practice by the laity cannot be overemphasized. Whether they meditate daily or not, the clients of meditation centers are popping in and out of their ordinary lay life with its worldly concerns, and it is inevitable that they soon come to regard meditation as something besides progress towards salvation: it can also help them to improve their lives. For the first time meditation is thus seen as *instrumental*, a means to success in ordinary life.

During Dharmapāla's lifetime meditation teachers were hardly available in Sri Lanka and certainly not for laymen. Modern meditation in Sri Lanka comes from Burma. This is hardly surprising in that the two "reformed" fraternities (Nikāya) founded in the nineteenth century, the Amarapura and the Rāmañña, both had their ordination traditions from Burma and their members would visit Burma on occasion for fresh religious inspiration. However, the kind of meditation that has recently been most influential in Sri Lanka derives from a distinctive recent Burmese tradition associated with the Burmese monk Mahāsī Sayādaw.[62] This kind of meditation already seems to have been taught in Sri Lanka in 1939;[63] but it was reintroduced there in 1955, when the prime minister, Sir John Kotelawela, brought three monks from Burma to teach it. The method had at that time the official backing of the Burmese government, and both governments were preparing to celebrate the twenty-five hundredth anniversary (by local reckoning) of the Buddha's death in 1956. At first the monks found little welcome,[64] and for a year they lived and began their teaching in a private home in Colombo, as guests of the widow and children of Mr. Sri Nissanka. But in 1956 a meditation center was founded at Kaňduboḍa by the Venerable Kahatapiṭiya Sumatipāla, a Sinhala monk who had studied meditation under Mahāsī Sayādaw.[65] The latter visited Sri Lanka in 1959.[66] Kaňduboḍa soon became an important center, not least because it provided meditation classes in English that were thus accessible to foreigners.

The meditation taught at Kaňduboḍa is known as "insight meditation"

[62] See, for example, Mahāsī Sayādaw, *Practical Vipassanā Meditation Exercises* (Rangoon: Buddhasāsanānuggaha Association, 1978).

[63] Bechert, *Buddhismus*, p. 39.

[64] We prefer this account by a participant to the rosier picture painted by U Nyi Nyi in Mahāsī Sayādaw, *Practical Vipassanā*, p. 8.

[65] Kaňduboḍa has already attracted scholarly attention. See Jacques Maquet, "Expressive Space and Theravāda Values: A Meditation Monastery in Sri Lanka," *Ethos* 3 (1975): 1–21; Jacques Maquet, "Meditation in Contemporary Sri Lanka: Idea and Practice," *Journal of Transpersonal Psychology* 7, no. 2 (1975): 182–96; Donald Swearer, "Lay Buddhism and the Buddhist Revival in Ceylon," *Journal of the American Academy of Religion* 68, no. 3 (September 1970): 255–75.

[66] On the topic of this section see also Richard Gombrich, "From Monastery to Meditation Centre: Lay Meditation in Modern Sri Lanka," in *Buddhist Studies, Ancient and Modern*, ed. Philip Denwood and Alexander Piatigorsky (London: Curzon Press, 1983), pp. 20–34.

Figure 1. Uttama Sādhu and his self-ordained monks, with begging bowls hidden under their robes.

Figure 2. The nuns of Uttama Sādhu's temple near Colombo. This group is engaged in rewriting the Buddhist scriptures intercepted by thought waves.

Figure 3. Pilgrims of all faiths and ethnic groups bathe in the purifying waters of the Mänik Gaṅga, which flows past Kataragama.

Figure 4. The statue of the Buddhist god Mahāsēna erected recently at Kataragama.

Figure 5. Vijeyaratna Sāmi, a distinguished theoretician of the spirit cults.

Figure 6. Gunaratna Sāmi, a Sinhala priest, being "dressed" by a Tamil priest at Kataragama.

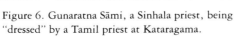

Figure 7. A Tamil *sāmi* (priest) who operates one of the stalls at Kataragama that rent *kāvaḍi* and instruments used for bodily mortification.

Figure 8. Children being socialized into the *kāvaḍi* dance at Kataragama.

Figure 9. Sinhala firewalkers at Kataragama dancing in honor of the god Skanda.

Figure 10. Young Sinhala priestess training for her vocation in a Colombo (Nāvala) shrine. Her preceptor, with his children, is watching from the side.

Figure 11. A new-style Sinhala priestess controls the demon in a patient with *īgaha*, the weapon of Vessamuni (Vaiśravaṇa), in a lower middle-class neighborhood in Colombo. This ritual is normally performed by male exorcists.

Figure 12. Sihavaṭuka, a demonic form of Śiva, popular in urban shrines in Sri Lanka.

Figure 13. The deity Hūniyam.

Figure 14. A new Buddhist temple near a working-class slum in Colombo 5. Note the visual anomaly in the juxtaposition of the traditional Hindu with Buddhist architecture.

Figure 15. A new shrine for Hūniyam in Baseline Road, Colombo. The mother's brother of the monk who founded the temple is installed as a guardian deity.

Figure 16. A new shrine for Hūniyam in Baseline Road, Colombo. The gods Vibhīṣaṇa and Gaṇeśa are worshiping the Buddha.

(*vipassanā bhāvanā*); but this obscures the fact that its distinctive feature lies in what tradition would call its "calming" techniques. Meditators at Kan̆duboḍa begin with concentration on their breathing, a standard technique in Indian meditative traditions in general and in Buddhist meditation in particular. Normally the distinctive feature of the Buddhist version had been that one must not try to control the breath or breathe abnormally, but observe it where it enters and leaves the nostrils. In Mahāsī Sayādaw's book he advises the meditator to breathe deeply and to focus his attention on the movements of his stomach and intestines; he may then attain a "momentary absorption" (*kṣaṇika samādhi*). The nature of this method we shall discuss in our last chapter; what primarily concerns us here is the laicization of meditation. It is possible to complete a course in meditation at Kan̆duboḍa and emerge with a kind of M.A. degree or *licentia docendi* ("license to teach"); one is then a *Kammaṭṭhānācārya*. This degree has been obtained by at least one layman, who calls himself Brahmacārin Āryatilaka. Brahmacārin, another title excavated from the Indian past, means "living in chastity" (see above) and in this context has the same meaning as Dharmapāla's title Anagārika.

In 1977 the government founded a training college at Mīrigama for teachers specializing in Buddhism. The Brahmacārin holds a post at this college to teach meditation to these teachers, who will then in turn teach it to their pupils. The first full meditation course for such teachers began in September 1978. Even before this, however, the Minister of Education, who also happened to be the lay custodian of the Temple of the Tooth in Kandy, had decreed that meditation was to be taught to all Buddhist schoolchildren. (He also had similar plans for the Hindus.) Wondering how meditation could be so routinized as to become an item on the school curriculum, we asked a girl in a Kandyan village school what her daily meditation consisted of. She explained that before the new order they used every day to put their hands together and say a Pāli verse before going home in the afternoon. (Every morning they take the Three Refuges and the five precepts in the same manner.) Now they do "meditation" instead: they say three times, "May all beings be free from sorrow, be free from sickness, attain bliss, and find release from sorrow." ("Siyalu sattvayō niduk vetvā nīrōgī vetvā suvapat vetvā dukin midetvā.") This is a version of the meditation on kindness, expressed in Sinhala, and it differs formally from the earlier practice, not just in the language, but also in the posture: instead of reciting with hands together (as in prayer) and eyes looking straight ahead, the hands are folded in the lap (the children standing) and the eyes cast down.

Protestant Buddhists, beginning with Dharmapāla, have encouraged schoolchildren to go to the temples on holy days to participate in the "meditation" traditionally engaged in by the elderly (see chapter 1); some school principals now order their pupils to do so. The pupils put on their white school uniforms and usually pin over them a strip of white cloth passing over the left shoulder and under the right arm, thus recalling the fall of a monk's robe. Such sartorial imitation is of course harmless. But we recall that one of the commonest traditional topics of meditation on such occasions is the loathsomeness of the body; so the question arises whether it is equally harmless for children to emulate those who have done with the world in systematically attempting to acquire a distaste for the body. One might guess that purveying meditation to a mass audience would result in nothing worse than its trivialization; but our case histories suggest that the results may be more dramatic.

The Venerable Balangoḍa Ānanda Maitreya (see Chapter 9) has predicted that in twenty years there will be no more monasteries (*pansal*), only meditation centers. Literally, this may be an exaggeration; symbolically, it puts the matter in a nutshell.

CHAPTER 7

The Creation of Tradition

The Protestant Buddhism that we have sketched in the previous chapter is in our view one of the great transformations in the history of Buddhism, as great as its transformations under the Emperor Asoka in India and the later development of the Buddhist state in Sri Lanka. For many urban Buddhists what we have defined as Protestant Buddhism *is* Buddhism, or at least part of a larger tradition of Sinhala Buddhism. The momentum created by Protestant Buddhism has spawned several innovations in Sri Lankan society. Here we are dealing with what Hobsbawm and Ranger call "the invention of tradition."[1] The new movements get their legitimation from tradition: each is explicitly perceived as a re-creation of a lost tradition or simply as an old tradition continuing. The tradition in question is "Buddhist," however that may be defined.

In the first chapter we used the phrase "important departures from tradition." It is now time to give this phrase greater precision. Sometimes the invented tradition bears little or no relation to the past as *we* see it; yet protagonists see it very differently. For them it is the re-creation or an expression of the past in the present. Is there any way in which we could legitimately discriminate between our sense of the tradition and theirs?

Some traditions are more fundamental to a culture than others: we may call them postulates.[2] Take a simple example: according to Sinhala Buddhist tradition there are, we noted earlier, four guardian deities of the realm who are also protectors of the teaching. This is a postulate underlying the tradition. Yet we noted in Chapter 1 that the actual guardian

[1] Eric Hobsbawm and Terence Ranger, *The Invention of Tradition* (Cambridge: Cambridge University Press, 1983).

[2] We borrow the term "postulate" from E. A. Hoebel, *The Law of Primitive Man* (Cambridge, Mass.: Harvard University Press, 1954), though we do not use the term in the somewhat rigid manner that Hoebel does.

deities (a less fundamental tradition) may vary according to time and place. Take a more complex postulate relevant to this chapter. Basic to both Theravāda doctrine and Sinhala Buddhism is a radical soteriological distinction between monk and layman. Built on this distinction are traditions, such as the one that keeps monks from participating in rites of passage except at death, and even formal rules, such as those that prohibit physical participation in economic production and social reproduction. These postulates and derivates of postulates have had a long run in the history of Sinhala Buddhism.

In this chapter we deal with two innovations in Sinhala Buddhism. One is an extremely important social movement—Sarvōdaya—that attempts to fashion a Buddhist social and economic ethic for modern Sri Lankan society. The other is a more spontaneous attempt to bring in Buddhist ritual and sometimes *sacralia* into that epitome of secular living, the marriage ceremony. Both are new in substance and, more importantly, both violate some basic postulates of Sinhala Buddhism. By contrast in the next chapter we discuss the resurrection of an old tradition—the revival of the nuns' order. Here there is no real violation of basic postulates. Buddhism recognized (reluctantly) that women could indeed achieve salvation (postulate) and consequently the Order of Nuns was a legitimate institution for the religion. It is true that the Order of Nuns had disappeared from the Theravāda tradition since the tenth century, but the postulates underlying the institution had *not* disappeared from the consciousness of Theravāda Buddhists. Theravāda Buddhists know the story of the original founding of the nuns' Order by the Buddha's foster mother; and many are familiar with stories of nuns from both folk traditions and the Sinhala religious literature. Thus the revival of nuns' orders, albeit with changes suitable to modern times, is fundamentally consonant with the postulates of the tradition. If, however, nuns try to combine their otherworldly soteriological goal with spirit possession (as some seem to do), or if the nuns' Order is structured on Catholic lines (as Western Buddhist nuns in Sri Lanka might soon be disposed to do), then the invented traditions have moved away from the basic postulates of the religion. If, furthermore, some of these pseudo-traditions are accepted by their protagonists and by significant numbers of the population, we may well speak of a Buddhism transformed.

A Buddhist Model of Development?

Sarvōdaya is a modern Buddhist movement that aims to foster a model of development consonant with Buddhist doctrine and ethics. It attempts to carve out a specifically Buddhist model of "development" and ipso facto to present a critique of Western capitalist and Marxist models. The movement has attracted considerable international attention and much of its success has depended on enormous sums of money given by foreign donors. The idea of an "indigenous model" of development has great appeal to donors, specially since such development, it is said, occurs within the framework of community participation rather than the notoriously wasteful framework of a government bureaucracy. Much of what has been written on Sarvōdaya is by good-hearted but naive Western intellectuals who see the movement in terms of their own utopian fantasies of a benevolent social order. The exception to this is Detlef Kantowsky's book, *Sarvodaya: The Other Development*, a sympathetic yet critical look at Sarvōdaya.[3] The founder of the movement, A. T. Ariyaratna, also a profuse writer, has recently distilled his experience in a pamphlet entitled *In Search of Development*.[4] In keeping with the educated Protestant Buddhist background of the founder, this work and most of his other writings are in English, which is effectively the language of communication of upper-class urban Buddhists.

That Sarvōdaya is rooted in the Protestant Buddhism of Dharmapāla is explicitly recognized by its founder, who dedicated a pamphlet he wrote in 1963 to Dharmapāla: "To the revered memory of Anagarika Dharmapala, patriot, nationalist and Buddhist revivalist, by one who is inspired by his life teachings. . . . We follow in his footsteps."[5] The footsteps appropriately begin at Nālandā College, a high school founded by Protestant Buddhists on the model of Christian missionary schools. A. T. Ariyaratna, a science teacher there, led a team of Colombo students to work in a depressed low-caste community in a remote area of Sri Lanka in 1958. The experience spiritually transformed Ariyaratna himself as well as his stu-

[3] Detlef Kantowsky, *Sarvodaya: The Other Development* (Delhi: Vikas, 1980).

[4] A. T. Ariyaratna, *In Search of Development* (Moratuwa: Sarvodaya Press, 1981), p. 21.

[5] Kantowsky, *Sarvodaya*, p. 186.

dents. The notion of selfless labor voluntarily given for communal welfare produced the beginnings of Sarvōdaya in Sri Lanka.

Soon Ariyaratna gave the movement cultural and philosophical justification. He formulated his own sentimental and idealized view of Sri Lankan villages, a view not unlike that of nineteenth-century Orientalists like Phear who saw the "Aryan Village" as organized on a "communistic" type model of sharing.[6] One of the theorists of Sarvōdaya, Professor Ratnapala, speaks of the necessity to have "farms cultivated on a communal basis following the pattern found in rural villages."[7] Nowhere in South Asia do villages display such a pattern, but nevertheless it remains a powerful model for Sarvōdaya. It is an attempt to give indigenous validation to communal farming on the communistic model. More important, Ariyaratna attributed to Sri Lankan villages the spirit of selfless giving of one's time and labor for fellow villagers that he saw in the institution of voluntary communal work groups known as *kayiya*. He believed that what he did was to inject new vitality into an old Buddhist custom of selfless communal labor. In reality *kayiya* was neither uniquely Buddhist nor uniquely Sri Lankan. Voluntary work groups like *kayiya* are found in many small-scale peasant societies all over the world. They are by no means selfless but, as Mauss notes for gift exchange, are based on an assumption of return. Social changes, however, are not produced by reformers on the basis of historical or sociological reality per se, but rather on the image they impose on that "reality." Ariyaratna's achievement was to impose his vision of reality on the world and have it accepted as true. His vision of selfless labor was expressed in terms of a powerful religious concept: *śramadāna*, the selfless gift of labor. The term was derived originally from Vinoba Bhave's essentially Gandhian Sarvōdaya movement. Ariyaratna soon translated it into the Buddhist idea of *dāna*, "giving." Ariyaratna is not the only one to use these work groups for communal "development": the Indonesian government has used similar work groups ("Gotong-Royong") for village development programs. But in 1958 *kayiya* had become rare in Sri Lankan villages. The lack of homogeneity in these villages owing to population increase and intervillage migration meant that it was difficult, except sporadically, to muster such communal resources. What Ariyaratna did was not to revive *kayiya* but to introduce into Buddhist Sri

[6] John B. Phear, *The Aryan Village in India and Ceylon* (London: Macmillan, 1880).

[7] Kantowsky, *Sarvodaya*, p. 139.

Lanka a concept of voluntary selfless giving of one's own labor for the uplift of the poor and the needy. It was a profound vision of involvement in the world, expressed in Buddhist terms. It has caught on and been taken up by other groups (including the government) in Sri Lanka. Undoubtedly this is the major and truly significant innovation of Ariyaratna and the high point of Protestant Buddhism—to inculcate in the laity a sense of Buddhist work for the welfare of others by the donation of selfless labor. In our view the rest of the Sarvōdaya program is both naive and unrealistic, with little hope of success once the massive support from aid donors is withdrawn.

Gandhi, who first used the term *sarvōdaya* (which is Sanskrit[8]), translated it "the welfare of all." It is significant that Ariyaratna, without any philological justification, translates *udaya* as "awakening."[9] This "awakening" is not primarily economic, but rather the moral development of the individual *and* the awakening of villages into self-sufficiency and prosperity. Ariyaratna says: "First, within one's own mind or thinking process there are certain defilements one has to recognize and strive to cleanse. Second, one has to recognize that there are unjust and immoral socio-economic chains which keep the vast majority of people enslaved."[10] Thus the goal of Sarvōdaya is personal and social development and economic development related to fundamental wants or needs. It is hoped that these spiritual and social goals can be achieved in a practical this-worldly asceticism of an altruistic rather than acquisitive nature. How are these goals supposed to be achieved in practical action?

1. Central to communal participation is the *śramadāna* ("gift of labor") camps. Through these camps, with their programs of communal activity, Sarvōdaya attempts to awaken in each participant "four principles of personality development" that Sarvōdaya (erroneously) believes lay at the roots of village society. These are the great Buddhist ethical principles of *mettā* ("compassion"), *karuṇā* ("kindness-empathy"), *muditā* ("sympathetic joy"), and *upekkhā* ("equanimity"). Initially the way to achieving these

[8] A compound composed of *sarva*, "all," plus *udaya*, "rising."

[9] Kantowsky, *Sarvodaya*, p. 40. An accurate (if rather unkind) translation of what Ariyaratna means by the title would be "universal uplift."

[10] A. T. Ariyaratna, *Collected Papers*, vol. 1 (Sarvodaya Research Institute, n.d.), p. 47. This recalls Gandhi's concept of the ideal society, Rāmrājya, in which personal morality and social justice are also intertwined. But Gandhi was a radical in action, not a conservative.

states is through eating, singing, and dancing together, which break down hierarchical barriers. Then one gives one's own time, thought, and energy (*śramadāna*) to help those who lack the basic essentials or needs for living. *Śramadāna* activities include repairing and building tanks, irrigation canals, and wells; soil conservation; clearing land for farming; cutting access roads to villages; construction of school buildings and latrines, community centers, and rural housing.

2. Kantowsky states: "Sarvōdaya is not an extension agency that hopes to improve the so-called 'quality of life' in certain rural areas through technical advice and capital aid. All the practical programmes started are only one of several means of achieving the ultimate end, namely the development in each individual of an insight into the true nature of things, thus relieving his suffering."[11] Therefore the ultimate goal of Sarvōdaya is "to awaken man's capacity for a correct understanding of the implications of this Buddhist doctrine of '*anatta*,' of No-soul or No-self; only then will he be able to free himself from the chains of craving (*tanha*), illusion (*moha*), and aggression (*dosha*) which yoke him to the endless cycle of existence and continuity."[12]

One can see why this transformation of Buddhism in a Protestant direction has an appeal to Westerners. The Buddha had a realistic view of human life in society: the achievement of the ultimate Buddhist goals cannot be realized in the world; it requires the arduous path of the homeless monk and systematic meditation. Buddhist ethics are, of course, relevant for living in the world, but these ethics were enshrined in popular stories of the Buddha's past births. The understanding of profound doctrine cannot be achieved by the laity, whose goal must be heaven, not *nirvāṇa*; decent living, not meditation; everyday kindness and generosity, not the noble eightfold path. By contrast, Sarvōdaya attempts to achieve the great goals of Buddhism by living in the world and participating in this-worldly activity. The doctrine which was "difficult to comprehend" and "against the current" for the Buddha is realized by Sarvōdaya through its work. It is not an accident that the most recent writings of Ariyaratna, referred to above, read like a Buddhist version of Moral Rearmament. At other times his language has unfortunately been tainted with a shallow social scientism, perhaps influenced by his acquaintance with members of that (social

[11] Kantowsky, *Sarvodaya*, p. 68.

[12] Ibid., p. 73.

science) species: "Gramodaya or village awakening go through several identifiable phases one after the other and some together with others. Very broadly these stages are (i) a psychological infra-structural stage where the members of the community start thinking together; (ii) a social infra-structural stage where they start getting organized together; (iii) a physical infra-structural stage where they start building on their own effort the material foundation for their new life; and (iv) a technological infra-structural stage where they upgrade their technological know-how without endangering their psychosocial and economic balance. All these stages have to be passed through within a strong spiritual and cultural framework."[13]

In order fully to understand the Sarvōdaya movement, one must examine the social composition of its governing body. It will be clear that much of the ideology of Sarvōdaya is neither peasant nor, for that matter, based on Buddhist doctrine per se but on the class interests and ideological views of the Sinhala Buddhist bourgeoisie, influenced by the reform of Anagārika Dharmapāla. The governing board of Sarvōdaya is the Sangamaya, well described by Kantowsky. In 1978 the Sangamaya had 358 members, seventy-three percent of them from the four southwestern coastal districts of Colombo, Kalutara, Galle, and Matara. "This is precisely the area that produced practically all the Sinhalese who were active in the early stages of the Buddhist resurgence and the Sinhalese nationalist movement. Two hundred and five members of the Sangamaya come from the Colombo district alone."[14] All are educated, with a secondary school certificate (forty-six percent) or a higher education certificate (forty-five percent), except for thirty-two who are on the board as employees of the Sarvōdaya movement! Twenty-four percent of the Sangamaya are educationists—professors, principals, lecturers, and teachers. "Generally one can say that most of the members of the Sangamaya represent the urban upper middle class, except for those who are employed as full-time Sarvōdaya workers within the Movement."[15] Unfortunately Kantowsky has not given us the caste background of the Sangamaya, but he has shown conclusively that the body that makes policy decisions for implementation in rural areas comes from an urban-educated bourgeoisie whose social morality and ethics are Protestant Buddhist. In the previous chapter we stated that Protestant Bud-

[13] Ariyaratna, *In Search of*, p. 6.

[14] Kantowsky, *Sarvodaya*, p. 187.

[15] Ibid.

dhism provided an ethic for what Sri Lankan society earlier lacked—an urban bourgeoisie. Sarvōdaya is one vehicle for communicating these values, originally confined to an educated elite, to villages and thereby helping to bring village culture in line with the bourgeois ethos of Sri Lankan society and to effect the dominance of the latter over the former. It is to these deeper implications of Sarvōdaya that we must now turn.

If the governing body of Sarvōdaya consists of an educated urban bourgeoisie, not so those who work in the field for Sarvōdaya. These actual agents of development are much less educated and generally poor. They have bourgeois values but do not come from the upper ranks; they communicate Sarvōdaya values to the villagers. Thus we have here one of the paradoxes of Sarvōdaya, a paradox that was apparent in Dharmapāla's own reform. This is that Sarvōdaya advocates a simple happy life for villagers, a life in conformity with the ten basic needs: a clear and beautiful environment, a clear and adequate supply of water, a minimum of clothing requirements, a balanced diet, basic health care, a modest house to live in, energy requirements, basic communication facilities, total education, spiritual and cultural requirements. However, it is doubtful whether any Sarvōdaya leader has lived and participated in village life for long. This is the basic difference between Sri Lankan and Indian Sarvōdaya. The Gandhian ideal was a way of life for all; by contrast Dharmapāla travelled first-class and always addressed social inferiors by derogatory pronouns, putting them in their place. Sarvōdaya believes in the importance of "insight"; this insight is entirely "spiritual," lacking a self-critical historical and social awareness. Its Buddhist intellectuals may justify this stance and say that historical and social knowledge is "knowing accordingly" whereas true insight is "deep knowing." But one would think that it is important to know the former before one can reach the latter!

Against this background let us examine the founder's (Ariyaratna's) social message as formulated in his recent pamphlet. It is a social morality for Sinhala Buddhists, no doubt meant to supersede or supplement the one formulated by Dharmapāla many years ago. Dharmapāla, however, had no illusions that this moral code was canonically sanctioned; by contrast Ariyaratna says that "in the social philosophy of Buddhism the duties of each person of the community towards others are described in great detail."[16] He then formulates several series of rules (mostly borrowed from Buddhist

[16] Ariyaratna, *In Search of*, p. 20.

texts) on a variety of topics: duties of parents to children and vice versa; of husband to wife and vice versa; duties to a friend and reciprocal duties; duties of an employer to employees and vice versa; and duties of laymen towards monks and vice versa. This is followed by thirty-eight rules for virtuous living. Much of the latter is not uniquely Buddhist but cites moral norms similar to those of other human societies.

However, some of Ariyaratna's rules reflect the class values of the Buddhist bourgeoisie. Consider the duties of a wife toward a husband. The first rule states, "To consider one's husband as a god and do herself everything to look after him with affection."[17] This is not a Buddhist idea but a Brahmanic ideal that Ariyaratna has resurrected as a norm for Buddhists. Nowhere has it been part of Sinhala peasant life; indeed, it has been ridiculed in folk literature. Even Dharmapāla firmly believed that Buddhism, unlike Brahmanism, was a liberating force for women; and he pointed out that in India, as contrasted with Sri Lanka, women were treated as slaves.[18] Nevertheless the introduction of this Brahmanic ideal fits in with the "puritan" sexual orientation of Protestant Buddhism—to effect domination over women and satisfy the narcissism of Sinhala males. Moreover, the wife is properly tied to her middle-class domesticity: her job is "to keep the house clean, look after food, clothing; household matters, children, relatives, and neighbours."[19] All this is fine, except that the urban Buddhist bourgeoisie are meanwhile educating their own daughters to be lawyers, doctors, and engineers and pushing them to win scholarships to receive an education abroad.

The attitudes prescribed for employees are again a good example of urban Buddhist values:

(1) To wake up before the employer and start work.
(2) To go to rest after the employer.
(3) Not to take anything with a stealthy mind besides what has been justly given by way of food and salaries by the employer.
(4) To do one's assigned duties to the best of one's ability.
(5) Always speak good of the employer and never speak evil.[20]

[17] Ibid., p. 21.

[18] Dharmapāla, *Return to Righteousness*, p. 77n.

[19] Ariyaratna, *In Search of*, p. 21.

[20] Most of the contents of Ariyaratna's ethics have been borrowed from the classic *Sigālovāda Sutta*. Yet the Buddha's own injunctions on wifely duty have not the slightest sex-

This ethic, especially rules 1–3, is irrelevant for most Sri Lankans—particularly the bourgeoisie—who are in the professions or in business. Clearly the model of the employee here is that of the domestic servant living in the employer's house and receiving food and salary—itself an institution created, for the most part, as a result of the rise of the bourgeoisie and the increase in the rural poor seeking domestic employment. In Sri Lanka most household servants are de facto slaves who have no fixed hours of work, no entitlement to leave, no room of their own, sleep on the floor, and are miserably paid. Many urban householders even employ children as servants. But nowhere is this social reality recognized in Ariyaratna's discourse. The notion that social and moral criticism must begin at home—in his own social class—and that such criticism must be more than platitudinous to be effective is rarely found in Ariyaratna, though this was not the case with Dharmapāla. Ariyaratna by contrast with Dharmapāla is not willing to rock the boat. He uses it to sail to another shore—the ideal Sinhala village.

Sarvōdaya's vision of village society and the past of Sri Lankan civilization is a projection of the bourgeoisie, a fantasy that has no social reality. "The mental culture found in Buddhist doctrine and practices is a unique quality that can be utilized in bringing about an economically and politically exploitation-free society. In fact such a society existed during the Anuradhapura and Polonnaruva periods in Sri Lanka."[21] This Ariyaratna probably believes; Dharmapāla also had a vision of the past, one in which the Sinhalas had built a monumental civilization (in its literal sense) and trounced the aliens, especially the Tamils. Ariyaratna's is not a true his-

ism: "In these five ways does the wife, ministered to by her husband as the western quarter, love him:—her duties are well performed, by hospitality to the kin of both, by faithfulness, by watching over the goods he brings, and by skill and industry in discharging all her business" (T. W. and C.A.F. Rhys Davids, *Dialogues of the Buddha*, Sacred Books of the Buddhists Series, pt. 3 [London: Oxford University Press, 1921], p. 182). Ariyaratna's views on the duties of employers and servants directly reflect the ethics of the *Sigālovāda Sutta*: "In five ways does an Ariyan master minister to his servants and employees as the nadir:—by assigning them work according to their strength; by supplying them with food and wages; by tending them in sickness; by sharing with them unusual delicacies; by granting leave at times. In these ways ministered to by their master, servants and employees love their master in five ways:—they rise before him, they lie down to rest after him; they are content with what is given them; they do their work well; and they carry about his praise and good fame" (Ibid., pp. 182–83).

[21] Ariyaratna, *In Search of*, p. 20.

torical consciousness; anyone familiar with history would know that you cannot compress 1,500 years (the Anurādhapura and Polonnaruva periods) into a single reality. The recent scholarly literature on that past, especially the literature on monastic landlordism, bears no resemblance to Ariyaratna's vision.[22] So is it with his model of the Sinhala village given to communal sharing, embodying Buddhist doctrinal values and familiar with the Dhamma, and so forth. Ariyaratna quotes several stanzas in Pāli and says: "These are stanzas known by every man, woman and child in a Buddhist village. They are the part of their tradition and daily mental culture."[23] The popularization of these stanzas in Sri Lanka is, for the most part, a product of very recent times, mainly due to the compulsory teaching of Buddhism in schools. They were not the vehicle by which Buddhist ethics were traditionally conveyed at the popular level. Ariyaratna's disembodied village has little recognition of social conflict, of the vice and folly that constitute part of our humanity and were clearly recognized by the great religious teachers of history, including the Buddha.

Having constructed his fantasy of the past, Ariyaratna goes on to state that *śramadāna* itself was found in its identical form in ancient Sri Lanka. "This form of sharing of labour was called 'Samudan' (i.e., *śramadāna*) by the ancient Sinhala. 'Samu' means a collection of people and 'Dana' means sharing."[24] This is Ariyaratna's invention; no such institution existed in the past and "samudan" is his own neologism. Here is an example of "symbolic traditionalization"; Milton Singer shows that in India innovative practices must be seen as traditional to be accepted by the people.[25] Ariyaratna proceeds to invent the past and give it symbolic validation. "Our ancients called it the Dhanyagara-Dharmadweepa ideal—the ideal of a land of economic prosperity and social righteousness."[26] Not only was ancient Sri Lankan society a bountiful place but it was characterized, Ariyaratna says, by political and social equality. " 'Samanthamatha' or equality was the fourth principle. Knee-deep in the mud in the paddy field the king and the commoner worked. There was not discrimination due to caste

[22] R.A.L.H. Gunawardana, *Robe and Plough: Monasticism and Economic Interest in Early Medieval Sri Lanka* (Tucson: University of Arizona Press, 1979).

[23] Ariyaratna, *In Search of*, p. 10.

[24] A. T. Ariyaratna, *Collected Papers*, vol. 2 (Sarvodaya Research Institute, 1980), p. 52.

[25] Milton Singer, *When a Great Tradition Modernizes* (New York: Praeger, 1972); see specially the discussion on "traditionalization," pp. 383–414.

[26] Ariyaratna, *Collected Papers*, vol. 2, p. 29.

at that time. . . . Every man, king or commoner, was considered equal before the law."[27] This is almost millennial in its vision, but projected into the past. Ariyaratna proceeds to elaborate his romantic view of the village. For example: "The language our people used in their day-to-day life among members of the family, villagers, the clergy, the elders, and children were so varied and pleasant that everyone's worth and dignity were well recognized."[28] One must conclude that Ariyaratna cannot have lived in a traditional village for any length of time. Indeed, ordinary spoken Sinhala had no polite form of a second-person pronoun until very recent times! "Even animals were addressed with pet names like 'son' and never in derogatory terms."[29] One wonders where this kind of information comes from! Ariyaratna seems to be totally unaware of such things as the privileged obscenity and abuse that characterize Sinhala village life and make it very different from the sterilized vision of a Protestant Buddhist.

The Monk and This-Worldly Asceticism

Kantowsky states: "Strong missionary influences during the eighteenth and nineteenth centuries have led to a Buddhist Renaissance in Sinhalese society that is manifesting itself today in a peculiar form of 'Buddhist Protestantism' among the middle classes of Sri Lanka, from which the hard core of the Sarvodaya propagators stem. Their movement does not promote the Anagārika ideal of the homeless monk and the seeker of truth, but tries to bring the Bhikkhu out of his ritual and scholastic isolation and back into society."[30] This is a radical and serious step that reminds one of the government-sponsored programs for Thai monks.[31] Dharmapāla clearly recognized that the monk's role was not suitable for such activity. He was a traditionalist in this regard, more like Luther than Calvin. Few realize that when Anagārika Dharmapāla became a monk late in life as Venerable Dēvamitta Dharmapāla, he also moved away from worldly involvement, as he felt befitted a monk.

[27] Ariyaratna, *Collected Papers*, vol. 1, p. 53.

[28] Ibid.

[29] Ibid.

[30] Kantowsky, *Sarvodaya*, p. 73.

[31] See Niels Mulder, *Monks, Merit, and Motivation*, Northern Illinois University: Center for Southeast Asian Studies, reprint no. 1, 1969; and Steven Piker, "Buddhism and Modernization in Contemporary Thailand," *Contributions to Asian Studies* 4 (1973): 51–67.

Sarvōdaya takes the opposite view: the monk must promote social and economic welfare. It is believed (as with the Thai program) that the monk's charisma and influence can be utilized for altruistic worldly activity. Thus Sarvōdaya co-opted the services of one of Sri Lanka's most erudite and influential monks, Venerable Henpiṭigedera Ñāṇasīha, the founder of the Pātakaḍa Bhikkhu Educational Institute for monks. This institute was converted into the Sarvōdaya Training Institute to produce a new generation of monks who would, said the Venerable Ñāṇasīha, involve themselves not only "in the emancipation of the individual but also the material development of the community as well."[32]

The spacious institute, financed with German development aid, "with comfortable boarding and lodging facilities" (in typical German but singularly un-Buddhist manner) was not much of a success. There was a gradual decline in members, and recruitment problems were serious. The leaders of Sarvōdaya have given various reasons for this but it is likely that the following were the significant ones:

(1) Some modern monks view the monkhood as a temporary state in which to obtain an education and later move into lay life. Sarvōdaya is not for them.
(2) Others may simply not be temperamentally suited to a life of this-worldly activity. Their motivation for joining the Order may be precisely to avoid such activity and to follow the classical ideal of the recluse.
(3) Some are probably aware of the public disapproval of worldly involvement by monks, even when such involvement is for the laudable goals of Sarvōdaya.

But failure has not daunted Sarvōdaya. Ariyaratna has decided to establish three more feeder institutions to train younger Buddhist monks. Joanna Macy, an ardent Sarvōdaya advocate from the United States, states that there are many monks (not trained at the institute) involved in grass roots development work.[33] It is difficult to figure from Macy's account whether in most cases the monk is a symbolic presence or actively participates in development work, including manual labor, which is forbidden by the rules of the Order. Some certainly do participate in forbidden activ-

[32] Kantowsky, *Sarvodaya*, p. 125.

[33] Joanna Macy, "Dharma and Development: Religion as a Resource in the Sarvodaya Self-Help Movement in Sri Lanka," mimeographed, 1981.

ities: "Monks at Shramadana have been known, not only to help roll boulders and pass buckets of dirt, but also swing the mamoty shovel in cutting a road. . . . This departure from tradition is more acceptable now than in the recent past."[34] This is not only a departure from Sri Lanka's past but also a violation of Theravāda monastic rules. Unhappily Macy has not obtained villagers' opinions about it, though public criticism is certainly there. "Some Sarvōdaya monks reflect ruefully on the relative lack of esteem accorded to socially active monks."[35] One monk told Macy: "At first there was criticism in the village. Some people didn't like it, the way I was walking around with the children and young people I got to help me."[36]

Macy thinks that these attitudes will change and the role of the monk will not be modelled on the Buddha and the *arhat*s but on the Mahāyāna tradition of the compassionate Bodhisattva who postpones his salvation for the welfare (in this case spiritual and material) of the people. We are skeptical about this, but we are not concerned here with predicting the future. (We postpone our own modest prophecies to the concluding chapter.) We can at least assume that changes in the role of the monk to approximate to the Bodhisattva ideal must lead to consequences unanticipated by those who advocate these changes.

The problem is a deep one: the notion that the monk could help to change the material conditions of society appeals to Western notions of worldly activity as it does at least to Sarvōdaya, if not to all lay Buddhists. It may also appeal to some monks and may motivate them to take part in development activity. But Sarvōdaya is wrong to claim that this has been the traditional role of the monk: the monk's aloofness is intrinsic to his charisma and the public perception of his role. Indeed the more aloof he is from worldly affairs, the greater his charisma; witness the enormous respect given to monks who live in remote hermitages. This view of monks, traditional among Sinhala Buddhists and Theravāda Buddhists in Southeast Asia, is based on the *arhat* ideal of the scriptures. It is very different from the Bodhisattva ideal of Mahāyāna.

The power of the old ideal has been recently discussed by Niels Mulder and Steven Piker in their criticism of the Thai government programs.[37] These criticisms ultimately amount to the view that to get the monks

[34] Ibid., p. 66.

[35] Ibid., p. 70.

[36] Ibid., p. 60.

[37] See n. 31 above.

involved in the world of material activity is to destroy the Theravāda order, because the strength of the monk's role lies in the fact that it is the opposite of the lay role. He is an image of detachment from worldly ties, from human social conflict, from crosscutting kin bonds that enmesh every one of us in our social existence. This was clearly recognized by the Buddha himself (long before Durkheim!) as the social function of the ascetic (*arhat*) role: the *arhat* by being aloof, by being homeless and detached, by living a simple life must be a model for the world-involved laity.[38] This does not mean that village monks, for example, took no part in lay affairs. Monks were counsellors; but the laity consulted them in their monasteries, not the other way around. Thus the question is not whether the monk can partake in the affairs of the world but *how*. The monk arriving in a Sarvōdaya camp and uttering a sermon of exhortation poses no problem, so long as he maintains his aloofness and goes back to his monastery. But if he gets involved in social and economic activity, which he is supposed to have renounced, he ceases to mirror our ideals.

The upshot of our remarks is that there is for the monk a real problem—how to maintain aloofness and detachment amid the ebb and flow of human activity. His posture of detachment might not be compromised by certain kinds of worldly activity in closed social arenas, away from everyday life. He might well be effective in hospitals, visiting sick wards and consoling the distressed, or in orphanages, homes for destitute people, asylums for the mentally ill or the lepers. It is indeed surprising that monks have not been encouraged to undertake such work. Maybe this is because movements like Sarvōdaya, contrary to accepted views, have not been sensitive enough to human pain and suffering.

Buddhist Marriage

One of the commonest features of the embourgeoisement of non-Western countries has been their adoption of Victorian sexual mores—an ideal of strict monogamy and the general repression of overt sexuality. In Sri Lanka this probably went further than in most countries. Dharmapāla made few direct pronouncements on sexuality, perhaps because he felt that it would be unseemly for him to do so. But his own puritanism comes out clearly in his pronouncements against women exposing the midriff and his urging

[38] See Obeyesekere, "Theodicy," esp. pp. 37–39.

schoolgirls to reject the skirt (that exposes the legs) in favor of the more decorous Kandyan "half sāri." Dharmapāla was also aware that some of these practices (exposing the midriff) were old peasant customs, but he foisted the blame on the influence of Kerala. It should be remembered that even in Dharmapāla's time it was perfectly acceptable for Sinhala peasant women not to cover their breasts, particularly in their own villages.

Missionary influence on sexual mores was especially strong. It was inculcated in all the mission schools and later adopted in toto by the Buddhist ones, which adhered to the model of the mission schools in everything from cricket to the curriculum. Sexual mores were, at least indirectly, enforced by new laws concerning marriage. Plural marriages (both polygyny and polyandry), which were accepted in Sinhala villages (and in Buddhist texts), were outlawed, and divorce, which was traditionally very flexible, was rendered extremely difficult. The embourgeoisement of Sinhala society came from a variety of sources, but it was Dharmapāla's reform that gave Buddhist legitimation to these new values and permitted later generations of the Sinhala Buddhist elite to introject them as quintessential Buddhist ethics.

In traditional Sinhala Buddhist society marriage was not a sacrament, and often divorce was by mutual consent. Much of this changed with the advent of British rule. The British, under a mistaken assumption that the Dutch had implemented Roman-Dutch law, enforced the rigid Roman-Dutch law of marriage in the courts. But this fact is not sufficient to explain why people *accepted* the new laws. Roman-Dutch law, with its tight divorce rules and the rigid sexual mores implicit in them, fitted the values of the new bourgeoisie. However, one thing was lacking: the Christian marriage was sacramental in character, with a minister performing the rites in church, whereas the Sinhala Buddhist was not. Thus the Sinhala marriage ceremony had to be "sacramentalized" in order to bring it closer to the Christian ideal and to make it more "respectable."

To understand the changes in the marriage ceremony we must know what happened traditionally.[39] We shall illustrate traditional marriage by

[39] We have not come across any descriptions of the marriage ceremony in Sinhala before modern times. This is not surprising since marriage ceremonies were simple and nonsacramental. However, a Sinhala rendering of a Sanskrit text (via Tamil) known as *Hariscandra Katāva* (The Story of Hariscandra), attributed to 1706 by W. A. de Silva, describes the wedding of Princess Candravatī.

> A great heap of renowned manifold gems was made
> When the king stood there with the lovely queen

giving the views of three British observers: the first by Robert Knox from the mid-seventeenth century and two other accounts from the early nineteenth century.

> But enough of the *Ribaldry*, let us turn away to more honest Practices. To speak of their Marriages, which make the Bed lawful. There are not many Ceremonies used in or about the same. Here is no wooing for a Wife. The Parents commonly make the Match, and in their choice regard more the Quality and Descent than the Beauty. If they are agreed, all is done. The Match being thus made, the man carrieth or sends to the Woman her Wedding Cloths; which is a Cloth containing six or seven yards in length, and a Linnen Wastcoat wrought with Blew and Red. If the man be so poor that he cannot buy a Cloth, it is the Custom to borrow one. In case the Man with his Friends goes and carries it himself, that Night they both sleep together to beget acquaintance one with the other. And then they appoint a day when he is to come and fetch her home; which is the *Marriage-Day*.
>
> The day being come, he attended with his Friends goes to her house, which is always in the Evening, and brings Provisions and Sweet-meats with him according to his Ability, towards the Charges of the *Wedding*. Which is never more than two Meals. Whereof *Supper* is the first. Then the *Bride* and *Bridegroom* both eat together in one Dish, which is to intimate that they are both of one rank and quality, and sometimes they tye their Thumbs together, but not always: and that Night go to sleep together.
>
> The next day having dined he taketh his *Bride*, and departeth home with her, putting her before him, and he following her, with some of her Friends to Conduct her. For it is the constant Custom and Fashion in this Land for the Husband to follow his Wife. The reason whereof is a Tradition among them, that a man once going

---

> An uncle [mother's brother], according to ancient rites, with a golden thread
> Joined the two lovely little fingers of their hands and tied them.
>
> Then with a golden pitcher was poured the water on the joined hands,
> The two walked in harmony thrice round,
> The golden chain was tied round the neck of the handsome queen.
> In this manner she was married to the world-renowned king.

See W. A. de Silva, "The Popular Poetry of the Sinhalese," *Journal of the Royal Asiatic Society, Ceylon Branch* 24, no. 68, pt. 1 (1917): 51.

foremost, it happened that his Wife was stoln away, and he not aware of it. Being come home the *Bridegroom* makes a Feast as he is able.

Some few days after, her Friends usually come to see her bringing a present of Provision with them. And sometimes they use this Ceremony, the Man is to stand with one end of the Woman's Cloth about his Loins, and she with the other, and then they pour water on both their Heads, wetting all their Bodies: which being done, they are firmly Married to live together, so long as they can agree.

The Elder sorts of People usually woe and conclude their Marriages as they are in Bed together. For when they have lost their Maidenheads, they fear not much what man comes to sleep with them, provided he be of as good quality as they, having nothing more to lose. And at the day appointed the man gives the Woman her Cloths, and so takes her home.

But their Marriages are but of little force or validity. For if they disagree and mislike one the other; they part without disgrace. Yet it stands firmer for the Man than for the Woman; howbeit they do leave one the other at their pleasure. They do give according to their Ability a *Portion* of Cattle, Slaves and Money with their Daughters; but if they chance to mislike one another and part asunder, this Portion must be returned again, and then she is fit for another Man, being as they account never the worse for wearing.

Both Women and Men do commonly wed four or five times before they can settle themselves to their contentation. And if they have Children when they part, the Common Law is, the Males for the Man, and the Females for the Woman. But many of the Women are free from this controversie, being *Childless*.[40]

The second account is from the papers of Alexander Johnston, chief justice of Sri Lanka from 1811 to 1819.[41]

Ceremony of Marriage as Practised in Ceylon

The manner of marrying, according to the Cingalese custom, is, when a bridegroom comes, together with his relations, to the house of the bride's parents, for the purpose of marrying, there shall be spread a white cloth upon a plank called Magoolporoewe, and upon that white cloth there shall be scattered a small quantity of fresh rice,

[40] Knox, *Historical Relation*, pp. 93–94.

[41] In Elwood Upham, *Budhist Tracts*, pp. 323–24.

> whereupon the bridegroom and the bride shall be put or carried upon the said plank by the uncle of the bride, who shall be on her mother's side—if there are none, by any other nearest relation—and afterwards there shall be delivered by the bridegroom to the bride a gold chain, a cloth, and a woman's jacket, besides which there shall be changed two rings between them; at the same time, the bridegroom gives a white catchy cloth to the mother of the bride, according to his capacity; after which ceremony, and while the bridegroom on the right and the bride on the left are standing upon the said plank, by the uncle of the bride, or by any of her nearest relations, as above stated, shall be tied the two thumbs, one of the bride and one of the bridegroom, by a thread, and under the knot of the said thumbs there shall be holden a plate, and some milk or water poured upon the said knot, and then shall the bride be delivered to the bridegroom. In some places, the two little fingers of the bride and bridegroom are tied, and the said ceremony performed; and, in some places, a chain shall be put by the bridegroom on the bride's neck, a cloth be dressed, and then rings be changed. In some places the marriage is performed without these last-mentioned ceremonies.

John Davy's account from the same period (published 1821) mentions the importance of parental decision, the age of marriage for males (eighteen to twenty years), caste endogamy, and the various formalities, including dowry (household goods and cattle), to be agreed upon by the two kin groups. He also mentions that the bridegroom and his family, carrying a load of provisions, jewelry and ornaments, and a white cloth go in procession to the bride's residence. There a festive hall has been constructed to entertain the guests.

> In the middle of the mandoo [festive hall], which is covered with mats, the men of both parties seat themselves round a large pile of rice, placed on fresh plantain leaves, and garnished with curries of different kinds; the ladies do the same, collected within the house. Both parties help themselves with their hands, and eat from the common pile. This mode of eating, peculiar to the marriage-feast, is esteemed proof of good fellowship; and, should any one hesitate to partake, he would be considered an enemy, and be driven away. After the repast the bridegroom enters the house, meets the bride attended by her friends; they exchange balls made of rice and cocoa-nut milk;

> and he presents her with the piece of white cloth and with the jewels and ornaments he has brought. All this having been transacted in silence, she retires, and he returns to the mandoo. The night is passed by the company in telling stories and in conversation; the next morning the bride, led by the bridegroom and accompanied by all their friends, is conducted to his father's house, where the ceremony is concluded with another feast similar to the preceding.[42]

These are ordinary marriages. But there is an addition in high-status marriages—a *pōruva* ceremony, as in Johnston's description. D'Oyly describes an even more elaborate ceremony of marriage among aristocratic families in the Kandyan Kingdom in the late eighteenth or early nineteenth century. We refer the reader to his lengthy account.[43] Contrasted to these high-status marriages and the marriages of ordinary folk are those of the very poor and perhaps low-caste people. "Amongst the people of the lowest rank," says Davy, "little attention is paid to the marriage ceremony."[44] It is likely that the marriages that Knox described were among such people.

All these accounts strike us as reasonably accurate; they are for the most part confirmed by our own fieldwork in the late fifties and sixties in remote Sinhala villages. Let us isolate five features of central importance.

1. Knox lived among ordinary Kandyan peasants and he describes their customs. His account does not mention the *pōruva*. This might be an oversight, but more likely the amount of ceremony varied with social status, and poorer people, such as those in Knox's village, had little of it. By all accounts only the first marriage has ceremony; later marriages have little or none.

2. The marriage ceremonies have no religious significance. There is no religious officiant; no texts are recited. Weddings are perceived as matters of this world, not as sacraments. The emphasis of the ceremonies is on the obligation of husband and wife to support each other and the unification by the marriage of two kin groups. The husband's obligations are expressed in the gifts of apparel he gives the bride; he sometimes drapes a cloth around his wife's waist. An important custom is for the groom to tie

[42] Davy, *An Account of the Interior*, pp. 213–14.

[43] Sir John D'Oyly, *A Sketch of the Kandyan Kingdom* (Colombo: Government Printer, 1929), pp. 82–83.

[44] Davy, *An Account of the Interior*, p. 214.

a necklace around the bride's neck. In Kandyan areas *māla bäňdīma* ("necklace tying") or *kara bäňdīma* ("shoulder tying") is a term for marriage.[45] Marriage is also referred to simply as *bäňdīma* ("tying"); this refers to the union of the bride and groom symbolized in the tying of the necklace or the tying together of their little fingers or thumbs by the mother's brother.

As in most societies outside the modern West, marriage brings two kin groups together. In Sri Lanka, as elsewhere, this is expressed by their eating together at a wedding feast, known in Sinhala as *magul kǟma*. The Western accounts have missed its full sociological and symbolic significance, but let us describe briefly an example from Laggala in the late fifties. At the *magul kǟma* relations (generally male) of the two groups sit at the same table. A representative of the bride's party known as *däna muttā* ("master of ceremonies") picks up a banana and later an oil cake (*kävun*) (both phallic symbols), takes a bite from each, and passes them around the table. All the relations eat of the same fruit and *kävun*, thus symbolizing their new unity as a single group of kinsmen brought together by the marriage of the young couple. Only after this ceremony do the guests eat their individual meals from a common table.

3. One element in the ritual of marriage that is common to all the accounts and to contemporary practice is the white cloth given by the bridegroom's kin to the bride's mother. A similar cloth is given at the funeral by the deceased's family to Buddhist monks. The symbolic significance of the custom is similar in the two cases. At the funeral the white cloth symbolically absorbs the impurity of the corpse; it then can be worn by monks, who, like the washerman, are immune to the effects of pollution. Similarly the white cloth worn by the bride on the night of the wedding recognizes the polluting nature of intercourse, especially from the rupture of the hymen; the cloth absorbs the pollution, in this case literally as well as figuratively. In some areas a ritual bathing of the couple ends the pollution. The polluted clothes are generally given to a woman of the washer caste. This caste, as Hocart pointed out, has a priestly role to play on these occasions.[46]

In the Low Country areas of Sri Lanka the cloth is used nowadays for a ritual virginity test. The washerwoman confirms (we know no cases of

[45] This custom was probably influenced by the South Indian Hindu rite of the *tāli*. It is likely that it received a boost when the Nayakkar dynasty ascended the Kandyan throne.

[46] A. M. Hocart, *Caste: A Comparative Study* (London: Methuen, 1950).

disconfirmation) publicly that the bride is a virgin. The Kandyan areas do not have such a virginity test, and we know of no source mentioning it anywhere in Sinhala society before modern times.

4. All the accounts confirm our ethnographic evidence from the late 1950s, namely, that the *pōruva* ceremony now integral to contemporary weddings was optional. It indicated a more formal union; though the custom was widespread, it was essential in high-status marriages only. Traditionally the *pōruva* was simply a flat board covered with a white cloth over which rice was sometimes sprinkled. At a propitious time the bride's "mother's brother" gives her away. The *pōruva* has strong fertility associations: Leach points out that outside the marriage context the *pōruva* is the flat board used for smoothing the muddied paddy field preparatory to the sowing of the seed.[47] It is converted into a marriage *pōruva* by the white cloth covering it. The symbolic connection between the two *pōruva*s would be apparent to any traditional villager. In addition, in some areas the *pōruva* plank is made of jak, a "milk-oozing" tree. The role of the mother's brother who ties the fingers of the bride and groom at the *pōruva* (symbolizing their union or *bäñdīma*) must be seen in the context of bilateral cross-cousin marriage, a phenomenon of long duration in Sinhala culture. In cross-cousin marriage the following equivalences hold: a woman marries a mother's brother's son or father's sister's son and these two could be the same person. Since the terminological system seems to assume a brother and sister exchange in the previous generation, a woman's maternal uncle is in fact her husband's father (or his brother). Hence *māmā* is both "mother's brother" and "husband's father" and consequently the ideal person to unite the couple. However, this ideal is rarely practiced since, even traditionally, many people marry a classificatory rather than an actual cross cousin.

5. If cross-cousin marriage was ignored in favor of marriage with an outsider (a strategic marriage), then by local custom the permission of the eligible cross cousin was required. The simplest ritualized expression of this is known as *kaḍulu tahanci* (from *tahanama*, "prohibition"): the bride and groom are prohibited from leaving the house by her eligible cross cousin, who blocks the exit, the stile or *kaḍulla*. The rituals can be highly elaborate in some areas, but the basic idea is the same: the bride and groom

[47] E. R. Leach, *Social Anthropology* (London: Fontana; New York: Oxford University Press, 1982), pp. 196–97.

have to ask permission from the bride's cross cousin by giving him a sheaf of betel leaves and worshipping him. Then the cross cousin lifts the prohibition and moves away from the stile.

The model sketched above can be elaborated or emended in a variety of ways. The custom of taking permission from the cross cousin was perhaps not universal in Sri Lanka and is now rare even in the Kandyan areas where it was once standard. Cross-cousin marriage itself is now very rare in the middle class and is fast disappearing even in rural areas. The terms for cross cousin have been replaced, both as address and as reference, by the terms for siblings. The *magul kǟma*, "eating the wedding food," was an ubiquitous custom but it too is obsolescent, though the wedding feast itself has become more important than ever and, in high-status marriages, is linked to complicated "gastro-politics," to use Appadurai's term.[48] The *pōruva* and its associated rites have become more important and highly elaborated everywhere in Sri Lanka. It is likely that even traditionally the *pōruva* was decorated with *gok* leaves and banana bark in high-status marriages, but not to the elaborate degree now seen in urban upper-class weddings. Nowadays it is decorated to resemble a "throne." The old term *pōruva* is used but its original fertility significance has been forgotten. English speakers, as well as advertisements in English, speak of the *pōruva* as the "wedding throne," which is how it is perceived by most people. The royal symbolism has received reinforcement from aristocratic Kandyan marriages in which the groom wears the traditional aristocratic garb and the bride is decked in the richest jewelry. When such couples stand on the *pōruva* it in fact appears to be a consecration of royalty. Moreover, in upper-class weddings there are festival drumming, dancing, and music to reinforce the imagery of the *pōruva* as a "throne."

These changes in the basic symbolic elements of the wedding are not surprising, and even the royal symbolism of the *pōruva* is not a radical change. Thus far marriage remains a secular contract, not a sacrament. In some Sinhala weddings, especially in the Western and Southern Provinces, Sinhala Buddhist brides used to wear a "veil." This was however only partly influenced by the Christian custom; the Christian habit was readily accepted, we think, because for Sri Lankans the ideal female was the God-

[48] Arjun Appadurai, "Gastro-politics in South India," *American Ethnologist* 5, no. 3 (1981): 494–511.

dess Pattinī, who wore a "veil."[49] But even this initial (and temporary) Christian influence did not produce a radical change. That change occurred when marriages came to be viewed as sacramental and consequently sanctified by Buddhist ritual.

In Sinhala tradition the color white has a peculiar ambiguity. It signifies purity; but precisely for this reason white cloths are used on polluting occasions: childbirth, puberty, marriage, and death. On such occasions white is a marker to indicate an event associated with pollution; hence white cloths cover the furniture during weddings and funerals. Thus the white cloth placed over the *pōruva* plank covers the possible impurities of the mundane object and marks the plank as a wedding *pōruva* and not the *pōruva* used for ploughing. The white cloth given to the bride has similar significance, we noted, and is in fact called *kili kaḍa hälla* ("white pollution cloth"). Besides purity, white is the color of chastity, sterility, and mourning. It is especially associated with death. The white flags that are put up at a house where someone has died and line the funeral route suggest the impurity of the corpse that has to be contained, but by association also allude to mourning. Widows and some widowers wear white. So do those who have taken a vow of chastity as part of the eight or ten precepts. To wear white clothes, therefore, denotes renunciation of sex—as we saw above in the context of the Anagārika role. In traditional weddings white is not used for wear; on the contrary, the bride and groom wear brightly colored clothes precisely to oppose the symbolism of whiteness. Yet nowadays the Christian custom that the bride wear white is widespread among the middle classes and is penetrating the villages.

But this is only the first of the actual *reversals* of traditional symbolism that is taking place. Such reversals become flagrant as soon as Buddhist *sacralia* are introduced into the ceremony—though to the modern Buddhist precisely such an introduction seems the natural way to solemnize the event.

It is now standard practice at weddings for a group of "maidens" (i.e., bridesmaids), little girls dressed in white like the bride, to chant a medieval Pāli text called the *Jayamangala Gāthā*. They do this when the *pōruva* ceremony has been concluded. The text consists of nineteen four-line stanzas (*gāthā*), each celebrating an auspicious victory (*jayamangala*) of the Buddha. By the power of the event recounted, the text says, may victory

[49] Obeyesekere, *Pattini*, pp. 538–39.

be mine. The ideal type of the *jayamangala* is Buddha's victory over Māra ("Death") and his daughters, who in the popular imagination represent sex and passion. In the *Jayamangala Gāthā* this event and others in which the Buddha triumphed over evil and passion are celebrated. Fundamentally its theme is Buddhist, the triumph of ascetic renunciation (*tapas*) and the power (*tejas*) it generates over the very values—sex and procreation—represented in marriage. Few people know the meaning of the Pāli words, but most people are familiar with the two key words, *jaya* ("victory") and *mangala* ("auspiciousness"), since they occur in ordinary Sinhala usage. *Mangala* in popular usage means "wedding," and consequently many people believe that these Pāli verses are appropriate for weddings and were in fact designed for that purpose. In reality in traditional village society praises of the Buddha's triumph over Māra, as well as over other worldly passions and forces, were sung at various types of communal religious festivals like postharvest thanksgiving for the gods (*gammaḍuva*) and exorcism rituals (*bali-tovil*). In these rituals the context is that malevolent forces are being banished, demons expelled, *vas-dos* ("misfortunes") eliminated.[50] To have those Buddhist verses sung by prepubertal (i.e., infertile) girls dressed in sterile white is a symbolic proceeding that from the standpoint of the traditional culture annuls the sexual and procreative aspect of marriage. It certainly ought to warm the hearts of family planners.

The majority of Sinhala Buddhists still find it strange for a monk to appear at a wedding at all, let alone take any part in the formal proceedings. A monk is traditionally associated with sterility and even with death, so that the mere sight of one is—or used to be—inauspicious in a secular context; for example, to see a monk as one sets out on a journey is a bad omen. By the same token weddings are always held on secular premises.

However, it is now gradually becoming popular to have monks recite *pirit*, the all-purpose rite of blessing, at middle-class weddings. It does not conflict with traditional practice for the bride or groom or both to make merit before the wedding by inviting monks to recite *pirit* and accept alms—though we suspect that even this is a relatively modern custom. However, it is decidedly innovative to have monks recite *pirit* at the wedding itself. A media resources catalogue on *Buddhism in Southeast Asia and Ceylon* published by Yale Divinity School in 1974 has several slides of *pirit*

[50] One of these texts, *Jayamangala Sāntiya*, for curing diseases, is referred to in Nevill, *Sinhala Verse* 2: 15.

being recited by monks as part of a wedding ritual that culminates with the monks' receiving "their gifts from the bride and groom and other guests."[51]

We can document two cases that approximate the Christian model even more closely in that a monk (the same in both instances) has organized the weddings *in his temple.*

The Venerable Māpalagama Vipulasāra is the incumbent of the Paramadhammacetiya Piriveṇa[52] in Ratmalāna, a suburb of Colombo. This monastic school was the first to be founded in modern times as a counterpart to Christian mission schools; it dates back to 1849.[53] The first impression one gets on entering the monastery is of a cross between a palatial mansion and an office; there are several telephones and much coming and going. Māpalagama Vipulasāra by no means cultivates the traditional image of a monk. A Buddhist monk customarily places strong emphasis on decorum. He is supposed to be clean-shaven and keep his robes close to his body, to move calmly and deliberately, to restrain his gestures and even his eye movements—in brief to present a picture of total control. When we have met him, Māpalagama Vipulasāra has had hair on his head (it resembles a crew cut) and his chin. He speaks and laughs loudly; he moves quickly and energetically so that his robes fly about him, and he is said even to run in public, traditionally unthinkable for a monk. Though we do not know the details of Mohoṭṭivattē Guṇānanda's deportment, the image of the monk as active and fast-moving is no doubt due to him. (A famous political monk, Yakkaduve Prajñānanda, at one time vice-chancellor of Vidyālankāra University, followed the same tradition when he regularly appeared with plenty of hair on his head and chin.) Guṇānanda was primarily engaged against Methodist and Baptist ministers and lay preachers. Vipulasāra's image is close to the stereotype of the jolly Church of England vicar.

Early in 1976 a young Danish artist had become engaged to a Sinhala Buddhist girl and had also come to know the Venerable Māpalagama Vipulasāra, who has claims to being a sculptor. The monk undertook to arrange his wedding. A newspaper report of the wedding begins: "Rarely

[51] *Buddhism in Southeast Asia and Ceylon*, prepared by Charles A. Kennedy, Media Resources Catalogue on Asian Religions, Visual Education Service, Yale Divinity School (New Haven, 1974), p. 13.

[52] *Piriveṇa* means Buddhist seminary.

[53] Bechert, *Buddhismus*, p. 45.

these days does one get to see a wedding conducted according to the instruction of the incumbent of a Buddhist village temple in accordance with the custom which has come down to us from the distant past. For a foreigner unfamiliar with these customs it is a rare event to have been married according to the instructions of one of our Buddha's sons"[54] (i.e., of a Buddhist monk). Though the words here are the reporter's, several informants told us that the claim that the involvement of Buddhist monks in weddings is an ancient custom was made by the Venerable Māpalagama Vipulasāra himself. The newspaper report tells us that immediately after the actual marriage rite the young couple worshipped the Buddha in the temple's Buddha shrine, then worshipped the Venerable Māpalagama Vipulasāra and other monks and listened to *pirit*. The Venerable Piṁburē Sōrata, head of the *piriveṇa* school (whereas Māpalagama Vipulasāra is incumbent of the temple), then preached a sermon to them.

This was not the first wedding the Venerable Māpalagama Vipulasāra had organized in his temple. In the previous year, 1975, he had similarly provided hospitality for the wedding of a Sinhala couple. On that occasion the monk himself designed and supervised the construction of the *pōruva*, the platform on which the couple stood for the ceremony. As soon as the actual acts of joining the couple (tying their fingers and pouring water) were completed, Māpalagama Vipulasāra came into the hall and gave them his blessings; then while they remained on the platform, he and other monks chanted *pirit*.

The above practices receive reinforcement from an unexpected source—from Sinhala Buddhist monks residing abroad. These monks have a Western lay following whose members *want* to sacramentalize their marriages. In the United States monks must sign marriage licenses and consequently must perform some kind of ritual, especially for those whom they call *hippi bauddhayō* ("hippie Buddhists"). One senior monk residing in the United States asks the couple to sit down while he chants *pirit* and *Jayamangala Gāthā*. He ties a *pirit* thread on the bridegroom's waist and instructs him to tie one on the bride's (since the monk cannot touch women). Thereafter the monk lustrates the couple with *pirit* water. These are the very basic rites: much more elaborate ones are invented for grander occasions. It is almost certain that these practices will be adopted by Sinhalas residing abroad and from there reinforce parallel customs being invented at home.

[54] *Siḷumiṇa*, Sunday, 25 April 1976, Reporter: Nimal Horaṇa.

In Sri Lanka itself these rites have not yet caught on and remain atypical. More typical of contemporary urban middle-class weddings is the introduction of a new kind of officiant, a Brahman-type figure. His first duty is to calculate the auspicious times for the various stages in the *pōruva* ritual. Traditionally time calculations were at best approximate or even ignored, but with the advent of the clock *exact* time calculations are possible. In traditional village society knowledge of the customs associated with marriage was the preserve of an older kinsman, generally known as *dänamuttā* ("the knowledgeable ancestor"), and his female counterpart, *dänamutu ammā*. In modern society this expertise is taken over by specialists. There is no one designation for the officiant of marriages but sometimes he is called *sāmi* or even *kapurāḷa* (the term for the priests of the *deva* cults as well as for the marriage broker). In fact the *kapurāḷa* or *sāmi* is a kind of officiating priest. Often he is bearded and wears what Sinhala people (erroneously) think is Brahman garb, thus appearing like the chaplain (*purohita*) of a Hindu king. He not only brings into the wedding ritual a seemingly priestly role, but also enhances thereby the symbolism of royalty in the *pōruva* ceremonies. In modern towns in Sri Lanka one can hire the *pōruva* itself as well as the services of such an officiant.

The changes in marriage ritual can best be illustrated by analyzing a high-status marriage officiated at by Mr. Tilakasena (age sixty-three), who calls himself *Sāmi*. He was born in a village in south Sri Lanka into a family of traditional demon exorcists (*kaṭṭāḍirāḷa*). In 1941 he came to Colombo for an exorcistic ritual and decided to stay on. In 1949 he realized that a skill that he possessed was in great demand—*gok kola* art. *Gok kola* are tender coconut leaves used for decorations (along with banana bark and other leaves), and Low-Country exorcistic rituals use them extensively. However the demand in Colombo was for decorating the ceremonial arches or pandals (*toraṇa*) often set up to welcome politicians. Soon Tilakasena's skills were in demand for the construction of *pōruva*s (which he does beautifully). But he graduated from this profession to become well known as an officiant at high-status weddings. Now he is a full-time specialist at wedding ceremonies held in smart hotels in Colombo. The new job has made him financially secure, though not wealthy. His two daughters are married to well-to-do people; one son has a clerk's job in a government corporation while another is employed in Switzerland.

We shall describe the standard ceremony Tilakasena performs at the weddings of upper-class, English-speaking Sinhala Buddhists. Every attempt is made to traditionalize the ceremonies so that the assembled guests believe that they are witnessing an ancient ritual. Needless to say the *pōruva* is the elaborate work of Tilakasena's *gok kola* art. At the four corners of the *pōruva* are four full pots and coconut oil lamps. The latter are lit and the rites of marriage commence. These are standard acts in auspicious ceremonies, and the full pots are traditional symbols of prosperity used in a variety of contexts. Tilakasena explains that the full pots represent the occasion of the Buddha's Enlightenment, when the Earth Goddess cursed Māra while holding aloft a full pot.[55]

The rituals commence with Tilakasena making a speech requesting the permission of the audience to commence the *pōruva* ritual. This again is standard practice in village rituals, except that his elocutionary style is influenced by contemporary political oratory. He says that they are assembled to perform a marriage ceremony "according to old customs and our religion" (*āgama*). He formally requests permission from the Buddha, the Dhamma, and the Sangha; from the major gods, the parents of the couple, and those assembled, and says, "May this occasion be a *jayamangala* for all." Note that this procedure is borrowed from village exorcistic and Pattinī rituals. The Buddhicization of the previously secular ceremony is clear from the very start. The couple is now summoned by him in front of the *pōruva*, with the parents and close kin from both sides. This occurs about ten minutes before the exact auspicious time (calculated in advance by Tilakasena) for climbing the *pōruva*. Then he utters *aṣṭaka*s, a key feature of contemporary wedding ritual. *Aṣṭaka*s are sets of eight Sanskrit couplets (*śloka*), generally uttered in highly formal style in village rituals. The *effect* is all that matters since the Sanskrit is quite ungrammatical and often completely garbled, for the language is generally unintelligible to Sinhalas. We do not know when these *aṣṭaka*s were formulated, but their introduction into the context of marriage probably occurred in the late nineteenth century. Some versions are published as popular manuals.[56] The *aṣṭaka*s contain a *namaskāra* or obeisance to the Buddha by praising him in grand style as befits the Supreme Sage. Then Tilakasena utters what he calls a *sanna* or "exposition"; traditionally the term refers to the Sinhala paraphrase of a Pāli text. This is also sung in the style of prose "plaints" (*kan-*

[55] According to Buddhist scriptures the earth only bore witness at the event, but popular Sinhala ritual texts refer to the Earth Goddess cursing Māra.

[56] One such manual is *Pōruve Cāritra Sahita Mangala Aṣṭaka* (The *Pōruva* Customs with Wedding *Aṣṭakas*) (Nugegoda: Modern Book Store, 1976).

nalavva) of the village ritual traditions. It is in high-flown language and describes the prototypical *pōruva* on which Prince Siddhārtha (the future Buddha) married Yaśōdharā, his wife. The beauty of this original *pōruva* is described in great detail, and the text also mentions that all the great gods (including Śakra, Brahmā, Īśvara, Viṣṇu, Maheśvara [*sic*], Garuḍa, Gandharva, and thirty-three *kōṭi* of gods) were present on this occasion. The nine planets were also present (they are named in the text), and the (Buddhist) Four Warrant Gods guarded the four corners of the *pōruva*. The text continues that Īśvara had a magic *pirit* thread hidden in the folds of his hair and with this he tied the little fingers of the Bodhisattva and his bride, while Brahmā Sahampati poured water on their hands from a golden pot (*keṇḍiya*) and thus they were brought to liberation (*vimukti*). By that great influence, Tilakasena now says, may this new couple step onto the *pōruva* after obtaining permission (*varam*) from the four Buddhas of our eon (*kalpa*)—Kakusañda, Kōṇāgamana, Kaśyapa, and Gautama—and the great gods in charge of Sri Lanka (named in the text) and all the other gods, the parents of this couple and the assembled relatives, guests and wellwishers. Then permission from the Earth Goddess is requested (since the *pōruva* is supposed to be constructed on the ground). There are only a couple of minutes left before the auspicious time for climbing the *pōruva* when Tilakasena sings the following verse.

Our Bodhisattva, knowing the right signs, was seated on his diamond throne
And at dawn achieved Enlightenment after destroying the *kleśa*s ("defilements") of this foul world.
With the sound of thunder he destroyed Vasavat Māra and by that power
Place the right foot on the *pōruva*, for it is now the auspicious time.

Now the fathers of the bride and the groom each hold their respective children by the hand and lead them to the *pōruva* while Tilakasena utters several Pāli stanzas (nowadays sung at the conclusion of *pirit* rituals). I quote one of them:

> May all blessings—the protection of the gods—
> The influence of all Buddhas—May all be mine forever.
> (*Mahā Jayamangala Gāthā*, verse 13)

Now follow the rites of the *pōruva*; we shall highlight those that seem to be wholly or partially innovative. The first act performed by the couple on the *pōruva* is to offer a sheaf of betel leaves as a *pūjā* to the Buddha (always referred to by Tilakasena with unconscious irony as Lovturā Muni, the transcendental, or otherworldly, sage). The theory underlying this act is a conventional one from popular Buddhism: the *pūjā* to the Buddha produces merit that is transferred to the gods, who then protect the couple as an expression of their gratitude. Soon after this rite, the couple seeks permission first from the bride's mother and then the groom's. The groom and bride give a gift of white cloth (*kacciya*) to the bride's mother while Tilakasena sings of the origin of this custom. An origin myth (which we are not familiar with) is recounted; it tells the story of a Brahman girl Somasiri who was reared with great suffering by her mother. The groom in the origin myth is so impressed by the mother's love that he gives her the gift of cloth. Then the groom holds the hand of the bride and puts a ring on the fourth finger of the left hand (a Christian custom). This must be done after getting permission from the Buddha, the gods, and both sets of parents since the groom, as yet, has no right to hold the hand of the girl. Then the groom ties a necklace on his bride (traditional custom) and gives her a gift of white cloth (traditionally given to her mother). Then comes the crucial act of the *pōruva* ritual: the father (traditionally, it would be the bride's maternal uncle) ties the right little finger of the bride to the left little finger of the groom (traditional custom), while the following *gāthā* ("stanza," nowadays translated "prayer") from the conclusion of the *Mahā Jayamangala Gāthā* is uttered (innovation): "By the influence of all the glorious Buddhas, Pacceka Buddhas, and *arhat*s I secure your protection in every way."

Now the bride's father pours *pirit* water from a pot onto the hands of the couple (according to the text an ancient custom initiated by Brahmā at Siddhārtha's wedding) while Tilakasena utters *ślokas* (couplets in folk Sanskrit) to ward off troubles from the planets, to secure for the couple the protection of the gods and the *pihiṭa* ("help") of the Buddha (all new ideas, including the strikingly unusual one of seeking the Buddha's help). The text says that the bodies of the groom and bride are divided into five parts with the influence of the Buddha resident in the head and that of the four guardian deities within the rest. It should be noted that the role of the father makes a great deal of sense in modern marriage, cross-cousin marriage being virtually defunct. The officiant told us, as a good British social anthropologist would have done, that all of this signifies the father's transference of his rights over the girl to the groom!

After this rite the virgins in white sing the *Jayamangala Gāthā* (the custom described above). Even Tilakasena thinks this custom is no more than one hundred fifty years old and was not included in the wedding of Siddhārtha and Yaśōdharā! Then the bride's mother feeds the new son-in-law with milk rice; then she feeds the daughter (a new custom but consonant with tradition). Then the groom and bride feed each other (traditional). Only a few more minutes are left before the auspicious moment determined for the couple to descend from the *pōruva*. The relations from both sides and selected guests come up to the *pōruva* and receive a betel leaf each from the couple (a variation of a custom practiced traditionally *after* the *pōruva* ritual). A lot of *aṣṭaka*s are recited by Tilakasena recalling various heroic acts of the Buddha, his past life as Vessantara in which he gave away his children and wife (acts that would appear to indicate a certain ambivalence about domestic life), and his Enlightenment and fight with Māra (when he overcame the passions, including the erotic blandishments of Māra's daughters). As the couple descends from the *pōruva*, Tilakasena utters a *śloka* asking permission (*varam*) from the Buddha, the past Buddhas, and the gods. The bride is escorted from the *pōruva* by the groom's father, assisted by her own father, while Tilakasena recites three stanzas ("prayers") from the *Mahā Jayamangala Gāthā*. As they step out a coconut is smashed (traditional custom) to banish effects of the evil eye, evil mouth, and evil thoughts and to obtain the blessings of Gaṇeśa and the Earth Goddess. Then after lighting a lamp for the Buddha the couple are ready to sign the marriage register (the modern legal act of marriage).

One source for the innovations in this ritual is Christian weddings. The other, here preponderant, is such traditional rites of the spirit religion as *bali-tovil* and the *gammaḍuva*. We recall that the officiant comes of a family of hereditary specialists in those rituals. Their usages are bound to strike an upper-middle-class Sinhala audience as authentically traditional. The selection from that tradition is judicious—not, for example, the passages of comedy or licensed obscenity, but the sonorous chanting of barely intelligible verses in archaic, high-toned language and the recounting of origin myths. In the village ritual tradition the origin of each rite is recalled by rehearsing the myth of a prototypical event. This is the model for the new myth that explains the origin of the *pōruva* and its rites by reference to the wedding of Siddhārtha and Yaśōdharā, a wedding witnessed by all the gods (including Īśvara and Maheśvara, who are of course both Śiva) at which Īśvara ties the sacred marriage knot. Īśvara is the

Hindu patron saint, as it were, of yogis, and one might think him an odd choice for that role; but evidently he is introduced because he is in vogue in Sinhala Buddhism today (see Chapter 3).

The strangeness of choosing Īśvara to preside at the marriage, however, pales into insignificance besides the irony of patterning the entire event after the (future) Buddha's own marriage. Everyone knows that the bridegroom in that marriage left his wife and later persuaded his son to join the Order, thus ensuring that his family line terminated. Marriage is the rite of creating a home and family; the Buddha stands for the higher value of renouncing all that. The paradox glares at us throughout the ritual. Vessantara went so far in rejecting the values of family life as to give away his family, ceding paramountcy to the absolute value of renunciation—hardly the ideal model for a marriage. It is no accident that in parts of Sri Lanka it used to be the custom to recite versions of the Vessantara story, not at weddings but at funeral wakes.

Such paradoxes are probably inevitable in any attempt to Buddhicize the marriage ceremony. Traditional Buddhism rests on recognizing that there are two sets of values, those of life in the world and those higher ones of leaving it. Protestantism is characterized by rejecting any such hierarchy: the same values are considered applicable to all people in all circumstances. "Religion must be made the work of your life; it must enter into everything; it must be seen by your children, and servants, and neighbours, that your heart is not here, but in heaven," wrote the missionary Spence Hardy in 1863.[57] How many Buddhists in Colombo today realize what influence this view has has among them?

[57] R. Spence Hardy, *The Sacred Books of the Buddhists Compared with History and Modern Science* (Colombo: Wesleyan Mission Press, 1863), p. 161.

CHAPTER 8

The Contemporary Resurgence of Nuns

The Order of Nuns (*bhikṣuṇī-sangha*) founded by the Buddha died out in Sri Lanka long ago, probably in the late tenth century,[1] and cannot be refounded unless the valid ordination tradition is reintroduced from a country which still has nuns—a Mahāyāna country. Scholars know that Theravāda and Mahāyāna are doctrinal currents that have no bearing on monastic traditions, so such a refounding would be legitimate in terms of Buddhist canon law. However, it could not prosper unless it was widely accepted, and most Sinhala Buddhists—including most nuns we have spoken to—are unclear about the distinction between doctrine and canon law and believe that the *bhikṣuṇī-sangha* in Mahāyāna countries is corrupt. The Theravādin Order, therefore, remains exclusively male.

Though there are thus no *bhikṣuṇīs*, there are now women who function, behave, and look like nuns, and many of them follow the discipline almost exactly as if they were nuns, omitting only the ceremonies (*kammavācanā*) to which they are not entitled because they do not have the higher ordination.

These nuns are of two kinds. To differentiate them clearly, we must recall the traditional gamut of religious observances and roles that is still available to men. A man can take the eight precepts. Traditionally this is strictly temporary, usually for twenty-four hours, and it is normal to wear white for the occasion. Or a man can take the ten precepts, which are really the same as the eight with the one important addition that he eschews the use of money. By custom the person who does this is old and assumes the status of pious layman permanently; he too wears white. But the ten precepts he undertakes are exactly the same as those undertaken by a boy on

[1] Gunawardana, *Robe and Plough*, p. 39.

entering the Order as a novice. The boy shaves his head and wears yellow robes, and unless he reverts to lay life the role is permanent until he takes the higher ordination. (The monastic code he then pledges himself to follow elaborates on the same basic principles.) Thus there are two sets of people who have taken the ten precepts: old men and boys. The boys always live in monasteries (or monastic schools), the old men usually do not. There are no institutions that have as their main purpose to house old pious laymen.

Though the situation of women is now rather more complicated, the reader should keep the same basic dichotomy in mind. At the beginning of the century, so far as we can tell, laywomen kept the eight or the ten precepts on the same terms as men. There were no female equivalents to either the male novices or the monks, though Copleston, writing shortly before the turn of the century, makes reference to pious laywomen (*upāsikā*) dressed in white "especially in Kandy, or on the way to Adam's Peak."[2] There are now women who take the ten precepts on the same general principles as male novices: they lack the higher ordination ceremony that would formally turn them into nuns, but they continue throughout adult life to live just as if they were full-fledged nuns. Old women no doubt still exist who take the ten precepts, wear white, and stay at home, but this category has become inconspicuous and perhaps small and does not figure in our story. What has happened to most of these women is that they too now shave their heads and put on yellow robes. Many of them have gone to live in nunneries or retreats, though some live singly or in pairs in caves, or in cells in their children's back gardens, and some even live at home just like their white-clad counterparts. They are much less organized than young nuns, often do not keep such a strict regimen, and even live in the nunneries on different terms. But from the official Buddhist point of view they are in the same category as young nuns, for their formal status is the same. Finally, some women now take the eight precepts permanently rather than the ten, and then live likewise in nunneries. In the strict modern nunneries for young women, postulants have this status, wear white, remain unshorn, and take only eight precepts; in these institutions, therefore, the eight-precept woman is to the ten-precept woman as a novice is to a monk on the male side. This is all

[2] R. S. Copleston, *Buddhism, Primitive and Present in Magadha and in Ceylon* (London: Longmans, 1892), p. 279.

very new, and the Sinhala language does not distinguish between these categories, except occasionally to mention whether a woman has taken eight or ten precepts. All alike can be known as "moral-precept mother," with various words being used for "mother" so that we encounter *sil mātāva*, *sil māṇiyō*, *sil māṇivaru*; they may also be known by the traditional village term of "lay-disciple mother" (*upāsikammā*, etc.). As this latter term has the connotation of advanced years, it is not usually used of the young nuns despite the fact that they too live in *upāsikārāma*, "retreats for female lay disciples." However, in *English*—and this is a true modernist touch—the young nuns do differentiate themselves, being known as "Sister," a title they never accord the older women.

Despite a few modernist touches and the lack of a proper higher ordination, the institution of the young nuns is not essentially new, but a revival closely comparable to the periodic revival of forest hermitages and strict ascetic life among monks documented and discussed by Carrithers.[3] The gathering of old women with shaven heads wearing yellow robes into retreats is likewise not wholly new, but is probably new to Sri Lanka: it seems to be an import from Burma. There the formal situation is just as in Sri Lanka, in that there are no true *bhikṣuṇī*, but there are large nunneries full of women who have become novices. There the women may be of any age, just as in a Christian convent.

In Sri Lanka the two categories coexist closely but rather uneasily. In 1976 we visited the Helen Ranavaka Bhikṣuṇī Ārāmaya in the outer Colombo suburb of Pannipiṭiya. About twenty nuns lived here under the charge of a woman who had earlier married into the Hēvāvitarana family (the family of Anagārika Dharmapāla). Except for this woman (whom we did not meet), all the inmates seemed to be either very young or very old. The nunnery contains a large house (given by Helen Ranavaka with the land), and at the bottom of the garden are cells, simple cubicles in a long low plain building. The young nuns, who have mostly taken the ten precepts between the ages of nine and twelve—of course with their parents' consent and more likely at their behest—live with the incumbent up in the main house. They reside there permanently but still go to school and are supported by voluntary donations from local supporters (possibly also from their relations). The old women all live in the cells at the bottom of the garden, and for such a cell, we subsequently discovered, they have to

[3] Carrithers, *Forest Monks*.

make a down payment of up to 1000 rupees (a huge sum for most pockets in 1976), depending on the quality of the accommodation. It is comparable to buying yourself into an old-age home; but it covers the cost only of lodging, not of board; the food they must normally somehow provide for themselves. Most of them leave the retreat for periods and go and stay in other retreats, go on pilgrimage, or even visit their families. They may perform some religious function such as saying *pirit* or preaching in private houses, but a nun of this category is not invited to preach publicly.

The precise history of the nuns' movement is not easy to recover, but it seems clear that there are two main phases. The first phase is that of direct Burmese influence, and in particular the influence of a Burmese nun called Mā Vicārī. This phase sees the establishment of retreats for laywomen and their occupancy by shaven ladies wearing yellow—though they may also be joined by ladies in white. The second phase is dominated by a Sinhala nun widely known as Sister Sudharmā, born in 1919; we shall see that Burma recurs in her story too. It is Sister Sudharmā and her sponsors who have started and established an organized body of young nuns who are trying to recover the way of life of the true nun, the *bhikṣuṇī*. Since the rise of the nuns' movement is a topic that now attracts much interest in the West, we shall include in the following paragraphs rather more historical detail than is strictly necessary for our subsequent analysis.

The first Sinhala nun whom we have been able to trace is Sister Sudhammācārī. She was born sometime in the 1860s. Her original name was Catherine de Alwis. The family was socially prominent. It had both Christian and Buddhist branches; her parents were Christian (Anglican). She converted to Buddhism in her twenties and then went to study in Burma.[4] She first studied in Burma for twelve years at Minging, six miles from Sagan; her teacher was a relative of King Mindon. She returned to Sri Lanka and took up residence in Kaṭukällē, Kandy, as the incumbent of the Lady Blake Upāsikārāmaya ("Retreat for Pious Laywomen"). This was founded for her in 1907 by Dhammavikrama Mohandiram and named after the wife of the Governor, Sir Henry Blake. She lived there till her

[4] Elizabeth Nissan, "Recovering Practice: Buddhist Nuns in Sri Lanka," *South Asia Research* 4, no. 1 (May 1984): 32–49. Biographical data on Sudhammācārī on p. 35. Most of our information is from Mā Vicārī (see below).

death in 1939[5] and taught Pāli in schools. In her old age she went blind. Her only pupil was a granddaughter of the retreat's founder called Sumanāvatī. Sumanāvatī, however, took only the eight precepts and thus wore white. According to Mā Vicārī, she was a bad-tempered (*sära*) woman who once made a pupil go deaf by hitting her on the ear. In 1939 she fell out with the supporters of the retreat, and they began a lawsuit to remove her. This lasted till 1946, when she was finally dislodged and went to live at Sanghamittārāma in Anurādhapura. Then Mā Vicārī was invited to come and take her place. Mā Vicārī has lived there, with one interruption, ever since.

Mā Vicārī was born in Burma in November 1894, in or near Sagan. One night in September 1911, when she was not quite seventeen, she was supposed to be asleep upstairs while on the ground floor her elder sister was giving birth to a child. What she overheard so scared her that she determined to leave the lay life and immediately cut off her hair with a pair of scissors.

In January 1927 the foundation stone was laid for a magnificent new building, paid for by the Burmese government, at the Palace of the Tooth Relic in Kandy. A large party came from Burma to attend this ceremony, among them twenty-five nuns. Mā Vicārī came and returned to Burma with this party, but came back to Sri Lanka the next year with her mother and younger sister, who was also a nun. As a result of the journey the mother too became a nun, for she was seasick on the crossing and vowed to give her hair to the Palace of the Tooth Relic if she arrived safely. The other two went home, but for some reason Mā Vicārī decided to stay behind. She first wanted to found a cell on Varanakanda, the hill where the Sinhala saint king Siri Saṅga Bō is supposed to have stayed, but that came to nothing. Instead she went to Anurādhapura, where she found a Burmese nun aged about eighty, who had been living there for some time leading a very strict life. We thus see that there were Burmese nuns in Sri Lanka before Mā Vicārī and perhaps even before Sudhammācārī went to Burma. The Venerable Ānanda Maitreya mentioned to us another who lived at Situlpavuva. But he said that none of them before Mā Vicārī was influential; they seem to have lived as hermits.

[5] We understood Mā Vicārī to say that Sudhammācārī died in 1932. But Nissan gives the date as 1939 and seems to derive this from a contemporary document. Mā Vicārī was very old when we interviewed her (she died soon thereafter) and her memory was perhaps not always clear.

Mā Vicārī became the pupil of the old Burmese nun, who began teaching her Sinhala. But very soon the old lady died. Mā Vicārī inherited her retreat, the Kuttampokuṇa Ārāma, and stayed there for two or three months. Then while worshipping at the *bō* tree she met a Sinhala monk who had studied in Burma and knew Burmese. He invited her to come to Horaṇa, some twenty miles south and east of Colombo, and for a short while she lived there in an ordinary house.

In October 1929 occurred what seems to have been the most important event in her life after becoming a nun. The younger sister of a schoolmistress who was her chief supporter at Horaṇa was training to be a schoolteacher at Musaeus College in Colombo, a famous Buddhist girls' school. She fell ill with measles, but suddenly recovered after meeting Mā Vicārī. Out of love for Mā Vicārī (by the latter's account) she herself took the robes at Rājagiri Upāsikārāma (in Colombo), despite the opposition of all her relatives. She lived with Mā Vicārī as her pupil and adjutant till her death in 1969 at the age of sixty-eight. Her name in religion was Dhammikā Sīlāvatī. Till 1946, when they came to Kandy, they lived in a residence (*āvāsē*) at Morontuḍuva, Vādduva, given to them by Sīlāvatī's parents. In that period Mā Vicārī had altogether six pupils, including one Nepali. She and Sīlāvatī visited Burma together three times; once she went by herself and Sīlāvatī was unable to eat in her absence. She can no longer visit Burma, she told us, because the former prime minister, U Nu, was a supporter of hers.

Since 1946 thirteen nuns have lived at Lady Blake's. For a while after her pupil's death Mā Vicārī lived elsewhere. She taught for two months in Balangoḍa at the invitation of Balangoḍa Ānanda Maitreya. In 1970 a wealthy lady from Colombo invited her to go and live at her expense in a cell on Väḍahiṭikanda at Kataragama. With three other nuns from Lady Blake she went for a trial period, but soon came back. (The interest of the patroness in Kataragama stemmed from a vow she had made to the god.) Despite the failure of this attempt, the lady then founded a retreat for nuns in Pannipiṭiya, a Colombo suburb. It is the very place where Ānanda Maitreya is now living (in 1976) and hoping to build a meditation center. The foundation stone was laid by the Burmese ambassador, and for a while Mā Vicārī lived there with her disciples. But when Mā Vicārī returned to Kandy, the others quarrelled and dispersed. (The patroness then gave the site to the Venerable Hädigalle Paññātissa of the Maha Bodhi Society, Colombo, who later passed it on to Balangoḍa Ānanda Maitreya.)

We are told that Mā Vicārī has had a career as a preacher and teacher of Pāli. We find this a little hard to understand, as her Sinhala seems to be very limited and spoken with a Burmese accent so strong as to hamper communication. She knows no English. But she undoubtedly knows a lot of Pāli and presumably learned a great deal by heart in her early days in Burma. She has had several disciples. Her career is mainly of interest, however, for what it tells us of the association of modern Sinhala Buddhism with Burma. She has been far less prominent and influential than Sister Sudharmā.

Sister Sudharmā decided to become a nun, she told us, at the early age of eleven. There were very few nuns in those days, she said. She was acquainted with an old pious laywoman from Kǟgalla called Dhammavatī, who used to come to her village, Varakapoḷa (just halfway on the main road between Kandy and Colombo), to learn Pāli from a layman. There were also monks in her family. She was inspired by the story of a servant of the Buddha's chief lay supporter, Anāthapiṇḍika, who supplied the Buddha with firewood. Her parents were strongly opposed to it and tried to prevent her from going to the temple. The day she cut off her hair, 12 March 1934, her mother rolled on the ground in agony. She was thirteen, and the ceremony took place at the local temple, Bodhirukkhārāma, Varakapoḷa.

Shortly after this she got to know Mr. Sri Nissanka, an important figure in recent Buddhist history (see Chapter 6). Sri Nissanka had been a monk for a while in a Burmese temple in Colombo and studied meditation in Burma. He became a successful attorney (advocate), and used to pass Varakapoḷa regularly on his way from Colombo to court at Kuruṇǟgala. In November 1936 he had refounded Biyagama, a retreat for nuns, and he also founded the famous forest hermitages at Salgala and Ruvangirikanda. He headed a board of trustees that bought ten acres of land at Biyagama. During the war, however, Biyagama was evacuated and stood empty, and the trustees later gave some of its land to a Buddhist orphanage.

On 23 February 1937 Sri Nissanka brought Sister Sudharmā and her family to Biyagama and installed them there for a while. Sister Sudharmā was instructed in Buddhist doctrine (*dharma* and *abhidharma*) by a Burmese nun who knew Sinhala and also studied Pāli and English. After two years, on 15 January 1939, she moved to Musaeus College, the very Buddhist girls' secondary school in Colombo where Mā Vicārī had found her chief disciple. She was brought there by Sri Nissanka, a Burmese woman, and Mr. and Mrs. J. R. Jayawardene. It was the future President of Sri Lanka who paid her fees. She began her preaching and teaching career at Musaeus College. Her first public sermon was given at Vesak in 1945 in a public hall in Kalutara (a large coastal town south of Colombo). Between then and 1966 she gave no fewer than 2,530 public sermons. She kept a record of them in her *pin pota* ("merit book"), at which she kindly allowed us to look. It begins with an address to the Buddha as "My immortal mother."[6]

In 1947 she entered the university, being the first Buddhist nun ever to do so. She obtained a first class in her B.A., having studied Pāli, Sanskrit, Sinhala and Buddhist civilization. She was taught some Mahāyāna Buddhism by a Chinese monk at the monastic university of Vidyālaṃkāra. While awaiting her university final examination results in 1951 she taught for six months at a girls' school run by the Buddhist Theosophical Society in Gampola near Kandy. Then Dr. G. P. Malalasekera, the famous Pāli scholar, asked her to go to Penang to teach Buddhism at the Penang Buddhist Association. She took a sapling of the *bō* tree, thus indicating that she was a missionary in the tradition of Sanghamittā, who brought a *bō* sapling from India to Sri Lanka in the third century B.C. She reached Penang in December 1951, and there taught in a girls' school and preached to the Penang Theosophical Society and in a leprosy hospital. However, she fell ill, and in 1952 returned to the school in Gampola. Her opinion of the Penang Buddhists is not unfavorable, but she finds that they have mixed up their Buddhism with Confucianism and Taoism and do not observe the monastic rule in such particulars as not eating after noon. However, she said, the belief current in Sri Lanka that Chinese nuns eat after sundown is incorrect.

The general manager of the school in Gampola asked her to start a new school in Ambalangoḍa on the southwest coast. She worked there as principal in 1953–1954 and got the school registered, that is, officially recognized by the government. It was here that she began to have disciples. She started a nunnery in 1954 with eight girls, of whom five (Sujātā, Sumedhā, Sumanā, Subhadrā, and Sunandā) became nuns. (Here Sister Sudharmā used the term *mahana vunā*, which definitely connotes entry into the Order.) All these girls were teenagers who had passed the senior

[6] For the Buddha as mother see chap. 11 and Gombrich's article cited in n. 14 of that chapter.

school certificate (S.S.C.), and she started them on a two-year training course. Later that year she went by invitation to the Sixth World Buddhist Council at Rangoon and toured Burma; she then meditated for ten days at a temple in Bangkok and toured Thailand. On her return to Sri Lanka, she was invited to take up residence in Musaeus College. She moved there in January 1955 and stayed till late 1976, when she returned to Biyagama. When we visited her in the summer of 1976, she lived in a separate small building next to the main school building, taught Buddhism at the school, and preached a sermon there once a week. She was paid a salary, received and spent for her by the school bursar and the girl in her residence who acted as her personal attendant. After the fashion of the forest-dwelling monks, her residence was known as a "cell" (*kuṭiya*), though it was of supracellular size.

At the same time that she moved to Musaeus College, she moved her pupils to Biyagama. During her absence Biyagama nunnery had been reoccupied by two or three fellow ascetics (*sahabrahmacāriyō*) and she would sometimes go and stay there during the holidays, but the place was not organized. When she brought her disciples there in 1955, Mrs. J. R. Jayawardene started a supporters' association, which she still heads. Biyagama is now the headquarters of an organization with ten branches, some of which are residential nunneries and some meditation centers. Till moving there in 1976, Sister Sudharmā visited it frequently, but spent her holidays every year meditating on the southeast coast at Kuṭumbigala near Pottuvil under the tutelage of the Venerable Tāṁbugala Ānandasiri, who kept a cave reserved for her.[7]

The most remarkable thing Sister Sudharmā told us was that she received between 200 and 250 letters a month from girls and young women who wanted to become nuns under her. She thought that they usually got her address from the newspaper *Taruṇī* ("Maiden"). She said her organization could not afford to admit many; it was too costly for the supporters. Moreover, she is keen to differentiate her nuns from the traditional old women who take the ten precepts. Therefore her organization will normally only take educated women who have studied Buddhism at school up to the seventh or eighth standard (i.e., till they are about fourteen) and have passed some examinations. After thirty people are hard to teach, so she normally admits women under thirty-five, she said; but she had re-

[7] For a full account of Ānandasiri, a most impressive figure, see Carrithers, *Forest Monks*, pp. 269–93.

cently admitted four rather older schoolteachers because they were highly educated. Postulants are admitted only after an interview and with the consent of their parents or guardian. She has herself ordained forty-eight and taught about 250, some of whom were later ordained elsewhere. Since 1970 she has delegated the selection and training of new arrivals to the nuns in charge of the individual nunneries. The young ladies are put through a period of probation before ordination and sent on a meditation course to Kaňduboḍa, but they do not have to pass that course to be "ordained." She said that some of those who write to her have suffered disappointment in love and mentioned cases in which girls had committed suicide because their parents had refused consent to a match. Sister Sudharmā did not mention this to us, but the card with which she answers first inquiries asks the applicant to forward (among other things) her horoscope.

In 1976 we visited the nunnery at Biyagama. In front of it there is a conspicuous inscription that records in English that this is the Vihāra Mahā Dēvī Upāsikārāma, Biyagama, opened by His Excellency Sir A. Caldecott, Governor of Sri Lanka, on 11 February 1908. However, when we spoke to the incumbent, Sister Sumanā, she was unaware both of the existence of this inscription and of its message. She only knew of the founding in the late 1930s by Sri Nissanka, J. R. Jayawardene, and Dudley Senanayake. Sister Sumanā, who was a member of Sister Sudharmā's first group of disciples, comes from Chilaw District and was forty-two when we met her. There were many monks in her family. When she was young she received much enlightenment from traditional Sinhala religious books such as the *Lō Väḍa Sangarāva*, *Subhāṣitaya*, and the translation of the *Dhammapada*. She heard of Sister Sudharmā from the newspapers and wrote to her. She took the eight precepts permanently when she was eighteen, the ten at twenty. Sister Sumanā called herself *sil mātāva* and referred to the other inmates as *sil mǟṇivaru*.

The nunnery is mainly for training nuns. When they enter it they take the eight precepts and are admitted to take the ten after a training course that on average lasts two years. The minimum age for taking the ten precepts, that is, becoming a nun, is sixteen. (But according to Jessica Wood,[8] who got her information from Sister Sudharmā, the age is twenty—the same age as that at which a male novice may become a

[8] Jessica Wood, "Buddhist Nuns in Sri Lanka," undergraduate dissertation for Lancaster University, 1977.

monk.) When we spoke to her, there were eight such trainees in residence; six were young, two retired schoolteachers (mentioned by Sister Sudharmā above) in their fifties; all were spinsters. On the whole the women were enclosed, though the rule is not rigid and they may sometimes go out after signing a book, if accompanied by another nun. Various monks come to preach. Meditation (*vidarśanā bhāvanā*) is taught daily by a nun who, like Sister Sumanā herself, learned it at Kaňduboḍa. Sister Sumanā was explicit that the meditation technique that they use is the breathing technique brought to Sri Lanka (and thus to Kaňduboḍa) by Burmese monks in the mid-fifties. Also every day they practice the four recollections: on the Buddha, on kindness, on impurities (i.e., the constituents of the body), and on death.

The nunnery has a temple, founded in 1956, but its decoration was still incomplete in 1976. The slow progress is symptomatic of a lack of interest in the gods (who are to be represented): Sister Sumanā said that she believed in their existence but made no requests of them as that was worldly. After going on pilgrimages she gives the merit to Maitreya, the future Buddha who is now a god in the Tusita heaven.

The nunnery received its food from the supporters. Unlike a monastery of comparable size, it has only one servant—plus a male watchman. The kitchen work is mainly done by the nuns themselves, working in pairs on a weekly rotation. Here is the daily timetable, copied from a notice in the nunnery:

4:00	wake up
5:00–5:30	worship of the Three Jewels
5:30–6:30	usual chores
6:30–7:30	offerings to the Buddha and breakfast
7:30–9:30	various business
9:00–10:30	bathing, etc.
10:30	offerings to the Buddha
11:00–11:45	midday meal
11:45–1:00	chores and leisure
1:00–1:30	worship
1:30–2:00	reading of religious books
2:00–3:00	lessons
3:00–3:30	refreshments and leisure
3:30–5:00	learning doctrine or meditation

5:00–6:30	chores
6:30	refreshments
6:45–9:00	worship of the Three Jewels and recitation of auspicious *pirit*
9:00–9:30	lessons
10:00	go to sleep

The meaning of some of these headings (notably, "various business") is not very clear. Sister Sudharmā supplied Jessica Wood with a rather more specific (and apparently rather more exigent) timetable in English, which we reproduce as an appendix to this chapter along with a copy of *The Rules of Biyagama Nunnery* from the same source.

What significance do we see in the rise of the nuns? As a religious phenomenon it is fair to remember that it is primarily a revival, consonant with traditional Buddhism, a renewed expression of religious piety comparable, *mutatis mutandis*, to the revival of the Order that centered on the recovery of the ordination tradition from Siam in 1753. All the present ordination traditions in Sri Lanka, except that one, spring from Burma, and the Burmese influence is thus no novelty; however, foreign influence is one of the catalysts for change that appears frequently in this book.

Obviously, the nunneries represent an advance in the religious status of women. For many a century women have had no public religious role in Sinhala society. Women who wanted to dedicate their lives to religion had to stay at home, where their inclinations gave them little or no prestige and were therefore probably difficult to translate into practice. To don the monastic uniform of yellow clothing and shaven head is to acquire a recognized place in society; and we have noted that even the old women are sometimes invited to chant or preach in people's houses. But some nuns go further, and here we must note new roles: to preach in public, as Sister Sudharmā and a few of her followers do, has hitherto always been a male prerogative. Again, for a woman to teach meditation is completely new. We have referred above to this happening within a nunnery; we hear that it also happens at Kan̆duboḍa, where a nun may even instruct male laymen.

Next we note the interesting small shifts in the formal role structure that we have explained above, especially in Sister Sudharmā's nunneries, where postulants take only the eight precepts and relate to ten-precept nuns as novices do to monks. The traditional status categories no longer correspond to the socially important distinctions. When English-speaking Buddhists say that "Sister Sudharmā was the first nun" in modern Sri Lanka, they ignore the old "ten-precept pious women"and thus cut across formal distinctions made by Sinhala and Pāli—but in so doing they are true to the spirit of the modern institutions.

A salient feature of the nuns' movement is the extraordinary degree of control exercised by the laity over some nunneries. The Suśīlārāmaya in Maharagama (another Colombo suburb), for example, is run by a committee of lay women, and they control both the admission on probation and the admission to full membership (which as usual is formalized by taking the ten precepts, shaving the head, and donning the yellow robe). The nuns may not go out of the nunnery without the committee's permission, and this is normally granted only for visits to meditation centers, arranged by the committee in advance. In a word, the committee exercises the functions one would expect to see exercised by a head nun (who in these institutions is simply called the "big mother" [*loku mǟṇiyō*]); when we investigated it, in 1978, Suśīlārāmaya had no such internal head. The laity justify their control by stressing that the enclosed ladies are not true nuns (*bhikṣuṇī*) and by the same token claim that it is unseemly for ten-precept women to go begging. Be that as it may, the committee exercises direct control over the religious lives of people who have undertaken more precepts than they have, and so have a higher religious status. This is a glaring departure from Buddhist tradition.

Some aspects of the way in which these institutions function also illustrate the loss of community and increasing impersonality of social life. Retreats that function as old-age homes are supplying a need that was not met—whether or not it was felt—in village society. Sister Sudharmā recruits largely through the mass media; her constituency is nationwide, and her criteria for admission have nothing to do with ascriptive status.

Sociocultural Background of the Rise of Nuns

How do the nuns fit into the themes of this book? Since we wrote the above account (in 1976 and 1978) Lowell Bloss has compiled an even more detailed history of this movement and we shall use some of his data in our analysis.[9] Initially we shall confine ourselves to the major organizations of nuns—effectively nunneries—described by us and by Bloss and then deal with little-known, small groups of nuns studied by us and also by Salgado.[10]

One can agree with Bloss that the initial impetus for founding what are effectively, but not theologically, orders of nuns came from people who were pillars of Protestant Buddhism, even though Dharmapāla did not anticipate this movement. The first major figure, Catherine de Alwis or Sister Sudhammācārī, came from a family related to the great Sinhala scholar, James de Alwis, a leading Sinhala Protestant; her parents mixed with the elite of Colombo society, both Buddhist and Christian. It is therefore no accident that Sister Sudhammācārī's convent initially combined several functions together: Lady Blake's was a shelter for orphans and the very old, *and* it was also a place for *dasa sil mǟṇiyō*. The latter feature became progressively more significant. The early lay Buddhists who patronized the nuns, like H. Sri Nissanka and Sir D. B. Jayatilleke, were also influenced by Dharmapāla's reform (though the latter was critical of Dharmapāla's violent anticolonialism). Nissanka and D. B. Jayatilleke did not see the *dasa sil mǟṇiyō* as nuns in the strict sense; they were interested in getting *dasa sil mǟṇiyō* to engage in social work, especially in the hospitals. Bloss notes that H. Sri Nissanka, visiting a Buddhist monk in a hospital, was appalled to see him nursed by a Catholic nun. Hence the idea of the lay Buddhist elite of Colombo was to produce a group of women, intermediate between nun and laity, who could take the place of Christian nuns in social work. Such a group would parallel the male *anagārika*, the role invented by Dharmapāla to be intermediate between laity and monk. In both cases the traditional sentiment remained: that monks, and nuns in the orthodox sense, by virtue of their vocation should *not* engage in economic or social work activity. Given this context it is not surprising that D. S. Senanayake, later the country's first prime minister, wrote in 1936: "Buddhists who speak so much of Ahimsa had not taken steps to educate women in the art of succoring the sick. Such work is done

[9] Lowell W. Bloss, "Theravada 'Nuns' of Sri Lanka: Themes of the Dasasilmattawa Movement," paper presented at the Association for Asian Studies, Sri Lanka Study Group Meeting, Washington, D.C., 23 March 1984.

[10] Nirmala S. Salgado, "Custom and Tradition in Buddhist Society: A Look at Some Dasa Sil Matas from Sri Lanka" (Colombo: International Centre for Ethnic Studies, n.d.), cyclostyled.

by Christian sisters, and it is high time women of that country work for the welfare of fellow human beings in a selfless way."[11]

Yet, says Bloss, in spite of these efforts yearly reports on the Biyagama "nunnery" from 1938 to 1940 showed that these nuns had little interest in social work and were not fired, as was Sister Sudhammācārī (Catherine de Alwis), with the spirit of public service. Initial attempts to introduce such practical activities as spinning and weaving were failures. Bloss interprets this in terms of the social backgrounds of nuns: those influenced by Protestant Buddhism were committed to an ethic of this-worldly activity while the overwhelming majority of nuns from the village areas modelled themselves on the village monk. There is some validity to this argument insofar as early founders like Sudhammācārī are concerned, but Sister Sudharmā, and others like her, were Western-educated women coming from elite girls' schools and the university and were fully imbued with the spirit of Buddhist modernism. Moreover, one cannot assume that women in village society were untouched by Protestant Buddhism; much depended on their education and status in village society. Dharmapāla, it should be remembered, fundamentally influenced a *village* intelligentsia whose members had advanced phenomenally by the middle of the century. Thus we have to probe deeper, not into village or Protestant Buddhism, but the nature of Theravāda Buddhism, be it of the village or reformist variety.

The village monk had a few priestly functions: attendance at almsgivings and *pirit* rituals in lay homes and performance of death rituals; he acted as teacher (for children who came to the temple) and as general counsellor. Active engagement in social work was not considered appropriate to his station. By contrast the movement of Protestant Buddhism (though not Dharmapāla himself) and the spirit of modern Buddhism in responding to the Christian challenge and criticism of Buddhism favored a this-worldly involvement for both monk and laity, as we have seen of Sarvōdaya. On the other hand, the same pressures have led modern Buddhists to take up meditation, especially the form of *vipassanā* meditation recently imported from Burma. But the practice of Theravādin meditation must produce its inevitable counterpart—detachment from the world and the web of social ties. Sister Sudharmā requires the women "she accepts at her nunneries (to) spend at least three months at the *vipassanā bhāvanā* center

[11] Bloss, "Theravada Nuns," p. 10.

at Kañduboḍa."[12] This introjection of the *arhat* ideal of Theravāda must ipso facto draw people away from worldly involvement. Thus, while it is not impossible for village monks (and some nuns) to work in closed arenas like orphanages and hospitals, that does become difficult for those who by meditation have introjected the ideal of world renunciation of the *arhat*. The Theravāda *arhat* simply *cannot* be a Mahāyāna Bodhisattva, and, unlike the gods of Hinduism, cannot work in the world for man's material well-being.

The Buddhist elite and bourgeoisie have felt it necessary to maintain and even elevate the *arhat* ideal, but have also wanted to create a group intermediary between lay and monastic life, one involved in social work. They especially hoped thus to create a corps of Buddhist nurses who could eventually replace Christian nuns, who were increasingly (and perhaps rightly) being criticized for exploiting their position to convert sick and dying Buddhists. Nuns seemed to be the answer; but not on the classical model of the *bhikṣuṇī*, who was associated with the ideal *arhat*. "Ten-precept mothers" were neither laymen nor orthodox nuns (who could not exist). If the *anagārika* status for men did not catch on, perhaps, they thought, a whole class of female religious specialists could take an analogous position and become this-worldly ascetics on the Protestant model.

But unhappily for those lay religious leaders, the nuns frustrated their plans. While the orthodox Order of *bhikṣuṇī*s was extinct in Sri Lanka, the new nuns, especially those with high education and higher ideals, wanted *effectively* to be nuns, though *in theory* they were "ten-precept mothers." They revived the *arhat* ideal. Bloss has pointed out that some nuns want to achieve *arhat*-hood in this very life through the meditative techniques enjoined by doctrine.[13] These nuns have modelled themselves not so much on the village monk, who expects to achieve Enlightenment in some future rebirth, as on the forest monk, whose movement has been revitalized in modern times. Thus contemporary nuns, especially in the organizations described in this chapter, have set up *vipassanā* meditation centers, while others are even meditation teachers. A recent study refers to a nun attached to a Buddhist temple who is in sole charge of a meditation center for women.[14]

[12] Ibid., p. 14.

[13] Ibid., p. 17.

[14] Ibid.; Salgado, "Custom and Tradition," p. 12.

Nevertheless, the conflict between the Protestant ideal of service and the Buddhist ideal of renunciation surfaces again and again. For example, Bloss records the recent popularity of a German nun, Sister Khemā, who has started another movement with the goal of this-worldly involvement for nuns: under her direction a modern nunnery based on Catholic orders has been started near Doḍanduva. The location itself is symbolic: Doḍanduva became famous early in this century for its hermitage for German and other foreign scholar-ascetic monks.[15] Thus under the inspiration of another German, a parallel institution is being set up for women. The architecture and symbolic spaces planned in the new nunnery are based on Catholic models, as might be expected.

It is not surprising that many bourgeois Sinhalas have given their full support to Sister Khemā, who herself admitted to Bloss that her skin color is one reason for her success. The extreme adulation given to white nuns, monks, and meditation teachers is a general feature of contemporary Buddhism in Sri Lanka. It parallels the desire that Sinhala people have for foreign goods. But beyond that perhaps lies a deeper malaise rooted in the colonial experience—an identification with the aggressor and wish to please and placate the Foreigner, who only a few years ago denigrated the indigenous cultural tradition. Thus the conversion of the Foreigner looks like a turning of the tables, though in reality it is so eagerly celebrated because of a much more complicated lack of confidence in oneself and one's own cultural tradition. It should be remembered that English-speaking Sinhala nuns have taken over the title "Sister" for both address and reference, though this term has no Buddhist equivalent or antecedents. The colonial conquest of the mind lasts much longer than the political domination.

In our previous work and in Carrithers's more recent documentation[16] the profound significance of the *arhat* ideal in the Buddhist societies of South and Southeast Asia has been demonstrated: it is, among other things, the measure by which people evaluate ordinary monks. The almost universal criticism of monks is that they are violating the *Vinaya* by being too involved in the world. Bloss records, as one would expect, that ordinary lay people view the nuns as *sīlavanta* ("pious," literally, "observing the precepts") while the temple monks are criticized for the luxurious and

[15] Bloss, "Theravada Nuns," p. 24; Carrithers, *Forest Monks*, pp. 27–29.

[16] Obeyesekere, "Theodicy"; Carrithers, *Forest Monks*.

worldly lives they lead.[17] The monks, with few exceptions, say that nuns should not try to be *bhikṣuṇīs*, either in theory or in practice; some opine that they should confine themselves to social work activities, while others are openly disapproving or at best ambivalent. According to Bloss, the nuns in his sample (who tend to be educated) do not want to reinstitute the older *bhikṣuṇī* Order, since by the *Vinaya* rules this would put them under the formal authority, and domination, of monks. Others, especially the smaller, little-known and little-educated groups, have taken over the monk's derogatory views and see themselves as inferior to monks. It is very likely that education and social class determine which of these attitudes is assumed.

In Chapter 5 we related the high level of underemployment and unemployment to the rational choices made by individuals (and their families) regarding marriage. People postpone marriage and many do not marry at all. We posited that these forces have lead to increased sexual frustration. In order to understand the increasing number of young nuns and the far greater number of young women who apply to Sister Sudharmā to join her order, we must bear in mind not only the rise in the age of marriage, but also another great social change—the boom in public education since 1945, when the farseeing Buddhist Minister of Education, C.W.W. Kannangara, introduced a state system of free education (primary, secondary, and tertiary).

> Between 1945 and 1970, school enrollments underwent a three-fold increase. The 1971 census recorded literacy rates for persons 10 years of age and older of 85.6 percent for males and 70.9 percent for females. Literacy rates were noticeably higher in the younger age groups, whose school-age years came after the educational expansion, and the differential between males and females, which was marked in the older age groups, narrowed substantially at the younger ages. Among persons aged 20–24 years, for example, 91.0 percent of males and 83.1 percent of females were literate, while 79.1 and 45.3 percent, respectively, of males and females aged 55–59 years were literate.[18]

[17] Bloss, "Theravada Nuns," p. 21.

[18] Robert N. Kearney and Barbara Diane Miller, "The Spiral of Suicide and Social Change in Sri Lanka," *Journal of Asian Studies* 45, no. 1 (1985): 86.

The expansion of education has led to higher aspirations among young people. Kearney and Miller refer to a study by Haputantri that indicates the increased pressure on students for educational achievement. "It was reported that 29 percent of students in government schools were attending private tutorial classes, and this proportion was even higher in the examination grades, the fifth, eighth, tenth, and twelfth."[19] But in a stagnant economy most hopes are frustrated, and many must become pessimistic about their chances. The nunneries appeal to the better-educated women, the ecstatic cults draw on the less well-educated groups.

Meanwhile, as Kearney and Miller have recently shown, the suicide rate in Sri Lanka has risen over a twenty-year period to one of the highest in the world.[20] The socioeconomic background renders the rise of these movements historically intelligible; it does not "explain" the rise of ecstatic cults, or of nuns, or of the suicide rate. Other information, both of a sociological and a deep motivational sort, is required if one is fully to understand the choices the individual makes against the larger socioeconomic and cultural backdrop. For the latter one requires case studies, but one can postulate sociocultural reasons for choosing to become a nun rather than an ecstatic priestess.

1. Education. The whole educational system plays down the spirit religion and extols Buddhist doctrine.

2. Social status. The cults of ecstatic priestesses require possession trances and orgiastic shaking of the body which, as we show in Chapters 1 and 6, are frowned on both by traditional Buddhism and the bourgeoisie, whereas meditation is acceptable and desirable. The priestess is assertive, the nun comparatively passive.

3. The role of nun requires (in all but leaders) subservience to authority. We guess that this propensity is inculcated in families that are stable and governed by a firm authority, either the father or the mother. Those in the ecstatic cults are more independent and have had the will to break away from the authority of the home—parents or husband. The style of life of ecstatics is also more individualistic: the Buddhist orientation of nuns requires a suppression of individuality, and we think that this requirement is anticipated in their family relationships. Open protest and rebellion

[19] Ibid.

[20] Kearney and Miller, "The Spiral of Suicide."

appear in the case studies of priestesses; we surmise that this is rarely true of nuns.

The basic distinction between the nuns described thus far and ecstatic priestesses pertains to their professional/religious specialism: the nuns have a vocation of salvation, priestesses a vocation of curing. The educated nuns in Bloss' and our sample will at best, out of courtesy almost, transfer merit to deities, but they do not care about them. This is not surprising: the goal of these nuns is Enlightenment. The gods, who have a say in worldly matters alone, have little significance for them. However, the gods are not easily banished. Even in the classical texts the meditating monk can be frightened by demons and evil spirits, and in fact the *Āṭānāṭiya Sutta*, a popular *pirit* text, was designed to ward off such malignant beings through the power of the word. But a god, in popular Sinhala thought, can also help people to keep demons at bay, and it is likely that some nuns, however steadfast their salvation quest, occasionally seek the protection of the gods. Furthermore, gods as well as demons can be related to one's emotional life,[21] and one must expect some nuns in our sample to have intimate relations with them. Thus one would expect empirically the existence of nuns who *combine* the orientations—the cult of the Buddha with the cult of the gods; the role of the renouncer seeking salvation with the role of the curer concerned with the welfare of those affected by demons. Such combinations are not without contradiction or conflict, but we shall see in Chapters 10 and 11 that they do now happen and may indeed indicate religious trends in the making.

One movement in which nuns are synthesizing the two orientations is reported in Chapter 10, in the section on Uttama Sādhu. Another, apparently more straightforward, comes from a pioneering, yet preliminary, study by Nirmala Salgado.[22] Salgado did not study the well-knit organizations with educated leaders and a cohesive soteriology, but focused on small groups (including one nun living in a monastery) led by leaders of various educational and social backgrounds. These small groups do not have the support of the elite, and consequently they are often harassed by monks, by influential men of the area, and also on occasion by the police. The local power structure, possibly owing to the work of influential monks, does not want them around, though they seem to have considera-

[21] Obeyesekere, *Medusa's Hair*.

[22] Salgado, "Custom and Tradition."

ble support among ordinary laymen. The group that synthesizes the two orientations consists of ten nuns led by Sumana Māṇiyō. Seven of them have taken new names from Buddhist hagiography and legend and suffixed to them the term *māṇiyō*, the formal term for "mother." The three who still have their lay names are not "ordained," that is, they have yet to take the ten precepts. Their ages range from twenty-eight to fifty-five, the modal ages are thirty-eight and fifty-five while the mean is forty. Half the members of the group have been married and presumably have left their families (with or without their consent) or joined the group at the death of the husband. Sumana Māṇiyō, like Jayanta in Chapter 11 below, was instructed by a god in a dream to go to a specific place and start an *ārāmaya* ("retreat"). This she did, and in spite of opposition from a monk, had the nine others join her.

The distinctive feature of this group is that while they emphasize meditation, they have also had experiences with demons, very much in the manner of ecstatic priestesses discussed in *Medusa's Hair* and in Chapter 2. Of the nine, excluding Sumana, the head, for whom no information is available, six experienced illnesses prior to joining the group: namely, fainting, loss of appetite, paralysis (conversion hysteria?), bodily pain. Even more remarkable from our point of view is that all (and perhaps even the leader) were afflicted by an evil spirit of a dead relative, exactly like the cases discussed in *Medusa's Hair*. Moreover, after they joined the group six of them were cured of this affliction; the three still tormented by the dead are those who have not yet been "ordained."[23] Thus two spiritual forces bind this group together: their common experience of affliction from dead ancestors and their ultimate goal in Buddhist salvation. The chief, Sumana Māṇiyō, through her powers of meditation can actually see the ancestral spirit afflicting a fellow nun and can force the recalcitrant spirit to obey her. The merit acquired by Buddhist practice is transferred to the dead, who then cease to afflict the living. The bonds that tie this group seem exceptionally strong: they believe that they have met before in their previous births and will meet again in the dispensation of the next Buddha, Maitreya. It is likely that nuns in Salgado's sample come from village backgrounds and are less educated than the nuns in Sister Sudharmā's group.

That similar groups who attempt to reconcile, if not synthesize, the two

[23] Ibid., p. 7.

orientations exist is also clear from recent trends in Kataragama. In our over fifteen years of experience at Kataragama we have noticed that Buddhist monks and *upāsaka*s who have taken the eight or ten precepts and laymen who want to feed the poor and acquire merit congregate at the stupa of the Kiri Vehera; while those interested in the this-worldly cult of Skanda congregate under and around the *bō* tree behind his shrine (see above). It would be rare to see a nun (*dasa sil mǟṇiyō*) of the more respectable new orders at the latter shrine; they would go to the premises of the Kiri Vehera. But in 1984, during the annual festival, we noted a new phenomenon: a group of about ten *dasa sil mǟṇiyō* clad in brown robes were congregated for several days at the Skanda shrine. Brown, the color worn also by Uttama Sādhu's followers, is supposed to indicate ascetic rigor.[24] Unfortunately we were not able to interview them, but their very presence there, given the spatial arrangements of Kataragama, has symbolic significance. They are, without doubt, devotees who have reconciled or attempted to reconcile their devotion to Skanda with the ascetic goal of Buddhist renunciation.

[24] Nur Yalman, "The Ascetic Buddhist Monks of Ceylon," *Ethnology* 1, no. 3 (1962): 315–28; Carrithers, *Forest Monks*, pp. 116–36.

APPENDIX[25]

Part 1
The Rules of Biyagama Nunnery

For the nuns who have undertaken Dasa Sil (the Ten Precepts) for the sake of Dhamma.

1. Three times daily you must contemplate upon the usefulness and beneficial consequences of observing Dasa Sil, and be satisfied if you have lived according to them, and thus maintained your Sil. If you have broken a precept, your anguish at this failing should lead you to make a determined effort not to break the precept again. Then you should renew your Sil.
2. You may not live apart from the other nuns, and you may not travel alone.
3. If you must leave the nunnery on important business, then you must first obtain permission from an elder nun, and be accompanied by another nun.
4. You must rise before twilight and wash. After paying homage to the Lord Buddha, and reciting the Triple Gem, you must begin the ceremonies to the Lord Buddha and chant pirit.
5. After twilight and the morning ceremonies, you may take breakfast.
6. Only if you are ill may you sleep until twilight or sleep at other times of the day.
7. If you visit a nearby temple, all of you must go together.
8. In the morning and at night, you must meditate, read books on Dhamma and attend the teachings given by the elder nuns.
9. You must do the walking meditation at least once daily.
10. In the evening and in the morning you must offer flowers to the Lord Buddha.
11. Nuns who need to leave the nunnery must return before dark.
12. You must not talk unless it is necessary.
13. You must do all that you can to assist a nun who is behaving incorrectly.

[25] Material cited in Jessica Wood, "Buddhist Nuns."

Part 2
Timetable

In outline:

4 A.M.	Rise: work: meditate. Chant Three Refuges and ten precepts.
5 A.M.	Prepare shrine for *Buddha Pūjā*.
	Perform *pān pūjā* and *mal pūjā* (offerings of lights and flowers).
6 A.M.	Domestic duties: tidy up rooms, sweep courtyard, etc.
7 A.M.	*Dāna* (alms) received from householders. *Buddha Pūjā*. Take morning meal.
8 A.M.	Bathe, wash clothes, individual tasks, work, study.
9:30 A.M.	Visit and receive visitors.
10:30 A.M.	*Buddha Pūjā*.
11 A.M.	Lunch. Clear up lunch.
12 noon	Rest.
1 P.M.	Study. Listen to Dhamma sermon on radio.
2 P.M.	Meditation.
3 P.M.	Sweep courtyard. Walking meditation.
4 P.M.	Teach juniors.
5 P.M.	*Buddha Pūjā. Gilam Pasa.**
5–8 P.M.	Domestic duties: sewing, letters, work.
8 P.M.	*Gilam Pasa.**
8–10 P.M.	Meditation and communal chanting of *suttas*.
10 P.M.	Rest.

* *Gilam pasa*: refreshments, which may not include food which has to be bitten or chewed; probably just a cup of tea.

CHAPTER 9

The Venerable Balangoḍa Ānanda Maitreya: Theosophy and Astrology

The Ven. Balangoḍa Ānanda Maitreya is undoubtedly one of the leading figures of contemporary Buddhism, not only in Sri Lanka but throughout the world. He has published books in both English and Sinhala and has travelled abroad extensively. He has explained Buddhism to the British public on television.[1] His prestige is such that when the Amarapura Nikāya decided to forge itself into an organizational unity, he became its first overall head. He was for many years professor of Buddhism at Vidyōdaya University and for a short while its vice-chancellor. He represented Sri Lanka at the Sixth World Buddhist Council in Rangoon and was one of those selected to recite the scriptures for the new recension of the Pāli Canon. If one had to select a single monk in Sri Lanka to present a model of Buddhist character and learning—and this is no doubt the advice the B.B.C. team received—one might do well to choose the Venerable Balangoḍa Ānanda Maitreya.

It is for that reason that we were anxious to meet the Venerable Ānanda Maitreya. We hoped for edification and were not disappointed. We explained that we were writing a book on contemporary religion in Sri Lanka and took notes throughout two delightful interviews. Ranging far beyond the scope of our questions, he volunteered the following information about his experiences and beliefs, and we consider it worthy of record.

He entered the Order in 1914, when he was fifteen, and while he was a novice he got to know the well-known German monk Ñāṇatiloka. Ñāṇa-

[1] Program in the series "The Long Search." He was shown being interviewed in his monastery at Pannipiṭiya, where we too interviewed him.

tiloka told him about the Englishman Allan Bennett,[2] who had become a monk in Burma under the name of Ānanda Metteyya. On becoming a monk he chose the same name for himself—though he spells it in the Sanskrit instead of the Pāli way.

In 1923 or 1924 he came to Colombo to teach Pāli in Ānanda College, the leading Buddhist school in the city and a Buddhist Theosophical Society foundation. At that time Anagārika Dharmapāla asked him to write a book attacking Theosophy. As he knew little or nothing about it, he joined the Theosophical Lodge at Borälla (in Colombo) and began reading in their library. In those days it was his custom to meditate daily at 8 P.M., controlling his breathing. (To us he used the general Sanskrit term *prāṇāyāma*, as well as the specifically Buddhist *ānāpāṇasati*.) He would sit thus meditating in the dark. One day while doing this he had a vision (*darśana*). A light came on in the room. He opened his eyes and sought its source. Gradually he perceived that it was coming out of the wall opposite him. Slowly it grew brighter, and an outline began to form, till he saw that it was a very beautiful man with a short black beard, looking like Jesus. The figure's eyes were "mystical" (the English word) and turned up so that one saw mainly the whites. Then he realized that it was Maitreya (the future Buddha). Behind Maitreya came many other figures, whom he realized to be the Mahatmas. As he was good at drawing he wished to sketch Maitreya, but as soon as he thought of doing so the light and the vision disappeared. He began to meditate again. The light came on again and the vision returned. He started to memorize the appearance of Maitreya, when Maitreya spoke in English and said to him, "Don't care for the shape, care for the truth." Thereupon the vision faded. He then drew the figure of Maitreya from memory and next day took his drawing to the Theosophical Society. The Dutch lady who was secretary of the lodge told him that this vision made him a member of the Inner Circle, and showed him a series of pictures in a book accessible only to the Inner Circle. His picture matched exactly the picture of Maitreya in that book. Members of the Theosophical Society frequently see visions, and these are valid, he told us.

In 1925, at the age of twenty-six, he went to India as a Buddhist missionary in Kerala for the Missionary Society (Lankā Dharmadūta Sabhā). He went via Madras, where he heard Krishnamurti's first lecture at Adyar,

[2] Alias Allan Bennett Macgregor. See Bechert, *Buddhismus* 2: 53 and 56.

at the Theosophical annual conference. He later returned to teaching Pāli at Ānanda College, where he had many famous pupils, and became professor of Buddhism at Vidyōdaya in 1958. However, he has been to India thirty-three times (this in September 1976). He has studied Hindu yoga for six weeks with Svāmi Nārāyaṇānanda, a Vedāntic yogi, at Kankehal near Rishikesh (the holy town where the Ganges leaves the Himalayas; it is full of Hindu ashramas). He also spent nine months at Sarnath (Benares) as incumbent of the Mahā Bodhi monastery there in the late sixties after his retirement from Vidyōdaya. However, most of his visits to India have been to consult the astrological bureau at Madras (see below).

He approves of the spread of meditation among laymen; he has himself founded a meditation center at Vāgirikanda near Gampola, where he placed his pupil in charge, and intends to found another where he is staying in Pannipiṭiya, a Colombo suburb. These centers cater mainly to Westerners—indeed it is essential to provide such modern comforts as running water—and he acquired this place because he felt he needed somewhere not too distant from the airport. Nowadays the average state of monks (*niyama bhikṣutattvaya*) is close to ordinary worldly life (*laukika jīvitaya*); the good monks are attracted away from the old monasteries to the meditation centers, and those monasteries that do not become meditation centers will have to close. This is good: it will improve the quality of the Sangha. At the moment there is no control: *tāpasa*s[3] can ordain themselves and be registered as monks by the state, while those who have been expelled for dire breaches of monastic discipline (*pārājika*) may be expelled from meetings of the Sangha but do not lose their monastic property rights. Many monks "go bad" at the university because they get mixed up in politics.

On meditation his views are catholic. Besides learning it from Hindu yogis he has meditated (in Colombo) with Goenka[4] and studied with a Burmese monk, U Sujāta, at Kaňduboḍa. The Hindu yogic breath control (*prāṇāyāma*) was very like the Buddhist *ānāpāṇasamatha*, but of course different from *ānāpāṇasati*. *Vipassanā* is absent from the Hindu tradition. The

[3] "Ascetics," in particular a movement of self-ordained monks briefly prominent in the 1950s. See Carrithers, *Forest Monks*, chaps. 6 and 7; also Chapter 10 n. 11.

[4] A famous Indian meditation teacher. Hindu by birth, he lived for many years in Burma and learned meditation there from a Buddhist layman. His meditation technique is Buddhist inspired but he claims that it has no connection with any religion and is suitable for anyone.

Kañduboḍa meditation is again somewhat different from both *ānāpāṇasamatha* and *ānāpāṇasati*; it is a meditation by the sensation of touch (*phassabhāvanā*, *vedanānupassanā*) by feeling the breath increase in one's belly. In *ānāpāṇasamatha* one concentrates on the breath passing through one's nostrils, and feeling (*vedanā*) develops later. But all come to the same in the end: like everything else in the world, the belly is a compounded thing (*saṃkhārayak*) and therefore impermanent.

Balangoḍa Ānanda Maitreya is learned in Māhāyana Buddhism and condemns Theravādin exclusivity. The Theravādin are "too orthodox" and cannot forget the ancient schism, nor do they accept monastic liturgy (*kammavācanā*) in any language but Pāli. He also has a long record of support for the nuns' movement.[5] It is true, he says, that some details of the discipline are different in China but that should be no bar to reinstating the full ordination of nuns in Sri Lanka by bringing it over from China. The ordination tradition of the Abhayagiri monastery of Anurādhapura has been preserved in China after the Abhayagiri monks were expelled by the Mahāvihāra; they are Sarvāstivādin. The disciplinary rules are of two kinds, *lokavajja* and *paññattivajja*. The former are *akusal*, real weaknesses—not *sins*—whereas the latter are just "society rules." Probably they are the "minor precepts" that the Buddha on his deathbed told Ānanda need not be observed. It is only in these conventions that the Sarvāstivādin discipline differs from the Theravādin. Monks are against the introduction of the higher ordination for nuns, we gather, because they are themselves not so virtuous and the nuns might show them up by contrast.

Theosophists believe in the *ātman* and the *paramātman* ("individual soul" and "supreme soul") of Vedānta, and this is contrary to Theravāda. But his personal view is that Vedānta came directly from Buddhism and that Śaṃkara wrote his commentaries on the Upaniṣads in the light of Buddhism. The Vedāntins just called *paramātman* what the Buddhists had called *nirvāṇa*, but they ascribed to their *paramātman* the characteristics that *nirvāṇa* has. Most monks in Sri Lanka believe that when one becomes an *arhat* the coming into being of one's components ceases ("skandha paramparāva hädīma navatinavā arhat velā"). But some think there is a "positive reality" (Balangoḍa Ānanda Maitreya, speaking in Sinhala, used the

[5] As recently as 1986 he passed the annual monastic retreat (*vas*) in Britain at Amaravati, the Buddhist "convent" (for want of a better term) established near London by the English Sangha Trust, which is claiming to ordain nuns there.

English words) beyond that. The majority view was just "negative"; but "this is a deception, not the truth, just relative" ("mēka rävatillak, ätta nǟ, nikam relative"). The true reality is beyond final *nirvāṇa* (at death) ("häbǟ tattvaya parinibbānen passe"). This true reality cannot be given a name, for to call it *paramātman* would lead to misunderstanding. But such advanced states as *sotāpatti* have *nirvāṇa* as their object of meditation, so it cannot be something empty (*his*); he only knows it is not a void (*śūnyatā-vak*). An old book, the *Saccasaṃkhepa*, says that *nirvāṇa* is not mere waning away (*khayamattaṃ na nibbānaṃ*). Jinarājadāsa, president of the Theosophical Society, wrote a book against the Theravāda view called *The Reign of Law*, and he agrees with that book. The original doctrine of the Buddha was close to Vedānta, as shown by the *Mūlapariyāya Sutta*,[6] but opinion in Sri Lanka has changed.

The Venerable Ānanda Maitreya has learned from other English sources besides those written by Theosophists. He has learned hypnotism from various English and American books, such as Verner's *Way to Success*. This hypnotism he has used to dispel physical pain, both in others and in himself, and to help students to study: every day for a fortnight he puts his hands on their heads to suggest that they can learn, and it works.

Nor have his visions been confined to the Theosophical context. In about 1956 he went to Kataragama with Venerable Nārada, a famous Buddhist monk of the Vajirārāma temple in Colombo, to see the firewalking. An hour before it began, he and Nārada both saw someone standing at the end of the fire pit near the main shrine, shaven-headed, his lower half wrapped in a brick-red cloth, his upper half bare but for a cloth over his left shoulder. After standing a while, the figure walked away from the shrine across the fire. He was blazing, but shook off the flames as he went. As he reached the gate at the far end of the enclosure he suddenly disappeared. They think that the figure was Kataragama himself, for some people always see him, or a sign of him, before they do annual firewalking. He was in any case a Buddhist god (see Chapter 12).

The Venerable Ānanda Maitreya learned astrology according to the Indian tradition when he was young. His own horoscope was examined to see whether he was suitable for the Order, and he does the same for his pupils. To become a monk one requires a conjunction called *pabbajjā yoga*.[7]

[6] *Majjhima Nikāya*, *sutta* 1.

[7] See Gombrich, *Precept and Practice*, p. 147. (*Pabbajjā* = *pävidi*.)

The Kaumāra Nāḍi Vākyam Astrological Bureau of Madras plays a great part in Ānanda Maitreya's life and thought. It has been his habit to visit this bureau about once a year, and he has published a magazine article about it.[8] He has three very thick notebooks in which he keeps the horoscopes and other answers they have given to his questions. These answers are in Tamil, a language he does not know, though it is easy for him to find an interpreter. What is the source of these Tamil dicta?

They are all prophecies. About six thousand years ago, when the Kali Yuga (our present degenerate age) was beginning, lots of seers (*ṛṣi*) did yoga for a thousand years. They gained the knowledge with which they started the sciences of medicine (*āyurveda*), astrology (*jyotiḥśāstra*),[9] and palmistry (*lekhāśāstra*). They also investigated what would happen to various virtuous people yet to be born; this knowledge of the future they gained both by asking Subramaniam and other gods and by using their yogically acquired power of the divine eye. These predictions they embodied in Sanskrit verses which their pupils then learned by heart. They were of two kinds: things which *would* happen, and things which *might* happen but might also be prevented. Two thousand years ago Tiruvangar, king of Trivandrum, had a thousand pundits translate the books into Telugu and Tamil; the originals and translations amounted to ten million palm leaf manuscripts and were deposited in the royal library. But about 150 years ago a king of Trivandrum had them thrown into the moat. A lot of them were saved by Brahmans. Of these, 100,000 went to Britain, 300,000 to the United States, and 300,000 to Germany. (These figures are from a book called *Celestial India*.) Many others survive in India: Telugu ones are in Mysore, Tamil ones in the Connemara Library in Madras, Sanskrit ones in a village ten miles from Kusinagara, and in private hands in Lucknow. A native of Madras studied these manuscripts and began to interpret them; some he possesses, others he consults in the Connemara Library. He set up the Nāḍi Vākyam Astrological Bureau. *Nāḍi* means a second of time; the system divides each astrological house into 400 parts. If given the exact second of birth the founder of the bureau could make anyone's horoscope; otherwise he could do it on the basis of examining your palm. From your horoscope he could give you your name. The prediction of public events was a separate department; answers are given in Tamil verse and cost

[8] "Aruma Puduma Nāḍi Grantha," *Rasavāhini*, August 1980, pp. 5–10.

[9] The word also covers "astronomy" but that seems irrelevant in this context.

twenty rupees each. But the founder of the bureau is now dead and his grandson is training to take over.

In 1951 the Venerable Ānanda Maitreya visited the bureau (for the first time?) and asked several questions. First, for five rupees, he had his palm examined. They correctly told him what his name had been as a layman, and his parents' names. They gave him his "life reading." He then asked about Jesus. It turns out that there were in fact two preachers of that name, whom the New Testament has confused and conflated. The first, who is somehow connected with the Dead Sea Scrolls, was a mystic saint who was crucified; the second, 125 years later, a revolutionary who was stoned to death. Christ was yet another man, who inspired the first, saintly, Jesus. That Jesus ran away from home and came to India with a caravan. Asking questions of the holy men there, he was not satisfied till he got to Kashmir, where he was converted by a learned Buddhist monk. He went still further north to meditate and then returned home and taught till he was crucified, sacrificing his life for the Dhamma. It may be that Messiah and Metteyya are the same word, as the Theosophists claim, said the Venerable Ānanda Maitreya. He can also not pronounce on the truth or falsehood of their claim that Jesus is now a Mahatma. The Theosophist Roerich found a life (*carita*) of Jesus under the name Hamis in manuscript in a Tibetan monastery and copied it—see his book, *Heart of Asia*.

In this account we are not quite clear how much the Venerable Ānanda Maitreya had learned from the Nāḍi Vākyam and how much from the Theosophists. We had hoped to infer it from the original Tamil oracle that he was kind enough to show to our research assistant, Mr. N. Shanmugalingam. The oracle is in three verses; here is Mr. Shanmugalingam's translation of them:

About Christ

1. In an earlier birth Ānanda Maitrī was the son of Mary. As a child in this birth he grew up trying to research into the noble ideas quoted in religious works.
2. In order to achieve a high and esteemed position he listened to the teachings of the great and learned Lord Buddha. He gained experience and benefit by this and then he established a religion of his own to teach his ideas.
3. When his religion spread, the bad deeds that collect sky-high like the mountains vanish away, never to return again. He was killed

on the crucifix, so that evil from this world would vanish away and his life would be an example for others to follow.

Note that according to this oracle the Venerable Ānanda Maitreya himself was Jesus in a former birth. He did not mention this to us in the interview, possibly out of modesty or for fear of shocking us. But he did give us other details of his former lives. During the lifetime of the Buddha he was the deity who lived in the tree under which the Buddha attained Enlightenment (*Bodhivṛkṣādhigṛhīta dēvatāva*). The *bō* tree was cut down in the time of Asoka, causing his own (i.e., the deity's) death. He was then reborn as the son of one of Asoka's ministers, was converted to Buddhism, helped Buddhist missions, and finally became a minister himself. His last life before this present one was in India as a Brahman priest, doing Hindu *pūjā*. He was good at Sanskrit and English. He quarrelled with some ministers and got them dismissed, then prevented their sons from getting a good education, but later repented. In this present life his previous knowledge of the languages helped him to improve his Sanskrit and English, but because of his fault in preventing others from getting educated he was born in a remote area with no good schools and had no opportunity to pass the examinations. Moreover, his life reading correctly predicted that he would participate in the Sixth World Buddhist Council and be head of the United Amarapura Nikāya. The prediction in the first case was, "In the highest of councils he will be chief"; in the latter, "among high people a very high individual."[10]

He asked the bureau about the fate of a pupil of his who had died and was told he had been reborn in Bihar. He actually went and met him. The rebirth had taken place after an interval (*antarābhava*).[11]

The Nāḍi Vākyam also gave Balangoḍa Ānanda Maitreya information about the god Kataragama or Subramaniam. He was a Buddhist deity (*dēvatāva*) and a follower of the Buddha. The Buddha, when about to visit Sri Lanka, told him to go to Rohaṇa (southern Sri Lanka) and await him. After some months the Buddha came to Kälaṇiya,[12] then to a mountain and

[10] Here we translate literally from the Venerable Balangoḍa's words; we did not see the Tamil oracle.

[11] Whether such a gap occurs between one life and the next was a point of controversy in ancient Buddhism. Many schools hold that it does, but the Theravādin position is that it does not.

[12] This identifies the visit with the Buddha's third visit to Sri Lanka as recounted in the

various other places, finally to Kataragama. People there were sacrificing animals. This the Buddha forbade. He then showed Subramaniam to the people and told them to build him a shrine. The present shrine is still on the same site. He told Subramaniam to look after the people; to live on the nearby hill of Väḍahiṭikanda but to come to the shrine to hear their requests. "After centuries," the Buddha predicted, "my Dharma will be here and the Buddhists will ask your help; you must give ear to them." So saying, he returned to India. Ānanda Maitreya believes that the Hindus have confused this Subramaniam with the Hindu god of the same name.

Here now is the original Tamil oracle, as translated by Mr. Shanmugalingam:

About Gugavell (Subramaniam)

1. The time of birth, the position of the planets at birth, etc., is given.

2. The son of Pandit Menkamy and Kiriappuhamy was sent to the Sinhala land in order to find out the way in which the people were living and also to find out about their attitudes to life in general. In a similar way Thevan[13] was sent to the same Sinhala land by Lord Buddha.

3. The Thevan who came was the radiant (*kathir*) and loving Gugavell.[14] On arriving in the Sinhala land he found that there was no unity among the people and also the people had very feeble and weak minds.

4. The people were very cruel to both man and beast alike, and this was told to the Lord Buddha by Thevan.

5. In order that the people should live together happily and honestly, Lord Buddha himself came to the Sinhala land and spread the religion of love, honesty, truthfulness, and justice. In order to commemorate this, a temple to Lord Buddha was built at Kataragama.

Mahāvaṃsa. The mountain, according to this well-known tradition, was Adam's Peak. The text also lists other places visited—but not Kataragama.

[13] *Thevan* is Tamil for *deva*, "god."

[14] This alludes to a folk etymology. In Tamil, Kataragama is called Kathirgāmam. This can be explained (religiously, not philologically) as the combination of "'Kathir' meaning effulgence (Jyotir) and 'Kāmam' implying Love. In short it is a place where the *light* of Muruga mingled with the *love* of Valli." Ratna Navaratnam, *Karttikeya, the Divine Child* (Bombay: Bharatiya Vidya Bhavan, 1973), p. 191.

The Nāḍi Vākyam predicts an atomic Third World War between 1980 and 1990. It will last three months, inflict vast destruction, and be settled by religious leaders (*āgamika nāyakayō*). However, if we follow Nehru's policies this war can be avoided. In either event, world government will follow in A.D. 2000; there will be peace for a thousand years, good health and long life, due to new drugs—possibly "atom drugs." There will be equality (*tulyatādharma*), not communism but maybe "religious socialist government."

Comment

Balangoḍa Ānanda Maitreya is of a venerable age and the influences on his thought are not entirely new. Clearly Theosophy and astrology are of paramount importance. A pillar of the Order, he holds traditional views on the role of monks and disapproves of monks in politics. He also did not approve of Māpalagama Vipulasāra officiating at a wedding ceremony. He strongly supports lay meditation, but seems to see its virtue mainly in improving the quality of the Order. However, some other characteristics of Protestant Buddhism are prominent. Though speaking to us in Sinhala he introduced English words at some highly significant points: when he referred to the eyes of Maitreya as "mystical" (indeed, it would be hard to translate that word into Sinhala); and, most interestingly, in talking of *nirvāṇa*, the very center of his religious life, when he had recourse to such words as "positive" and "relative." Whether his views have been formed by Theosophy and/or European scholarship is here of less interest than the mere fact that he feels that English best expresses them.

The Buddhicization of Jesus comes from the central Theosophical doctrine that both the Buddha and Jesus were members of the line of great religious Masters, Mahatmas, who all preach the same thing. On the other hand, the Buddhicization of Kataragama is a theme close to the heart of this book. On more levels than one this story shows direct Indian influence: is it not attributed to a Tamil astrologer and through him to ancient Indian seers? But the story also represents a strong Sinhala Buddhist reaction: the cult was founded by the Buddha, and Kataragama was originally a Buddhist deity. In laying claim to a Buddhist origin for Kataragama this story is an ideological parallel to the new custom (see Chapter 12) of having Buddhist monks chant blessings at the inception of the great annual firewalking there. It is not unique. An educated Kandyan girl told us that she had read a newspaper article by a monk who had conversed with Kataragama; Kataragama told him that his father, Īśvara, was a Hindu, but he was a Buddhist and the Buddha had entrusted to him the care of the Buddhist religion. This last claim neatly transfers to Kataragama the function that the ancient chronicle of Sri Lanka, the *Mahāvaṃsa*, ascribes to Viṣṇu.

The Venerable Balangoḍa Ānanda Maitreya is popular, influential, and respected among educated Sinhala Buddhists (and wider afield). To what extent is he likely to have influenced others directly, and in what respects does he merely represent a (possibly extreme) example of trends? We would guess that his views on the character of Kataragama, which he is unlikely to have kept to himself, have been more influential than his Theosophically-inspired vision and opinions on *nirvāṇa*, which he knows to be heterodox. Nor is he likely to have publicized the astrological oracles about himself that he so eagerly sought. On the other hand, these matters do stand at the center not merely of his personal life as a monk but also of his professional life as a scholar. Moreover, we are reliably informed that another famous scholar monk, the Venerable Nārada, declared in a sermon that he had received predictions from the Nāḍi Vākyam and that all had come true except the date of his death.

Astrology is an ancient component of South Asian civilization, so we must ask to what extent the Venerable Balangoḍa's obsession with the subject bears the marks of modernism. Although in the Canon the Buddha condemns as "beastly sciences" various forms of prognostication and forbids their practice to monks, knowledge of astrology has always been a part of traditional learning in Sri Lanka[15] and as such a common part of the intellectual repertory of monks. Probably it was only its practice for money that was considered improper. On the other hand, the casting of horoscopes—a complex branch of the subject—seems to have been rare in Sinhala village life until recent times, certainly much less common than in India. Moreover, the calculation of precise auspicious moments was only possible in traditional society where there were clocks (of traditional kinds)—presumably only at court and in major temples. For enterprises that required auspicious beginnings, astrology predicted auspicious and

[15] For astrology in traditional Sinhala Buddhism, and in particular its relation to other systems of causal explanation, see Gombrich, *Precept and Practice*, pp. 146–50.

inauspicious days rather than precise times. Life crises, events in the agricultural cycle, public works, and rituals had to begin on a suitable day: nothing could start on a Tuesday, marriages best took place on Thursdays, rituals for the gods avoided Buddhist holy days. Village society was also much concerned with omens. A bad omen, or obstacle (*bādā*), encountered for example as one left home, caused one to turn back and postpone the enterprise. There were texts (called *bādāvali*) that listed such bad omens: inauspicious people and animals one might meet and sounds one might hear. *Suba* and *asuba*, the "auspicious" and the "inauspicious," were matters for much concern; but the terms related not merely to astrological phenomena—days and omens—but also to other categories such as pollution.

The terms *suba* and *asuba* now refer almost exclusively to astrological time. Concern is not only with auspicious days, but with precise auspicious moments, measured to the minute. The system of obstacles is now little used. It appears naive and unsophisticated; in a city one rarely encounters the cry of a woodpecker, and modern life does not permit postponement of journeys: the office manager will not accept *bādā* as an excuse for late arrival at work nor will the plane wait. Uncertainty about the outcome of one's expedition requires more sophisticated consultation. Whereas it is still permissible to arrive two hours late for a social appointment, all enterprises on which anxiety may focus are timed to the minute. Since cross-cousin marriage is now the exception rather than the rule, and one may be marrying a stranger, the best one can do to ensure success is to examine the partners' horoscopes with elaborate care and then to marry them at the best possible moment. Even important political decisions are timed by consulting astrologers, who base their advice both on the individual politician's horoscope and on the almanac, thus buttressing the traditional notion that political outcomes depend on the ruler's personal fortunes. In modern Sinhala society auspicious dates and times are most commonly established by consulting a single annual almanac, the *Ǟpā Pañcāngalita*, which began publication in 1893.

There appear to be several reasons for the increased popularity of astrology. It is not just that now nearly everyone has a watch. Increased contact with India and an educated awareness of Sinhala cultural roots have produced enthusiasm for what is seen as an Indian contribution to human knowledge that can plumb secrets inaccessible to Western science. Astrological literature, both books and newspapers, is in great demand not only for practical use but to cater to the hunger for information and understanding of the world which there are few other Sinhala publications to satisfy. At the same time, as we have shown above, the state of society and the economy produce much more anxiety and uncertainty these days than used to be current; there is a vast demand for reassurance about the future.

What links this to Protestant Buddhism is that it often takes the form—as in our case above—of a demand for reassurance about the *past*. Neither knowledge of one's own former lives nor knowledge of the former lives of others is a traditional topic of astrology. In the Canon both those kinds of knowledge are said to be acquired, purely by cultivating the mind, in the final stages on the road to Enlightenment. According to doctrine one's luck is determined by one's past moral actions, one's *karma*; but that *karma* one cannot normally know directly. However, it can be reified in one's horoscope: in this way an astrologer can show you what you have coming to you.

Venerable Ānanda Maitreya's faith in astrology is probably reinforced by the influence of Theosophy and other forms of Western occultism—his study of hypnosis points in the same direction. Theosophy is normally associated with a belief in astrology. Āpā Appuhāmi, the founder of the almanac mentioned above, was an early member of the Buddhist Theosophical Society. Dharmapāla wrote: "My father was taught astrology and he was an expert in the science."[16] Evidently he too believed in it, but had a bad conscience about using it. One diary entry records: "I thought of consulting an astrologer; but Buddha has condemned this."[17]

The Venerable Ānanda Maitreya suffers no such ambivalence. While Dharmapāla (late in life) set him on to *attack* Theosophy, there seem to be striking similarities in the influence Theosophy has exerted on the two men. Dharmapāla believed in Theosophy's occult predictions: "Medhankara Priest who left us in 1887 August will appear again in August, 1901, and preach Buddhism. In 1900 the Masters will again appear publicly and teach the Dharma."[18] The diary entry for the day before this remark was penned[19] records a vision: "Last night I gazed attentively at the candle from 9 to 10; again from 11 to 2 p.m.[20] I saw a light at the foot of the

[16] Quoted from his *Diary* by Amunugama, "Anagarika Dharmapala," p. 701.

[17] Diary entry, 18 April 1895, in *The Maha Bodhi* 61, no. 8, August 1953, p. 303.

[18] Diary entry, 6 August 1897, *The Maha Bodhi*, 65, no. 7, July 1957, p. 297.

[19] Diary entry, 5 August 1897, *The Maha Bodhi* 65, no. 7, July 1957, p. 296.

[20] *Sic*, presumably for A.M.

bed but I did not care to examine it. It was after I had laid down after extinguishing the candle." Ānanda Maitreya's vision of the Buddha whose name he bears was of course more spectacular. That this Buddha looked like Jesus—with whom Ānanda Maitreya later discovered himself to have, to say the least, an affinity—shows that he lacks the anti-Christian animus that made Dharmapāla reject that aspect of Theosophical doctrine. In Buddhist terms Ānanda Maitreya is more modest than Dharmapāla: the closest he came to the Buddha was to be the deity in the *bō* tree; Dharmapāla, on the other hand, seems at times to have identified with the Buddha. "Had a cold and hot bath. The Bodhisat at his birth had first a cold and then a hot bath."[21] At Bodh Gaya he wrote in his diary:[22] "Under the Bo tree I pledged: *Gautama namin Budu vemva. Me demavpiyo jatiyak pasama demavpiyo vetva.*" The editor, Sri D. Valisinha, has annotated this:[23] "Sinhalese sentence which means: 'May I become Buddha, Gautama by name, may my present parents be my parents in all lives to come.' " This preserves the ambiguity of the original: *budu vemvā* could just mean "may I be Enlightened," but that is here excluded by the name Gautama; on the other hand the sentence can mean "may I become *the* Buddha called Gautama" or "may I become *a* Buddha called Gautama." Since *the* Buddha called Gautama, namely the historical Buddha, is past, ordinary logic might seem to exclude the former interpretation; but doctrine does not speak of a future Buddha of the same name, and indeed it would seem to be pointless to refer to Gautama Buddha unless one meant the obvious Buddha of that name. We deduce, therefore, that Dharmapāla's aspiration was to become identified with Gautama Buddha, whom he believed in some sense still to exist and hence be capable of such identification. Evidently he had taken to heart his father's blessing, "Go, then, and aspire to be a *Bodhisatva*."[24]

We recall that Ānanda Maitreya is learned in the Mahāyāna and believes in a positive reality beyond death. According to Mahāyāna Buddhism the Buddha is absolute reality, eternal truth. Hindu Vedānta goes a step further by holding that salvation consists in realizing one's identity with God, the only reality. While in pure nondual Vedānta, the school of Śaṃkara, God is impersonal in the final analysis, most Hindus, including

[21] Diary entry, 9 July 1898, *The Maha Bodhi* 69, no. 9, September 1961, p. 275.

[22] Diary entry, 4 April 1895, *The Maha Bodhi* 61, no. 8, August 1953, p. 301.

[23] Ibid.

[24] Dharmapāla's account, quoted in Obeyesekere, "Personal Identity," p. 234.

Vedāntins, conceptualize a personal form of God with whom they strive to realize their identity. Dharmapāla's religious aspiration sounds very like a form of this idea of salvation expressed in Buddhist terms. He was evidently influenced by the great Hindu revivalist (Protestant Hindu) Svāmi Vivekānanda. Dharmapāla had been with Vivekānanda two years earlier at the World Parliament of Religions in Chicago, where it was Vivekānanda, representing Hinduism, who had made the greater impression, and the two remained in touch; moreover Dharmapāla was at the time living in India and frequently visited Calcutta, Vivekānanda's base. In fact the diary entry recorded only two days earlier[25] refers to someone as "my good Brother, brother-chela [disciple] of Vivekananda," which proves that at this time Dharmapāla considered himself Vivekānanda's disciple. This is by no means the first time in history that Buddhism has been influenced by a Hindu soteriology.

Theosophy has a concept of salvation much like that of Vedānta (by which it has been influenced), though vaguer.[26] As a scholar and intellectual the Venerable Ānanda Maitreya is able to express himself much more precisely. We quoted above two passages from the *Buddhist Annual* for 1932; Ānanda Maitreya inhabits the same universe of discourse. In the first passage the Theosophist neo-Buddhist Alexandra David-Neel talked of "mysticism." Shortly after the passage quoted from the second article, Sri Nissanka talks of the spiritual elite for whom he is founding a forest hermitage, "those, be they monks ordained or otherwise, laymen or women, who, having utterly finished with ritual and ceremonial, devote all that time [on earth] or a part of it, to real contemplation upon the *absolute*."[27]

[25] Diary entry, 2 April 1895, *The Maha Bodhi* 61, no. 8, August 1953, p. 301.

[26] "Theosophists also maintained that the Buddhists had misunderstood the teachings of the Buddha especially with regard to the soul and in their view of *Nirvana*. Far from preaching *An-atma*, or the theory of the absence of a soul, the Buddha too had followed Hinduism and accepted the soul as an indestructible entity, which after death was reabsorbed into a supreme life or self which the Hindus called *Brahman*. The Theosophists equated this condition with *Nirvana* or *Nibbana*, and declared that it was a mark of sectarianism to say that *Nibbana* is not *Brahman*." L. A. Wickremeratne, "Annie Besant, Theosophism, and Buddhist Nationalism in Sri Lanka," *Ceylon Journal of the Historical and Social Sciences*, n.s. 6, no. 1 (January–June 1976): 79.

[27] *Buddhist Annual of Ceylon*, p. 206. See chap. 6 n. 43 and n. 44.

CHAPTER 10

Three Buddhist Leaders

Meditation and Possession: The Case of the Pereras

Mr. and Mrs. Perera are a highly educated and intelligent couple, perfectly fluent in English. He is a pleasant, good-looking man of about fifty; she is a few years younger. He attended a famous Buddhist school and is a university graduate. By profession he is a teacher in an institute of higher education; though originally appointed in another subject, he now teaches Buddhism. In his teaching he uses both English and Sinhala, and he is just as happy speaking about his religion in the one language as in the other. To us (in 1978) he spoke mainly in English, so that we have been able to report him largely in his own words. This use of English was not unusual for him because he had lodging in his home a young university teacher from another country in Asia, a Buddhist, who did not know Sinhala but participated in the religious activities and had come to share the beliefs we are about to describe.

When teaching Buddhism professionally, Mr. Perera includes in his classes—he began to do so in 1977—instruction in meditation. He was free to draw up his own syllabus, and got it approved by the Ministry of Education. The meditation he teaches is of the "calming" type, to acquire concentration; he calls it "tranquil meditation." The subjects he uses are common ones: breathing, kindness, recollection of the Buddha. He does not teach insight meditation (*vipassanā*) in that context. The instruction is not directed toward attaining *nirvāṇa*, but aims to give the ability to concentrate. In our terms, for those pupils it is purely instrumental. Mr. Perera also teaches meditation regularly to another group that consists entirely of intellectuals, and in this activity he acquired the sponsorship of an important lay Buddhist charitable foundation. Neither to his pupils where he is employed nor to this latter group does he impart any of the esoteric teachings of which he told us; but both classes include some members of his own society, which we shall here call the Friends of the Dhamma.[1]

Before we describe this esoteric society, a few more words on Mr. Perera's exoteric views on meditation. They are not unusual for a modern Buddhist. "The idea of meditation is to make a success of lay life," he said. "We [here he refers to the members of his society] want to make meditation a part of daily living, to practise the Dharma way of living." Though he is certainly attached to Buddhist moral principles, by "the Dharma way of living" he means practice in the sense of realization achieved by meditation. If one fully understands the moral precepts of Buddhism one will follow them automatically. Meditation helps in lay life because it leads to nonattachment. Inefficiency is mostly due to craving, and Dhamma is to limit craving. We asked about business. Even business can benefit from the Dhamma, for earning is secondary. One should know where to draw the line and earn only enough to support one's dependents. If one keeps the Dhamma principles one can hardly become a millionaire: "I think all businessmen exploit." We asked Mr. Perera whether there are any businessmen in his society; he thinks not.

To meditate, then, it is not necessary to leave the lay life, except for short intensive spells of *samatha*—what we might call retreats. But even that is like going to a library to read a book; one can also read books at home. For his society Mr. Perera in fact conducts occasional "meditation camps" lasting a week. At the same time, however, the lay meditator makes spiritual progress towards *nirvāṇa*. "I firmly believe it is possible to reach the highest as a layman." At one point in our interview Mrs. Perera said to her husband in English, "So you are trying to do it, no?—to be an *arhat*?" One can measure one's progress on the path by one's increased detachment. One can also check one's progress by referring to the *Visuddhimagga*. Grasping ceases—there is a moment of freedom. Then one retraces the sequence of thought that led up to that moment, the insight that all things are transient, and one can recapture the experience. One sees various truths through a series of intuitive flashes. But it is not necessary to recollect one's former lives (*pubbenivāsānusmṛti jñāna*). If at the point of death one grasps no more, there is no rebirth.

[1] Nothing that we were told or shown was said to be confidential. Nevertheless, since the movement has an Inner Circle that does not seek publicity, we have used pseudonyms and made one other small change, otherwise inconsequential, to conceal identity.

We asked Mr. Perera what kind of meditation he taught and practiced, and he said he followed the *sati-paṭṭhāna*. (This is the method which is the basis of the insight [*vipassanā*] tradition.) When we asked him how he learned it he smiled, checked for a moment, and then explained. He first read books about it, discussed things with people, and meditated himself, but seemed to make no progress. "Then somehow I came in touch with the occult." A brother of his, a bus inspector, became a medium for someone from another world. At first this manifested itself in automatic writing. His brother would get up at night and write messages and then, following instructions from above, mail them to Mr. Perera in the morning without even being aware of their content. After this the brother developed "direct mediumship" so that Mr. Perera could converse through him with the deities in the other world. He himself developed contact with these deities, not through a trance but while sitting in meditation; however, the instructions he received himself were generally less clear, and for details he had to resort to his brother. On this basis Mr. Perera founded his "Friends of the Dhamma" society.

Unfortunately his brother, who was unmarried when he first became a medium, has recently taken to drink. If he is sober he can still act as a medium and "what comes through is fairly genuine," whereas "earlier it was perfect." His brother is still the only true medium, but both Mr. and Mrs. Perera have the "power of communication." They have both done exercises for over two years to develop this faculty, by drawing power (*śaktiya*) from nature (*svabhāvaya*). Indeed, all members of the Inner Circle (see below) are taught to "develop contacts" for themselves. The group did try to find another medium but the deities told them not to. Mrs. Perera has very good powers of clairvoyance, and Mr. Perera only a little. We gather that lack of a medium does not hamper the group's work under Mr. Perera's leadership; we also deduce from what we saw (see below) that Mrs. Perera's powers of clairvoyance now play an important part.

When Mr. Perera founded his society, he advertised it in the newspapers and received some replies in this way. Its membership he describes as predominantly young and exclusively lay, consisting mainly of teachers and government servants. (To this we may add intellectuals.) As stated above, there are no business people. A few of the members are very poor—one woman made money to attend a camp by breaking stones—but we infer that these are a small minority. There is no subscription and the society has no standing funds, but members contribute the cost of their upkeep at meetings. There are sixty-five in all, and of these about forty are members of the Inner Circle. Mr. Perera recommends members for the Inner Circle; then through the medium the deities give him instruction on how to interview the candidate in the presence of the others.

The meetings seem to be of two kinds. There are "meditation camps," lasting a week; and there are meetings of just one or two days, usually at a member's house. These latter meetings Mr. Perera first said were for "discussions"; but we gather that the discussions are based on séances. At the "camps" there is contact, but it is not through a medium. (Presumably Mr. and Mrs. Perera can always have contact.) Once a year a "meditation camp" is held at Situlpavuva, an ancient Buddhist site near Kataragama. The group first offers *pūjā* at the shrine at Kataragama, then goes to the ancient stupa and meditates in the open air. Why Situlpavuva? It is a very peaceful, holy place, a lay member told us; in ancient times there were twenty thousand *arhat*s there.

Who are the deities who guide the group? They are a group of deities who live in the Tusita heaven.[2] Most of them are female. They live in a particular *maṇḍala* (circle, sphere of influence), the forty-second, and their chief is exoterically called Sarasvatī.[3] In fact it is not really Sarasvatī but a goddess under Sarasvatī, whose name must be kept a secret. None of the goddesses who speak to them are generally widely known. Before speaking they announce their names. Some of them, but by no means all, were connected with members of the group in previous lives and can tell them about those lives; Mr. Perera has received such information. The chief deity can dispatch whomever she wishes to convey messages to them—one, two, or three deities at a time. The deities specialize in particular topics; thus one is for science, one to help members with their ailments, and so forth. The deity who communicated with them first, however, remains their chief teacher; she is the instructress in the Buddhadhamma, which she heard from the Buddha himself, as she was a deity in his lifetime.

The deities have ruled that their names and other details may not be

[2] According to ancient Buddhist cosmology, this is one of the six "god-heavens" directly above our world—the third from the bottom. What distinguishes it is that in it the next Buddha lives his last life before being born on earth; that is, each Bodhisattva in turn must be born there. The Tusita heaven plays no part in standard Sinhala religious practice.

[3] The Hindu goddess of learning, not active in the traditional Sinhala pantheon. See chap. 3.

revealed to nonmembers because those not genuinely interested in the Dhamma may ridicule their messages—especially as some of those messages may deviate from what is generally considered to be the Buddha's word. There is a hierarchy in heaven and a rule that a deity may not act in a way derogatory to the dignity of his or her seniors. The major deities such as Viṣṇu know of what is going on and have approved it. All other members have to take an oath of secrecy; only Mr. Perera is permitted to divulge the information at his own discretion.

The advice of the goddesses enabled Mr. Perera to make progress in his meditation: he saw things in a new light and shifted from bookish learning to the contemplation of nature. Nature plays a considerable part in his thought: the society's emblem shows the sun rising over water and thus symbolizes both the light of illumination spreading over the ocean of *saṃsāra* and the power of the sun in nature. The exercises he now undertakes are threefold: concentration, mindfulness, and *mantra*. (The first two of these correspond to *samatha* and *vipassanā*; we note that the third has its antecedents in Tantric Buddhism.) The power of nature is great and its misapplication could lead to insanity. However, it is the goddess who has shown him how to use it. Its main purpose is to get one to *nirvāṇa*. Healing is only incidental and comes from another source, Hippocrates. Hippocrates, the father of medicine, is now a very high god, "a god in his own right." He lives in an area other than that inhabited by the deities with whom they are in regular contact, but can be contacted through them. If a member of their family falls ill, Mr. and Mrs. Perera get in touch with him, and he has given them remarkable medicines, telling them what herbs to gather and how to prepare them. Healing too, however, is not the exclusive prerogative of Mr. and Mrs. Perera; other members of the Inner Circle have also been informed by the deities that they can heal if they wish. Moreover, Hippocrates operates under his own rules and requires the permission of no superior deity, so his advice is not secret.

In theory it is possible for certain very advanced human beings, not just gods, to communicate with initiates. Mr. Perera believes that there are two such men in India and three in China or Mongolia. But they have not yet been in touch with them.

The deities are not greatly concerned with the externals of morality. Members of the society of course are asked to keep the Five Precepts, which include abstaining from alcohol, and vegetarianism is recommended, but enforced only during meetings. Similarly, such habits as smoking and chewing betel are prohibited to members only during meetings. But the external act of "taking the precepts" is not favored by the deities, and at the camps the eight precepts are never formally taken; it is understanding that the deities stress, because once we understand that something is bad we will not do it. The deities also avoid the normal technical terminology of Buddhism: they always stick to ordinary Sinhalese words (e.g., *ällīma* for *taṇhā*).

The techniques of meditation that Mr. Perera teaches to his meditation classes are based in the first place on *haṭha yoga*. His knowledge of *haṭha yoga* derives from two sources: English books and his acquaintance with a Sri Lankan Tamil called Swami Varuṇānanda. This swami is "a real yogi" with miraculous powers "like a *ṛṣi*." Once before founding the society Mr. Perera was assailed by doubts, but his wife was trying to make him believe. Within three months of this attack of skepticism he came across the swami. The swami was the pupil of an Indian guru (whom he had found in a cave on the Malabar coast); he wore brown robes and was fine to look upon. He would fast for whole months at a time and had a large following. Mr. Perera did a lot of meditation with him. The swami first developed his miraculous powers while meditating on the *cakra*s (centers of power in the body, according to Tantric mystical physiology). On emerging from a trance one day he found a ring in his hand; considering, he remembered that it was a ring he had lost and thought of before entering the trance. He was thereafter able to make objects materialize, move toward him, etc. However, he somehow came to owe this power to a devil (*bhūta*) whom he had to feed with his blood once a month. If he missed the day he would immediately have an accident and cut himself. He then wished to get rid of the power and pass it on; however, the taker would have to go on giving blood to the devil. He offered Mr. Perera the power, but he refused it—even though when the offer was first made the concomitant disadvantage was not explained; the swami only confided in him later. The swami knew the Dhamma and could preach a good sermon, but was later saddled with that devil, so his guru came and disrobed him and took him back to India.

Mr. Perera knew another Tamil, Swami Premānanda, who could produce sandalwood ash from his bare hands, an ounce or more at a time. He was "a born psychic." In response to a challenge from the manager of a (named) bank he made the notes from the locked bank vault appear in front of the manager.

Mr. Perera has also been to see Uttama Sādhu (see below) and thinks well of him. "Something has opened there also. A lot of knowledge is coming through to him." A friend of his, who is a devotee of Uttama Sādhu, has told him that before ordaining himself Uttama Sādhu used to walk on fire after pouring oil over his body and setting it alight. "Something creditable, no?" says Mr. Perera. It shows devotion to "the fire deities," *gini kurum̆bara dēvatā*.

Before describing a rite that we witnessed at the end of our interview, we pause for comment. Again, as in Chapter 9, we find here the influence of Theosophy—the Inner Circle, the Mahatmas (though not by name and not really operative), discreet séances with a Theosophical flavor. Equally pronounced is the Indian/Tamil influence, some of it direct, some of it mediated through English books (no doubt both Theosophical and other). We shall see another aspect of this Hindu influence below, as well as further evidence of the importance to the movement of goddesses and women.

The Protestant Buddhist features are pronounced and by now mostly familiar. The laicization of meditation can go no further. In his distrust of businessmen Mr. Perera gives direct expression to the anti-acquisitive ethic[4] that in its criticism of capitalism has so often made common cause with socialism.[5] Fundamentalism is prominent: one checks one's progress against the *Visuddhimagga*; the deities contacted are from the Tusita heaven, straight out of the Pāli scriptures. Mr. Perera calls these deities *deva*, using the Sanskrit/Pāli term, not the Sinhala. He teaches in English and spoke in English.

In some respects this movement is more Protestant than any of the Protestant Buddhism we have encountered so far. The rejection of form for substance, of the outward show of taking the precepts for the internalizing of their meaning, signifies a shift to a religion of the heart that recalls the Protestant Christian appeal to the individual conscience. Along with this

[4] "The Theravada Buddhist notion that worldly affluence and salvation striving are polarized is widely accepted in Ceylon, and thus the amassing of wealth is considered an activity which is inimical to spiritual progress." This makes "people feel guilty about wanting to make money, and therefore, by resorting to projection, condemn as amoral those who have succeeded in becoming affluent; the most popular scapegoats being the village *Mudalali* (trader) and the urban businessman." Tissa Fernando, "The Western-Educated Elite and Buddhism in British Ceylon," pp. 18–29, in *Tradition and Change in Theravada Buddhism*, ed. Bardwell L. Smith, Contributions to Asian Studies, vol. 4 (Leiden: E. J. Brill, 1973), p. 29. This universalization of an ultimate value of course characterizes *Protestant* Buddhism.

[5] Bechert, *Buddhismus* 1, chaps. 17, 20, and 22.

goes rejection of the hieratic Pāli terminology of Buddhist dogmatics for simple everyday language, whether in Sinhala or English; this recalls the Protestant rejection of Latin and even the "plain speech" of early Protestant sectarians. Like lay meditation, it implies spiritual egalitarianism. And this trend is indeed important in Mr. Perera's society, despite its esotericism. We have so far not mentioned Mr. Perera's concern over the problem of his leadership. Clearly he is the leader of the movement and regarded by at least some (probably all) members as a guru. This ascription obviously causes him great unease. The aim of his spiritual exercises is to diminish the ego, he said. At another point he said that the guru tradition is very dangerous, as the ego gets inflated. He interprets the yoga precept that one should not accept gifts in a broad sense and allows no one to worship him. We notice also his assigning leading roles to his wife and brother and his insistence that all members of the Inner Circle can learn to contact the deities and acquire healing powers. Here there is a genuine modesty.

Two members of the society, both of them teachers of Buddhist subjects at major institutions of higher education, were about to go abroad. A rite (*pūjā*) was held for them, and we were allowed to witness it. It had been intended that more members should attend, but there was a failure of communication. In any case, no more could have squeezed into the very small shrine room in a corner of Mr. Perera's house. This room contains an altar, some five feet above the ground, on which there are prints of Sarasvatī and of Skanda/Kataragama with his two wives—both prints of Tamil, not of Sinhala, origin. On the altar lay a peacock feather (emblem of Skanda), a conch, and oil lamps. A little higher, on another wall, is a very small altar in front of a picture of the Buddha. The other pictures on the walls are a printed photograph of an ancient Indian Buddha image, a photograph of an Indian yogin, a print of the *arhat* Sīvali (a very common object in Sinhala Buddhist households), and the society's emblem, described above. There was a large sign saying SILENCE in English. On the floor were mats and cushions; there was only just room for five people to sit there, with a couple more similarly accommodated in a tiny anteroom.

The material for the *pūjā* was supplied by one of the beneficiaries, who had come expecting a full meeting of the esoteric group. Two identical trays of offerings were prepared. Each was covered with a purple cloth. On each were neatly arranged seven separate bananas, four mangosteens with the top of the husk removed, a dish of milk rice dyed pink, a little lamp of clarified butter, and red and purple flowers. Betel leaves were placed under each lamp but were said not to be part of the offering. Mr. Perera changed out of his trousers into a plain white *veṭṭi* (the cloth worn by Tamil men[6] around the lower body) and Mrs. Perera changed into a white blouse and purple sari. She wore her hair down. Naturally all had bare feet.

Joss sticks and an oil lamp were lighted before the picture of the Buddha and oil lamps before the deities. Mr. and Mrs. Perera and the two beneficiaries made the usual salutation with joined palms before the picture of the Buddha and then sat down in silence, palms still joined. Mr. Perera had his eyes shut and appeared to be silently speaking (we might say "praying"). Then under Mr. Perera's guidance the two beneficiaries each lit a lamp containing clarified butter (*ghee*) before the deities. Resuming his former attitude, Mr. Perera then in a low tone made a statement in Sinhala ("I remind you . . ." [*matak karami*]) of why the group was there. After a pause he then said to his wife in Sinhala, "Talk in Sinhala." She had her eyes shut too. After another pause she began to say what she could see. She came up to a very ancient Hindu temple. At first there was no one around, but as she passed inside she came upon a figure dressed in white and gold. It turned out to be a beautiful woman carrying a musical instrument, with a child in her arms. The figure was motherly and welcoming. Now she saw a very different figure, black and blue, with a face so dark that at first she could not make it out. Then she saw two huge blue eyes in the face, a long nose, and a red mouth out of which lolled a great tongue dripping blood. The figure was even more frightening than the image at Munnēssarama. This too was no statue, but a living figure (*jīvamāna*). She dwelt at length, without raising her voice, on the gory details, especially the mouth with its red lips, flashing teeth, and bleeding tongue. The beautiful woman was Pattinī, the frightful figure Bhadra Kālī. She realized that the frightful goddess too would not hurt her; both figures were necessary (*avaśyatāva*). She folded her hands in worship to Bhadra Kālī, and blood from the tongue dripped onto them.

At this point Mr. Perera explained in English, as one of the beneficiaries did not understand Sinhala, "She wants you to offer to Bhadra Kālī." Both the beneficiaries then rose and offered their trays, which were lying on the altar, before the picture of Sarasvatī. Mr. Perera took the two bunches of

[6] Buddhist laymen observing the eight precepts also may wear such a garment, in which case it is known as a "white cloth" (*sudu redda*).

betel leaves from the altar and told both that he had written their names on the leaves in sandal paste. He then appeared to pierce each bunch with a needle, tied them together with red thread, and gave them to the two beneficiaries. Mrs. Perera had her eyes shut throughout. She then told the beneficiaries to fold their leaves, put them in an envelope, and keep them with them always; they would provide safety. It was not necessary to carry them everywhere, but once in a while they were to touch them. The instructions were translated into English by Mr. Perera. Both beneficiaries were then asked whether they had any special questions or requests; discretion forbids us to report on this episode, which lasted for more than ten minutes. Reassurance was conveyed. Both were then told to begin their journey with devotion (*bhaktiya*) and trust (*viśvāsaya*) for they had Her blessing (*unvahansēgē āśīrvādaya*). Mr. Perera then announced that on the forehead of each of the beneficiaries a drop of blood had fallen from Kālī's tongue. This was taken as a consummating benediction. All rose, briefly worshipped the images, and returned to the living room.

We asked Mr. Perera whether the terrifying vision was of Sohon Kālī (see Chapter 4) and he said no. Sohon Kālī is just one of the seven aspects of Kālī in her retinue. Sarasvatī is another. There are seven Kālīs and seven Pattinīs (and they are not entirely different?), but all this is a deep mystery (*tada gupta tänak*). To understand it one must consult the *Mūlapariyāya Sutta*.[7]

What struck us most about the above rite was that whereas all our previous conversation had prepared us for intercourse with purely Buddhist deities, the rite turned out to be entirely centered on Kālī. This was not the inspiration of the moment: the shrine room has the picture of Sarasvatī, and the colors of the offering and Mrs. Perera's sari, red and purple, prepared one for this Hindu deity. However, there may still be a close connection between the two: we could not be told the name of the Buddhist goddess, but we recall that she comes under Sarasvatī, and now we learn that Sarasvatī is a subordinate aspect of Mahā Bhadra Kālī. We see repeated the recurrent Indian development of the mother goddess: she splits into two, a benign and a frightening aspect, and yet it is the terrifying aspect that is truly worshipped and gives the potent blessings. The

[7] It can hardly be a coincidence that this sermon was also singled out by the Venerable Ānanda Maitreya; but to noninitiates like ourselves the point is obscure. It may be relevant that a foreign monk in Sri Lanka, Bhikkhu Bodhi, was at the time preparing a new translation of the text.

terrifying one acquires the name one would expect for the benign one, and then the process is ready to start on another cycle.

It is not necessary to stress that though Christians may sing of their hope to be washed clean in the blood of the Lamb, to traditional Buddhists such imagery is abhorrent. How far the frame of mind of the participants in this ritual differed from that normal for Buddhists old or new may be gauged from the following. One of the beneficiaries was asked whether he was going to do what one would normally expect of a religious middle-class Buddhist these days—hold a *pirit* ceremony before leaving for abroad. He was startled and said that really the questioner was quite right, but it simply had not occurred to him to do so. The difference in affect between a *pirit* ceremony and the blessing we witnessed needs no underlining.

Authority in religious matters used to rest in the Sangha. The typical Sinhala villager, if asked a question about Buddhism, would refer one to a monk. If Buddhism is equally accessible to all, however, where does authority lie? In the scriptures, surely. But they are not a social reality: living interpreters are required. Thus the laicization that is the hallmark of modern Buddhism contains within itself the seeds of sectarianism. Mr. Perera, a religious leader *malgré lui*, locates authority at one level in the civilized past or cultural tradition (gods of the Tusita heaven, Hippocrates), at another level in his close relations. For a while he had a guru (Swami Varuṇānanda), but it seems that his guru played him false. His own reluctance to be a guru may partly explain the secrecy surrounding the group and inhibit its growth.

We have suggested that Protestant Buddhism is part of a movement to demystify the world. Influenced by modern knowledge, it aims at cognitive rationality. Mr. Perera, highly educated, attempts to build his experiences of contact with the "occult" into a coherent system, a cosmology compounded of both doctrinal Buddhist and modern scientific elements. But this striving for cognitive rationality is startlingly associated with a reversion to irrationality (in the Weberian sense) in practical action, in other words to thaumaturgy. This again recalls the course of the Protestant Reformation. In England, Keith Thomas records, post-Reformation theologians laid stress on natural remedies (i.e., instrumental rationality); prayer was to be used only as a last resort. (Hence the adage "God helps those who help themselves.") But when sects burgeoned during the crisis of the Civil War, many of them claimed "to provide that supernatural solution to earthly problems which the makers of the Protestant Reformation had so sternly rejected. The sects revived the miracle-working aspect of medieval Catholicism without its Roman and hierarchical features."[8] Mr. Perera's movement perhaps falls just short of being a sect because of his modesty; and its thaumaturgy, as befits educated, even intellectual, circles, is discreet. But in the two movements that follow, both of which appeal to rather less elite, though still mainly middle-class, groups, we find not only a full-blown sectarian assertion of separateness but also a florid display of miraculous powers combining with what we have come to regard as Protestant characteristics.

Mr. Perera is a professional teacher of Buddhism and an educated and intelligent man. It is therefore not surprising that he preserves the distinction between using Buddhist meditation for salvation and the gods for worldly concerns. In the next two movements we shall find that distinction somewhat blurred: in them "Buddhism" assumes functions traditionally associated with the spirit religion. We should first note, however, that Mr. Perera's spirit religion is idiosyncratic. For that part of it that is more instrumental than expressive, the séances for healing and advice, he applies elements of learned, doctrinal tradition to new purposes. For devotion and the procurement of blessings he turns to the Hindu Kālī. We have recorded above how a young man moved from the intensive practice of Buddhist meditation to making his living by possession as a priest. The apparent affinity between lay meditation and possession is a major theme of this book. In Mr. Perera we find an interesting variation on the theme: he himself does not get possessed but his wife does and they act in partnership, so that in effect he is the officiant but without sacrificing Buddhist decorum. This use of a female medium to achieve contact with the divine has deep roots in Indian tradition. We have met it in the partnership between the Venerable Visuddhānanda and Mrs. C. E. de Silva, and we meet it again in the symbiosis of Uttama Sādhu and his female entourage, to which we now turn.

Uttama Sādhu, the Self-ordained Buddha

The main sect we are about to describe had its origin in a breakaway from a thaumaturgic cult headed by Mr. M.D.S. Samaravīra, a Sinhala busi-

[8] Keith Thomas, *Religion and the Decline of Magic* (London: Weidenfeld and Nicholson, 1971), p. 125.

nessman in Maradana, a crowded, mainly working-class part of Colombo. Mr. Samaravīra called himself Pinvatā, "the Meritorious One," and called his three chief disciples Silvatā, "the Virtuous One," Guṇavatā, "the Excellent One," and Näṇavatā, "the Knowledgeable One." Pinvatā seems to have begun his cult in the 1950s; he died in 1976 and we did not meet him. His followers believe that he was Enlightened, or rather that he was a Buddha. We have pointed out in Chapter 9 that Sinhala has an important ambiguity: *budu venavā* can mean "to become Enlightened" or "to become a Buddha." In a traditional environment this formal ambiguity would be of no importance because the context would always make clear which was meant: after all, the number of Buddhas is delimited by scripture. But in the new sects the ambiguity can be exploited: initiates or followers understand the term in its strongest sense, but to outsiders who are shocked by so unorthodox a claim it can be represented, tacitly or explicitly, as merely (though still not inconsiderably) a claim to Enlightenment. Thus when a follower told us that he became *budu* we could take it to mean that he attained Enlightenment like the saintly disciples of the Buddha; but the clue that more was meant came in the next statement: that Pinvatā gave a *vivaraṇa* to each of his three chief disciples. A *vivaraṇa* is a classical term for a revelatory prediction made by a Buddha to a follower that the latter will in turn become a Buddha. (In the classical case this will come to pass after a vast lapse of time.) Pinvatā, then, was considered by some, and presumably considered himself, a Buddha, and promised his three chief disciples that they too would become Buddhas. All were laymen at the time. Silvatā, the senior disciple, broke with Pinvatā in 1962 and around that time took the title Uttama Sādhu, "the Supremely Holy." He also put on monastic robes and proclaimed himself a self-ordained monk. Though one informant thought that the new title was bestowed by Pinvatā, the logic of the situation suggests that he took it himself after the break, as a claim to be superior to his teacher (whom he no longer acknowledged) and perhaps to coincide with his subsequent shift from the white apparel of the pious layman to the monk's robes.

Guṇavatā and Näṇavatā continue to practice as healers in and near Colombo, and from their proceedings one can probably deduce the character of Pinvatā's cult, as they claim to be carrying on in his tradition. They provide services for the usual range of contingencies—healing, averting general misfortune, etc.—with performances that combine elements from Buddhism and the spirit religion, especially the cult of Kataragama in the modern style; and all this is wrapped up in a good deal of semi-intelligible grandiloquence and pseudoscientism. The one performance we witnessed combined *pirit* (the traditional recital of certain Pāli texts); firewalking, said to demonstrate devotion to Kataragama or any other deity one chose; and lime cutting, the traditional centerpiece of rites to avert misfortune caused by demons. We were told that the charcoal of the fire pit was a disinfectant, that limes produce electricity, and so forth. Buddhist *sacralia* were more involved in the ritual than is traditional, and some considered that the power harnessed was that of the Buddha directly rather than that of gods. The Three Refuges, to Buddha, Dhamma, and Sangha, were taken in the normal way, and then those Three Jewels were invoked in the most elaborate Sanskritized Sinhala, the high-toned language used to invoke deities—but never the Buddha—in traditional spirit cults. Then seven lamps were lit: four for the four guardian deities and one each for the Three Jewels. The healers acquire the mental power (*cittabalaya*) to walk the fire by attaining the first *jhāna*. But they do not seem to believe that they are or are about to become Buddhas themselves, and their cult practices are syncretic in a way that by now we have come to expect in working-class Colombo. This fits what a follower of theirs told us: Pinvatā had a worldly and a supramundane side (*koṭasa*) and these two carry on the worldly side, by which they make a living. The supramundane side, according to the same informant, is carried on by Uttama Sādhu. But the informant—whose son became a monk under Uttama Sādhu but left him after three years to live in a cell by himself near Kataragama—was evidently ambivalent about Uttama Sādhu. He said that his powers had declined. Uttama Sādhu, he said, had promised to rise cross-legged in the air,[9] but did not; perhaps this was because he or some of his disciples worked for gain. This informant was evidently still guided by the traditional distinction between Buddhist religious professionals, who never work for money and are thus "above the world" in both senses, and officiants of the spirit religion, who both cater to the needs of this world and take fees for doing so.

When we last saw Uttama Sādhu, in 1979, he headed an order of five monks and thirty-seven nuns: most of the nuns were well under thirty,

[9] In India this would be a commonplace yogic accomplishment (*siddhi*). But in a Theravādin context it suggests emulation of the Buddha's levitation at his father's ploughing festival (*vap magula*)—or so we are led to think by Uttama Sādhu's self-image (see below).

the youngest only six. We use the monastic terms for convenience; from the orthodox point of view there are no "monks" or "nuns" because Uttama Sādhu is self-ordained and has himself ordained the rest. He uses special terminology; but all of them do shave their heads and wear monastic robes and so present themselves like orthodox clergy. In particular the style is modelled on that of reformist forest dwellers. Self-ordination is not legitimate in the Buddhist tradition, nor is it unprecedented in Sri Lanka: Carrithers[10] has traced a case in 1898—though in that case it was done by a regularly ordained monk who had renounced his robes as a gesture of protest. That monk, Subodhānanda, started a small protest movement that became important briefly in 1954 because of its influence on another self-ordaining[11] protester, Vǟbaḍa Tāpasa Himi, and his group of followers. We shall see that Tāpasa Himi in turn has influenced Uttama Sādhu, but so far as we are aware neither Tāpasa Himi nor anyone else proceeded to invent his own form of ordination, let alone to bestow it on girls. Nor did those earlier protest groups claim to produce new versions of the Pāli Canon. Yet, despite the strangeness of these proceedings, Uttama Sādhu and his nuns command the respect, adherence, and even devotion of a fair number of people, many of them well educated. An article about them has appeared in the English-language press;[12] its tone is respectful and it contains no hint of criticism or comment on their being unorthodox in any way. This acceptance makes the movement much more than a curiosity.

Uttama Sādhu does not like to speak about his life before ordination; he explained to us that on becoming a monk one gives up everything,[13] even a name. (He also claims to have no citizenship.) From his followers we were however able to glean a few facts. He was born in 1921 or 1922 in Karavanälla, near Ruvanälla in the Kǟgalla District. He lived in Colombo, where he owned or managed—accounts differ—a textile shop and owned a fleet of about a dozen taxis. He has also worked as a newspaper reporter. Before leaving the lay life, he had a wife and a son.

This last fact he too mentioned to us. Otherwise he would talk of his earlier life only in terms of his religious quest. He never mentioned Pin-

[10] Carrithers, *Forest Monks*, p. 104.

[11] It appears that these other men only gave themselves the lower ordination (*pabbajjā*); we shall see that Uttama Sādhu deals in both.

[12] "Young Women Going the Buddha Way," text, H. W. Abeypala, pix [*sic*], Bernard Chandrasekera, *Weekend*, Sunday, 15 January 1978, p. 10.

[13] Except of course the canonical eight requisites: bowl, robes, dwelling, etc.

vatā to us, but said that he travelled all over Sri Lanka, trying various teachers and practices. He went to one teacher who had forty pupils, and when the teacher said "Hum" they all got possessed; he himself tried it and swung his head around, but his consciousness did not alter. He went to Kataragama, put pins through his lips and cheeks and hung on hooks, but he was fully conscious even though he felt no pain. He also visited many monasteries and hermitages, but found no place satisfactory for ordination: the monasteries nowadays are just kindergartens (*montessōri skōla*) where people learn Pāli and read books, but do not *do*. The Buddha instituted the ordination ceremony because there were unsuitable applicants and screening was necessary; but if one is pure one may ordain oneself. So that is what, some time in the late sixties, he did.

The myth that Uttama Sādhu has conceived about himself may not be very close to the actual facts. We know that at first he did have a teacher, Pinvatā. It is possible that he hung on hooks at Kataragama since a few Sinhala seem to have begun this practice recently. It is certain that like his teacher he used to go firewalking; we recollect that Mr. Perera commended his performance. We shall see that Uttama Sādhu considers himself a Buddha; he has modelled his past accordingly. Like the Buddha he has left a wife and young son to embark on a religious quest in which he has found all existing institutions wanting; finally he has ordained himself and founded a Teaching.

In 1962 (when he left Pinvatā), he settled on a small piece of ground in Battaramulla, an outer suburb of Colombo. He had a cement cell put up. He first lived there as an *anagārika*; he wore white, meditated, and healed. He called his organization, which consisted merely of himself and a few lay supporters, "The Board for Propagating the Doctrine of the Church" (*Sasuna Dharma Pracāraka Maṇḍalaya*), incorporating in its title the words that denote Buddhism both as the righteous truth (*Dharma*) and as an empirical phenomenon (*Sasuna*). It was here at Battaramulla that we first visited him, in 1975. It was easy to find him: one simply had to get off the bus on the main road and ask for the ascetic monk. "Ah," said people, "you mean the one who walks like this"—and they indicated a slow measured tread with minimal body movement and the eyes cast down in a grave, impassive gaze. Thus we could see immediately that Uttama Sādhu had hit on the crucial characteristic of a monk's public image, the representation of total control.

Carrithers's account of Vābaḍa Tāpasa Himi[14] makes it plain that in most respects he was—and is—quite a different character from Uttama Sādhu. But besides their self-ordination there are two important similarities in their public careers. Both have or are believed to have had episodes in their early development that echo episodes in the early life of Gautama Buddha.[15] And both have captured the imagination by their controlled demeanor.[16] In fact we shall see that Uttama Sādhu has taken this feature to its very limit in his disciples.

We ourselves were impressed. Like other hermit monks he was only accessible to the public at certain hours (in his case 9–11 A.M. and 3–5 P.M.) and we called on him after nine one morning. He evidently had a steady trickle of visitors, people calling to seek his advice and assistance. These visitors had included several prominent political figures, not all of them Buddhists. When we arrived, three young women who had come to consult him were with him. We waited at a shrine that contained only a stupa, no images—again suggestive of ascetic rigor. When they left, we were conducted up an incline to where he was sitting on a mat under a tree, both shoulders covered by a dark brown robe, so motionless that we did not immediately see him. Our attention was first caught by a nun in yellow robes, who turned out to be in attendance on him. When we had recovered from our surprise at discovering a second figure and greeted him, he silently indicated that we should move to another position, where he sat on elevated ground under another tree, and we sat on the ground a couple of feet below him on a sheet of dark brown plastic. At first Uttama Sādhu spoke very quietly and gravely, but as he warmed to his theme he talked fast and fluently and his features became animated. He is a man of considerable vitality. On the other hand he sat cross-legged for two and a half hours, barely moving his body, and several times alluded to this fact, contrasting it to our recurring need to change position. His lack of movement was not due to listlessness or low spirits, but was self-conscious and intentional.

At this first interview Uttama Sādhu gave us a long discourse on his teaching. His main point was that practicing Buddhism was a question not just of learning but of doing. Educated people like us, he said, could do

[14] Carrithers, *Forest Monks*, chap. 7.

[15] Ibid., p. 120.

[16] Ibid., p. 121.

it in three months, as he taught a short method (*keṭi kramayak*). *What* one could do in three months was not yet clear to us. He continually used the simile of passing examinations. One does not go on visiting a teacher after one has passed one's examinations; that is why he no longer needs to worship Buddha images, though he allows such worship to his lay followers. In the Canon the way to Enlightenment is divided into four stages, each in turn divided into "path" and "result." Uttama Sādhu compared the "path" to taking a B.A. examination and the "result" to passing it. But he evidently saw something beyond the final "result" (*rahat phala*) of Enlightenment, the normal goal of the Theravāda Buddhist.

Uttama Sādhu's sermon to us consisted largely of disquisitions on Buddhist terms and formulae central to the Teaching, the stock in trade of most sermons: he discussed the Three Refuges (the Buddha, the Dhamma, the Sangha), the five precepts, the noble eightfold path, the nine spiritual attainments (*samāpatti*), and similar formulaic summaries of Buddhist doctrine. We cannot and need not report the details of these teachings. We cannot, because to make them intelligible would require lengthy explanations of Theravādin orthodoxy; and we need not, because we shall soon see striking proof that the precise content of what he says has no relevance to an understanding of the movement. Nor are we convinced that these doctrinal details are stable. The point is simply that the discourses sound impressive, and we repeat that we were impressed—at first. Gradually it dawned on us that Uttama Sādhu's exposition was not merely unorthodox: it was wildly idiosyncratic. In illustration we need give only a short extract from our voluminous notes. There is a famous Pāli formula listing the virtues of the Buddha (*Buduguṇa*) in which the Buddha is given nine epithets.[17] Uttama Sādhu analyzed the formula to show that the first three epithets refer to the Buddha, the next three to the Doctrine, and the last three to the Order. He said that when one goes to the Buddha for refuge in the Pāli formula *Buddhaṃ saraṇaṃ gacchāmi*, the word *Buddha* is neuter and the reference is to one's own intelligence (*buddhi*). *Sangha* he derived

[17] The formula is called the *Iti pi so gāthā*. Its recitation constitutes the meditation of "recollecting the Buddha" (*Buddhānussati*). In our account of traditional Buddhism in a Kandyan village, we wrote: "What *pirit* is in public, the *Iti pi so gāthā* is in private. . . . The *Buduguṇa* are the most frequently employed spell in white magic. . . . The ex-headman said that in an *apalē* (astrologically dangerous period) one should just recite the *Buduguṇa*, and not bother about *bali-tovil* and such ceremonies." See Gombrich, *Precept and Practice*, pp. 206–8.

from Pāli *sanghaṭṭana*, "clashing," and made it mean "the whole world." *Bhagavā* received a long exposition to show that *bhaga*, "private parts," is left below; *bhava*, "becoming," is left above; and the Enlightened One somehow sails through the middle.

This kind of discourse has borrowed two surface features from the mass of Sinhala sermons. It plays with numbered lists; and it deals largely with etymologies, from which it claims to draw remarkable truths. Both features the Sinhala sermons have, of course, inherited from ancient exegetical literature, from the Pāli commentaries and indeed from large parts of the Canon itself; they are typical of scholasticism everywhere. Here there is an added ingredient. Uttama Sādhu is revealing to his audience, not through etymologizing alone, arcane interconnections between all the Buddhist terms and concepts with which they are familiar or half familiar. The discovery that everything links up is profoundly satisfying to the puzzled seeker, and if the link is somewhat esoteric he can add to his intellectual satisfaction pride in being one of the few elect who are in the know. Uttama Sādhu's discourse is full of Sanskrit and Pāli terms and discussions of those terms, though to us he denied knowledge of both languages; we shall soon see the significance of this denial. In fact he must know some Pāli, for in a sense he understands the terms he discusses; and indeed he has published a Sinhala translation of the *Dhammapada*. This translation is no doubt based (as is the work of orthodox scholars) on preceding translations and is unlikely to embody research, but from our knowledge of his movement's structure we are confident that his publications are his own work.

Uttama Sādhu claims that his teaching—which is Buddhism, correctly understood—is not incompatible with any religion (*āgama*); on the contrary, it in some sense includes them all. The doctrinal details of this claim are not spelled out, but for example in a small booklet[18] that Uttama Sādhu has produced for children, there is a page addressed to Christian children and another to Muslim children. They contain harmless moral platitudes. Hindu children are ignored, perhaps because they are assumed not to read Sinhala. We shall report below the claim that Jesus, Mary, and Mohammed have declared themselves in sympathy with the movement.

Uttama Sādhu and his followers lay great emphasis on their strict veg-

[18] *Harimaga*, published by *Hoňda Ḷamayingē Saṃvidhānaya*, "Sasuna Senasuna," Rattanapiṭiya, Boralāsgamuva, 2520 nikiṇi (i.e., 1976).

etarianism. (Abstention from alcohol is taken for granted.) They often point out that they abstain even from the Maldive (dried) fish which, crushed to fragments, is widely used as a seasoning. When at our first meeting we asked Uttama Sādhu how many followers he had he said there were about twenty thousand,[19] and immediately added that since they were strict vegetarians they were all in good health. Uttama Sādhu began his public religious career as a healer, and the provision of good health to his adherents is still an essential feature of the movement. He also used to exorcise, and his view of this is traditional: possession is always done by spirits (*bhūtayō*), never by gods, though a possessing spirit may claim to be a god. He strongly recommends belief in the gods—of which more below.

As one would expect, Uttama Sādhu is dismissive of the Sangha (as the term is conventionally understood). Thus we may remind the reader that although his movement is monastic in form, it displays most of the main features of Protestant Buddhism. Everyone is urged to meditate and seek *nirvāṇa*—though in this case under Uttama Sādhu's guidance. The traditional monastic role is strongly criticized in the light of puritan values such as vegetarianism. The style of exposition is pseudoscientific. The message overcodes all hitherto established religions—a point to which we shall return in our comments at the end of the chapter. Above all the movement is fundamentalist—though in a novel manner. For it produces two kinds of preaching. Uttama Sādhu's, to which we were exposed on our first visit, is but one of these. The other consists of the original canon as enunciated by the Buddha, not as corrupted by the clergy; this canon is picked out of the atmosphere, as it were on radio waves, enunciated and recorded by his nuns. Let us put this activity in its setting.

Uttama Sādhu has two headquarters, at Battaramulla and at Rattanapiṭiya, another of Colombo's outer suburbs, and he divides his time between them, but in recent years has spent more and more time at Rattanapiṭiya. Here his establishment is far more impressive. In a large garden there stand a preaching hall (again containing an aniconic shrine with only a stupa) and two rows of cement cells (*kuṭi*), one for monks (including Uttama Sādhu himself) and one for nuns, as well as several detached cells. The compound also contains an ordinary dwelling house—in fact, it is built in that house's garden. The house is owned and occupied by an el-

[19] We warn the reader that there is no substance to this claim.

derly couple; the lady we would judge to be the same age as Uttama Sādhu, that is, about fifty-five in 1976 (when we first met her), her husband perhaps a couple of years older. He had retired from his job as a medical technician; the lady was still employed as the vice-principal of a large school in Colombo. This couple had given the movement their land—and their youngest daughter, now in her early twenties. The husband was accorded the title of "chief supporter" and yet he described himself to us as "just like an outsider"; he was not a member of the committee of management. It was his wife, evidently a lady of strong character, who was of real importance. Though she still used her lay name, as she led a normal lay life when away from home, within the movement she was known as Mātā, the Pāli word for "mother." She wore white and practiced complete chastity. Uttama Sādhu explained her position thus. He was the earth which is necessary for a tree to grow; taking his essence (*sāraya*) grew the tree which is Mātā, the Mother of the Teaching; from that tree grew the fruit and flowers (*geḍimal*) which were the nuns.

Mātā's husband gave this account of their first meeting with Uttama Sādhu. In 1966 the lady was very ill, and their son went and sought his help. Uttama Sādhu knew that Mātā's husband reared chickens, so he said, "Do you want chickens or your mother?" They then tried to get rid of the chickens—who were in any case dying off. Their attempts to sell them were unsuccessful and Mātā's condition deteriorated daily. Finally in desperation the son took the last eight surviving chickens and dumped them on a prospective buyer; then he disinfected his home. Ever since the family has been strictly vegetarian and none of them has ever fallen ill. (Soon after recounting this he complained of a cold and a headache.)

By Uttama Sādhu's account he cured Mātā as he has cured other people, by passing his hand over her abdomen, though without touching her. His hands emitted hot rays, which burnt up her insides. Mātā now cannot sleep under the same roof as any male, even a child; were she to do so she would swoon and die. She therefore sleeps in a detached cell. In February 1976 Uttama Sādhu had gone to Battaramulla when she swooned and was about to die; she wrote several pages of "last words" (*avasāna vākya*), ending with worship of Uttama Sādhu. He returned in the nick of time to pass his hand over her and revive her.

The couple gave their land to Uttama Sādhu in 1967, we think before he had ordained himself. Who first became a nun we do not know, but in 1974 the couple's fifth and youngest child became a nun at the age of twenty. She is now at the head of the nuns' hierarchy, for Uttama Sādhu describes her role as analogous to that of Mahā Pajāpatī, the Buddha's stepmother, whose pleading (according to the Canon) persuaded the Buddha to institute the Order of Nuns. Like Mahā Pajāpatī, he said, she is self-ordained and now ordains others. Every day she sends a portion of her food to her parents.

Originally, we were told, there was only one cement cell, for Uttama Sādhu; now there is a short range of such cells on one side of the garden for him and five more monks, and a longer range opposite for the nuns. There seems to be accommodation for about twenty nuns. For the rest of the thirty-seven claimed to be in the movement there was clearly no room and we gather that they live scattered, probably on the premises of their families like the apostate daughters of Mr. Amarasinghe (see below). On the day that we first visited Rattanapiṭiya we counted one monk (besides the leader) and nineteen nuns in residence. The nuns varied greatly in age, but several of them were only children. At about 11:30, when it was time for their meal, the nuns filed silently out of their cells, completely swathed in their dark robes, holding begging bowls beneath the outer garment; they then were fed by a row of laity, headed by Mātā, while they stood in line; the two monks were fed apart. We gather that on some days the nuns go on alms rounds in the neighborhood. We were there on a Buddhist holy day and counted about eighty laymen. They wore white and passed the day in meditation and listening to sermons, as they would if they took the eight precepts at an ordinary temple. One of Uttama Sādhu's sermons came to them over an excellent public address system.

The movement, we were told, was administered by a committee[20] of three people chosen by Uttama Sādhu: Mātā, a headmaster (who said he had learned of Uttama Sādhu from another headmaster), and a worker in the Agricultural Department, who said (in 1976) that he had known Uttama Sādhu about fifteen years. This last gentleman estimated that the Pāli "airwaves" began only in about 1971. He began by taking the Buddhist moral precepts from Uttama Sādhu. His only daughter, who was fifteen, was having fainting fits. Uttama Sādhu recited some spells (*set kavi*) for her and made her become a strict vegetarian. He then cured her by putting his hands on her head. After two or three years (we gather that

[20] The chief supporter vehemently denied to us that the committee functioned, saying it was just "for discussion." We detect bad feeling.

the cure was a slow process) she too began to take the moral precepts from Uttama Sādhu. She never had the slightest inclination to marry—her father was emphatic on this point—and last year at the age of twenty-six said that she wanted to become a nun, to which he said both parents were happy to agree.

We were able to talk to the parents of the six-year-old nun, who were both present taking the precepts. They were probably in their early thirties. The father used to drive his own lorries but now drives for others—we gather he has come down in the world. They live as a nuclear family and have two daughters and a son, the youngest child. When the eldest child, the elder daughter, was three years old she used to faint. Uttama Sādhu cured her. She went for two years to kindergarten and then started school, but was not learning well. After a few months Uttama Sādhu took her as a nun, and since that time they have only talked to her twice, though they come about once a week. We gather she is now eight. The next daughter, about two years younger, began to preach to her parents at home about the unsatisfactory nature of life in the world (*sasara duka*). Her father told her to go to school and become a nun when she was over twenty, but she replied that she had already "passed the final examination" (we recall that this was a favorite metaphor of Uttama Sādhu's) and left to become a nun after only three months of primary school. (Uttama Sādhu however said she had not yet been to school and could not read or write.) The son, now aged five, was there taking the precepts with his parents.

Another layman present taking the precepts[21] told us he was the vice-principal of a high school. His initial contact with the movement came when Uttama Sādhu cured him of a stomach complaint he had had for four years. He then practiced *samatha* meditation under Uttama Sādhu's guidance, using a clay disc as his object, and attained *jhāna*. This enabled him to see underground into the world of ghosts (*bhūtalōkē*) and to the two lowest heavens but no higher. He told us the Pāli names of these heavens (correctly) and explained that he had studied not only Buddhism but also a little Sanskrit and Pāli; he could not read Pāli, but understood it "generally" when he heard it. After marriage he lost his power to meditate but learnt the "Indian method" of hypnotism from a book and with its power had cured some two hundred patients.

We were also able to talk to a youth aged twenty who was the president

[21] He described himself as a "disciple" (*śrāvakayā*).

of the Good Children's Organization that published and distributed the free booklet mentioned above. He studied science at Nālandā College. He claimed that the organization had close to a thousand members, equally divided between the sexes. The three committee members who ran the organization came here every Saturday; other children frequently came to ask Uttama Sādhu questions and were accorded personal interviews. He himself had found that other monks had given him less satisfying answers than Uttama Sādhu. The aim of the organization was to improve society and to become aware of the teaching (*sāsanē avabōdha venavā*)—a phrase he kept using. He said that children, mostly from Colombo, kept asking for their booklets—we assume that his estimate of the membership was in fact a readership estimate. He was not taking the eight precepts that day, for the interesting reason that he started getting ill when he did so and Uttama Sādhu had explained to him that if he took the precepts he would have to become a monk.

The vice-principal too told us that Uttama Sādhu had stopped several schoolmasters from taking the eight precepts with him, saying that if they did so they would find themselves unable to remain laymen. This was indirectly confirmed by Uttama Sādhu himself when he told us that his officeholders had all attained the "fruit of once-returners" (*sakadāgāmiphala*), second in the canonical four degrees of sanctity. (Later he said that the president of the Good Children's Organization was a "nonreturner" (*anāgāmin*), the third stage, only just short of Enlightenment; we suspect that he is not consistent.) To advance further they would have no choice but to take the robe. If they did that there would be no one to look after affairs and spread the word. He will give the officeholders of the Good Children's Organization permission to attain higher states when they are older. Even Mātā still has worldly thoughts (*laukika hita*), which enable her to look after him, but her supramundane thoughts preponderate so that if she should die she will go up and not down. She has however attained the five supernormal powers (*abhiññā*) as evidenced by her automatic writing.

One may deduce from the above that those who have entered the order under Uttama Sādhu can no longer participate in worldly affairs. This is far from the traditional view of the Sangha, even of its spiritually advanced members; but it certainly reflects what we observed, for Uttama Sādhu's monks and nuns seem to be in a state of passivity verging on catatonia.

Uttama Sādhu gave us his own account of the process of recruitment.

On full moon days his followers and other people who have heard of his prowess gather at Rattanapiṭiya. He has the power of mind reading and is therefore able to identify those among them who are "stream enterers" (*sōvan*)—the first degree of sanctity according to the Canon. (These could be children like the six-year-old nun.) Once one has reached that stage it is highly desirable and may even be necessary to enter the order. On this occasion he explained to us that the meaning of the word Sangha is "fittingness" (*gälapīma*) or "suitability" (*sudusubava*), so that anyone qualified is ipso facto a member of the Sangha. This reminds us of the canonical concept of the ideal Sangha, that is, those who have attained one of the four degrees of sanctity beginning with stream entry, which is opposed to the conventional Sangha, those in robes. Seen in this historical perspective, Uttama Sādhu's apparently arbitrary attribution of states of spiritual advance starts to make sense: it is a fundamentalist claim that his Sangha is not the one of human convention but the true spiritual elite of whom the Buddha spoke. Incidentally, the Agricultural Department worker specifically denied to us that his daughter was a stream enterer, claiming in a common-sense way that she had become a nun at her own wish; but no doubt for Uttama Sādhu that wish itself established her sanctity.

We noted above that when we visited Uttama Sādhu he had only one male in robes with him. We discovered that he has in the past dismissed at least four male pupils—some females too, but more males in proportion to those admitted. He may have found it harder to cow them into total subservience. Moreover—and to an outsider this may appear another facet of the same fact—his male pupils rarely become inspired with the texts that are now the movement's most distinctive product. We know of only one adolescent monk who receives texts. Though he did not say so, Uttama Sādhu is evidently interested mainly in recruiting nuns, not monks, and it is mainly of nuns that he spoke to us.

The girls are inducted by Mātā's daughter, the men by Uttama Sādhu. This induction is the equivalent of the orthodox *pabbajjā*, the "lower ordination" that makes one a novice. After this all keep their heads shaved (including the eyebrows) and wear dark brown robes of the usual monastic type, covering both shoulders. Like Uttama Sādhu they walk silently, with measured steps, their heads down and their gaze fixed, conveying a sense of remoteness. They are subject to a strict regime, apparently with no leisure or "time off" of any kind, and spend most of their time "meditating" in the cramped cement cubicles in which they also pass the night, though during the day they also "meditate" elsewhere on the premises. When Uttama Sādhu talks he becomes quite lively, and his activity is much more varied; but his acolytes seem to be frozen into a state of impassivity.

Again like Uttama Sādhu, all who enter his order lose their names and histories. He gives them new names—as also happens in the orthodox Sangha. Among the nuns[22] he has created a fairly elaborate hierarchy, and several of them have been accorded titles, such as *Sāsanajoti*, "Light of the Teaching." On induction they are "novices" (*sāmaṇerī*); then they graduate to being "nuns" (*bhikkhuṇī*). Both are names of traditional statuses. But one does not become a "nun" by full ordination, but earlier. Full ordination confers the status of *sikkhamānā* (a Pāli word meaning "trainee"). So far only three nuns, all young women, have attained that status. For this higher ordination it is necessary to have attained the spiritual state of a "nonreturner." There is no public ceremony for the ordination; it consists of Uttama Sādhu reading out a passage from the *Anguttara Nikāya* three times. (This is a part of the Pāli Canon, a collection of sermons that has nothing to do with any orthodox rite.)

What degree of sanctity lies beyond, awaiting the "nonreturner trainees"? We gather that none of them has yet achieved Enlightenment itself; perhaps this would make them totally inoperative. They are however promised Enlightenment, and at one point Uttama Sādhu said to us, "We are all Enlightened" ("Api okkoma budu").[23] This seemed to mean "we are all certain to become Enlightened." About his own condition Uttama Sādhu is either inconsistent or perhaps deliberately obscure. He told us that when he first met the Mother he was "only" a nonreturner. On that occasion he went on to compare himself to a radio without batteries, the batteries being desire (*āsāva*); his body is just the radio case, and at his death it will dissolve and he will go to *nirvāṇa*. Earlier he had also claimed to have passed all his examinations. But on another occasion he explicitly denied that he was an *arhat* (i.e., Enlightened); if he were, he said, he could not help the Teaching. No, he had fulfilled the Perfections[24] and would become

[22] Collectively he calls them *meheṇinvahansēlā*, "female clergy."

[23] We recall however the ambiguity of *budu*—see chap. 9 n. 23.

[24] *Pāramī*. These are moral qualities that a future Buddha has to bring to perfection in the course of countless lives. A future Buddha cannot become Enlightened in an earlier life because then he could no longer be reborn. Hence, no doubt, Uttama Sādhu's vacillation:

a Buddha. There was a prediction in the Canon, repeated in the time of Diyasēna (which he said was in the Kōṭṭe era),[25] that after 2,500 years someone would be born to reestablish the Teaching and hold a *Saṃgīti*, a council to reestablish the text of the scriptures. He is that person. He will become a Buddha, but only in the next life.

This last statement, which is clear enough, allows us to trace the origin of Uttama Sādhu's ideas to the late 1950s, when the Theravādin world celebrated the 2500th anniversary of the Buddha's Enlightenment—and hence of the founding of the Teaching—by their chronology. That date fell in 1956 and brought the Sinhala Buddhist nationalist S.W.R.D. Bandaranaike to power. We have recorded above that some saw in him the millenarian hero Diyasēna. At the same time the Burmese government sponsored a great council of scholars from all over the Theravāda Buddhist world (the Venerable Ānanda Maitreya attended) to prepare a new recension of the Canon. Theravāda Buddhists believe that the Canon was originally formed at such a council shortly after the Buddha's death and that to rehearse the scriptures in such a synod is the best way to preserve and purify Buddhism. The Rangoon council was however only the sixth in Theravādin history. The newest recension, that being compiled by Uttama Sādhu's nuns, is, he told us, "the last council."[26]

The ability to preach in Pāli originated in the movement with Uttama Sādhu himself. The words of the Buddha are in the atmosphere like radio waves or electricity. He can stand with his hand on a main current without coming to any harm; on the contrary, he can preach like that. But though he can preach in Pāli, his words are not written down. (We noted however that his sermons are recorded and tapes sent as far afield as Australia; but these may have been his sermons in Sinhala.) That prerogative is reserved for the messages received by the nuns and by Mātā; we deduce that here Uttama Sādhu allowed himself to be superseded by Mātā's daughter, the senior-ranking nun. Sometimes nuns literally plug into the current: on one occasion, he told us, a nun had her finger stuck in an electric fixture for fifteen minutes, till Mātā switched off the current, and was unscathed. But this is not how their inspiration usually proceeds. Once the nuns have been ordained they are tuned into the waves at all times. Their meditation consists in tapping them.

he would like to be higher than a nonreturner, but traditional doctrine will not allow him to combine that with being a future Buddha.

[25] Fifteenth-sixteenth centuries.

[26] *Pacchimā saṃgāyanā*.

In 1976 the messages received were of several kinds. One nun was receiving all the current news in Pāli and knew when the Russians and Americans were sending up rockets. She wrote down the bulletins and he interpreted them. Another was reading off ancient Sinhala inscriptions that exist as yet undiscovered in various parts of Sri Lanka. Uttama Sādhu showed us a large book in which were recorded various such messages, including some complicated diagrams. These messages had been received by Mātā, many of them on the bus going to school; they were mostly in "Pali," a few in "English." Some were from gods, among whom were included Jesus and Mohammed. The latter, Mohomed-Al-Deva, communicated in "English"; Kristu Devo spoke "Pali," addressing Uttama Sādhu as Uttamāvuso.[27] Christ, said Uttama Sādhu, is a god in the *Brahmaloka*.[28] We give the names of the languages in quotes, because in fact the messages are gibberish; they merely sound superficially like real language. As a sample here is a message received by a nun called Dhammasīlā Therī from the local Roman Catholic saint, St. Mary of Madhu, who in this version is called Madumātā[29] Marin. It is entitled "Whats go Swarga[30] Nibbana": "Beyond the harshful words are beings are the three world. How much they are uncomparable thinking to use neither good thinking for useful throwing to does wrong view as far as normally thought dies to the Something for is not decay. All beings are very unkind haughty for display killing the have these prayers and runeetha problem Soon after his mind unkind the throwing the flux to the decay. Mode inliving so always dicaring for it."

The "Pali" is analogous. It has the right hieratic ring and contains real Pāli words, but no meaning whatsoever. Uttama Sādhu explains that Pāli[31] has no grammar and only "masters" (*ācāryayō*) know it properly.

When we returned in 1978 we found that the messages were being put to better coordinated use. While some of the nuns, such as the six-year-

[27] *Āvuso* is a correct Pāli term of address for monks.

[28] A very high Buddhist heaven. The idea is not entirely new. "I have seen it stated in a controversial tract, written by a Buddhist priest of Matura not 15 years since [i.e., in about 1835], that probably Christ in a former state of existence was a God residing in one of the six heavens." Daniel Gogerly, quoted in Malalgoda, *Buddhism*, p. 210.

[29] It was in English script, so we assume Madumata is Madu-mātā, "Mother of Madhu."

[30] *Swarga* is Sanskrit/Sinhala *svarga*, "heaven."

[31] For accuracy we should add that Uttama Sādhu always refers to Pāli as "Māgadhī." This is in fact the name of the language in the premodern Buddhist tradition. It again shows that Uttama Sādhu has "a little learning."

old, still impressed the adherents by delivering impromptu Pāli sermons, the three most senior, the *sikkhamānā*, were slowly writing out the entire Canon—in its original, authentic version.

The 1978 newspaper article reports on "thirty-nine Buddhist nuns" in the following terms.

> The nuns are women who have given up worldly pleasures and through meditation has brought hapiness [*sic*], comfort to their ardent believers. They are no fortune tellers, but many have been the instances when they have been able to correctly forecast the present, past and the future of a firm believer. Housed in a building which affords little in the form of comfort these nuns have developed supernatural powers solely through the sustained practice of meditation. The nuns believe that meditation is the answer to many a problem that has engulfed the world. . . .
>
> These Buddhist nuns say that they have discovered parts of the Dhamma preached by the Lord Buddha but not recorded in Buddhist scriptures. The nuns have collected them and transformed them into written work.
>
> People possessed come to the "Senasuma"[32] in search of relief. The nuns with a mere wave of their hands drive the spirits away. The nuns say this is possible through meditation. [They also cure chronic illness and snakebite.] . . . The nuns offer any type of assistance with no reward accepted.

Before discussing this movement we must briefly describe its penumbra. We mentioned above that Uttama Sādhu has expelled several monks and nuns from his order. He told us that they were guilty of *pārājika* offenses. In the Buddhist tradition these are the four acts that automatically disbar a monk from the order: sexual intercourse, killing, stealing, falsely claiming supernormal powers. Uttama Sādhu said that the four girls and four boys he had expelled had claimed that "stream enterers" no longer needed to observe the monastic discipline (*Vinaya*).

We gather however that not all these people returned to lay life. Some, at least, continued the same mode of living elsewhere and have different versions of why they have separated. In other words Uttama Sādhu, like all sectarian leaders, has suffered schism.[33]

[32] *Sic* (for *senasuna*).

[33] We briefly paid a visit to Uttama Sādhu in March 1987 after our manuscript was

It was sheer chance that brought us to the house of Mr. D. C. Amarasinghe in Pannipiṭiya, not far from the Venerable Ānanda Maitreya's monastery in outer Colombo. We were walking along the road and spotted the nuns in his garden. There were three cement cells of the familiar type and on closer inspection each contained a brown-swathed young nun. We asked the householder whether these were his daughters. No longer, came the reply; but they had been. Now they were Her Reverence Sangharakkhitā, Queen of the Sangha,[34] Her Reverence Dhammalocanā, and Her Reverence Dhammasārikā. He was now their chief supporter. Were he too to take the robe, who would look after their affairs? We recognized the influence of Uttama Sādhu.

Mr. Amarasinghe, now fifty-seven, had recently retired from his job as record keeper in the General Post Office in Colombo. He was brought up very much under the influence of a grandmother who had taken the eight precepts for life and lived alone. He started taking the eight precepts himself at the age of twelve and all his life undertook them rigorously (*rūkṣa pratipattiya*). He had four daughters (of whom the eldest is married) and two sons. The (ex-) daughters in the garden were all in their twenties when we saw them.

In 1971, when the present Queen of the Order was seventeen and had left school, he was saying an invocation (*stōtra*) to Kataragama when the god's gaze fell on her and she became possessed. She said this was her last life (*antima ātmaya*) and began to preach to the family. This frequently recurred: she would preach to them while possessed by Kataragama. Though he was a lifelong vegetarian (and teetotaler) already, she converted him out of taking Maldive fish. Kataragama predicted through her that she would die at nineteen, saying she had the Buddha's revelatory prediction (*vivaraṇa*) that she would be born as an *arhat*. In 1973 her father took her to Uttama Sādhu, after she had persisted in wildly demanding monastic robes. He had known Uttama Sādhu earlier as an expert in handling

complete. All but two of the nuns had left the premises. The head of the order, the daughter of Mātā, was still there. There were six monks, several of whom could receive through airwaves the original Buddhist texts. We do not know why there was a mass exodus (or expulsion) of nuns, but Uttama Sādhu was adamant that nuns were unable to control their sexual desires. He also told us that most of them had not reverted to lay life but had become "mothers of the ten precepts" living in other nunneries or in their own homes.

[34] *Sangharājāninvahansē*. The term is a bold invention. *Sangharāja*, "King of the Order," was a medieval office; the last monk to hold it died in the eighteenth century.

demons (*bhūta vidyāve ācārya*). Maybe he was hoping to have her exorcised. Be that as it may, she in fact soon became a nun with Uttama Sādhu.

Her elder sister at that time had passed her senior school certificate (S.S.C.) and also all her *abhidharma*[35] examinations in Buddhist Sunday school. She had no job and did not feel like marrying. She began to meditate at Rattanapiṭiya and mastered the eight attainments (*samāpatti*).[36] Soon she asked her father's permission to enrobe and did so on 2 April 1974. Her younger sister, who was still at school and studying for the senior school certificate in science, followed her in December. Once they became nuns, Kataragama and all the other gods had to stay clear of them. There are Enlightened spirits, *arhat*s, in the pure abodes (*suddhāvāsa*) at the very top of the universe and somehow his daughters are working in conjunction with them, but how is not clear to us worldly people. They use their "power of persistence" (*adhiṣṭhāna-balaya*) to cure people—though only good people—and also to recite *pirit*.

Uttama Sādhu's teaching is good, says Mr. Amarasinghe, but he is a cruel man and lacks "realization" (*avabōdha*). One gathers that there was a quarrel and that Uttama Sādhu expelled the sisters; Mr. Amarasinghe accuses him of jealously having tried to poison them. Uttama Sādhu was the Queen's "worldly teacher" (*laukika guruvarayā*). Her proud father is emphatic that she started up by herself. She has had several pupils, including males. Two of her pupils are old ladies who now live similarly in privylike cement cubicles, and at least one of these (named to us) is Enlightened. Here, says Mr. Amarasinghe, Buddhist philosophy is fully realized.[37] Monks just follow the Buddhist religious custom.[38] The Teaching has declined. Now is the Teaching of the female clergy.[39]

Mr. Amarasinghe named to us about a dozen people who, he said, gave him financial assistance for the upkeep of Their Lady Reverences. They included a school principal, a district magistrate, accountants, university administrators, and a man in the film industry.

We were not able to visit the elderly pupils of the Queen of the Order, but we did visit a university administrator whose seventy-two-year-old mother-in-law had been ordained by Uttama Sādhu two years earlier and

35 Buddhist scholastic philosophy.

36 Canonical stages of *samatha*, including the four *jhāna*.

37 "Bauddha darśanē avabōdha karanavā."

38 "Nikam bauddha āgam sirita."

39 "Dän pirihīna śāsanē. Dän meheṇi sasuna."

who now lived in a cement cubicle at the bottom of his garden. The old lady, though rather deaf, told us that her grandfather was an exorcist and is now a tree deity, while her brother constantly gets possessed and gives cures and oracles but is *not* an exorcist.

By now we have met enough women crouching in cement cubicles. But we must record one more opinion of Uttama Sādhu, that delivered by the retired principal of the government police training college, who is a keen meditator and reader of Buddhist literature, about which he is happy to talk at length. Twelve years ago, he told us, Uttama Sādhu came to meditate for four or five days with a married friend of the principal and the friend's wife. He told the couple that one of the Brahmas[40] was anxious to be reborn in this world, so he gave up the Brahma world and was conceived in the lady's womb. When he was eight he went and was ordained by Uttama Sādhu, with his parents' consent. He has psychic powers. When he sits in meditation he sees a white patch and through it can see a vision of any world he chooses. "A very quiet priest," said the principal. At Rattanapiṭiya what they practiced was "pure *vipassanā* meditation." It was the only place in Sri Lanka where the nuns' Teaching (*therī-sāsana*) had distinctly developed. Uttama Sādhu has been able by dint of his own mental development to assess the mental attainments of others and thus to select those who achieved so much in their previous births that they need very little attention in order to develop further and attain Enlightenment. The nuns had developed the supernormal powers (*abhiññā*) and it is clear, in his own estimate, that the leading nun was a nonreturner and the others at least stream enterers. Through their powers they were getting the original text of the *Vinaya* complete with the commentaries, and also certain sermons (*sutta*) not in the *Sutta Piṭaka* but "completely in line." He had gone to ask the nuns a point of doctrine, though they do not discuss things at length. He had trouble with the Pāli term *anidassana samādhi*. Uttama Sādhu interpreted it for him but it was still not clear. So Uttama Sādhu called the third-ranking nun and told her to get into higher *samādhi*. She did so and then explained it in Pāli. Uttama Sādhu asked her to give a Sinhala interpretation so she wrote it out in Sinhala. Then he understood it.

We should make clear that this gentleman, who spoke to us in English, was by no means an exclusive devotee of Uttama Sādhu. He regularly ob-

[40] The highest kind of god, not active in traditional Sinhala religion.

serves the eight precepts at the Kalutara *bō* tree. But he is a true Protestant Buddhist layman. In his opinion, one can start learning meditation from anyone experienced, but once one has begun to develop, "the spirit of Dhamma makes you realize your defects and it is for you to adopt your own system of meditation to overcome those defects." Religious individualism can go no further. The principal's "own system" had led him to the startling conclusion that "*viññāṇa* is in my opinion the creator of evil in man." It is "the source of *nibbāna* and of hell too." *Viññāṇa* is the Pāli word for "consciousness"; if the principal thinks that consciousness, rather than desire, is the root of all suffering, no wonder he gets in a muddle.

The material presented above graphically illustrates two of the themes outlined in the first chapter: the religious rise of women; and the increasing importance of possession states, conceptualized here, however, as achievements of Buddhist meditation. The traditional hierarchies of meaning and activity have also been badly disturbed: elements of Buddhism plucked straight from the Canon are used for all kinds of worldly purposes; Kataragama first possesses the Queen of the Order and reveals her to have a prediction of sanctity from the Buddha, then is treated as a low spirit and (with the other gods) has to stay clear of her because of her high spiritual state. Moreover, to have all these Buddhas and near-Buddhas around is itself a flagrant violation of the traditional hierarchic structure. Strikingly odd in this sense is the fact that the senior nun daily sends her parents some of her food. Traditionally anything offered to a member of the Sangha thereby becomes taboo for lay consumption. But food offered to a god does not; on the contrary, it is then consumed as blessed (*prasāda*).

What about our theme of Hinduization? We have not found *bhakti* in this movement or had reason to suspect Indian influence. Yet the movement centers on women sitting in cement cells so cramped that they have to sleep curled up in foetal positions; and these women are the oracles who deliver the Truth, albeit in a hieratic language that has to be decoded for the public.

The essence of Indian *tantra* is the worship of Power, which is feminine and is incarnate in women. It is the masculine principle that represents authority, but without power authority is barren and inert. This seems to us to represent very well the relationship between Uttama Sādhu and the women surrounding him. Moreover, the not-quite-intelligible "Pali" utterances are an apt Theravādin echo of the powerful and generally not-quite-intelligible Sanskrit *mantra* that are an essential component of Tantric practice.

To the outsider it appears that Uttama Sādhu's pupils, many of whom wear glazed expressions, are pathologically withdrawn or suffering from severe depression. As we shall see again in the next chapter, none of the women seems to have taken the robe in the prime of life; the majority have done so some time between the onset of puberty and the age when they would normally marry—though a few remarkable exceptions are younger. We take all possibility of direct influence to be excluded, but believe that we can cite a striking Tantric parallel.

As a young man the famous professor of Sanskrit R. C. Hazra was a devotee of a female Tantric saint of his native East Bengal. This woman must have been born late in the last century. We know very little about her. But the essence of her story is that she was married at a very early age, as was then the custom, and at the age of eleven was already living with her husband's family. She became possessed and insisted that the family construct a small cave for her in their garden. She proceeded to live in the cave for eight years, never coming out by daylight or when anyone could see her—even her natural functions she performed in secret at the dead of night. She had no contact with anyone: her food was left for her at the mouth of the cave. When she finally emerged from the cave (as if reborn from a womb) she was a *siddhā*, a living goddess, so of course married life was out of the question. Thereafter she lived a long, pious and successful life as an object of veneration.[41]

Evidently similar crises may produce similar results. The problem is that Theravādin culture has no ready-made role like that of female saint that can offer these "nuns" an escape from the reconstructed (but uncomfortable) womb.

Uttama Sādhu's disciples are women, but a few of them are also children. At first we found this puzzling. We then noticed that the belief in religious infant prodigies—for which the culture offers no antecedents and which is not traditional in Hinduism either—is becoming quite widespread. For example, in Kandy some extremely well-educated and intelligent women, who were also very pious, told us that the son of a servant woman in town had known the Buddha's first sermon ("The Turning of

[41] We owe this story to Dr. Sanjukta Gupta Gombrich. She had it from Professor Hazra, who showed her the saint's photograph.

the Wheel of the Law") by heart at the age of four or five though he had had no opportunity ever to hear it—in this life—and frequently went into "deep trance"; the explanation for this was that he had been present and learned the sermon when the Buddha preached it. In Colombo a boy called Prasanna Jayashanta was considered similarly gifted and was invited to preach sermons at the age of thirteen (for example, on 15 December 1982 at the Young Men's Buddhist Association headquarters). We think that very few Buddhists in Colombo would venture to scoff at this. It is in part the result, we surmise, of the much publicized investigations of prominent Buddhist laymen, notably the late Professor K. N. Jayatilleke, into cases of alleged rebirth in Sri Lanka. Though belief in such rebirth is of course fundamental to Buddhist doctrine, no one in the culture, before these recent investigators, thought that it could be empirically verified by unearthing actual cases of children who remember past lives.

However, the full reason for the acceptance of infant religious prodigies was revealed to us by the interview with the retired police college principal. It is the result of following the logic of Buddhist doctrine rather than its traditional manner of acceptance. Let us explain.

Traditionally it was held in Sri Lanka that for a very long time no one had attained *nirvāṇa*, and there was even general skepticism about the possibility of attaining what the Canon defines as the first formal stage of spiritual advance and becoming a "stream enterer" (*sōvan*). According to the Canon, such a "stream enterer" will attain *nirvāṇa* in seven lives at the most and is no longer liable to be reborn in a state below the human. The idea that spiritual advance is no longer possible these days (for which there is indeed no canonical justification) is naturally anathema to Protestant Buddhists and seems to have gone out of fashion even among the Sangha, who cannot wish to sound defeatist in the face of lay zeal. But it did raise some monastic eyebrows a few years ago when a monk, the Venerable K. Sumangala, publicly claimed to be a *sōvan*. It was perhaps the public claim that they found inappropriate. On the other hand, the Venerable K. Sumangala[42] published an article in which he argued, with perfect logic, that since people in the past have undoubtedly become *sōvan*, there must be people being born who are already at that stage at birth. This funda-

[42] Venerable Pandit K. Sumangala, "Attainment to the First Stage of Sanctity, the Sotāpatti Stage," *World Fellowship of Buddhists Review* 18, no. 5 (Rains Retreat Number, September–October 2526/1981): 9–13. The Venerable Sumangala's address is there given as Veluvanārāmaya, Kannimahara, Waturagama, via Gampola. He has since died.

mentalist argument would make it reasonable to believe in religious infant prodigies; and again, the more assiduously one is keeping up with Buddhist writings, the more likely one is to have encountered the argument and so to acquire the belief.

Though Uttama Sādhu wields authority as a leader, his success is only possible in a wider climate of do-it-yourself religion. The inhabitants of that climate do not care if he has ordained himself, any more than they seem to care about the bizarre anomaly, in traditional terms, of a "coed" monastery.[43] But all innovation has to appear as restitution, as rediscovered tradition; and fundamentalism ensures that the Canon (most of which is after all not available in intelligible Sinhala) provides the charter. It is significant that the nuns are reconstituting the Canon without the commentary, as the principal told us: even that source, hitherto the guide to all canonical exegesis, is now suspect! It is also significant, and sad, that several of Uttama Sādhu's followers are schoolteachers. One of them told us that he had studied some Pāli and had a "general" understanding of it. The chief supporter told us that the nuns' Pāli was not as complex as what is in the books, but intelligible even after studying Sinhala—thus indicating that he understood what is in fact pure gibberish. Mr. Perera said that the Pāli of Uttama Sādhu is in fact "old style" Prakrit. Last but not least, even a university teacher in the field did not condemn it as nonsense, but said it was "very bad" Sinhalicized Pāli. There are educators everywhere who equate incomprehensibility with profundity.[44] If we have been forthright in calling the texts of this movement gibberish, it is because we wish to distance ourselves from that position.

What is perhaps most interesting about Uttama Sādhu's movement from the sociological point of view is that there is a contemporary move-

[43] Mr. Perera neatly turned this around, saying of Uttama Sādhu, "He's very observant of the *Vinaya*—has to be because there are *bhikkhunīs* there."

[44] The consonance between the wisdom of Uttama Sādhu and that of the wider society is especially poignant in the matter of the hallucinated inscriptions from the island's distant past. In his dotage the senior government epigraphist, Professor S. Paranavitana, who had been a great scholar in his prime, began to hallucinate inscriptions from which he derived all kinds of new and surprising information. Unfortunately he also proceeded to publish this "information" and theories built upon it and finally went so far that he published photographs of some of these alleged inscriptions, photographs that revealed plain, uninscribed rock surfaces. It was some time before anyone ventured publicly to impugn the hallucinations, with the result that for years the historiography of early Sri Lanka was bedeviled by the intrusion of "facts" that could ultimately be traced back to them.

ment in another Theravādin society, Thailand, that shares some of its most salient features. It is never possible to be absolutely certain in such cases that there has been no influence of one movement on the other, but both the chronology and the general circumstances of the two movements do make that seem unlikely: similar circumstances seem rather to have produced strikingly similar effects.

The Thai movement[45] is called Santi Asoka. Its founder and leader is known as Phra Bodhiraksa and he was born in the early 1930s. Before founding Santi Asoka, in about 1971, he was a television announcer; he also composed several highly successful popular songs. He entered the Sangha and spent a period in each of the two main sects of the Thai Order, the Mahā Nikāya and the Dhammayuttika Nikāya, but was dissatisfied with both and left. In the latter sect he was a pupil of the famous meditation master Achaan Lee, who was however disappointed in him. When he left, he handed back his official monastic record (*sūcipatra*), thus repudiating his monastic career.

That career had caused controversy. He began to preach soon after ordination, an act of presumption that drew criticism from his monastic colleagues. More dramatic was his appearance on television, the medium that had already made him famous, to talk about his ordination. He claimed that one day, while he was still a layman, he had become enlightened while urinating. It was this that had made him feel the need to be ordained. The program was banned and not allowed to be repeated.[46]

The first headquarters of Santi Asoka were in the town of Nakhon Pathom, west of Bangkok, but it soon spread to Bangkok and that is where it is strongest. The movement is predominantly middle-class and urban. Its ordained members, who are drawn from both sexes, are now to be numbered in hundreds, its lay followers in tens of thousands. It was influential among university students at an early date, and in about 1974 Phra Bodhiraksa organized students to stage a polemical exhibition called "Dissecting Buddhism."

Polemics and austerity are the movement's two main characteristics. Phra Bodhiraksa is hostile to other religions and in particular holds Buddhism as it exists outside his movement to be utterly corrupt. In his

[45] We owe our information on Santi Asoka and its leader to the Venerable Mettanando of Wat Phra Dhammakaya in Prathumthanee (near Bangkok), to whom we are extremely grateful. Neither of us has worked in Thailand.

[46] The Venerable Mettanando has seen a videotape of the program.

preaching he draws conclusions from the (alleged) etymologies of Pāli words; he explains that *sīla*, "moral behavior," is derived from *silā*, "rock," and from this draws the moral that one should be hard as rock in one's attitude both toward sensuality and toward other religions.

Phra Bodhiraksa lives in a hut and is famous for his austerity. Santi Asoka is rigorously puritanical. Followers are not merely vegetarian but avoid all animal products to the point of eschewing both milk and the fish sauce that is a standard ingredient of Thai cooking. The laity do not wear the white customary for pious Buddhist laymen but dark or dull clothes, and both sexes cut their hair very short; some wear no shoes. Similarly, those ordained do not wear the usual orange robes but dark ones; unlike the Thai Sangha, they do not shave their eyebrows, but they do shave their heads. The laity is encouraged to be celibate and live extremely simply. The movement opposes the worship of images, the use of amulets, and all rituals such as chanting. Phra Bodhiraksa himself may however be worshipped.

The movement practices a distinctive form of "meditation." They say it is corrupt to close your eyes while meditating because if you close your eyes you cannot know the world. They just sit quietly with their eyes open and look around.

Phra Bodhiraksa had to achieve Enlightenment by his own efforts and ordain himself because no uncorrupted alternative was available. He now ordains others, though strictly speaking this is illegal: his ordinations are not recognized by the state. Those ordained live together in ordinary houses; the sexes are not segregated. They now occupy between ten and twenty houses. Phra Bodhiraksa ordains candidates when they have been approved by a vote of his Sangha. He has many titles and grades. The women he ordains he calls *sikkhamānā*, "trainees." He also grades his followers according to the traditional fourfold scheme of the path to Enlightenment: those who take the five precepts are "stream enterers"; those who take the eight are "once-returners"; those whom he ordains are "nonreturners"; and some of those are Enlightened (*arhat*). Though he himself explicitly claims only Enlightenment, his followers consider him a *pratyekabuddha*. We may comment that according to tradition a *pratyekabuddha* is one who achieves Enlightenment by himself, when the Teaching is not extant; this fits the claim that there is no real Buddhism in the world today. On the other hand, tradition likewise differentiates a *pratyekabuddha* from a Buddha, the founder of a Teaching, in that the former does not preach. Since Phra Bodhiraksa does preach, the lesser claim may be no more than a politic move not to provoke the state into banning the movement.

The Teaching would not be defunct if the Buddha's word were still available. Phra Bodhiraksa claims that the Pāli Canon is a forgery. By virtue of his Enlightenment he has access to what the Buddha actually preached, and with this knowledge he is writing a new canon—the original canon. This version is however in Thai.

The Mayor of Bangkok, General Jamlong Srimoung, and his wife are members of Santi Asoka. The couple claims to have had no sexual relations for several years. They sleep on the floor and sometimes go barefoot. General Srimoung has waged a successful campaign against a parliamentary bill to legalize abortion. He used to be the prime minister's secretary but was dismissed for using his position to further Santi Asoka. This did not however prevent him from being elected mayor and he is widely considered to have done a good job of cleaning up the city.

The most important difference between the two movements is that the Thai one has been far more successful. Uttama Sādhu does not have any really prominent adherents. Indeed, his lay followers do not constitute a distinctive sect: as we have shown, they follow the pattern traditional for Buddhist laity and generally do not have an exclusive loyalty to one leader or institution. In this important respect Santi Asoka is more like a Christian sect.

It is unnecessary to point out the Protestant character of Santi Asoka and its appeal to the educated middle class. It is the coincidence of some of the idiosyncracies of the two movements that is most remarkable. Both flout traditional proprieties by having monks and nuns share lodgings; presumably they are so ascetic that the very thought of sex has been banished. The asceticism is strikingly similar in style—dark robes, extreme vegetarianism (we are told that for a Thai to renounce the ubiquitous fish sauce is previously unheard of). The style of preaching, on the basis of alleged Pāli etymologies, seems also to be the same. Very similar use is made of Pāli terms denoting stages in the spiritual hierarchy. Most striking of all is the fundamentalism so radical that the Canon has to be recomposed. That such movements, which in Buddhist terms must border on blasphemy, should command widespread admiration tells us how far the middle-class inhabitants of the two capital cities have moved from their roots.

The Sun Buddha

One day in August 1973, at 11:45 A.M., in a Buddhist shrine room in Colombo Fort, Mr. D. A. Jayasuriya, a port superintendent earning 1500 rupees a month,[47] realized the Truth. He was the first to do so since Gautama Buddha, and in certain respects his Enlightenment was even more striking. Since then Mr. Jayasuriya, out of his benevolence toward mankind, has devoted himself to promulgating, gratis, the truth that earlier religious leaders have known about but hidden. It is not so much a doctrine, in fact, as a practice that he wishes to promulgate: this meditative practice, which he has discovered, will lead to everlasting bliss. At one time, he says, his followers numbered 150, but many were weak and fell away. When we met him in 1979, there were thirty, scattered over Sri Lanka and mostly women; they met at weekends in a cottage on a hilltop in Alavva (some forty miles from Colombo, on the way to Kandy) to practice under his leadership. He had assumed no name or title, but his followers, who could see the Buddha rays emanating from him, know him as Sūrya Buddha ("Sun Buddha"), and he accepted the ascription of Buddhahood. The fact that "sun" appears in his surname (which means "Sun of Victory") may have suggested this name; but a leading disciple, a dental nurse, gave quite another explanation: "Prince Siddhārtha removed the mind from matter when the moon was high. *He* removed the mind from matter when the sun was high." We shall see that this has Theosophical resonances.

Followers have also expressed it more poetically:

> Prince Siddhartha enlightened by looking at the moon
> Lord Surya saw the light as the sun was high at noon
> Sun is brighter than the moon with light
> Sun has ability of lighting up the universe bright.[48]

Thirty may not seem a very impressive following—and indeed his followers are at pains to demonstrate that the world is always slow to recognize greatness. But much about Mr. Jayasuriya is paradigmatic for trends with which this book is concerned, so we shall explore his case in more detail.

Three of Mr. Jayasuriya's followers compiled a pamphlet in English

[47] A decent middle-class salary at the time.

[48] Verse 186 of SHOT—DART; see below and n. 54.

called *Realization of the Truth for the First Time in Sri Lanka* (Colombo, 1978).[49] From its first page we can learn that Mr. Jayasuriya at the time of his Enlightenment had behind him a long career as a lay Buddhist activist. He had been a committee member and officeholder in many Buddhist organizations, some of them important political pressure groups in their day. For instance, he was for nineteen years treasurer of the Varāya Bauddha Bala Maṇḍalaya, the Buddhist activist movement in the port of Colombo; and he specifically mentioned in his talk that he played an active part in promoting the erection of the stupa that still looms unfinished over the corner of Colombo at one end of the harbor. He was a committee member of the Siṃhala Jātika Sangamaya[50] (Sinhala National Association) and the Bauddha Balavēgaya[51] (Buddhist Power, an extremist pressure group); in his talk (see below) he mentioned that he worked for the political victory of S.W.R.D. Bandaranaike in 1956 and for the cause of the Sinhala language. At that time, when he was in his thirties, he was surely typical of those who spearheaded the MEP's (later the SLFP's) seizure of political power, a Protestant Buddhist zealot.

"When this Great Guru was President of the Harbour Buddhist Association, 292 sermons were delivered by prominent bhikkhus to the members of that Society. . . . It was his own Private Vehicle that was used for the transport of the prominent priests for the sermons." However: " 'None of the above activities were able to direct man towards eternal peace,' was not mentioned by any of the accepted and educated priests; but it will come as a great surprise to see this Great Guru's acquired knowledge through actual realization. He knows that one must practice and train the mind to end birth and suffering in Sansara. To attain this he did not require a robe, nor leave his employment, or give up living as a layman. Neither did he memorize the big books on Abhidhamma, etc., nor did he go to the forest, nor leaned against a sacred tree. He was able to win the battle conquering death in the Buddhist shrine room in a crowded place in Colombo Fort; and set his mind free from enslavement with the realization of the Truth." About a month later this was allegedly announced by a monk on the radio. "None of those in robes was able to attain this

[49] Compiled by Mr. V. C. Dassanayake, Department of Inland Revenue, Colombo; Mr. Ranal Yahampath, Traffic Police Headquarters, Echelon Square, Colombo; Miss Indra Shanthi Viridunada, D.N.T.S. Maharagama. Published by Mr. S. J. Withanawasam and Mrs. P. Withanawasam, Posts and Telecommunications Department, Colombo 1, 1978.

[50] See Bechert, *Buddhismus*, p. 319.

[51] See Bechert, *Buddhismus*, p. 303.

state. But this great Guru was able to realize the Truth, while remaining a layman, and within a short period as two weeks. Now he has devoted his whole life to spiritual service."

"The Dhamma mentioned in books as the teachings of Gautama Buddha is limited only to a group of people known as Buddhists. But the Great Guru makes it clear that this teaching is common to all, free of national or religious differences. The person striving to realize the Truth has been enslaved to the following three factors all along. That is listening as others do. Saying as others do, and doing as others do. By stopping this one becomes the master of oneself."

"He is the brightest scientist living today having the complete knowledge of the three worlds. He has the ability to travel past all worlds in the universe and give guidance to others also to practise the way of doing so."

"Prince Siddhartha . . . struggled for six long years and attained Buddhahood. But this Great Guru did not require such things. While attending to the normal routine work of his employment, and also those of his lay needs; within a short period as two weeks, after training the mind and defeating the five desires realized the truth. . . . Those who went to the forest with the intention of finding the truth has [*sic*] not yet come out, because they have not realized the truth."

Monks have only taught people how to be reborn "in Heaven or in the material world. As a result of this the human population on earth increased immensely. The clergy do not know that this is the cause of the terrific growth in the world population with the most difficult growing human problems without solutions daily."

"Buddhists in Sri Lanka were clinging on to a religion that has been misinterpreted. These misled people utter words without seeing the true meaning of the word like suffering in Samsara. . . . The Great Guru who saw this situation was plunged into an unutterable spiritual sorrow. Giving up all his worldly belongings, he now spends a homeless life doing the spiritual service of guiding the innumerable people along the spiritual path." There follows a list of public events that includes: "Special Events: On 14.8.76 at 33/5 Egodawatta at the house of Mr. Wilson Sugathapala. After one round of meditation Mrs. P. W. Fernando saw the Aura around Suriya Buddha and this was made known to all the others present." The "Special Events" section also includes as "a miracle of Suriya Buddha" the sighting of this same golden halo around his head by the dental nurse, after they had been meditating at the Ruvanväli Sāya at Anurādhapura.

The pamphlet ends with seven pages of reproduced correspondence, most of it an unsuccessful attempt by him and a disciple to open a correspondence with Lobsang Rampa, author of *The Third Eye*. There are also two letters complimentary to Mr. Jayasuriya. One is from a convicted murderer in prison (he had lectured to the prisoners), who says, "You can be considered as a Divine Being." The other is less directly flattering, but more significant; it is from a foreign monk, who has spent forty years in Sri Lanka, to the dental nurse—here called "one of our Yoginee"—whom he addresses as "Daika," that is, *dāyikā*, "lay supporter." He encourages her to "take all the tourists and foreigners" to her Guru "to be initiated in a kind of Dhamma different from the traditional teaching in books. We need such change, as our too orthodox expositions do not inspire the hearers." The letter contains this remarkable paragraph: "After 65 years of reading and 45 years of studying the Dhamma from books, I really feel that if all the books in our library in 20 languages were put into a heap and set fire to, the bonfire would not make me sorry. Away from reading one ought to realise the deathless Nibbana. I admire your devotion to your 'Guru.' As one grows older one realises that there are other ways away from books." If the nurse was a supporter of a senior foreign monk—a most prestigious figure—who held such radical views in the Protestant tradition of "doing your own thing" and cared nothing for the accumulated wisdom of the past, it becomes easier to understand how she could accept Mr. Jayasuriya's claims.

We ourselves were "initiated in a kind of Dhamma different from the traditional teaching" in 1979 when Mr. Jayasuriya was invited to address a small group of intellectuals who met regularly on a campus of the University of Sri Lanka to study and discuss Buddhism, as well as to learn meditation. We subsequently visited his home in Colombo, a typical middle-class dwelling. He was not at home on that occasion, but we were able to talk to his wife, a psychiatric nurse. She was not an active member of her husband's group, but was kind enough to give us valuable information.

As a result of this visit Mr. Jayasuriya and several followers called on us in Kandy, just as we were about to leave Sri Lanka.[52] But our contact did not end there. Back in England we received a letter from a woman doing graduate work in chemical engineering at a British university; she told us

[52] Recorded thus: "Recently in a house in Kandy we met / With a professor from Oxford in this country we sat / With him a Spiritual discussion we all had / About liberation of the mind many facts were said." SHOT—DART, verse 637.

that she was "among that group of Yogis" for two years and sent us more literature, in both Sinhala and English, about her "Great Guru." Over a year later we received a letter and still more literature from the dental nurse, Miss Viridunada. The literature is an excellent source for the movement's ideas, but none of it is by Mr. Jayasuriya himself, though it must have his imprimatur. The greater part of it consists of a Sinhala poem,[53] issued in five installments, by Mr./Venerable Wariyagoda S.D. Somaratne and its translation into English verse by Miss I. S. Viridunada, which is published as a single pamphlet of exactly a hundred pages.[54] Unlike much of Uttama Sādhu's literature it is perfectly intelligible, but it is easier to follow once one has some familiarity with the subject matter. We shall accordingly use it alongside our oral sources.

Mr. Jayasuriya was born on 12 March 1919 at Dēvālagama near Kǟgalla. His father, who died in 1956, was a keen meditator. He was educated in the Sinhala medium but learned English. He came to Colombo at the age of twenty-six and evidently made quite a lot of money while employed as a white-collar worker in the port. The poem expresses this more romantically:

> 192. In the Island of Lanka, Pearl of the Indian ocean
> In the province of Kegalle, Devalagama village known
> Lived a Sinhala couple of country style simple
> Lucky father Jayasuriya had a son with a little dimple.

[53] Title: *Vedilla—vidilla*. This means "Shooting—hitting." It was explained to us as "shooting the impure mind." That refers to the suddenness of realization (or, as we might say, of conversion). The author's vacillation between Mr. and Venerable is idiosyncratic; he is a layman. The publishers are the same as for the translation. The fascicles are undated but we think they came out in 1979–80.

[54] *SHOT—DART by a Ray of Cosmic Light*, published by Mr. S. J. Withanawasam and Mrs. P. Withanawasam, No. 37, 6th Lane, Nelumpura, Ratmalana, n.d. (1980?). This is both more and less than the Sinhala poem. More, in that the last part, verses 553–673, is Miss Viridunada's own additional composition. Less, in that quite a number of verses have been omitted. We also have a carbon copy of a typescript of the translation of the first two fascicles, kindly given us by Miss Viridunada, which corresponds perfectly to the Sinhala original. The numeration of the published translation runs straight through, whereas the original (and the typescript) is in several parts, each numbered separately. We have quoted a few of the unpublished verses from the earlier, fuller version; we have prefixed their numbers with an asterisk and given footnote references to the pages of the original on which they occur. Where we have two versions of a verse, the typescript and the published, and there are discrepancies, we have simply made our own choice of reading.

193. The sun[55] he had after a long wait
Has come down to earth for an everlasting feat
Infant born was brought up with care great
Giving education at college of Saint Marys' to start.

194. Having educated well in his home town
Came down to the city only carrying his hands and feet
Found employment through efforts of his own
A lonesome life for sometime did he lead.

195. A lonesome life for a while he lead
He entered marriage at his choice and wish
His just earnings he spent and built
Three big mansions like palaces plush.

196. The couple was gifted with a daughter bright
He became a father of three sons beloved
Attended to families duties he never failed
Many an example was set to those he associated.

197. Holy deeds so many he did according to worldly beliefs
Offices he held in societies and organizations wide
A Dagaba was erected in the harbour so splendid
Sermons he arranged by priests to the harbour crowd.

No doubt it is a coincidence that Prince Siddhārtha too had three palaces.

In 1971 his wife suggested they visit a Sai Baba *bhajan* group; he went reluctantly. (We think that only later, in 1976, did he go to see Sai Baba himself; he dismissed him as "just magic.") Though he declared himself unimpressed, he was probably influenced by the experience. As is the Hindu tradition, Sai Baba's devotees say *mantras* 108 times over. This magical number is also employed in popular Sinhala tradition. Mr. Jayasuriya adapted it to his Buddhist context. He took to reciting the Pāli formula listing the virtues of the Buddha (*Buduguṇa*) (see above and note 17) 108 times (telling them off on a rosary); more unusual is his contemplating a small statue of the Buddha he had above a door in his living room while reciting this formula. His wife recalls that he would stare fixedly at the image for long periods, then shut his eyes. After a period he

[55] The printed edition reads "son," which translates the Sinhala accurately. Maybe the translator intended a pun.

came to have the image before his eyes at all times. He also claimed to smell the fragrance of jasmine flowers at night. One day he was doing his recitation before the Buddha image for the third time that day when he swooned. She asked him to stop the practice but he would not. It was soon after this that he had an "out-of-the-body" experience in the Young Men's Buddhist Association shrine room in Colombo Fort and realized Enlightenment.

198. His wife mentioned a rumour she heard
That Bhajans of Sai Baba was holy and powerful
She begged of him to go in search and find
So went he after yogi Practices without a will

199. Looking at the picture of Sai Baba holy
Devotees chanted hundred and eight times daily
The secret theory of physics in this he was at
Back at home he started before the Buddha Statue he had

200. At port he was employed and while he worked
Five times daily at Fort he practiced
None of the home duties he ever neglected
Giving prominence to his mind courageously practiced

201. The half hour at home when he meditated
With tightened chest he fell down on to the ground
"Are you trying to kill yourself" his wife reprimanded
It was through fear she had for her husband beloved

202. However much preached he never gave ear
It was like trumpeting to a deaf elephant near
Ears and eyes closed he lived with the mind
Sooner the result, he did find

203. Never feeling lazy he went for his work
Driving his car at his own wish and choice
Whatever others said his mind never shook
Through courage continued, the rarest eye he attained

204. Day by day his mind grew stronger
A wisdom unknown came rising in his mind
Five times of half Hour daily he did eager
One day he devoted three quarters of an hour to this task

205. In nineteen seventy three November nineteenth[56]
In the shrine room was he in war with death
All pains of death there he suffered
Into the air he took his mind from body separated

By the Sun Buddha's own account, he came from his office in the docks that morning at about 11 A.M. and sat contemplating the Buddha image in the public shrine room while repeating very rapidly the word *arahaṃ* ("Enlightened"), which appears in the *Buduguṇa* formula. A vibration began in his legs and moved up his body. He had an acute sensation of burning. He passed out (*sihi nätuva*). Then he found himself above his body, looking down at it. From up there he joined his palms in the gesture of worship. He then felt as if someone else were in his body and he sat in amazement, unable to move. Finally when he went out everything looked different. On the bus home he was laughing and crying simultaneously, "crying because I came to body to suffer," laughing because he had no more rebirth. When he got home he scared his wife by his demeanor.

Despite her strong opposition, said his wife, he then gave up his job, having lost all interest in possessions. He also gave up marital relations. However, he remained a smoker and a nonvegetarian.

Miss Viridunada told us, in Mr. Jayasuriya's presence, that his wife used to say, "I have more virtue than him." She would attend *abhidhamma* classes and he would say, "You go to university with *abhidhamma*." When the family went to the temple he would take them but stay outside. Evidently there was some religious rivalry between the couple. On the other hand, the disciple's poem seems to continue with a eulogy of her role:

206. To denounce the desire for life which isn't worth
To go to the forest in search of the truth
The woman was a help just like mother earth
She was Yasodhara to our guru in this birth[57]

207. Siddhartha in the past young women he associated
To balance this for six years in forest he suffered
The realization he attained in the moonlight
Was valuable dowry to the Bharatha woman enslaved[58]

[56] Our other sources all put the event in August.

[57] Yaśōdharā was Gautama's wife before his Enlightenment.

[58] Bhārata is India.

208. To be born on earth is Impossible without woman
The beauty who bears the weight of life and worldly pain
To attain Buddhahood too isn't possible without woman[59]
She is cleverer in attaining the eternal light of mind

209. In Bharatha's famous Prince Siddhartha then
Finding fruitlessness of joy among herem women
Unable to find happiness over and over again
Away into the forest in search of truth he ran

It is not clear how Mr. Jayasuriya initially interpreted his "out-of-the-body" experience or indeed whether he interpreted it at all. If he told his wife that he was a Buddha, she, as an orthodox Buddhist, naturally does not care to say so. By her account he began to read English books about Tibet. In other words he read Theosophical literature. Theosophy has played an important part in forming his ideas and in particular in determining how his followers (literally) see him. To introduce these topics let us return to the occasion on which we first encountered him, on the university campus.

Mr. Jayasuriya arrived with a small group of supporters, all but one of them women. He and Miss Viridunada, who clearly was the informal leader of the supporters, wore white; he was wearing trousers, not national dress, and so was not presenting himself as the normal "pious layman." His face was deeply furrowed and he had a fine head of wavy hair, neatly and symmetrically combed up from the head, and turning gray. His general demeanor gave an impression of anxiety rather than calm, but his behavior was very controlled; he moved and spoke quietly and inexpressively, as is culturally expected of one who is spiritually advanced.

Before he began his talk, Miss Viridunada took considerable care with the seating arrangements. We all sat on cushions around the walls of a shrine room (which was a fairly large room in what was built as a private house) and had to sit so that we had a good frontal view of Mr. Jayasuriya against an "undisturbed background." She told us, with his approval, that if we now fixed our attention on him while he spoke, looking without interruption "just above the silhouette of the hair," we would "see the

[59] For this sentiment in traditional Sinhala folk poetry see Richard Gombrich, "Feminine Elements in Sinhalese Buddhism, II: Buddha by His Mother's Blessing," *Wiener Zeitschrift für die Kunde Südasiens XVI*, 1972, pp. 78–93.

aura." She later referred to the halo as "cosmic rays" and he as "Budu räs," that is, a Buddha's halo. She said we would see it when he was "in samādhi," that is, in a trance, which we expected him to enter before our eyes. Certainly his manner during the talk completely altered; but he himself stated, "I am always in the trance—twenty-four hours." We shall see what lies behind the apparent inconsistency in defining his "trance."

As there were two foreigners present who did not know Sinhala (Mr. Jayasuriya was expecting that), he said he would give an introduction in Sinhala and then switch to English. What in fact happened was that as he went on he gradually used more and more English words and phrases, but he was not consistent, and at no point could one have followed his talk without knowing any Sinhala. Moreover, his English was not very correct and we suspect that he cannot speak it really fluently. On the other hand, he used so much English that we can present his talk largely through direct quotation without needing to translate.

Having got us all to join our palms and say "Sādhu," as is normal before a sermon, Mr. Jayasuriya himself maintained that posture, his legs lightly crossed in front of him, and shut his eyes and sat for a few seconds in silence. He then opened his eyes and addressed us as "Pinvatnī," which is how a monk addresses the congregation at a sermon. Then, however, came an abrupt change of style. Mr. Jayasuriya spoke with vehemence and large histrionic gestures. When talking of monks, he mimicked their way of talking. He glared at his audience and several times shouted at the top of his voice. One could well imagine him on a political platform of the Bauddha Balavēgaya, and we have little doubt that addressing mass meetings must have formed his oratorical style. However, a still more important comparison remains to be made.

He began his talk (which lasted more than an hour) by saying that he was speaking from his own experience. Indeed, this simple point was the one that recurred so often in his speech as to constitute its leitmotiv—*däkīmen dänīma*, knowing by seeing. So he would first tell us how his experience came about. "I am a Buddhist" ("mama Buddhāgamkārayek"). When he was small he regularly went with his mother to the temple and offered flowers before the Buddha image, but his mind was not right. At school he asked whether the books on religion were written by the Buddha himself (and thus successfully cast doubt on them). He briefly mentioned his activities as a political Buddhist, detailed above, and also said that at the instance of a friend he had been to see Sai Baba, but was unimpressed.

He then spoke of his Enlightenment experience, which we have described above. In this exposition he stressed its suddenness. He said he had no previous experience of meditation and did not even allude to the two weeks of effort mentioned in the movement's literature. Some time after the experience he went to call on the Venerable Balangoḍa Ānanda Maitreya to ask his advice. Unfortunately he was out, but a pupil of his told Mr. Jayasuriya that he had reached "the ninth stage"[60] and had no further use for books; he advised him to tell no one about it. Mr. Jayasuriya proceeded to visit every prestigious Buddhist institution and leader in Sri Lanka, each encounter confirming him in his view that his experience was unique and everyone else was merely parroting what they had heard from books. Of these encounters his visit to Kan̆duboḍa is typical. He was met there by the chief monk, the Venerable Sumatipāla. The latter was wearing dark glasses. This showed that he recognized Mr. Jayasuriya (who emits bright light—see below). When he heard of Mr. Jayasuriya's attainment he told him he had won a great treasure and should make sure that it did not slip away through the five doors of his senses. To guard it he suggested that Mr. Jayasuriya take a week's holiday and come to meditate at Kan̆duboḍa. At this Mr. Jayasuriya asked the monk some questions he could not answer (but to which Mr. Jayasuriya knew the answers because of his superior realization), whereupon he left in disgust. He concluded that Kan̆duboḍa was "commercial basis, to make money."

After his account of his salvific experience, Mr. Jayasuriya's talk consisted of a rather disjointed combination of self-glorification, mainly through accounts of these encounters, and a very unsystematic exposition of the Truth he had discovered, in which his own experience was always central. He told us often about the seven *cakra*s (power centers) in his body, but clearly stated that he had learned about them from a friend only *after* his Enlightenment, and the same may well be true of other components in his interpretation.

The most basic feature of his interpretation—and no doubt the earliest—is that "Mr. Jayasuriya finish." (We should thus apologize for having so referred to him till now without warning the reader of this important qualification—but Mr. Jayasuriya does not object to it as a matter of convenience.) "Mind has taken over matter." "When you make up the seven

[60] This presumably means the ninth *samāpatti*, "cessation of perception and feeling," which is how the Canon defines the highest state of *samatha* meditative concentration.

centers, *bodhi* [Enlightenment], but you in the air." Mr. Jayasuriya's body was and is the universal mind, and this is his first birth on earth. Unlike Gotama Buddha, who came up from the bottom, he has come down from the top. By the same token he has reversed the normal order of things, so that in him the physical development (of *cakra*s, etc.) has come only after Enlightenment, rather than as a stage on the road to Enlightenment. The latter was the case with Gautama Buddha, who practiced *yoga-śāstra*[61] and roused the "kuṇḍalānī" [*sic*], the serpent sleeping at the bottom of the spine.[62] This is the serpent popularly called Mucalinda, who is supposed to have sheltered the Buddha in the sixth week after his Enlightenment.[63] Mr. Jayasuriya has another interpretation of those seven weeks, as well as of the seven lotuses on which the Buddha trod when he was born, and the fact that Prince Siddhārtha first entered a trance at the age of seven; in each case, the number seven is really an allusion to the seven *cakra*s in the body. The seven weeks, *sat satiya* in Sinhala, he reinterprets as the seven awarenesses (from Pāli *sati*). In Mr. Jayasuriya the *kuṇḍalānī* has risen "automatically"—one might say as an epiphenomenon of his Enlightened state; nor does he teach his disciples to strive to rouse it. They just let it happen.

We may here interpose Miss Viridunada's gloss on a later occasion: you feel the snake coiling around your spine, the cobra hood above[64] protecting you, and rain pouring down upon your skin. (This is modelled on Mucalinda, not on the Tantric tradition.)

There is conscious, subconscious, and unconscious mind (*uḍa hita*, *yaṭa hita*, *no dannā hita*), and we must get from the higher to successively lower levels. Only one-tenth of mind is normally on top, and we must connect with the nine-tenths underneath. This connection is what "practice" consists in, and it cannot be adequately explained in mere words, but will be approved experientially. The greater connection of mind manifests itself in increasing vibration. Finally matter becomes antimatter, dissolving into light at the height of vibration. Increasing the vibration, though essential for Enlightenment, is dangerous unless undertaken under proper supervision (i.e., Mr. Jayasuriya's). The adept comes gradually to realize the unity of mind and matter and thus to increase his power. This is because all mind is one—all minds (*hita*) are common—Mr. Jayasuriya's, the Buddha's, everyone's. "Unlimited knowledge, unlimited value; no one

[61] "The science of yoga."

[62] Such a snake, called *kuṇḍalinī*, appears in Tantric mystical physiology.

[63] See Gombrich, *Precept and Practice*, pp. 95–96.

[64] For another cobra hood on an ecstatic lady see Obeyesekere, *Medusa's Hair*, p. 28.

can value your mind." Once you know your mind to be the Buddha's mind, you are Buddha, Enlightened. *Budu vunā*, said Mr. Jayasuriya of himself. "Your mind is Buddha; pure mind is Buddha."

When you join the one-tenth of mind up to the submerged nine-tenths, a light goes on (he mimes connecting two wires). One must practice for half an hour a day or at least a few minutes, even if ill; make a habit of it like going to the toilet, from which nothing can stop you. "When you do the practice daily you get the light." First you get the silver light, "that is called the astral world." Then you get the golden light, *nirvāṇa*, "everlasting bliss."

Though Mr. Jayasuriya did not say so in his talk, this recalled the explanation that Miss Viridunada gave of his title as Sun Buddha and associates Gotama Buddha with the lesser, astral light. In a later leaflet[65] she coordinates this Theosophical doctrine of auras with the Mahāyāna Buddhist doctrine of the three bodies of a Buddha;[66] naturally Mr. Jayasuriya has all three and they become progressively visible to the adept.

Mr. Jayasuriya stressed his soteriological mission. "Unworldly service I am doing it, not worldly." "I am doing a service for the invisible. Why I have come to the physical body? As an example." "You must go to the other world and come back to the body." But this has involved him in great suffering: "I went and came back, but the pain on returning then unspeakable as it developed." "You must experience the death *märenṭa issara* [before dying], withdrawing the mind from the body." As SHOT—DART says, "He died consciously suffering every pain."[67]

Mr. Jayasuriya has as little time for the traditional forms of Buddhism as for their retailers, the Order. He pours scorn on the monks, who are all dying in their sins. They tell people "do the merit," but "by giving bribes you can't escape." Asoka the Fierce (Caṇḍāsoka) built 84,000 stupas but at his death he became a python; "I am telling in *their* books—you can't change what you have done." To that extent his view of *karma* is orthodox. Only "when you go to the highest vibration there is no *karma*." So much for morality: it is no way to Enlightenment. As for traditional meditation, "*Ānāpāṇa* bugger all." He does not believe in the traditional stages of Enlightenment such as *sōvan* as they do not correspond to his experience.

65 A single leaf, dated from Kodapalu Mountain Ashram, Wariyagoda, Alavva, 2 October 1980.

66 The *nirmāṇakāya*, *saṃbhogakāya*, *dharmakāya*. They correspond to his body, "similar to that of man with five senses," his silver shadow, and his golden shadow respectively.

67 Verse 172.

Other traditional tenets fare no better. He is the first to realize that there are not four truths[68] but one—"Truth is one." He has corresponded with a German professor who has admitted he is right about this. The one truth is "birth is suffering" (*ipadīma dukayi*). "Always I speaking on the root, not on the branches or leaves." Then, who believes in *anicca dukkha anatta?*[69] We volunteer as the fall guy and get laughed to scorn. "What a nonsense!" The Buddha "gave it for information, not to repeat it like parrots." (Mr. Jayasuriya seems to mean that it is no more than a pointer on the way.) The *Jātaka* too are all *boru* (lies). Though the *Vessantara Jātaka* is everywhere depicted, we cannot believe it. There is no need to give up one's wife. But attachment, "desire for the material," ceases in the adept: "When you reach this stage you can give your wife and children, but not by word, by practicing."

His practice would not conflict with any other religion—if that religion were rightly understood. Though his general tone was polemical and he criticized almost everyone he mentioned, in theory his position was eirenic: "Api kāṭavat äṭṭäk karanne nǟ" ("We attack no one"). More specifically, he stressed that everyone should remain in the religion they were born to and commended faith as a prerequisite for his practice. "*Särdhāva hō bhaktiya* [faith or devotion]—faith, it is hitting you. Therefore I am totally against changing of religion."

His view on religious authority was uncompromising and necessarily paradoxical. "Tamā tamāgē nāyakayā," he said several times: one is one's own master. "You are the master. Think yourself. . . . You know what you are doing. I explain the facts; decide yourself whether is right or wrong." Unbiased independent inquiry would lead one to become a follower of Mr. Jayasuriya. But only as a means to one's goal: once one has arrived one needs no guide.

A very important point is Mr. Jayasuriya's position on memory. The Sinhala word for this is *sihiya*, which in some contexts also means consciousness. We recall that at his Enlightenment he lost his *sihiya*. He lays great stress now on having no memory: "What I am saying I don't know because I don't have memory." That, he says, is why he is speaking so violently (*särin*). Memory is somehow part of the body, which he has transcended: "Memory is concrete." He has no reason. "I am not in the

[68] The allusion is to the Four Noble Truths preached in the Buddha's first sermon.

[69] Impermanence, unsatisfactoriness, lack of essence. It is a cardinal Buddhist doctrine that these characterize all phenomenal existence.

senses." "Talking without thinking, acting without thinking."[70] He describes himself as permanently *ārūḍha*, which normally means "possessed," but he renders it in English as "trance."

His followers are keen to lose their memories. When we mentioned a well-known point of Buddhist doctrine to Miss Viridunada she said she did not know it because she had no memory. We were told that another disciple, a policeman,[71] had succeeded in erasing his memory and that the rest of them were doing so. This doctrine (the origin of which we trace below) serves an anti-intellectual turn: the author of SHOT—DART "is not a so called educated university don full of temporary memory in the brain, but he is a village lad fully endowed with the limitless foundation of wisdom from the universe, attained through diligent practice he has done in the process of realizing the self."[72] Merit too must be erased from the mind. The senses are limited but mind is not: mind-to-mind talk is unlimited. The erasures serve to clear the mind for unimpeded realization.

Mr. Jayasuriya's views are strongly favorable to women. Males were always busy, he said, their minds scattered; women were more concentrated. This explained the preponderance of women in his following. "Books say Buddhahood only for the men; I say no." Further, "Buddhism's root is get rid of the difference"—so one should realize that ultimately there is no difference between the sexes. He recommended an experiment to prove this: take five men and five women, cut off their hair, and stand them at a distance in a line with their backs to you, and you will not be able to tell which are which. "No difference with the subconscious."

At one point early in his talk Mr. Jayasuriya shouted, "Anyone can see my body," and offered to take his shirt off to demonstrate his physical development. At the end we reminded him of the offer. He removed shirt and vest and stood with his back to us. His followers, led by the nurse, told us that we could see four *cakra*s going up his spinal cord, as well as the *kuṇḍalānī*, and his skull pulsating in a certain rhythm. When he turned to face us we could see the *cakra* where his brows joined; we gather that the last two, called Hōrā and Nētrī, were just over his head, one to each side, in the halo. Mr. Jayasuriya added that when it was dark one could see his skeleton, or rather the light that had entirely replaced it: "Light has pierced through the bones, bones are all filaments."

[70] "Sitīmak näti katāvak, sitīmak näti kriyāvak."

[71] In SHOT—DART he earns the charming subheading: "For the first time in Sri Lanka a Police Constable sees the vision of the Enlightened One" (p. 32).

[72] Viridunada, "Forward," SHOT—DART, p. 4.

It is evident that there is some divergence between the sect's theory and its practice. In theory each member is to realize his/her mind. In practice the goal—to attain which apparently confirms one as a full member of the sect—is to see the Sun Buddha's aura. At our last meeting he presented us with a photograph of himself in which his outline is somewhat blurred and he appears to be surrounded by light. We recall that the first pamphlet mentioned as a "Special Event" how a woman saw the aura "after one round of meditation." The results are not purely visual. On one occasion, we were told, forty-five of them went to meditate at Anurādhapura. The Sun Buddha felt as if a huge rock were on his head. The power of their concentration set up such air suction that the trees shook—even the cows noticed it. This was the result of a clash between negative and positive charges. The Sun Buddha is one hundred percent positive. When he concentrated, the clash with the negative charges of those less advanced was so violent that four of them were physically thrown backwards out of the circle by the shock.

As we have seen, Mr. Jayasuriya has no respect for Buddhist traditions of meditation. However, the techniques the group uses are evidently in the *samatha* tradition and related to his own experience. To start meditation faith is essential, and one is to meditate on the object of one's own faith. So a Buddhist may begin by visualizing the Buddha; then her mind will tell her what to visualize. At the same time one should mentally repeat some word, such as *arahaṃ*, "to increase the vibration." The aura is six feet around one; one should keep visualizing a point beyond that and four feet above the ground, at one's eye level (presumably when seated). At the same time, explained some disciples, one gets the "force" from the Sun Buddha. It seemed to us that the disciples fixed their gaze on *him*—which enables them after a while to see the aura.

Most of the disciples are from the Sinhala-educated lower middle class, much the same background as Mr. Jayasuriya though not as wealthy. (They are much impressed by his worldly success, stressing that he had three houses and two cars.) But not Mr. S. D. Somaratne, who was in his late twenties when he met the Sun Buddha at Alavva. At the time he was making a living from dealings in illegal liquor and gambling. Since becoming the movement's bard and chronicler he has taken the title of Venerable, but this is sarcastic: he says he was "lord" (*himi*, also = monk) of various criminalities.[73] His poem begins with an account of his conversion, a document that seems to us worthy of reproduction in extenso.

[73] *Veḍilla—vidilla* fascicle 1, p. 31.

1. The rumour I heard in a country house
   That a group has come to the āshram cave
   Though I was absorbed in gambling and drinks
   Pricked my ears to the news of the cave.

2. Some said that they were some thieves
   Some said that they were insurgents
   May be in search of happiness
   Oh! the Colombo guys, what comments!

3. Hearing these from the country folk
   On a day in the Sinhala New Year's eve
   Hoping to get at the truth of this talk
   I met the group that came to the cave.

4. Elderly gent' on an armed chair
   May be the leader I saw sitting there
   Not only males but sat the sex fair,
   What kind of meditation I searched with care.

5. Why only the leader up on a chair,
   While all the rest were down on a mat
   Sooner I thought, he was up from the chair
   Now all were equal as he sat on the mat.

6. Listened and discussed and shared a smoke
   You will become your own master he spoke
   I only lend you a hand at death
   These to my face with force he said.

7. To know who I am practice your mind
   There are no leaders at death to find
   I am no leader but came to guide
   These attracted and encouraged me quite

8. The mind from body he has separated
   All other realms seen he narrated
   Takes the mind to the point he soughr
   Why can't I do this within a week I thought.

9. Empty words are uttered by all
Learning books makes parrots all
Thought and said, you say, you thought and did
Show me the person living consciously with the mind.

10. Somethings he says like Greek to me
From time to time he frowns at me
There is something unusual here I feel
Will find through practice never I fail.

11. Thus started I, on mind practice
Week-ends from Colombo they came ready to guide
Now I have put in several days of practice wide
Change of sight in my eyes were visible quite.

12. Never did I have such qualities people praised
Nor was I in life disgusted
Keen to find out the truth myself
Harder tried I to know my mind myself

13. My mind centred at my Guru at the cave
I saw a white light that shined bright
It gradually turned into a golden hue
I saw round his head the aura bright . . .

18. One day my Guru went for a nature's call
With water to clean I was at his heel
Seeing such a wonderful milk white form
I saw the great splendour of your evolved form.

19. Clearer and clearer became the sight of my mind
Education and eye sight with defeat got behind
A wisdom I never had came shining a-new
No doubt you are the Buddha now I know.

20. Good or bad to me it is one
Seen the eternal light doubts I have none
Let there be the mightiest opposition even
   from the King of Devas
Treading the path of the liberated
   mind I have no fears.

Saw through thee I the real self.

Of all the movements discussed in this book, this is the most like a Christian Protestant sect. We referred above to both this movement and that headed by Uttama Sādhu as "sects." By comparing them we can clarify the problem in transferring that concept to a Buddhist society. A Christian sect is characterized not only by a distinctive body of belief and practice, but by a clear demarcation between members and nonmembers. In traditional Theravāda such a line of demarcation in religious status has been reserved for the division between cleric and laity (and divisions among the clergy). The laity forms rather into cult groups. Clearly there is a good deal of similarity between the urban cult groups described in the first half of this book and the followings of Uttama Sādhu and Mr. Jayasuriya. Unlike cult groups, however, sects preclude plural allegiance.

Uttama Sādhu cannot admit or expel a lay follower. Evidently quite a few middle-class Buddhists occasionally come to hear him preach or pass the day in meditation at his hermitage, but another Buddhist holy day will find them, say, at the *bō* tree at Kalutara. Uttama Sādhu has no hold on them. What does correspond to a Christian sect is his Order, which he entirely controls. Here we find formal admission, expulsion, even schism. Membership is not merely exclusive, but a total commitment. Yet, keeping within the local tradition, the sectarian Order depends for its daily maintenance on a wider movement or cult group.

This dependence means, it seems to us, that there is some kind of limit to how violently Uttama Sādhu can proclaim himself at odds with the wider society. There is a surprising flexibility in what he can do and say. But his success is due to a masterly sense of style, a feeling for decorum. We have noted that he and his Order present the perfect picture of ideal monastic deportment. Another aspect of this decorum is that although Uttama Sādhu is clearly at odds with the entire monastic establishment, he does not attack others. Occasionally, if asked, he will pour scorn on them, but that is as far as he will go. Similarly, although he claims Buddhahood, he never compares himself to the Buddha to the Buddha's disadvantage, as does the Sun Buddha.

Mr. Jayasuriya, by contrast, does not merely possess an extremely distinctive doctrine and practice, but constantly proclaims his distinctiveness with opprobrious comparisons. Claiming as he does to overcode rather than directly compete, he also asserts that he is eirenic and open to followers of all religions, who are not to renounce their faiths. But in fact his message is directed at Buddhists:

80. A statue of clay believed to be the Buddha
A heap of books upheld as the Dhamma
A robed figure with shaven head called Sangha
A triple refuge of the blind believer is of this nature.

This is so extreme that multiple allegiance is in practice unthinkable. In Buddhist terms he is blasphemous, not only in his occasionally dubious remarks about the Buddha but also in his coarse denunciation of traditional meditation. (His claim that he and his followers have superseded the need for merit is a heresy with more respectable antecedents; nor does this antinomian theory lead to antinomian practice.) There are no formal rites of admission or expulsion, though his power to expel those who do not wholly believe in him is strongly hinted at in the story of the negative charge bowling over novice members meditating at Anurādhapura. However, the sect is so firmly centered on his person and personality that it could in any case hardly grow beyond those who can maintain regular personal contact with him—the chemical engineer notwithstanding. It remains to be seen whether his charisma can be inherited, but nothing in the movement makes that seem probable. This is the weakness of a sect that builds its soteriology on a *practice* that in turn rests on a guru—as meditative practice is almost bound to do.

Formal considerations apart, Mr. Jayasuriya's followers display the true sectarian spirit of being pitted against the world. SHOT—DART is full of vivid denunciations and even social protest.

490. Before the living Lord, seated in front,
Today's clergy posing as saints great
Holding a knife, hidden behind in their hand,
Like stabbing the Lord having come from behind.

645. Prophet Mohammed was thrown into a pit of burning coal
Jesus Christ onto a cross was fixed by nail
Did those mighty leaders hold their positions for ever
Nail me too now, why keep silent under cover.

646. Politicians, educated clergy and leaders of this country
All their tricks and schemes exposed to the world freely

The curtain of differences I have pierced and damaged
You are your own master, secrecy of this fact is unveiled.

217. There are the poor who do not have a roof
But walls are put up around Bo trees, very fine
Many people in hunger in this country we find
But tasty foods are offered to trees and rocks blind.

219. One master taught all these people the path
Now we find divisions amongst lay and clergy both
Caste system too has crept in fast
These quacks are supposed to be showing the spiritual path.

220. Composing charms casting charts and horoscopes
There are quack doctors wearing the holy yellow robes
Underhand transactions carried behind collection sheets
Society's tiny prawns are caught by these stealthy sharks.

221. The children suffering from malnutrition
Do not get such nourishment, to monks given . . .

These are angry voices.

It will not have escaped the reader's notice that the similarity is indeed to a *Christian* Protestant sect. As is true of the sentiments just quoted, this is not just an individual idiosyncrasy, for we are hearing the voices of three quite different people: Mr. Jayasuriya, Miss Viridunada, and Mr. Somaratne.

171. Before a situation none would face he had no hesitation
Suffering all pains of death he found victory.

The English is by Miss Viridunada, but the substance is Mr. Somaratne's; and it derives from his leader's "Why I have come to the physical body? As an example." He has died to save us. The Sun Buddha, educated at St. Mary's Convent School, has a good dash of Christ in him. Christ—as distinct from Christians—gets a favorable press:

310. Those who follow Christ are rare in this world
Greater respects are given to saints and are highly beheld

People do not follow the path that Christ showed
Giving prominence to outward show sing hymns well tuned.

311. The body of Christ was nailed on to a cross
Those days the cross was used as a gallows . . .

312. Like a helpless pauper he got onto the road
To help the suffering poor all his time he devoted . . .

313. The chiefs and clergy who lived those days
Receiving slave services and such arrangements
The rulers hoarded money becoming the wealthy
I appreciate His fight against these factions guilty.

Christian doctrine is partially assimilated to the system:

315. Christ taught the super conscience as the son
And the subconscious as the father of the son
Act according to your conscience he said then
He told these to make man a universal and unselfish being.

But Christians, like Buddhists, have not got everything right:

319. Buddhists speak of soullessness
There is no rebirth, the Christian says
This belief a big mistake they realize only at death
Both parties together to the soulless realm goeth.

The Sun Buddha evidently believes in rebirth of the (unliberated) soul on the Theosophist/Hindu model.

Another way in which this movement is like a Christian Protestant sect—and so carries to extremes the trends analyzed early in Chapter 6—is in its absolute denial of validity to the spirit religion. The gods, we were told, are really mind (*deviyō kiyanne hita*). We have quoted above an attack on monks who practice astrology, but other traditional specialists too are savaged, and the king of the gods is criticized for indecency:

*139. Sakra the king of two heavenly realms
Believed to have powers and majestic charms
Been pulling a dame's garments at Devram Ashram
Has performed duties no one will ever dream

*140. Scissors of witch doctors with powers of driving evil out
Today they cut lime as the villagers conduct
Such is the background of false teachings told . . .

*136. Who has ever realized by seeing such nonsense
Why so much struggle to see lower spirits
The marijuana boys in most of our towns
Not one but they see them in many heaps.[74]

The literature does not refer to Mr. Jayasuriya as a healer or thaumaturge, and we have seen that he has come for "unworldly service, not worldly." He did, however, allude in his talk to the "mind force" that enables him to effect cures by merely saying *suvapat vēvā*—"may you be happy"—a standard blessing traditionally given by monks to laity. His cures were not really miracles, he explained, for miracles were just *karma*; and even he could not help the wicked. Since his disciples are striving to realize that they are pure mind, we suppose that they assign physical problems to the mental/spiritual realm. When Mr. Jayasuriya went to a Transcendental Meditation meeting he told them, he said, that meditating for worldly ends was a crime. His practice would make worldly matters come easier, but that was not its purpose.

The Sinhala spirit religion is not however shaken off so easily. To us outside observers it seems that the Sun Buddha has brought the religion of the gods into a fundamentally Sinhala Buddhist soteriology. He identifies as a Buddhist, talks to Buddhists, and uses their language. But—by his own account—he talks as one possessed. His Enlightenment experience—the burning sensation, the shaking moving upwards from the legs, and finally the sensation that someone else was in his body—was just like the onset of the ecstatic trance of possession. The only respect in which it seems to have differed experientially from normal Sinhalese possession is that there the sensation of the ego is lost, that is, it is just possession rather than ecstasy in the strict sense, whereas Mr. Jayasuriya experienced both possession *and* ecstasy. He describes himself with the standard Sinhala term for "possessed," *ārūḍha*. This is a Sanskrit word that literally means "mounted," though few users may know that. Mr. Jayasuriya is not mounted by a god or spirit but by "universal mind," but that may make little difference either experientially or behaviorally. Here we can resolve

[74] Fascicle 1, p. 28.

the ambiguity, mentioned above, about when he is in trance. As he has lost his memory permanently and is no longer Mr. Jayasuriya but universal mind inhabiting Mr. Jayasuriya's body, his trance is, of course, permanent. On the other hand, when he performs he switches roles from the pious Buddhist layman to the priest in trance. It is this model that essentially underlies the unbridled display of emotion and histrionics, the shouting, the grandiloquence, and above all the aggression. "What I am speaking I don't know": he is a medium for a greater power and therefore not responsible for what comes out.

As was true of Uttama Sādhu, the Hinduization that Mr. Jayasuriya represents is more a move toward *tantra* than toward *bhakti*—though the Great Guru clearly has his followers' devotion. Like the Venerable Ānanda Maitreya his ideas owe much to Theosophy—Paul Brunton is mentioned by name in SHOT—DART. Another source, however, underlies one of his most distinctive tenets, the depreciation of memory. This belief must be influenced by Krishnamurti's theory that what he calls "psychological memory" is a spiritual hindrance; this is nowhere acknowledged as a source, but one of the leaflets is an open letter to Krishnamurti on another topic, which proves the contact. There is however likely to be a more interesting dimension to this matter. We remarked above that the Sinhala of Protestant Buddhism is at times a calque on English. The Sinhala word *sihiya* means both "consciousness" and "memory." The sect is founded on the leader's experience of losing his *sihiya*—as he himself put it. So in losing consciousness he lost "memory."

Among the characteristics of Protestant Buddhism we listed, between a polemical style and the influence of the English language, the fundamentalism and the denial that Buddhism was a religion. Here again it is worth comparing Mr. Jayasuriya and Uttama Sādhu. Both have found ways of taking fundamentalism to extremes. Uttama Sādhu has gone back even beyond the Canon to the alleged original text; the Sun Buddha too, in childhood, questioned the authenticity of the scriptures. (Maybe a Christian missionary had suggested this to him.) But mostly the fundamentalism of his followers takes the more typical Protestant form of denouncing the Church for corrupting the Teaching. We have quoted some criticisms of the Buddha, but mostly he is praised—and contrasted with his followers, such as "Brahmin Buddhaghosa."[75]

[75] Verse 104 of the same section as the last quotation. It is an ancient tradition that the great exegete was born a Brahman and converted.

Though Mr. Amarasinghe said that what Their Lady Reverences had realized was Buddhist *philosophy* (*darśanē*), the denial that Buddhism is a religion is not always an assertion that it is a philosophy. There are variations on this theme. We quoted above an article in which Sri Nissanka wrote that his hermitage was open to applicants without distinction of "caste, creed or sect." As he went on to say that the applicants had to be ordained Buddhist monks, one suspects that the word "creed" is a slip of the pen or a mere rhetorical flourish—until one comes to the end of the article. For Sri Nissanka concludes: "The Lord Buddha belongs to no religion. He is only one in an ordinary succession of saviours." The line of saviours, drawn from various cultural traditions, is a heritage from Theosophy; but here the implication of Sri Nissanka's words, and indeed his actions, is that it is the Buddha who has shown the way to Enlightenment for all, regardless of their religious affiliation. Thus when Uttama Sādhu says, "Religions are various, the Teaching is one,"[76] he is saying nothing new, however new the content of the Teaching turns out to be. For the Sun Buddha's followers "there are no caste, creed or colour bar divisions" (verse 526). But since both Uttama Sādhu and Mr. Jayasuriya are themselves Buddhas, the Buddhas for our time, they hold that "Buddhism" (*Buddhāgama*) as apprehended by the vulgar is a *mere* religion, not the Truth.

Uttama Sādhu's claim to teach a "short method" (*keṭi kramayak*) has similar neo-Buddhist resonances. In a 1932 article entitled "What is Buddhism?" Madame Alexandra David-Neel rejected both the notions that it might be a religion and that it might be a philosophy, to arrive at the answer that Buddhism is a *method*—for attaining liberation. Mr. Jayasuriya certainly would agree with that sentiment. And like Uttama Sādhu, he not only preaches a *practice*, the direct road to Enlightenment, but a *short cut*. He seems to have begun his own meditations one or two years before his Realization; in the literature this is shortened to two weeks; in his talk even those two weeks were somehow elided. One of the points in his favor, compared with the Buddha, was that he was *faster*. This is not untypical of sectarian fervor anywhere; but perhaps it is particularly typical of the modern world. Our leaders are leading the search for the short cut.

We return finally to trying to place this small and apparently eccentric sect in the main line of development that we are tracing through the Protestant revolution of Buddhist embourgeoisement into an uncertain future. If one may venture the comparison on our small scale, Dharmapāla was a

[76] "Āgam venayi, sāsanē ekayi."

Luther whereas the Sun Buddha might be analogous to one of the sectarian enthusiasts of the seventeenth century.

In striking contrast to Protestant Buddhists from Dharmapāla to Mr. Perera, the Sun Buddha values earning money and family life. He said to us, "Gautama never earned but I am thirty years hard earning."

> 53. Gautama had all the luxuries free
> Our Guru didn't have them from the heavenly tree . . .

On the other hand:

> 336. Gautama Buddha denounced[77] all kingly comforts
> He gave prominence to the mind purest
> The present day monks give prominence to meals
> Proving this they carry the begging bowls.

The story of Vessantara is dismissed as a fabrication. Nor could Gautama have been so heartless as to go out riding when his wife was about to give birth to their first child, as the story has it:

> *74. Yasodara in labour pains for Rahul
> A husband beloved enjoying in parks royal
> An act that a normal husband never does
> For tales like this people applaud and praise.[78]

Of course, when one has attained Enlightenment one is no longer attached to such things. Verse 53, cited above, concludes

> The wealth he earned through hard work and toil
> Denounced[79] like a drop of spit upon the soil.

In a Buddhist society it could hardly be otherwise (and our selection of remarkable verses should not obscure the fact that the main source for the sect's literature is the Buddhist tradition itself). Nevertheless, we think it would be crass to see in this nothing but the traditional hierarchy of values, the lower tier being for those in the world and the higher tier for those who have left it. Here it is only the Enlightened (so far, only Mr. Jayasuriya) who have left the world; leaving it is not a *means* to salvation.

[77] We suspect that "denounce" may be confused with "renounce"—or is it intentional?

[78] Fascicle 1, p. 21.

[79] See n. 77.

It is indeed pointless, for "while attending to one's work . . . one can practice meditation daily."

The sect is of course fully aware that by wearing trousers the Sun Buddha is not conforming to the cultural stereotype for spirituality.

61. He wears no rosary or a yellow robe
Nor carries a board of halo painted
Like the Gautama practice there's no uniform clad
You got to recognize him by the vision of pure mind.

335. When Gautama Buddha attained enlightenment
Costume of the times he wore without excitement
If someone attains the same status today
Must he wear a costume approved by the majority?

Protestant Buddhists are the target as often as traditionalists.

338. As temples became unpopular Ashrams came into fashion
Majority went in for this latest fashion
Not even a hedgehog had a cave to live in
A useless crowd for both realms came into being.

*35. Inflation and deflation by breathing is meditated
They say from Burma to this country brought
When and who did in Burma realize?
From the day they were born still they bloat.[80]

345. Over the lives of goats, pigs and poultry tame
The compassionate people seem to have no feeling for them
Maybe they feel for their own kind
That they protest against beef eating as unkind.[81]

226. To show an eternal light[82] to the people abroad
Collection sheets are circulated among our folks
To erect buildings and revive religious societies abroad
Local donkeys are tied to pull these useless Yorks.[83]

[80] Fascicle 1, p. 17.

[81] In Sri Lanka it is the ox that is proverbial for stupidity.

[82] The original (fascicle 2, p. 6, verse 15) says *nivanak*, "a nirvana."

[83] Yorks is obscure to us—but expressive.

The sect condemns all traditional hierarchies and authority structures. Egalitarianism is the only reason we can discern for the almost feminist note occasionally sounded:

191. Young women waking up by his rays of wisdom
Having power of awakening the worlds human kingdom
Defeating all men these fountains of wisdom
Turning all minds Lanka's rising women come.

It is of course possible that this has a primarily psychological rather than an ideological or sociological explanation. But even more significant may be the sarcastic comment on Duṭugämuṇu's killing Tamils:

*103. Prince Gamini intending to save the country
Killed many a Tamil in Lanka's history
He paid for this act by his death so early
Kings by killing went to heaven, was it really?[84]

This is a long way from the Sinhala Buddhist pressure groups of Mr. Jayasuriya's earlier years.

The crux of the matter lies in the abolition of all external authority. Miss Viridunada told us in the guru's presence and with his approval, "Actually he is not our guru, he is only the guide. Guru is the mind." Sometimes liberation is described in terms very close to traditional orthodoxy:

287. You are your own master in all three realms
If you see the eternal light free from all thoughts
All are the same when they realized this truth
There is no 'I' or 'mine' the mind understands the truth.

The last line is of course quintessentially Buddhist. Yet the sect has turned this into a kind of Buddhist liberation theology, for the next verse reads:

288. For those who are trampled, hopeless and crushed
The helpless and simple folks in this world
To know a fact I tell their mind
If you practice there is a value yourself will find.

[84] Fascicle 1, p. 24.

This sect reminds one that extreme Protestantism has in the West been a stage on the way to secularization. At one level the sect is bizarre and is suitably ranged as a specimen to illustrate our themes. Yet at the same time so much of SHOT—DART reads like a highly critical commentary on our subject matter that it is difficult to desist from quoting it.

85. The learned professors of the Buddhist philosophy
The titled fools sunk in mires so muddy
What happens after death and where goes one
Without insight what philosophy the proud jackals seen.

Readers of our next chapter will bear in mind:

*11. By nun Sanghamitta a Bo sapling brought
And an order of nuns in Lanka established
Bodhi is wisdom it lies in the spinal cord
Oh! for what purpose Bo saplings were brought?[85]

*51. With offerings to Bo trees and singing prayers faithful
Donkeys hope to reach the kingdom eternal
Not in the milky trees; wisdom lies below in spinal cord
Never try elsewhere when there sits the lord.[86]

Should we turn up our noses at the grammar, even that has been anticipated:

142. Today there's a language used by the educated class
If we write they say the grammar is not right
But these guys jabber in the same language we use
Why can't they talk in the language they write?

*9. The big university dons all sank in books
To have experience of practice by these folks
Reminds me the curry smearing all over face
By going to use fingers instead of the fork.[87]

We hope we have not got too much egg curry on our faces.

[85] Fascicle 1, p. 6.
[86] Fascicle 1, p. 11.
[87] Fascicle 1, p. 14.

PART FOUR

Toward a New Synthesis?

CHAPTER 11

The Bōdhi Pūjā

Around 1976 a new form of Buddhist ritual came to public notice. It was a form of *Buddha pūjā* devised, and at that time generally conducted, by a young monk called Pānadurē Ariyadhamma. The Venerable Ariyadhamma[1] is a forest-dwelling monk who began his meditation training, while still a layman, at Kañduboḍa and received his higher ordination there. His *Buddha pūjā* revitalizes a traditional form of *Buddha pūjā*, almost obsolete, in which offerings of the kind usual at 6 P.M.—flowers, lamps, incense, etc.—were made before images of the twenty-eight Buddhas (twenty-seven former ones and Gotama) to the recitation of a few Pāli verses. Another traditional element that the ritual revives is the custom of honoring the *bō* or Bōdhi tree as a symbol of the Buddha's Enlightenment.[2] The latter element led rapidly to the new ritual's becoming known as *Bōdhi pūjā*. In August 1978 a month of *Bōdhi pūjā*s held in Galle culminated with a crowd reliably estimated at nearly 100,000.

The *Bōdhi pūjā*, as we shall call it in deference to popular usage, has already attracted scholarly attention. Gombrich has already published a description of the ritual, the Venerable Ariyadhamma's own view of it, and the full text (with translation) of his service.[3] Another article has been published by H. L. Seneviratne and Swarna Wickremeratne.[4] The two articles were written at the same time without knowledge of each other and are largely complementary.

[1] The Venerable Ariyadhamma died, at a tragically early age, in 1986, but we have not changed the tenses accordingly.

[2] For a historical account of the worship of the *bō* tree in Hindu and Buddhist tradition see Lily de Silva, *The Cult of the Bodhi-Tree*, Ceylon Studies Seminar Paper no. 55, 1975, cyclostyled.

[3] Richard Gombrich, "A New Theravādin Liturgy," *Journal of the Pali Text Society* 9 (1981): 47–73.

[4] H. L. Seneviratne and Swarna Wickremeratne, "*Bodhi-puja*: Collective Representations of Sri Lanka Youth," *American Ethnologist* 7, no. 4 (November 1980): 734–43.

In 1979 Gombrich wrote, "It is not yet possible to say whether the service can become popular without {Ariyadhamma's} participation as its leader." Events have proved that the *Bōdhi pūjā* has indeed become popular but, in spreading, has changed its form and its meaning to the participants with astonishing rapidity. Its story vividly illustrates the principle that innovations stem from individuals, but what becomes of them is what the many other individuals who constitute society make of them and often has little to do with the intention of the original innovator. In this case the *Bōdhi pūjā* has been adapted to become something of a bridge between Buddhism proper and the spirit religion, which was not Ariyadhamma's intention. This will be fully illustrated below in a case history that thus neatly straddles our expository distinction between the spirit religion and Buddhism. First, however, we must briefly recapitulate our account of Ariyadhamma's original invention while referring the reader to the published material for the full version of his text, and then indicate the general lines along which the institution has been changing.

We have referred to the *Bōdhi pūjā* as a "service" advisedly. Its form is quite new. A traditional *Buddha pūjā* involves the participation only of the person, whether monk or layman, who is making the offering; he recites (often sotto voce) a few set Pāli verses. There is almost no set ritual and the event takes only a couple of minutes. The new *Bōdhi pūjā*, by contrast, takes well over an hour,[5] and throughout that time the congregation are actively involved; they are reciting words, both Pāli and Sinhala, after or along with the person who conducts the service. They also know what to recite because the words of the *Bōdhi pūjā* are recorded in readily available printed pamphlets. It is clear that many people already know the words of this fairly long liturgy by heart. We shall see below, however, that important variants have rapidly crept even into the published texts.

In Sinhala Buddhism it is an innovation to have an actively participating congregation at all. A crowd may come to hear a monk preach, but their only role is to listen and express approbation. Another new feature in the *Bōdhi pūjā* is that the leader, who early on was always the Venerable Ariyadhamma or another monk, positions himself so as to appear one of the congregation. Normally when a monk preaches or administers the pre-

[5] In its original form the full service took two to three hours because the *Bōdhi pūjā* proper was interrupted by a full-length sermon and some other interventions by the officiating monk.

cepts he faces the laity, is seated on a higher level, and is treated with great formal respect. The monk conducting the *Bōdhi pūjā* sits as a member of the congregation, like them facing the Buddha image in an attitude of humility. In this respect he behaves more like a Muslim prayer leader in a mosque than a traditional monk. This is not to say that either Islam or Christianity has supplied a conscious model for the *Bōdhi pūjā*. However, it is possible that Ariyadhamma was influenced by the Christian service without being aware of it, since Panadura, Ariyadhamma's home, had a powerful Protestant elite and also churches and Christian schools, and moreover, was the venue for the famous controversy between Christians and Buddhists.

The most fundamental innovation, which affects both form and content, is the use of Sinhala. Traditionally only Pāli has been used in Buddhist liturgy. Though most laymen certainly have a general idea of what is being said, hardly any of them actually know Pāli so that the words in that language can have no emotional immediacy for them. The *Bōdhi pūjā* uses not only Sinhala prose but also Sinhala verses of the traditional type, which are not spoken but chanted melodically. In fact the most famous feature of the original *Bōdhi pūjā* was the Venerable Ariyadhamma's mellifluous chanting of the verses he had composed. This is not to say that their content was not of the greatest importance; but his presentation gave them an aesthetic as well as a purely emotional appeal. He told us that his motive for composing the service was a desire to offer young people an attraction to compete with films and pop songs. In this he certainly enjoyed at least a brief success. While he agreed, when we put it to him, that the comfort people derive from the *Bōdhi pūjā* might meet the needs that drive them to worship the gods, the spirit religion was not in his mind when he composed it. Already when we interviewed him in 1978 he was unhappy about the uses to which his invention was being put.

It has been the innovation in content, itself the main reason for the *Bōdhi pūjā*'s initial success, that has contained the seeds from which these other growths have sprouted. The Sinhala text of the service has been used to express emotions hitherto unexpressed by the congregation in Sinhala public ritual of any kind. Everyday emotion may be expressed in everyday language in traditional rituals of the spirit religion, but only by the officiants; and in Buddhist ritual, we have seen, the language is Pāli. In the *Bōdhi pūjā* everyone present expresses *ādara*, the ordinary word for love, for all creatures and the hope to be forgiven for all faults. The Buddha is referred to in emotional language as both father and mother. And the most famous passage is a pair of Sinhala verses that express the hope for comfort and consolation:

> To see the Lord Buddha's statue is consolation to the eyes,
> To bow before the Lord Buddha is consolation to the limbs,
> To think of the Lord Buddha's virtues is consolation to the mind,
> To take the path the Lord took is consolation for becoming.
>
> In life there is trouble truly every day
> And to death we approach ever a little closer,
> Only doing good is at least a little appropriate;
> For all of us it is *nirvāṇa* that is the consolation.

These verses are followed by the words "May all beings be happy," repeated several times, first by the monk and then by the congregation, each time a little softer, till they die away in a whisper. There is a profound silence, as everyone attempts to suffuse his own thoughts, and thence the whole world, with kindness. The silence is finally broken, on the monk's cue, with a loud exclamation of "Sā!" and everyone breaks into a loud, fast repetition in a monotone of the *Metta Sutta*, the scriptural and thus the traditional liturgical form given to the same sentiments.

The Venerable Ariyadhamma told us that when Mahā Pajāpatī, the Buddha's stepmother, became a nun, she said to him, "You are now my Buddha mother and give me the milk of immortality";[6] the story makes him weep with emotion. The words constantly on his lips and featuring prominently in his service are kindness, compassion, pity, and above all comfort and consolation. He also frequently mentions equability, both as a quality of the Buddha and as a condition to aspire to. But it has been his genius to realize that between the layman walking in off the street and this ideal state of calm there lies a gap that requires some emotional bridge. Not innovating, but bringing into unwonted prominence an element from the tradition, he stresses both the parental love that the Buddha felt for all suffering creatures and that we may legitimately still project onto him and the love, of the same quality, that we in our turn must cultivate. In recalling these qualities of the Buddha, he said to us, people's thoughts become broader and open out like a flower blossoming. The main message

[6] This seems not to be an accurate quotation; see Gombrich, "A New Theravādin Liturgy," n. 4.

of the sermon we heard him give at a *Bōdhi pūjā* was that everyone should meditate daily on the qualities of the Buddha and practice kindness. We recall here that the same meditation—recollection might be a better word—on kindness has been made part of the daily routine of Sinhala schoolchildren. The same traditional value embodied in the same meditative practice can become almost unrecognizable as its context changes. Of this the *Bōdhi pūjā* affords a dramatic example.

The element in the *Bōdhi pūjā* that first led to its popular reinterpretation is the series of Sinhala verses in which the worshipper contemplates the Bōdhi tree. The tree under which the Buddha attained Enlightenment by defeating Māra, the personification of death and desire, has always been a popular symbol in Sinhala Buddhism. Immediately after the Enlightenment, the Buddha is supposed to have remained a week in the bliss of meditation and then a second week in unwinking contemplation of the *bō* tree, as an expression of gratitude. There is a tradition, going back to ancient India, that all important trees are inhabited by spirits, and this naturally applies also to *bō* trees. We saw that the Venerable Balangoḍa Ānanda Maitreya believes that he was the spirit (*dēvatāva*) in the original *bō* tree at the time of the Enlightenment. This spirit is never explicitly identified with the Buddha, but our material will disclose a close psychological connection between the two, a connection perhaps originally fostered by the fact that in early Indian representations of the Enlightenment only the tree is shown, not the Buddha.

The Sinhala chronicles record that soon after Buddhism itself was brought to the island a cutting of the original *bō* tree was planted in Anurādhapura and that cuttings from that tree in turn were then planted in temples all over the island. The Anurādhapura *bō* tree is still one of the most important national shrines. Virtually every temple has a *bō* tree; in fact, its presence—for some grow wild—often determines the site of a temple. In a temple it is customary to build a low protective rampart around the tree, sometimes in two tiers, and to pave or at least flatten the ground around the rampart so that worshippers can circumambulate the tree; it is also often adorned with pennants. However, the ancient custom of ritually watering the tree by bathing its roots in scented milk or water was, for the most part, obsolete before the *Bōdhi pūjā* revived it.

The verses in the *Bōdhi pūjā* celebrate in turn the original *bō* tree, the Anurādhapura *bō* tree, and the local *bō* tree—for religiously all are one. They do not explicitly mention the deity in the *bō* tree—though it would not have been unorthodox to do so—but the *bō* tree is personified in this stanza:

> I pass to and fro on this enclosure,
> I tread on the roots and leaves of the Bō tree;
> Forgiving me, it does away with my sin;
> The king Bō tree grants me permission [to worship it].

The Venerable Ariyadhamma assured us that he envisaged no special regard for the *bō* tree deity. His attitude to all the gods is that there must be mutual respect, but he asks no favors of them and merely follows the normal custom of offering merit to all of them without distinction. He regarded *Bōdhi pūjā* as a misnomer for his service and did not approve of the ritual worship of the tree which, he was aware, was already tending to accompany it. In the services he conducted, the only offerings made were of flowers and incense before images of the twenty-eight Buddhas (or fewer, standing for the twenty-eight) and of the traditional "eight requisites" to members of the Sangha present at the end of the service. Nor did the service have to be held in the vicinity of a *bō* tree; the tree is addressed in imagination only.

The Metamorphosis of the Bōdhi Pūjā

The *Bōdhi pūjā* diffused extremely rapidly. In the late 1970s the Venerable Ariyadhamma's tours, on which he held series of *Bōdhi pūjā*s in large towns, received a lot of newspaper publicity. The congregations tended to be young and middle class so that tape recordings of the services began to circulate. Meeting demand, several new editions of the text were soon printed—three of them are in our possession. Such *Bōdhi pūjā* leaflets are now on sale in stalls and on pavements at pilgrimage centers, to some extent superseding the Sinhala verse versions of *Jātaka* stories and similar popular ballad literature, which seem to have gone out of fashion. These leaflets did not have to be, and surely were not, authorized by the Venerable Ariyadhamma. The ritual instructions and glosses they contain would certainly not have met with his approval, for they instruct worshippers how to use the *Bōdhi pūjā* for worldly ends.

At the same time, the *Bōdhi pūjā* has become something of a national ritual for Sinhala Buddhists. By this we do not mean that it forms part of civic religion or is associated with the state. We mean that while its emotional appeal makes it attractive to almost all Sinhala Buddhists, it has no association with any particular status group or faction within the society, but seems to belong to all Sinhala Buddhists equally. From this point of view it is not surprising, though deeply ironic, that services have been held with the express purpose of bringing success to the Sinhala army waging war against the Tamils in the north and east. But some officiants consider this very wrong. The incumbent of the Sat Bōdhi temple in Narahēnpiṭa in Colombo told us: "That principle [performing the *Bōdhi pūjā* for military success] is all wrong. All of mankind is the same. The Lord Buddha did not divide people in terms of race, or of upcountry and low, or of tall and short, or of American and English. Humankind is distinguished in terms of goodness. Goodness is goodness whether it exists in the Catholic, the Muslim, or among gods and laymen. Gold does not change, whoever wears it. To do a *Bōdhi pūjā* to win a war with the Tamils or Muslims—that is flatly opposed to the Dhamma of the Buddha. Such actions also do not befit a civilized mind." This monk did not, of course, derive his moral stance from the *Bōdhi pūjā*, but from his upbringing as a Buddhist and his training as a monk. Yet he sees the *Bōdhi pūjā* as a fine means to communicate Buddhist values and has therefore introduced it in his temple.

He has, however, profoundly modified it in a conservative direction by using only Pāli. The problem that this change is designed to meet is the use of music. All members of the Sangha must, ideally, abstain from witnessing displays of dancing, singing, and instrumental music, and those who take the eight precepts on *pōya* days make the same vow. Pāli verses are always chanted, not sung. There is of course no clear line between chanting and singing; but the Venerable Ariyadhamma's rendition of the Sinhala verses in his service comes closer to singing. It has even been suggested that his style has been influenced by that of a certain popular singer.[7] In his own view there is no music in the service because it does not employ instruments. One might add that he breaks up the quatrains into separate lines, each being repeated by the congregation, which enhances the liturgical effect. Moreover, in traditional acts of public worship at Buddhist temples there is always a certain amount of drumming and other instrumental music performed by hereditary specialists and no one

[7] Seneviratne and Wickremeratne, "*Bodhi-puja*," p. 740.

objects to that. Nevertheless, some monks do see the singing of the Sinhala verses as a problem. The incumbent at Narahēnpiṭa was aware that by restricting to Pāli the *Bōdhi pūjā* that he introduced as part of his temple's daily evening service he was sacrificing immediacy, but felt constrained by his tradition.

One might ask whether less scrupulous officiants may not move in the opposite direction and abolish Pāli altogether. We are, however, not aware of an instance of a text entirely in Sinhala. Pāli sounds sonorous and impressive; as the traditional language of Theravādin liturgy its use imparts dignity, even solemnity. We recall the pseudo-Pāli compositions of Uttama Sādhu's disciples. No version of the *Bōdhi pūjā* has similar Pāli-sounding gibberish; but one of our pamphlets has added, for example, the following verse in a kind of dog Pāli to be recited while circumambulating the *bō* tree.

Buddhaṃ Buddhaṃ Buddhaṃ vande
Dhammaṃ Dhammaṃ Dhammaṃ vande
Sanghaṃ Sanghaṃ Sanghaṃ vande
Cetiṃ Bodhiṃ sambhaṃ vande.

Allowing for mistakes in the last line, this translates as:

I worship the Buddha, the Buddha, the Buddha
I worship the Dhamma, the Dhamma, the Dhamma
I worship the Sangha, the Sangha, the Sangha
I worship every stupa, every *bō* tree.

If on the one hand the *Bōdhi pūjā* has been taken up by Sinhala Buddhists as a nation to serve their common purposes, it is on the other being still more commonly used specifically by individuals to serve their private worldly ends. It is being simultaneously universalized and parochialized. We now turn to the latter.

The *Bōdhi pūjā* is increasingly being performed for clients by priests of the spirit religion, whether old-style *kapurāḷa* or new-style *sāmi*, at their shrines. Of this we shall give an illustration in the case of Jayanta, reported below. The service is being adapted to the traditions of Sinhala spirit worship. Most strikingly, it no longer requires public participation, but may be performed for individuals or groups of clients. Its instrumental character is moreover clearly explained in the leaflets. In effect it has become for many a rite of worship of the *bō* tree for particular ends, a piece of white magic. At the same time, as we shall see, it has not lost but rather enhanced its expressive character, so that it has a two-sided appeal.

The ritual procedure laid down in our three pamphlets is basically the same, though there are minor variations in such details as the quantity and type of ingredients to be used. Typically the worshipper is instructed to bring baskets of flowers and coconut or mustard oil for lamps, these items being for the worship of Buddha images; and for the worship of the tree, the same plus panic grass, sesame oil, white sandalwood, parched rice, colored pennants, and white sand to sprinkle on the ground. In the early days of enthusiasm some people revived the practice of bathing the tree in milk, but it has been decided that this is bad for the tree and is now actively discouraged, so our texts do not mention it.

The worshipper is instructed to come first to the compound in which the tree stands and to clean and tidy it up. He is then to go to the temple and offer flowers and light lamps before the Buddha image or images there. He is to take the Three Refuges and five precepts (in Pāli, as usual), and return to the tree. He is now to bathe it in water perfumed with various prescribed ingredients and pour pots of water over its roots. Trays of flowers and the other offerings are to be placed at the foot of the tree. One then recites (repeats after the officiant) Pāli and Sinhala verses from the *Bōdhi pūjā* text. (As a line in one of our printed texts has it, "Ghosts (*prēta*) and demons quake on seeing the Bodhi.") One then remains silent in a meditative posture and repeats a wish (*prārthanāva*) in Sinhala. We reproduce part of the prayer given in one of our texts. "The Bodhi tree that helped the Buddha of the three worlds to attain omniscience; the tree that protected the Bodhisattva from the enemies known as the moral defilements (*kleśa*) . . . this Bo tree, descended from the glorious Great Bodhi of India, which protected the Lord Buddha; may it banish all our sufferings and sorrows, the ill effects of planets, the evil eye and evil mouth, illnesses and the machinations of enemies; and may it fulfill our wishes and give us boundless wealth." After circumambulating the tree, the worshipper is then to take home the items that have been offered to the tree (insofar as they are recoverable) to use them for further protective rites. Here are some of the instructions for these.

> For misfortunes caused by demons and *prēta*s recite the *Ratana Sutta* over the white sand and then sprinkle it around the house.

> For diseases recite the *Metta Sutta* over the panic grass and put it under the patient's pillow.
>
> For nightmares follow the same procedure but put the grass in the patient's hands.
>
> For appointments with government officials, for court cases, for taking part in public meetings, rub the sandalwood on a stone to make a paste of it, recite the *Mahā Mangala Sutta* over it, and make a mark with it on the center of your forehead.
>
> For your rice crop recite the *Metta Sutta* over the mustard oil and sprinkle it on the paddy field.
>
> To scare away snakes, or beetles attacking coconut trees, follow the same procedure.
>
> To counteract sorcery recite the *pirit* text of the twenty-eight Buddhas over the mustard oil, sesame oil, and panic grass and put them in small pots at the four corners of the house.

Similar instructions are given for planetary troubles, sores, stomachaches, eczema, fear of demons, epilepsy, domestic disharmony, sprains, house construction, and reuniting separated families. The *Bōdhi pūjā* thus covers every contingency requiring white magic for which it has been customary to use the spirit religion. This change has been accepted by many Sinhala people. The chief monk at Narahēnpiṭa, whom we mentioned above, told us that *Bōdhi pūjā* is for well-being (*yahapata*) in this world and specifically referred to protection from planetary evil, divine anger, and infectious diseases.

There is of course a Sinhala Buddhist tradition of using the recitation of sacred texts for such protective purposes: the very word *pirit* etymologically means "protection." Moreover, while there is a much longer classical collection of *pirit* texts for large ceremonies, the quintessential texts (collectively known as *Maha pirita*, "The Great *Pirit*") are just three: the *Ratana*, *Metta*, and *Mahā Mangala Sutta*s. So we see that the author of the above instructions is consciously tagging onto an ancient tradition. The recital of the *Metta Sutta* is already part of Ariyadhamma's *Bōdhi pūjā*, and it is quite natural that those three famous texts should be reprinted in *Bōdhi pūjā* pamphlets. The list of names of the twenty-eight Buddhas, which is not a traditional *pirit* text, is derived from the same source.

A traditional *pirit* ceremony consecrates water and thread that are then used for protective purposes. People may wear the thread around their wrists and sprinkle the water on themselves and around their houses. Are there then any important differences between the *Bōdhi pūjā* as laid down in our pamphlets and the traditional use of *pirit*?

Pirit is traditionally a public ceremony and normally recited by monks—usually several of them. It is often held in private houses, but everyone around is free to come and participate and so gain merit. Moreover, though the occasion for holding a *pirit* ceremony is almost always quite specific, it is deemed to work in a general, unspecific way. About how it works there are several, mutually compatible theories. The most sophisticated and perhaps also the most impeccably orthodox is that the texts are in fact sermons being preached to convert malign spirits to Buddhist ethics so that they will give up doing harm. Another orthodox theory simply assimilates the recital and hearing of the scriptural texts into the general category of meritorious actions: the merit gained by the participants is offered to the gods in a formula at the end, and in return they afford their protection. Other theories, pan-Indian rather than specifically Buddhist in origin, ascribe automatic efficacy to the sacred word or to the power of enunciated truth (*satyakriyā*).

Some texts of the *Bōdhi pūjā* and many people we have interviewed use the latter type of theory to account for its efficacy: it has "power vibrations" (*balavēgaya*) that derive from the fact that the tree sheltered the Buddha during his fight for Enlightenment. But in its magical use it has moved from the *pirit* to the spirit religion model. It is more laicized than *pirit* and more specific. It is being performed by priests for clients and in this form is a more private affair than *pirit*. Instead of the unspecific use of water and thread, highly specific ingredients from the magical tradition here appear. For example, the scattering of mustard seed to ward off demons seems to be a pan-Indian magical practice; here we have mustard oil as a local variant.

However, the greatest difference between the *Bōdhi pūjā* and *pirit* lies in the appeal of the former to the emotions. To this expressive aspect of the text we shall return below after further considering its functional use. Because of this appeal the more orthodox *Bōdhi pūjā* too, the one employing monks and a public congregation, is eroding the sphere of *pirit* on such occasions as the birthdays of public figures and events of more serious national concern.

There seems to be a widespread feeling that the *Bōdhi pūjā* is a particularly appropriate remedy when one's troubles are due to the planets, that is, to a bad horoscope. Traditionally the countermeasure for such trouble is a rather elaborate ritual known as *bali* performed by specialists, but in many parts of the country *bali* rituals have become scarce.

In our earlier article we reported that already in 1978 a woman had seen in her daughter's horoscope that the daughter was about to pass through an unlucky period, so to avert misfortune she had watered a Bōdhi tree with milk perfumed with turmeric and sandal every day for a week and given the merit to her daughter. This again illustrates the mechanism by which the *Bōdhi pūjā* is deemed to work: its performance creates good *karma*, a fund of merit that can be called on at need.

Some printed editions of the *Bōdhi pūjā* include a text called *Nava Guṇa Śāntiya*, "The Blessing of the Nine Virtues," which is for warding off the bad influence of the nine planets by invoking the Buddha's nine virtues or qualities. This has strong roots in tradition. The nine virtues are the *Buduguṇa* (see Chapter 10 and note 17 in that chapter), a Pāli formula. A passage in the original *Bōdhi pūjā* text dwells on the same formula, so the connection is evident. What appears to be new is again a certain specificity, matching the virtues to the planets. The first three virtues are *arahaṃ*, *sammā-sambuddho*, *vijjā-caraṇa-sampanno* (the meanings are not relevant here). The first three verses of the *Nava Guṇa Śāntiya* translate:

By the virtues of the *arahaṃ* Buddha
May the Sun's ill effects disappear;
Without fear of disease or pain
May happiness and joy approach me

By the effulgent power of *sammā-sambuddho*
May the Moon's ill effects disappear;
May deathly hindrances be prevented
And my wishes be fulfilled.

By the power of *vijjā-caraṇa*
May Saturn's ill effects disappear;
The effects of poison verses and calamities [brought by] enemies
May they not approach me.

This use of the *Bōdhi pūjā* is justified in an English-language newspaper article[8] by a learned monk, the Venerable Kaduvälle Dhīrānanda. "The

[8] *Sunday Observer*, 8 July 1984.

Trinity of Brahma, Vishnu and Maheshwara preside over Time, according to the science of astrology," he writes.[9] Each god takes his turn in controlling the universe for a twenty-year period known as *viṃśatiya*. The *viṃśatiya* of Brahma is uniformly propitious, that of Viṣṇu contains both good and bad, but the sway of Īśvara is so maleficent that it even cancels out the benign results produced by his predecessors. The year 1984 is an especially bad part of Īśvara's *viṃśatiya*.

> This year is described in astrology as a dark period of upheaval and destruction marked by murders, kidnappings, rapes, civil strife, droughts, famines, floods, robberies, lootings, drug abuse, instability of religious institutions, disaffection with gods, manifestations of divine wrath and inhuman acts resulting from hate, cruelty and vengeance. . . . Following in the steps of the Buddha, Ven. Meetiyagala Gunaratana, the chief Sangha Nayaka of Jayawardhanapura, inaugurated the 1095 Bodhi poojas commencing on May 1 to ward off calamities and protect the people from inexplicable harm. . . . Astrology stipulates that a Bodhi pooja is a vital and essential "shanti karma" [rite of blessing] for overcoming malefic planetary influences, the wrath of the gods and achieving one's cherished ambitions.[10]

Having invented an astrological charter for the *Bōdhi pūjā*, the Venerable Dhīrānanda turns to its Buddhist side: "It should be remembered that the Buddha was the first ever to hold the Bodhi pooja . . . during the second week after Enlightenment . . . as a mark of gratitude to the tree that helped him in his quest. It was unique because it was a week-long visual concentration on an inanimate object."[11] Dhīrānanda thus adds a mythical Buddhist justification to his astrological pseudotradition (note "stipulates") and in so doing legitimizes a blatantly Hinduized astrological doctrine, perhaps also a recent invention, by connecting it with Buddhism, despite the Buddha's well-known injunction to monks to steer clear of such "beastly arts."

We have mentioned that the success of the *Bōdhi pūjā* has led to its being taken up by priests of the gods and adapted to their own traditions. Some of them have reduced the rite to the literal meaning of its popular title,

[9] Ibid.

[10] Ibid.

[11] Ibid.

"Worship of the Bō Tree," and have dispensed with the text altogether. When a client comes with a problem, the priest simply makes offerings to the *bō* tree, bathes it, returns to the god's shrine, transfers the merit to the god, and utters a traditional invocation asking the god to help his devotee with the problem.

The Venerable Dhīrānanda's theorizing has brought a Hindu touch into Sinhala Buddhism; the practice of *kapurāḷa*s has had an even more Hinduizing effect. By tradition all Buddhist *sacralia* are accessible to both sexes at all times, and menstruating women are not ritually impure when it comes to Buddhist worship, as they are in Hindu culture and in Sinhala tradition for the purposes of the spirit cults. Now a notice has appeared at the great *bō* tree behind the main shrine at Kataragama forbidding women access to the inner rampart around the tree, and this restriction is being emulated at other sites. This is a drastic, and to our knowledge completely unprecedented, infringement of the Buddhist principle of sexual equality in worship. It seems that the deity in the tree objects not merely to menstrual pollution, as other gods do, but to the presence of women altogether. If this trend spreads, we shall have to change the view we have expressed above that the *Bōdhi pūjā* "seems to belong to all Sinhala Buddhists equally" and rewrite "Buddhists" as "Buddhist males." However, some *kapurāḷa*s are emphatic that the exclusion of women is wrong, and one will have to wait to see which party carries the day.

Having described the current ritual uses of the *Bōdhi pūjā*, we return to consider the texts and the emotions they express. If the *Bōdhi pūjā* is tending to supersede *pirit*, we have suggested, that is largely due to the appeal of the text. The *pirit* texts, besides being in Pāli, are not devotional in tone and never evoke the image of the Buddha. By contrast a line in one of the Venerable Ariyadhamma's Sinhala verses says, "I make my heart into a cool Fragrant Hut," the term Fragrant Hut being a technical term for wherever the Buddha is staying.[12] The sentiment is not new to the literature: an older Pāli verse that is used in the service says much the same; but the point is that now it is expressed in the speaker's mother tongue.

In Ariyadhamma's text the worship is directed to all twenty-eight Buddhas, but this does not affect the emotional tone. We quote a few sample verses from the newer printed versions that elaborate on this theme.

[12] This verse was not used in the version of the service recorded in our earlier article.

1. With the power of alms-merit he brought blessings on the world,
Sage Taṇhaṃkara, I worship you. Sādhu!

3. Giving away his children as alms, he defeated Māra.
Sage Saraṇaṃkara, I worship you. Sādhu!

14. Removing doubt, he opened the way to liberation.
Royal Sage Sumedha, I worship you. Sādhu!

21. He defeated the assembled host of Māra.
Sage Phussa, I worship you. Sādhu!

However, when Gautama, "our" Buddha, is addressed in these texts, the tone becomes still warmer:

> The world is bathed in the lovely rays of the Buddha;
> The Buddha monk uttered such good sermons.
> With full heart I offer lights at your blessed feet.
> My sorrow and sin destroyed, may I inherit content.
>
> Like the full moon seen from the mountain top,
> Wearing a golden robe and giving forth light,
> Showing compassion to the three worlds,
> Behold the beauty of our Lord Buddha.

Another short sequence from one of our variant versions expresses traditional Buddhist themes in simple language; it states the purposes of the ritual:

> To spread compassion to beings in all the worlds,
> To release from suffering those near and far,
> To obtain happiness for all in this world,
> For my mother and father to achieve *nirvāṇa*.
>
> To live without trouble from our enemies,
> To live in harmony with our friends,
> To live in happiness forever—
> May our friends and enemies achieve *nirvāṇa*.
>
> To be born in an honorable caste (*kula*),
> To possess as much wealth as one wishes,
> To build stupas without limit
> May I be born like King Dahaṃsoñḍa.

King Dahaṃsoṅḍa, "Dharma Addict," was, according to an apocryphal story, the future Buddha Gautama in one of his former births. He was so avid to hear the Dhamma preached that he gave his life for it, though luckily the sacrifice proved to be illusory. In a similar vein this version goes on with verses in which the devotee asks to have the wisdom of Mahauṣadha (the Buddha in another former birth), the health of the monk Bakkula, and the divine eye (clairvoyance) of the Buddha's disciple Mugalan.

The less traditional themes in our variant versions are three: references to the magical and almost exorcistic uses of the ritual dealt with above; the focusing of worship on the tree; and adoration of the Buddha as a mother figure. The first two of these themes cannot be entirely disentangled in our examples.

The text used by Jayanta has a series of stanzas addressed to the *bō* tree that are strongly reminiscent of exorcistic verse. In that tradition it is customary to expel the badness (*dōsa*) from the patient, moving systematically from his head down to his feet.

O Lord Bō, who gave [the Buddha] tenfold power and wisdom,
By the merit of past births we have come to worship here.
May all planetary ills and calamities be banished
From the face, ears, and tongue.

O Lord Bō, who gave tenfold power and wisdom,
We worship you to calm the fires of sorrow.
Through the two legs and from the soles
May all planetary ills and calamities disappear.

O Lord Bō, who gave tenfold power and wisdom,
We have come to deck you with lovely flowers and worship you.
From the waist, intestines, kidneys, and so on
May all planetary ills and calamities disappear.

O Lord Bō, who gave tenfold power and wisdom,
We have come to offer you lights and lovely flowers.
Such things as poisons, venoms, and tying [by black magic],
May such bad planetary ills and calamities be banished.

Expel and banish badness caused by the nine planets.
May we be blessed by the power of the ninefold Sangha.
O Lord Bō, who destroyed the power of Māra,
May we obtain the help (*pihiṭa*) of the Fully Enlightened One.

We mentioned above that at the climax of Ariyadhamma's service everyone repeats several times, "May all beings be happy." The predicate of the sentence, *suvapat vetvā*, is so vague as to be hard to translate; one might also translate it, for example, as "attain bliss." Jayanta, however, has given that point in the service a decided twist by inserting the word "physical" (*kāyika*) at one of the repetitions; one would therefore translate the climax of *his* service as "May all beings be well, / May all beings be physically well, / Be well, be well."

Everyone we have interviewed maintains the traditional theory that the Buddha cannot directly intercede in current affairs or help the worshipper and equally maintains that the Bōdhi tree is a king by virtue of the divinity living in it and presiding over it. Clearly if there is an agency that can grant the worshipper's requests, it can only, according to the doctrine, be that divinity. But the last stanza cited above shows that in this context the tree, the tree spirit, and the Buddha himself have all but merged in the mind of the devotee. The standard traditional formula is "The Buddha for refuge, the gods for help"; yet in the verse above the same term "help" from that formula is used to request assistance from the Buddha.

In many verses (we choose three separate ones at random) the *bō* tree is said to shine with the Buddha's own halo or effulgence (*räs*):

> By simply gazing our eyes awaken [to truth],
> By worship and offerings the roots of sin are washed,
> By hearing his name the path to liberation unfolds,
> The Buddha's rays shine in the compound of the glorious victorious
> Bōdhi.[13]

> In every house may there be a Buddha image
> And may it shine with scented flowers and lamps,
> And may I get the comfort and protection of the gods,
> And may the Buddha rays shine from the King Bō.

> May the power of the blessed Gautama Buddha appear,
> May the blessed Lord Bō protect this country,
> May the power of the Bodhisattvas here appear
> And may the Buddha rays radiate from the blessed Tooth Relic.

We mentioned above that already in the original text by the Venerable Ariyadhamma the Buddha is referred to as both father and mother. This is

[13] "Victorious," because of Buddha's victory over Māra.

somewhat unusual. In Sinhala the Buddha is usually referred to as "lord" or "king," much less frequently as "father." We are not aware that in the Pāli liturgy he is ever referred to by a kinship term. Gombrich has published elsewhere[14] a premodern Sinhala text of uncertain date in which the Buddha is compared to a mother in an elaborate metaphor, but this was worth drawing attention to precisely because it was exceptional. As pointed out in that article, it is much less unusual to attribute to one's mother the qualities (namely, the compassion) of the Buddha. Occasionally the compassion of the mother is attributed to the Buddha. Thus in the Buddha legend as recorded in the thirteenth-century Sinhala text *Pūjāvaliya* a repentant person addresses the Buddha as "compassionate mother."[15] But in public utterance the Buddha has always been referred to and addressed with a certain distance and formality.

Now we find Jayanta singing, with his audience as chorus:

> O Mother, the mother guru of all the worlds,
> O Mother, the mother guru of human beings,
> O Mother, full of goodness and truth,
> Worship the fully Enlightened Buddha-Mother.

Here what was hitherto a private emotion in Sinhala culture has been given public expression. In the traditional pantheon there was only one important goddess, namely Pattinī, so she was the only being onto whom the Sinhala worshipper could project maternal feelings. Her cult is now in decline for other reasons, and her place as a *good* mother is not being taken by the ambivalent Kālī. Possibly, though we would not wish to press the point, the Buddha is here moving into an emotional gap left by Pattinī's withdrawal. Be that as it may, the officiants of the *Bōdhi pūjā* are, as Lévi-Strauss[16] has argued, abreacting their own past and opening a breach in the public culture by permitting the emotion of mother love to emerge from individual consciousness into the public cult of the Buddha. We should perhaps add, at the risk of saying the obvious, that none of the worshippers is denying that the Buddha is male; his "motherhood" is metaphorical. It is nonetheless felt for that.

In the *Bōdhi pūjā* texts (including that of Ariyadhamma) we also find

[14] R. Gombrich, "Feminine Elements in Sinhalese Buddhism, I: 'Buddha Mother,'" *Wiener Zeitschrift für die Kunde Südasiens XVI*, 1972, pp. 67–78.

[15] Kiriällē Ñāṇavimala, ed., *Pūjāvaliya* (Colombo: Gunasena, 1986), p. 643.

[16] Claude Lévi-Strauss, "The Sorcerer and His Magic," in *Structural Anthropology* (New York: Basic Books, 1963), pp. 167–85.

the word *bhakti*, "devotion," which though not unknown to the Theravādin tradition is hardly typical of it. In devotional Hinduism *bhakti* is passionate love of God; as in Christian mystical tradition the model, implicit or explicit, is often sexual love. The *bhakti* in the *Bōdhi pūjā* lacks sexual connotations; it refers to the mother's warmth and nurturance and the child's grateful dependence. The Hindu analogue of this Buddhist sentiment is the feeling for the cow. It may be no accident that one printed text of the *Bōdhi pūjā* tells the worshipper not to eat beef, though it enunciates no other food taboo or more general injunction to vegetarianism.

We sum up the emotional development of the *Bōdhi pūjā* with an illustration. Any offering of flowers before a Buddha image is normally accompanied by a Pāli stanza that naturally almost everyone knows by heart. It means: "I make offering to the Buddha with this flower, and by this merit may there be release. Just as this flower fades, so my body goes towards destruction." In other words the offering is made an occasion for recalling the cardinal Buddhist principle of impermanence. The Sinhala equivalent of this verse given in one printed version preserves the main idea but strikes a more hopeful note:

> Like these flowers may my mind be pure;
> May these flowers make me aware of the body [as impermanent];
> May these flowers become an offering for the Sage,
> And like these flowers may my mind blossom to *nirvāṇa*.

Yet another Sinhala verse now current says:

> Brimming with the scent of goodness,
> To the fully Enlightened Buddha-Mother (*ammā Sambudunhaṭa*),
> Overflowing with scent and color
> I offer these flowers. Sādhu! Sādhu!

Jayanta, a Priest of the Bōdhi Pūjā

We shall now illustrate the above social and psychological themes with a case study of a young man who has adopted a new role—priest of the *Bōdhi pūjā*.

We interviewed Jayanta in December 1984, when he was twenty-one. We write as of that date. He was born in 1963 in Kapugama near Mātara into a patrilineage of exorcists. His parents are both about fifty-four years old; they married when they were fifteen or sixteen. They had eleven children, of whom five boys and four girls are alive today. The oldest sibling is thirty-four. Jayanta is the seventh child. He had only a very elementary education, but he can read and write. He proudly proclaims that he comes of a family of exorcists "going back a hundred generations." His father is still active in that profession and all his brothers follow it. Yet Jayanta is even prouder to affirm that he has broken away from demon exorcism into what he calls "the gods' department" (*dēva aṃsaya*).

Jayanta works at the Saman shrine on the premises of the ancient Viṣṇu shrine at Devundara or Devinuvara ("City of the God"). This shrine, on the south coast near Matara, has traditionally been considered Viṣṇu's chief seat on the island. Conforming to the common pattern of the Buddha plus four guardian deities, the site now also has a Buddhist temple with resident monks and subsidiary shrines for the gods Saman, Pattinī, and Kataragama. Each shrine has its own priests. The chief priest of the Saman shrine, seeing the popularity of the *Bōdhi pūjā* conducted by a monk at the temple, invited young Jayanta to assist him by conducting *Bōdhi pūjā* rituals at his shrine, which is near a *bō* tree. Jayanta's performance quickly became enormously popular and overshadowed that of the monk. However, Jayanta's neighbor at work, the priest of the Pattinī shrine, is openly contemptuous of the *Bōdhi pūjā* and declares it to be an innovation devoid of efficacy. Jayanta believes that his *Bōdhi pūjā* is taking custom away from the traditional priests, but the Pattinī priest vehemently denies it.

Jayanta's case history recalls those described in *Medusa's Hair*. When he was fifteen or sixteen he fell ill: he would start shaking and fall down, sometimes twice in a day. His father, the demon exorcist, would give him some charmed water that would cure him for the moment. To this household of exorcists the diagnosis was obvious: Jayanta was possessed by the spirits of his dead sisters.

Jayanta had no recollection of the two sisters who had died at the ages of nine and seven, when he was three, but their dramatic deaths were often talked about by everyone in the household. Jayanta's father had been performing a piece of sorcery (*guru kama*) on behalf of a client. For this purpose he had to instill life (*jīvan*) into, that is, magically activate, three eggs in his home by repeating (*japa*) spells for a certain length of time. While he was doing so one of the eggs fell, broke, and spilled all over the threshold. Without telling anyone, the father rubbed the debris off with his feet; but two sisters had accidentally stepped over some of this ensorcelled material. One girl died twenty-one days after this event and the other two days later.[17] The eldest girl in the family (now thirty-four) also fell ill but soon recovered. The father got scared. He had fellow exorcists perform rituals to protect the members of his household. But they could not completely cancel ("cut") the effects of his black magic because he had performed such a complicated series of spells (*mantra*), including deadly Malayalam magic. Moreover, according to the theory of magic one cannot oneself cancel the effects one has produced. So the father explained the complicated procedure to his brother, who then, under his instruction, performed a special "cutting" rite (*käpilla*) and destroyed the effects of the spilt egg once and for all. For this rite all members of the household except the eldest sister were put in a special room under magical custody. The eldest sister was placed in front of the ritual paraphernalia, and the "poison" in her body was transferred into the body of a chicken.

While Jayanta was suffering from his malady, the god Kataragama appeared to him in a dream wearing a crown and the Kandyan-style costume of a Basnāyaka Nilamē, the traditional lay custodian of an important shrine to a god. Jayanta says the god appeared in a single guise (*tani ves*), in other words with one face rather than the six with which he is normally represented. The god said to him: "Child, you possess a meritorious life (*pin jīvita*). Do not make it miserable (*kālakanni*). I shall teach you a program of work and you must do as I tell you." Further instructions followed. The god told him to practice *Bōdhi pūjā* in order to banish planetary ills (*apala*) and to light lamps with sesame and mustard oil for the twenty-eight Buddhas. In his rituals he was to pay homage to the Buddha, the Dhamma, and the Sangha and mentally worship the main spiritual centers of Sinhala Buddhism. Then he was to transfer the merit to the nine planetary deities and make the wish (*prārthanāva*) that all the patient's ills disappear. He was to rotate a coconut around the patient's head, then smash it on the ground while wishing that all the patient's misfortunes be smashed with it.

In such situations it is the custom to seal one's compact with a deity by lighting a lamp in his honor. Jayanta built a small shrine for a lamp (*pahan kūḍuva*) outside the house, but instead of following convention by lighting

[17] The number 21 is from 3 times 7, both magical numbers in Indo-European tradition.

a lamp for the gods he performed a ritual service (*tēvāva*) for the Buddha. Then on the site of the shrine he lit a lamp for the god (*deviyō*) Hūniyam, who would be his personal guardian deity. Lighting the lamp for Hūniyam, doing *pūjā*s to the Buddha, and transferring the merit to the gods completely cured his illness.

A few months after his illness, still following Kataragama's instructions, he built a small Buddha shrine (*budugē*) in the compound of his house; it took him less than a month. He insisted that this was not a shrine for the gods (*dēvālē*). At its ceremonial inauguration a miracle occurred. "The time was about 8:45 P.M. I had worshipped the Buddha and lit a lamp for him. Then, as I was reciting the *Karaṇīya Metta Sutta*, a beautiful effulgence emanated from that lamp and spread all over the shrine. . . . Others who were present also saw it. My mother felt it over her head and had to bow down."

Now that the shrine was dedicated, he began regularly to pray to the Buddha and to light lamps for the gods and to transfer merit to them and to his dead sisters. He stated very clearly to us that his father had no interest in all this, as he was a demon exorcist. But he was not opposed to it.

Once he had begun to transfer merit to his dead sisters they came to appear regularly in his dream visions. They assumed adult guise, wearing white saris. "They praised me for doing the work of the Buddha (*budungē väḍa*) and urged me to get them some merit by taking refuge in the Buddha. They said they would protect me. I could feel their look (*bälma*) over me." The sisters informed him that they were not in a bad place, but still lacked a little merit to improve their condition. If he were to transfer merit to them they could go to "a good place." Jayanta constantly used the expression *räka gannavā*, "to protect," a term used, for instance, to describe a bird protecting its eggs or its brood; it connotes a comforting protectiveness. "They tell me of two things regularly: their lack of merit and their protection if merit is given them." He feels that his sisters' *diṣṭi* (literally "look" or "gaze," in effect "energizing force") falls on him. To develop this "power vibration" (*bala vēgaya*) he must worship the Three Jewels and ask the help of the gods so that he may have the power to heal all beings, to banish their planetary ills, and to send them on the right path. Once they achieve a higher condition his sisters will become intermediaries between him and the gods. He seals his compact with his sisters by putting aside two balls of rice (*bat guli*) before eating his main meals.

Jayanta was convinced that all his experiences indicated that he should become a priest of the *Bōdhi pūjā* cult. In 1980 he therefore went to a Buddhist monk, a relation of his, at Pādukka, about a hundred miles from his home. The monk was a friend of the Venerable Ariyadhamma and knew his *Bōdhi pūjā*. He urged Jayanta to become a novice, but Jayanta had no wish to join the Order. He stayed three months in Pādukka and there memorized the text and learned the ritual procedure of *Bōdhi pūjā*.

Once he had memorized the text, he went to Kataragama to obtain the god's permission (*varama*) to perform the *Bōdhi pūjā* professionally, that is, as a *kapurāḷa*. This did not entail possession or firewalking, as it would with ecstatic neophytes, but only doing a *pūjā* to the god. He went back home and continued to memorize verses (from other versions of the text?).[18] Now another extraordinary thing happened: his voice changed "from rough to soft" and became very "feminine." "My voice became beautiful after I started work. In my dreams I sing the *Bōdhi pūjā* songs in this same tone of voice in the Buddha shrine. My two sisters sit in the corner of the shrine and listen. Divine damsels (*surangana*) with blue shawls come up to me and lustrate me with water (*pän*) and make wishes that my voice should become beautiful." Jayanta does indeed sing in a soft, mellifluous voice; his gait and all his mannerisms are feminine. The *diṣṭi* of the sisters has given him their essence and transformed him into a feminine person.

Jayanta's first major *Bōdhi pūjā* was at Kataragama. He went with some relatives from Colombo in 1981, and having worshipped at the stupa there, the Kiri Vehera, he performed a *Bōdhi pūjā* for them at the great *bō* tree behind the god's main shrine. In all likelihood this was one of the first *Bōdhi pūjā*s held at Kataragama. No wonder some of the priests attached to the shrine, always open to new religious ideas, watched it with interest. They invited the young man into the main shrine for the 10:30 A.M. *pūjā*s and invoked the blessings of Kataragama on him. One of the priests even urged Jayanta to stay with him and perform a *Bōdhi pūjā* for his mother, who was troubled by planetary ills. Jayanta came home with that same priest to get permission from his parents to be a priest (*kapurāḷa*). The priest reassured his parents and urged them to agree. Jayanta's first truly professional *Bōdhi pūjā* was in due course held for the mother of this ben-

[18] Jayanta claims that the text of the *Bōdhi pūjā* he learned at Pādukka is Ariyadhamma's own version. But this is doubtful as he uses verses (and ideas) not found in Ariyadhamma's.

efactor. He stayed in the latter's house at Kataragama for three years performing *Bōdhi pūjā*s and occasionally assisting the priests at the main shrine. He was the only one among the priests there who could do the *Bōdhi pūjā*. He had become a specialist of the *Bōdhi pūjā* cult.

Jayanta had a classificatory uncle (mother's brother) who was the priest of the Saman shrine at Devinuvara. One day Jayanta's father mentioned to him that he had a son who was performing *Bōdhi pūjā* at Kataragama. The priest took the hint and urged the father to bring Jayanta along. So his father brought him home from Kataragama and put him in the care of his uncle. Thus on 2 January 1984 he became his uncle's assistant at the Saman shrine.

There Jayanta performs both *Bōdhi pūjā*s and the conventional rituals for Saman that the other priests too perform. He tends to combine the two. Thus he may ask a client first to have a *Bōdhi pūjā* and then to come to the Saman shrine, where he transfers the merit to Saman and then utters the standard kind of plaint (*kannalavva*) asking the god to grant the client favors.

How does Jayanta see the future? He wants to develop both the *Bōdhi pūjā* and the rituals for the gods. He admits that for the *Bōdhi pūjā* no shrine for the gods is necessary, but he also feels that he has a power that is most appropriate for the cult of the gods. When he is performing the *Bōdhi pūjā* his body tends to shake. "I feel that I am destined to receive a garland of authorizations (*varam mālāva*) from the gods," he says. This is a standard concept among the new-style *sāmi* who congregate at Kataragama; but Jayanta is not following their route. He is not doing penance or firewalking to legitimize his ecstasy. He believes that as he goes on doing *Bōdhi pūjā*s he will be able to develop the divine spark within him to the point where he will eventually obtain the "mouth warrant" (*muka varama*), that is, the ability to deliver oracles. The warrant will come from the dead sisters, who will speak through him and act as liaison between him and the gods. This oracular gift is useless for *Bōdhi pūjā*, he says, but essential for the work of the gods. When he obtains it he will return to the Kiri Vehera and light as many lamps as he is years old and transfer the merit to Kataragama, who will be responsible for the warrant, and to his late sisters. By that time they will be in a better place and consequently capable of possessing him and acting as mediators between him and Kataragama. Once he obtains this gift he will be able to convert people who are on the wrong track to the true spirit of Buddhism and also to help them through *Bōdhi pūjā*, in particular to overcome bad planetary influence. Possession by his sisters will also enable him to perform rites to cancel out the evil effects of sorcery, not by enlisting the aid of demons as his father does, but by the help of the gods who hold kingly sway over the demons. To achieve and keep these powers he must lead an exemplary life. He must be a strict vegetarian, abstain from sex, and refuse to charge his clients but accept only what they freely give. After many years of service to the gods they might permit him to marry, but that will also herald the decline of his powers.

Jayanta's case recapitulates many themes not only of this chapter but of earlier ones too. The *Bōdhi pūjā* has passed from monks to be shared by other religious specialists. The younger generation has been attracted by Ariyadhamma's attempt to soften the dominant Protestant Buddhism into a religion of the heart. Jayanta, the poorly educated son of a village exorcist, is not from the social stratum in which one expects to find the influence of Protestant Buddhism at its strongest; yet in building his own Buddha shrine in the compound of his house and servicing it himself he is acting in a truly Protestant manner—without benefit of clergy. He wants to act as a priest for the Buddha and even convert people to the true spirit of Buddhism, but sees no reason to join the Order to do so.

Jayanta is in passive rebellion against his father, a very traditional specialist of the demon cults. Those cults now have little appeal to the youth of any social class in Sri Lanka. Traditionally they cope mainly with disease; perhaps their decline has been hastened by the now universal awareness of the methods of modern medicine and indeed by some of its successes. Be that as it may, we have shown both in this book and in *Medusa's Hair* that the traditional exorcist is being superseded by the modern *sāmi*. The *sāmi* is generally possessed by the spirit of a dead relative, who mediates between him and his god. He generally has to legitimate that possession by some display of devotional (*bhakti*) religiosity such as firewalking or hanging from hooks.

Jayanta's history is like that of the typical *sāmi* in that he fell ill, was found to be possessed by dead relatives, had his possession brought under control, and aspired to become a god's vehicle. But his religious devotion is for the Buddha, and his primary cultic practice is the *Bōdhi pūjā*. However, this creates a problem. As he is well aware, possession has nothing to do with Buddhism. Moreover, a traditional Buddhist like his father defines a possessing spirit as a *prēta*, a disgusting and morally inferior spirit who should be exorcised. It is the milieu of the *sāmi* that has redefined the possessing spirit as benign. But since he does not want to go the way of the *sāmi* and channel his devotion toward a god, Jayanta must change the theology of possession. Note that it is Kataragama himself who "tells" Jayanta to change his life style and take up the *Bōdhi pūjā* cult. In effect the god is telling Jayanta to direct his devotion to the Buddha rather than to himself. So Jayanta goes to Kataragama, but does not perform the legitimation procedures of the *sāmi*; he just follows the traditional Buddhist practice and offers the god the merit of his Buddhist worship. Similarly, if he gets the gift of tongues he plans again to go to the Kiri Vehera and just give Kataragama the merit. Indeed, he told us that it is only if one is possessed by a *prēta* that one has to undergo penance at the god's shrine. That is what one might expect a traditional Buddhist like his father to say; any *sāmi* would deny it with vehemence. It is no accident that Jayanta calls himself a *kapurāḷa* and explicitly denies that he is a *sāmi*. It also fits his Buddhist orientation that he says that his sisters will achieve a better state, but entirely through his acts of merit transfer; this is the Buddhist rationale for transferring merit to the dead, though it is not traditional thus to operationalize the belief.

It is not merely that the *Bōdhi pūjā* lacks the "vulgarity" of traditional exorcisms. As we have suggested above, it also has an appeal to Sinhala Buddhists as such, an appeal they may not be able consciously to articulate. For many young people like Jayanta it is presumably a Sinhala Buddhist ritual that differentiates them from Tamil Hindus. While Jayanta may not know as much as scholars do about South Indian religious traditions and their decisive influence on the new *sāmi*, he certainly must have become aware at Kataragama that some of the Sinhala *sāmi* had Hindu Tamil gurus and that their practices had Hindu antecedents. In the current political climate, this may well have influenced him to become a *kapurāḷa* rather than a *sāmi*.

Yet by traditional standards he is a very odd *kapurāḷa*. For him the gods are effectively subsidiary. The primary power lies in the *bō* tree, and it is his role to harness it for individual purposes and the common good. Jayanta holds that the *Bōdhi pūjā* can help people to find jobs, whereas any traditional priest will hold that such worldly concerns are a matter for the gods and have nothing to do with Buddhist worship.

Jayanta's course may have been negatively influenced by the too-Hindu image of the *sāmi*; but the positive attraction of the *Bōdhi pūjā* must have been far more decisive. Here a psychological hypothesis seems to be appropriate. Jayanta is not like the more guilt-ridden female ascetics in *Medusa's Hair*: the dead relatives who possess him have never been punitive spirits.[19] They just jolt him to make him aware of his obligations as a Buddhist, the message that Kataragama then conveys directly in a dream. He recognizes this lack of a tormented relation with his dead relatives, for he told us that though he could not remember them himself his mother had told him that they had truly loved him. He has no problems with them.

It is the idea of the Buddha as mother that has profound emotional meaning for Jayanta. His father was not an authoritarian person. True, he used to drink and occasionally hit the children; but Jayanta said he loved his father. Yet clearly in his adolescence he reacted against him by renouncing his profession, despite the weight of family tradition. Still that renunciation was halfhearted; his own profession is rather a reformed version of his father's. Toward his mother, however, Jayanta had little ambivalence: "Even if father hits us for some fault my mother scolds him. Mother is full of kindness. . . ." Later he bluntly told us, "I love my mother more than I do my father." He was quite conscious of the association: "The honor (*satkāra*) I pay my mother I also pay the Buddha." Probably his feminine identification with his sisters is based on a more primordial identification with his mother.

For Jayanta, then, the mother is the Buddha, as the Buddha is the mother. Since the Buddha has not usually been explicitly likened to a mother in traditional Sinhala culture, the direction of metaphorical transfer is probably from the family to the religious context. The *Bōdhi pūjā* movement must have received its momentum from several factors. It provides a more respectable substitute for the old, rural exorcistic traditions; it reaffirms Sinhala Buddhist cultural identity. But the most important single motivating force must come from its transfer of love for the mother to the Buddha himself.

[19] See esp. Obeyesekere, *Medusa's Hair*, pp. 76–83.

CHAPTER 12

Sinhala Firewalkers and the Buddhist Appropriation of Kataragama

Chapter 5 introduced the topic of how Sinhala Buddhists have in recent times virtually taken over the shrine of Kataragama and its principal religious activities and in so doing absorbed the *bhakti* religiosity of the Tamils they have ousted. Part of that topic has however been postponed to this late stage in the book; for we wish to show how the takeover has interacted with the Protestant Buddhism of some leading religious innovators, themselves drawn from the Sinhala middle classes. In particular we regard as highly significant the myths that these innovators have invented to justify the Sinhalicization of the cult. Such inventions (which we certainly do not believe to be knowingly fraudulent) give us a vivid illustration of how the past is constantly remade to suit the present. More than that: our material here shows how the assimilators are affected by what they have assimilated. A Buddhism that has appropriated Kataragama cannot remain unaffected by it.

In Chapter 5 we introduced Vijeyaratna Sāmi, the first Buddhist to walk the fire. He plays a large role in this chapter too. It was however another Sinhala Buddhist, Mutukuḍa Sāmi, who was responsible for converting the ritual into one dominated by Sinhala Buddhists. Born in 1910 in Kalutara, Western Province, Mutukuḍa was from a respectable Sinhala Buddhist family. He was educated in Sinhala schools but had a fair knowledge of English. In the mid-1930s he visited India, where he stayed for four years studying the "occult sciences." He came back to Sri Lanka, but in 1940 enlisted in the Royal Army Service Corps. He went first to Bombay; after four months he was sent to Egypt. He participated in the battle of El Alamein; from there he was sent to Tobruk, Tripoli, and then Sicily. The critical event occurred when Lieutenant Mutukuḍa led a convoy of seventeen vehicles in the attack on Monte Cassino. The following is his own graphic English rendering of the events: "When we were convoyed through Monte Cassino . . . then Italians came and raided. They raided us with bombs and the machine guns. Drivers and vehicles were being destroyed. At that time only myself and my driver escaped. Italians came and machine-gunned and I crept under my vehicle. I remember at once god Kataragama. All these are fire, the bombs are also fire, I thought. If I escape from this raid I will go back to Sri Lanka and go to Kataragama and do firewalking. This was my vow." He returned to Sri Lanka in 1945, a captain in the army. True to his vow, he came to Kataragama in 1947; but unfortunately he arrived after the firewalking was over. Depressed, he went to the sacred river Mäṇik Gaṅga to bathe; there an old man who looked like his dead uncle (father's younger brother) told him: "Son, do not be afraid; you come next time. You must put an end to eating fish and meat. Bathe, purify yourself, and be ready for walking the fire next time." This apparition was, of course, the god himself.

In 1948 he returned to Kataragama and successfully walked the fire under the guidance of Selliah Sāmi, the Hindu mendicant. In the following three years he was joined by three or four acquaintances of his, among them two government officials: an accountant in the government Railways Department and the chief of the Colombo fire-fighting unit. This period coincided with the emerging political dominance of Sinhala Buddhists and strong resentment against Tamil Hindus. Thus in 1951 the Sinhala lay trustee of the shrine gave Mutukuḍa the title of chief firewalker, displacing the Hindu Selliah Sāmi. Thereafter the Sinhala was known by his Hinduized name, Mutukuḍa Sāmi. No more Hindus have been nominated to this post since then.

Soon the mass media highlighted the prowess of firewalkers, and Mutukuḍa Sāmi came to have an almost national reputation. He resigned his position in 1962, in an argument with the lay trustee on the timing of the ritual. Vijeyaratna Sāmi took his place till 1969; he also resigned after an argument with the lay trustee, a disagreement over a change in venue of the firewalking ritual from the small compound facing the main shrine to a larger area opposite the trustee's own official residence. Subsequently the position fell to various persons: a carpenter and part-time priest, a priest of a Colombo shrine, the chief inspector of the public transport system of the city of Ratnapura. In 1975 a young liberal member of Parliament was elected lay trustee by the Kataragama electoral college. He reinstated Vijeyaratna Sāmi (although the firewalking site, over which the latter had originally resigned, was not changed back).

Vijeyaratna Sāmi was, like Mutukuḍa, a well-educated, cultured, and frail-looking gentleman. He was born in about 1908. As a young man he went to India on the advice of Anagārika Dharmapāla, to whom he was related. Apparently the original idea, under the influence of the Gandhian movement, was for him to study textile manufacture as a cottage industry. In fact he still makes his own clothes and has taught spinning, weaving, and natural dying in Sri Lanka. In India he conceived the desire to become a monk. Anagārika Dharmapāla was not the only family influence here: his parallel cousin became the incumbent of Tissamahārāma. He spent two years and seven months at Bodh Gayā, the site of the Buddha's Enlightenment. However, he could not realize his ambition to be a monk because while in India he lost the use of one eye, and such blindness is a disqualification from joining the Sangha. Thus frustrated, he took a vow of chastity (*brahmacarya*) (as Dharmapāla had done). He did, however, marry later, at the age of forty-two, at his mother's insistence and fathered five children.

In India he also became interested in occult science (*gupta vidyā*). He said that he first went firewalking at a Śiva temple in Benares. His subsequent career as a firewalker we have recorded above. He told us that there are two kinds of occult science, the Indian and the Californian, and that the latter is superior; he is a corresponding member of a Californian society of occultists and owes some of his discoveries (recorded below) to exercising that art.

Both Vijeyaratna and Mutukuḍa introduced a variety of innovations in the firewalk, effectively giving it a Sinhala Buddhist orientation. Most important was the development of myths associating the firewalk with the great Sinhala king, Duṭugämuṇu; we return to them below. Mutukuḍa initiated the practice that firewalkers go in procession to the Buddhist stupa, the Kiri Vehera, before the firewalking to pay homage to, and seek the permission (*avasara*) of, the Three Refuges—the Buddha, the Dhamma, and the Sangha. Moreover, Mutukuḍa got the monks from the somewhat unorthodox Buddhist temple, the Abhivanārāmaya, to chant *pirit* immediately before the actual firewalking. Blessing the firewalkers gave their walk Buddhist legitimation. It was, however, unorthodox, since Buddhist monks are supposed to keep aloof from the worship of the gods (beyond giving them merit). Monks were in fact reluctant to participate, and the practice has been only sporadic. It was resurrected by Vijeyaratna Sāmi in 1975; but in 1979 monks did not attend, and laymen under the leadership of Väligallē Sāmi, a respected firewalker, recited *pirit* at the head of the fire trench. This is known as *gihi pirit* (*pirit* by laymen). But the very next year monks came back on the scene and it is likely that *pirit* recitation at the firewalk will become a standard practice. All these innovations were justified in the new myths that we will discuss below.

Innovators like Mutukuḍa and Vijeyaratna Sāmi belonged to the class influenced by Dharmapāla. When Mutukuḍa broke the Tamil domination of the firewalk several people of this same class joined him. They were Sinhala- and English-educated bureaucrats, merchants, and schoolteachers. It is no accident that these people followed Dharmapāla's patriotic views in the Sinhala Buddhicization of the firewalk. However, they illustrate the failure of one aspect of Dharmapāla's program—his contempt for the Hindu-derived gods of the Buddhist pantheon. It is possible for monks as well as renouncers of Dharmapāla's type ("this-worldly ascetics") to dispense with the gods, but not for laymen, for whom the gods serve a variety of nonsoteriological needs. Moreover, the tradition of occultism was far too entrenched in Sinhala and South Indian culture to be abolished by exhortation. So Mutukuḍa Sāmi and Vijeyaratna Sāmi and their successors, having captured the firewalk, as good Protestant Buddhists systematically gave it Buddhist legitimation. Mutukuḍa made it clear that firewalking did *not* require *bhakti*: it only needed concentration in a Buddhist sense, and a life of Buddhist piety (*sil*). Vegetarianism was for him a Buddhist way of life; he also urged the observance of the ten precepts on Buddhist holy days. So did Vijeyaratna Sāmi. It is not *bhakti* but *patipatti* (practice of Buddhist morality) that is important. Yet both Mutukuḍa and Vijeyaratna, like all other firewalkers, believed in *gupta vidyā*, "the occult sciences." These were for them true rational sciences parallel to the ethical and philosophical rationality of Buddhism. Vijeyaratna Sāmi, for example, told us that those who get burnt are not pious and possess a weak moral character. If one practices the Buddhist precepts (*sil*) one will not get burnt; however, one can also walk across the fire by the power of occult formulas (*mantra*). Mutukuḍa asserted that Hindus practice purity, and his mentor Selliah Sāmi practiced abstinences to purify and sacralize (*pē*) his body for seven days. But the Buddhists need not go to such extremes; crucial is *pin-daham* ("merit and morality") to send you unscathed across the fire. Vijeyaratna Sāmi insists that one must be fully conscious and self-possessed when walking over the coals—the state of mind that Buddhism opposes to ecstasy. He claims that before the walkers step into the fire he looks into their eyes to see whether they are possessed or in trance. Only if they are fully conscious and aware will he apply to their brows the sacred ash that is Skanda's blessing and protection. That may be his perception; but we doubt whether it would be how other observers would interpret what they see happening.

It is curious to find in a chief firewalker, of all people, a disapproval of emotional display and lack of self-control. But it is a hallmark of Protestantism, including Protestant Buddhism, that moral prescriptions are removed from specific context and generalized to all situations: if some thought or emotion is bad, it is always bad. The Buddhist puritan streak in Vijeyaratna Sāmi showed itself in another way. He, like others of similar background, strongly disapproved of the entire atmosphere in which the Kataragama festival was being conducted. He said he despised the communal aspect of *kāvaḍi* dancing, all the noise and confusion—people were acting like uneducated savages (in fact he said like Väddas). However most of the rank and file of firewalkers have radically different attitudes. Some lower-class firewalkers (especially males) may reiterate Vijeyaratna Sāmi's view that a meditative self-awareness in the Buddhist sense is the right attitude to walking across the fire, but only a few will adopt his anti-emotionalism.

Ethical changes in Sinhala society at large are anticipated and worked out at Kataragama. We have explained in Chapter 5 why it should be under the aegis of this particular god that these changes occur. Not only in 1765 did Buddhist monks class Skanda as a chthonic (and so morally inferior) god; we know that many monks hold an equally low opinion of him today. Traditional priets (*kapurāḷa*s) at Kataragama have even used the canonical term *mithyā dṛṣṭi*, "heretical," to describe him, because they cannot accept as fully Buddhist his willingness to abdicate moral judgment when it comes to helping his devotees or his sexual immorality. Let us look at two such ethical changes before turning to change on a higher level of generality—the assumption of the entire site and cult, past as well as present, as exclusively Sinhala cultural property.

1. Our first example is the *kāvaḍi* dance. Before the encroachment of Protestant Buddhism communal dancing, drumming, and singing were

common in Sinhala village life, but men and women were segregated. Women's dancing, even their singing at harvest, and the tradition of playing the flat drum have practically vanished from village life today. In some areas, as Knox as well as contemporary anthropologists have noted, marriage rules and sexual mores were flexible before Sinhala culture was practically swamped by the puritan sexual ethic of Protestant Buddhism. But the *kāvaḍi* dance is cracking this ethic. *Kāvaḍi*, insofar as both sexes join together, is not only unthinkable in traditional dance but also provokes the ire of Protestant Buddhists. It is ethically not right, but it is this moral ambiguity that makes it appropriate for Kataragama. We noted that the *kāvaḍi* dance may anticipate the emergence of a more relaxed sexual code and closer intersex communication.

2. The second example is the moral ambiguity of the role of Buddhist monks at Kataragama. Monks are not supposed to participate in rituals for the gods, as that violates the classic Sinhala Buddhist distinction between the Buddha for salvation and the gods for the world. Moreover, traditional rituals for gods and demons involve dancing, singing, and obscenity that not only upset monastic decorum but also violate the precept that forbids the witnessing of displays. In practice drumming and music, and an occasional drama enacting a Buddhist legend, took place in temples, but such displays were extremely sedate, quite unlike the rituals for deities and demons. Moreover, these displays occurred on the temple premises, not in a clearly "secular" environment. Now not only are monks officiating in the firewalk but they are increasingly to be seen on the premises of the main shrine. It is clear therefore that they are witnesses to shows like the *kāvaḍi* dance. Though not yet common, it may indicate a move toward public recognition that monks will increasingly be seen at *secular* performances *outside* Kataragama. Monks have started going into theaters, but as yet rarely to the cinema.

Ethically even more dubious is the unabashed practice of occult arts by monks at Kataragama. These arts were viewed as "vile and false" in the scriptures, and in Sinhala society it was rare for a monk to practice sorcery or dispense magical medicine. Astrology was permitted in practice (not in scripture) since it was not harmful and was viewed as a kind of "science" that delineated a person's *karma*. One famous monk was a well-known sorcerer at Koṇḍādeniya; but the Buddhist public, though standing in awe of him, did not consider him to be a "genuine monk." We noted that his pupil continued the practice after the teacher died, but disrobed himself. But consider what happens at Väḍahiṭikanda, now occupied by the monk Venerable Siddhārtha. As one climbs the mountain one hears over the loudspeaker advertisements for selling magical medicines of various sorts and a charmed thread that can protect you from snake bites. If worn around the waist it can free you from nightmares. An extra donation will enable you to purchase charmed packets of incense, while twenty rupees will buy you the *kan̆da kumāra vaśī yantra*—"Skanda's magical diagram for gaining influence over others"—presumably for success in love. Politicians come here in droves before an election to purchase *yantra*s that will bring them success. All of this reflects what is happening in the larger society, but it is also a recognition and acceptance of behavior by monks that the Buddhist public used to consider morally unsuitable.

Recent Myths of Skanda and Vallī Ammā

The *sāmi*s of Kataragama are theoreticians whose views seem to anticipate changes in the religion of the Sinhalas. Consequently their versions of myths must be significant. At Kataragama there are many *sāmi*s coming out with their own versions of Skanda myths; hence it would be wrong to treat any of the myths quoted in this section as "dominant," "normative," or "standard." Quite the contrary: they express debates going on in Kataragama and in the nation on what *we* might call problems of Sinhala cultural identity. Most Sinhala *sāmi*s possess myths that are close to very basic South Indian myths—that of Skanda and Gaṇeśa's conflict over their mother's mango, Skanda leaving India for Sri Lanka and his falling in love with Vallī, the woman of the hunters. The *sāmi*s we quote here are educated people, economically well off and belonging to the Sinhala intelligentsia influenced by Dharmapāla's reform. They are thus unlike most of the *sāmi*s and firewalkers, who come from lower-class backgrounds. But insofar as they are leaders we assume that their views are not fortuitous, but indicate the future reshaping of the Kataragama shrine complex.

Sinhala Version I: Mutukuḍa Sāmi

When Skanda left his spouse Dēvasēnā in India he decided to go and live in heaven. But one needs a residence in heaven, otherwise one has no place to live. In order to create such a residence Skanda had to meditate for six years. He saw with his divine eye that Väḍahiṭikanda was a pure ground [*suddha bhūmi*] for meditation. He landed in Devinuvara in the south of Sri Lanka and from there he came to Väḍahiṭikanda. From that day the soil of that area became converted into *vibhūti* [sacred ash]. While Skanda was engaged in meditation in the forest, Viṣṇu and other gods thought that if he came to heaven he would create trouble since he was a bit of a *caṇḍiyā* [tough guy] and also wayward. So the divine assembly [*sabhā*] decided to keep him in the human world. Since Skanda left India owing to his disappointment with a woman, Viṣṇu and other gods decided that another woman would be able to keep him in the human world. Thus they sent Vallī down to earth to be born there in an *opapātika* manner [spontaneously, not by normal procreation]. When Väddas were out hunting they saw the little infant and decided to raise her.

There is in heaven a trickster [*sellakkārayā*] named Nārada who was sent to Kataragama by the gods. He said: "What are you doing here? I know that you are meditating well, but there is a nice girl around here, so let's go see her." Skanda replied, "I don't care for that kind of thing. . . . I am disappointed with those things." But Nārada insisted, "For my sake come and see her." Nārada was a real nuisance since he would not leave and Skanda was forced to comply. They went into the forest and saw Vallī. The god forgot his meditation and fell in love with Vallī. He sent Nārada back to heaven and stayed on. Now he goes to Väḍahiṭikanda at night and spends the day chatting with Vallī at Sella Kataragama.

One day he asked Vallī whether she was agreeable to marrying him. "Yes," she said, "but I have to ask my parents." However she wanted *him* to seek their permission. [Mutukuḍa said: "You see the problem; a god cannot ask someone for favors, but he can take things by force. But to take something by force is wrong and does not entitle you to it. Someone must offer (*oppu*) a gift to god."] So Skanda was despondent owing to this dilemma. Then Gaṇeśa, his older brother, came up to him and asked him the cause of his despondency. When Gaṇeśa heard the story he told him to inquire from Vallī which animal she was most afraid of. Soon Skanda learned from Vallī that she was most afraid of elephants. Gaṇeśa told Skanda: "Come into the forest. When you are there ask Vallī for some water to clear your throat. I'll do the rest."

Now Skanda, taking the guise of an old man, was waiting in the forest for Vallī. When she arrived he accosted her and told her that he was hungry and wanted some food. Vallī said, "Sir, I have only some rice that I have made for my parents, and that is all we have." "Give it to me," he said. When this was done he ate it and then shouted, "It's stuck in my throat!" Then she tried to give him water from his water pot but it was empty. Vallī said, "Go to the river and drink some water," but the old man said he did not know where the river was. When Vallī was leading him there, Gaṇeśa, in the guise of an elephant, came crashing through the forest. Vallī got frightened and begged Skanda to save her. He said, "What will you promise me if I save you?" "I'll promise you anything," she said. "Will you come and live with me?" She agreed and then Skanda reassumed his youthful form. There is a statue of Gaṇeśa and also an elephant sculpture at Sella Kataragama to remind us even today about these events.

The Väddas pursued him. On one occasion, in order to escape them, he changed into a rock; on another into a tree. Ultimately the Väddas prepared for war, but Skanda killed all 500 of them. This war is known as the war between the *sura*s and *asura*s. The Väddas are *asura*s. Now Vallī cried and cried, saying, "You have killed my parents and kinsmen." In compassion for her he sprayed on them some water from the Mäṇik Gaṅga and they awoke. From that day onwards the Väddas treated him like a king and performed a *perahära* ["procession"] for the nuptial celebrations. This is what we commemorate today also. Even today we offer the same foods that the Väddas gave them that day—rice flour and bees' honey.

We think that the water sports have to do with the same thing, though it is a secret and not revealed to any of us [by the priests]. The secret is this: the area is screened off and the nuptial clothes are washed. Then the clothes are rinsed and the water taken to the temple. That's what *we* think the secret is. The god and his mistress are separate now; they will be reunited again next year. The festival of Kataragama is also over after this event.

Sinhala Version II: Käppiṭipola Sāmi

The god Skanda was born in India, and on the same day was born Tēvānī Ammā, his future wife. It was the custom of his *kula-gotra* ["caste and clan"] to get their children married as infants. This was done but Skanda never saw his legitimate wife after that. Ultimately he came to Sri Lanka and was meditating in Väḍahiṭikanda when the war between King Duṭugämuṇu and the Tamil Elāra broke out. [At this point Käppiṭipola Sāmi went on to describe the god's role in this war. This account is presented below. After the war was over Skanda resumed his meditation at Kataragama.]

Now Skanda was happily in residence in his chamber [shrine] at Kataragama [presumably still as a *yogi* and still a human being]. One day he thought of going upstream for *vinōda* ["pleasure," "fun"]. That day he saw Vallī singing in a sesame field, and she was very beautiful. He spoke to her; she remained silent, and he did not continue the conversation. On another occasion he saw her bathe [a sensuous scene for Sinhalas]. Prince (S)Kanda thought, "If I have great power [*bala mahima*] and the possibility of divine apotheosis [*dēvatva*], this woman must be *vaśi* [subjugated through a hypnotic type of power] for me." He then stepped into the river and she came running toward him, fell at his feet, worshipped him and said, "I am agreeable to anything!" The only garment she was wearing above her waist was a strap to cover her breasts; it is to commemorate this that the female servitors of the god at Kataragama wear breast straps [*tana poṭa*].

Now he had to marry her. He saw the seeds used to make rosaries float downstream and with these he made a necklace and placed it round her neck and married her. Then he came back to his chamber and lived happily with her. But remember he has not seen his legitimate wife yet. So meanwhile Tēvānī Ammā, his legitimate wife, thought, "I can neither go with another man nor can I find my man." So she made an amulet called the *Skanda kumāra maha vaśi yantra* ["the Prince Skanda amulet for seduction-domination"] with the following intentions—that Prince Skanda might not see Vallī Ammā; that the *vaśi* power would make him love Tēvānī Ammā; that he would return to India to join her.

Tēvānī Ammā sent this amulet to Sri Lanka with a Brahman who was familiar with magical arts. This Brahman saw the couple at Kataragama, but he had no way of placing the amulet around Skanda's head without Vallī seeing it. Then he went into the forest and made a huge garland of flowers, smuggled the *yantra* into the garland, and waited outside the door of the god's chamber [shrine]. Meanwhile Skanda, the prince, had the foreknowledge that today was to be his final day on earth as a human being and that he would achieve apotheosis [*dēvatva*] and become invisible. Now Skanda and Vallī emerged from the doorway. The Brahman was so excited that when he tried to place the garland on them, it fell down, and the couple vanished from his sight [they were now divinities]. The Brahman went inside the chamber and he saw the bed on which they slept. He placed the garland and gold amulet there and performed a *yāga-homa* [classical Hindu ritual] as best he could. He could feel their presence but they could not be seen by him. He also brought fruit and rice and all manner of things, but they still did not reveal themselves. Unsuccessful, he went upstream to a rock where he died while washing his clothes. This place is now called *salugala* ["clothes rock"].

The god and his mistress were no longer seen now. One day some members of the Okkampiṭiya *paramparāva* [the lineage of the priests of Kataragama] came wandering here in search of their cattle and saw the chamber-palace. Then they heard a voice: "I am Prince Kanda of Kataragama. From today the service [*tēvāva*] for me is in your charge." Thus they have served him to this day.

Commentary on the Sinhala Myths of Skanda and Vallī Ammā

The two myths recorded above indicate a thoroughgoing attempt to break away from the Tamil Hindu background of these myths, while at the same time maintaining the basic core of the triple relationship between Skanda, his legitimate wife Tēvānī Ammā (Dēvasēnā), and his mistress Vallī Ammā. We will note how the Sinhalicization of the myths occurs.

1. One striking feature of both myths is that they do not deal with Skanda's relation with his father and mother (Śiva and Pārvatī alias Umā) at all. Both informants know the myth of the mango, but refused to quote it. The reasons are political (though the two *sāmi*s were not aware of that). Both Śiva and Umā connect Skanda with the Hindu pantheon. Their elimination opens the way to a further Sinhalicization of Skanda in other myths to be quoted later in this chapter.

2. Older Sinhala ritual texts, such as those quoted in *The Cult of the Goddess Pattinī*, clearly recognize Skanda as the vanquisher of *asura*s. As

the leader of the divine army he is also known as Mahāsēna.[1] However note the recent Sinhalicization of the war between the *suras* ("gods") and *asuras* ("titans"): according to Mutukuḍa Sāmi it was the war between Skanda and the Väddas! Käppiṭipola Sāmi told us that Skanda killed a Tamil leader called Asurayā (Titan)!

3. Both myths retain the powerfully erotic character of the Skanda-Vallī relationship, since this is what is emphasized in the evening procession (*perahära*) held during the annual festival. Both play down Tēvānī/Dēvasēnā, but treat her as the legitimate spouse who is ignored or abandoned by Skanda. Myth II however transforms the triple relationship in a very Sinhala manner. In this myth Skanda and Dēvasēnā/Tēvānī Ammā were married as infants, but thereafter they did not see each other. Thus they never consummated the marriage. By contrast the sensuality of his life with Vallī the mistress is glorified. This echoes the theme of the myths of the goddess Pattinī, in which Kōvalan̲ or Pālan̄ga could not or did not have intercourse with his legitimate wife Pattinī. He also abandoned her for the courtesan Mādēvi, his mistress. Later on, repentant, he came back to Pattinī and the myths and rituals glorify this legitimate wedded relationship. The Skanda-Vallī relationship, as we noted, is the reverse of the coin, idealizing the love life of the god with his mistress. The first set of ritual dramas is enacted in villages; the other in the impersonal, central shrine of the god at Kataragama.

Thus there is a core theme to the myth that remains and is in fact intensified: the erotic aspect of the Skanda-Vallī relationship, obviously important for Sinhala personality and culture. The other myths that envelop this core are for Käppiṭipola Sāmi political parameters that must be changed. For both Buddhists and Hindus the core myth is erotic and oedipal in significance. However, for the Sinhalas this is all there is to it, whereas Hindus can invest the relationship with philosophical significance. For Buddhists this is impossible, since any attempt to accept Hindu philosophical meanings would undermine Buddhist soteriology, and there is no way in which an erotic relationship could be given philosophical and soteriological significance in Theravāda Buddhism. In South Indian thought the philosophical development occurs on an erotic base. Shulman notes: "According to Śaiva Siddhānta, Tēyvayānai symbolizes the *kriyāśakti* (Tamil, *kiriyācatti*, the power of works or motivation), while Vaḷḷi

[1] See for example Obeyesekere, *Pattini*, pp. 80, 191, 208.

embodies the *icchāśakti* (Tamil, *iccācatti*, the power of desire). Even on the level of abstract symbolism, Vaḷḷi is connected with the human experience of desire (*icchā*)."[2]

4. The motivation to Sinhalicize the myths is political. But for the myths to be widely accepted, they must also act as a charter for the ritual activities of Kataragama. Elements of the myth must tie in with the shrine and the sacred geography of the area. What we see here is a myth charter, in Malinowski's sense, being constructed. Thus, for example, Mutukuḍa Sāmi's view is that the myth accounts for such things as the annual festival, the water sports, and the offering of rice and bees' honey to Skanda and Vallī (rice for the agricultural Sinhalas and honey for the hunting and gathering Väddas). But it is in myth II that we see a systematic attempt to relate the newly invented elements of the myth to older continuing practices of Kataragama. We quote Käppiṭipola Sāmi's own interpretations here:

> We place garlands in the "offerings tray" (*pūjā vaṭṭi*); thus we remember the old garland sent by Tēvānī Ammā. When we offer fruits we give a portion to the deity and keep the rest; this is exactly what Tēvānī Ammā's Brahman emissary did. God Kataragama wanted to enjoy his wedding (*magul*) with Vallī and he had a hall (*maḍuva*) for this. We commemorate this by planting the *kapa* ("bough") for the *magul maḍuva* ("wedding hall"). At that time Vallī showed the power of her chastity by jumping into the fire unscathed—and this is what we do at the firewalk. The culmination of their wedding was in water sports and this is our *diya keliya* (water sports). The procession every night recaptures their wedding: here the god and his mistress unite for the duration of the festival and thereafter they part until the following year. In this procession what is carried ceremoniously on the back of the elephant is the *vaśi yantra* (the amulet) and the rosarylike necklace the god placed around Vallī Ammā's neck during the marriage ceremony.

5. One aspect of the charter of myth II is especially striking, namely its preoccupation with magic and occultism. We believe that this part of the myth is influenced by the occult practices of the heterodox monks in and around Kataragama. It says that on the instructions of Tēvānī Ammā, the

[2] Shulman, *Tamil Temple Myths*, p. 282.

god's legitimate spouse, a Brahman tried to place a *vaśi yantra* to subjugate Skanda's erotic will and make him return to Tēvānī Ammā. The Brahman smuggled the *yantra* in a garland but failed to place it around the god's neck. Instead he placed it on his (empty) nuptial bed. It is this *yantra* and garland that are ceremoniously carried on the back of the elephant during the god's grand parade to visit Vallī Ammā. But neither the priests (*kapurāḷa*) of Kataragama nor any Hindus will accept this explanation, since the *yantra* is an abstract representation of the god himself. Myth II is perfectly consonant with the activities of the Buddhist monks at Kataragama, especially at Väḍahiṭikanda, namely, that amulets with magical power, and especially ones that can subjugate a recalcitrant man or woman, are available here. True, Tēvānī's magic failed; that was not however due to the inefficacy of the magic but to the incompetence of the Brahman. This part of the myth expresses, even if it does not justify, the existence of a booming business in charms by Buddhist monks. Every Buddhist knows that such activities violate doctrinal ethics; but they do not violate the ethics of the Kataragama cult. We even think that the invention (or resurrection) of this part of the myth might have been a response to the well-known activities of a leading Buddhist monk in Kataragama who is noted for the number of women who "work" for him. It is popularly believed that the wills of these women have been subjugated by the monk through *vaśi*, especially by his magical ability to control their possession trances and bring them under his control.

The Coming of King Duṭugämuṇu

We have noted the erosion of myths in which the great Hindu deities, Śiva and Pārvatī, appear. Yet the core myth of Skanda-Vallī-Tēvānī is retained. We also noted that the erotic relationship between Skanda and Vallī is Sinhalicized. However, there is no Buddhist significance given to the core myth; we suggested that it is difficult to give eroticism Buddhist meaning. To replace the Hindu myths that have been dropped one might expect the development of new myths by Sinhala *sāmi*s around the core Skanda-Vallī-Tēvānī myth. This has indeed happened, so that there are at least two sets of "parameter myths" that are thoroughly Sinhala Buddhist. One set links Skanda with the Buddhist hero Duṭugämuṇu; the other tells us that Skanda was a reincarnation of an ancient Sinhala Buddhist king! Let us now consider how the great Buddhist hero, King Duṭugämuṇu, the vanquisher of the Tamils and the defender of the Buddhist faith, enters into the myths of Kataragama.

Duṭugämuṇu's entry is recent, though the exact date cannot be determined. Pāli and Sinhala chronicles deal with King Duṭugämuṇu and his wars with Tamils, wars fought, according to the *Mahāvaṃsa*, not for the joys of sovereignty but for the glory of Buddhism. Yet no chronicle before the eighteenth century, as far as we know, refers to his association with Kataragama, the place or the deity. The *Kahakurulu Sandēśaya* ("The Golden Oriole's Message," ca. 1710–1739) in stanza 150 refers to "the god's mansion on the northern side built by King Duṭugämuṇu," but it is the nineteenth-century *sandēśa*s that develop this theme. The *Kirala Sandēśaya* ("The Lapwing's Message"), written about 1815, is very significant in this regard. It condemns Śrī Vikrama Rājasiṃha, the last king of Kandy and a Tamil, and praises his enemy the Sinhala chieftain Ähälēpola. In stanza 169 an explicit reference is made to King Duṭugämuṇu, who destroyed the Tamils owing to a "warrant" given to him by the god Kataragama; the context makes it clear that both king and god are being used in a propaganda campaign against the Tamil king. The same story is repeated in other nineteenth-century poetry, for example, *Mayūra Sandēśaya* ("The Peacock's Message," ca. 1859), stanza 186.[3] A similar reference occurs in the *gammaḍuva* rituals of the Pattinī cult. The consecration ceremonies of the *gammaḍuva* have a ritual known as "the planting of the festival bough" (*magul kapa*) where the priests sing of the origin of the bough. One set of songs relates the bough to the inauguration of the Pattinī rituals and to the life of the goddess herself. This we think is the older version. Several scattered stanzas sung during this ritual also state that Duṭugämuṇu planted the festival bough at Kataragama, presumably to commemorate his victory (*magul, mangaḷa*). This is the only reference to Duṭugämuṇu in the cycle of *gammaḍuva* rituals, and even this is known only to a few priestly traditions. The conclusion is irresistible that this is also a post-eighteenth-century interpolation; it probably developed in the nineteenth century because of the increasing Tamil presence at Kataragama.

[3] See, *Kirala Sandēśaya*, ed. Charles Godakumbura (Colombo: Gunasena and Company, 1961); *Kahakurulu Sandēśaya*, ed. Henpiṭigedera Piyānanda (Colombo: Gunasena and Company, 1954); *Mayūra Sandēśaya*, ed. Charles Godakumbura (Colombo: Gunasena and Company, 1961).

Whatever the origin of the Duṭugämuṇu myth, it has been elaborated at Kataragama and from there spread to other parts of the Sinhala country. Even zealous Hindus seem to have accepted it, though perhaps unaware of its political implications.[4] This myth, in its present detailed versions, was elaborated, if not invented, by the Sinhala ecstatics at Kataragama as a charter for the Sinhala Buddhist takeover of the shrine and the cult and has contributed to the larger interethnic debate in national politics. In view of their importance we shall present three Sinhala versions of the myth by the new *sāmi*s of Kataragama.[5]

Version 1 by Mutukuḍa Sāmi

It is King Duṭugämuṇu who built the shrine at Kataragama and implored the god to reside there. How did this come about?

Duṭugämuṇu's father was King Kāvantissa, the ruler of Ruhuṇa, the Southern Kingdom. His son Prince Duṭugämuṇu went out to fight the Tamils and Elāra, their king. King Duṭugämuṇu had his ten warriors and Elāra also had a host of warriors. During this war the "power" [he uses the English word] of Elāra's warriors was greater than Duṭugämuṇu's. Elāra also had a war elephant known as Parvata ätā ["mountain tusker"] while Duṭugämuṇu's was Kaḍol [Kaṇḍula]. Duṭugämuṇu knew that there was no way of winning this war.

At that time transport was in caravans of pack bulls [*tavalam*]. The road to Anurādhapura [Elāra's capital in the north] was from Tissa [Duṭugämuṇu's residence] to Kataragama to Mahiyangana and then to Anurādhapura. A few miles from Tissa is Divurungala. Duṭugämuṇu rested here and then moved toward the river, Mäṇik Gaṅga [which flows past Kataragama]. While he was crossing the river, the god Kataragama appeared in human guise before him and inquired, "What goods are in your caravan?" He responded, "We carry *uňdu* [a lentil]," though they had other foodstuffs also. When Duṭugämuṇu had finished resting on the riverbank he noticed that all the goods in

[4] Navaratnam, *Karttikeya, the Divine Child*, pp. 228–29.

[5] An early version of the kind of Duṭugämuṇu myths reported from Kataragama is reported by Covington in 1875 and reprinted in Herbert White, *Manual of Uva* (Colombo: Government Printer, 1893), pp. 45–53. In this account Duṭugämuṇu performed acts of devotion to the god before embarking on his war against the Tamils, and the god himself, in the form of a Tamil mendicant (*paṇṭāram*), prophesied victory. The prince made a vow to build a shrine in honor of the god after his return from Anurādhapura.

his caravan had changed into *uňdu*. Duṭugämuṇu, who was with his full army, was puzzled and said: "Someone asked me what are in these carts and I said *uňdu* and now everything has changed into *uňdu*. There seems to be no good reason for this." He then lay on a slab of rock and rested. Soon he fell asleep and in his sleep he felt a shaking of his body [*gässīma*]. He saw someone in his dream, and Duṭugämuṇu addressed the stranger thus, "I am here to develop Buddhism [*Buddha sāsana*] and unite the country, and yet I feel I won't be able to do it." Then the stranger put a sword in his hand and said: "Take this sword and swear as I instruct you. Make this vow: this war is not for royal ambition but to develop Buddhism. You ['thou,' inferior address] take this sword and fight the Tamils. Thou shalt surely win for I shall protect thee. But in order to remember me build me a small hut." [This meant, said Mutukuḍa, "construct a shrine for me."]

Then Duṭugämuṇu went north to fight the Tamils and destroyed the fort of Vijitapura and straightaway came back to Kataragama to fulfill his vow. He first came to Väḍahiṭikanda, but there was no shrine there yet. Duṭugämuṇu's best warrior shot an arrow from Väḍahiṭikanda, and it fell in the present site of the great shrine [*mahā dēvālē*] of Kataragama. On the king's orders they constructed a road to this place [from Väḍahiṭikanda] and built a shrine with three golden domes and three golden pillars. It was named the *ruvan māligāva* ["the golden palace"]. In front were four pillars to support the roof, which was covered by an overhang of branches. Even now we remember this in our customs. During the festival we bring four banana trunks and cover the roof with forest branches. Hence this structure is called *atu säla* ["branch hall"]. When Duṭugämuṇu had finished building the shrine he went to Väḍahiṭikanda and asked the god to reside in his new palace. Since then the god is present in person [*jīvamānava*] in the great shrine of Kataragama.

Ever since the god has resided there it has been necessary for him to be given *puda-satkāra* ["offerings and care"]. One of Duṭugämuṇu's warriors was Nandimitra, whose father was an *adikāram* ["royal official"]. He was given the task of developing *pūjā*s—at 5 A.M., 11 A.M., and 5 P.M., just before we human beings eat and drink. King Duṭugämuṇu also gave to the temple several villages as fiefs. Now all religions—Muslim, Hindu, Buddhist—accept this schedule of *pūjās*. Thus this *dēvālē* is from Duṭugämuṇu's time and we can date it from history [*itihāsa*]. The shrine is unchanged through time. It cannot be enlarged or changed in any way. Once a high official of the Public Works Department decided to enlarge it, but the god threatened him in a dream, and he desisted through fear.

Version 2 by Käppiṭipola Sāmi

Elāra's troops came to Kataragama in order to mobilize the Tamils who were in the Southern Kingdom, Ruhuṇa. They gathered a large host and when they were ready to depart a huge rain fell and the river became flooded. They had no way of crossing the river and were going here and there in consternation when they beheld a person meditating near the "water-cutting ferry" [*diya kapana toṭa*]. Elāra's people asked his advice regarding a place where they could ford the river and the *yogi* said, "If you build me a place to rest I'll show a path." They agreed and the *yogi* parted the waters. The Tamil army crossed over but they ran, for they were afraid of Duṭugämuṇu's warriors who were pursuing them. They consequently did not keep their promise to the god [the *yogi*]. ["You see," Käppiṭipola Sāmi told us, "a person expecting to be a god (*dēvatvaya*) cannot claim any part of the earth as his, and devotees must build a place for him."]

A few weeks passed. Duṭugämuṇu heard that the Tamils of Ruhuṇa had gone to Anurādhapura. The Sinhalas have a bad habit: whenever they see their enemies they want to kill them! So Duṭugämuṇu kept pursuing the Tamils to kill them, but they had gone. Duṭugämuṇu then rested a while at the *asṭhaphala bō* tree (the present *bō* tree near the shrine, one of eight sacred trees) while his tracker was looking for a path through the forest and river. The tracker came across a Brahman-yogi under a huge *kum̆buk*[6] tree, and he told the *yogi* his problem. The *yogi* said, "I will control the waters if you build me a place to stay." The tracker told all this to the king, who ordered a soldier to cut a branch and plant it on the spot where the present shrine lies. He then told his servitors [*sēvaka*] to build a hut of leaves and he himself went in search of the *yogi*. He accosted Skanda [the *yogi*], who saw a *yantra* on the king's golden crown on which was inscribed a Buddhist stanza. Skanda blessed him and added: "You have a better blessing than mine inscribed on your crown. You will

[6] Terminalia glabra.

undoubtedly be victorious, a victory that generations before you could not accomplish." While Skanda was blessing Duṭugämuṇu, the leaf hut [*atupäla*] was complete.

Duṭugämuṇu asked Prince Skanda to reside in the leaf hut until he returned victorious from the war. And he was victorious. Now Duṭugämuṇu thought, "I made a promise and now I must go back to Ruhuṇa and fulfill it." He therefore came back to Kataragama and built a chamber suitable for the god. He also wrote a letter of authority [*sannasa*] in golden sheets that the whole area around the river Mäṇik Gaṅga is for Skanda—from Buttala in the north to Yāla (the present game sanctuary) on the east. All this area rightfully should belong to the *maha dēvālē* ["great shrine"].

[The rest of the myth told by Käppiṭipola Sāmi did not deal with Duṭugämuṇu, but with Skanda's relation with Vallī Ammā, his mistress; it has been quoted above.]

Version 3 by Vijeyaratna Sāmi

Vijeyaratna Sāmi's account of Duṭugämuṇu was, he said, from an ancient book of religious ordinances (*katikāvata*) that the Sinhala priests of the shrine had hidden. Vijeyaratna however was able to retrieve the contents of the book through occult science (*gupta vidyā*), generally by getting a gifted seer to peer into a magic light (*anjanam eliya*) and then asking him questions. The knowledge of the past thus acquired produced an unusual and unabashedly political myth.

Before leaving for the war against Elāra, Duṭugämuṇu thought thus: "Alas, Elāra has many giants; he also can get his armies from India. But I have only Väddas. If we want to have revenge on the Tamils for destroying Buddhism we must abandon hopes of retreat. But alas we have no one to help us."

Duṭugämuṇu's armies were not very experienced. So he exhorted his people to sacrifice their lives for the sake of religion. Consequently even monks joined him and so did housewives. The king and all his hosts came to Kataragama on a *pōya* day.

Since it was *pōya*, Duṭugämuṇu observed the eight precepts, and then he also implored the god to help him. Next day he secretly went to the river and clambered up a rock from where he could see Väḍahiṭikanda [the god's first abode]. He soon went there to make a vow [*bāra*], but remember there was no shrine there at that time. He prayed to the god thus: "It is not for the greed of kingship [*rāja lōbhaya*] but for the glory of Buddhism that I fight Elāra." While he was praying thus he saw a herdsman with a *ketēri* [an ax with a long handle and small head], who confronted him face to face. "With whose permission darest thou enter this place?" The king thought, "No one has yet addressed me as 'thou,' so this surely must be a result of my wish." The god then said: "I was waiting for someone like you to come. We gods are weak [hearted?] and incapable of fighting humans. We must get a real man to fight this war. Be not afraid; proceed undaunted into battle. I'll be at your side always." Thus the god instilled determination into Duṭugämuṇu. He also gave Duṭugämuṇu a sword and said, "You shall only strike a king with this, not others." The god also gave the king a giant [*yōdayā*] as his representative [*niyōjitayā*].

King Duṭugämuṇu captured the Tamil fortress of Vijitapura and destroyed the city. He took much booty from its treasury and carried it on the backs of elephants. He established his government there and came back to Kataragama with gold, silver, and copper and ordered them to be deposited at the shrine. He then observed the eight precepts and entered into a *dhyāna* ["meditative trance"] state. But he could not obtain a vision of the god through trance. He had planned to deliver the giant personally to the god at a huge celebration of victory he held, but he was puzzled that the god did not appear even on this occasion. He then asked his goldsmith to forge a statue of the god in gold. Since this statue had to be installed somewhere, he made a wish that night that the god instruct him where to place the statue. Still no instructions from the god. Despondent, he asked his astrologers to calculate a good time and place. Meanwhile the king was wandering up and down, disconsolate, when a large golden arrow flew past him and landed at the site of the *bō* tree. This is where the statue was installed. Thus the present shrine is not the site of the original one according to "the book of rules" [*katikāvata*].

Commentary on the Duṭugämuṇu Myths

All three versions of the myth effectively convert Kataragama, the shrine, into a Sinhala Buddhist one from which Tamils are excluded. These myths are deliberately constructed charters to justify the Sinhala Buddhist hegemony over the place and in the nation. These myths reaffirm Malinowski's insight that origin myths, at least of one type, are sociological charters. However, in conventional sociological analysis of myth, the charter is generally viewed as a function (effect) of the myth for the social system at large. The Duṭugämuṇu myths clearly show that some myths are *intended* to be charters by those who invent them.

Myths 1 and 2, or versions thereof, are well known in Kataragama and from there have spread. How are they constructed? The hero is Duṭugämuṇu, whose exploits as recorded in the Pāli and Sinhala chronicles are well known to everyone in Sri Lanka. These myths have added an important element to the life of the hero—his association with Kataragama. In these two myths the hero meets the god as a stranger or a *yogi*, which is exactly how the *sāmi*s of Kataragama themselves have seen the god. When Duṭugämuṇu falls asleep in myth 1 he experiences a *gässīma* or "shaking"; everyone knows that this is how Skanda rouses people in their sleep. The conversion of all the goods into *uňdu* is the kind of mischievous miracle that the god indulges in. These kinds of intimate detail exist side by side with Duṭugämuṇu's Sinhala patriotism culled from the chronicles: he is waging war not for personal gain but for the glory of Buddhism. Both myths have to account for the fact that during the festival the roof of the shrine is covered with branches in order to convert it into a leaf hut (*atupäla*). It is likely that the leaf covering had a different significance originally: as a symbolic device to bring the Väddas into the Kataragama festival. We know that Väddas (and also Sinhala people living in remote areas) used temporary shrines made with branches of trees. In Vädda culture these rituals as well as the structure were called *kola maḍuva* ("leaf hall").[7] Placing branches on the rooftops of all the shrines in Kataragama (not just the main shrine) was originally a symbolic action indicating that the cult was the common religion of these two groups. But this action is now associated with Duṭugämuṇu, which of course makes more sense to contemporary Sinhalas. There are no Väddas nowadays in the region around Kataragama, for they have been fully assimilated into the Sinhala social structure. Myth 1 also denies the older genealogy of the priests of the shrine, who have traditionally claimed descent from the Väddas or from local wild people in the area. They have now become descendants of one of Duṭugämuṇu's warriors. Myth 2 also ties up the past with the present: all significant present customs at Kataragama are simply commemo-

[7] For a description see Seligmann and Seligmann, *The Veddas*, pp. 267–69, 306–17.

rations of past events in the life of King Duṭugämuṇu and the god Skanda. To quote its narrator: "What does water cutting mean? It is the parting of the waters by Skanda for Duṭugämuṇu's army to cross the river. And why do Tamils pierce their body with hooks and suffer pain? Because they broke their promise to the deity. Why do we place branches over all the roofs of shrines here at Kataragama? To commemorate Duṭugämuṇu's building the shrine for the god."

Myth 3 represents an extraordinary departure, for it ignores many events of the previous myths and introduces radically new features. The inventor of the myth is Vijeyaratna Sāmi, a paradoxical figure. On the one hand he was a protégé and kinsman of the Buddhist reformer Dharmapāla, and on the other he is a devotee of the gods, a facet of Sinhala religion that Dharmapāla stigmatized as un-Buddhist. Vijeyaratna Sāmi is self-consciously proud of both aspects of his religious identity and the myth is an attempt to reconcile them. The narrators of myths 1 and 2, Mutukuḍa and Käppiṭipola, also come from the middle class that Dharmapāla influenced. We have seen that it was these middle-class firewalkers who wrested the leadership of the firewalk from the Tamils and rationalized it in Buddhist terms: they expressed the view that firewalking required not *bhakti* but meditation and observance of the Buddhist precepts. Nevertheless myths 1 and 2 were not invented by the narrators; they were developed at Kataragama anonymously. At most the narrators added or changed details. The myths tie present practices to the past in a systematic manner that gives plausibility both to the myth and to the practices. Elements are culled from other myths. Thus the parting of the waters by Skanda for Duṭugämuṇu to cross the river is the origin of the present water cutting; this derives from a previous water-cutting myth in the Sinhala repertoire—the older view that the water-cutting ritual is a commemoration of King Gajabāhu parting the waters of the ocean.[8] Myths 1 and 2 are self-consciously Buddhist and Sinhala but they do not reject present practice. For example, Mutukuḍa told us that it is only right that Buddhists should recite *pirit* before the firewalking, but he cared little about justifying the practice in his version of the myth. Not so with Vijeyaratna Sāmi.

Vijeyaratna Sāmi's myth, as far as we know, has not had popular acceptance yet, but it perhaps indicates the shape of the myths to come. It starts with Duṭugämuṇu's statement that Elāra has help from Tamils in

[8] Obeyesekere, *Pattini*, pp. 364–72.

India, but he has only Väddas. The king also speaks of revenge on the Tamils for destroying Buddhism. What is remarkable about the first part of Duṭugämuṇu's statement is that nowhere in Pāli chronicles is there a reference to Elāra getting troops from India, but it is perfectly consonant with the current Sinhala view that the Sinhalas have only themselves (and a few Väddas!) while the Tamils have a large body of native Tamil speakers in South India. The Tamils as destroyers of Buddhism appear in Sri Lankan chronicles, but the king's wish for revenge is probably Vijeyaratna's innovation. The idea that Duṭugämuṇu's armies were not experienced is not found in the *Mahāvaṃsa* or other texts, but fits the public perception of the present-day Sri Lankan army. The exhortation to give their lives for religion is also a current slogan. It is true that monks joined Duṭugämuṇu's campaign according to ancient sources, but they did not participate in the fighting; urging housewives to join the fray has been, we think, influenced by local newspaper reports of female fighters in recent wars in the Middle East. It is important to remember that Vijeyaratna's myth was invented in the early seventies, before the upsurge of warfare between the Sinhala army and Tamil guerrillas. Kataragama once again anticipates the shape of events, and it would not surprise us if politicians started urging monks and housewives to join the Sinhala forces to vanquish Tamils.[9]

In Vijeyaratna's version, as in the others, Duṭugämuṇu's famous statement (found in the ancient texts) that he is fighting for the glory of Buddhism rather than for sovereignty is *localized* in Kataragama. Vijeyaratna Sāmi's localization is very specific: the statement was made at Väḍahiṭikanda (where the god first landed), and we are also told "there was no shrine there at that time." The contemporary context gives considerable significance to that statement: it implicitly accepts the usurpation of Väḍahiṭikanda by the Venerable Siddhārtha as perfectly legitimate and consonant with the past. It was here that Duṭugämuṇu made his statement on his motivation to fight Elāra; there was no shrine there at that time; so any Tamil shrine subsequently built is really without justification; Venerable Siddhārtha's action in establishing a Buddhist temple and shrine for the god is consonant with "history" (as spelled out in the myth).

One of the most interesting features of myth 3 is Duṭugämuṇu's Bud-

[9] This in fact has happened recently! In a speech reported in the *Daily News*, 1 February 1985, Mrs. Wimala Kannangara, Minister of Rural Development, says, "The womenfolk of this country should learn the use of guns and ammunition for the defense of the country."

dhist piety. In the classic texts his piety was expressed in the Buddhist monuments he constructed. One Pāli text, the *Sumangalāvilāsinī*, mentions that he once observed the eight precepts to cure his insomnia.[10] But here he is presented like a contemporary good Buddhist layman, taking the eight precepts regularly on holy days, though that practice was traditionally confined to the old. He also enters into a Buddhist form of meditative trance (*dhyāna*). Vijeyaratna Sāmi (like Mutukuḍa and Käppiṭipola) eschews possession, so Duṭugämuṇu's piety is just like his own. But it is the conclusion of the myth that is truly remarkable. In the previous accounts an arrow falls on the site of the present shrine to Skanda, or the present shrine is the site of the original one. Not so with myth 3. The arrow falls near the *bō* tree behind the present shrine; the location of the original shrine containing a golden icon of the god was at this *bō* tree and not at its present site. This clearly implies the association of the god and his shrine (and Duṭugämuṇu who built the shrine) with the *bō* tree, which ipso facto means an identification with Buddhism. The present shrine is too much associated with Hinduism and the Tamils.

If Vijeyaratna's version (myth 3) is not yet popularly accepted, not so with his views of the firewalk (also gleaned through occult science). He told us that it was Duṭugämuṇu who first walked the fire after his victory over Elāra; then Duṭugämuṇu's father's younger brother. This part of Vijeyaratna's invention of the past is accepted by many firewalkers: it makes sense to them. The Tamils are the usurpers, and the Sinhala takeover of the firewalk is a reassertion of their ancient legitimate right. Vijeyaratna also stated that Duṭugämuṇu gave his *māmā* ("mother's brother") charge of the *pūjā* for the god; the present *kapurāḷa*s are their descendants. Vijeyaratna Sāmi himself is a descendant of Duṭugämuṇu's father's brother, who was an *adhikāri* ("manager") with administrative control over the shrine. We do not know whether the priests at Kataragama accept this version of their ancestry, but the myths at Kataragama have begun to enhance the status of the priests, and who would not be flattered to be told that they are related to a great king and national hero instead of lowly Vädda or wild people of Okkampiṭiya?

The Duṭugämuṇu myths quoted above, in attempting to give Katara-

[10] Cited in J. D. Dhirasekera, "Text and Traditions—Warped and Distorted," in *Nārada Felicitation Volume* (Kandy, Sri Lanka: Buddhist Publication Society, 1979), pp. 69–70.

gama an exclusive Sinhala Buddhist legitimacy, have to face the problem that almost all the historical and mythic associations of the god are with India and Hinduism. The fact that Hindus do worship him cannot be denied, and his many Tamil Hindu names (Murugan, Arumukam, Subramaniam, Kathiravel) are familiar to most Sinhalas. In Sinhala mythology he is generally known as Kanda Kumāra (Mountain Prince), but Sinhala origin myths also, at least till recently, relate his birth to a well-known South Indian myth of Śiva's encounter with Basma, the Asura.[11] What most recent myths have done (e.g., myths 1 and 2) is to say that the Tamils betrayed Skanda, and consequently Skanda supported Duṭugämuṇu. Moreover, Skanda punishes the Tamils to this day for their betrayal of him by forcing them to engage in painful penances. These solutions however are not radical enough to deny all legitimacy to Tamil association with Kataragama.

That, however, can be done by claiming that the original Kataragama was pure Sinhala, but Hindus/Tamils have confused him with their own god. We have met the Venerable Ānanda Maitreya's view that the Subramaniam at Kataragama was appointed by the Buddha to stop animal sacrifice there and is not really the Hindu god at all. A more influential myth has developed in Kataragama in very recent times: that Kataragama was in fact a Sinhala king, Mahāsēna by name, albeit in a previous birth. This myth, unlike Vijeyaratna Sāmi's myth of Duṭugämuṇu, is widely known and accepted in Kataragama. We quote a well-known version from Käppiṭipola Sāmi.

Myth of King Mahāsēna

Skanda in a previous birth was King Mahāsēna, who built the Buddhist stupa at Kataragama, known as the Kiri Vehera. It is called Kiri Vehera because it was the site of *kihiriya* trees[12] that he cleared in order to build this stupa. He also planted the *bō* tree at the back of the Kataragama shrine, and this is one of the eight saplings from the great *bō* tree at Anurādhapura. King Mahāsēna protected these two like his own heart and worshipped them. He had a great desire (*āsāva*) to be their protector forever and thought: "How shall I continue to protect these after I die? I will make a wish (*prārthanā*) that

[11] See Obeyesekere, *Pattini*, pp. 113–14.

[12] Acacia sundra.

after I die I may become a god in order to protect this place." After he died, he was born in Daṁbadiva (India) into a Brahman caste, which is the destiny of all meritorious persons! The Brahmans wanted to give him a name, and since they knew that he would do heroic things and end up possessing a heap of heads they called him Iskanda ("mountain of heads"). These Brahmans also had a caste custom of finding a girl born on the same day as a spouse. This was to protect their chastity. Hence they chose Tēvānī Ammā and they tied a *tāli* around her neck. The couple grew up without ever seeing each other.

Iskanda as a young man committed all sorts of *vīrakriyā* ("heroic acts") and a lot of *daruna väḍa* ("terrible things"). The king of the city became afraid. He built a ship and loaded it with foodstuffs and requisites and floated it with Iskanda aboard. Now Iskanda by the power of his past merit (*pin*) landed in Devundara (at the southern tip of Sri Lanka). From Devundara he went on foot eastwards a long, long way or *katara*. After he walked one *katara* ("a long distance") he came to a village, which henceforth was called Kataragama. When he came up here he saw, once again, the *bō* tree and the Kiri Vehera. He felt a sense of peace. He gave up his bad ways. He went up the river and became a *yogi*, practicing meditation (*bhāvanā*).

At that time in Kataragama there dwelt a Tamil man named Asurayā (*asura*), who was very cruel. Since Asurayā didn't give up his evil ways, Iskanda held him by the neck and shook him and Asurayā's head came off. This is what you see in paintings with Iskanda holding Asurayā's head in his hand.

This myth is a clear invention of a new charter for Sinhala dominance. Skanda was a Sinhala Buddhist king, who planted the great *bō* tree and built the stupa at Kataragama. His birth as Skanda was simply to guard the Buddhist shrines; consequently he is a Buddhist guardian deity (not a Hindu god). His coming to Sri Lanka had nothing to do with the competition with his brother over mother's golden mango, but was due to his powerful rebirth wish. The manner in which he obtained his six heads is simply ignored in Käppiṭipola's version. (Vijeyaratna Sāmi told us that the six heads were a symbolic way of expressing his power. Skanda had only one head and artists and craftsmen confused the symbolism with the reality.) Basma, the Asura ("Titan") whose heroic exploits are recounted and enacted in Hindu ritual, is just a bad Tamil fellow. Skanda actually did not kill him (he was a *yogi* by now), but Asurayā's head simply fell off when Skanda shook him (to frighten him, no doubt). The myth of Skanda's birth and coming to Sri Lanka has been radically rationalized in a Buddhist direction.

The mythmaker often does not invent a myth de novo, but puts together pieces from earlier myths and fuses them into a new conception. The myth of Mahāsēna is especially interesting because we can show precisely the sources used by the mythmaker to construct the new myth.

The term Mahāsēna ("having a big army") is one of the designations of Skanda in Sanskrit sources and well known in Sinhala ritual texts such as those of the Pattinī cult. This is one important datum. Mahāsēna is also a well-known Sinhala king (A.D. 274–301) who built large reservoirs (tanks), including the Minnēriya tank near Polonnaruva, and was subsequently deified by locals as God Minnēriya. To this day there are shrines for him in that region. Datum two then is the existence of a deified Sinhala king, Mahāsēna. However, Käppiṭipola Sāmi, as one would expect from his background, was educated enough to know the rough dates of this king and told us that the King Mahāsēna of his myth lived much earlier. The *Mahāvaṃsa*, composed in the sixth century, refers to the nobles of Kataragama (Pāli: Kājaragāma) who were present when the sapling from the tree of Enlightenment was brought to Sri Lanka by Asoka's missionaries, Mahinda and Sanghamittā, and planted in Anurādhapura in the third century B.C.

> The great thera Mahinda and the bhikkhuṇī Saṃghamittā went thither with their following and the king also with his following. The nobles of Kājaragāma and the nobles of Candanagāma and the Brahman Tivakka and the people too who dwelt in the island came thither also by the power of the gods, (with minds) eagerly set upon a festival of the great Bodhi-tree. Amid this great assembly, plunged into amazement by this miracle, there grew out of the east branch, even as they gazed, a faultless fruit.
>
> This having fallen off, the thera took it up and gave it to the king to plant. In a golden vase filled with earth mingled with perfumes, placed on the spot where the Mahāāsana (afterwards) was, the ruler planted it. And while they all yet gazed, there grew, springing from it, eight shoots; and they stood there, young Bodhi-trees four cubits high.

> When the king saw the young Bodhi-trees he, with senses all amazed, worshipped them by the gift of a white parasol and bestowed royal consecration on them.
>
> Of the eight Bodhi-saplings one was planted at the landing-place Jambukola on the spot where the great Bodhi-tree had stood, after leaving the ship, one in the village of the Brahman Tivakka, one moreover in the Thūpārāma, one in the Issarasamaṇārāma, one in the Court of the First thūpa, one in the ārāma of the Cetiya-mountain, one in Kājaragāma and one in Candanagāma. But the other thirty-two Bodhi-saplings which sprang from four (later) fruits (were planted) in a circle, at a distance of a yojana, here and there in the vihāras.[13]

Datum three then is the presence of the nobles of Kataragama at the planting of the sacred *bō* tree (a sapling of the tree under which the Buddha achieved enlightenment) at Anurādhapura. On this occasion eight shoots miraculously sprouted from the tree and one of them was planted at Kataragama. Nowadays the huge *bō* tree behind the main shrine is identified with this ancient tree and is consequently known as the *aṣṭhaphala bō* ("eight-sprouted *bō*").

What this text does *not* say is that a ruler named Mahāsēna was present at these celebrations, though two late compendia of edifying tales refer to both a King Mahāsēna and a god Mahāsēna in legends associated with the Buddha.

The *Saddharmālaṃkāraya* ("Ornament of the True Doctrine"), a fourteenth-century Sinhala collection of Buddhist stories, refers to a King Mahāsēna who reigned in Pāṭaliputta (modern Patna) sometime after the Buddha's death.[14] He practiced the ten virtues of kingship. To show his true devotion he went to North Madhurā to work in the household of a merchant in order to offer to the monks what he had earned by his own toil. This tale however makes no reference to Kataragama or Sri Lanka; North Madhurā is presumably Mathurā. No Sinhala or Pāli chronicle of royal dynasties refers to this king, so it is unlikely that he has any relevance for our topic.

The deity Mahāsēna is mentioned in the fifteenth-century Sinhala work

[13] *Mahāvaṃsa*, pp. 132–33, chap. 19, verses 53–63.

[14] "Mahāsēna Vastuva" (The Story of Mahāsēna) in *Saddharmālaṃkāraya*, edited by Makuloluvē Piyaratana (Colombo: Gunasena and Company, 1971), pp. 322–26.

Dhātuvaṃsa[15] ("The History of the Relics"), based on an earlier Pāli work no longer extant. In his third visit to Sri Lanka, according to popular tradition, the Buddha placed the imprint of his foot on the peak of Saman (Samanaḷa, Sumanakūṭa, Adam's Peak), and then arrived at Dīghavāpī on the east coast with five hundred disciples. According to the *Dhātuvaṃsa* (but not according to earlier texts), this was when the stupa at Dīghavāpī was being constructed. The Buddha entered into a state of *samādhi* ("meditative trance") and the earth quaked. He then appointed a *divya putra* (god) named Mahāsēna to be the guardian of the place.

Sinhala poetry of the eighteenth and nineteenth centuries such as the *Kahakurulu Sandēśaya* and the *Nīlakobō Sandēśaya* ("The Message of the Blue Dove") says that the Buddha in fact visited the Kiri Vehera at Kataragama. It was therefore relatively easy to transfer the god Mahāsēna from Dīghavāpī to Kataragama. However the time sequence of the two Mahāsēnas of legend had to be transposed so that initially there was a *king* Mahāsēna at Kataragama, and this king, in a subsequent birth, was deified as Mahāsēna. One must not expect minor chronological anomalies to trouble the mythmakers of Kataragama.

This identification or fusion was facilitated by a very important historical development. We noted in Chapter 5 that the great shrine complex for Viṣṇu at Devinuvara was destroyed by the Portuguese in 1588. This meant that the shrine centers for the major gods—Viṣṇu, Vibhīṣaṇa, Nātha, and Pattinī—were in areas under Portuguese (and later Dutch) control. All except Saman and Kataragama. Saman, even in the sixth century when the *Mahāvaṃsa* was composed, was viewed as an entirely benevolent god, a pious disciple of the Buddha, and consequently uninvolved in the affairs of the world. This leaves Kataragama, whose cult center became increasingly popular till it also felt the impact of British imperial power in 1817. In the *Sandēśa* (or epistle poetry) written after the seventeenth century the bird who carries the poet's message inevitably takes it to Kataragama; and after the eighteenth century the god is referred to most commonly by his well-known Sanskrit epithet, Mahāsēna.[16] We think it

[15] *Dhātuvaṃsa*, edited by Makuloluvē Piyaratana (Colombo: Gunasena and Company, 1941), p. 8.

[16] Some of the relevant texts are *Kahakurulu Sandēśaya* (The Message of the Golden Oriole) and *Kaṭakirili Sandēśaya* (The Message of the Female Rice Bird), both written in the eighteenth century; and *Diyasävul Sandēśaya* (Message of the Waterfowl) and *Kirala Sandēśaya* (The Lapwing's Message), written in the early nineteenth century.

likely that this substitution was based on the resentment felt by the poets of this period against the Tamil Nayakkar kings, whom they felt to be Śaivites at heart (and patrons of Kataragama as Murugan). We know that the myths associating the god Kataragama with King Duṭugämuṇu originated during this period (perhaps at the Kataragama shrine itself) but we are not sure whether a similar development occurred in respect of the Mahāsēna myths at that time. Their later elaboration and spread are, as we said earlier, a feature of our own times. This contemporary transformation of Skanda-Kataragama into an ancient Sinhala king Mahāsēna obliterates the Tamil names of the deity and traces his ancestry to the history of the Sinhala nation. Thus Vijeyaratna Sāmi put the matter very bluntly: "Mahāsēna was a Sinhala king of Kataragama during the time of the Buddha. When the Buddha came to Sri Lanka on his third visit he visited the Kiri Vehera. Mahāsēna listened to the sermons of the Buddha and achieved the first stage on the path to *nirvāṇa* (*sotāpanna*). In a later birth Mahāsēna was named Skanda and lived in India."

The Emergence of a Popular Historical Consciousness

In the preceding discussion we noted Käppiṭipola's assertion that the Mahāsēna of his myth lived some time before the King Mahāsēna of Minnēriya (A.D. 274–301) of the Pāli chronicles. This statement, we believe, implies an awareness of historical time and of the chronological devolution of events, in contrast to genealogical time. What is striking about Theravāda Buddhism in South and Southeast Asia is its sense of history, by which we mean the following:

1. The existence of a determinate event viewed as the beginning of history. In Buddhism this event is the *parinibbāna* ("the passing away") of the Buddha.
2. All subsequent events are chronologically related to this first determinate event. There is a sense of chronological devolution, and Buddhist chronicles faithfully record events subsequent to the death of the founder. The writing of chronicles is inevitably associated with this chronological sense.
3. As in all historical writing, the events that are recorded are selec-

tively chosen. But unlike in modern historiography the selection is not based on a variety of premises, values, and methodological assumptions, but rather on a single consistent viewpoint: the movement of events is inextricably related to the unfolding of Buddhist history. In monotheistic religions history is the unfolding of the Divine Will. In Buddhism this is not possible and history has to be *constructed* and then chronicled by learned monks, the guardians of the Buddhist tradition. In this endeavor they enter into a coalition with kings, who are viewed as guardians of the faith. The unfolding of Buddhist history is the work of Buddhist monks in alliance with the king. Ordinary people for the most part are outside it all. The central concern of this monastic historiography is to establish the authenticity of the monastic tradition by tracing correct pupillary succession from the Buddha to the present.

4. Unlike modern historical writing, this tradition of Buddhist history is not hostile to myth and miracle. But myths are subordinated to history in that they are placed chronologically in the historical framework. Miracle is selectively used to herald events that have cultural significance for Buddhist history, such as the miracles associated with the planting of the *bō* tree at Anurādhapura.

The construction, preservation, and dissemination to the masses of this special type of historical consciousness were the work of the literati of Buddhist society, the Sangha. It must be assumed that this historical sense was never uniformly instilled in the laity, but must have varied with literacy and closeness to the learned tradition. Where oral tradition predominates it is difficult to retain a deep chronology, for here the past is expressed in myth (which often has a timeless character) and in terms of genealogy. Genealogical time however is quite different from historical time; in it there is no past determinate event from which subsequent events take their bearing. One does not move from the past to the present, but rather from the present to the past. An individual or his family or clan traces connections backwards, generally to a founder. This contrast can be nicely illustrated from a concrete case.

The Pāli chronicle, *Mahāvaṃsa*, records the arrival of Prince Vijaya, the founder of the Sinhala race in Sri Lanka, and notes among other things his first marriage with a demoness, from which union sprang the Väddas of Sri Lanka. This was obviously an origin myth that existed in the popular tradition before the *Mahāvaṃsa* was compiled and was incorporated into it. The mode of incorporation is however significant: Vijaya landed in Sri Lanka on the very day the Buddha died. Before dying, the Buddha predicted his arrival and the flowering of the Buddhist religion in Sri Lanka. The Vijaya myth is thus incorporated into Buddhist chronology and into a Buddhist vision of history. But insofar as the Vijaya myth is an origin myth it also exists *outside* this history. Thus in 1958 we met a Vädda shaman in the (then) remote Laggala region. He simply mentioned Vijaya as his *muttā* ("great-grandfather," "ancestor") who, according to his genealogy, lived only a few generations ago. Genealogical time, even among groups with long genealogies, is necessarily shallow in comparison with historical time owing to the limitations of memory and the absence of a chronological record of events. A fascinating example comes from Marguerite Robinson's work in Kotmalē, where, according to the chronicles, the hero Duṭugämuṇu spent his youth. The people of Kotmalē trace genealogical (affinal) links with Duṭugämuṇu, but if we try to give any chronological meaning to their genealogies, Duṭugämuṇu, like Vijaya, can have lived only a few generations ago.[17] In myths of preliterate people time past is related to time present in a direct manner without an intermediate chronology of events; in their genealogy time present moves backwards into the past until it is anchored to an ancestor traceable through precise or vague kinship links. Modern myths of Duṭugämuṇu are very much like myth charters of nonliterate people in form and function, except that they are also governed by a sense of history that is absent in the former and quite uncharacteristic of genealogy.

The three informants who recounted the myths of Duṭugämuṇu are literate, well educated in Sinhala, and also cultured gentlemen. They are products of a variety of historical forces, beginning with the Dharmapāla reform, that glorified a Buddhist sense of history and made it popular. With the advent of mass education people have access to their past from school texts and the popular media. This new popular historical consciousness does not mean that mythmaking declines. On the contrary, the propensity to mythmaking may in fact increase, except that now there occur a historicization of myth and a mythicization of history. In both, myth is

[17] Marguerite Robinson, " 'The House of the Mighty Hero' or 'The House of Enough Paddy'? Some Implications of a Sinhalese Myth," in *Dialectic in Practical Religion*, ed. E. R. Leach (Cambridge: Cambridge University Press, 1968), pp. 122–52.

given a historical context and seen in terms of a past that takes its bearing from a determinate event and gets ordered in a chronological sequence. We can only demonstrate the emergence of this form of myth in modern Sri Lanka. The full implications of this popular form of historical consciousness (in Sri Lanka and in the modern West) must be reserved for future writing.

Afterword: Mahāsēna in 1987

In July 1987 the prime minister, Mr. Ranasingha Premadasa, opened the annual *gam udāva* ("village-awakening") celebrations at Kataragama. *Gam udāva* is Premadāsa's pet project and it is directly influenced by Sarvōdaya. Under this program new housing projects are built all over Sri Lanka ostensibly for poor villagers, but in reality for supporters (or would-be supporters) of the ruling party. Every year a *gam udāva* celebration is held in some chosen spot in Sri Lanka where a new "town" and a kind of Sri Lankan Disneyland are built at enormous expense. Thus out of nowhere an impressive town emerged in Kataragama, illustrating the irrevocable embourgeoisement and politicization of Kataragama. The traditional ethos of Kataragama described in Chapter 5 is fast becoming a thing of the past.

Two features of the new Kataragama are relevant to our study. First, a new stupa named after Duṭugämuṇu's mother, Vihāra Mahā Dēvī, has been built at the *gam udāva* site. Second, two statues of Mahāsēna have been erected, one at the Vihāra Mahā Dēvī premises (along with other kings of the ancient southern kingdom of Ruhuna) and the other at the entrance to the road leading to Väḍahiṭikanda, the mountain where the god Kataragama first resided. An ancient statue found in the Kiri Vehera premises has also been identified as that of Mahāsēna. Till very recently the Kiri Vehera statue was popularly identified as that of Däḍimuṇḍa or Dēvatā Baṇḍāra, the god of Alutnuvara and at one time a guardian of that shrine. With the acceptance of the Mahāsēna myth this "guardian" was, quite appropriately, renamed Mahāsēna a few years ago. Moreover a Pāli *gātha* or prayer for Mahāsēna has been printed and prominently displayed for those who come to worship the Kiri Vehera. It is now known as "the *gātha* for worshipping the Kiri Vehera":

The lord of Sages, the ascetic, seated,
Taught the sublime Doctrine to the deities all around.
I worship the site of the Kataragama stupa,
That is worthy of the respect of the god (or king) Mahāsēna.

The new history has been politically legitimated and religiously sanctioned as true history.

CHAPTER 13

Conclusion

The Nature of Authority in Sinhala Religious Tradition

In the first century B.C. the Sangha in Sri Lanka formally recognized what must in fact have been the case from the beginning—that they had the duty to preserve and interpret the scriptures, the Pāli Canon. This decision was taken when they first committed the Canon to writing. Although in principle written texts are accessible to anyone who can read, in practice it was the Sangha who wrote the manuscripts, kept them in their monasteries, and transmitted their contents to the laity. The Pāli Canon was not printed till the late nineteenth century. The monks of the Sangha were the educators of the Sinhala people. Literacy was taught primarily at village temples and its materials were Buddhist. Insofar as the laity had anything to read, it was Sinhala Buddhist texts that they read.

The Canon was in Pāli, a classical language, and from the fifth century onwards the commentaries too were in Pāli. In the same century were composed the two texts, also in Pāli, that lie at the heart of the Sinhala Buddhist tradition. The *Visuddhimagga* ("Path to Purity") by Buddhaghosa, the monk who compiled the most important Pāli commentaries, is a compendium of doctrine and instructions for practicing meditation, written for monks. Also written by monks, and primarily for monks, is the *Mahāvaṃsa* ("The Great Chronicle"). Its first part, which covers the period from the Buddha's lifetime till the late fourth century A.D., was composed by Mahānāma early in the sixth century on the basis of older materials; further installments have carried it down to modern times. The *Mahāvaṃsa* is a history of organized Buddhism in Sri Lanka, but identifies the fortunes of Buddhism with those of the Sinhala people. It has played a crucial role in forming Sinhala national consciousness.

Very few members of the laity can ever have learned Pāli. From the first, monks expounding Buddhist texts to the laity must have done so in the vernacular. Early Sinhala literature, which began in the late tenth century, is Buddhist in content and mostly parasitic on the Canon and Pāli commentaries. However, little of the Canon was translated or even paraphrased in Sinhala texts. The Sinhala literary texts for the most part contain stories of the Buddha in his former lives and his final existence, stories which, besides being excellent entertainment, served to inculcate Buddhist values. From the earliest times the Sangha had reserved to itself doctrines like the theory of no soul (*anātmavāda*); the laity was not to be bothered with such difficult abstractions. Besides this didactic story literature, Sinhala literature included historical works related to the *Mahāvaṃsa*.

The more formal literary texts, in their turn, were probably not available or perhaps even fully intelligible to everyone. However, those texts that dealt with the past lives of the Buddha legend were recited by educated laymen at pilgrimage centers on Buddhist holidays for an interested village audience. Their contents also reached a wider public through ballads. Manuscripts of such ballads date back as far as the sixteenth century, but early in this century this primarily oral literature became universally available in cheap printed leaflets (*kavikoḷa*). This ballad literature draws both on the texts so far specified and on ritual texts concerning gods and demons. This literature and allusions in the more formal texts constitute our evidence for popular religion in premodern times.

The structure of the authority that determines Sinhala Buddhist orthodoxy is thus fairly unproblematic. Authority lies in "the word of the Buddha," that is, the Pāli Canon, as mediated by the Sangha and to some extent also by texts deriving from that tradition. The tradition explicitly states that when it has fallen on hard times it is restored by learned monks who repeat and transmit the scriptures. No doubt the full content of those scriptures was rarely known or understood by more than a few learned monks; but their message was conveyed at several different levels of sophistication. Even uneducated villagers heard and regarded as authoritative the texts used on ritual occasions. Though many of these deal with spirits and transactions not found in the Pāli literature, they conform to its ethicized cosmology and do not violate fundamental canonical doctrines.

The integrity of the Sangha is conceived to rest not so much on its orthodoxy as on its orthopraxy. The Buddhist tradition is that monks guilty of certain grave offenses against their disciplinary code are deemed ipso facto to have left the Order. However, the secular power of the king used to be called upon to expel malefactors, and sometimes kings have even taken the initiative in so "purifying" the Sangha. In the nineteenth century the British government refused to assume responsibility for enforcing ecclesiastical decisions, a refusal that led to their being accused of causing the decline of Buddhism. Since Independence prominent Buddhists both within and outside the government have been much concerned with the problem of state regulation of the Sangha. Nowadays the state does exercise a good deal of control, for instance by keeping a register of valid ordinations and by putting the temporalities of rich monasteries in the charge of the Public Trustee. On the other hand, under a representative system of government that recognizes religious pluralism, the President or Prime Minister can hardly play the traditional role of the Sinhala king as protector of the Sangha.

The Sangha has not been radically affected by the developments that we have discussed in this book. Individual monks have figured in these pages, but for the most part the Sangha is rather bypassed by what is happening. It continues to recruit overwhelmingly from the countryside. Though monks assume various roles in the cities and suburbs, the ratio of temples to Buddhist laity in urban areas is very low, especially in Colombo. Whatever their personal piety, villagers are acquainted with their local Buddhist monks; few city dwellers can claim such acquaintance.

Sinhala Buddhism is Theravāda, "the Doctrine of the Elders," that is, of the Sangha. But can that title still be justified? The Sangha began to lose its monopoly as the fountainhead of cultural values and information in the middle of the nineteenth century, when the British introduced state education on the Western model. Though the first schools were all Christian, most of the syllabus was secular. All over the world the scientific and technical achievements of the West have sown doubts about the monopolistic position of traditional sources of knowledge. In the Sinhala case, this effect was reinforced by the fact that the new education was purveyed in English and associated with the political power of the day. Even Western Orientalism contributed to decreasing the importance of the Sangha, for the Pāli Canon was translated into English, and thus made accessible to the educated Sinhala laity without clerical intermediacy, long before it was translated into Sinhala. The laity came to regard English as the best medium for studying Buddhism. We have quoted above Mr. S.W.R.D. Bandaranaike's statement to Parliament in 1944 that for studying Buddhism

English might be more useful than Sinhala. Mr. Bandaranaike claimed that it was at Oxford that he first learned about Buddhism.

Since Independence the government has sponsored a translation of the Canon into Sinhala by monks, but the language they have employed is so learned and archaic that even we, who are relatively well educated, can barely understand it. The Sangha's tradition that it alone can master the scriptural language dies hard. It is significant that the few intelligible published translations of Pāli texts into Sinhala are mostly by laity. No less significant is the fact that *What the Buddha Taught*, the best-selling account of Buddhism by a Sinhala monk, the Venerable Walpola Rahula, was originally written in English and published in England; only several years later was it translated into Sinhala and published in Sri Lanka. What is printed in Sinhala in newspapers, books, and above all in school textbooks derives largely from the English-language Orientalist view of Buddhism.

Without further research it is not possible to say from what sources the typical modern Sinhala urbanite derives his knowledge of religious matters. But what can be said with assurance is that he draws his impressions from a wide range of sources and perceives the Sangha as just one source among many. What tends to survive from the past is a feeling that authority lies in sacred texts, available perhaps only to initiates. This feeling competes with respect for the latest advance in technology that has arrived from the Western world.

With the exception of some modern forms of Christianity, religious traditions always claim to present to their adherents a view of the world that is eternally valid. To accommodate what outsiders perceive as change they employ various strategies. Fundamentalist ideologies, such as some Protestant sects and certain movements in modern Islam, present themselves as rejections of latter-day accretions in favor of a return to a pristine purity to be found in the basic text, the Bible or the Koran. The Sinhala case is slightly different, perhaps because precisely what constitutes the basic text is not so clear to the layman. Here too the only kind of change admitted to occur is a lapse from original ideals. Innovations are incorporated by claiming that they are only restorations of things forgotten or malevolently suppressed for a time. In particular, nowadays virtually any innovation is attributed to a remote past, which if specified dates to the Polonnaruva or Anurādhapura periods or even earlier, and is usually connected to some culture hero. While we know that Colonel Olcott invented the Buddhist flag in the late nineteenth century, people believe that it is ancient and some date it to the time of Duṭugämuṇu (second century B.C.). Typically an innovation is said to have authority in an ancient text, such as the *Mahāvaṃsa*, not perhaps in the version publicly available but in some more authentic recension. Thus Vijeyaratna Sāmi has discovered a text kept hidden in the main shrine at Kataragama that gives the place's true history. The invention of a Buddhist wedding ceremony (Chapter 7) is ascribed to the time of Prince Siddhārtha himself, though we know not only that it is new but also that it goes against the tradition that Buddhist *sacralia* play no part in life-cycle ceremonies except at death. Similar fanciful attributions to ancient custom are frequently to be read in the press. We note at the time of writing that a proposal to institute compulsory military service is said to revive ancient practice. An advocate of the study of Indian music is reported to rest his case on the claim that Sri Lanka excelled in that field in the time of Rāvaṇa. Rāvaṇa was the demon king of the island in the Sanskrit epic, the *Rāmāyaṇa*, but hitherto Sinhala history has ignored him; nevertheless, his rule is now being assigned to the primordial time before the Buddha. Thus the past is not merely being credited with ever more inventions, but also extended back beyond what has always been regarded as the point of origin of the Sinhala people. Modern conditions appear to have stimulated the popular mythopoeic imagination.

Such instances of inventing tradition (what Malinowski called charters) must worry the historian by posing the question whether similar inventions have not been occurring throughout history. We are not claiming either that there were no changes earlier or that changes were never endowed with a spurious authority. But, as explained in the previous chapters, we see some of the developments recorded in this book as contravening the underlying postulates of the Sinhala religious tradition. And we believe not only that the pace of change has greatly accelerated, but that while religious authority lay with the Sangha alone it must have exercised considerable control over additions to the tradition and greatly restricted the possibilities for its fabrication.

The Emergence of a New Syndrome?

This book has fallen roughly into two halves. The first half, up to Chapter 5, treated developments in the spirit religion, the second, Chapters 6 to 11, in Buddhism proper. We must stress that the distinction is made within the society by our subjects, not just by us. But it also has an added convenience for exposition, in that the matter of the first half has largely concerned religious innovation among lower-class people, the second half innovations affecting the middle class. This division by class is however not hard and fast. It applies better to the second half, in that some urban proletarians have little contact with organized Buddhism—even if their children must pick up a few of its ideas at school. The developments in the spirit religion, on the other hand, affect the lives of most of the population of all social classes, and its leading theoreticians, in particular, tend to have educated middle-class backgrounds.

In Chapter 11 we presented a case study of a development in Buddhism and showed how it is being variously adapted to the requirements of the spirit religion; in Chapter 12 we showed Buddhism and the spirit religion interacting at Kataragama. We shall now venture some more general observations on what connects the two sets of developments.

The socioeconomic problems of contemporary Sri Lanka have been sketched in our early chapters. One facet of these changes is the loss of the traditional community. Protestant Buddhism started as the Buddhism of those who had left the village community. They no longer had local deities to worship or local rituals to support. The Twelve Gods became obsolete. They and the Four Gods were traditionally propitiated in collective village rituals determined by the agricultural cycle, rituals that contained song and dance and adopted a familiar tone toward the gods that at times reached irreverence, humor, or obscenity. For middle-class city dwellers such collective rituals could have little meaning, and their tone conflicted with the high moral tone and solemn attitude toward the sacred adopted by Protestant Buddhism from Christianity. Since tradition thus failed to provide rituals for worshipping the gods appropriate to the new social context, Hindu customs helped to fill the gap.[1] The time and place for worship and the deities to be addressed had hitherto been determined by local custom. Once uprooted from the locality, one could focus one's religious life on two levels: the national and the private. The national level meant visiting one of the few pilgrimage centers traditionally visited by Sinhala Buddhists from every area. The best example is Kataragama. On the pri-

[1] Indian villagers can be as disrespectful to the gods as Sinhalese, but the type of Hinduism imported is again the supralocal *bhakti* religion. See chap. 3, n. 8.

vate level one could set up a shrine in one's own home for one's own guardian deity (*iṣṭa dēvatā*). Moreover, the spiritual egalitarianism of Protestant Buddhism has implications for worship of the gods as well: if each man is told that he is responsible for his own salvation, he is the less likely to allow others to determine for him whom and how he shall worship, and the fundamentalism he learns in the Buddhist context he can transfer to the sphere of worshipping gods. The two levels interact: Kālī appeals to many as an *iṣṭa dēvatā*, and thus her shrine at Munnēssarama becomes one of the principal pilgrimage sites on the national level. But as the socially mobile flex their muscles as individuals in economic competition, deities' shrines are no longer everything: the spiritual corollary of privatized religion is that the deity's true temple is in one's heart.

An obvious contrast between the new lower-class and the new middle-class religiosity lies in the emotional and psychological states that they cultivate. While both are attempting to restore meaning and enchantment to life, the mystical model that is essentially contemplative has little appeal to the lower classes, who either live in poverty and squalor themselves or feel their imminent threat. They fall back on the less quiescent mode of ecstatic religiosity and devotion. Can the contemplation of the Buddhist meditator bear any relation to such ecstasy?

The Buddhist tradition prescribes that meditation be learned within the Sangha from a senior monk (or nun) who is one's constant guide and companion (*kalyāṇa-mitra*). This meditative tradition flourishes in Sri Lanka today. Michael Carrithers, in his fine account of the contemporary hermitage movement, has shown what this great monastic tradition means, and has probably always meant, to its practitioners. The Buddhist, like other Indian traditions, holds that a meditation teacher must exercise constant supervision because to embark on this uncharted sea by oneself is dangerous and may lead to mental derangement. There has traditionally been little institutional support for lay meditation.

Assigning to the laity support of the Order as their principal function shows a realistic appraisal of the needs of the society and polity. And the traditional division of labor between monks and laity shows a realistic acceptance of the emotional needs and spiritual capacities of mankind. To be on the path to *nirvāṇa* is no longer to be prey to any human emotion. Those who were supposed to cultivate a sublime equanimity had no worldly, and in particular no family, ties so that the conflict, for example, between parental grief at the death of a child and the ideal of calm detachment simply did not arise. Sexuality is an unavoidable problem in normal people, but monks were helped to maintain chastity by rigid seclusion from women.

Nowadays lay Buddhists influenced by Dharmapāla's reform try to live in the world while not being of it. Some of them go so far as to practice complete sexual abstention while still living with their husbands or wives. Our informants, whose anonymity must be respected, have provided us with instances. Those who seek *nirvāṇa* while still sexually active have the hardly less difficult problem of constantly switching from attachment to detachment and back again. Sex is but a paradigm case. Either one is completely detached toward one's own husband or wife, one's parents and children, or again one oscillates. Economic activity immediately becomes problematic for the salvation seeker. Is not moneymaking the prime cause of greed? Some talk of "the middle way" and say one should make just enough for one's needs, but what are those needs and what is enough? Moreover, it is notoriously hard to run a business or professional career on such principles. When it comes to meditation, psychological problems crop up—just as the tradition envisages. The meditation of serious Protestant Buddhists is not the ten minutes a day of Transcendental Meditation said to be so helpful to Western businessmen, but a matter of long sessions in meditation centers on Buddhist holy days, weekends, and holidays and an attempt to practice awareness of one's movements, thoughts, and feelings throughout daily life. At the meditation center they receive some guidance, but most of the time they are meditating on their own. The Buddha is not a deity who can intercede to help them, and the ideology of Buddhist meditation is that one has no self, and by realizing this one abolishes one's dependency needs. This contrasts with theistic meditation in which the self is yoked to or merged with the supreme deity. Thus Buddhist meditators who are inadequately prepared must feel themselves spiritually lonely and isolated. It is no surprise if someone so situated looks for a human guru like Sai Baba or Uttama Sādhu, or a divine protector. The increasing number of Buddhists who go to meditate in India are primarily aware of a wish to renew contact with the best traditions of Indian spirituality by visiting the land of the Buddha; but in fact they probably are also seeking gurus and no doubt finding them. But to find Indian gods it is not necessary to travel: they have come to Sri Lanka. Among Protestant Buddhists devotion to the gods—often to one particular god—carries the charge of all the emotion not allowed expression elsewhere and fills the spiritual void left by a forced detachment from the world.

This outcome seems paradoxical. One sets out to cut oneself off from the world, and one becomes devoted to a god—who according to Buddhist ideology is as much of the world as is anything else. But the god is no longer so conceived. The Protestant Buddhist meditator, if he faces the paradox at all, sees his religious emotion as "pure" *bhakti*, devotion free from all the taints of normal human feelings. He has come to worship a Hindu god in a true Hindu spirit.

No observer can fail to be struck by the extraordinary prevalence in contemporary Sri Lanka of interest in and even attainment of altered states of consciousness: possession, trance, "higher" states reached by meditation. Eliade draws a distinction between ecstasy, in which the subject's true self leaves the body, and enstasis, in which the self is so concentrated within that all contact with the outside world of sense experience is lost.[2] This latter state is typified by the absorption (*samādhi*) of Indian meditative traditions. In fact the form of ecstasy prevalent in Sri Lanka is not the shamanic departure from the body, but the body's temporary takeover by another spirit. This kind of ecstasy and enstasis do seem prima facie polar opposites. In possession awareness of the self is obliterated and there is complete dissociation from normal experience, so that the person possessed is afterwards not aware of what has been going on. Enstasis, on the other hand, is supposed to be a condition of control; whether or not it entails an altered state of consciousness (we have seen that in this the tradition is ambiguous), it entails a heightened awareness of one's own experience, and memory of the condition persists afterwards. Cultural prestige attaches to enstasis, and we have shown in Chapter 1 that traditionally ecstasy, since it is an extreme form of loss of self-control, was condemned and indeed not allowed except for certain special purposes. Our data show a strong tendency for the lower classes to practice ecstasy, the middle classes to strive for enstasis. But these two forms of escape from normal experience are sometimes not easy to differentiate. This is admittedly but a guess by laymen with no experience of these states, but we feel emboldened by a famous controversy between experts. In Chapter 6 we have given some account of the founding of the meditation center at Kan̆duboḍa and of its

[2] Mircea Eliade, *Yoga, Immortality, and Freedom*, 2d ed., trans. Willard R. Trask (New York: Bollingen Foundation, 1969), esp. p. 337.

importance in recent Buddhist history, so its methods are of great relevance. Mahāsī Sayādaw had published a book in Burmese about his method; parts of it were translated into English and published by the Sri Lanka government in 1955.[3] Monks at Vajirārāma, a famous Colombo monastery, who had themselves studied *vipassanā* meditation in Burma but according to a more traditional method, attacked the method used at Kaňduboḍa.[4] They quoted Mahāsī Sayādaw himself to show that the deep breathing he recommended could lead to strange physical sensations, swaying, trembling, and even loss of consciousness, and they went on to point out that these were results of excess oxygen in the blood.[5] What they did not say, but must strike anyone who has seen possession in Sri Lanka (or perhaps any shamanic trance), is that the technique and result are those used for entering trance states. Over the last twenty years Kaňduboḍa has no doubt played down this aspect, but it has by no means renounced allegiance to the teachings of Mahāsī Sayādaw. We think therefore that the monks, nuns, and pious laity in these pages who have trained in meditation at Kaňduboḍa have been learning a technique which, however in fact applied, could if followed to the letter take them into trance states very like possession.

Returning to our case studies, we are struck by how ecstasy has been converted by a little social pressure into enstasis or the appearance of it—which change is construed as spiritual development. Speaking "the language of the gods" is held to be unsuitable for a Buddhist meditator, but speaking the language of the Buddha, like Uttama Sādhu's nuns, is interpreted as a supernormal power acquired by practicing enstasis. Without investigating in depth the psychology of the individuals who have these experiences we cannot say more about how these differently interpreted states of consciousness may be related. However, on the societal level it is almost banal to observe that seeking refuge from normal consciousness is a response to intolerable stress. Here the sociologist's commonplace echoes the Buddha's wisdom, for he recommended the practice of meditation to

[3] *Lessons of Practical Basic Exercises in Satipatthana Vipassana Meditation by Mahasi Sayadaw*, published at the request of the Lanka Vipassana Society by the Lanka Bauddha Mandalaya, Ministry of Home Affairs, Colombo 7, 1955. There was later a Sinhala translation too.

[4] Foreword by Kassapa Thera, *A Collection of Articles on Meditation* (Colombo: Henry Prelis, 1957).

[5] Kassapa Thera, "Foreword," p. iv.

free one from the pain and sorrow present throughout the phenomenal world. Meditation is but one form that flight from a harsh outer world may assume, and it is practiced only by a minority, though an influential minority. Possession too, in every society where it occurs, happens only to a few. The form it takes in modern Sri Lanka is an extreme expression of devotion to a god. Firewalking is another. More widespread as an expression of such devotion, though restricted to public occasions, is the *kāvaḍi* dancing discussed above. Possession, firewalking, and *kāvaḍi* dancing are however all merely manifestations of a pervasive religious temper, devotion to a personal god or gods. Like traditional Sinhalese Buddhists, these devotees look to the gods for material benefits and ply them with specific requests for help; but unlike the traditional worshippers, they expect from their gods constant guidance, consolation, and love. Their gods are always in their hearts, ready to soothe their anguish (an anguish that has risen out of the social and political changes discussed in this book).

Though this book has been about Buddhists, this *bhakti* religion is found among all classes and members of all religions in the modern society we have characterized, and its celebration cuts across social distinctions. Hindus, Muslims, and Christians are devoted to Kataragama, Kālī, and Hūniyam and light lamps to them daily in shrines both private and public. For Hindus of course this represents no deviation from orthodoxy. Among Muslims and Christians we know of many cases, but we are not in a position to say what proportion of them worships these alien gods; we suspect rather that among them the same mood prevails, but that the orthodox majority may honor the saints of their own traditions in this spirit of devotion.

The Buddhist devotees still believe that all gods are beneath the Buddha and that it is Buddhist doctrine that points the only true way to final salvation. Yet neither Buddhist doctrine nor the Buddhist practices that have developed in Sri Lanka have made the Buddha the kind of god who intervenes in human affairs, nor have they supplied the interceding Bodhisattvas found in Mahāyāna societies. The Buddha is traditionally seen as unequivocally benevolent, but without any active role in the world he has left. Yet for modern devotees the figure of the Buddha is inadequate to their emotional needs. Though they remain irrelevant for salvation, it is the gods who dominate the emotions. But a minority contrive to cobble theistic devotion into the frame of orthodox soteriology: when Sai Baba, both god and guru, is identified as a Buddha, the latter has come down to intercede for his devotee.

Contemporary Buddhism in Comparative Perspective

We are aware that ecstatic religion and thaumaturgic cults have appeared in many parts of the world in response to the kind of socioeconomic changes we have described in this book. Similarly religious pluralism and the spread of literacy have in many areas led to the dissolution of traditional certainties and the formation of sects. Rather than making comparisons on so grand a scale, it may be more rewarding if we try instead to locate these developments within the Indian religious tradition.

In taking this approach we hope to respond in some measure to the appeal made several years ago by Sri Lankan social scientists for a non-Western sociology/anthropology. The authors of this appeal never progressed from program to practice. Yet it seems to us that religion can indeed be analyzed usefully in terms derived from the intellectual tradition of India rather than in Western terms. If the religion in question is South Asian, this is hardly controversial: to analyze a culture in the terms set by its own reflective tradition is no more than to take what anthropologists (borrowing from linguists) have called the "emic" (as opposed to the "etic") approach; others call this "ethno-methodology." We would in fact be prepared to go further. In the field of religion, at least, the subtlety and sophistication of the Sanskrit tradition have produced concepts that we think can be usefully applied to the discussion of *any* religion. Just as we have used the Christian concept of Protestantism to analyze modern Buddhism, Indian religious concepts can well be applied, for example, to put the European Reformation into comparative perspective. The difficulty, obviously, is that the non-Indian reader has first to be taught the Sanskrit religious vocabulary before he can appreciate how it is being put to use. For this reason our final analysis, while using Indian concepts, does so for the most part unobtrusively, rendering them into English. *Bhakti* and *tantra* are Sanskrit terms with established usages in the South Asian religious tradition; to extrapolate those usages into modern times is hardly daring but may be enlightening. Even without using any Sanskrit we can remain within indigenous traditions of analysis by insisting, for example, on the rigid distinction between this-worldly goals (*bhukti*) and salvation (*mukti*) as motives for religious practice.

All over the South Asian cultural area, from Burma to what is now Pakistan and from Nepal to Sri Lanka, the religion of villagers seems from the earliest times to have centered on cults in which contact is established with spirits by means of possession. The normal pattern is for such possession to be routinized by certain individuals, who then can use their divine contacts to help the community by healing, recovering lost objects, averting misfortune.

The great classical religions of India—Brahmanism, Buddhism, and Jainism—by contrast, inculcated self-control and decorum. Buddhism and Jainism taught from the beginning that salvation comes through attaining complete mastery of the senses, appetites, and emotions; and in this they were later followed by the soteriologies that Brahmanism admitted as orthodox. Possession is of course the very converse of self-control and is normally accompanied by the display of violent emotion. One could say that the Indian classical religions precisely censored out possession and opposed emotionalism. The scheme of values they set up was one of calm and dignified conduct, *civilized* behavior as opposed to rustic license.

Naturally these great religions could not suppress the folk religion and probably never tried to do so. But they compartmentalized experience of the divine. The folk religion of possession they categorized as a vulgar affair fit only for the problems of this world. Any deity who could enter an impure human body must be vulgar. The spiritual aristocrat observed these practices of the common crowd from a distance; his aim was to detach himself from such mundanity. In Sri Lanka traditional Theravāda Buddhism has probably coexisted with the spirit religion from time immemorial, but its scriptures and practices show barely a trace of it.

In South Asia, as elsewhere, the textual religions, the "great traditions," have been guarded and officially preserved by men. To this rule the Buddhist Order of Nuns, while it was still extant, hardly constituted an exception, for all evidence suggests that such public roles as preacher were reserved for monks. It has been the male clergy, or clerical class, that has opposed the folk religion of possession, and the latter has been typically, though not exclusively, the preserve of women. Actually in South Asia we tend to find a hieratic structure with several levels. This can be illustrated in terms of language. The scriptures are preserved in a classical language, such as Sanskrit or Pāli, which until modern times was the main or only language of literacy. A folk religion, which typically but not always originates with social protest against the hierarchies of sex and gender, adopts a vernacular language, but as it in turn ossifies the social hierarchies creep back and its literature, once recorded, is in a language that after a few generations is no longer generally intelligible. Thus Jaina Prakrit, for example, or the medieval vernaculars of Hindu *bhakti* literature, have become even less accessible than Sanskrit, for they are not in the classical language generally taught in schools. The old ballads and liturgies of Sinhala priests, the literature of the spirit religion, are suffering the same fate. While they are still genuinely oral literature the language is probably updated in use; but once they are recorded (a process that hardly began before the nineteenth century) their language rapidly passes into obscurity. But at the opposite end from the classical scriptures preserved by the clerics we find the nonliterate religious activities of those at the other end of the social scale, the low caste, the poor, the women.

This situation has interesting implications for rates of change. The classical scriptural tradition—in Sri Lanka, Theravādin orthodoxy—is conservative, for it continually reverts to authoritative texts that command general acceptance. This does not rule out shifts in selection and interpretation; but certainly such a tradition is likely to be far less volatile than a religion without scriptures. It is quite possible that the arrival of modern recording media, not least the tape recordings and writings of anthropologists, will give a little more permanency to the religions of the oppressed; but of course this will happen only insofar as the oppressed themselves have access to the records. For the moment we can safely predict that the spirit religion of the Sinhalas will go on changing faster than their Buddhism proper. At the same time one must be aware that the less official religions sometimes erupt from below, so to speak, and affect the character of the learned tradition, the dominant orthodoxy.

In India Sanskrit sources for many centuries remained as silent about religious ecstasy as the Pāli sources have remained in Sri Lanka. It is hard to date the breakthrough from the vernacular strata into Sanskrit, the language of Brahmans, of practices that accord a soteriological value to possession: we cannot be more precise than to put it somewhere around the middle of the first millennium A.D. The religious movement to which we are alluding is *tantra*. In Hindu *tantra*[6] (from which we believe that other

[6] The best introduction to *tantra* is Sanjukta Gupta, Dirk Jan Hoens, and Teun Goudriaan, *Hindu Tantrism* (Leiden and Köln: E. J. Brill, 1979).

forms of *tantra* derived), the practitioner aims to realize his identity with God and the universe (the universe being but an aspect of God) by means of meditation that must accompany a complex ritual practice. To undertake this practice he must be initiated by a guru, who is also identical to God. Early Tantric texts show that this identity was ritually enacted by the guru at initiation: he made the pupil open his mouth wide, took out the pupil's soul and put it in his own body while depositing his own soul in the pupil's heart. The Sanskrit Tantric texts have evolved a most elaborate theology and exegesis of the ritual, but do not entirely disguise the fact that the sought-after identity between the practitioner and God is also based on an idea of being possessed by the deity.

The earliest Tantric texts are Brahmanized, to the extent that salvation is for them an experience from which normal human emotions have been systematically eliminated by the practice of yoga. But later *tantra*s are affected by the other great current that has made Hinduism: emotional theism. According to this doctrine of *prapatti*, "self-surrender," salvation comes from God to his worshippers as an act of pure grace. While it cannot be constrained, the correct human attitude is to devote oneself entirely to loving God as emotionally as possible. Indeed, in some versions emotion is so much prized as the means to salvation that even *hating* God can be salvific. The ideal devotee loves God so much that he forgets all normal rules of decorum and may even act like a madman. Anything he suffers as a result of his wild behavior can only strengthen his claim on God's compassionate attention.

The Sanskrit text that first preaches this emotional theism and is its basic charter is the tenth book of the *Bhāgavata Purāṇa*, composed in southern India ca. A.D. 900. We now know that crucial parts of this text are taken from earlier Tamil poems by Vaiṣṇava poet saints, the Āḻvārs.[7] The personal form God takes in these sources is Kṛṣṇa. He is worshipped above all as an adolescent, irresistibly seductive. The wives of the cowherds among whom he is brought up all fall passionately in love with him, a love all the more exciting for being adulterous. In subsequent centuries the cult of Kṛṣṇa spread to Bengal and other parts of India. Generally it has an erotic character, and devotees imagine themselves in the place of the milkmaids who long for Kṛṣṇa's embrace.

The majority of Tamils are not Vaiṣṇava but Śaiva. The erotic character

[7] Friedhelm Hardy, *Viraha-Bhakti: The Early History of Kṛṣṇa Devotion in South India* (New Delhi, Oxford University Press, 1983), pt. 5.

that Vaiṣṇavas attributed to Kṛṣṇa the Śaivas attributed to Skanda. Thus the character that Kataragama is acquiring at his main shrine, as described in Chapter 5 above, is not new. A thoroughly Tamil religious tradition is being adopted by many Sinhalas. But there is of course one crucial difference. The *Bhāgavata Purāṇa* theologized Kṛṣṇa, presenting him as identical with the Absolute; he grants salvation. No Sinhala Buddhist, bar the stray eccentric, believes that a god can grant salvation. Thus the theorizing about Kataragama rapidly reaches a cutoff point; myths can grow around him, but no true theology can emerge from the myths.

A distinctive feature of *tantra* is that it is practiced at the same time for spiritual and for material ends. A practitioner may not even attempt to reach the ultimate goal of identity with the supreme God. He may be content instead to identify with a lesser spirit and so attain its powers. Thus *tantra* for many people becomes simply a system for practicing magic both white and black.

Emotional theism and Tantric magic have had a long run in India; both permeate Hindu culture to this day. This suggests to us that once *bhakti* religiosity and black magic have permeated Sinhala culture, it may prove hard to dislodge them. The question is whether they can continue to coexist with Buddhist soteriology without much affecting it. Already the emotional climate of Sinhala religiosity has changed. Are more tangible changes on the way?

We cannot pretend to be able to answer this question; we prefer to wait and see. We would however hazard one negative prediction. In ancient India around the turn of the Christian Era, early Buddhism acquired an element of thaumaturgy and devotion when the cult of future Buddhas, Bodhisattvas, began the great movement called Mahāyāna. We do not think Sri Lanka will go the same way. A few scholars, like the Venerable Ānanda Maitreya, have been taking an interest in Mahāyāna, and this consorts well with our perception of the change in religious temper. But the Sinhala Buddhist identity has been grounded in the belief that their form of Buddhism, the Theravāda, is the pure one and that it is they who have preserved that purity for the world. In the popular imagination Mahāyāna has long been tantamount to heresy. Thus it is not surprising, though noteworthy, that although the Dalai Lama has been invited to visit and preach in many Western countries, he has not come to Sri Lanka and the government has rejected private suggestions that it associate itself with an invitation to him.

Can such apparently incongruous partners as Theravādin soteriology and emotional theism continue to coexist, not merely in one society but even in one breast? Again the Indian parallel may prove instructive. As Louis Dumont has pointed out,[8] Brahmanism reached an accommodation with *bhakti* emotionalism. In Dumont's terms, *bhakti* was internalized. Its sentiments were recognized and permitted, provided that they were restricted to private life and not allowed to disturb public practice, for example, by following through their egalitarian implications to the extent of upsetting caste rules. In other words the experience of the divine was again compartmentalized. Emotional *bhakti* was perfectly all right for the lower castes, insofar as they were outside the purview of Brahmanical theory. For Brahmans and the high castes who emulated them, the compartmentalization had to take place within individual lives. Adoration of God was added to the older tradition of ritual obligations but was not allowed to interfere with them.

The role of the Brahmans as cultural elite and pacesetters in India fell to the Buddhist Sangha in Sri Lanka. But whereas India is so vast and heterogeneous that Brahmanism has always had to recognize cultural pluralism and allow, at least implicitly, that its norms were only fully applicable to those at the top of the hierarchy, namely Brahmans, Sinhala society is small and relatively homogeneous and the doctrines of Buddhism are universalistic (the same ideas of right and wrong apply to all), so the hegemony of the Sangha has been absolute. Not that hierarchy has been totally absent. In Brahmanical style, for example, black magic and traffic with demons have been countenanced, but to practice them professionally brings low social status.

The crucial difference between Brahmanism and Buddhism has however remained what it was at the outset: Brahmanism places all its emphasis on correct ritual behavior, whereas the Buddha saw the world and correct behavior primarily in ethical terms. For the Brahmans, *karman*, literally "act," referred primarily to rites; for the Buddha, to action that was morally right or wrong because of the good or bad intention behind it. Thus the gravamen of the Sangha's hegemony lies not in details of the cosmology or similar specifics, but in Theravāda Buddhism's ethical values.

The new Sinhala ecstatics, the *sāmi* and *mǟṇiyō*, have at least not aban-

[8] Louis Dumont, "World Renunciation in Indian Religions," *Contributions to Indian Sociology* 4 (1960): 33–62.

doned this ethical framework. When they acquire their powers, they one and all proclaim, and no doubt sincerely believe, that their aim is to use those powers for the good of the world. In this we suspect that they may be somewhat different from the ecstatics and miracle workers in city slums in, say, South America or the Caribbean. While all in fact work for particular clients, our subjects locate themselves *ethically*, however confused they may be doctrinally, within the local great tradition of Buddhism.

For this reason the new ecstatic religiosity need not of itself pose a threat to the leadership of the Sangha and the continuation of the tradition it represents. It can be compartmentalized, both within society—being left to the laity—and, apparently, within individual lives. From this point of view the developments within Protestant Buddhism described in Chapter 10 present the Sangha with a greater threat.

Buddhism has been infiltrated by devotional religiosity and magical practices before, in India in the early centuries of the Christian Era. It quite lost its original antiritualistic character when it developed its own version of Tantrism, the Vajrayāna. We think that this came about as a result of a change in its formal organization. Earlier, as is still true of Theravāda, religious knowledge was publicly transmitted to all members of the Sangha. But Tantric Buddhism follows the Hindu model: religious teaching is given esoterically after initiations imparted one-to-one. The relation of teacher to pupil cross-cuts and in some ways supersedes the old clerical/lay distinction. Thus religious teaching and practice are no longer supervised by a public body, and this leads to the fragmentation and mystification of the tradition. Therefore the lay leadership of sectarians like Mr. Perera and the Sun Buddha does pose a threat to tradition. Mr. Perera and Uttama Sādhu do at least still recognize the supreme authority of the Buddha and claim to be fulfilling his program better than the Sangha. It is the Sun Buddha's claim that he is the Buddha for our age that is truly subversive. However, he has few followers and probably not many emulators. Maybe such extreme apostasy will remain a marginal phenomenon.

Even if he accepts our analysis, our theory of the compartmentalized coexistence of Buddhist ethical principles and religious emotion, the reader may still be wondering what the flagrant incongruities involved can look like in practice in an educated person. But we think that here too history has precedents. In the great Indian religious movements that arose early in the Christian Era we find a common pattern: a severely abstract view of ultimate reality, a view that can be fully realized only by meditation, coexisting with a belief in loving gods, or Bodhisattvas, who may intercede and perhaps even take one to salvation by a shortcut. The great Mahāyāna Buddhist devotional poet, Śāntideva, was at the same time a follower of Nāgārjuna and his doctrine of the voidness (lack of essence) of all things, including ultimately even the doctrines of Buddhism. The great systematizer of nondual Vedānta, Śaṃkara, who argued the purest possible monism, is also plausibly credited with hymns to the very mother goddess whom we know as Kālī. And the authors of the *Bhāgavata Purāṇa* toyed endlessly with the paradox that the dark-skinned erotic cowherd Kṛṣṇa was at the same time the Absolute. Therefore, if the psychological compatibility we see between Protestant Buddhism with its ascetic quest for *nirvāṇa* and an emotional devotion to colorful Hindu gods seems paradoxical, the paradox is not new. The sixteenth-century Vedāntin philosopher Madhusūdana Sarasvatī wrote long books to prove that nothing in the world was real but the One, which had no attributes but Existence, Consciousness, and Bliss. He also wrote at a crucial point in his exposition:[9] "If yogis, their minds subjected by practicing meditation, behold that supreme Something, a light devoid of qualities and actions, they are welcome to it. But long may that delight my eyes, that dark luster which runs along the sandbanks of the Jumna." The dark luster was Kṛṣṇa stealing the clothes of his girlfriends while they bathed.

[9] The beginning of his commentary on *Bhagavad Gītā* 13.

BIBLIOGRAPHY

Abeypala, H. W., text; Chandrasekera, Bernard, pix [*sic*]. "Young Women Going the Buddha Way." *Weekend*, Sunday, 15 January 1978, p. 10.

Abeysekera, Dayalal. "Being Realistic about Age at Marriage and Fertility Decline in Sri Lanka." *Ceylon Journal of the Social Sciences* 5, no. 1 (1982): 1–10.

Administration Reports: Report of the Assistant Government Agent, Hambantoṭa District. Colombo: Government Press, 1975.

Amunugama, Sarath. "Anagarika Dharmapala (1864–1933) and the Transformation of Sinhala Buddhist Organization in a Colonial Setting." *Social Science Information* 24, no. 4 (1985): 697–730.

Ānanda Maitreya, Balangoḍa. "Aruma Puduma Nāḍi Grantha." *Rasavāhini*, August 1980, pp. 5–10.

Appadurai, Arjun. "Gastro-politics in South India." *American Ethnologist* 5, no. 3 (1981): 494–511.

Ariyapala, M. B. *Society in Medieval Ceylon*. Colombo: Government Press, 1968.

Ariyaratna, A. T. *Collected Papers*. Vol. 1. Sarvodaya Research Institute, n.d.

———. *Collected Papers*. Vol. 2. Sarvodaya Research Institute, 1980.

———. *In Search of Development*. Moratuwa: Sarvodaya Press, 1981.

Barnes, Michael. "The Buddhist Way of Deliverance: A Comparison between the Pāli Canon and the Yoga Praxis of the Great Epic." M.Litt. thesis, Oxford, 1977.

Barnett, L. D. "Alphabetical Guide to Sinhalese Folklore from Ballad Sources." *The Indian Antiquary* 45 (1916): appendix, pp. 1–116.

Bechert, Heinz. *Buddhismus, Staat und Gesellschaft in den Ländern des Theravāda Buddhismus*. Vol. 1, Frankfurt and Berlin: Alfred Metzner, 1966; vols. 2 and 3, Wiesbaden, 1967 and 1973.

Bell, Daniel. "The Return of the Sacred." In *The Winding Passage*, pp. 324–54. New York: Basic Books, 1980.

Bell, H.C.P. *Report on the Kegalle District.* Colombo: Government Printing, 1892.

Bloss, Lowell W. "Theravada 'Nuns' of Sri Lanka: Themes of the Dasasilmattawa Movement." Paper presented at the Association for Asian Studies, Sri Lanka Study Group Meeting, Washington, D.C., 23 March 1984.

Burlingame, E. W. *Buddhist Legends*, part 1. London: Routledge and Kegan Paul, 1979 (1921), reprinted for the Pali Text Society.

Carrithers, Michael. *The Forest Monks of Sri Lanka.* Delhi: Oxford University Press, 1983.

Census of Population 1971, Sri Lanka: General Report. Colombo: Department of Census and Statistics, 1978.

Clothey, Fred W. *The Many Faces of Murukan.* The Hague: Mouton, 1978.

———. "*Skanda-Saṣti*: A Festival in Tamil India." *History of Religions* 8, no. 3 (1969): 236–59.

Copleston, R. S. *Buddhism, Primitive and Present in Magadha and in Ceylon.* London: Longmans, 1892.

Dassanayake, Mr. V. C., Department of Inland Revenue, Colombo; Yahampath, Mr. Ranal, Traffic Police Headquarters, Echelon Square, Colombo; Viridunada, Miss Indra Shanthi, D.N.T.S. Maharagama, comps. *Realization of the Truth for the First Time in Sri Lanka* (Colombo, 1978). Published by Mr. S. J. Withanawasam and Mrs. P. Withanawasam, Posts and Telecommunications Department, Colombo 1, 1978.

Davy, John. *An Account of the Interior of Ceylon and of Its Inhabitants with Travels in That Island.* London, 1821, reprinted in the *Ceylon Historical Journal* 16 (1969).

de Silva, Lily. *The Cult of the Bodhi-Tree.* Ceylon Studies Seminar Paper no. 55, 1975. Cyclostyled.

de Silva, W. A. "The Popular Poetry of the Sinhalese." *Journal of the Royal Asiatic Society, Ceylon Branch* 24, no. 68, pt. 1 (1917): 27–66.

de Silva Gooneratne, Dandris. "On Demonology and Witchcraft in Ceylon." *Journal of the Ceylon Branch of the Royal Asiatic Society* 4 (1865): 1–117.

Dewaraja, L. S. *The Kandyan Kingdom, 1707–1760.* Colombo: Lake House Publishing Company, 1972.

Dharmadasa, K.N.O. "The Sinhalese-Buddhist Identity and the Nayakkar Dynasty in the Politics of the Kandyan Kingdom, 1739–1815."

Ceylon Journal of Historical and Social Studies, n.s. 6, no. 1 (1976): 1–23.

Dharmapāla, Anagārika. *Dharmapāla Lipi* (Dharmapāla Letters). Edited by Ānanda W.P. Guruge. Colombo: Government Press, 1963.

———. Diary. In *The Maha Bodhi* 61, no. 8, August 1953.

———. Diary. In *The Maha Bodhi* 65, no. 7, July 1957.

———. Diary. In *The Maha Bodhi* 69, no. 9, September 1961.

———. Diary. In *The Maha Bodhi* 72, no. 2, February 1964.

———. *Return to Righteousness*. Edited by A. Guruge. Colombo: Government Press, 1965.

Dhātuvaṃsa. Edited by Makuloluvē Piyaratana. Colombo: Gunasena and Company, 1941.

Dhirasekera, J. D. "Text and Traditions—Warped and Distorted." In *Nārada Felicitation Volume*, pp. 68–75. Kandy, Sri Lanka: Buddhist Publication Society, 1979.

Djurfeldt, Goran, and Lindberg, S. *Pills against Poverty*. Studentlitteratur. London: Curzon Press, 1975.

D'Oyly, Sir John. *A Sketch of the Kandyan Kingdom*. Colombo: Government Printer, 1929.

Dumont, Louis. "World Renunciation in Indian Religions." *Contributions to Indian Sociology* 4 (1960): 33–62.

Egan, Michael. *The Configurational Analysis of a Sinhalese Ritual*. Ph.D. thesis, Cambridge University, 1969.

Eliade, Mircea. *Yoga, Immortality, and Freedom*. 2d ed. Translated by Willard R. Trask. New York: Bollingen Foundation, 1969.

Elkana, Yehuda. "The Emergence of Second-Order Thinking in Classical Greece." Manuscript, 1984. German version published in Y. Elkana, *Anthropologie der Erkenntnis*, Frankfurt, 1986.

Fernando, Tissa. "The Western-Educated Elite and Buddhism in British Ceylon." In *Tradition and Change in Theravada Buddhism*, edited by Bardwell L. Smith, pp. 18–29. Contributions to Asian Studies, vol. 4. Leiden: E. J. Brill, 1973.

Freud, Sigmund. "Obsessive Acts and Religious Practices" (1907). In *The Standard Edition*. Vol. 9. London: Hogarth Press, 1959.

Geiger, Wilhelm. *Culture of Ceylon in Medieval Times*. Wiesbaden: Otto Harrassowitz, 1960.

———, trans., assisted by Mabel H. Bode. *Mahāvaṃsa: The Great Chronicle of Ceylon*. London: Pali Text Society, 1912.

Gombrich, Richard. "Feminine Elements in Sinhalese Buddhism, I: 'Buddha Mother.' " *Wiener Zeitschrift für die Kunde Südasiens XVI*, 1972, pp. 67–78.

———. "Feminine Elements in Sinhalese Buddhism, II: Buddha by His Mother's Blessing." *Wiener Zeitschrift für die Kunde Südasiens XVI*, 1972, pp. 78–93.

———. "From Monastery to Meditation Centre: Lay Meditation in Modern Sri Lanka." In *Buddhist Studies, Ancient and Modern*, edited by Philip Denwood and Alexander Piatigorsky, pp. 20–34. London: Curzon Press, 1983.

———. "A New Theravādin Liturgy." *Journal of the Pali Text Society* 9 (1981): 47–73.

———. *Precept and Practice: Traditional Buddhism in the Rural Highlands of Ceylon*. Oxford: Clarendon Press, 1971.

Gooneratne, W., and Gunawardena, P. J. "Poverty and Inequality in Rural Sri Lanka." In *Poverty in Rural Asia*, edited by Azizur Rahman Khan and Eddy Lee, pp. 247–71. Bangkok: International Labour Organization, 1984.

Gunasekera, Tamara. "Deity Propitiation in Urban Sri Lanka." M.A. thesis, Edinburgh, 1974.

Gunawardana, R.A.L.H. *Robe and Plough: Monasticism and Economic Interest in Early Medieval Sri Lanka*. Tucson: University of Arizona Press, 1979.

Gupta, Sanjukta; Hoens, Dirk Jan; and Goudriaan, Teun. *Hindu Tantrism*. Leiden and Köln: E. J. Brill, 1979.

Handleman, Don. "On the Desuetude of Kataragama." *Man* n.s. 20, no. 1 (1985): 156–59.

Hardy, Friedhelm. *Viraha-Bhakti: The Early History of Kṛṣṇa Devotion in South India*. New Delhi: Oxford University Press, 1983.

Hardy, R. Spence. *The Sacred Books of the Buddhists Compared with History and Modern Science*. Colombo: Wesleyan Mission Press, 1863.

Harimaga, published by *Hoňda Ḷamayingē Saṃvidhānaya*. "Sasuna Senasuna," Rattanapiṭiya, Boraläsgamuva, 2520 nikiṇi (i.e., 1976).

Hassan, M.C.A. *The Story of Kataragama, Mosque and Shrine*. Colombo: United Printers, 1968.

Hill, Christopher. *The World Turned Upside Down*. London: Temple Smith, 1972.

Hobsbawm, Eric, and Ranger, Terence. *The Invention of Tradition*. Cambridge: Cambridge University Press, 1983.

Hocart, A. M. *Caste: A Comparative Study*. London: Methuen, 1950.

Hodge, M. C. *Buddhism, Magic, and Society in a Southern Sri Lankan Town*. Ph.D. thesis, Victoria University of Manchester, 1981.

Hoebel, E. A. *The Law of Primitive Man*. Cambridge, Mass.: Harvard University Press, 1954.

Jayatilleke, K. N. *Early Buddhist Theory of Knowledge*. London: Allen and Unwin, 1963.

———. *Facets of Buddhist Thought*. Kandy: Wheel Publications, 1971.

Kahakurulu Sandēśaya. Edited by Henpiṭigedera Piyānanda. Colombo: Gunasena and Company, 1954.

Kantowsky, Detlef. *Sarvodaya: The Other Development*. Delhi: Vikas, 1980.

Karunaratne, David. *Anagārika Dharmapāla* (in Sinhala). Colombo: M. D. Gunasena, 1964.

Kassapa Thera. Foreword to *A Collection of Articles on Meditation*. Colombo: Henry Prelis, 1957.

Kearney, Robert N., and Miller, Barbara Diane. *Internal Migration in Sri Lanka and Its Social Consequences*. Boulder, Colo.: Westview Press, 1987.

———. "The Spiral of Suicide and Social Change in Sri Lanka." *Journal of Asian Studies* 45, no. 1 (1985): 81–101.

Kemper, Steven. "Buddhism without Bhikkhus: The Sri Lanka Vinaya Vardhana Society." In Bardwell L. Smith, *Religion and the Legitimation of Power in Sri Lanka*, pp. 212–35. Chambersburg: Anima Publishers, 1978.

Kennedy, Charles A., preparer. *Buddhism in Southeast Asia and Ceylon*. Media Resources Catalogue on Asian Religions, Visual Education Service, Yale Divinity School, New Haven, 1974, p. 13.

Kirala Sandēśaya. Edited by Charles Godakumbura. Colombo: Gunasena and Company, 1961.

Kirthisinghe, Buddhadasa P. "Colonel Henry Steele Olcott, the Great American Buddhist." In B. P. Kirthisinghe and M. P. Amarasuriya, *Colonel Olcott: His Service to Buddhism*, pp. 1–20. Buddhist Publication Society, Wheel Publication no. 281, Kandy, 1981.

Knox, Robert. *An Historical Relation of the Island of Ceylon*. London: Richard Chiswell, 1681.

Leach, E. R. *Pul Eliya: A Village in Ceylon*. Cambridge: Cambridge University Press, 1961.

———. *Social Anthropology*. London: Fontana; New York: Oxford University Press, 1982.

Leacock, Seth, and Leacock, Ruth. *Spirits of the Deep*. New York: Anchor Books, 1975.

Lessons of Practical Basic Exercises in Satipatthana Vipassana Meditation by Mahasi Sayadaw. Published at the request of the Lanka Vipassana Society by the Lanka Bauddha Mandalaya, Ministry of Home Affairs, Colombo 7, 1955.

Lévi-Strauss, Claude. "The Sorcer and His Magic." In *Structural Anthropology*, pp. 167–85. New York: Basic Books, 1963.

Lewis, Ioan. Paper delivered to a conference on religious pluralism at Bristol, United Kingdom, in April 1987.

Macy, Joanna. "Dharma and Development: Religion as a Resource in the Sarvodaya Self-Help Movement in Sri Lanka." Mimeographed, 1981.

Mahāsī Sayādaw. *Practical Vipassanā Meditation Exercises*. Rangoon: Buddhasāsanānuggaha Association, 1978.

Malalgoda, Kitsiri. *Buddhism in Sinhalese Society, 1750–1900*. Berkeley and Los Angeles: University of California Press, 1976.

Maquet, Jacques. "Expressive Space and Theravāda Values: A Meditation Monastery in Sri Lanka." *Ethos* 3 (1975): 1–21.

———. "Meditation in Contemporary Sri Lanka: Idea and Practice." *Journal of Transpersonal Psychology* 7, no. 2 (1975): 182–96.

Mayūra Sandēśaya. Edited by Charles Godakumbura. Colombo: Gunasena and Company, 1961.

Mendelson, E. M. *Sangha and State in Burma*. Ithaca and London: Cornell University Press, 1975.

Merton, Robert K. "Social Structure and Anomie." In *Social Theory and Social Structure*, pp. 121–60. Glencoe, Ill.: Free Press, 1957.

Metraux, Alfred. *Voodoo in Haiti*. New York: Schoken, 1972.

Mudiyanse, N. *The Art and Architecture of the Gampola Period (1341–1415 A.D.)*. Colombo: M. D. Gunasena, 1965.

Mulder, Niels. *Monks, Merit, and Motivation*. Northern Illinois University: Center for Southeast Asian Studies, reprint no. 1, 1969.

Navaratnam, Ratna. *Karttikeya, the Divine Child*. Bombay: Bharatiya Vidya Bhavan, 1973.

Nevill, Hugh. *Sinhala Verse*. Vol. 2, Colombo: Government Press, 1954; vol. 3, Colombo: Government Press, 1955.

Nissan, Elizabeth. "Recovering Practice: Buddhist Nuns in Sri Lanka." *South Asia Research* 4, no. 1 (May 1984): 32–49.

Obeyesekere, Gananath. *The Cult of the Goddess Pattini*. Chicago: University of Chicago Press, 1984.

———. "The Firewalkers of Kataragama: The Rise of Bhakti Religiosity in Buddhist Sri Lanka." *Journal of Asian Studies* 37, no. 3 (1978): 457–76.

———. "The Idiom of Demonic Possession: A Case Study." *Social Science and Medicine* 14: 97–111, reprinted in *Labelling Madness*, edited by Thomas T. Scheff. Englewood Cliffs, N.J.: Prentice Hall, 1975.

———. *Land Tenure in Village Ceylon: A Sociological and Historical Study*. Cambridge: Cambridge University Press, 1967.

———. *Medusa's Hair: An Essay on Personal Symbols and Religious Experience*. Chicago: University of Chicago Press, 1981.

———. "Personal Identity and Cultural Crisis: The Case of Anagarika Dharmapala of Sri Lanka." In *The Biographical Process*, edited by Frank Reynolds and Donald Capps, pp. 221–52. The Hague: Mouton and Company, 1976.

———. "Psychocultural Exegesis of a Case of Spirit Possession from Sri Lanka." *Contributions to Asian Studies* 8: 42–89, reprinted in *Case Studies in Possession*, edited by Vincent Crapanzano and Vivian Garrison. New York: John Wiley, 1977.

———. "Religious Symbolism and Political Change in Ceylon." *Modern Ceylon Studies* 1, no. 1 (1970), reprinted in *Two Wheels of Dhamma*, edited by Bardwell Smith, pp. 58–78. AAR Monograph no. 3. Chambersburg, 1972.

———. "Sinhala-Buddhist Identity in Ceylon." In *Ethnic Identity: Cultural Continuities and Change*, edited by George de Vos and Lola Ross, pp. 229–58. Palo Alto: Mayfield Publishing Company, 1975.

———. "Social Change and the Deities: The Rise of the Kataragama Cult in Modern Sri Lanka" *Man*, n.s. 12 (December 1977): 377–96.

———. "Sorcery, Premeditated Murder, and the Canalization of Aggression in Sri Lanka," *Ethnology* 14, no. 1 (1975): 1–23.

———. "Theodicy, Sin, and Salvation in a Sociology of Buddhism." In *Dialectic in Practical Religion*, edited by E. R. Leach, pp. 7–40. Cambridge: Cambridge University Press, 1968.

Obeyesekere, Ranjini, and Obeyesekere, Gananath. "The Story of the Demoness Kālī: A Thirteenth-Century Text on 'Evil.' " *History of Religions*, forthcoming.

Olcott, H. S. *From Old Diary Leaves. Olcott Commemoration Volume*. Edited by S. Karunaratne. Colombo: Gunasena Press, 1967.

Paranavitana, S. "The Civilization of the Period: Buddhism." In *History of Ceylon*. Vol. 1, pt. 2, pp. 745–67. Colombo: University of Ceylon Press, 1960.

Paranavitana, Senarat. "Mahayanism in Ceylon." *Ceylon Journal of Science* 2, no. 1 (December 1928): 35–71.

Phear, John B. *The Aryan Village in India and Ceylon*. London: Macmillan, 1880.

Pieris, P. E. *Notes on Some Sinhalese Families, Part IV: Ilangakon*. Colombo: Times of Ceylon Company, n.d.

———. *Sinhalē and the Patriots, 1815–1818* ("Kataragama Deviyo and the Ritual of Worship," Johnson manuscript no. 13 of the Colombo Museum). Colombo: Colombo Apothecaries, 1950.

Piker, Steven. "Buddhism and Modernization in Contemporary Thailand." *Contributions to Asian Studies* 4 (1973): 51–67.

Pillai, Elamkulan Kunjan. *Studies in Kerala History*. Kottayam: National Book Stall, 1970.

Pōruve Cāritra Sahita Mangala Aṣṭaka (The *Pōruva* Customs with Wedding *Aṣṭakas*). Nugegoda: Modern Book Store, 1976.

Pūjāvaliya. Edited by Kiriällē Ñāṇavimala. Colombo: Gunasena, 1986.

Rahula, Walpola. *History of Buddhism in Ceylon: The Anurādhapura Period*. Colombo: M. D. Gunasena, 1956.

Rhys Davids, T. W. *Buddhism*. London, 1887.

Rhys Davids, T. W., and Rhys Davids, C.A.F. *Dialogues of the Buddha*. Sacred Books of the Buddhists Series, part 3. London: Oxford University Press, 1921.

Rickmers, C. Mabel, trans., from the German translation by Wilhelm Geiger. *Cūlavaṃsa, Being the More Recent Part of the Mahāvaṃsa*. 2 vols. Colombo: Department of Information, 1953.

Robinson, Marguerite. " 'The House of the Mighty Hero' or 'The House of Enough Paddy'? Some Implications of a Sinhalese Myth." In *Dialectic in Practical Religion*, edited by E. R. Leach, pp. 122–52. Cambridge: Cambridge University Press, 1968.

Saddharmālaṃkāraya. By Dharmakīrti. Edited by Makuloluvē Piyaratana. Colombo: Gunasena and Company, 1971.

Saddharmaratnāvaliya. By Dharmasēna Mahāsāmi. Edited by Kiriällē Ñāṇavimala. Colombo: Gunasena and Company, 1971.

Salgado, Nirmala S. "Custom and Tradition in Buddhist Society: A Look at Some Dasa Sil Matas from Sri Lanka." Colombo: International Centre for Ethnic Studies, n.d. Cyclostyled.

Seligmann, C. G., and Seligmann, Brenda Z. *The Veddas*. Cambridge: Cambridge University Press, 1911.

Seneviratne, H. L., and Wickremeratne, Swarna. "*Bodhi-puja*: Collective Representations of Sri Lanka Youth." *American Ethnologist* 7, no. 4 (November 1980): 734–43.

Shulman, David. *Tamil Temple Myths*. Princeton: Princeton University Press, 1980.

Singer, Milton. *When a Great Tradition Modernizes*. New York: Praeger, 1972.

Somaratne, Mr./Venerable Wariyagoda S.D. *SHOT—DART by a Ray of Cosmic Light*. Translated by Miss I. S. Viridunada. Published by Mr. S. J. Withanawasam and Mrs. P. Withanawasam, No. 37, 6th Lane, Nelumpura, Ratmalana, n.d. (1980?).

Srinivas, M. N. *Remembered Village*. Berkeley: University of California Press, 1976.

Sumangala, Venerable Pandit K. "Attainment to the First Stage of Sanctity, the Sotāpatti Stage." *World Fellowship of Buddhists Review* 18, no. 5 (Rains Retreat Number, September–October 2526/1981): 9–13.

Swearer, Donald. "Lay Buddhism and the Buddhist Revival in Ceylon." *Journal of the American Academy of Religion* 68, no. 3 (September 1970): 255–75.

Thomas, Keith. *Religion and the Decline of Magic*. London: Weidenfeld and Nicolson, 1971.

Thurston, E. *Castes and Tribes of Southern India*. Vol. 6. Madras: Government Press, 1909.

Turner, Victor. "Conflict in Social Anthropological and Psychoanalytical Theory: Umbanda in Rio de Janeiro." In *On the Edge of the Bush*, pp. 119–50. Tucson: University of Arizona Press, 1985.

Upham, Elwood. *Budhist Tracts*. London: Parbury, Allen, and Company, 1833.

Wallace, A.F.C. "The Institutionalization of Cathartic and Control Strategies in Iroquois Religious Psychotherapy." In *Culture and Mental Health*, edited by M. K. Opler, pp. 63–96. New York: Macmillan, 1959.

Weber, Max. "Social Psychology of the World Religions." In *From Max Weber*, edited by Hans Gerth and C. Wright Mills, pp. 267–301. New York: Oxford University Press, 1976.

White, Herbert. *Manual of Uva*. Colombo: Government Printer, 1893.

Wickremeratne, L. A. "Annie Besant, Theosophism, and Buddhist Nationalism in Sri Lanka." *Ceylon Journal of the Historical and Social Sciences*, n.s. 6, no. 1 (January–June 1976): 62–79.

Wilson, Bryan. *Religion in Sociological Perspective*. Oxford and New York: Oxford University Press, 1982.

Wirz, Paul. *Exorcism and the Art of Healing in Ceylon*. Leiden: Brill, 1954.

———. *Kataragama: The Holiest Place in Ceylon*. Translated from the German by Davis Berta Pralle. Colombo: Lake House, 1972.

Wood, Jessica. "Buddhist Nuns in Sri Lanka." Undergraduate dissertation for Lancaster University, 1977.

Yalman, Nur. "The Ascetic Buddhist Monks of Ceylon." *Ethnology* 1, no. 3 (1962): 315–28.

———. *Under the Bo Tree*. Berkeley: University of California Press, 1967.

Zelditch, Morris. "Role Differentiation in the Nuclear Family." In Talcott Parson and Robert Bales, *Family Socialization and Interaction Process*. Glencoe, Ill.: Free Press, 1955.

Zvelebil, Kamil. "The Beginnings of *Bhakti* in South India." *Temenos* 13 (1977): 223–57.

INDEX